Opening Doors

Understanding College Reading

SEVENTH EDITION

Janet Elder   **Joe Cortina**

Richland College
Dallas County Community College District

McGraw Hill

Connect
Learn
Succeed™

The McGraw·Hill Companies

Connect
Learn
Succeed™

OPENING DOORS

Published by McGraw-Hill, a business unit of The McGraw-Hill Companies, Inc., 1221 Avenue of the Americas, New York, NY, 10020. Copyright © 2014 by The McGraw-Hill Companies, Inc. All rights reserved. Printed in the United States of America. Previous editions © 2011, 2008, 2005, 2002, 1998, and 1995. No part of this publication may be reproduced or distributed in any form or by any means, or stored in a database or retrieval system, without the prior written consent of The McGraw-Hill Companies, Inc., including, but not limited to, in any network or other electronic storage or transmission, or broadcast for distance learning.

Some ancillaries, including electronic and print components, may not be available to customers outside the United States.

This book is printed on acid-free paper.

1 2 3 4 5 6 7 8 9 0 QTN/QTN 1 0 9 8 7 6 5 4 3

ISBN: 978-0-07-351351-5 (Student edition)
MHID: 0-07-351351-2 (Student edition)

ISBN: 978-0-07-753138-6 (Instructor's edition)
MHID: 0-07-753138-8 (Instructor's edition)

Senior Vice President, Products & Markets:
  Kurt L. Strand
Vice President, General Manager: *Michael Ryan*
Vice President, Content Production & Technology
  Services: *Kimberly Meriwether David*
Managing Director: *David Patterson*
Director: *Paul Banks*
Executive Brand Manager: *Kelly Villella*
Senior Director of Development:
  Dawn Groundwater
Editorial Coordinator: *Dana Wan*
Senior Marketing Manager: *Jaclyn Elkins*
Market Development Manager: *Suzie Flores*
Director, Content Production: *Terri Schiesl*

Senior Production Editor: *Carey Eisner*
Full Service Project Manager:
  Melanie Field, Strawberry Field Publishing
Senior Buyer: *Laura Fuller*
Designer: *Matt Diamond*
Cover/Interior Designer: *Laurie Entringer*
Cover Image: © *Getty Images*
Content Licensing Specialist: *Jeremy Cheshareck*
Photo Researcher: *Ira Roberts*
Digital Product Manager: *Janet Smith*
Media Project Manager: *Angela Norris*
Typeface: *10.5/12 Times Roman*
Compositor: *MPS Limited*
Printer: *Quad/Graphics*

All credits appearing at the end of the book are considered to be an extension of the copyright page.

Library of Congress Cataloging-in-Publication Data

Elder, Janet.
  Opening doors / Janet Elder, Joe Cortina. — 7th ed.
    p. cm.
  Includes bibliographical references and index.
  ISBN-13: 978-0-07-351351-5 (alk. paper)
  ISBN-10: 0-07-351351-2 (alk. paper)
  ISBN-13: 978-0-07-753138-6 (alk. paper)
  1. College readers. 2. Reading (Higher education) I. Cortina, Joe. II. Title.
PE1122.C637 2014
428.6—dc23

                           2013045075

The Internet addresses listed in the text were accurate at the time of publication. The inclusion of a website does not indicate an endorsement by the authors or McGraw-Hill, and McGraw-Hill does not guarantee the accuracy of the information presented at these sites.

www.mhhe.com

About the Authors

Janet Elder

Joe Cortina

Janet Elder and **Joe Cortina** began their writing collaboration as colleagues in the Human and Academic Development Division at Richland College, a member of the Dallas County Community College District. Professor Elder now writes full time; professor Cortina currently teaches both developmental reading and honors English courses at Richland, and serves as the developmental reading program coordinator. Both are trained reading specialists and are highly experienced in teaching basic and advanced reading improvement and study skills courses. Their combined teaching experience spans elementary, secondary, and undergraduate levels, as well as clinical remediation.

Dr. Elder and Dr. Cortina began collaborating in 1985. Their first textbook was *Comprehending College Textbooks: Steps to Understanding and Remembering What You Read.* Their beginning-level textbook, *New Worlds: An Introduction to College Reading,* is now in its fifth edition. Dr. Elder is also the author of an introductory-level text, *Entryways into College Reading and Learning,* and an intermediate- to upper-level college reading improvement textbook, *Exercise Your College Reading Skills: Developing More Powerful Comprehension,* second edition. Both authors are long-standing members of the College Reading and Learning Association (CRLA) and the National Association for Developmental Education (NADE). Dr. Cortina is also a member of the Texas counterparts of these national organizations, Texas-CRLA and TADE, and Dr. Elder has given numerous presentations at their conferences over the years.

Janet Elder was graduated summa cum laude from the University of Texas in Austin with a B.A. in English and Latin, and is a member of Phi Beta Kappa. She was the recipient of a government fellowship for Southern Methodist University's Reading Research Program, which resulted in a master's degree. Her Ph.D. in curriculum and instruction in reading is from Texas Woman's University where the College of Education presented her the Outstanding Dissertation Award. After teaching reading and study skills courses at Richland for several years, she implemented the college's Honors Program and directed it for six years before returning to teaching full time. She was a three-time nominee for excellence in teaching awards. Disability Services students also selected her three times as the recipient of a special award for "exceptional innovation, imagination, and consideration in working with students with disabilities." She is a recipient of the National Institute for Staff and Organizational Development's Excellence Award. In fall 2004, she left teaching in order to write full time, but she continues her affiliation with Richland as a professor emerita.

Joe Cortina earned his B.A. degree in English from San Diego State University and his master's degree and doctoral degree in curriculum and instruction in reading from the University of North Texas. He has taught undergraduate teacher education courses in reading at the University of North Texas and Texas Woman's University. In 2010 Dr. Cortina received Richland College's Excellence in Teaching Award for Full-Time Faculty. In 1994, 2009, and 2011 he was a recipient of the Excellence Award given by the National Institute for Staff and Organizational Development. And in 1992 he was selected as an honored alumnus by the Department of Elementary, Early Childhood and Reading Education of the University of North Texas. In addition to teaching, Dr. Cortina conducts in-service training and serves as a mentor to both new full-time and adjunct faculty at Richland College.

Brief Contents

Contents

CHAPTER 2   **Approaching College Reading and Developing a College-Level Vocabulary** 67

	CONNECT Reading 2.0 Personalized Learning Plan CORRELATION GUIDE	
Unit	**Topic in PLP**	**Relevant Learning Objectives**
Unit 5: Study Techniques	Flexible Reading Rates	• Understand the skill of reading with flexible reading rates • Understand the 5 reading rates and when to use each
Unit 1: Vocabulary Skills	Vocabulary: Context Clues	• Understand the skill of using context clues • Recognize 6 types of context clues • Recognize clue words and signals for 6 types of context clues • Use context clues to determine a word's meaning • Use context clues to select the appropriate dictionary definition
Unit 1: Vocabulary Skills	Vocabulary: Word-Structure Clues	• Understand the skill of using word-structure clues • Identify and know the meaning of common prefixes • Identify and know the meaning of common roots • Identify and know the meaning of common suffixes • Use one or more word parts to unlock a word's meaning
Unit 3: Interpreting	Author's Tone and Figurative Language	• Understand 4 common figures of speech and the skill of interpreting them • Interpret 4 common figures of speech

CHAPTER 3   **Approaching College Assignments: Reading Textbooks and Following Directions**   143

CONNECT Reading 2.0 Personalized Learning Plan CORRELATION GUIDE		
Unit	**Topic in PLP**	**Relevant Learning Objectives**
Unit 5: Study Techniques	Using Textbooks Effectively	• Understand the skill of using the SQ3R study technique

CONNECT Reading 2.0 Personalized Learning Plan CORRELATION GUIDE		
Unit	**Topic in PLP**	**Relevant Learning Objectives**
Unit 2: Comprehension	Main Idea	• Differentiate between the topic and main idea • Understand the skill of locating the stated main idea of a paragraph • Locate the stated main idea in a paragraph • Locate the overall stated main idea of a longer selection

CHAPTER 5   Formulating Implied Main Ideas   273

CONNECT Reading 2.0 Personalized Learning Plan CORRELATION GUIDE		
Unit	**Topic in PLP**	**Relevant Learning Objectives**
Unit 2: Comprehension	Main Idea	• Differentiate between the stated and implied main ideas • Understand the skill of formulating the implied main idea of a paragraph • Formulate the implied main idea of a paragraph • Formulate the overall implied main idea of a longer selection

CHAPTER 6   Identifying Supporting Details   341

CONNECT Reading 2.0 Personalized Learning Plan CORRELATION GUIDE		
Unit	**Topic in PLP**	**Relevant Learning Objectives**
Unit 2: Comprehension	Supporting Details	• Understand the connection between main ideas and supporting details • Understand the types of information in supporting details • Apply the skill of identifying supporting details • Use signal words to identify supporting details • Distinguish between major and minor details

CHAPTER 7   **Recognizing Authors' Writing Patterns**   411

CONNECT Reading 2.0 Personalized Learning Plan CORRELATION GUIDE		
Unit	**Topic in PLP**	**Relevant Learning Objectives**
Unit 2: Comprehension	Authors' Writing Patterns	• Understand the skill of identifying organizational patterns • Understand 6 common organizational patterns • Recognize clue words and signals for 6 organizational patterns • Identify the organizational pattern in a paragraph
Unit 2: Comprehension	Sentence Relationships	• Understand the skill of identifying within-sentence relationships • Understand common types of within-sentence relationships and their clue words • Interpret within-sentence relationships • Understand common types of between-sentence relationships and their clue words, and the skill of identifying between-sentence relationships • Interpret between-sentence relationships

CHAPTER 8   **Reading Critically**   513

CONNECT Reading 2.0 Personalized Learning Plan CORRELATION GUIDE		
Unit	**Topic in PLP**	**Relevant Learning Objectives**
Unit 3: Interpreting	Author's Purpose and Intended Audience	• Understand 4 common purposes and the skill of identifying author's purpose • Understand how to identify or reason out the author's purpose • Apply the skill of determining the author's purpose in paragraphs
Unit 3: Interpreting	Intended Purpose and Intended Audience	• Understand 3 types of audiences and the skill of determining author's intended audience • Understand clues to identifying the author's intended audience • Apply the skill of identifying the author's intended audience
Unit 3: Interpreting	Author's Point of View	• Understand the skill of author's point of view • Understand clues that reveal the author's point of view • Identify the author's point of view in passages
Unit 3: Interpreting	Author's Tone and Figurative Language	• Understand the skill of author's tone and clues that reveal it • Understand common types of tone and the words that signal them • Identify the author's tone in passages

CHAPTER 9   **Thinking Critically**   591

CONNECT Reading 2.0 Personalized Learning Plan CORRELATION GUIDE		
Unit	**Topic in PLP**	**Relevant Learning Objectives**
Unit 4: Reading Critically	Fact and Opinion	• Understand fact and opinion • Understand the skill of distinguishing facts from opinions • Identify facts and opinions in paragraphs • Distinguish well-supported opinions from poorly-supported and unsupported opinions
Unit 4: Reading Critically	Inferences and Conclusions	• Understand the skill of making inferences and drawing conclusions • Apply the skill of making inferences • Find the faulty inference • Apply the skill of drawing conclusions • Identify stated conclusions and the words that signal them
Unit 4: Reading Critically	Evaluating an Author's Argument	• Understand the skill of evaluating an author's argument • Understand the process of evaluating an author's argument • Evaluate an author's argument

PART THREE   Systems for Studying Textbooks: *Developing a System That Works for You*   685

CHAPTER 10   **Selecting and Organizing Textbook Information**   687

CONNECT Reading 2.0 Personalized Learning Plan CORRELATION GUIDE		
Unit	**Topic in PLP**	**Relevant Learning Objectives**
Unit 5: Study Techniques	Using Textbooks Effectively	• Understand the skill of using the SQ3R study technique
Unit 5: Study Techniques	Using Textbooks Effectively	• Understand the skill of using textbook features
Unit 5: Study Techniques	Study Skills	• Understand the skill of marking and annotating textbooks • Recognize correctly marked and annotated textbook passages • Mark supporting details in textbooks • Record supporting details in notes
Unit 5: Study Techniques	Study Skills	• Understand the skill of outlining textbook information • Recognize a correct outline of a passage • Understand the skill of mapping • Recognize a correct map of a passage • Understand the skill of summarizing • Recognize a correct summary of a passage • Understand the Cornell note-taking method and its advantages
Unit 5: Study Techniques	Using Textbooks Effectively	• Understand 4 types of graphic aids and how to interpret them • Understand 4 types of visual aids and how to interpret them

Preface

Opening Doors . . .
Moving Students into College-Level Reading

OPENING DOORS PAIRED WITH CONNECT READING 2.0 OFFERS PERSONALIZED LEARNING

Powered by Connect Reading, students gain access to our groundbreaking personalized learning plan, which supports differentiated instruction. With a simple diagnostic test that assesses student proficiencies in five core areas of Vocabulary Skills, Understanding, Interpreting, Reading Critically, and Study Techniques, students' responses generate a self-guided, adaptive plan of contextualized reading lessons, videos, animations, and interactive exercises tailored to their specific needs.

Embedded reading selections across the academic disciplines prepare students for future coursework, and real-world videos and examples bring relevance to the students' work to further engage them and generate in-class discussion. Informed by metacognitive learning theory, the personalized learning plan continually adapts with each student interaction, while built-in time management features make students more productive, keep them on track, and ensure that they progress steadily to achieve course goals.

Built around common national learning objectives and designed to increase student readiness, motivation, and confidence, Connect Reading may be used in conjunction with any course material. This flexible content and format works well in traditional course settings, hybrid and online courses, or redesign models including accelerated courses, supplemental instruction, and emporium/lab-based environments. Instructors may assign individual learning topics in the personalized learning plan for weekly coursework or the holistic personalized learning plan for individualized instruction.

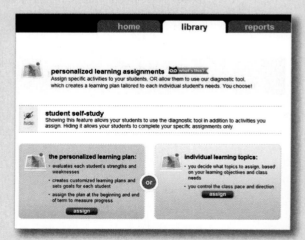

Chapter 14. Learning and the Brain

Your Brain: A User's Manual

Introduction
Building a Better Brain Is Within Every Student's Power
Myths or Facts about the Brain?
Your Brain: A User's Manual
The Truth about Multitasking
Learning and the Brain, Part 1
Learning and the Brain, Part 2
Emotion, Attention, and the Brain
Stress and the Brain
Memory

Additionally, the Connect Reading eBook contains 12 modules on learning and the brain in Chapter 14.

In *Opening Doors,* personalized learning plan icons appear next to the first heading of any chapter with related content.

The detailed table of contents for this book includes Connect Reading 2.0 Personalized Learning Plan Correlation Guides for each chapter. These guides beneath each chapter title provide instructors with a list of units, individual learning topics, and learning objectives in the personalized learning plan that relate directly to content in the chapter.

OPENING DOORS EMPHASIZES PRACTICE

This new edition of *Opening Doors* contains more practice exercises. The new Checkpoint feature allows students to gain experience and practice with skills before they move to the Test Your Understanding sections. Ten new Essential Skills Review Tests (at the back of the book) allow students to apply multiple skills to 3- to 5-paragraph passages.

Extensive and varied exercises accompany every reading selection in *Opening Doors* to prepare students to read the selection and, afterward, give them opportunities to apply comprehension, vocabulary, and study skills.

CHECKPOINT
Locating the Stated Main Idea

Directions: To determine the stated main idea, read each paragraph carefully and then ask yourself, "What is the most important point the author wants me to understand about the topic of this paragraph? (Notice that you are told the topic of each paragraph.) Then select the answer choice that expresses the main idea and write the letter in the space provided.

1. This paragraph comes from a United States government textbook:

One area in which African Americans have made substantial progress since the 1960s is elective office. Although the percentage of black elected officials is still far below the proportion of African Americans in the population, it has risen sharply over recent decades. There are now roughly 600 black mayors and more than 40 black members of Congress. The most stunning advance, of course, was the election of Barack Obama in 2008 as the first African American president.

Source: Adapted from Thomas E. Patterson, *The American Democracy,* Alternate Edition, 10e, p. 137. Copyright © 2011 by The McGraw-Hill Companies, Inc. Reprinted with permission of The McGraw-Hill Companies, Inc.

The topic of this paragraph is *African Americans in elective office.*

What is the stated main idea of this paragraph?
   a. The most stunning advance, of course, was the election of Barack Obama in 2008 as the first African American president.
   b. There are now roughly 600 black mayors and more than 40 black members of Congress.
   c. One area in which African Americans have made substantial progress since the 1960s is elective office.
   d. African Americans are still underrepresented in elective office.

2. This paragraph comes from a wellness textbook:

People often ask, "What makes a good marriage?" Is there a key trait that characterizes a successful marriage? Researchers have identified several patterns in "high-quality," or well-balanced, marriages. Some of these married people tend to focus their energies on joint activities. Their strongest wish is to spend time together, yet they also strike a balance between privacy and togetherness. Other couples focus their energies on being parents and on raising their children. Some dual-career couples, although they spend much of their energy on their individual careers, develop intimacy by sharing what is going on in their work.

Source: Adapted from Marvin R. Levy, Mark Dignan, and Janet H. Shirreffs, *Targeting Wellness: The Core,* p. 122. Copyright © 1992 by The McGraw-Hill Companies, Inc. Reprinted with permission of The McGraw-Hill Companies, Inc.

218

OPENING DOORS EMPHASIZES ENGAGING READINGS

Reading selections were chosen for their excellence, student relevance, and value in helping students expand their knowledge base in a variety of academic subjects and on a variety of contemporary topics. In addition to updating introductions for a number of selections, the following new and updated reading selections include accompanying exercises, quizzes, and activities:

1.1 "Why Go to College?" *(Student Success)*

4.2 "Classes without Walls: Distance Learning" *(Student Success)*

6.2 "Quacks and Quackery" *(Health)*

9.2 "Your Financial Wellness" *(Health)*

9.3 "Our Ecological Footprint: Do We Consume Too Much?" *(Environmental Science)*

---

660   PART **2**   Comprehension

SELECTION 9.2: YOUR FINANCIAL WELLNESS

Wellness is a term that is often used to refer to a person's health, fitness, and lifestyle activities. And there are, indeed, many dimensions of wellness: physical wellness, emotional wellness, intellectual wellness, interpersonal wellness, spiritual wellness, and environmental wellness. But have you ever considered assessing your financial wellness? In this selection from a health textbook, the authors explain the basic elements of financial wellness and discuss how you can become financially "healthy."

1   With the news full of stories of home mortgage foreclosures, credit card debt, and personal bankruptcies, it has become painfully clear that many Americans do not know how to manage their finances. Are such stressful experiences inevitable in today's world? Not at all. You can avoid them—and gain financial peace of mind—by developing the skills that contribute to financial wellness.

2   What exactly is financial wellness? Basically, it means having a healthy relationship with money. It involves such skills as knowing how to manage your money, using self-discipline to live within your means, using credit cards wisely, staying out of debt, meeting your financial obligations, having a long-range financial plan, and saving. It also includes managing your emotional relationship with money and being in charge of your financial decisions. If you haven't developed these skills yet, now is the time to start.

Learn to Budget

3   Although the word "budget" may conjure up thoughts of deprivation, a budget is really just a way of tracking where your money goes and making sure you're spending it on the things that are most important to you. Basic budgeting worksheets are available online, but you can also just use a notebook with lined paper. On one page, list your monthly income by source (for example, job, stipend, or parental aid), and on another, list your expenditures. If you're not sure where you spend your money, track your expenditures for a few weeks or a month. Then organize them into categories, such as housing (rent, utilities), food (groceries, eating out), transportation (car, insurance, parking, public transportation), entertainment

Annotation Practice Exercises

Directions: For each of the exercises below, think critically to answer the questions. This will help you gain additional insights as you read.

Practice Exercise

Do the authors present a statement of *fact* or *opinion* in the last sentence of paragraph 2?

_____

The best way to avoid credit card debt is to have just one card, to use it only when necessary, and to pay off the entire balance every month.

WHAT ELSE IS NEW IN THIS EDITION

In addition to incorporating the Connect Reading personalized learning plan, increasing the number of exercises, and updating the reading selections, *Opening Doors* includes the following enhancements:

- Thirteen new single-paragraph **Embedded Exercises** in Chapters 4 through 9. These excerpts are accompanied by open-ended, respond-in-writing exercises that provide immediate application of the skills presented in each chapter.

- Six new 5-question **Checkpoint** assessments, one each in Chapters 4 through 9. Multiple-choice exercises check students' understanding of the skills presented in each chapter. Because they target specific chapter skills, these easy-to-score activities provide additional practice and helpful feedback to both students and instructors.

- Ten new 10-question **Essential Skills Review Tests** at the end of the book. Each of these multiple-choice tests encompasses the vocabulary skills presented in Chapter 2 and the comprehension and critical reading skills presented in Chapters 4 through 9. This recursive review and/or assessment of essential skills allows students to strengthen and refine their skills, as well as see their progress. Tests can be assigned as homework or supplemental work, or used as collaborative in-class activities.

- Six new 10-question **Test Your Understanding** comprehension exercises, one each in Chapters 4 through 9. These open-ended, respond-in-writing exercises target the skills presented in each chapter. Because these are open-ended, they simulate what students must do when they deal with actual textbooks. They also provide opportunities for students to become more precise in their writing.

- Updated "Read More about This Topic Online" section at the beginning of each reading selection. These suggest key search words to encourage students to discover more about each topic on their own. Also included is an introduction to conducting online searches and evaluating websites.

- New **Reading Skills Competency Chart.** This comprehensive, color-coded chart is conveniently placed at the beginning of the text. It allows instructors and students to quickly locate specific reading, vocabulary, critical thinking skills, and study skills wherever they occur in the book. Specific competencies can be easily accessed for targeted instruction, review, and preparation for standardized or state-mandated tests.

- New **Assignment Sheet and Progress Record.** Located on the inside back cover, this score summary sheet allows students to record their scores and track their progress on the text's assessment exercises, reading selections, and multiple-skills tests.

HALLMARK FEATURES

Designed to help students who read at a precollege level to move into college-level reading, the seventh edition of *Opening Doors: Understanding College Reading* teaches a systematic way of approaching college textbook material. While the scope of this book is broad, the focus is on the most crucial skill for successful college reading: comprehension. Comprehension skills are introduced early in the text and are integrated throughout the subsequent chapters. This enables students not only to learn the skills but also to practice extensively with them.

Although *Opening Doors* is designed for developmental readers, we continue to use primarily college textbook excerpts and other materials of the type students are likely to encounter in their content-area courses. We present selections that not only are interesting and appropriate but also help students expand their knowledge base in a variety of academic subjects and on a variety of topics.

Effective teaching hinges on providing the delicate balance between challenge and support. Some selections may be a slight stretch for students. This is intentional: It provides the opportunity for growth. With coaching and guidance from the instructor, students can comprehend the selections. They appreciate dealing with college-level material; they know it is what they will encounter in their other college courses. This type of practice enables them to transfer skills to other courses and gain the confidence that comes from experience.

The following hallmark features have been retained in the seventh edition:

- Direct instruction and scaffolded approach provide clear explanations and understandable examples.
- Recursive, integrated application of skills provides ample practice.
- Comprehensive coverage of reading for understanding, critical thinking, vocabulary, and study skills is incorporated.
- Numerous **textbook excerpts and longer passages** allow for application of reading and study skills.
- **Chapter Review Card** activity following each chapter provides a structured review of the essential concepts presented.
- The **Test Your Understanding** exercises appear in Chapters 4 through 9. These multiple-choice and open-ended exercises provide immediate feedback on students' understanding of chapter concepts. Students can check their comprehension immediately after completing the chapter and before starting the reading selections.
- Thorough treatment of **authors' writing patterns** is provided, including *list pattern* (division/classification), *sequence/time order pattern* (process), *definition pattern* (definition-example), *comparison-contrast pattern* (ideas in opposition), *cause-effect pattern,* and *spatial order pattern* (place order).
- Thorough treatment is given to **other writing patterns.** Many standardized tests, such as state-mandated ones and course exit tests, include patterns beyond the basic ones; the patterns now addressed are the *addition pattern,* the *generalization and example pattern,* the *statement and clarification pattern,*

the *summary pattern*, and the *mixed pattern*. Patterns beyond the basic ones are introduced in a separate section giving instructors flexibility as to whether they use them and to what extent. Awareness of writing patterns also enhances students' own writing.

- Thorough treatment is given to **relationships within and between sentences,** including *clarification, example, addition, sequence, comparison-contrast, cause-effect, problem-solution, spatial order, summary/conclusion,* and *concession.*

- **Twenty-seven full-length reading selections** are included (3 in each of the first nine chapters)

- **Reading Selection Quizzes** are included for the 27 reading selections in Chapters 1 through 9.

  These 25-question quizzes contain three parts:

  Comprehension
  Ten questions much like those that a content-area instructor (such as a psychology professor) would expect students to be able to answer after reading the selection.

  Vocabulary in Context
  Ten questions that test students' ability to determine the meaning of a word by using context clues.

  Reading Skills Application
  Five questions that test the ability to apply certain reading skills to the material in the selection. These are the types of questions that appear on standardized reading tests, exit tests, and state-mandated basic skills tests.

- Annotation Practice Exercises and Respond-in-Writing Exercises that accompany each reading selection integrate writing and reading by calling for written responses and the formulation of the selection's overall main idea. Respond in Writing Exercises include collaborative options.

- Thorough treatment of the SQ3R Study System and an enhanced section on the Three-Step Process for Reading and Studying Textbooks are included. SQ3R, a familiar, long-standing study system, is introduced in Chapter 3; this is followed by an in-depth presentation of an effective three-step process in Chapter 10. This comprehensive approach provides effective, step-by-step procedures for approaching college textbook reading assignments (Chapters 3 and 10) and preparing for tests (Chapter 11).

- Thorough treatment of Interpreting Graphs and Visual Aids is offered in Chapter 10. Coverage of this topic is now more comprehensive, which is especially important since more people today get news and information from the Internet and increasingly in graphic form. Younger college students in particular get their information this way and need help in interpreting and evaluating it.

- A chapter-length Reading Selection (in Chapter 10) includes annotation, outlining, mapping, and note-taking exercises.

- Vocabulary and study skills are presented as they relate to learning from college textbooks and other college-level materials.
- Coverage of all skills typically included on state-mandated reading competency tests, as well as tips for scoring well on standardized reading tests, is provided.
- Consistency in philosophy and approach with *New Worlds* and *Exercise Your College Reading Skills,* other reading improvement textbooks in the Elder/Cortina series, is maintained.

SUPPLEMENTS TO *OPENING DOORS*

Annotated Instructor's Edition (AIE)

The AIE contains the full text of the student edition of the book with answers as well as an Instructor's Guide at the front, marginal Teaching Tips, Timely Words, and relevant quotations.

Downloadable Instructor Supplements

A revised **Online Learning Center** contains a list of readings organized thematically and correlated with Connect Reading eBook readings, updated PowerPoints for each chapter, an updated instructor test bank with chapter quizzes, and the following **Supplemental Reading Selections** with questions that may be assigned as extra practice exercises or used as tests:

"America's Most Popular Drug: Caffeine"
From *Having Our Say: The Delany Sisters' First 100 Years*
"Latinos: An Emerging Influence in the United States"
"The Decision to Marry"
"Diabetes"
"Cultural Diversity: Family Strengths and Challenges" (chapter-length reading selection)

Full-Length Textbook Chapters and Pedagogy to Customize *Opening Doors*

With **McGraw-Hill Create™**, you can easily arrange your book to align with your syllabus, eliminate chapters you do not assign, integrate material from other content sources, and quickly upload content you have written, such as your course syllabus or teaching notes, to enhance the value of course materials for your students.

Through **Create™ ExpressBooks**, you may choose from the following seven author-selected, full-length textbook chapters from career-oriented disciplines to customize this text. You may also choose to incorporate any of the three supporting pieces of pedagogy for each chapter: Introduction, Post-Selection Apparatus, and Practice Quiz.

	Textbook/Edition/Author/Copyright/Content Area	Chapter Number and Title	No. of pages
#1	**Choosing Success in Community College and Beyond,** 1st Ed., 2012 by Rhonda Atkinson and Debbie Longman *(Student Success)*	Ch 12: "Exploring Career Options and Opportunities," pp. 276–95	20
#2	**Business and Administrative Communication,** 10th Ed., 2013 by Kitty Locker and Donna Kienzler *(Business)*	Ch 1: "Succeeding in Business Communication," pp. 2–24	23
#3	**Emergency Medical Technician,** 2nd Ed., 2011 by Barbara Aehlert *(Allied Health)*	Ch 16: "Scene Size-Up," pp. 310–23	14
#4	**Computing Essentials 2013: Making IT Work for You,** Introductory Ed. by Timothy O'Leary and Linda O'Leary *(Information Technology)*	Ch 1: "Information Technology, the Internet, and You," pp. 2–28	27
#5	**Think Criminology,** 1st Ed., 2012 by John Fuller *(Criminology)*	Ch 1: "Thinking Critically about Crime," pp. 2–15	14
#6	**Think: Critical Thinking and Logic Skills for Everyday Life,** 2nd Ed., 2012 by Judith Boss *(Critical Thinking)*	Ch 10: "Marketing & Advertising," pp. 308–37	30
#7	**Connect Core Concepts in Health,** 12th Ed., Brief, 2012 by Paul Insel and Walton Roth *(Health)*	Ch 15: "Conventional and Complementary Medicine," pp. 362–83	22

McGraw-Hill Create™ ExpressBooks facilitate customizing your book more quickly and easily. To quickly view the possibilities for customizing your book, visit www.mcgrawhillcreate.com and enter "Opening Doors" under the Find Content tab. Once you select the current edition of this book, click on the "View Related ExpressBooks" button or ExpressBooks tab to see options. ExpressBooks contain a combination of pre-selected chapters and readings that serve as a starting point to help you quickly and easily build your own text.

Go to www.mcgrawhillcreate.com and register today!

ACKNOWLEDGMENTS

The quality of *Opening Doors* is a testament to the skills and abilities of so many people. We are grateful to the following reviewers for their insightful suggestions for this edition:

Sandra Brady, St. Louis Community College at Meramec
Rhonda Carroll, Pulaski Technical College
Lisa R. Mizes, St. Louis Community College at Meramec
Christine Padberg, St. Louis Community College at Meramec
Carolyn E. Rubin-Trimble, University of Houston, Downtown
Marion Ruminski, Belmont College
Lori Eggers Saxby, University of Southern Indiana

Alan Shuttleworth, Sierra College

Deborah Spradlin, Tyler Junior College

Karen Taylor, Belmont Technical College

Melanie Ward, Tyler Junior College

Christine Wittmer-Moore, University of Southern Indiana

We wish you success in using *Opening Doors* to prepare your students to read textbooks effectively and to be more successful in college. We hope the endeavor will be enjoyable and rewarding for both you and your students.

A new edition of any textbook is the result of the efforts of many talented individuals, and we are fortunate to have worked with so many uniquely skilled and dedicated people. We are grateful to our new editor, Executive Brand Manager Kelly Villella-Canton, who deftly picked up the reins mid-project and applied her considerable energy, insight, and technological savvy to the enterprise. We thank Dawn Groundwater, Senior Director of Development, for graciously stepping in during the interim between editors. Also instrumental in the early stages was Development Editor Anne Leung, who helped get the project off to a successful start. Nor could we have asked for a more competent, congenial, and astute production team than Senior Production Editor Carey Eisner and Full Service Production Manager Melanie Field. From start to finish, working with them was a joy. We also thank copy editor Thomas Briggs for braving the many complex changes to this new edition. The efforts of Senior Designer Matt Diamond and Cover/Interior Designer Laurie Entringer are reflected in the pleasing new design and format of this edition of *Opening Doors*. In addition, we greatly appreciate the contributions of Text Permissions Editor Lori Church, Content Licensing Specialist Jeremy Cheshareck, photo researcher par excellence Ira Roberts, Marketing Manager Jaclyn Elkins, and Editorial Coordinator Dana Wan, who cheerfully handled various matters along the way. And, as ever, we are grateful to our longtime McGraw-Hill friend, the multi-talented Paul Banks, Director of Developmental English.

Janet Elder
Joe Cortina

Orientation

*Preparing and Organizing Yourself
for Success in College*

CHAPTERS IN PART ONE

1

Making Yourself Successful in College

In this chapter, you will learn the answers to these questions:

- What do successful college students do?
- How can I motivate myself to do well in college?
- How can I set goals for myself?
- How do I prefer to learn?
- How can I manage my time more effectively?

SKILLS

Doing What Successful Students Do

Motivating Yourself

Setting Your Goals

Identifying How You Prefer to Learn

Managing Your Time

- Setting Up a Weekly Study Schedule
- Making the Most of Your Study Time
- Planning Further Ahead: Creating a Monthly Assignment Calendar and Using a Daily To Do List

CREATING YOUR SUMMARY

Developing Chapter Review Cards

READINGS

Education is our passport to the future, for tomorrow belongs to the people who prepare for it today.

Malcolm X

Keeping up is always easier than catching up.

(Unknown)

Bumper sticker: "Aggressive learners hit the books."

I can accept failure, but I can't accept not trying.

Michael Jordan

Many of life's failures are people who did not realize how close they were to success when they gave up.

Thomas Edison

DOING WHAT SUCCESSFUL STUDENTS DO

Some students are more successful than others. Why? One reason is that successful students know how to motivate themselves, set goals for themselves, and manage their time. They also have identified their learning style, the way they learn best. In this chapter, you will learn how to do these things. If you start now and consistently apply the techniques and strategies in this chapter, you will become a more successful college student. Getting off to a good start is important because, as the proverb says, "Well begun is half done." This is just a way of saying that a good beginning goes a long way toward your ultimate success.

Moreover, the Greek philosopher Aristotle observed, "We are what we repeatedly do. Excellence then is not an act, but a habit." This is valuable advice. If you make good study techniques and time management a habit, you can become a better, more effective student each semester.

It is helpful to look at exactly what successful students do. One especially interesting research study involved college students who were highly effective *despite the fact that they did not have high entrance scores.* In other words, anyone looking at these students' test scores would not have predicted that they would do well in college. Researchers learned that these students all identified and shared five important characteristics:

1. **Effective students are highly motivated.** Successful students have an inner drive to do well. They are goal-oriented; they have specific careers in mind. They believe that they are responsible for their own success or failure; they attribute nothing to "good luck" or "bad luck."

2. **Effective students plan ahead.** Successful students are organized. They develop good study habits. They establish a study schedule and stick to it. They study at the same time each day, and in the same place.

3. **Effective students focus on understanding.** Successful students use instructors' oral and written feedback to monitor their progress and make necessary

changes. They assess their strengths and weaknesses on the basis of instructors' comments in class, evaluations of homework assignments, and test grades. If they start to do poorly or fall behind, they spend more time on it, and they immediately seek help from an instructor, a tutor, or a friend. Moreover, they know how they learn best, and they use study techniques that capitalize on their learning style.

4. **Effective students are highly selective.**   Successful students concentrate on main ideas and important supporting details when they read. They pay attention to how paragraphs are organized and to signals and clue words. They do not try to memorize everything. They use instructors' suggestions, course outlines, textbook features, and class lectures to help them identify important information.

5. **Effective students are involved and attentive.**   Successful students focus on their academic work in class and outside of class. In class, they pay attention, take notes, and participate in discussions. They arrive early, and they sit near the front. Outside of class, they study in appropriate, distraction-free places. They put academic work ahead of social life, and they limit time spent watching television, playing video and computer games, and surfing the Internet. They find a "study buddy" or join a study group so that they can study with others who are serious about school. They take advantage of their college's tutoring center and other resources. They concentrate on the present rather than worrying about the past or daydreaming too much about the future.

Source: Adapted from John Q. Easton, Don Barshis, and Rick Ginsberg, "Chicago Colleges Identify Effective Teachers, Students," *Community and Junior College Journal,* December–January 1983–1984, pp. 27–31.

Notice that with planning and determination, any student can make these behaviors part of his or her own life in college. There is nothing that is especially complicated or difficult about them.

Another, more recent study also looked at students who had low high school grades and low college entrance exam scores. Although these students were not expected to do well in college, half of them achieved a relatively high college grade point average (GPA). The rest were on scholastic probation after several semesters. Researchers wanted to know, What was the difference between those who succeeded and those who did not?

Careful interviews with all the students revealed these characteristics of the successful students:

1. They attend and participate in class.
2. They are prepared for class.
3. They perceive instructors as experts.
4. They adhere to an organized study routine.
5. They develop a repertoire of study skills and strategies.
6. They take responsibility for their own learning.

Sounds familiar, doesn't it? The findings are strikingly similar to those of the earlier study. The unsuccessful students "readily admitted that they did not engage in these behaviors and explained that their social lives held higher priority." Clearly, practicing these obvious "success behaviors" and making your college education a priority can make you more successful too.

Source: JoAnn Yaworski, Rose-Marie Weber, and Nabil Ibrahim, "What Makes Students Succeed or Fail? The Voices of Developmental College Students," *Journal of College Reading and Learning,* vol. 30, no. 2 (Spring 2000), pp. 195–221.

MOTIVATING YOURSELF

In college, you are responsible for motivating yourself. Developing an interest in and a commitment to your studies is not your instructors' responsibility; it is yours. Developing the discipline and commitment to make yourself successful is not your parents' responsibility; it is yours. If you assume the responsibility, then you can feel justifiably proud when you succeed, because the credit goes to you. The truly valuable and worthwhile things in life are seldom easy, but that is part of what gives them value.

Fortunately, motivating yourself is easier than you think. For one thing, college is a stimulating place to be! As you progress through college, you will find how pleasurable and satisfying learning can be. Also, there are specific, effective self-motivation techniques you can use. Here are a dozen to help you get motivated and stay motivated throughout the semester:

1. **Write down your educational goals for the semester.** Writing out semester goals can be motivating in and of itself. Clear goals can also motivate you to use your time well. Specific goals for class attendance and participation, home-work, and grades help you select activities that move you toward your goals. In addition, achieving any worthwhile goal is deeply satisfying and will motivate you to achieve more goals. (Goal-setting is discussed on pages 9–11.)

2. **Visualize your success.** Visualize outcomes that you want to make happen, such as earning a high grade on an assignment or completing the semester successfully. Then visualize the future further ahead: Imagine yourself in a cap and gown being handed your college diploma; imagine an employer offering you the job you've dreamed of. Make your mental images as sharp and vivid as possible. Imagine the feelings as well, such as the happiness and pride you will feel in your accomplishment.

3. **Think of classes as your easiest learning sessions.** If you spend three hours a week in class for a course, view those hours as your *easiest* hours of learning and studying for the course. Remind yourself of this when you feel frustrated by a course or when you are tempted to skip class. Your instructor, who is an expert, is there to explain and to answer questions. Adopting this perspective can make a big difference.

4. **View your courses as opportunities.** If a course is difficult, approach it as a challenge rather than a problem or an obstacle. The brain grows only when it is challenged. Accept the fact that you are required to take a variety of courses to broaden your educational background. Later in life, you will most likely come

Simply doing the things that successful students do can enable you to succeed in college.

to appreciate these courses more than you can now. Taking the "long view" can be motivating.

5. **Develop emotional strategies for dealing with difficult courses.** To keep from feeling overwhelmed, focus on the material you are studying rather than worrying about what is coming next. Consider the feelings of accomplishment and pride that will come from succeeding at a challenging subject. Realize, too, that you can enjoy a subject even if you never make a top grade in it.

6. **Seek advice and study tips from good students in your courses.** Ask them what they do to be successful. If they like a subject that seems difficult or boring to you, ask them why they enjoy it. Ask them how they approach assignments and prepare for tests.

7. **Choose the right friends.** "Right" friends means friends who support and encourage your class participation and studying. Find a study buddy or form a small study group with others who are serious about college. It is also helpful to find a mentor (a wise and trusted counselor or instructor) who can give you advice, support, and encouragement.

8. **Divide big projects into smaller parts.** To motivate yourself, break large projects into manageable tasks. For instance, a 20-page reading assignment can be divided into shorter readings of 5 pages each, which you could read during short study sessions on two different days.

9. **Give yourself rewards.** Reward yourself for successfully completing a challenging homework assignment or studying for a test. For example, have a healthy snack or take a short walk.

10. **Make positive self-talk a habit.**   Say encouraging things to yourself, such as "I can do this assignment, even though it might take a while" and "If other students can do this, I can too." Over time, this actually changes your beliefs. Also, use a technique called *thought stopping* to shut off negative self-talk, such as "I'll never learn this!" or "This test is impossible." When you realize you are giving yourself negative feedback, just say "Stop!" and substitute some *positive* self-talk. Don't let frustration overcome you and destroy your productivity. Recognizing that frustration is a normal part of learning (and life) will help you develop tolerance for it.

11. **Feel satisfied if you have done your best.**   If you truly do your best, you can feel satisfied, regardless of the outcome. You will never have to wonder whether you could have done better if only you had tried harder. This means you will have no regrets.

12. **Remind yourself that motivation and success reinforce each other.**   Motivation and success go hand in hand. Motivation leads to success; success increases motivation; increased motivation leads to more success; and so on! Celebrate each small success, and use it as a springboard to even greater success.

From this list, pick at least two strategies that are new to you that you think would work for you. Add them to your short-term goals list, and then use them throughout the semester to sustain your motivation.

Some students who are having a difficult time in a subject mistakenly believe the subject is easy for those who are doing well in it. They do not realize that those students are successful *because* they are working very hard. Some students who struggle in a course tell themselves they just don't have the ability to do well, so there is no reason to try. Of course, the way you become better at a subject is by working at it. Thinking that a subject is easy for everyone else or that you simply don't have the ability is just an excuse for not trying. Don't fall into this self-defeating trap.

SETTING YOUR GOALS

Most successful students (in fact, most successful people) establish goals, and they put them *in writing*. They write down *what they want to accomplish* and the *length of time* in which they plan to accomplish it. Putting your goals in writing is a simple, but powerful technique to help you turn wishes into reality.

There are several reasons you should write your goals. First, unwritten goals are not much better than wishes ("I wish I had a college degree"; "I wish I had a career I enjoyed"), and they will probably remain just wishes. Second, writing your goals helps you make a commitment to them. If a goal is not important enough to write down, how likely do you think you are to accomplish it? Third, writing out your goals gives you a written record you can use to measure your progress. Finally, you don't want to look back and feel regret about things you might have done or accomplished but didn't. When your life is over, what do you want to be remembered for?

Surely that is important enough to write down. Another way to think about goals is to ask yourself what you *don't* want to be doing a year from now, several years from now, or several decades from now.

You will find it helpful to put your goals into categories, such as educational, financial, spiritual, personal (including family matters), physical (health and fitness), and career. An educational goal might be "To complete my courses this semester with at least a B in each"; a financial goal might be "To save enough money next year to make a down payment on a car."

Sometimes you must choose between two or more competing goals, such as attending college full time and working full time. You would have to give up the second goal to have enough time for studying. Or you could modify both goals, deciding to do both part time. Competing goals do not always require giving up a goal, but they do require being realistic, setting priorities, and adjusting your time.

A famous expert in time management, Alan Lakein, gives these recommendations for setting goals:

- **Be specific.**   An example of a specific goal is "I will exercise for 30 minutes five days a week for the next three months." A vague, unhelpful goal is "I will get more exercise."
- **Be realistic.**   "I will exercise for 30 minutes five days a week" is also an example of a realistic goal. An unrealistic goal would be "I will exercise two hours a day for the rest of the year." Unrealistic goals are not helpful, and they can be frustrating and discouraging.
- **Revise your goals at regular intervals.**   People change, and so do their situations and priorities. Therefore, it is important to review your goals regularly and revise them as needed.

Source: Alan Lakein, *How to Get Control of Your Time and Your Life* (New York: Signet, 1973), pp. 30–37, 64–65.

long-term goal

Goal you want to accomplish during your lifetime.

intermediate goal

Goal you want to accomplish within the next 3 to 5 years.

short-term goal

Goal you want to accomplish within 3 to 6 months.

Lakein also recommends grouping goals based on the amount of time required to accomplish or achieve them. **Long-term goals** are ones you want to accomplish during your lifetime; **intermediate goals** are ones you want to achieve within the next three to five years; **short-term goals** are ones you want to accomplish within three to six months. (As a student, you may find it helpful to think of short-term goals as ones you want to accomplish during the semester.) Your short-term goals should help you achieve your intermediate goals, which in turn should help you achieve your long-term goals. For instance, improving your reading skills is a short-term goal that contributes to the intermediate goal of earning a college degree, and ultimately to the long-term goal of a successful career. Of course, some goals will fall between half a year and three years. Regardless of the precise length of time, it's still helpful to think in terms of long-term, intermediate, and short-term goals.

In the following box, record some of your long-term, intermediate, and short-term goals. Keep your goals where you can see and read them: at the front of a notebook, for instance, or on your desk. Some goals will be achieved quickly and removed from your list, but others will remain on it for a long time, perhaps even a lifetime.

PUTTING YOUR GOALS IN WRITING

Take a few minutes to write down at least three goals for each category. (Goals are personal and private, and they do not have to be shared with anyone.)

What are three long-term goals you want to accomplish and achieve during your lifetime?

1. *Get my graduate-level Certificate in pharmacy*
2. *Pass my board and get a stable job*
3. *Be happy and make my family happy*

What are three intermediate goals you want to accomplish during the next 3 to 5 years?

1. *Work on my credit to get good credit*
2. *To achieve good grades in my courses*
3. _____

What are three short-term goals you want to accomplish this semester?

1. _____
2. _____
3. _____

IDENTIFYING HOW YOU PREFER TO LEARN

In addition to managing your study time and setting goals, you need to identify the way you prefer to learn. To gain insight into this, complete the inventory below. Total your responses before reading the rest of this section.

HOW DO YOU PREFER TO LEARN?

To gain insight into how you prefer to learn, answer the following questions. For each item, circle all the answers that describe you.

1. When I go someplace I have not been before, I usually

   A.   trust my intuition about the right direction or route to take.

   B.   ask someone for directions.

   C.   look at a map.

2. I like to go to places where

   A.   there is lots of space to move around.

   B.   people are talking or there is music that matches my mood.

   C.   there is good "people watching" or there is something interesting to see.

(continued on next page)

(continued from previous page)

3. If I have lots of things to do, I generally

A. feel nervous or fidgety until I get most of them done.

B. repeat things to myself so I won't forget to do them.

C. jot them down on a list or write them on a calendar or organizer.

4. When I have free time, I like to

A. work on a handicraft or hobby, or do an activity such as play a sport or exercise.

B. listen to a tape, a CD, or the radio, or talk on the phone.

C. watch television, play a computer or video game, or see a movie.

5. When I am talking with other people, I typically

A. pay attention to their gestures or move close to them so I can get a feel for what they are telling me.

B. listen carefully so I can hear what they are saying.

C. watch them closely so that I can see what they are saying.

6. When I meet someone new, I usually pay most attention to

A. the way the person walks or moves, or the gestures the person makes.

B. the way the person speaks, what the person says, and how his or her voice sounds.

C. the way the person looks and is dressed.

7. When I select books, magazines, or articles to read, I generally choose ones that

A. deal with sports or fitness, hobbies and crafts, or other activities.

B. tell me about something that happened or tell a story.

C. include lots of photos, pictures, or illustrations.

8. Learning something is easier for me when I can

A. use a hands-on approach.

B. have someone explain it to me.

C. watch someone show me how to do it.

Total up your A's, then total up your B's, and your C's.

_____ A's _____ B's _____ C's

If your highest total is A's, you are a tactile *or* kinesthetic *learner.*

If your highest total is B's, you are an auditory *learner.*

If your highest total is C's, you are a visual *learner.*

---

learning preference

The modality through which an individual learns best.

visual learner

One who prefers to see or read information to be learned.

auditory learner

One who prefers to hear information to be learned.

Learning preference refers to the modality through which an individual prefers to learn because learning is easier and more efficient that way.

Three primary modalities for learning are seeing (visual modality), hearing (auditory modality), and touch (tactile modality) or movement (kinesthetic modality). **Visual learners** prefer to see or read the material and benefit from books, class notes, concept maps, review cards, test review sheets, and the like. **Auditory learners** prefer to hear the material in the form of lectures and discussions. They benefit from reciting material or reading aloud to themselves and participating in

tactile or kinesthetic learner

One who prefers to touch and manipulate materials physically or to incorporate movement when learning.

study groups. **Tactile learners** benefit from touching and manipulating materials, while **kinesthetic learners** benefit from physical movement. Tactile learners prefer laboratory work and other hands-on projects. Kinesthetic learners like to "go through the motions" of doing something; even writing things down can be helpful. (The three basic learning preferences are summarized in the box below.)

Of course, people learn in more than one way, and most use some combination. And even though most people use one modality more heavily, how they learn can change as they acquire more practice in using other modalities.

Did your results on the learning preference survey surprise you, or did they simply confirm what you already knew about how you like to learn? If you know your learning preference, you can put yourself in situations in which you learn best; you can utilize study techniques and strategies that take advantage of your strengths. Moreover, when material is presented in a way that does not match the way you like to learn, you can take steps to work around the problem by studying the material the way *you* learn best.

There is one other aspect of learning you should think about: whether you prefer to work by yourself or with others. If you prefer studying alone, make it a priority to find a place where you will not be disturbed. Self-paced courses, computer-assisted instruction, telecourses, or other online or distance-learning options may work well for you. On the other hand, if you find it advantageous to study with others, join a study group or work with a study partner. When selecting study partners, choose classmates who are serious and motivated. Also, keep in mind that participating in a study group does not guarantee success. You must prepare yourself to work with a group by reading and studying on your own first.

THREE LEARNING PREFERENCES

If This Is Your Learning Preference . . .	Then These Activities Are the Most Helpful to Your Learning
Visual learner (prefers to read or see information)	Reading textbooks and seeing information in print Reviewing class notes and concept maps Reading chapter review cards Studying test review sheets
Auditory learner (prefers to hear information)	Listening to class lectures and discussions Reciting material (saying it out loud) Reading aloud to yourself Listening to audiotapes Participating in study groups
Tactile or kinesthetic learner (prefers to manipulate materials physically or incorporate movement)	Taking notes from lectures and from textbooks Making concept maps Rewriting lecture notes after class Preparing study cards Doing laboratory work (computer labs, science labs, etc.) Actually going through steps or procedures in a process Taking hands-on classes (science, computer science, engineering, and other technical or vocational subjects)

MANAGING YOUR TIME

Time, like money, is valuable, and, like money, it should be spent wisely. Managing your time means making good decisions about how you spend your time. The numbers in the box below reveal how much decision making is necessary in order to manage your time.

HOW DO YOU CHOOSE TO SPEND YOUR TIME?

- There are 168 hours in a week.
- If you sleep 8 hours a night, you spend 56 hours a week sleeping.
- If you spend 1 hour at each meal, you spend 21 hours a week eating.
- If you have a full college schedule, you spend about 12 to 20 hours a week attending classes and labs.

This leaves you about 70 hours a week, or 10 hours a day, for everything else: studying, work, recreation, personal chores, and so on.
For at least 10 out of every 24 hours, you must make decisions about how you will spend your time.

Fortunately, there are strategies that you can use to manage your time. In this section, you'll learn how to set up a weekly study schedule and make the most of your study sessions. You'll also look at two other important planning tools: a monthly calendar and a daily To Do list.

Setting Up a Weekly Study Schedule

study schedule

Weekly schedule with specific times set aside for studying.

If you tell yourself you will study "whenever you find time," you may never "find time," or at least not *enough* time. To be effective, you must set aside time specifically for studying. A weekly **study schedule** is just what it sounds like: a weekly schedule with specific times set aside for studying. A realistic, well-thought-out weekly schedule assures you of ample study time.

Most college students cite too much to do in too little time as their number one source of stress. Scheduling your time can reduce stress, tension, worry, and inefficiency. A realistic schedule lets you make the best use of your time because it frees you from constant decision making—and indecision!

It's important to balance study time and leisure time, but here's the rule successful students go by: Study first; then relax or have fun. If you stick to this rule, you will have more free time, and you will genuinely enjoy that free time because you won't feel guilty about unfinished work.

To create a weekly study schedule, use the planning form on page 17 and follow these steps:

- **Step 1: Identify times that are already committed to other activities** (such as classes, meals, and work) since those times are not available for study. Write them in the appropriate places on the schedule (type them in if you keep your schedule on your computer, smart phone, or PDA).

- **Step 2: Identify other times when you probably would not be able to study** (for example, times devoted to household and personal chores, family, and leisure activities). Post these on your schedule. These are more flexible since you have more control over when you do many of them.

- **Step 3: Identify the best general times to study.**   On the list below, circle the time periods when you are most alert and energetic:

  Early morning (6–9 A.M.)

  Midmorning (9 A.M. to noon)

  Early afternoon (12–3 P.M.)

  Late afternoon (3–6 P.M.)

  Early evening (6–9 P.M.)

  Late evening (9 P.M. to midnight)

  Late night (after midnight)

  You will accomplish more in less time if you study during daylight hours and when you are alert and rested. Schedule as much studying as possible, however, during the hours you identified as *your* best times.

- **Step 4: Determine how much study time you need.**   Allow a *minimum* of one hour of study time for each hour spent in class. (For a typical three-credit course, that means a minimum of three hours of study time per week; difficult courses will require more time. Allow more study time if you are a slow reader or have not yet developed efficient study skills.) Set aside an appropriate number of study hours for each course; it is better to overestimate than to underestimate. College students are expected to be much more independent in their learning than high school students, and many new college students are surprised at how much time studying takes. To be safe, plan as much study time as you think you might need.

- **Step 5: From the times still available, select the specific times you will study, and mark them on your schedule.**   Be specific about what you intend to study at each time (such as "Study psychology" or "Computer science homework" rather than "study"). You may want to highlight the times you plan to study. The schedule on page 16 shows you how a completed study schedule might look.

When you have created your schedule, keep it where you can see it—*then follow it*. Allow three weeks to become accustomed to it because it takes that long to establish a new habit or break an old one. Don't get discouraged if using a schedule feels awkward at first. That's normal.

If your work schedule changes weekly or if other activity times vary, you should update your schedule weekly. Successful students generally feel great satisfaction from organizing their time. As you gain experience in managing your time, it will become easier to "find" enough study time.

SAMPLE WEEKLY STUDY SCHEDULE

Here is a sample of a weekly study schedule that has been completed according to the directions on pages 14–15. Notice that *specific study times have been identified for each course*. Use the blank form on page 17 to create your own weekly study schedule.

Time	Sunday	Monday	Tuesday	Wednesday	Thursday	Friday	Saturday
6:00 A.M.				Get ready for school			
7:00				Travel to school			
8:00		Computer Science	Read English	Computer Science	Review English	Computer Science	Workout
9:00		History	English	History	English	History	Tennis
10:00	Family time	Sociology		Sociology		Sociology	
11:00		Lunch	Biology	Lunch	Biology	Lunch	
12:00 noon		Computer Science homework		Computer Science homework	Biology	Computer Science homework	Work
1:00 P.M.		English assignment	Lunch	English assignment	Lunch	English assignment	
2:00	Workout	Study biology	Biology lab		Biology study group	Snack	
3:00	Tennis			Study biology	study group		
4:00		Dinner		Dinner	Workout	Work	
5:00		Work	Read history text	Work	Read history text	Work	Spend time with friends
6:00	Read biology assignment		Dinner				
7:00					Dinner		
8:00	English assignment		Read sociology text		Read sociology text		
9:00							
10:00	Sleep	Relax/watch TV	Relax/go online	Relax/video games	Relax/TV	Go out	
11:00		Sleep	Sleep	Sleep	Sleep	Sleep	
12:00 midnight							Sleep
1:00 A.M.							

WEEKLY STUDY SCHEDULE

Time	Sunday	Monday	Tuesday	Wednesday	Thursday	Friday	Saturday
6:00 A.M.							
7:00							
8:00							
9:00							
10:00							
11:00							
12:00 noon							
1:00 P.M.							
2:00							
3:00							
4:00							
5:00							
6:00							
7:00							
8:00							
9:00							
10:00							
11:00							
12:00 midnight							
1:00 A.M.							

Remember: Adjust your weekly schedule if you need to, but then make every effort to stick to it. Each time you deviate from your schedule, returning to it becomes harder. Following a schedule gets you past one big obstacle to studying: simply getting started. Using a study schedule is one key to becoming a more effective, successful student.

Making the Most of Your Study Time

Once you have set up a weekly study schedule, you need to make your study time as productive as possible. Try these proven techniques:

1. **Find or create a suitable place to study.**   It can be at home, in the library, or in another quiet place on campus. Have at hand any materials and supplies you will need. *Use your study place* only *for studying.* This reinforces the message that when you are in your study place, you are there to study!

2. **Study in the same place at the same time every day.**   This helps you get into studying immediately. It makes studying automatic, a habit. Knowing when, where, and what you are going to study keeps you from indecision and procrastination.

3. **Make your study sessions more productive, not longer.**   Strive for one or two productive study hours rather than three or four unproductive hours. To be productive, you must stay focused. Sitting at a desk is not studying, and looking at a book is not reading. If you find yourself daydreaming, stop and refocus. If you begin to tire and lose focus, take a five-minute break or switch to another subject. Be sure, however, to take your break at a logical stopping point—not in the middle of a task that is going well. Stand up or stretch at least every half hour while you are studying. Drink a glass of water.

4. **Study as soon as possible after lecture classes.**   One hour spent studying immediately or soon after class develops your understanding and recall of the material as much as several hours of studying would a few days later. Review and tweak your lecture notes while they are still fresh in mind. Start assignments while your understanding of the material is still accurate. Take steps immediately to clear up points you do not understand. Look up unknown words, make a note to ask about something that confused you, and so on.

5. **Take advantage of short periods of free time for studying.**   Students often waste brief periods of time (for instance, 15 to 45 minutes before, between, and after classes). Instead, use them to study or review. Before a lecture class begins, spend a few minutes reviewing your notes from the previous lecture or the reading assignment. When you look for short periods of free time to use, keep in mind that (in general) daytime study is more efficient than nighttime study.

6. **Don't try to study your most difficult subject last.**   It is tempting to focus on your favorite subjects first and leave the harder subjects until last. But if you do this, you may run out of time or be too tired to be effective. Study difficult subjects while you still have the time and energy to do a good job on them.

7. **If you can't study at your scheduled time, take time from another nonstudy activity.**   When unexpected events take time scheduled for studying, decide immediately when you can make up the study time, and make a temporary adjustment in your schedule. Don't overlook weekends. Use part of them for productive, unhurried study times.

8. **Experiment to develop study strategies and techniques that work for you.**   Try techniques that capitalize on your learning preferences and make learning easier. Be creative. If you get sleepy when you read your textbooks, walk back and forth as you read. Try reading out loud or taking notes. Try reviewing your week's class notes and textbook markings to help you learn and remember the material. Study hard for 45 minutes, then take a 15-minute break. The key is to discover what works for you.

9. **Don't let friends, the phone, computer, television, or other media interfere with study time.**   Students say over and over again that along with working too many hours, these are the main reasons they do not get their studying done. Every time you interrupt your study session, you make it longer and less effective. Honor your commitment to your study time.

10. **Improve your concentration.**   Deal immediately with any external and internal distractions. To deal with external distractors in your environment, you may need to find a place that is quieter or has better light, adjust the room temperature, and so on. To deal with internal (emotional) distractors, you need strategies to reduce worrying and daydreaming. The last section of the box on page 72 in Chapter 2 describes some techniques. Your instructor or a counselor can give you additional suggestions.

Planning Further Ahead: Creating a Monthly Assignment Calendar and Using a Daily To Do List

monthly assignment calendar

Calendar showing test dates and due dates in all courses for each month of a semester.

To Do list

Prioritized list of items to be accomplished in a single day.

Two useful tools for planning ahead are a monthly assignment calendar and a daily To Do list. A **monthly assignment calendar** shows test dates and due dates in *all* your courses for each month of the semester. This helps you plan ahead, meet each deadline, produce better work, feel more in control, experience less stress, and enjoy the semester more!

As you receive syllabi for your courses, transfer all the test dates and due dates (for projects, papers, oral reports, etc.) to *one* calendar. When a test or due date is announced, add it to your calendar. If several due dates coincide in one week, plan to finish some of the projects ahead of time. If several tests coincide, begin reviewing well ahead of time.

Another effective time management and productivity tool is a daily **To Do list,** a prioritized list of things to be done in a single day. Prioritizing helps you resist the temptation to do easy, unimportant tasks first rather than the important ones, and, of course, it helps you avoid procrastination. Keep it with you to refer to throughout the day. Check off items as you complete them.

Here are the steps for making a daily To Do list:

- **Step 1: Write down everything you would like to accomplish today** (or tomorrow, if you make the list the night before). Some activities will be school related; others will not. Do not include routine activities (such as "go to work").

- **Step 2: Rate each item as being an A (very important to complete that day), B (moderately important), or C (less important).**   In other words, set priorities. This step is crucial.

- **Step 3: Set final priorities by ranking all your A's, then your B's, and then your C's.**   Rank the A's and label them A-1, A-2, A-3, and so on, according to the importance of each. Do the same for the B's and C's. This gives you the *overall* order in which you should do the items on the list. Try to do all of your A items first, starting with item A-1. When you complete it, tackle item A-2. When you complete your A items, start on the B items, and so forth. Even if you can't complete your list, you will have accomplished the most important items. If some still need to be done, carry them over to the next day's list.

DEVELOPING CHAPTER REVIEW CARDS

Review cards, or *summary cards,* are an excellent study tool. They are a way to select, organize, and review the most important information in a textbook chapter. Creating review cards helps you organize information in a meaningful way and transfer it into long-term memory as you prepare for tests (see Part Three). The review card activities in this book give you structured practice in creating these valuable study tools. Once you have learned how to make review cards, you can create them for textbook material in your other courses.

Now complete the seven review cards for Chapter 1 by answering the questions or following the directions on each card. When you have completed them, you will have summarized (1) what successful college students do, (2) ways to motivate yourself, (3) important information about setting goals, (4) three learning styles, (5) ways to make the most of your study time, (6) how to develop a monthly assignment calendar, and (7) steps in making a To Do list. Print or write legibly. You will find it easier to complete the review cards if you remove these pages before filling them in.

Doing What Successful Students Do
What are five things successful college students do? (See pages 5–6.)
1. Motivate themselves
2. Set goals
3. Manage time
4. Highly selective
5. Get involved
Card 1   Chapter 1: Making Yourself Successful in College

Motivating Yourself

What are 12 ways to motivate yourself? (See pages 7–9.)

1. Write down educational goals for each semester

2. Visualize your success

3. Think of classes as your easiest learning session

4. View your courses as opportunity

5. Develop emotional strategies

6. Seek advice and study tips

7. Choose the right friend

8.

9.

10.

11.

12.

Card 2   Chapter 1: Making Yourself Successful in College

Setting Goals

1. Why should goals be written down? (See page 9.)

Help to make a commitment

2. What are Lakein's three recommendations for setting goals? (See page 10.)

(a) Be specific
(b) Be realistic
(c) Be willing to revised

3. List and define the three types of goals. (See page 10.)

(a) Short term goals
(b) Intermediate goals
(c) long-term goals

Card 3   Chapter 1: Making Yourself Successful in College

Learning Preference

Briefly describe these three types of learners. (See pages 11–13.)

Visual learners: _prefer Read or see information_

Auditory learners: _prefer to hear information_

Tactile or kinesthetic learners: _prefer to manipulate materials physically or incorporate movement._

Card 4   Chapter 1: Making Yourself Successful in College

Making the Most of Your Study Time

What are 10 ways to make the most of your study time? (See pages 18–19.)

1.
2.
3.
4.
5.
6.
7.
8.
9.
10.

Card 5   Chapter 1: Making Yourself Successful in College

Developing a Monthly Assignment Calendar

How can you prepare a monthly assignment calendar? (See page 19.)

1. What should you do as soon as you receive the syllabi for your courses?

2. What should you do if several project or test dates coincide? (See page 19.)

Card 6   Chapter 1: Making Yourself Successful in College

Making a To Do List

Describe briefly the three steps to follow in making a daily To Do list. (See page 20.)

Step 1:

Step 2:

Step 3:

Card 7   Chapter 1: Making Yourself Successful in College

FINDING INFORMATION ONLINE USING BOOLEAN SEARCHES

In the *Opening Doors* reading selections, you are encouraged to learn more about the selections' topics online. This can be done before you read to enhance your background knowledge, or it can be done after you have read the selection to learn even more about the topic.

Conducting a Boolean (pronounced BOO-lee-un) search can be extremely helpful when you search for information on the Internet. It lets you target your search and more quickly locate the information you need. According to About.com, with a *Boolean search*, you "combine words and phrases using the words AND, OR, NOT and NEAR (otherwise known as boolean operators) to limit, widen, or define your search." It continues, "Most Internet search engines and Web directories default to these Boolean search parameters anyway, but a good Web searcher should know how to use basic Boolean operators" (http://websearch.about.com/od/2/g/boolean.htm; accessed 3/22/12).

For an excellent tutorial on how to conduct these types of searches, go to Internet Tutorials at www.internettutorials.net. The website is maintained by Laura B. Cohen, a former academic librarian at the State University of New York (SUNY) at Albany. Start with "Boolean Searching on the Internet: A Primer in Boolean Logic" (http://www.internettutorials.net/boolean.asp). After you have read it, click on "Basic Search Techniques" (http://www.internettutorials.net/basic-search-techniques.asp). You can actually try the searches as you go!

In writing and English classes, instructors tell students to "narrow your topic." In other words, they are telling you that before you can begin gathering information, you must narrow the subject to a manageable aspect of a more general topic. For instance, an overly broad topic such as "voter turnout in US presidential elections" would be unmanageable. However, a more precise topic, such as "voter turnout among 18- to 20-year-olds in the 2008 and 2012 presidential elections" would be manageable. Knowing how to conduct Boolean searches can save you time and frustration when you need to locate information online.

EVALUATING INTERNET SOURCES

Whenever you gather information from a website, especially if you are doing research, it is a good idea to evaluate the website and the information it contains. For example, you should ask yourself questions such as these:

- Who sponsors this website?
- Is the information at this website current (up to date)?
- Is the website trustworthy?

Robert Harris, Ph.D., describes himself as "a writer and educator with more than 25 years of teaching experience at the college and university level. He has written on the use of computers and software in language and literature study, using the Web as a research tool, the prevention of plagiarism, creative problem solving, and rhetoric." At his website, VirtualSalt.com, you can read his clear, complete explanation of how to evaluate Internet research resources. He uses the memory peg "CARS" for his evaluation checklist: Credibility, Accuracy, Reasonableness, and Support. This chart from his website summarizes the checklist:

Credibility	Trustworthy source, author's credentials, evidence of quality control, known or respected authority, organizational support.
	Goal: an authoritative source, a source that supplies some good evidence that allows you to trust it.
Accuracy	Up to date, factual, detailed, exact, comprehensive, audience and purpose reflect intentions of completeness and accuracy.
	Goal: a source that is correct today (not yesterday), a source that gives the whole truth.
Reasonableness	Fair, balanced, objective, reasoned, no conflict of interest, absence of fallacies or slanted tone.
	Goal: a source that engages the subject thoughtfully and reasonably, concerned with the truth.
Support	Listed sources, contact information, available corroboration, claims supported, documentation supplied.
	Goal: a source that provides convincing evidence for the claims made, a source you can triangulate (find at least two other sources that support it).

Source: Robert Harris, "Evaluating Internet Research Sources," *VirtualSalt*, 22 November 2012. Web. 2 April 2011.
http://www.virtualsalt.com/evalu8it.htm.

Evaluate Internet sources carefully. As Dr. Harris points out, infomation is power—but only if the information is *reliable*.

Student Success

Why Go to College?

From *P.O.W.E.R. Learning: Strategies for Success in College and Life*
by Robert S. Feldman

Prepare Yourself to Read

Directions: Do these exercises *before* you read Selection 1.1.

1. Read and think about the title of this selection. Why are *you* going to college? Write 1, 2, and 3 next to the *three most important* reasons that you have for attending college:

   _____ I want to get a good job when I graduate.

   _____ My parents want me to go.

   _____ I couldn't find a job.

   _____ I want to get away from home.

   _____ I want to get a better job as soon as possible.

   _____ I want to gain a general education and appreciation of ideas.

   _____ I want to improve my reading and study skills.

   _____ I want to become a more cultured person.

   _____ I want to make more money.

   _____ I want to learn more about things that interest me.

   _____ A mentor or role model encouraged me to go.

   _____ I want to prove to others that I can succeed.

   How do you think your reasons compare with those of other first-year students?

   _____

   _____

   _____

   _____

2. Next, complete your preview by reading the following:

   Introduction (in *italics*)

   Chart

   First sentence of each paragraph

   On the basis of your preview, what does the selection seem to be about?

   _____

   _____

   _____

   _____

3. **Build your vocabulary as you read.** If you discover an unfamiliar word or
   key term as you read the selection, try to determine its meaning from the way
   it is used in the sentence.

Internet Resources

Read More about This Topic Online

Use a search engine, such as Google or Yahoo!, to expand your existing knowledge
about this topic *before* you read the selection or to learn more about it *afterward.*
Use search terms such as "benefits of attending college" or "advantages of attending
college." If you are unfamiliar with conducting Internet searches, read pages 25–26
on Boolean searches. You can also use Wikipedia, the free online encyclopedia, at
www.wikipedia.com. Keep in mind that when you visit any website, it is a good
idea to evaluate the site and the information it contains. Ask yourself questions such
as "Who sponsors this website?" and "Is the information it contains up to date?"

read 29-31

SELECTION 1.1: WHY GO TO COLLEGE?

According to the U.S. National Center for Education Statistics (U.S. Department of Education), 20 years ago, there were 14.1 million students in U.S. colleges and universities. By 2000, there were 15.3 million, and by 2009, 18.8 million. For fall 2011, the estimated number was up by nearly a million, to a record 19.7 million students. Females were expected to make up the majority of college students, and more students were expected to attend full time than part time. Increasing numbers and percentages of black and Hispanic students are attending college. Why are so many people willing to devote the effort, time, and money a college education requires? What would your answer be if you were asked the question "Why are you going to college?"

This selection comes from the student success textbook P.O.W.E.R. Learning: Strategies for Success in College and Life *by Robert S. Feldman, professor of psychology at the University of Massachusetts at Amherst. (The POWER acronym stands for <u>P</u>repare, <u>O</u>rganize, <u>W</u>ork, <u>E</u>valuate and <u>R</u>ethink, a system designed to help people reach their goals.) Professor Feldman presents the reasons that first-year college students cited most frequently when they were asked, "Why are you going to college?" Then, to support his belief that "the value of college extends far beyond dollars and cents," he presents seven other important reasons for going to college that first-year students may be unaware of.*

1   Congratulations. You're in college.

2   But *why?* Although it seems as if it should be easy to answer why you're continuing your education, for most students it's not so simple. The reasons that people go to college vary. Some people want to go to college for practical reasons ("I want to get a good job"). Other reasons range from to the lofty ("I want to learn about people and the world"), to the unreflective ("Why not?—I don't have anything better to do").

3   Surveys of first-year college students show that almost three-quarters say they want to learn about things that interest them, get training for a specific career, land a better job, and make more money (see Figure 1). And, in fact, it's not wrong to expect that a college education will help people find better jobs. On average, college graduates earn about 75 percent more than high school graduates over their working lifetime. That difference adds up: Over the course of their working lifetimes, college graduates earn close to a million dollars more than those with only a high school degree. Furthermore, as jobs become increasingly complex and technologically sophisticated, college will become more and more of a necessity.

4   But the value of college extends far beyond dollars and cents. Consider these added reasons for pursuing a college education:

5   **You'll learn to think critically and communicate better.** Here's what one student said about his college experience after he graduated: "It's not about what you major in or which classes you take. . . . It's really about learning to think and to communicate. Wherever you

Figure 1

Choosing College

These are the most frequently cited reasons that first-year college students gave for why they enrolled in college when asked in a national survey.

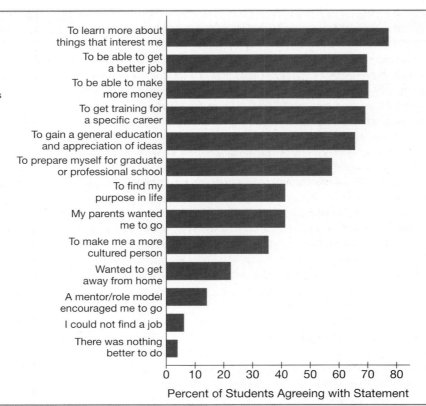

Percent of Students Agreeing with Statement

end up, you'll need to be able to analyze and solve problems—to figure out what needs to be done and do it." Education improves your ability to understand the world—to understand it as it now is, and to prepare to understand it as it will be.

6   **You'll be able to better deal with advances in knowledge and technology that are changing the world.** Genetic engineering . . . drugs to reduce forgetfulness . . . computers that respond to our voices. . . . No one knows what the future will hold, but you can prepare for it through a college education. Education can provide you with intellectual tools that you can apply regardless of the specific situation in which you find yourself.

7   **You'll learn to adapt to new situations.** College is a different world from high school. It presents new experiences and new challenges. Your adjustment to college culture will prepare you for future encounters with new situations.

8   **You'll be better prepared to live in a world of diversity.** The racial and ethnic composition of the United States is changing

rapidly. Whatever your ethnicity, chances are you'll be working and living with people whose backgrounds, lifestyles, and ways of thinking may be entirely different from your own. You won't be prepared for the future unless you understand others and their cultural backgrounds—as well as how your own cultural background affects you.

9   **You'll learn to lead a life of community service.** In its broadest sense, community service involves making contributions to the society and community in which you live. College provides you with the opportunity to become involved in community service activities, in some cases even getting course credit for it—a process called *service learning*. College also allows you to develop the skills involved in acting toward others with civility and respectful, courteous behavior.

10   **You'll make learning a lifelong habit.** Higher education isn't the end of your education. Education will build upon your natural curiosity about the world, and it will make you aware that learning is a rewarding and never-ending journey.

11   **You'll understand the meaning of your own contributions to the world.** No matter who you are, you are poised to make your own contributions to society and the world. Higher education provides you with a window to the past, present, and future, and it allows you to understand the significance of your own contributions. Your college education provides you with a compass to discover who you are, where you've been, and where you're going.

12   In short, there are numerous benefits of attending college.

Source: Adapted from Robert S. Feldman, *P.O.W.E.R. Learning: Strategies for Success and Life,* 5e, pp. 2–5. Copyright © 2011 by The McGraw-Hill Companies, Inc. Reprinted with permission of The McGraw-Hill Companies, Inc.

Obika pascaliu

Student Success
(continued)

Reading Selection Quiz

This quiz has several parts. Your instructor may assign some or all of them.

Comprehension

Directions: Items 1–10 test your understanding of the selection. They are the type of questions a content area instructor (such as a student success professor) might ask on a test. You may refer to the selection as you answer the questions. Write your answer choice in the space provided.

As an example, the answer to the first item and an explanation for it are given below.

True or False

_____F_____ **1.** Professor Feldman believes that the value of a college education should be measured mainly in terms of dollars and cents.

Explanation:

In paragraph 4, Professor Feldman states, "But the value of college extends far beyond dollars and cents." He then goes on to present seven other important reasons for pursuing a college education. Consequently, this statement is false because Professor Feldman does *not* believe that "the value of a college education should be measured mainly in terms of dollars and cents."

_____T_____ **2.** On average college graduates earn about 75 percent more than high school graduates over their working lifetime.

_____F_____ **3.** According to the national survey results presented in Figure 1, first-year college students most frequently cited being able to make more money as their reason for enrolling in college.

_____T_____ **4.** According to Figure 1, approximately 67 percent of first-year college students cite gaining a general education and appreciation of ideas as their reason for enrolling in college.

_____T_____ **5.** Professor Feldman believes that college can help you develop your capacity to think critically and communicate better.

Multiple-Choice

_____b_____ **6.** Of the following, which is cited least as a reason for enrolling in college?
  a. the ability to make money
  b. there was nothing better to do
  c. to improve my reading and study skills
  d. to get away from home

d   **7.** According to the author, adjusting to college life prepares you to:

  a.   have a career in genetic engineering.

  b.   make learning a lifelong habit.

  c.   engage in service learning.

  d.   be able to adapt to new situations in the future.

b   **8.** The author states that college will become more and more of a necessity because:

  a.   higher incomes will be required in the future.

  b.   jobs are becoming increasingly complex and technologically sophisticated.

  c.   the economy of the United States is becoming global.

  d.   there will be fewer jobs in the future.

 9. The racial and ethnic composition of the United States:

  a.   does not differ from that of other major countries.

  b.   is becoming less diverse.

  c.   makes it easy to understand others' cultures.

  d.   is changing rapidly.

d   **10.** Higher education can enable you to:

  a.   become less civil.

  b.   avoid service learning.

  c.   work only with students whose background is similar to your own.

  d.   contribute to society and the world.

SELECTION **1.1**

Student Success

(continued)

Vocabulary in Context

Directions: Items 11–20 test your ability to determine a word's meaning by using context clues. *Context clues* are words in a sentence that allow readers to deduce (reason out) the meaning of an unfamiliar word in the sentence. They also help readers determine the meaning an author intends when a word has more than one meaning. Each item below consists of a sentence from the selection, with the vocabulary word *italicized*. It is followed by another sentence that uses the same word in the same way. Use context clues to deduce the meaning of the *italicized* word. Be sure the meaning you choose makes sense in *both* sentences. Write each answer in the space provided. *Note:* Chapter 2 presents the skill of using context clues.

Because the skill of using context clues is not introduced until the next chapter, the answer to the first vocabulary item and an explanation are given below.

___d___   **11.** The reasons that people go to college *vary*.

Prices of new homes *vary* depending on their size and location.

vary (vâr′ ē) means:
a. disappear
b. decrease
c. remain the same
d. differ

Explanation:
- Answer choice **a,** *disappear* (meaning *to vanish* or *to cease to exist*), does not make sense in either sentence.
- Answer choice **b,** *decrease* (meaning *to grow smaller*), also does not make sense in either sentence.
- Answer choice **c,** *remain the same* (meaning *does not change*), does not make sense in the second sentence.
- Answer choice **d,** *differ* (meaning *to be different*), is the only choice that makes sense in *both* sentences: "The reasons that people go to college *differ*" and "Prices of new homes *differ* depending on their size and location."

_____   **12.** Some people want to go to college for *practical* reasons ("I want to get a good job").

Patricia's *practical* knowledge of Spanish helped her on business trips to Mexico City.

practical (prăk′ tǐ kəl) means:
a. private
b. useful
c. enjoyable
d. limited

_____   **13.** Consider these added reasons for *pursuing* a college education.

In *pursuing* his goal to become a commercial airline pilot, Ted spent many years training.

pursuing (pər so͞o′ ǐng) means:
a. chasing or running after
b. attending
c. studying
d. striving to gain or accomplish

14. You'll be able to better deal with *advances* in knowledge and technology that are changing the world.

During the last two decades, there have been many scientific *advances* in understanding how the brain functions.

advances (ăd văns′ əz) means:

a. steps or moves forward

b. money given ahead of time

c. preparation before the appearance of a public figure

d. disappointments

15. *Genetic* engineering . . . drugs to reduce forgetfulness . . . computers that respond to our voices. . . . No one knows what the future will hold, but you can prepare for it through a college education.

Genetic testing was used to determine whether the baby inherited sickle cell anemia from his parents.

genetic (jə nĕt′ ĭk) means:

a. related to languages

b. related to education

c. related to genes

d. related to geography

16. Education can provide you with the *intellectual* tools that you can apply regardless of the specific situation in which you find yourself.

Cassandra preferred *intellectual* activities such as playing chess and bridge, reading, working crossword puzzles, and writing poetry.

intellectual (ĭn tə lĕk′ cho͞o əl) means:

a. helpful

b. interesting

c. pertaining to the ability to learn

d. challenging; difficult to grasp

17. You'll be better prepared to live in a world of *diversity.*

New York City is famous for the *diversity* of its ethnic restaurants—Italian, Chinese, French, Indian, Russian, Vietnamese, you name it!

diversity (dĭ vûr′ sĭ tē) means:

a. opportunity

b. variety

c. difficulty

d. quantity

18. College also allows you to develop the skills involved in acting toward others with *civility* and respectful, courteous behavior.

    Members of Congress are often criticized for their lack of *civility* toward members of the opposing political party.

    civility (sĭ vĭl′ ĭ tē) means:
    a. a pleasant tone of voice
    b. a refusal to discuss matters
    c. politeness
    d. enthusiasm

19. No matter who you are, you are *poised* to make your own contributions to society and the world.

    After graduating from college, Kim was *poised* for the challenges and responsibilities of her first full-time job.

    poised (poizd) means:
    a. afraid
    b. positioned
    c. required
    d. allowed

20. Your college education provides you with a *compass* to discover who you are, where you've been, and where you're going.

    Most gang members seem to have no moral *compass* to help them distinguish between right and wrong.

    compass (kŭmp′ əs) means:
    a. range or scope
    b. sense of personal direction
    c. hinged device for drawing circles
    d. enthusiasm

SELECTION **1.1**

Student Success

(continued)

Reading Skills Application

Directions: Items 21–25 test your ability to *apply* certain reading skills. You may not be familiar with all the skills yet, so some items will serve as a preview. As you work through *Opening Doors,* you will practice and develop these skills. These are important skills, which is why they are included on the state-mandated basic skills tests that some students must take. Write each answer in the space provided.

21. In paragraph 11, the author uses the word *window* to mean:

  a.   an opening.

  b.   a pane of glass.

  c.   a way of learning about.

  d.   an opportunity.

22. According to the selection, *service learning* refers to:

  a.   understanding others and their cultural backgrounds, as well as how your own cultural background affects you.

  b.   discovering who you are, where you've been, and where you're going.

  c.   making your own contributions to society and the world.

  d.   courses that allow students to engage in community service activities while getting course credit for the experience.

23. Which of the following statements from the selection represents an opinion rather than a fact?

  a.   Surveys of first-year college students show that almost three-quarters say they want to learn about things that interest them, get training for a specific career, land a better job, and make more money.

  b.   On average, college graduates earn about 75 percent more than high school graduates over their working lifetime.

  c.   Over the course of their working lifetime, college graduates earn close to a million dollars more than those with only a high school degree.

  d.   Furthermore, as jobs become increasingly complex and technologically sophisticated, college will become more and more of a necessity.

24. The author's primary purpose in writing this selection is to:

  a.   persuade all students to attend college.

  b.   broaden students' understanding of the value of college.

  c.   encourage more research on the value of college.

  d.   convince first-year college students to study hard.

25. In paragraph 5, the author uses which of the following patterns to organize the information?

  a.   cause and effect

  b.   comparison and contrast

  c.   sequence

  d.   list

Respond in Writing

Directions: Refer to the selection as needed to answer the essay-type questions below. (Your instructor may direct you to work collaboratively with other students on one or more items. Each group member should be able to explain *all* of the group's answers.)

1.   In paragraph 4, Professor Feldman states, "But the value of college extends far beyond dollars and cents." He then goes on to present seven other important reasons for pursuing a college education. In the space below, list these seven reasons.

_____

_____

_____

_____

_____

_____

_____

_____

2.   What are *your* reasons for attending college? How do they compare with other college students' reasons (based on information in the bar graph)?

_____

_____

_____

_____

_____

_____

_____

_____

3.   Which of the seven reasons Professor Feldman gives for attending college were new to you? In other words, which reasons were ones that you had not thought about before? How might becoming aware of those reasons benefit you?

_____

_____

_____

_____

_____

_____

_____

_____

4. **Overall main idea.** What is the overall main idea the author wants you to understand about reasons for attending college? Answer this question in one sentence. Notice that the phrase *attending college* appears in the overall main idea sentence.

　　Because this is the first time you are asked to write an overall main idea, the answer and an explanation are given below. (Chapters 4 and 5 present the skills of identifying and expressing main ideas. These chapters include examples and practice exercises.)

There are numerous benefits of attending college that go far beyond dollars

and cents.

_____

Explanation:

　　Notice that this sentence expresses the one most important point the author wants readers to understand after reading the *entire* selection.

SELECTION **1.2**

Business

Getting Ready for Prime Time: Learning the Skills Needed to Succeed Today and Tomorrow

From *Understanding Business*

by William Nickels, James McHugh, and Susan McHugh

Prepare Yourself to Read

Directions: Do these exercises *before* you read Selection 1.2.

1. First, read and think about the title. What do you already know about the skills that are needed for success?

_____

_____

_____

2. Next, complete your preview by reading the following:

     Introduction (in *italics*)

     Headings

     All of the first paragraph (paragragh 1)

     First sentence of each of the other paragraphs

On the basis of your preview, what two kinds of success are the authors addressing?

_____

_____

_____

_____

3. **Build your vocabulary as you read.** If you discover an unfamiliar word or key term as you read the selection, try to determine its meaning from the way it is used in the sentence.

Internet Resources

Read More about This Topic Online

Use a search engine, such as Google or Yahoo!, to expand your existing knowledge about this topic *before* you read the selection or to learn more about it *afterward*. Use search terms such as "career success" or "professional etiquette." If you are unfamiliar with conducting Internet searches, read pages 25–26 on Boolean searches. You can also use Wikipedia, the free online encyclopedia, at www.wikipedia.com. Keep in mind that when you visit any website, it is a good idea to evaluate the site and the information it contains. Ask yourself questions such as "Who sponsors this website?" and "Is the information it contains up to date?"

SELECTION **1.2**

SELECTION 1.2: GETTING READY FOR PRIME TIME: LEARNING THE SKILLS NEEDED TO SUCCEED TODAY AND TOMORROW

You've probably done it lots of times: arranged your evening in order to watch prime time TV. But have you ever thought about getting ready for the "prime time" of your life? In other words, are you preparing yourself for the most important or significant time in your life—your future? Writer Christopher Morley once said that the three ingredients in a good life are "learning, earning, and yearning." This selection from the preface to a business textbook affirms Morley's assertion and addresses the challenge of preparing yourself to succeed. In it, the authors present a variety of techniques and behaviors you can adopt in order to be successful both in college and in your career. As you will discover when you read this selection, taking a business course can be beneficial even if you are majoring in a different subject. The suggestions in this selection can help any student, and not just students who are majoring in business.

1   Your life is full. You're starting a new semester, perhaps even beginning your college career, and you're feeling pulled in many directions. Why take time to read this introductory section? Because your success is no joking matter. The purpose of this introduction is to help you learn principles, strategies, and skills for success that will help you not only in this course but also in your career and entire life. Whether or not you learn these skills is up to you. Learning them won't guarantee success, but not learning them—well, you get the picture.

Succeeding in This Course and in Life

2   Since you've signed up for this course, we're guessing you already know the value of a college education. But just to give you some numerical backup, you should know that the gap between the earnings of high school graduates and college graduates, which is growing every year, now ranges from 60 to 70 percent. According to the U.S. Census Bureau, the holders of bachelor's degrees will make an average of $40,478 per year as opposed to just $22,895 for high school graduates. That's a whopping additional $17,583 a year. Thus, what you invest in a college education is likely to pay you back many times. See Figure 1 to get an idea of how much salary difference a college degree makes by the end of a 30-year career. That doesn't mean that there aren't good careers available to non–college graduates. It just means that those with an education are more likely to have higher earnings over their lifetime.

3   The value of a college education is more than just a larger paycheck. Other benefits include increasing your ability to think critically and communicate your ideas to others, improving your ability to use

Figure 1
Salary Comparison of High School versus College Graduates

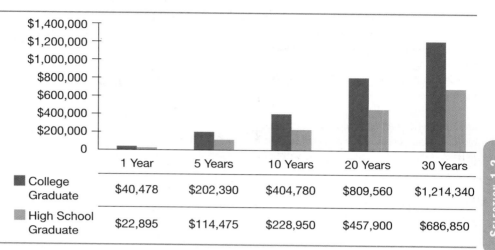

	1 Year	5 Years	10 Years	20 Years	30 Years
■ College Graduate	$40,478	$202,390	$404,780	$809,560	$1,214,340
■ High School Graduate	$22,895	$114,475	$228,950	$457,900	$686,850

Many people return to college to improve their skills in areas such as computers and writing. Others return because they realize, once they enter the marketplace, how important a college education is. Can you see the advantage of going back to school periodically during your career to keep your skills current?

technology, and preparing yourself to live in a diverse world. Knowing you've met your goals and earned a college degree also gives you the self-confidence to continue to strive to meet your future goals.

4   Experts say it is likely that today's college graduates will hold seven or eight different jobs (often in several different careers) in their lifetime. There are many returning students in college today who are changing their careers and their plans for life. In fact, 41 percent of the people enrolled in college today are 25 or older. More than 1.6 million students are over 40. Talk to them and learn from their successes and mistakes. You too may want to change careers someday.

SELECTION 1.2

Often, that is the path to long-term happiness and success. That means you will have to be flexible and adjust your strengths and talents to new opportunities. Many of the best jobs of the future don't even exist today. Learning has become a lifelong job. You will have to constantly update your skills if you want to achieve and remain competitive.

5   If you're typical of many college students, you may not have any idea what career you'd like to pursue. That isn't necessarily a big disadvantage in today's fast-changing job market. There are no perfect or certain ways to prepare for the most interesting and challenging jobs of tomorrow. Rather, you should continue your college education, develop strong computer skills, improve your verbal and written communication skills, and remain flexible while you explore the job market.

Using This Course to Prepare for Your Career

6   One of the objectives of this course is to help you choose an area in which you might enjoy working and in which you might succeed. This textbook and this course together may be one of your most important learning experiences ever. They're meant to help you understand business so that you can use business principles throughout your life. You'll learn about production, marketing, finance, accounting, management, economics, and more. At the end of the course, you should have a much better idea about what careers would be best for you and what careers you would *not* enjoy.

7   But you don't have to be in business to use business principles. You can use marketing principles to get a job and to sell your ideas to others. You can use your knowledge of financial planning to invest wisely in the stock market. Similarly, you'll be able to use management skills and general business knowledge wherever you go and whatever career you pursue—including government agencies, charities, and social causes.

Learning to Behave Like a Professional

8   Good manners are back, and for a good reason. As the world becomes increasingly competitive, the gold goes to the individuals and the teams that have an extra bit of polish. The person who makes a good impression will be the one who gets the job, wins the promotion, or clinches the deal. Manners and professionalism must become second nature to anyone who wants to achieve and maintain a competitive edge.

9   Often, students focus on becoming experts in their particular field and neglect other concerns, including proper attire and etiquette. Their résumés look great and they may get through the interview process, but then they get in the workplace and may not succeed.

Their behavior, including their verbal behavior, is so unacceptable that they are rejected by their peers.

10   The lesson is this: You can have good credentials, but a good presentation is everything. You can't neglect etiquette, or somewhere in your career you will be at a competitive disadvantage because of your inability to use good manners or to maintain your composure in tense situations. You must constantly practice the basics until they become second nature to you. Such basics include saying "Please" and "Thank you" when you ask for something. They also include opening doors for others, standing when an older person enters the room, and using a polite tone of voice. You may want to take a course in etiquette to learn the proper way to act at a formal party, and so on. Of course, it is also critical that you are honest, reliable, dependable, and ethical at all times.

11   You can probably think of sports stars who have earned a bad reputation by not acting professionally (for example, swearing or criticizing teammates in front of others). People in professional sports are fined if they are late to meetings or refuse to follow the rules established by the team and coach. Business professionals also must follow set rules. Many of these rules are not formally written anywhere, but every successful businessperson learns them through experience.

12   You can develop the habits *now* while you are in college so that you will have the skills needed for success when you start your career. These good habits include the following:

13   *Making a good first impression.* An old saying goes, "You never get a second chance to make a good first impression." You have just a few seconds to make an impression. Therefore, how you dress and look are important. Take a clue as to what is appropriate in a college classroom or at any specific company by studying the people there who are most successful. What do they wear? How do they act?

14   *Focusing on good grooming.* Be aware of your appearance and its impact on those around you. Consistency is essential—you can't project a good image by dressing up a few times a week and then show up looking like you're getting ready to mow a lawn. Wear appropriate, clean clothing and accessories. For example, revealing shirts, nose rings, and such may not be appropriate in a work setting. It is not appropriate for men to wear hats inside buildings. It is also not appropriate, usually, to wear wrinkled clothing or to have shirttails hanging out of your pants. Many businesses are adopting "business casual" policies, but others still require traditional attire, so it may be helpful to ask what the organization's policies are and choose your wardrobe accordingly. What is business casual to some may not be acceptable to others, but there are a few guidelines most

organizations accept. First of all, casual doesn't mean sloppy or shabby. For women, casual attire includes simple skirts and slacks (no jeans), cotton shirts, sweaters (not too tight), blazers, low-heeled shoes or boots (always with socks or stockings). For men, acceptable casual attire includes khaki trousers, sport shirts with collars, sweaters or sport jackets, casual loafers or lace-up shoes (no athletic shoes).

15 *Being on time.* When you don't come to class or to work on time, you're sending a message to your professor or boss. You are saying, "My time is more important than your time. I have more important things to do than be here." In addition to the lack of respect tardiness shows to your professor or boss, it rudely disrupts the work of your colleagues. Promptness may not be a priority in some circles, but in the workplace promptness is essential. But being punctual doesn't always mean just being on time. You have to pay attention to the corporate culture. Sometimes you have to come earlier than others and leave later to get that promotion you desire. To develop good work habits and get good grades, it is important to get to class on time and not leave early.

16 *Practicing considerate behavior.* Considerate behavior includes listening when others are talking—for example, not reading the newspaper or eating in class. Don't interrupt others when they are speaking. Wait for your turn to present your views in classroom or workplace discussions. Of course, eliminate all words of profanity from your vocabulary. Use appropriate body language by sitting up attentively and not slouching. Sitting up has the added bonus of helping you stay awake! Professors and managers get a favorable impression from those who look and act alert. That may help your grades in college and your advancement in work.

17 *Practicing good "netiquette."* Computer technology, particularly e-mail, can be a great productivity tool. The basic courtesy rules of face-to-face communication also apply to e-mail exchanges. As in writing a letter, you should introduce yourself at the beginning of your first e-mail message. Next, you should let your recipients know how you got their names and e-mail addresses. Then you can proceed with your clear but succinct message, and finally, close the e-mail with your signature.

18 *Practicing good cell phone manners.* Cellular phones are a vital part of today's world, but it is important to be polite when using a phone. Turn off the phone when you are in class or a business meeting unless you are expecting a critical call. If you are expecting a critical call, turn off the audible phone ring and use the vibrating ring if your phone has that feature. If you do have to have your cellular phone turned on, sit by the aisle and

near the door to leave if the phone rings. Leave the room before answering the call. Apologize to the professor after class and explain the nature of the emergency. Most professors are more sympathetic when you explain why you left the room abruptly.

19   *Being prepared.* A business person would never show up for a meeting without reading materials assigned for the meeting and being prepared to discuss the topics of the day. *To become a professional, you must practice acting like a professional.* For students, that means reading assigned materials before class, asking questions and responding to questions in class, and discussing the material with fellow students.

20   From the minute you enter your first job interview until the day you retire, people will notice whether you follow the proper business etiquette. Just as traffic laws enable people to drive more safely, business etiquette allows people to conduct business with the appropriate amount of dignity. How you talk, how you eat, and how you dress all create an impression on others.

Doing Your Best in College

21   The skills you need to succeed in college are the same skills you need to succeed in life after college. Career, family, and hobbies all involve the same organizational and time management skills. Applying these skills during your college years will ensure that you will have the life skills you need for a successful career. We will try to help you hone your skills by offering hints for improving your study habits, taking tests, and managing your time.

22   Success in any venture comes from understanding basic principles and having the skills to *apply* those principles effectively. What you learn now could help you be a success—for the rest of your life. If you use the suggestions we've presented here, you will not simply "take a course in business." Instead, you will be "getting ready for prime time" by participating in a learning experience that will help you greatly in your chosen career.

Source: Adapted from William G. Nickels, James M. McHugh, and Susan M. McHugh, *Understanding Business,* 7e, pp. P-3, P-4, P-6–P-9. Copyright © 2005 by The McGraw-Hill Companies, Inc. Reprinted with permission of The McGraw-Hill Companies, Inc.

Reading Selection Quiz

This quiz has several parts. Your instructor may assign some or all of them.

Comprehension

Directions: Items 1–10 test your understanding of the selection. They are the type of questions a content area instructor (such as a business professor) might ask on a test. You may refer to the selection as you answer the questions. Write your answer choice in the space provided.

1. A college education will:
   a. guarantee that you will be able to find a high-paying job.
   b. give you the self-confidence to continue to strive to meet your future goals.
   c. enable you to keep the same job for your entire career.
   d. provide you with a salary that is 41 percent higher than that of a high school graduate.

2. According to the salary comparison in Figure 1, by the end of a 30-year career a college graduate is likely to earn:
   a. $22,895.   *b.* $40,478.   *c.* $686,850.   *d.* $1,214,340.

3. Students who graduate from college will:
   a. prepare themselves to live in a diverse world.
   b. increase their ability to think critically and communicate their ideas to others.
   c. improve their ability to use technology.
   d. all of the above

4. College graduates should remain flexible throughout their careers and adjust their strengths and talents to new opportunities because:
   a. this is the path to the highest salaries.
   b. they may want or need to change careers someday.
   c. this is the only way to keep a good job.
   d. there will be fewer jobs in the future.

5. What percent of college students today are 25 or older?
   a. 4%   *b.* 10%   *c.* 25%   *d.* 41%

6. In addition to being reliable, dependable, and ethical, behaving like a professional requires you to:
   a. have a great-looking résumé and to present yourself well during an interview.
   b. use good manners and maintain your composure in tense situations.

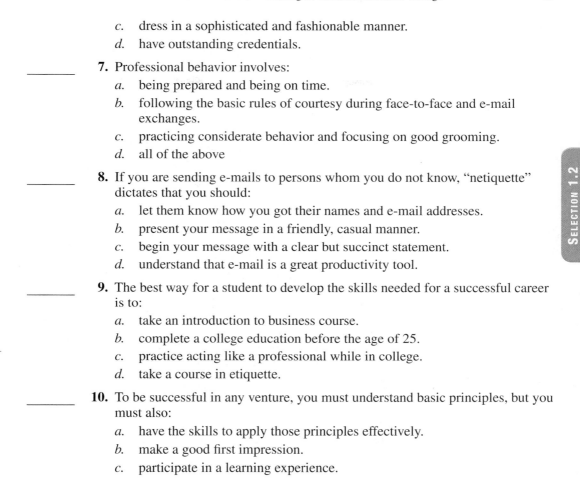

      c.   dress in a sophisticated and fashionable manner.

      d.   have outstanding credentials.

7. Professional behavior involves:

      a.   being prepared and being on time.

      b.   following the basic rules of courtesy during face-to-face and e-mail exchanges.

      c.   practicing considerate behavior and focusing on good grooming.

      d.   all of the above

8. If you are sending e-mails to persons whom you do not know, "netiquette" dictates that you should:

      a.   let them know how you got their names and e-mail addresses.

      b.   present your message in a friendly, casual manner.

      c.   begin your message with a clear but succinct statement.

      d.   understand that e-mail is a great productivity tool.

9. The best way for a student to develop the skills needed for a successful career is to:

      a.   take an introduction to business course.

      b.   complete a college education before the age of 25.

      c.   practice acting like a professional while in college.

      d.   take a course in etiquette.

10. To be successful in any venture, you must understand basic principles, but you must also:

      a.   have the skills to apply those principles effectively.

      b.   make a good first impression.

      c.   participate in a learning experience.

      d.   enjoy what you are doing.

SELECTION **1.2**

Business

(continued)

SELECTION 1.2

Vocabulary in Context

Directions: Items 11–20 test your ability to determine a word's meaning by using context clues. *Context clues* are words in a sentence that allow readers to deduce (reason out) the meaning of an unfamiliar word in the sentence. They also help readers determine the meaning an author intends when a word has more than one meaning. Each item below consists of a sentence from the selection, with the vocabulary word *italicized.* It is followed by another sentence that uses the same word in the same way. Use context clues to deduce the meaning of the *italicized* word. Be sure the meaning you choose makes sense in *both* sentences. Write each answer in the space provided. *Note:* Chapter 2 presents the skill of using context clues.

_____   **11.** But have you ever thought about getting ready for the *prime* time of your life?

Our retired neighbor, Fred Thomas, said that the time he served as mayor of our city was the *prime* experience of his career.

prime (prīm) means:

   a.   earliest
   b.   easiest time in a person's career
   c.   most important period or part ✓
   d.   most exciting

_____   **12.** Other benefits include increasing your ability to think critically and communicate your ideas to others, improving your ability to use technology, and preparing yourself to live in a *diverse* world.

Most first-time visitors are amazed by the *diverse* collection of artwork displayed at the Museum of Modern Art in New York City—sculpture, paintings, drawings, collages—something for every taste!

diverse (dĭ vûrs′) means:

   a.   complicated
   b.   modern
   c.   having variety in form ✓
   d.   involving many styles and preferences

_____   **13.** Knowing you've met your goals and earned a college degree also gives you the self-confidence to continue to *strive* to meet your future goals.

Pamela will *strive* to pay off her student loan in less than three years, even if it means postponing buying a new car and riding the bus to work.

strive (strīv) means:

   a.   to accomplish
   b.   to budget
   c.   to prepare for the future; to plan
   d.   to exert much effort; to struggle ✓

_____   **14.** Rather, you should continue your college education, develop strong computer skills, improve your *verbal* and written communication skills, and remain flexible while you explore the job market.

A telemarketing salesperson must have good *verbal* skills in order to catch and keep your interest and discourage you from hanging up the phone.

verbal (vûr′ bəl) means:

   a.   grammar skills
   b.   spoken rather than written; oral
   c.   computer and communication skills
   d.   keeps your attention; interesting

_____ **15.** Similarly, you'll be able to use management skills and general business knowledge wherever you go and whatever career you *pursue,* including government agencies, charities, and social causes.

My two-month internship at a hospital during high school persuaded me to *pursue* a degree in nursing.

pursue (pər sōō′) means:

a. to chase; overtake

b. to study or examine

c. to strive to accomplish or attain

d. to volunteer; participate

_____ **16.** You can't neglect etiquette, or somewhere in your career you will be at a competitive disadvantage because of your inability to use good manners or to maintain your *composure* in tense situations.

When a flight is delayed, airline ticket counter personnel must try to maintain their *composure* and assist annoyed and impatient customers.

composure (kəm pō′ zhər) means:

a. advantage

b. behavior

c. interest

d. calmness ✓

_____ **17.** You may want to take a course in *etiquette* to learn the proper way to act at a formal party, and so on.

Because Charles' mother and father insisted that he learn rules of *etiquette,* he felt comfortable at business functions, banquets, and other social events.

etiquette (ĕt′ ĭ kĕt) means:

a. speech communication

b. behavior

c. rules for business

d. good manners

_____ **18.** Of course, it is also critical that you are honest, reliable, dependable, and *ethical* at all times.

Although Cecilia was tempted to keep the wallet she found, she knew that the *ethical* thing to do would be to contact the owner and return it.

ethical (ĕth′ ĭ kəl) means:

a. dependable

b. likely to be successful

c. honorable

d. safe

SELECTION 1.2

_____ **19.** Be aware of your appearance and its *impact* on those around you.

My brother's study habits and excellent grades throughout college had a powerful *impact* on my desire to become a successful student.

impact (ĭm′ păkt) means:

a. awareness

b. influence

c. desire

d. habit

_____ **20.** Then you can proceed with your clear but *succinct* message.

Because our professor's explanation of the computer log in was so *succinct* and easy to understand, we began working immediately and had plenty of time to finish the assignment.

succinct (sək sĭngkt′) means:

a. clear

b. successful

c. challenging

d. brief

S ELECTION **1.2**

Business

(continued)

Reading Skills Application

Directions: Items 21–25 test your ability to *apply* certain reading skills. You may not be familiar with all the skills yet, so some items will serve as a preview. As you work through *Opening Doors,* you will practice and develop these skills. These are important skills, which is why they are included on the state-mandated basic skills tests that some students must take. Write each answer in the space provided.

_____ **21.** What is the meaning of the word *clinches* as it is used in paragraph 8?

a. misses; loses

b. closes; finalizes

c. creates; invents

d. proposes; presents

_____ **22.** What is the main point of paragraph 7?

a. You can use your knowledge of financial planning to invest wisely in the stock market.

b. You can use marketing principles to get a job and to sell your ideas to others.

c. You'll be able to use management skills and general business knowledge wherever you go.

d. You don't have to be in business to use business principles.

23. The information in paragraph 17 is organized using which of the following patterns?

    a. cause-effect

    b. comparison-contrast

    c. sequence

    d. problem-solution

24. Which of the following statements represents an opinion rather than a fact?

    a. Holders of bachelor's degrees will make an average of $40,478 per year.

    b. The gap between the earnings of high school graduates and college graduates is growing every year.

    c. High school graduates will make an average of $22,895 per year.

    d. What you invest in a college education is likely to pay you back many times.

25. The authors' purpose in writing this selection is to:

    a. convince students that they must find a suitable career when they graduate.

    b. persuade students to select a job that they can keep for a lifetime.

    c. present principles, strategies, and skills for success that will help students not only in their college courses but throughout their careers and entire lives as well.

    d. prove to students that a college degree is required in order to obtain a job with a good salary.

SELECTION **1.2**

Business
(continued)

Respond in Writing

Directions: Refer to the selection as needed to answer the essay-type questions below. (Your instructor may direct you to work collaboratively with other students on one or more items. Each group member should be able to explain *all* of the group's answers.)

1. Do you agree with the authors' point of view that success requires you to "behave like a professional"? Explain why or why not.

2. Create a "Top 10" list of behaviors or techniques that you believe can help
    people succeed in college as well as in their careers. You may use some or
    all of the suggestions included in the selection, or you may include your own
    suggestions. (Item 1 on your list should be what you view as the *most* impor-
    tant success behavior.)

    1. _____

    2. _____

    3. _____

    4. _____

    5. _____

    6. _____

    7. _____

    8. _____

    9. _____

    10. _____

3. **Overall main idea.** What is the overall main idea the authors want the reader
    to understand about the skills that are needed for success? Answer this ques-
    tion in one sentence. Be sure to include the words *success* (or *succeed*) and
    professional in your overall main idea sentence.

    _____

    _____

    _____

    _____

    _____

    _____

    _____

    _____

SELECTION **1.3**

Literature

Saved

From *The Autobiography of Malcolm X*

As told to Alex Haley

Prepare Yourself to Read

Directions: Do these exercises *before* you read Selection 1.3.

1. First, read and think about the title. What do you already know about Malcolm X?

   _____

   _____

   _____

2. Next, complete your preview by reading the following:

   Introduction (in *italics*)

   First paragraph (paragraph 1)

   All of the last paragraph (paragraph 19)

   On the basis of your preview, what aspect of Malcolm X's life do you think will be discussed?

   _____

   _____

   _____

3. **Build your vocabulary as you read.** If you discover an unfamiliar word or key term as you read the selection, try to determine its meaning from the way it is used in the sentence.

Internet Resources

Read More about This Topic Online

Use a search engine, such as Google or Yahoo!, to expand your existing knowledge about this topic *before* you read the selection or to learn more about it *afterward*. Use search terms such as "Malcolm X" or "Malcolm X and reading." If you are unfamiliar with conducting Internet searches, read pages 25–26 on Boolean searches. You can also use Wikipedia, the free online encyclopedia, at www.wikipedia.com. Keep in mind that when you visit any website, it is a good idea to evaluate the site and the information it contains. Ask yourself questions such as "Who sponsors this website?" and "Is the information it contains up to date?"

SELECTION 1.3

Malcolm X has been described as one of the most influential African Americans in history. Born Malcolm Little in 1925, Malcolm X was a member of the American Black Muslims (1952–1963), an organization that advocated separatism and black pride, but before Malcolm X became a prominent Black Muslim and political leader, he served time in prison.

In this selection, Malcolm X describes a life-changing experience he had while he was in prison. His desire to write letters to Elijah Muhammad during this time motivated Malcolm X to make a profound change in his life. (Elijah Muhammad, a black American, was an activist and leader of the Nation of Islam from 1934 to 1975. He favored political and social equality, as well as economic independence for black Americans.)

However, Malcolm X eventually separated from the Black Muslims and converted to orthodox Islam, a religion that believes in the unity of the human race. He founded the Organization of Afro-American Unity in 1964. He made a pilgrimage to Mecca, and he traveled throughout the Middle East and Africa. In 1965, at age 39, Malcolm X was assassinated in Harlem as he was about to give a speech. At a Harlem funeral home, thousands of people came to pay their respects.

In 1992 Warner Studios produced the film Malcolm X, *directed by Spike Lee and starring Denzel Washington. And in 1995 A&E Network produced a documentary on Malcolm X for its* Biography *series. In 1999 the United States Postal Service issued a stamp in honor of Malcolm X (El-Hajj Malik El-Shabazz).*

1   It was because of my letters that I happened to stumble upon starting to acquire some kind of a homemade education.

2   I became increasingly frustrated at not being able to express what I wanted to convey in letters that I wrote, especially those to Mr. Elijah Muhammad. In the street, I had been the most articulate hustler out there—I had commanded attention when I said something. But now, trying to write simple English, I not only wasn't articulate, I wasn't even functional. How would I sound writing in slang, the way I would say it, something such as, "Look, daddy, let me pull your coat about a cat, Elijah Muhammad—"

3   Many who today hear me somewhere in person, or on television, or those who read something I've said, will think I went to school far beyond the eighth grade. This impression is due entirely to my prison studies.

4   It had really begun back in the Charlestown Prison, when Bimbi first made me feel envy of his stock of knowledge. Bimbi had always taken charge of any conversation he was in, and I had tried to emulate him. But every book I picked up had few sentences which didn't contain anywhere from one to nearly all of the words that might as well have been in Chinese. When I just skipped those words, of course, I really ended up with little idea of what the book said. So I had come to the Norfolk Prison Colony still going through only book-reading motions. Pretty soon, I would have quit even these motions, unless I had received the motivation that I did.

5   I saw that the best thing I could do was get hold of a dictionary — to study, to learn some words. I was lucky enough to reason also that I should try to improve my penmanship. It was sad. I couldn't even write in a straight line. It was both ideas together that moved me to request a dictionary along with some tablets and pencils from the Norfolk Prison Colony school.

6   I spent two days just rifling uncertainly through the dictionary's pages. I'd never realized so many words existed! I didn't know which words I needed to learn. Finally, just to start some kind of action, I began copying.

7   In my slow, painstaking, ragged handwriting, I copied into my tablet everything printed on that first page, down to the punctuation marks.

8   I believe it took me a day. Then, aloud, I read back, to myself, everything I'd written on the tablet. Over and over, aloud, to myself, I read my own handwriting.

9   I woke up the next morning, thinking about those words — immensely proud to realize that not only had I written so much at one time, but I'd written words that I never knew were in the world. Moreover, with a little effort, I also could remember what many of these words meant. I reviewed the words whose meanings I didn't remember. Funny thing, from the dictionary first page right now, that "aardvark" springs to my mind. The dictionary had a picture of it, a long-tailed, long-eared, burrowing African mammal, which lives off termites caught by sticking out its tongue as an anteater does for ants.

10   I was so fascinated that I went on — I copied the dictionary's next page. And the same experience came when I studied that. With every succeeding page, I also learned of people and places and events from history. Actually the dictionary is like a miniature encyclopedia. Finally the dictionary's A section had filled a whole tablet — and I went on into the B's. That was the way I started copying what eventually became the entire dictionary. It went a lot faster after so much practice helped me to pick up handwriting speed. Between what I wrote in my tablet, and writing letters, during the rest of my time in prison I would guess I wrote a million words.

11   I suppose it was inevitable that as my word-base broadened, I could for the first time pick up a book and read and now begin to understand what the book was saying. Anyone who has read a great deal can imagine the new world that opened. Let me tell you something: from then until I left that prison, in every free moment I had, if I was not reading in the library, I was reading on my bunk. You couldn't have gotten me out of books with a wedge. Between Mr. Muhammad's teachings, my correspondence, my visitors — usually Ella and Reginald — and my reading of books, months passed without my even thinking about being imprisoned. In fact, up to then, I never had been so truly free in my life.

Malcolm X (1925–1965)

12   The Norfolk Prison Colony's library was in the school building. A variety of classes was taught there by instructors who came from such places as Harvard and Boston universities. The weekly debates between inmate teams were also held in the school building. You would be astonished to know how worked up convict debaters and audiences would get over subjects like "Should Babies Be Fed Milk?"

13   Available on the prison library's shelves were books on just about every general subject. Much of the big private collection that Parkhurst had willed to the prison was still in crates and boxes in the back of the library—thousands of old books. Some of them looked ancient: covers faded, old-time parchment-looking binding. Parkhurst, I've mentioned, seemed to have been principally interested in history and religion. He had the money and the special interest to have a lot of books that you wouldn't have in general circulation. Any college library would have been lucky to get that collection.

14   As you can imagine, especially in a prison where there was heavy emphasis on rehabilitation, an inmate was smiled upon if he demonstrated an unusually intense interest in books. There was a sizable number of well-read inmates, especially the popular debaters. Some were said by many to be practically walking encyclopedias. They were almost celebrities. No university would ask any student to devour literature as I did when this new world opened to me, of being able to read and *understand*.

15   I read more in my room than in the library itself. An inmate who was known to read a lot could check out more than the permitted maximum number of books. I preferred reading in the total isolation of my own room.

16   When I had progressed to really serious reading, every night at about ten P.M. I would be outraged with the "lights out." It always seemed to catch me right in the middle of something engrossing.

17   Fortunately, right outside my door was a corridor light that cast a glow into my room. The glow was enough to read by, once my eyes adjusted to it. So when "lights out" came, I would sit on the floor where I could continue reading in that glow.

18   At one-hour intervals the night guards paced past every room. Each time I heard the approaching footsteps, I jumped into bed and feigned sleep. And as soon as the guard passed, I got back out of bed onto the floor area of that light-glow, where I would read for another fifty-eight minutes—until the guard approached again. That went on until three or four every morning. Three or four hours of sleep a night was enough for me. Often in the years in the streets I had slept less than that. . . .

19   I have often reflected upon the new vistas that reading opened to me. I knew right there in prison that reading had changed forever the course of my life. As I see it today, the ability to read awoke inside me some long dormant craving to be mentally alive. I certainly wasn't seeking any degree, the way a college confers a status symbol upon its students. My homemade education gave me, with every additional book that I read, a little bit more sensitivity to the deafness, dumbness, and blindness that was afflicting the black race in America. Not long ago, an English writer telephoned me from London, asking questions. One was, "What's your alma mater?" I told him, "Books." You will never catch me with a free fifteen minutes in which I'm not studying something I feel might be able to help the black man.

Source: "Saved," from *The Autography of Malcolm X* by Malcolm X and Alex Haley, pp. 171–74, 179. Copyright © 1964 by Alex Haley and Malcolm X. Copyright © 1965 by Alex Haley and Betty Shabazz. Reprinted by permission of Random House, Inc.

SELECTION 1.3

Reading Selection Quiz

This quiz has several parts. Your instructor may assign some or all of them.

Comprehension

Directions: Items 1–10 test your understanding of the selection. They are the type of questions a content area instructor (such as a literature professor) might ask on a test. You may refer to the selection as you answer the questions. Write your answer choice in the space provided.

True or False

_____ 1. There were a small number of well-read inmates at the prison in which Malcolm X served time.

_____ 2. Despite Malcolm's initially limited ability to read and write, he was a person capable of learning.

_____ 3. Norfolk Prison Colony liked prisoners to exhibit an interest in rehabilitating themselves.

_____ 4. Malcolm's prison experience provided him with no opportunity to improve his reading or writing skills.

Multiple-Choice

_____ 5. What did Malcolm X mean when he said, "In fact, up to then, I had never been so truly free in my life"?
   a. He had been freed from prison.
   b. He was able to explore a "new world" of books and ideas even though he was in prison.
   c. He could devote as much time as he wanted to learning.
   d. He felt carefree.

_____ 6. According to Malcolm X, he felt a need to begin to acquire more education because of:
   a. his inability to express himself well in conversation.
   b. his desire to write letters and his envy of Bimbi.
   c. the influence of Parkhurst.
   d. the encouragement of a certain prison guard.

_____   **7.** Prison inmates who were outstanding debaters were:
     a.   looked down on by other inmates.
     b.   regarded almost as celebrities by other inmates.
     c.   ignored by other inmates.
     d.   disliked.

_____   **8.** The Norfolk Prison Colony was exemplary because of:
     a.   its strong emphasis on rehabilitation.
     b.   its unusually large library.
     c.   the quality of instructors in the prison school.
     d.   all of the above

_____   **9.** Parkhurst was:
     a.   the prison warden.
     b.   a teacher who taught at the prison.
     c.   the donor of the library books.
     d.   Malcolm's cellmate.

_____   **10.** The dictionary was the book that opened the door of learning for Malcolm X. He used it:
     a.   as a miniature encyclopedia, which provided background knowledge about a variety of subjects.
     b.   to improve his penmanship by copying its pages.
     c.   to improve and expand his vocabulary.
     d.   all of the above

SELECTION **1.3**

Literature
(continued)

SELECTION 1.3

Vocabulary in Context

Directions: Items 11–20 test your ability to determine a word's meaning by using context clues. *Context clues* are words in a sentence that allow readers to deduce (reason out) the meaning of an unfamiliar word in the sentence. They also help readers determine the meaning an author intends when a word has more than one meaning. Each item below consists of a sentence from the selection, with the vocabulary word *italicized*. It is followed by another sentence that uses the same word in the same way. Use context clues to deduce the meaning of the *italicized* word. Be sure the meaning you choose makes sense in *both* sentences. Write each answer in the space provided. *Note*: Chapter 2 presents the skill of using context clues.

_____ **11.** I became increasingly frustrated at not being able to express what I wanted to *convey* in letters that I wrote, especially those to Mr. Elijah Muhammad.

I am sorry that I won't be able to attend your uncle's funeral; please *convey* my sympathy to your aunt on his death.

convey (kən vā′) means:

a.   remember

b.   achieve

c.   write

d.   communicate

_____ **12.** In the street, I had been the most *articulate* hustler out there—I had commanded attention when I said something.

Former Prime Minister Winston Churchill was so *articulate,* his speeches are considered some of the finest ever given.

articulate (är tĭk′ yə lət) means:

a.   using clear, expressive language

b.   liking to talk

c.   talking extensively

d.   talking rapidly

_____ **13.** Bimbi had always taken charge of any conversation he was in, and I had tried to *emulate* him.

Parents should be good role models since children often *emulate* them.

emulate (ĕm′ yə lāt) means:

a.   surpass by diligent effort

b.   try to equal or excel, especially through imitation

c.   reject

d.   ridicule or make fun of

_____ **14.** In my slow, *painstaking,* ragged handwriting, I copied into my tablet everything printed on that first page, down to the punctuation marks.

Rebuilding and restoring antique furniture is a *painstaking* process.

painstaking (pānz′ tāk ĭng) means:

a.   involving great speed and dexterity

b.   involving significant physical pain

c.   involving considerable boredom

d.   involving great effort or care

15. With every *succeeding* page, I also learned of people and places and events from history.

In the years *succeeding* his presidency, Bill Clinton wrote his memoir and devoted time to humanitarian causes.

succeeding (sək sēd′ ĭng) means:

a. coming next or after

b. coming before

c. inserted or inserted in

d. preceding

16. I suppose it was *inevitable* that as my word-base broadened, I could for the first time pick up a book and read and now begin to understand what the book was saying.

It is *inevitable* that summer follows spring.

inevitable (ĭn ĕv′ ĭ tə bəl) means:

a. likely to happen

b. uncertain

c. incapable of being prevented or avoided

d. unreasonable

17. Much of the big private collection that Parkhurst had *willed* to the prison was still in crates and boxes in the back of the library—thousands of old books.

Since my grandmother is no longer alive, I treasure the piano she *willed* to me, and I play it often.

willed (wĭld) means:

a. kept in storage

b. taken back

c. received as a gift

d. granted in a legal will; bequeathed

18. As you can imagine, especially in a prison where there was heavy emphasis on *rehabilitation,* an inmate was smiled upon if he demonstrated an unusually intense interest in books.

It took three months of *rehabilitation* for the actor to recover fully from his drug and alcohol addiction.

rehabilitation (rē hĭ bĭl ĭ tā′ shən) means:

a. regaining useful life through education or therapy

b. hard physical labor

c. rest and relaxation

d. cooperation

SELECTION 1.3

_____ 19. Fortunately, right outside my door was the *corridor* light that cast a glow into my room.

When the fire alarm sounded, students quickly left their classrooms and walked down the *corridor* to the exit.

corridor (kôr′ ĭ dər) means:
a. door that leads to an exit
b. large room
c. passageway with rooms opening into it
d. an open area outside a building

_____ 20. Each time I heard the approaching footsteps, I jumped into bed and *feigned* sleep.

Have you ever *feigned* illness so that you wouldn't have to go to work?

feigned (fānd) means:
a. endured
b. experienced
c. pretended; gave a false appearance of
d. suffered or felt pain

S ELECTION **1.3**   *Reading Skills Application*

Literature
(continued)

Directions: Items 21–25 test your ability to *apply* certain reading skills. You may not be familiar with all the skills yet, so some items will serve as a preview. As you work through *Opening Doors,* you will practice and develop these skills. These are important skills, which is why they are included on the state-mandated basic skills tests that some students must take. Write each answer in the space provided.

_____ 21. What is the meaning of *devour* in paragraph 14?
a. eat greedily
b. read large quantities of
c. destroy
d. copy by hand

_____ 22. According to this selection, Malcolm X's formal education ended
a. after 6th grade.
b. with the 8th grade.
c. after high school.
d. after his first year of college.

_____ **23.** Which of the following conclusions can be logically based on the selection?

 a. Malcolm X would probably have returned to the same type of life he led before prison if he had not spent the time in prison reading and educating himself.

 b. Malcolm X could have qualified for a college scholarship if he had not gone to prison.

 c. Malcolm X was envied and disliked by the other prison inmates because he became so knowledgeable.

 d. Malcolm X willed his books to the Charlestown Prison library when he died.

_____ **24.** The writer's primary purpose for telling about his experience is to

 a. instruct others about how to improve their reading skills.

 b. persuade young men to stay out of prison.

 c. describe what life in prison is like.

 d. persuade readers of the value of reading and education.

_____ **25.** Which of the following best expresses the writer's point of view in this selection?

 a. Education can change lives.

 b. Prisons should offer inmates educational courses.

 c. Prisoners should be allowed to read as late at night as they like.

 d. No one should ever be sent to prison.

SELECTION 1.3

S E L E C T I O N **1.3**

Literature
(continued)

Respond in Writing

Directions: Refer to the selection as needed to answer the essay-type questions below. (Your instructor may direct you to work collaboratively with other students on one or more items. Each group member should be able to explain *all* of the group's answers.)

1. List at least three surprising or interesting facts you learned about Malcolm X.

_____

_____

_____

_____

_____

_____

_____

_____

_____

_____

2. Although Malcolm X may not have realized it, he used many of the same study and learning techniques that effective college students use. What were some of them?

_____

_____

_____

_____

_____

_____

_____

_____

3. What are at least two ways in which Malcolm X's prison experience may have "saved" him while he was in prison and after he was released?

_____

_____

_____

_____

_____

_____

_____

_____

4. **Overall main idea.** What is the overall main idea the author wants the reader to understand about Malcolm X's experience in prison? Answer this question in one sentence. Be sure to include the words _Malcolm X_ and _saved_ in your overall main idea sentence.

_____

_____

_____

CHAPTER 2

Approaching College Reading and Developing a College-Level Vocabulary

In this chapter, you will learn the answers to these questions:

- What do I need to know about the reading process?
- How can I improve my reading?
- Why should I make predictions as I read?
- How can I monitor my comprehension while I read?
- What do I need to know about adjusting my reading rate?
- How can I develop a college-level vocabulary?
- What are denotations and connotations?
- What is figurative language?

SKILLS

Understanding the Reading Process

Improving Your Reading

- Predicting as You Read
- Monitoring Your Comprehension
- Adjusting Your Reading Rate

Developing a College-Level Vocabulary

- Using Context Clues
- Using Word-Structure Clues
- Understanding Denotations and Connotations of Words
- Understanding Figurative Language

CREATING YOUR SUMMARY

Developing Chapter Review Cards

TEST YOUR UNDERSTANDING: CONTEXT CLUES, PARTS 1 AND 2

TEST YOUR UNDERSTANDING: WORD STRUCTURE: ROOTS, PARTS 3 AND 4

TEST YOUR UNDERSTANDING: FIGURATIVE LANGUAGE, PARTS 5 AND 6

READINGS

Selection 2.1   "Making It Happen: Creating Positive Change to Become a Peak Performer"
   from *Peak Performance: Success in College and Beyond*
   by Sharon K. Ferrett (Student Success)

Selection 2.2   "Terrorism in a Global Age"
   from *Nation of Nations: A Narrative*
   History of the American Republic
   by James Davidson et al. (History)

Selection 2.3   "A Whale of a Survival Problem"
   from *The Nature of Life*
   by John Postlethwait and Janet Hopson (Biology)

How is reading complex text like lifting weights? Just as it's impossible to build muscle without weight or resistance, it's impossible to build robust reading skills without reading challenging text.

Timothy Shanahan, Douglas Fisher, and Nancy Frey

To read without reflecting is like eating without digesting.

Edmund Burke

A synonym is a word you use when you can't spell the word you first thought of.

Burt Bacharach

When we read too fast or too slowly, we understand nothing.

Blaise Pascal

UNDERSTANDING THE READING PROCESS

Understanding the reading process can make you a better reader and help you study more effectively. You should be aware of these important points about reading:

1. **Reading is a form of thinking.** Although the eyes transmit images to the brain, it is the brain that does the reading, not the eyes. (To understand this, consider a blind person reading Braille: The fingertips transmit input to the brain.) Therefore, improving your reading means improving your *thinking*. Meaning resides in the reader's mind, not in symbols printed on a page. It is the readers who construct meaning by associating their knowledge and experience with what is on the printed page.

2. **Reading requires no unique mental or physical abilities.** The processes you typically use when you read, such as vision, reasoning, and memory, are the same processes you use in other areas of your daily life.

3. **The reading process includes three stages.** The three stages of reading are *preparing yourself to read, processing information,* and *reacting to what you read.* These stages overlap, but all three are needed for the reading process to be complete. In Chapter 3, this process will be explained as it applies to college reading.

4. **Effective reading is active and interactive.** Effective reading requires that you interact with the material you are reading. One way to interact with an author's ideas is to mentally ask yourself questions as you read and then seek the answers. Another way is to relate the author's ideas to your own experience and knowledge. Reading actively also means being aware of how the material is organized. Finally, active reading means that you *monitor your comprehension* as you read and that you take steps to correct the situation when you are not comprehending. (Monitoring your comprehension will be discussed later in this chapter.)

5. **Comprehension problems often result from a reader's lack of background knowledge.** Reading comprehension problems occur when a reader does not possess enough information about a subject to understand what an author is saying about it. When you have difficulty understanding new or unfamiliar material, you may need to increase your background knowledge. (For example, you could

Developing strong reading and vocabulary skills will make you more successful in college.

read a simplified explanation online first.) Finding out more about an unfamiliar topic often clears up this kind of problem. The greater the amount of background knowledge you have, the more you can understand. Every bit of information you acquire can help you learn new information more efficiently and easily.

6. **Comprehension, background knowledge, and reading rate are interrelated.** The more you know about a topic and the better you understand the material, the faster you can read it. Conversely, if you know very little about a topic, you must reduce your reading rate. This is why it is meaningless to try to improve your reading rate by artificial means, such as moving your eyes or hand down the page in a certain manner. Reading rate is a by-product of comprehension. To be precise, the goal is to *comprehend* more rapidly (efficiently). This is the work of the brain and does not depend on special eye or hand movements.

7. **Certain factors make text difficult to read.**   In addition to the reader's background knowledge, these factors can make text complex: the level of vocabulary, the coherence (how words, ideas, and sentences connect with each other), and the overall pattern of organization (such as cause-effect in a science text or flashback in fiction).

8. **Your reading strategies should fit your purpose for reading.**   You read for many different purposes, and your reason for reading any particular material affects the way you approach it. (For example, your approach to reading a newspaper article or an e-mail from a friend will be different from reading and studying a textbook.) You should choose reading strategies that fit your purpose.

With these things in mind, let's look at general ways you can improve your reading and your reading rate.

Predicting as You Read

predicting

Anticipating what is coming next as you read.

Predicting means anticipating or making educated guesses about what is coming next as you read. Predicting is a natural part of reading, and you need to do it when you read college textbooks. As you read an assignment, you should make a conscious effort to anticipate not only what is coming next but also the author's writing pattern. (Chapter 7 discusses authors' writing patterns.)

Of course, when you preview a chapter or reading selection, you are predicting in a general way what it will be about and how the material is organized. (The title or heading usually tells you or gives you a clue.) When you actually read it, you should continue to make predictions instead of passively waiting to see what comes up next. For example, if an author presents one side of an issue, you might predict that he or she is going to discuss the other side as well. If a paragraph in a psychology textbook begins with the question "Why do people have nightmares?" you expect the author to explain the reason or reasons.

Predicting helps you concentrate and comprehend. It focuses your attention because it makes you want to keep reading to see if your prediction is correct. In other words, predicting helps you stay actively involved with the material.

Monitoring Your Comprehension

monitoring your comprehension

Evaluating your understanding as you read and correcting the problem whenever you realize that you are not comprehending.

Monitoring your comprehension means periodically evaluating your understanding as you read and correcting the problem whenever you realize that you are not comprehending. With difficult material, you may need to monitor your comprehension paragraph by paragraph. At other times, you may need to stop and monitor at the end of each section.

To monitor your comprehension, follow this procedure:

- Ask yourself, *"Am I understanding what I am reading?"*
- If you do not understand what you are reading, ask yourself, *"Why* don't I understand?"
- Once you determine why you are not comprehending, do whatever is necessary to correct the situation.

Specific types of comprehension problems and strategies for correcting them are listed in the box on page 72. Make monitoring your comprehension a habit. After all, unless you comprehend what you are reading, you are not really reading.

Adjusting Your Reading Rate

Have you ever been asked, "What's your reading rate?" The fact is that each reader has, or should have, *several* reading rates. Reading everything at the same rate is a sign of poor reading. "Reading" at any rate without comprehending, even if the rate is a fast one, isn't really reading.

COMPREHENSION MONITORING: STRATEGIES FOR CORRECTING COMMON COMPREHENSION PROBLEMS

Problems	Solutions
I am not understanding because the subject is completely new to me, and I do not have enough background knowledge. College reading frequently introduces you to subjects you have not learned about before. Textbooks frequently contain a great deal of new information.	• Keep reading to see if the material becomes clearer. • Ask for a brief explanation from someone who is knowledgeable about the topic. • Read supplemental material or simpler material on the same topic (perhaps another textbook, a book from the library, or an online source) in order to build background knowledge.
I am not understanding because there are too many words I do not know. College material contains unfamiliar words and specialized or technical vocabulary that you must learn. Also, college textbooks in general are written at a higher level than other materials.	• Try to use the context (the rest of the sentence or paragraph) to figure out the meaning of an unfamiliar word. • Look up unfamiliar words in a dictionary or in the glossary at the back of the textbook. Online dictionaries, such as www.thefreedictionary.com, make this simple to do. • Ask someone the meaning of unfamiliar words.
I am not understanding because I am not concentrating as I read. I am allowing distractors to interfere with my concentration. Your mind may sometimes wander while you are reading long or difficult passages.	• Identify what is bothering you. Is it a *physical distraction* (such as a noisy room or being tired), or is it a *psychological distraction* (such as being worried or daydreaming)? • Take some action that will help you deal with environmental distractions. For example, close the door or move to a quiet room. Turn off the television, music, and your cell phone. Move out of sight of the computer screen. • If you are worrying about finding time for other important tasks or errands, jot the items on a To Do list. Then, after studying, tackle your To Do list. If you are worrying about a personal problem, tell yourself, "I'll deal with this after I finish studying." The point is to take some action to prevent distractors from interfering with your concentration. • Make a conscious decision to concentrate on what you are reading. Concentration does not happen automatically.

Having a range of reading rates and developing flexibility in using them is an important skill. The following information provides a brief introduction to adjusting your reading rate. The box on the next page presents various reading rates and tells when to use each.

Factors Influencing Reading Rate: Purpose and Difficulty

To be a flexible, efficient reader, you must adjust your reading rate according to two factors: your *purpose* for reading and *how difficult* the material is for you.

FLEXIBLE READING: INFORMATION-GATHERING RATES AND READING RATES

	Approximate Rate (wpm)	Uses
Information-gathering rates:		
Scanning	1,500 words per minute (wpm) or more	To find a particular piece of information (such as a name, date, or phone number)
Skimming	800–1,000 wpm	To get an overview of the highlights of the material
Reading rates:		
Rapid reading	300–500 wpm	For relatively easy material; when you want only important facts or ideas; for leisure reading
Average reading	200–300 wpm	For textbooks, complex magazines and journals, and literature
Study reading	50–200 wpm	For new vocabulary, complex concepts, technical material, and retaining details (such as legal documents, material to be memorized, and material of great interest or importance)

Obviously, you read for many different purposes: to understand and learn material for a test, to locate a specific bit of information (such as a name in an index), or just for pleasure.

The vocabulary level, writing style, and idea density determine how difficult material will be for you to read. The most important factor, however, is your *background knowledge,* or how much you already know about the subject. The less you know, the more difficult the material is likely to be.

When you read a textbook chapter, preview it first. Ask yourself why you are reading it and how much you already know about the subject. If the topic is new to you, you will need to read more slowly. If it is very familiar, you can read much faster. The point is to read flexibly, adjusting your rate as needed. The following lists describe when to slow down or speed up.

Slow down your reading when:

- You know little or nothing about the topic.
- It is complicated or technical material you need to learn.
- There are details you need to remember.
- There is new or difficult vocabulary in the selection.
- There are directions that you must follow.

- There are charts or graphs you must shift your attention to as you read.
- You must visualize something (for example, a heart valve as you read a biology text).
- Artistic, descriptive, or poetic writing invites you to linger on each word.
- There are ideas you want to consider carefully (such as philosophical, religious, or inspirational writing).

Speed up your reading when:

- The whole passage is easy (no complicated sentences, complex ideas, or difficult terms).
- There is an easy passage in a longer, more difficult section.
- There is an example of something you already understand.
- You are already knowledgeable about the topic.
- You want only main ideas and are not concerned about details.

DEVELOPING A COLLEGE-LEVEL VOCABULARY

Developing a powerful vocabulary takes time, but every time you read, you have an opportunity to expand your vocabulary. The more you read, the better your vocabulary can become—*if* you develop a real interest in words and their meanings. Remember that writers take special care to select words that convey precisely what they want to say.

Improving your vocabulary will make your college work easier, and your speech and your writing will become more interesting and precise. Your increased vocabulary may even lead to a higher salary: Research tells us that the size of a person's vocabulary is correlated with income. Thinking of each word you learn as "money in the bank" may be an incentive to pay attention to new words and add them to your vocabulary! And, needless to say, a broad vocabulary creates a favorable impression in a job interview.

Here are three techniques for developing and expanding your vocabulary as you read:

1. **Use context clues.**   This means that you reason out the meaning of an unfamiliar word from clues provided by the surrounding words and sentences.
2. **Use word-structure clues.**   That is, determine a word's meaning on the basis of its parts (prefix, root, and suffix).
3. **Use a dictionary.**   Use a dictionary to determine a word's meaning (and perhaps pronunciation) as it is used in the passage you are reading.

The vocabulary exercises that follow each reading selection in *Opening Doors* give you ongoing opportunities to use context clues and practice pronouncing words correctly.

context clues

Words in a sentence or paragraph that help the reader deduce (reason out) the meaning of an unfamiliar word.

Comprehension-Monitoring Question for Vocabulary in Context Clues

Are there clues within the sentence or surrounding sentences that can help me deduce the meaning of an unfamiliar word?

word-structure clue

Roots, prefixes, and suffixes that help you determine a word's meaning.

Word-structure clues are also known as *word-part clues.*

root

Base word that has a meaning of its own.

Using Context Clues

Writers want you to understand what they have written. When they use a word they think might be unfamiliar to readers, they often provide clues in the rest of the sentence so that the reader can deduce (reason out) the meaning of the word. Such clues are called **context clues.** (The word *context* refers to the sentence and the paragraph in which the word appears.) Since context clues can help you figure out the meaning of an unfamiliar word, think of them as gifts the writer gives you to make your job easier.

How can you take advantage of these "gifts"? By reading the sentence carefully and by paying attention to the words and other sentences surrounding the unfamiliar word. The most common types of context clues are summarized in the box on page 76.

Using Word-Structure Clues

Although context clues will be your greatest aid in determining the meaning of unknown words, **word-structure clues** or *word-part clues* can help you determine meanings, as well as confirm the educated guesses you made based on context clues. An extensive list of important and useful word parts appears in Appendix 2.

To use word-structure clues, examine the unfamiliar word to see if it has any of the following word parts:

- **Root:** Base word that has a meaning of its own.
- **Prefix:** Word part attached to the beginning of a root that adds its meaning to the meaning of the root.
- **Suffix:** Word part attached to the end of a root word.

Prefixes and suffixes are also called *affixes,* since they are "fixed" (attached or joined) to a root or base word. Words may consist of a:

Root only (such as the word *graph*)

Prefix and root (such as the word *telegraph*)

Root and suffix (such as the word *graphic*)

Prefix, root, and suffix (such as the word *telegraphic*)

Learning about prefixes and suffixes not only increases your vocabulary but can also help you improve your spelling. For instance, if you know the meaning of the prefix *mis* ("bad" or "wrong"), then you will understand why the word *misspell* has two *s*'s: One is in the prefix (*mis*), and one in the root word (*spell*).

Roots are powerful vocabulary-building tools because whole families of words in English come from the same root. For example, if you know that the root *aud* means "to hear," then you will understand the connection between *audience* (people who come to *hear* something or someone), *auditorium* (a place where people come to *hear* something), *audit* (enrolling in a course just to *hear* about a subject, rather than taking it for credit), *auditory* (pertaining to *hearing,* as in auditory nerve), and *audiologist* (a person trained to evaluate *hearing*). Knowing the meaning of a word's root also makes it easier to remember the meaning of the word.

USING CONTEXT CLUES TO DETERMINE THE MEANING OF UNFAMILIAR WORDS

Example	Type of Clue	What to Ask Yourself	What to Look for
The psychological term **interiority** is *defined* as a tendency toward looking within during middle age.	*Definition clue*	Are there *definition clues* and a definition?	Phrases that introduce a definition, such as *is defined as, is called, is, is known as, that is, refers to, means, the term;* a term that is in bold print, italics, or color; or certain punctuation marks that set off a definition or a term. (See page 476.)
The garden was **redolent,** or *fragrant,* with the scent of roses.	*Synonym clue*	Is there a *synonym* for the unfamiliar word? That is, is the meaning explained by a word or phrase that has a *similar meaning?* The synonym may be set off by commas, parentheses, a colon, dashes, or brackets. (See page 476.)	Phrases that introduce synonyms, such as *in other words, or, that is to say, also known as, by this we mean, that is.*
I did the physical therapy exercises incorrectly, *but instead of helping* my back, they were actually **deleterious.**	*Contrast clue*	Is there an *antonym* for the unfamiliar word? That is, is the unfamiliar word explained by a contrasting word or phrase with the *opposite meaning?*	Words and phrases that indicate opposites: *instead of, but, in contrast, on the other hand, however, unlike, although, even though.*
The campers *were warned that hiking up that steep mountain trail* would **enervate** even the fittest members of their group.	*Experience clue*	Can you draw on your *experience and background knowledge* to help you deduce (reason out) the meaning of the unfamiliar word?	A sentence that includes *a familiar experience* (or information you already know), which can help you figure out the meaning of the new word.
He enjoys **aquatic** sports, *such as swimming, scuba diving,* and *water skiing.*	*Example clue*	Are there *examples* that illustrate the meaning of the unfamiliar word?	Words that introduce examples of the meaning of the unfamiliar word: *for example, such as, to illustrate, like.*
When studying for his final exams, the student was told to **eschew** television. "*Just give TV up!*" was his roommate's advice.	*Clue from another sentence*	Is there *another sentence* in the paragraph that explains the meaning of the unfamiliar word?	*Additional information in another sentence* that may help explain the unfamiliar word.

prefix

Word part attached to the beginning of a root word that adds its meaning to that of the base word.

suffix

Word part attached to the end of a root word.

Comprehension-Monitoring Question for Word-Structure Clues

Are there roots, prefixes, or suffixes that give me clues to the meaning of an unfamiliar word?

etymology

The origin and history of a word.

denotation

Literal, explicit meaning of a word—its dictionary definition.

connotation

Additional, nonliteral meaning associated with a word.

Prefixes change the meaning of a root by adding their meaning to the meaning of the root. For example, adding the prefix *tele* ("distant" or "far") to the root word *scope* ("to see") creates the word *telescope,* a device that lets you *see* things that are *far* away. Try adding the prefixes *pre* ("before") and *re* ("back") to the root *cede* ("to go" or "to move"). *Precede* means "to go before" something or someone else; *recede* means "to move back."

Think of roots and prefixes as puzzle parts that can help you figure out the meaning of an unfamiliar word. Remember, however, that although a word may begin with the same letters as a prefix, it does not necessarily contain that prefix. The words *malt, mall, male,* and *mallard* (a type of duck), for example, have no connection with the prefix *mal* ("wrong" or "bad"), as in words such as *malnourished* or *maladjusted.*

Suffixes are word parts that are attached to the end of a root word. Some add their meaning to a root. Others change a word's part of speech or inflection. For example, consider these forms of the word *predict:* predic*tion,* predict*ability,* predic*tor* (nouns); predict*able* (adjective); predict*ably* (adverb). Examples of suffixes that serve as inflectional endings include adding *s* to make a word plural and *ed* to make a verb past tense.

Suffixes are not as helpful as roots or prefixes in determining the meaning of unfamiliar words because many suffixes have similar or even the same meanings. Also, some root words change their spelling before a suffix is added. For instance, when suffixes are added to *happy* the *y* becomes an *i: happier, happiness, happily.*

The most common and helpful roots, prefixes, and suffixes in English come from Latin and ancient Greek. These Latin and Greek word parts not only help you figure out the meaning of a word but also serve as built-in memory aids that make it easy to recall the meaning. In particular, a considerable number of scientific, medical, and technological terms are derived from Latin and Greek.

A word's **etymology** (origin and history) shows whether it contains Latin or Greek word parts. Because the etymology can help you understand and remember a word's meaning, dictionaries typically include the etymology in brackets [ ] before or after the definition. When you look up a word in the dictionary, take an extra minute to check its etymology for word parts that you might recognize.

Familiarize yourself with the common roots, prefixes, and suffixes in Appendix 2, and then watch for them in new words you encounter. Use word-structure clues whenever possible to help you determine the meaning of an unfamiliar word or confirm your educated guess from context clues.

Understanding Denotations and Connotations of Words

The literal, explicit meaning of a word—its dictionary definition—is called its **denotation.** But many words also have connotations. A **connotation** is an additional, nonliteral meaning associated with a word. For example, the two words *weird* and *distinctive* have similar denotations (both describe something that is different or out of the ordinary). It is their connotations that cause us to choose

EXAMPLES OF DENOTATIONS AND CONNOTATIONS

Similar Word with Negative Connotation	Denotation (Neutral)	Similar Word with Positive Connotation
Sofia has *weird* tastes.	Sofia has *different* tastes.	Sofia has *distinctive* tastes.
When I was younger, I was *skinny*.	When I was younger, I was *thin*.	When I was younger, I was *slender*.
I purchased a *secondhand* car.	I purchased a *used* car.	I purchased a *preowned* car.
Joe changed *jobs*.	Joe changed *occupations*.	Joe changed *professions*.
His behavior was *peculiar*.	His behavior was *abnormal*.	His behavior was *unusual*.
She *craves* power.	She *wants* power.	She *desires* power.
Lou spent time in a *penitentiary*.	Lou spent time in *jail*.	Lou spent time in a *correctional facility*.
Hector has joined a *gang*.	Hector has joined a *club*.	Hector has joined an *association*.
The patient *croaked*.	The patient *died*.	The patient *passed on*.

Comprehension-Monitoring Question for Connotative Meaning

Is there a positive or negative association in addition to the literal meaning of a word?

one word instead of the other when describing someone or something. You might describe the traits of someone you admire as *distinctive* but those of someone you dislike as *weird,* because *distinctive* has a positive connotation and *weird* has a negative one. Most people, for example, would rather be thought of as having *distinctive* clothes than *weird* clothes. *Distinctive* and *weird* have opposite connotations: *distinctive* is associated with positive qualities; *weird* is associated with negative ones.

As explained above, many words have positive or negative connotative meanings beyond their more neutral denotative meanings. The middle column in the chart above presents a sentence containing an italicized word whose denotation is neutral. In the other two columns, the italicized word has been replaced by other words that have a similar denotation, but have a positive or negative connotation.

Careful readers ask themselves, "Does this word have a connotation as well as a denotation?" That is, "Is there a positive or negative association in addition to the word's literal meaning?"

figurative language

Words that create unusual comparisons or vivid pictures in the reader's mind.

Figurative expressions are also known as *figures of speech.*

Understanding Figurative Language

Figurative language is language that uses imagery—unusual comparisons or vivid words that create certain effects—to paint a picture in the reader's or listener's mind. Figurative expressions are also called *figures of speech.* You use figurative language every day, although you may not know it by that name. Whenever you say something such as "That chemistry test was a monster" or "My mother is a saint," you are using figurative language.

Because figures of speech do not literally mean what the words say, you must *interpret* their meaning. If you say, "My supervisor is a prince," you do not actually or literally mean that he is royalty. You expect your listener to interpret your words to mean that you appreciate your supervisor, perhaps because he is patient and cheerful. If you say, "My supervisor is a rat," you do not literally mean that he is a rodent. You expect your listener to understand that you dislike your supervisor, perhaps because he has proved to be harsh or unfair.

Four common figures of speech are *metaphor, simile, hyperbole,* and *personification.* Let's look at each of these.

Metaphors and similes both make comparisons. A **metaphor** is an implied comparison between two things that seem very different from each other on the surface yet are alike in some significant way. A metaphor usually states that one thing is something else. For example, in the sentence "Ann's *garden is a rainbow,*" the writer makes a comparison between a garden and a rainbow to help the reader envision the garden's colorful array of flowers. To interpret this metaphor correctly, the reader must determine what a garden and a rainbow have in common: a multitude of colors. The author does not mean that the garden is literally a rainbow. As noted, a metaphor usually states that one thing is something else (in this case, that a garden *is* a rainbow).

A **simile** is also a comparison between two essentially dissimilar things, but instead of saying that one thing *is* something else, the author says that one thing is *like* something else. A simile is usually introduced by the word *like* or *as*: "The marine stood at attention *as rigid as an oak tree.*" In the example, a marine, because of his stiff posture, is compared with an oak tree. To repeat: A simile says that one thing is *like* another. To understand a simile, determine which things are being compared and the important way in which they are similar.

Another type of figurative language is **hyperbole** (pronounced hī *pĕr′* bə lē), in which obvious exaggeration is used for emphasis. "My parents will explode if I get one more speeding ticket!" is an example. The parents would not literally "explode," but the exaggeration conveys how angry they would be.

In **personification,** nonliving or nonhuman things are given human characteristics or qualities. "My car groaned, coughed, and wheezed, then crawled to a stop" gives human attributes to a car to suggest it made strange noises and then quit running. Cars, of course, cannot groan, cough, wheeze, and crawl in the same sense a person would. That's what makes it personification.

Careful readers ask themselves, "Is the author using figurative language?" "What things are being compared, and how are they alike?" "What exaggeration is being made, and why?" "Which human traits are being given to a nonliving thing?"

The chart on page 80 summarizes metaphor, simile, hyperbole, and personification, and presents examples of each.

Understanding figurative language can help you grasp an author's message, and it makes material more interesting and enjoyable to read.

metaphor

Figure of speech suggesting a comparison between two essentially dissimilar things, usually by saying that one of them *is* the other.

simile

Figure of speech presenting a comparison between two essentially dissimilar things by saying that one of them is *like* the other.

hyperbole

Figure of speech using obvious exaggeration for emphasis and effect.

personification

Figure of speech in which nonhuman or nonliving things are given human traits or attributes.

Comprehension-Monitoring Question for Figurative Language

Should these words or this expression be interpreted figuratively?

FOUR TYPES OF FIGURATIVE LANGUAGE

Figures of Speech	Examples
Metaphor	
Implied comparison between two essentially dissimilar things, usually using the word *is* or *was*.	My grandfather's face is a raisin. Shyness was my prison. One person's trash is another person's treasure. The midnight sky was diamonds on black velvet. His desk is a mountain of paper.
Simile	
Stated comparison between two essentially dissimilar things, usually introduced by the word *like* or *as*.	After the party, Ted's apartment looked as if it had been hit by a tornado. Monica's closet is like a shoe store. The hockey player looked as if he'd gone 10 rounds in a boxing ring—and lost. My allergies made my head feel like a block of wood. The sleet hit our faces like tiny knives.
Hyperbole	
Obvious exaggeration for emphasis and effect.	I'm so hungry I could eat a horse! Smoke came out of the coach's ears when the penalty was called. My grandmother's biscuits are so light they float off the plate. I'm buried in homework this weekend. My backpack weighs a ton.
Personification	
Attribution of human characteristics or qualities to nonhuman or nonliving things.	The ATM machine ate my debit card! The cans danced on the shelves during the earthquake. When the theater lights dimmed, the cell phones couldn't wait to begin screaming. Even though it once seemed far off and unlikely, a college degree has always beckoned me.

A WORD ABOUT STANDARDIZED READING TESTS: CONTEXT CLUES AND FIGURATIVE LANGUAGE

Many college students are required to take standardized reading tests as part of an overall assessment program, in a reading course, or as part of a state-mandated basic skills test. For example, these include the Nelson-Denny Reading Test, COMPASS, ASSET, ACCUPLACER, THEA (in Texas), and Florida's state-mandated test. A standardized reading test typically consists of a series of passages, each of which is followed by multiple-choice reading skill application questions. The test is often timed. That is, students are permitted to work for only a specified amount of time.

The tips below, along with the ones in each chapter in Part Two, can help you earn higher scores on standardized reading tests. The tips for this chapter deal with context clues and figurative language. Many tests include context clue questions, and some have figurative language items as well.

On tests, vocabulary-in-context questions will be worded:

As used in line [#], the word [—] means . . .

As used in paragraph [#], the word [—] means . . .

The [vocabulary word] in the first paragraph means . . .

In the fifth paragraph, the meaning of [word] is . . .

As used in the last paragraph, [the term] means . . .

To determine the correct answer, ask yourself, "What would this word have to mean in order to make sense in this sentence?" Most words have more than one meaning, so be sure to refer to the sentence in which the word appears. Reread the sentence and, if necessary, the sentences immediately before and after it. Look for definition clues, synonym clues (including punctuation clues), contrast clues (antonyms), experience clues, example clues, and clues from other sentences. You may be able to use word parts (prefixes and roots) to help confirm your answer choice. Keep in mind that you may occasionally be asked the meaning of a phrase in context. For example, in context, the phrase *to take a swing at it* might mean *to attempt* or *to try.* The process for determining the correct meaning will still be to ask yourself what the phrase would have to mean in order to make sense in the sentence. Be sure to read all the answer choices before choosing one.

Figurative language questions might be worded:

The author uses the metaphor of a ship to represent . . .

In paragraph 2, the author compares old age to . . .

In the selection, *winter* is personified as being . . .

In using the simile "Peace negotiations are like a high-stakes chess game," the author is suggesting . . .

In the metaphor in paragraph 4, a smile is compared with . . .

The comparison between the brain and a computer is an example of which figure of speech?

To find the right answer, think about the type of figure of speech. If it is a *simile* or *metaphor,* decide which two things are being compared and how they are alike. If it is a *hyperbole,* decide what effect the author is trying to achieve—humor, shock, persuasion, and so on. If it is *personification,* decide what inanimate object is being compared with a person and the important way it might be like a person. Be sure to read all the answer choices before choosing one.

DEVELOPING CHAPTER REVIEW CARDS

Review cards, or *summary cards,* are an excellent study tool. They are a way to select, organize, and review the most important information in a textbook chapter. Creating review cards helps you organize information in a meaningful way and transfer it into long-term memory as you prepare for tests (see Part Three). The review card activities in this book give you structured practice in creating these valuable study tools. Once you have learned how to make review cards, you can create them for textbook material in your other courses.

Now complete the eight review cards for Chapter 2 by answering the questions or following the directions on each card. When you have completed them, you will have summarized important information about (1) the reading process, (2) predicting as you read, (3) monitoring your comprehension, (4) adjusting your reading rate, (5) using context clues to determine the meaning of unfamiliar words, (6) using word-structure clues, (7) interpreting figurative language, and (8) monitoring your understanding of vocabulary. Print or write legibly. You will find it easier to complete the review cards if you remove these pages before filling them in.

Understanding the Reading Process

List eight important points about the reading process. (See pages 69–70.)

1.

2.

3.

4.

5.

6.

7.

8.

Card 1   Chapter 2: Approaching College Reading and Developing a College-Level Vocabulary

Predicting as You Read

1.   What is predicting? (See page 71.)

2.   Why is predicting helpful? (See page 71.)

Card 2   Chapter 2: Approaching College Reading and Developing a College-Level Vocabulary

Monitoring Your Comprehension

1.   What does monitoring your comprehension mean? (See page 71.)

2.   Describe the three-part procedure for monitoring your comprehension as you read. (See page 71.)

First:

Second:

Third:

Card 3   Chapter 2: Approaching College Reading and Developing a College-Level Vocabulary

---

Adjusting Your Reading Rate

Efficient readers adjust their rate according to two factors. List them. (See page 72.)

Factor 1:

Factor 2:

List several situations in which it is appropriate to *slow down* your reading rate. (See pages 73–74.)

List several situations in which it is appropriate to *speed up* your reading rate. (See page 74.)

Card 4   Chapter 2: Approaching College Reading and Developing a College-Level Vocabulary

---

Using Context Clues to Determine Meanings of Words

What are *context clues*? (See page 75.)

Describe six types of context clues. (See the box on page 76.)

1.   Definition:

2.   Synonym:

3.   Contrast:

4.   Experience:

5.   Example:

6.   Clue from another sentence:

Card 5   Chapter 2: Approaching College Reading and Developing a College-Level Vocabulary

---

Using Word-Structure Clues

Define the following terms. (See pages 75–77.)

Word-structure clues:

Root:

Prefix:

Suffix:

Etymology:

Card 6   Chapter 2: Approaching College Reading and Developing a College-Level Vocabulary

---

Four Types of Figurative Language

Define the following terms. (See pages 78–79.)

Figurative language:

Metaphor:

Simile:

Hyperbole:

Personification:

Card 7   Chapter 2: Approaching College Reading and Developing a College-Level Vocabulary

Monitoring Your Understanding of Vocabulary

1. What question should you ask yourself in order to take advantage of context clues? (See page 75.)

2. What question should you ask yourself in order to take advantage of word-structure clues? (See page 77.)

3. What question should you ask yourself in order to understand the connotation of a word? (See page 78.)

4. What question should you ask yourself in order to understand figurative language? (See page 79.)

Card 8 Chapter 2: Approaching College Reading and Developing a College-Level Vocabulary

Directions: Answer the following questions. In some, you will be asked about the *type* of context clue in the sentence. In others, you must use context clues to *determine the meaning* of the underlined word.

_____ 1. Internships are typically one-time work experiences related to your program of study or career goal in which you work in a professional setting with on-site supervision.

   The type of context clue in the sentence above is:
   a. a synonym clue.
   b. a definition clue.
   c. a contrast clue.
   d. an example clue.

_____ 2. Some people have <u>eclectic</u> tastes in music, yet others strongly prefer one certain genre or type.

   As used in the sentence above, the word *eclectic* means:
   a. hard to understand.
   b. consisting of a variety of styles.
   c. unusual; out of the ordinary.
   d. sophisticated; cultured; refined.

_____ 3. When you are in debt, you spend most of your time <u>scrambling</u> to make up for the past rather than planning for the future.

   As used in the sentence above, the word *scrambling* means:
   a. waiting patiently.
   b. jumbling things together.
   c. struggling frantically.
   d. collapsing in despair.

_____ 4. The extent to which market economies rely on **specialization** is extraordinary. It is the use of resources of an individual, region, or nation to produce one or a few goods or services rather than the entire array of goods and services.

   In the passage above, the type of context clue is:
   a. an example clue.
   b. a contrast clue.
   c. a synonym clue.
   d. a clue from another sentence.

_____ 5. *Acid rain* is the term generally used for pollutants that are created by burning fossil fuels and that change chemically as they are transported through the atmosphere and fall back to Earth as acidic rain, snow, fog, or dust.

   In the sentence above, what are the clue words that indicate a definition is being presented?
   a. is the term
   b. used for pollutants
   c. transported through the atmosphere
   d. fall back to Earth

_____ 6. Many people are unaware that they engage in *drug misuse*. For instance, they use prescription drugs for purposes other than those for which they were prescribed or in greater amounts than prescribed. Another example is using nonprescription drugs or chemicals for purposes other than those intended by the manufacturer.

In the passage above, which type of context clue reveals the meaning of *drug misuse*?
a. definition clue
b. synonym clue
c. contrast clue
d. example clue

_____ 7. It is not surprising that negative thinking goes hand in hand with pessimism, the tendency to expect the worst possible outcome.

As used in the passage above, the word *pessimism* means:
a. something that is not surprising.
b. positive thinking.
c. going hand in hand.
d. the tendency to expect the worst possible outcome.

_____ 8. Recently, cases of methicillin-resistant *Staphylococcus aureus*—or MRSA— have been associated with tattooing.

In the sentence above, which two things have the same meaning?
a. MRSA and tattooing
b. methicillin-resistant *Staphylococcus aureus* and tattooing
c. MRSA and cases
d. methicillin-resistant *Staphylococcus aureus* and MRSA

_____ 9. The *Type A behavior pattern* is a cluster of behaviors involving hostility, competitiveness, time urgency, and feeling driven, while the *Type B behavior pattern* is characterized by a patient, cooperative, noncompetitive manner.

Which type of context clue appears in the sentence above?
a. definition clue
b. synonym clue
c. contrast clue
d. example clue

_____ 10. The less you study, the worse you do academically, and the worse you do academically, the less inclined you are to study: It's a vicious cycle.

In the passage above, the meaning of *vicious cycle* is:
a. a "solution" to one problem creates a new problem and makes it harder to solve the original one.
b. not studying when you should.
c. doing poorly academically because you do not like to study.
d. going around and around in circles.

Directions: Answer the following questions. In some, you will be asked about the *type* of context clue in the sentence. In others, you must use context clues to *determine the meaning* of the underlined word.

1. A favorable change in <u>consumer tastes</u> (preferences) for a product means more of it will be demanded at each price.

   In the sentence above, what is the meaning of *consumer tastes*?
   a. a favorable chance
   b. preferences
   c. a demand at each price
   d. a product

2. The active pumping of air in and out of the lungs is called **breathing.**

   In the sentence above, what are the clue words that indicate a definition context clue?
   a. active pumping
   b. in and out of the lungs
   c. is called
   d. breathing

3. **Body image**—the mental representation that a person has of his or her own body, including perceptions, attitudes, thoughts, and emotions—is strongly influenced by culture.

   In the sentence above, which clues indicate a definition is being presented? *Choose all that apply.*
   a. commas
   b. hyphens
   c. dashes
   d. bold print

4. <u>**Disordered eating behaviors**</u> are common and widespread. They include restrictive dieting, binge eating and purging, and laxative abuse.

   As used in the passage above, the term *disordered eating behaviors* means eating behaviors that are:
   a. common.
   b. widespread.
   c. unhealthy.
   d. restrictive.

5. Complementary goods are products that are used together and thus are typically demanded jointly, such as computers and software, or cell phones and cellular service.

In the sentence above, which words signal an example context clue?
a. complementary goods
b. computers and software
c. cell phones and cellular service
d. such as

_____ **6.** Risk of injury and death, hardship, and prolonged separation from loved ones during tours of duty are examples of the <u>vicissitudes</u> of a military career.

As used in the sentence above, the word *vicissitudes* means:
a. difficulties.
b. benefits.
c. rewards.
d. promises.

_____ **7.** Rather than writing a positive, complimentary review of the novel, the critic made only <u>pejorative</u> comments about it.

As used in the sentence above, the word *pejorative* means:
a. favorable; approving.
b. insightful; thoughtful.
c. widely quoted.
d. belittling; showing a low opinion.

_____ **8.** Because accidents at that intersection are a <u>recurrent</u> problem, they are installing a traffic light.

As used in the sentence above, the word *recurrent* means:
a. happening repeatedly.
b. annoying.
c. cannot be prevented.
d. rarely reported.

_____ **9.** Self-confidence comes from a sense of *self-expectancy,* or in other words, the belief that you are able to achieve what you want in life.

Which words in the sentence above announce a synonym or restatement clue?
a. Self-confidence
b. a sense of self-expectancy
c. or in other words
d. the belief that you are able to achieve what you want in life

_____ **10.** <u>Strait-laced</u> parents do not permit their children to say or do anything they consider inappropriate.

As used in the sentence above, the word *strait-laced* means:
a. relaxed and easygoing.
b. uncaring, feeling.
c. excessively strict and proper.
d. insecure and anxious.

Directions: Study the following roots and their meaning. Then use these important word parts, along with context clues, to determine the meaning of the underlined word in each sentence.

Root	Meaning	Example Words
bio	life, living	biology, biography, bionic
chrono	time	chronology, chronometer
flect, flex	bend	reflection, reflex, flex
magn	big, great	magnify, magnificent
manu	hand, make, do	manufacture, manicure, manuscript
mit, miss	send, put	submit, transmit, emission
patri, pater	father	patriotic, patron, paterfamilias
pel, puls	push, drive	repel, compel, expulsion
ven, vene, vent	come	prevent, event, intervention
vid, view, vis	see, look	visible, review, videodisc, vision

1. When you receive a bill, the invoice indicates the date by which you must <u>remit</u> payment.

   Remit means:
   a. refuse.
   b. calculate.
   c. send in.

2. The pathologist examined a liver <u>biopsy</u> in order to determine whether cancer cells were present.

   Biopsy means:
   a. examining the liver.
   b. a tissue sample from a living body for diagnostic purposes.
   c. work done by a doctor.

3. A dozen of the world's wealthiest oil <u>magnates</u> held an international meeting in Switzerland.

   Magnates are:
   a. objects that attract other objects.
   b. people to whom other people are attracted.
   c. powerful people in an industry.

4. Parishioners approach the church's altar, <u>genuflect</u>, cross themselves, and then take their seats.

   Genuflect means to:
   a. walk down the main aisle of a church.
   b. make eye contact with other church members.
   c. bend the knee or touch one knee to the floor.

_____   **5.** Many world travelers keep a journal in which they <u>chronicle</u> their trips to various destinations.

Chronicle means to:
a. make a detailed record of events in the order they occurred.
b. keep close track of one's time.
c. brag about places you have been.

_____   **6.** Hard work and a positive attitude can <u>propel</u> you to success.

Propel means to:
a. guarantee; assure.
b. be a factor in.
c. move forward or ahead.

_____   **7.** Digging with a shovel and chopping wood are examples of <u>manual labor</u>.

Manual labor refers to:
a. physical labor done by people.
b. labor done by machines.
c. work done on weekdays rather than weekends.

_____   **8.** The international agency helps <u>repatriate</u> war refugees.

Repatriate means to:
a. help locate one's family members.
b. return to one's fatherland (country of birth or citizenship).
c. become national leaders.

_____   **9.** When the garden hose freezes, it becomes stiff and <u>inflexible</u>.

Inflexible means:
a. lighter in color.
b. easy to break.
c. not easily bent.

_____   **10.** Because of the recession, many Americans experienced <u>chronic</u> financial problems for several years.

Chronic means:
a. intermittent or periodic.
b. lasting for a long period of time.
c. minor or of little significance.

_____   **11.** Abraham Lincoln and Mother Teresa are viewed as <u>magnanimous</u> individuals.

Magnanimous means:
a. courageously noble in mind and heart; large in spirit.
b. extremely well regarded throughout the world.
c. important historical characters.

12. As the aging actor told the story of his life, his <u>amanuensis</u> jotted down every word.

Amanuensis means a person who is:
a. a highly trained butler.
b. employed to take dictation.
c. a fellow actor.

13. There are government regulations that control pesticides and other <u>biocides</u>.

Biocide means a:
a. government regulation.
b. government regulation that controls pesticides.
c. chemical agent that is capable of destroying living organisms.

14. Active duty military service <u>intervened</u>, and it was two years before the Army reservist could return to college.

Intervened means:
a. was completed.
b. came between two things.
c. offered educational benefits.

15. Several members of his church have served as <u>missionaries</u> in foreign countries.

Missionaries refers to people who:
a. undertake dangerous military assignments in other countries.
b. are sent to do religious or charitable work in other countries.
c. handle diplomatic relations with other nations.

16. Taking a speech course can help <u>dispel</u> a student's fears of public speaking.

Dispel means:
a. improve or enhance.
b. share.
c. drive away.

17. The student government <u>convenes</u> every other Tuesday afternoon at 3:00 P.M.

Convene means:
a. comes together for an official purpose.
b. votes on a variety of issues.
c. sets the agenda for the coming meeting.

18. Apple's founder, Steve Jobs, will always be considered a <u>visionary</u>.

A *visionary* is a person who:
a. sees the significance of events before they occur.
b. amasses a fortune by creating new technology.
c. donates significant amounts of money to charity.

19. In the Greek creation epic, Zeus commits <u>patricide</u> by poisoning his father, Cronus.

Patricide means:
a. being the main character in a Greek epic.
b. ruining family relationships.
c. killing one's father.

20. When writing a formal paper, you should allow ample time to <u>revise</u> it.

Revise means to:
a. complete the necessary research.
b. look at it again in order to reconsider and modify it.
c. ask questions about material you do not understand.

Directions: Study the following roots and their meaning. Then use these important word parts, along with context clues, to determine the meaning of the italicized word in each sentence.

Root	Meaning	Example Words
leg, legis	law	legislature, legitimate, legalize
loc, loco	place, area	location, locomotion, locus
mania	madness	mania, manic, kleptomania, pyromania
matri, mater	mother	maternity, matron, matrimony, maternal
mob, mot, mov	move	mobile, motor, motility, movable, remove
nov	new	nova, innovate, renovate, novice
poli	city	cosmopolitan, politics, police
rupt	break	interrupt, disrupt, eruption, abrupt
terr, terra	earth, terrain	territory, terrain, terrarium, terrier
vit, vita, viva	life, alive	revive, vivid, survive, vitamin

_____ 1. A *ruptured* pipe is one that is:
    a. broken.
    b. made of metal.
    c. flexible.
    d. pushed into the ground.

_____ 2. If something is *vital,* it is:
    a. new and untested.
    b. found in only one place.
    c. able to be easily bent.
    d. essential for life.

_____ 3. To *motivate* someone is to:
    a. move the person to do something.
    b. control the person.
    c. observe or see the person.
    d. drive the person crazy.

_____ 4. *Local* anesthesia prevents pain in:
    a. a patient's entire body.
    b. the place where it is injected or is applied.
    c. surgeries done in a particular hospital.
    d. patients of a certain doctor.

_____ 5. A *metropolis* is a:
    a. place filled with life.
    b. newly settled area.
    c. city.
    d. region that is isolated.

6. A *novel* idea is one that is:
  a. about a book.
  b. ridiculously impractical.
  c. new and strikingly unusual.
  d. about the earth or terrain.

7. A *matriarch* is a highly respected woman who is a:
  a. politician.
  b. city-dweller.
  c. lawyer.
  d. mother.

8. A *legal* holiday is one that:
  a. is authorized by law.
  b. occurs once a year.
  c. is celebrated only in certain parts of the country.
  d. is celebrated by all Americans.

9. To *inter* a dead body is to:
  a. bury it in a city cemetery.
  b. bring it back to life.
  c. move it to a different gravesite.
  d. place it into the ground for burial.

10. A homicidal *maniac* is a killer who is:
  a. overly attached to his mother.
  b. able to move easily from one place to another.
  c. insane.
  d. from a city.

11. A *renovated* house has been:
  a. moved to a different location.
  b. built in a city.
  c. made like new.
  d. raised above the ground.

12. A *legitimate* complaint is one that is:
  a. crazy-making.
  b. lawful.
  c. broken.
  d. lively.

13. A *terrier* is a dog that was originally developed to:
  a. move quickly.
  b. hunt in a certain area.
  c. live in a city rather than in the country.
  d. drive game from burrows in the ground.

14. A *vivacious* person is one who is:
  a. lively and spirited.
  b. insane.
  c. law-abiding.
  d. rude and abrupt.

15. A *corrupted* computer hard drive is:
  a. illegal.
  b. damaged or broken.
  c. extremely fast.
  d. used or secondhand.

16. A *politico* is a:
  a. thief.
  b. politician.
  c. executive.
  d. military leader.

17. *Egomaniacs* are:
  a. skillful with their hands.
  b. able to move in unusual ways.
  c. overly attached to their mothers.
  d. crazy about themselves.

18. *Locomotion* refers to the ability to:
  a. motivate others.
  b. survive.
  c. move from place to place.
  d. pass laws.

19. A *maternal* instinct is one that is characteristic of a:
  a. mother.
  b. soldier.
  c. researcher.
  d. psychic.

20. An object that is *immobile:*
  a. is shiny.
  b. cannot be broken.
  c. needs to be replaced.
  d. does not move.

Directions: Identify the *type* of figurative language (figure of speech) in each sentence below.

_____ **1.** "Life is like a game of cards. The hand you are dealt is determinism; the way you play it is free will." —Jawaharlal Nehru, former prime minister of India
   a. metaphor
   b. simile
   c. hyperbole
   d. personification

_____ **2.** "Opportunity is missed by most people because it is dressed in overalls and looks like work." —Thomas Edison, inventor
   a. metaphor
   b. simile
   c. hyperbole
   d. personification

_____ **3.** "Life's a voyage that's homeward bound." —Herman Melville, author
   a. metaphor
   b. simile
   c. hyperbole
   d. personification

_____ **4.** "When humor goes, there goes civilization." —Erma Bombeck, humorist
   a. metaphor
   b. simile
   c. hyperbole
   d. personification

_____ **5.** "You can't deny laughter. When it comes, it plops down in your favorite chair and stays as long as it wants." —Stephen King, author
   a. metaphor
   b. simile
   c. hyperbole
   d. personification

_____ **6.** "Music is the strongest form of magic." —Marilyn Manson
   a. metaphor
   b. simile
   c. hyperbole
   d. personification

_____ **7.** "Striving for success without hard work is like trying to harvest where you haven't planted." —David Bly
   a. metaphor
   b. simile
   c. hyperbole
   d. personification

101

8. "He runs a mile in nothing flat. / He can run right out from under his hat."

   —John Ciardi, "Speed Adjustments" (poem)

   a. metaphor
   b. simile
   c. hyperbole
   d. personification

9. "Analyzing humor is like dissecting a frog. Few people are interested, and the frog dies of it."   —E. B. White, author

   a. metaphor
   b. simile
   c. hyperbole
   d. personification

10. "Laughter is an instant vacation."   —Milton Berle, comedian, actor

   a. metaphor
   b. simile
   c. hyperbole
   d. personification

Directions: Interpret the *meaning* of the figurative language in each sentence below.

1. _____ "You can never get a cup of tea large enough or a book long enough to suit me."   —C. S. Lewis, British writer
  a. The writer greatly loves drinking tea and reading books.
  b. The writer thinks most teacups are too small and most books are too short.
  c. The writer is impossible to please.

2. _____ "Indecision and delays are the parents of failure."
                                                    —George Canning, British statesman and politician
  a. Parents should avoid indecision and delay.
  b. Indecision and delays result in failure.
  c. Parents fail unless they teach their children to be decisive and not procrastinate.

3. _____ "The best university of all is a collection of books."
                                                    —Thomas Carlyle, British historian and essayist
  a. A person can become educated by reading widely.
  b. A university's library is important to students' education.
  c. A university graduate should eventually put together a large, personal book collection.

4. _____ "Worrying is like shoveling smoke."   —Unknown
  a. It is useless to worry.
  b. Worrying can go away just as quickly as it begins.
  c. Worrying about smoke is useless.

5. _____ "Sometimes in this river of life, the best thing to do is just float."   —Unknown
  a. Sometimes it is better to accept things rather than struggle against them.
  b. Life can wash a person away.
  c. It is important to know what to do when you are in the water.

6. _____ "Example has more followers than reason." —Christian Nevell Bovee, author and lawyer
  a. It is important always to set a good example.
  b. If you want to be a leader, you must give reasons that are logical.
  c. People pay more attention to what someone does than to what he or she says.

7. _____ "Ideas are like rabbits. You get a couple and learn how to handle them, and pretty soon you have a dozen."   —John Steinbeck, novelist, Nobel laureate
  a. Our thoughts often jump around.
  b. It can be very difficult to manage our thoughts.
  c. Once you begin to get ideas, more of them follow.

8. "I have seen this river so wide it had only one bank."

—Mark Twain, American writer and humorist

   a. You should never take a boat on a river that has only a single bank.

   b. The river can flood so much that one bank seems to have disappeared.

   c. The river is not really a river, but instead is a lake.

9. "Courage doesn't always roar. Sometimes courage is the quiet voice at the end of the day saying, 'I will try again tomorrow.'" —Mary Anne Radmacher, American writer

   a. Courage can be shown in small ways, and not just in dramatic ones.

   b. It takes courage to speak in a quiet voice.

   c. Courage can be defined as trying again.

10. "Life is my college. May I graduate well, and earn some honors."

—Louisa May Alcott, American writer

   a. Life teaches us many lessons; I hope to learn them and live a worthwhile life.

   b. No one is ever too old to start or continue a college education and be successful at it.

   c. College is not helpful in a person's life; you can earn honors without going to college.

SELECTION 2.1

Student Success

Making It Happen: Creating Positive Change to Become a Peak Performer

From *Peak Performance: Success in College and Beyond,* 5th ed.
by Sharon K. Ferrett

Prepare Yourself to Read

Directions: Do these exercises *before* you read Selection 2.1.

1. First, read and think about the title. What do you know about making positive changes and becoming a peak performer?

   _____

   _____

   _____

   _____

   _____

2. Next, complete your preview by reading the following:
   First paragraph (paragraph 1)
   Headings
   Bold print
   Last paragraph (paragraph 20)

   Now that you have previewed the selection, what points do you think the author is making about creating positive changes?

   _____

   _____

   _____

   _____

   _____

3. **Build your vocabulary as you read.** If you discover an unfamiliar word or key term as you read the selection, try to determine its meaning by using context clues.

Internet Resources

Read More about This Topic Online

Use a search engine, such as Google or Yahoo!, to expand your existing knowledge about this topic *before* you read the selection or to learn more about it *afterward*. Use search terms such as "changing habits" or "breaking habits." If you are unfamiliar with conducting Internet searches, read pages 25–26 on Boolean searches. You can also use Wikipedia, the free online encyclopedia, at www.wikipedia.com. Keep in mind that when you visit any website, it is a good idea to evaluate the site and the information it contains. Ask yourself questions such as "Who sponsors this website?" and "Is the information it contains up to date?"

SELECTION 2.1: MAKING IT HAPPEN: CREATING POSITIVE CHANGE TO BECOME A PEAK PERFORMER

The first paragraph of this selection serves as an introduction.

1   You can use many strategies for doing well in your school, career, and personal life. Many techniques are also available on how to manage your time, how to succeed at taking tests, and how to develop healthy relationships. Reading about and discussing them is one thing, but actually making these techniques and strategies part of your everyday life is another. You will find that embracing them will prove rewarding and helpful as you begin developing and working on your goals. Knowing that you have the motivational skills to succeed in school and in your career can give you the confidence to risk, grow, contribute, and overcome life's setbacks. You have what it takes to keep going even when you feel frustrated and unproductive. This selection will show you how to take strategies and turn them into lasting habits. It will also look at the importance of effort and commitment, without which there is no great achievement. Look at great athletes. The difference in their levels of physical skill is often not dramatic, but their sense of commitment is what separates the good from the truly great. Peak performers also achieve results by being committed.

Prediction Exercises

Directions: At each of the points indicated below, answer the question "What do you predict will be discussed next?"

Making a Commitment to Change Your Habits

2   Most people resist change. Even when you are aware of a bad habit, it is difficult to change it. Consequently, you may find it hard to integrate into your life some of the skills and strategies that you know would benefit you.

3   Old habits become comfortable, familiar parts of your life. Giving them up leaves you feeling insecure. For example, you want to get better grades, and you know it's a good idea to study only in a quiet study area rather than while watching television or listening to music. However, you have always read your assignments while watching television. You might even try studying at your desk for a few days, but then you lapse into your old habit. Many people give up at this point rather than acknowledge their resistance. Some find it useful to take stock of what common resistors, or barriers, keep them from meeting their goals. However, as a potential peak performer, you will begin to adopt positive techniques to help change your old habits.

Prediction Exercise

What do you predict will be discussed in this section?

_____

_____

Using Strategies for Creating Positive Change

4   If you have trouble making changes, realize that habits are learned and can be unlearned. Adopting new habits requires a desire to change, consistent effort, time, and a commitment. Try the following ten strategies for eliminating old habits and acquiring new ones.

Prediction Exercise

What do you predict will be discussed in this section?

_____

_____

5 1.   **You must want to change.** To change, you must have a real desire and see the value of the change. It helps to identify important goals: "I really want to get better grades. I have a real desire to graduate from business college and start my own small retail business. I see the benefit and value in continuing my education." Your motivation has to be channeled into constructive action.

6 2.   **Develop specific goals.** Setting specific goals is a beginning for change. Statements such as "I wish I could get better grades" or "I hope I can study more" are too general and only help to continue your bad habits. Stating goals such as "I will study for 40 minutes, two times a day, in my study area" are specific and can be assessed and measured for achievement.

7 3.   **Change only one habit at a time.** You will become discouraged if you try to change too many things about yourself at the same time. If you have decided to study for 40 minutes, two times a day, in your study area, then do this for a month, then two months, then three, and so on, it will become a habit. After you have made one change, move on to the next. Perhaps you want to exercise more, or give better speeches, or get up earlier.

8 4.   **Be patient.** It takes at least 30 days to change a habit. Lasting change requires a pattern of consistent behavior. With time and patience, the change will eventually begin to feel comfortable and normal. Don't become discouraged and give up if you haven't seen a complete change in your behavior in a few weeks. Give yourself at least a month of progressing toward your goal. If you fall short one day, get back on track the next. Don't expect to get all A's the first few weeks of studying longer hours. Don't become discouraged if you don't feel comfortable instantly studying at your desk instead of lying on the couch.

9 5.   **Imagine success.** Imagine yourself progressing through all the steps toward your desired goal. For example, see yourself sitting at your desk in your quiet study area. You are calm and find it easy to concentrate. You enjoy studying and feel good about completing projects. Think back to a time in your life when you had these same positive feelings. Think of a time when you felt warm, confident, safe, and relaxed. Imagine enjoying these feelings and create that same state of mind. Remember, the mind and body produce your state of mind, and this state determines your behaviors.

10 6.   **Observe and model others.** How do successful people think, act, and relate to others? Do students who get good grades have certain habits that contribute to their success? Basic success principles produce successful results. Research indicates that successful students study regularly in a quiet study area. They regularly attend classes, are punctual, and sit in or near the front row. Observe successful students. Are they interested, involved, and well prepared in class? Do they seem confident and focused? Now model this behavior until it feels comfortable and natural. Form study groups with people who are good students, are motivated, and have effective study habits.

11 7.   **Self-awareness.** Sometimes paying attention to your own behavior can help you change habits. For example, you may notice that the schoolwork you complete late at night is not as thorough as the work you complete earlier in the day. Becoming aware of this characteristic may prompt you to change your time frame for studying and completing schoolwork.

12 8.   **Reward yourself.** One of the best ways to change a habit is to reward yourself when you've made a positive change. Increase your motivation with specific payoffs. Suppose you want

to reward yourself for studying for a certain length of time in your study area or for completing a project. For example, you might say to yourself, "After I outline this chapter, I'll watch television for 20 minutes," or "When I finish reading these two chapters, I'll call a friend and talk for 10 minutes." The reward should always come after the results are achieved and be limited in duration.

13 **9. Use affirmations.** Talking to yourself means that you are reprogramming your thoughts, a successful technique for making change. When you have negative thoughts, tell yourself, "Stop!" Counter negative thoughts with positive statements. Replace the negative thought with something like "I am centered and focused. I have control over my thoughts. When they wander, I gently bring them back. I can concentrate for the next 40 minutes, and then I'll take a short break."

14 **10. Write a contract for change.** Write a contract with yourself for overcoming your barriers. State the payoffs for meeting your goals: "I agree to take an honest look at where I am now and at my resistors, my shortcomings, my negative thoughts, the ways I sabotage myself, and the barriers I experience. I agree to learn new skills, choose positive thoughts and attitudes, and try new behaviors. I will reward myself for meeting my goals." You may want to discuss this with a study partner.

Making a Commitment to Contribute

15   As a peak performer, you can make a contribution to the world. By improving yourself, giving to your family, and volunteering your time in the community, you will make the world a better place. You will be leaving a legacy that is positive and inspiring to others. Try to focus on more than just financial success, possessions, prestige, and career advancement. Your family and friends will think of you as being a giving and service-minded person. Consider the contribution you make, the kind of person you want to be, and ways in which you can make a positive impact in your community and personal life.

Prediction Exercise

What do you predict will be discussed in this section?

_____

_____

_____

Making a Commitment to Develop a Positive Attitude

16   Achieving excellence is a combination of a positive attitude and specific skills. When you commit yourself to being successful, you learn to go with your own natural energy and strengths. You learn to be your own best friend by working for yourself. You begin by telling the truth about who you are: your current skills, abilities, goals, barriers, and both good and bad habits. You learn to be aware of the common barriers and setbacks that cause others to fail. Then you set goals to focus your energy on a certain path. Next, you create the specific thoughts and behaviors that will produce the results you want.

Prediction Exercise

What do you predict will be discussed in this section?

_____

_____

_____

17   Everyone gets off course at times; thus, it is important to build in observation and feedback so that you can correct and modify. You will learn to alter your actions to get back on track. Even when you are equipped with the best skills, self-understanding, and a motivated attitude, you will still face occasional setbacks and periods of frustration. At times you may question your decisions, become discouraged, and feel your confidence and self-esteem dip. Focus on the positive and learn to be resilient.

Making a Commitment to Be Resilient

18   The key to being a peak performer is to make adversity work for you. Successful people see their failures as temporary setbacks and learning experiences; unsuccessful people see their failures as barriers and dead ends. Use the power of reframing to see your setbacks as stepping-stones to your final goal. Children have a natural resiliency and can bounce back after a disappointment. You can reclaim resiliency by using your creativity to see what options are still available.

Making a Commitment to Be a Person of Character and Integrity

19   The word integrity comes from the Latin word *integer,* meaning "a sense of wholeness." It is important to use the *whole* of your intelligence for school and job success. When you have a sense of wholeness, you are confident about thinking, speaking, living, and taking the right path. You know that you can trust yourself to do the right thing, keep your commitments, and play by the rules. You are a complete human being when you use your skills, competencies, and essential personal qualities, such as integrity. You have effective communication skills, strive to be sociable and personable, but you put character first. It is not difficult to work out a code of ethics or a moral code that most of us can agree on. Most people believe in core values of honesty, truthfulness, fairness, kindness, compassion, and respect for others. Doing the right thing is a decision and a habit. The key is to assess your integrity as you would any skill and use critical thinking to reflect on your actions.

20   As an adult, you teach values by example. To choose to teach deliberately and consistently is the challenge. Becoming a responsible, motivated, emotionally mature person makes you smarter than you think. You may have a high IQ, talent, skills, and experience, but if you lack responsibility, effort, commitment, a positive attitude, interpersonal skills, and especially character and integrity, you will have difficulty in college, in the workplace, and in your relationships.

Prediction Exercise

What do you predict will be discussed in this section?

_____

_____

_____

Prediction Exercise

What do you predict will be discussed in this section?

_____

_____

_____

Student Success

(continued)

Reading Selection Quiz

This quiz has several parts. Your instructor may assign some or all of them.

Comprehension

Directions: Items 1–10 test your understanding of the selection. They are the type of questions a content area instructor (such as a student success professor) might ask on a test. You may refer to the selection as you answer the questions. Write your answer choice in the space provided.

True or False

_____ **1.** The difference between good athletes and great ones is often their commitment and not their levels of physical skill.

_____ **2.** Changing several habits at once is more effective and efficient than changing them one at a time.

_____ **3.** It takes approximately a month to change a habit.

_____ **4.** A goal of "I will work out for an hour three times a week" is more likely to lead to positive change than a goal of "I will get in better shape physically."

_____ **5.** Peak performers, like other successful people, view failures as temporary setbacks and as opportunities to learn.

_____ **6.** As an adult, you teach values by telling others how to think and behave.

Multiple-Choice

_____ **7.** Using affirmations refers to:
  a. being around others who are positive models.
  b. being patient with yourself while you make changes.
  c. saying positive things to yourself to reprogram your thoughts.
  d. visualizing yourself being successful.

_____ **8.** To be a peak performer, it is important to commit to contribute and to commit to:
  a. develop a positive attitude.
  b. be resilient.
  c. be a person of character and integrity.
  d. all of the above

_____ **9.** When writing a contract for change, it is important to:
  a. state the payoffs for meeting your goals.
  b. include affirmations.
  c. observe and model others.
  d. be patient.

_____ **10.** When you use the strategy of imagining success, you should:
  a. be with other people who are motivated.
  b. alter your actions to get back on track rather than become discouraged.
  c. reward yourself for having a positive attitude.
  d. visualize yourself progressing through the steps to your goal.

Vocabulary in Context

Directions: Items 11–20 test your ability to determine a word's meaning by using context clues. *Context clues* are words in a sentence that allow readers to deduce (reason out) the meaning of an unfamiliar word in the sentence. They also help readers determine the meaning an author intends when a word has more than one meaning. Each item below consists of a sentence from the selection, with the vocabulary word *italicized*. It is followed by another sentence that uses the same word in the same way. Use context clues to deduce the meaning of the *italicized* word. Be sure the meaning you choose makes sense in *both* sentences. Write each answer in the space provided. *Note:* Chapter 2 presents the skill of using context clues.

_____ **11.** *Peak* performers also achieve results by being committed.

Florists report *peak* sales on Valentine's Day and Mother's Day.

peak (pēk) means:
a. well-known; well-documented
b. less than expected
c. busy
d. approaching the highest or maximum

_____ **12.** You might even try studying at your desk for a few days, but then you *lapse* into your old habit.

Dieters should remove inappropriate food in the house so that they do not *lapse* into unhealthy eating habits.

lapse (lăps) means:
a. to fall to a previous or lower level
b. to improve upon
c. to refuse to cooperate or go along with
d. to struggle against

_____ **13.** Your motivation has to be channeled into *constructive* action.

Because of the new coach's *constructive* criticism, the team's morale was the best ever, and they won the college championship.

constructive (kən strŭk′ tĭv) means:
a. creating negative feelings
b. nonstop; continuous
c. helpful; intended to result in improvement
d. hurtful; insulting

_____ **14.** The reward should always come after the results are achieved and be limited in *duration*.

The audience lost interest quickly, but politely suffered through the *duration* of the guest speaker's long presentation.

duration (dŏo rā′ shən) means:

a. period of time something lasts
b. final few minutes
c. excitement
d. a brief period of time

_____ **15.** *Counter* negative thoughts with positive statements.

During a trial, the defense attorney's job is to *counter* the charges and evidence presented by the prosecuting attorney.

counter (koun′ tər) means:

a. to ignore; to dismiss as unimportant
b. to oppose; to offer in response
c. to reveal
d. to accept; to welcome

_____ **16.** I agree to take an honest look at where I am now and at my resistors, my shortcomings, my negative thoughts, the ways I *sabotage* myself, and the barriers I experience.

The soldiers were shocked when a member of their unit attempted to *sabotage* their mission.

sabotage (săb′ ə täzh) means:

a. to defeat by betraying faith or trust
b. to cause to happen
c. to complete alone without aid
d. to celebrate

_____ **17.** You will be leaving a *legacy* that is positive and inspiring to others.

Because my grandfather often took us camping and hiking, part of his *legacy* to us was a deep love for nature.

legacy (lĕg′ ə sē) means:

a. written document that explains or describes
b. something passed from one generation to another
c. time spent oneself
d. outdoor activities

_____ **18.** Try to focus on more than just financial success, possessions, *prestige,* and career advancement.

Because of her *prestige* in the community, she is often asked to lend her name to charitable causes and to chair important civic projects.

prestige (prĕ stēzh′) means:

a. lack of respect
b. living in the same place for a long time
c. a person's high standing among others
d. questionable reputation

_____ **19.** The key to being a peak performer is to make *adversity* work for you.

For children who live in poverty, hunger, and danger, *adversity* is a never-changing way of life.

adversity (ăd vûr′ sĭ tē) means:
a. sadness; unhappiness
b. lack of money
c. depression
d. misfortune; hardship

_____ **20.** Children have a natural *resiliency* and can bounce back after a disappointment.

Writer William Faulkner expressed the *resiliency* of the human spirit in his Nobel Prize acceptance speech when he said, "I believe that man will not merely endure: He will prevail."

resiliency (rĭ zĭl′ yən sē) means:
a. tendency to give up easily
b. ability to stretch
c. ability to recover quickly from misfortune
d. tendency to deceive oneself

SELECTION **2.1**

Student Success

(continued)

Reading Skills Application

Directions: Items 21–25 test your ability to *apply* certain reading skills. You may not be familiar with all the skills yet, so some items will serve as a preview. As you work through *Opening Doors,* you will practice and develop these skills. These are important skills, which is why they are included on the state-mandated basic skills tests that some students must take. Write each answer in the space provided.

_____ **21.** Based on the information in the selection, it can be inferred that the author believes that:
a. only people with high IQs can become peak performers.
b. talent, skills, and experience are the most important factors in becoming a peak performer.
c. it takes several years to become a peak performer.
d. anyone can make positive changes and become a peak performer.

_____ **22.** In paragraph 3, the writer says, "Some find it useful to take stock of what common resistors, or barriers, keep them from meeting their goals." *To take stock of* means:
a. change
b. eliminate; do away with
c. assess; take an inventory of
d. ignore; pay no attention to

_____ **23.** Which pattern is used to organize the information in paragraph 10?
a. definition
b. comparison

    c.   sequence

    d.   cause-effect

24. The information in the selection is based on which of the following assumptions held by the author?

    a. It is very difficult to persuade other people to change their habits.

    b. Only a few people can successfully change their own habits and attitudes.

    c. Making positive changes is more trouble than it is worth.

    d. People have a desire to make positive changes and perform at higher levels.

25. As an example of how observing and modeling others can be helpful, the author mentions:

    a. imagining yourself enjoying studying and feeling good about completing projects.

    b. giving to your family and volunteering time in the community.

    c. forming study groups with motivated students who have effective study habits.

    d. striving to be sociable and personable.

SELECTION **2.1**

Student Success

(continued)

Respond in Writing

Directions: Refer to the selection as needed to answer the essay-type questions below. (Your instructor may direct you to work collaboratively with other students on one or more items. Each group member should be able to explain *all* of the group's answers.)

1. In your opinion, how realistic is the author's approach for making changes? What do you base your opinion on?

_____

_____

_____

_____

_____

2. Write one habit you would like to change, and then describe how you could use at least three of the strategies in the selection to accomplish that change.

_____

_____

_____

_____

_____

3.   Which of the four commitments—to contribute, to develop a positive attitude, to be resilient, to be a person of character and integrity—do you think is most important for success? Why do you think that?

_____

_____

_____

_____

_____

_____

4.   In addition to the 10 strategies described in the selection, what are at least two other strategies that could help a person create positive changes?

_____

_____

_____

_____

_____

_____

5.   **Overall main idea.** What is the overall main idea the author wants you to understand about "changing habits and making positive changes"? Answer this question in one sentence. Be sure that your overall main idea sentence includes the topic (*changing habits and positive change*) and tells the overall most important point about it. Do *not* begin your sentence with "The overall main idea is . . ." or "The author wants us to understand . . ." Just *state* the overall main idea.

_____

_____

_____

_____

_____

_____

SELECTION 2.2

History

Terrorism in a Global Age

From *Nation of Nations: A Narrative History of the American Republic*
by James Davidson et al.

Prepare Yourself to Read

Directions: Do these exercises *before* you read Selection 2.2.

1. First, read and think about the title. What comes to mind when you think about the word *terrorism*?

   _____

   _____

   _____

   _____

   _____

2. Next, complete your preview by reading the following:

   Introduction (in *italics*)

   Headings

   Captions accompanying the photographs

   Now that you have completed your preview, what aspects of fighting terrorism does this selection seem to be about?

   _____

   _____

   _____

   _____

3. Most adults say that they can remember where they were or what they were doing on the morning of September 11, 2001. How did you learn of the news that planes had struck the World Trade Center and the Pentagon?

   _____

   _____

   _____

   _____

4. **Build your vocabulary as you read.** If you discover an unfamiliar word or key term as you read the selection, try to determine its meaning by using context clues.

Internet Resources

Read More about This Topic Online

Use a search engine, such as Google or Yahoo!, to expand your existing knowledge about this topic *before* you read the selection or to learn more about it *afterward.* Use search terms such as "terrorism United States" or "World Trade Center Memorial." If you are unfamiliar with conducting Internet searches, read pages 25–26 on Boolean searches. You can also use Wikipedia, the free online encyclopedia, at www.wikipedia.com. Keep in mind that when you visit any website, it is a good idea to evaluate the site and the information it contains. Ask yourself questions such as "Who sponsors this website?" and "Is the information it contains up to date?"

SELECTION 2.2: **TERRORISM IN A GLOBAL AGE**

During the past few years, significant terrorist conspiracies have been uncovered in the United Kingdom, Germany, and Denmark, among other places. Daniel Benjamin, a scholar on terrorism, American foreign policy, and international security, views terrorism as "a problem of small numbers and large consequences"—in other words, a relatively small number of terrorists who cause large-scale death and destruction. He sees the greatest threat not as the numerous, isolated, smaller-scale attacks, but the "catastrophic attacks" that may happen years apart. Warning against complacency, he cautions further, "And that threat isn't going away" (www.brookings.edu/opinions/2008/0530_ terrorism_ benjamin.aspx?p=1).

The attack on the World Trade Center and the Pentagon on September 11, 2001, reoriented American priorities. President George W. Bush's administration initiated a war on terror both at home and abroad. While an invasion of Afghanistan in October 2001 received widespread support, the decision to invade Iraq in March 2003 without the support of the United Nations signaled a more controversial foreign policy. (Iraqi leader Saddam Hussein was captured in December 2003 and hanged three years later; in December 2011, U.S. troops pulled out of Iraq completely. In May 2011, U.S. Navy Seals and CIA operatives killed Osama bin Laden in Pakistan.)

This selection from a U.S. history textbook explains how a world already connected in so many ways found those connections challenged and shattered by a terrorist movement that was itself global. During the past decade, the fight against terrorism has become an increasingly more challenging and complex national priority.

1   Along the northeast coast of the United States, September 11, 2001, dawned bright and clear. One New Yorker on the way to work remembered that it was the day of the Democratic mayoral primary. He decided to vote before going to his job at the World Trade Center. There, at about the same time, Francis Ledesma was sitting in his office on the sixty-fourth floor of the South Tower when a friend suggested they go for coffee. Francis seldom took breaks that early, but he decided to make an exception. Almost everyone makes similar small choices every day. But this was no ordinary day, and the choices proved to be life-saving.

2   In the cafeteria Francis heard and felt a muffled explosion. He thought a boiler had burst, but then saw bricks and glass falling by the window. Although he intended to head back to his office for a nine o'clock meeting, his friend insisted they leave immediately. Out on the street Francis noticed the smoke and gaping hole where American Airlines Flight 11 had hit the North Tower. At that moment a huge fireball erupted as United Airlines Flight 175 hit their own South Tower. "We kept looking back," Francis recalled as they escaped the area, "and then all of a sudden our building, Tower 2, collapsed. I didn't believe what I had seen; I really thought that it was a mirage."

Prediction Exercises

Directions: At each of the points indicated below, answer the question "What do you predict will be discussed next?"

Prediction Exercise

What do you predict will be discussed in this section?

_____

_____

_____

_____

_____

The Cold War of the 1950s had imagined a Manhattan like this: debris everywhere, buildings in ruin, the city shrouded in smoke and fumes. On September 11, 2001, however, disaster on such a large scale came not from confrontation with another superpower but through the actions of international terrorists. The attack made clear that in a post–Cold War world, global threats could come from small groups as well as powerful nations.

3   Both planes had left Boston's Logan Airport that morning carrying passengers—and a full load of jet fuel—for their flights to Los Angeles. Once the planes were aloft, terrorists commandeered their controls and turned them into lethal missiles. And that was only the beginning of the horror to follow. American Airlines Flight 77 to San Francisco left half an hour later from Dulles Airport in Washington, D.C. Shortly after takeoff it veered from its path and crashed into the Pentagon, the headquarters of the United States Defense Department. News of the terrorist attacks began to spread. Several passengers on United Airlines Flight 93 from Newark to San Francisco heard the news over their cell phones. But hijackers seized that plane as

well. Rather than allow another disaster, several passengers stormed the cockpit. Moments later the plane crashed into a wooded area of western Pennsylvania. The 38 passengers, 5 flight attendants, and 2 pilots, as well as the hijackers, all died instantly.

4   President Bush was in Sarasota, Florida, that morning to promote educational reform. He learned about the attacks while reading to schoolchildren. Aides rushed him to Air Force One, which then flew to a secure area at Barksdale Air Force Base in Louisiana. There the president addressed a shaken nation. He called the crashes a "national tragedy" and condemned those responsible. "Freedom itself was attacked this morning by a faceless coward, and freedom will be defended," he assured the American people.

5   The attack on the World Trade Center left New York City in chaos. The airports shut down, tunnels and bridges closed, and masses of people struggled to leave lower Manhattan. Fearing a potentially staggering loss of life, 10,000 rescue workers swarmed to the scene, where as many as 50,000 people had worked. Firefighters and police, arriving just after the explosions, did what they were trained to do with little regard for their personal safety. They rushed into the burning towers hoping to save as many people as they could. Some victims trapped on the top floors jumped to their deaths to escape the deadly flames. Then, with little warning, the two towers collapsed, one after the other, trapping inside thousands of office workers. With them died nearly 100 Port Authority and city police officers and some 343 fire fighting personnel.

6   At the Pentagon in Washington rescue workers struggled with similar heroism to evacuate victims and extinguish the intense flames. Eighty-four people died there along with the 64 people aboard Flight 77.

Global Dimensions of the World Trade Center Attack

7   In an age of instant global communications, the entire world watched as the tragedy unfolded. Three minutes after the first plane hit the World Trade Center's North Tower, Diane Sawyer of *ABC News* announced that an explosion had rocked the towers. British television was already covering the fire when the second plane reached its target at 9:03. Japanese networks were on the air with coverage of the Pentagon crash about an hour later, around midnight their time. *TV Azteca* in Mexico carried President Bush's statement from Barksdale Air Force Base, and China Central Television was not far behind. For this was, indeed, an international tragedy. The aptly named World Trade Center was a hub for global trade and finance. Citizens of more than 50 nations had died in the attack, hailing from states as diverse as Argentina and Belarus to Yemen and Zimbabwe. Expressions of sorrow flowed in from around the world. Paraguay, for example, issued a stamp memorializing the event, with the slogan "No to Terrorism."

In 2002 Paraguay issued a stamp memorializing the events that occurred on September 11, 2001, with the slogan "No to Terrorism."

Prediction Exercise

What do you predict will be discussed in this section?

_____

_____

_____

_____

_____

_____

_____

8   The events of September 11, 2001, changed the United States profoundly. Not since the surprise attack by the Japanese on Pearl Harbor in 1941 had the nation experienced such a devastating attack on its homeland. Most directly, the attack on the World Trade Center claimed approximately 3,000 lives. Some 2,000 children lost a parent in the attack. More than 20,000 residents living nearby had to evacuate their homes. Officials estimated the cost to the New York City economy at over $83 billion.

Economic Downturn and Threats to National Security

9   Before September 11 the booming economy of the 1990s had already shown serious signs of strain. Shares in many once high-flying dot-com Internet companies had plummeted, sending the stock market into a sharp decline. Telecommunications companies were among the biggest losers. Having spent vast sums on broadband connections for the Internet, they found themselves awash in debt they could not repay. The disruptions of September 11 and its aftermath shocked and, in many ways, weakened an economy already sliding into recession.

10   Added to those economic worries were new fears for American security. The attacks seemed to be the work not of enemy nations but of an Islamic terrorist group known as al Qaeda, led by a shadowy figure, Saudi Arabian national Osama bin Laden. Members of al Qaeda had moved freely around the United States for years, attended flight training schools, and found jobs. How many more undetected terrorist cells were preparing to commit acts of sabotage? Malls, high-rise buildings, and sports stadiums all loomed as possible targets.

11   What had also changed was the nature of the threat. Following World War II, the possibility of atomic war reduced American confidence that the United States could remain safely isolated from the great-power conflicts of the Old World. The attack on the World Trade Center proved that nations were no longer the only threat to our national security. Smaller groups—subnational or international—possessed the capability of using weapons of mass destruction to make war against the most powerful nation on Earth.

Wars on Terrorism

12   But September 11 changed perspectives both at home and around the world. "This is not only an attack on the United States but an attack on the civilized world," insisted German chancellor Gerhard Schroeder, while French Prime Minister Lionel Jospin expressed his feelings of "sadness and horror." Even normally hostile nations like Cuba and Libya conveyed their shock and regrets. At

Prediction Exercise

What do you predict will be discussed in this section?

_____

_____

_____

_____

_____

_____

Prediction Exercise

What do you predict will be discussed in this section?

_____

_____

_____

_____

_____

_____

home President Bush seemed energized by the crisis. In a speech to the nation he vowed that "the United States will hunt down and punish those responsible for these cowardly acts." At the same time he was careful to note that Americans would wage war on terrorism, not the religion of Islam. He distinguished between the majority of "peace loving" Muslims and "evil-doers" like Osama bin Laden. This war would produce no smashing victories nor a quick end, he warned, but the adversary's identity was clear: "Our enemy is a radical network of terrorists and every government that supports them." Other countries now had a simple choice: "Either you are with us or you are with the terrorists." The war would end only when terrorism no longer threatened the world.

13   But a war with so many shadowy opponents was not always easy to reduce to an *either/or* proposition, because it was not always easy to agree on which radical groups or even which nations threatened American security directly. The "radical network of terrorists" worked underground, communicated secretly, and was spread across dozens of nations. Even the states most hospitable to al Qaeda proved hard to single out. Afghanistan was an obvious target, as it had long been a haven to bin Laden and the seat of the Taliban Islamic fundamentalists who ruled the country. Yet 15 of the 19 hijackers in the World Trade Center attacks hailed from Saudi Arabia, long an ally of the United States. During 2003 and 2004, as the administration widened its campaign to root out terrorism, there seemed to be not one war on terror but several—waged both abroad and at home.

14   Over forty years earlier President John F. Kennedy had warned against a global mission that overreached the nation's powers. With only 6 percent of the world's population, our nation could not readily impose its will on the other 94 percent, he observed. Nor could the United States "right every wrong or reverse every adversity." In the end, "there cannot be an American solution to every world problem," he concluded. Only time would tell whether our nation could act successfully to police an uncertain world.

Source: Adapted from James Davidson et al., *Nation of Nations: A Narrative History of the American Republic,* 5e, pp. 1136–138, 1141–142, 1150. Copyright © 2005 by The McGraw-Hill Companies, Inc. Reprinted with permission of The McGraw-Hill Companies, Inc.

Reading Selection Quiz

This quiz has several parts. Your instructor may assign some or all of them.

Comprehension

Directions: Items 1–10 test your understanding of the selection. They are the type of questions a content area instructor (such as a history professor) might ask on a test. You may refer to the selection as you answer the questions. Write your answer choice in the space provided.

True or False

_____ **1.** Two planes that left Boston's Logan Airport on September 11, 2001, crashed into the Pentagon half an hour later.

_____ **2.** Both planes that had departed from Boston's Logan Airport were scheduled to land in Los Angeles.

_____ **3.** Fifteen of the 19 hijackers involved in the World Trade Center attacks hailed from Afghanistan.

_____ **4.** The disruptions of September 11, 2001, and its aftermath weakened the U.S. economy.

_____ **5.** The attack on the World Trade Center proved that smaller, subnational groups possessed the capability of using weapons of mass destruction to wage war against the United States.

Multiple-Choice

_____ **6.** On September 11, 2001, United Airlines Flight 93 from Newark to San Francisco crashed into:
  a. the World Trade Center, South Tower.
  b. the World Trade Center, North Tower.
  c. the Pentagon.
  d. a wooded area in western Pennsylvania.

_____ **7.** The al Qaeda leader Osama bin Laden was born in:
  a. Saudi Arabia.
  b. Afghanistan.
  c. Iraq.
  d. Libya.

_____   **8.** Fighting international terrorism is especially difficult because terrorists:

   a. work underground and communicate secretly.

   b. have networks that are spread across dozens of nations.

   c. sometimes hail from countries that are allies of the United States.

   d. all of the above

_____   **9.** The World Trade Center attack and its aftermath shocked the U.S. economy, which was:

   a. already sliding into recession by the end of the 1990s.

   b. remarkably strong as a result of the dot-com Internet industry.

   c. experiencing a telecommunications boom.

   d. all of the above

_____   **10.** One reason Afghanistan was an obvious target in the war against terrorism was because:

   a. it was the birthplace of Osama bin Laden.

   b. most of the hijackers were citizens of Afghanistan.

   c. it was the seat of the Taliban Islamic fundamentalists who ruled the country.

   d. all of the above

S E L E C T I O N **2.2**

History
(continued)

Vocabulary in Context

Directions: Items 11–20 test your ability to determine a word's meaning by using context clues. *Context clues* are words in a sentence that allow readers to deduce (reason out) the meaning of an unfamiliar word in the sentence. They also help readers determine the meaning an author intends when a word has more than one meaning. Each item below consists of a sentence from the selection, with the vocabulary word *italicized*. It is followed by another sentence that uses the same word in the same way. Use context clues to deduce the meaning of the *italicized* word. Be sure the meaning you choose makes sense in *both* sentences. Write each answer in the space provided. *Note:* Chapter 2 presents the skill of using context clues.

_____   **11.** Once the planes were aloft, terrorists commandeered their controls and turned them into *lethal* missiles.

   The college freshman died from drinking a *lethal* amount of alcohol at a party.

   lethal (lē′ thəl) means:

   a. dangerous

   b. terrorist

   c. deadly

   d. exploding

12. American Airlines Flight 77 to San Francisco left half an hour later from Dulles Airport in Washington, D.C. Shortly after takeoff it *veered* from its path and crashed into the Pentagon, the headquarters of the United States Defense Department.

Lilian's career path *veered* from sales and marketing to management last summer when she was invited to participate in her company's management training program.

veered (vîrd) means:

a. crashed
b. took off
c. improved rapidly
d. changed course

13. The *aptly* named World Trade Center was a hub for global trade and finance.

Our glamorous and stylish sister was *aptly* nicknamed "Ms. Diva."

aptly (ăpt′ lē) means:

a. suitably
b. frequently
c. poorly
d. jokingly

14. The events of September 11, 2001, changed the United States *profoundly.*

When the president was fired after 20 years with the company, it affected him *profoundly.*

profoundly (prə found′ lē) means:

a. intellectually; mentally
b. suddenly
c. deeply; thoroughly
d. positively

15. Shares in many once high-flying dot-com Internet companies had *plummeted,* sending the stock market into a sharp decline.

The temperature *plummeted* when an Arctic cold front blew into our area.

plummeted (plŭm′ ə təd) means:

a. dropped sharply
b. lost value
c. froze
d. rose suddenly; skyrocketed

SELECTION 2.2

_____ 16. How many more *undetected* terrorist cells were preparing to commit acts of sabotage?

Jennifer's diabetes had remained *undetected* for years but was discovered when she finally went to her doctor for a physical exam.

undetected (ŭn də tĕkt′ dĭd) means:

a. controlled

b. undiscovered

c. dangerous

d. secret

_____ 17. He *distinguished* between the majority of "peace loving" Muslims and "evil-doers" like Osama bin Laden.

Professor Martin *distinguished* between his students who were attentive and eager to learn and those who were indifferent.

distinguished (dĭ stĭng′ gwĭshd) means:

a. acknowledged a difference

b. judged to be outstanding

c. disliked

d. compared

_____ 18. This war would produce no smashing victories nor a quick end, he warned, but the *adversary's* identity was clear: "Our enemy is a radical network of terrorists and every government that supports them."

Procrastination is often a college student's greatest *adversary*.

adversary (ăd′ vĕr sĕr ē) means:

a. problem

b. challenge

c. identity

d. enemy

_____ 19. Afghanistan was an obvious target, as it had long been a *haven* to bin Laden and the seat of the Taliban Islamic fundamentalists who ruled the country.

When Joey was in his early teens, the Boys' Club was a *haven* from his dangerous neighborhood and his overcrowded school.

haven (hā′ vən) means:

a. obvious target

b. place of safety; refuge

c. secret hiding place

d. dangerous environment

_____ **20.** Nor could the United States "right every wrong or reverse every *adversity.*"

Learning how to overcome *adversity* is an important part of maintaining happiness and success in life.

adversity (ăd vûr′ sĭ tē) means:

a. misfortune; hardship

b. evil; wrong

c. reversal; change of attitude

d. decision; commitment

SELECTION **2.2**

History
(continued)

Reading Skills Application

Directions: Items 21–25 test your ability *to apply* certain reading skills. You may not be familiar with all the skills yet, so some items will serve as a preview. As you work through *Opening Doors,* you will practice and develop these skills. These are important skills, which is why they are included on the state-mandated basic skills test that some students must take. Write each answer in the space provided.

_____ **21.** In paragraph 14, the authors use the word *police* to mean:

a. to hire security officers

b. to eliminate threats of terrorism

c. to regulate and keep in order

d. to find a solution to a problem

_____ **22.** Which of the following best expresses the main idea of paragraph 8?

a. More than 3,000 people lost their lives and 2,000 children lost a parent in the attack on the World Trade Center.

b. Officials estimated the cost to the New York City economy at more than $83 billion.

c. More than 20,000 residents living near the World Trade Center had to evacuate their homes.

d. The events of September 11, 2001, changed the United States profoundly because the nation had not experienced such a devastating attack on its homeland since the attack on Pearl Harbor in 1941.

_____ **23.** The authors mention Diane Sawyer of *ABC News,* British television, and *TV Azteca* in Mexico to show that:

a. we are living in an age of instant global communications.

b. the war against terrorism is a war against "faceless cowards."

c. television networks were slow to report information about the World Trade Center attacks.

d. it was difficult to agree on which terrorist groups were responsible for the attacks.

_____ **24.** Which writing pattern did the authors use to organize the main idea and supporting details in paragraph 3?

    a. chronological order

    b. comparison-contrast

    c. definition

    d. listing

_____ **25.** Which of the following expresses an opinion rather than a fact?

    a. One hundred Port Authority and city police officers and 343 fire fighting personnel died when the World Trade Center towers collapsed.

    b. Firefighters and police rushed into the burning towers to save as many people as they could.

    c. The tragic attack on the World Trade Center caused widespread chaos and panic throughout New York City.

    d. Following the attack on the World Trade Center, New York airports shut down, and tunnels and bridges were closed.

SELECTION **2.2**

History

(continued)

Respond in Writing

Directions: Refer to the selection as needed to answer the essay-type questions below. (Your instructor may direct you to work collaboratively with other students on one or more items. Each group member should be able to explain *all* of the group's answers.)

1. On the morning of September 11, 2001, 19 hijackers commandeered four planes almost simultaneously. In the spaces below, list the facts given for each aircraft that was involved in the attack.

American Airlines Flight 11:

_____

_____

_____

United Airlines Flight 175:

_____

_____

_____

American Airlines Flight 77:

_____

_____

_____

United Airlines Flight 93:

_____

_____

_____

_____

2. On September 11, President Bush said, "Freedom itself was attacked this morning by a faceless coward." List several reasons terrorist attacks against the United States are so difficult, and likely impossible, to prevent.

_____

_____

_____

_____

_____

3. In the early 1960s President John Kennedy warned that "there cannot be an American solution to every world problem." What message did he hope to convey to both Americans and other nations with this remark?

_____

_____

_____

_____

4. **Overall main idea.** What is the overall main idea the author wants the reader to understand about the relationship between terrorism and the September 11 attacks? Answer this question in one sentence. Be sure to begin your sentence with the phrase "The attack on the World Trade Center and the Pentagon on September 11, 2001 . . ." and include the word *terrorism* in your overall main idea.

_____

_____

_____

_____

SELECTION **2.3**

Biology

A Whale of a Survival Problem

From *The Nature of Life*

by John Postlethwait and Janet Hopson

Prepare Yourself to Read

Directions: Do these exercises *before* you read Selection 2.3.

1. First, read and think about the title. What kinds of things do you think threaten the survival of blue whales?

   _____

   _____

2. Next, complete your preview by reading the following:

   Introduction (in *italics*)

   First paragraph (paragraph 1)

   First sentence of each paragraph

   Words in *italics*

   Diagram

   All of the last paragraph (paragraph 4)

   On the basis of your preview, what specific problem of blue whale survival do you think will be discussed?

   _____

   _____

   _____

3. **Build your vocabulary as you read.** If you discover an unfamiliar word or key term as you read the selection, try to determine its meaning by using context clues.

Internet Resources

Read More about This Topic Online

Use a search engine, such as Google or Yahoo!, to expand your existing knowledge about this topic *before* you read the selection or to learn more about it *afterward*. Use search terms such as "blue whales" or "blue whale survival." If you are unfamiliar with conducting Internet searches, read pages 25–26 on Boolean searches. You can also use Wikipedia, the free online encyclopedia, at www.wikipedia.com. Keep in mind that when you visit any website, it is a good idea to evaluate the site and the information it contains. Ask yourself questions such as "Who sponsors this website?" and "Is the information it contains up to date?"

SELECTION 2.3: A WHALE OF A SURVIVAL PROBLEM

Blue whales are the largest animals on earth. Until harpoon cannons became available, 19th-century whalers were unable to hunt these powerful, swift creatures, and until the start of the 20th century, blue whales could be found in abundance in almost every ocean. Before whaling began, there were an estimated 275,000 blue whales. By the 1960s, the population had dropped to an estimated low of 650 to 2,000. Valued for their oil, meat, and other body parts, they were hunted almost to extinction and have now been on the endangered species list for many years. Although a precise count is not possible, it is estimated that the blue whale population worldwide is now between 8,000 and 14,000. During summer and fall, the world's largest concentrations of these whales can be seen feeding along the central California coast.

During the past few decades, whale hunting has decreased, and blue whale populations are beginning to recover. However, human predators have not been their only problem. Their size alone presents unique challenges for survival. This textbook selection explores the biological adaptations this immense creature has had to make in order to survive.

1   An intrepid visitor to the perpetually frozen Antarctic could stand at the coastline, raise binoculars, and witness a dramatic sight just a few hundred meters offshore: a spout as tall and straight as a telephone pole fountaining upward from the blowhole of a blue whale (*Balaenoptera musculus*), then condensing into a massive cloud of water vapor in the frigid air. The gigantic animal beneath the water jet would be expelling stale air from its 1-ton lungs after a dive in search of food. Then, resting at the surface only long enough to take four deep breaths of fresh air, the streamlined animal would raise its broad tail, thrust mightily, and plunge into the ocean again. The observer on shore might see such a sequence only twice per hour, since the blue whale can hold its breath for 30 minutes as it glides along like a submarine, swallowing trillions of tiny shrimplike animals called krill.

2   It is difficult to comprehend the immense proportions of the blue whale, the largest animal ever to inhabit our planet. At 25 to 30 m (80 to 100 ft) in length, this marine mammal is longer than three railroad boxcars and bigger than any dinosaur that ever lumbered on land. It weighs more than 25 elephants or 1600 fans at a basketball game. Its heart is the size of a beetle—a Volkswagen beetle. And that organ pumps 7200 kg (8 tons) of blood through nearly 2 million kilometers (1.25 million miles) of blood vessels, the largest of which could accommodate an adult person crawling on hands and knees. The animal has a tongue the size of a grown elephant. It has 45,500 kg (50 tons) of muscles to move its 54,500 kg (60 tons) of skin, bones, and organs. And this living mountain can still swim at speeds up to 48 km (30 mi) per hour!

Prediction Exercises

Directions: At each of the points indicated below, answer the question "What do you predict will be discussed next?"

The blue whale is the largest creature on earth.

3   Leviathan proportions aside, it is difficult to grasp the enormous problems that so large an organism must overcome simply to stay alive. For starters, a blue whale is a warm-blooded animal with a relatively high metabolic rate; to stay warm and active in an icy ocean environment, it must consume and burn 1 million kilocalories a day. This it does by straining 3600 kg (8000 lb) of krill from the ocean water each day on special food-gathering sieve plates. In addition, each of the trillions of cells in the whale's organs must exchange oxygen and carbon dioxide, take in nutrients, and rid itself of organic wastes, just as a single-celled protozoan living freely in seawater must do. Yet a given whale cell—a liver cell, let's say—can lie deep in the body, separated from the environment by nearly 2 m (6 ft) of blubber, muscle, bone, and other tissues. For this reason, the whale needs elaborate transport systems to deliver oxygen and nutrients and to carry away carbon dioxide and other wastes. Finally, the galaxy of living cells inside a whale must be coordinated and controlled by a brain, a nervous system, and chemical regulators (hormones) so that the organism can function as a single unit.

Prediction Exercise

What do you predict will be discussed in paragraph 3?

_____

_____

_____

SELECTION 2.3

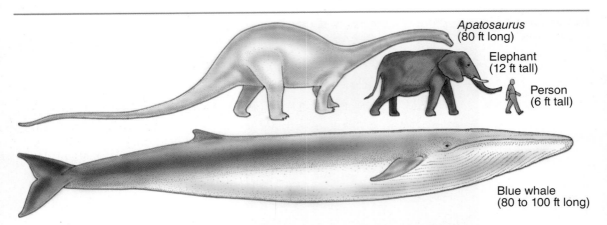

A whale to scale. A blue whale is longer and far heavier than an elephant or even an *Apatosaurus* (formerly *Brontosaurus*), the longest land animal that ever lived.

4   Although blue whales are the largest animals that have ever lived, they share with all other animals the same fundamental physical problems of day-to-day survival: how to extract energy from the environment; how to exchange nutrients, wastes, and gases; how to distribute materials to all the cells in the body; how to maintain a constant internal environment despite fluctuations in the external environment; how to support the body; and how to protect it from attackers or from damaging environmental conditions. Blue whales have evolved with unique adaptations of form and function that meet such challenges and leave the animals suited to their way of life.

Prediction Exercise

What do you predict will be discussed in paragraph 4?

_____

_____

_____

Source: John H. Postlethwait and Janet L. Hopson, *The Nature of Life,* 2e. New York: McGraw-Hill, pp. 430–31. Copyright © 1992 by John H. Postlethwait and Janet L. Hopson. Reprinted by permission of Janet L. Hopson.

SELECTION **2.3**

Biology
(continued)

SELECTION 2.3

Reading Selection Quiz

This quiz has several parts. Your instructor may assign some or all of them.

Comprehension

Directions: Items 1–10 test your understanding of the selection. They are the type of questions a content area instructor (such as a biology professor) might ask on a test. You may refer to the selection as you answer the questions. Write your answer choice in the space provided.

True or False

_____ **1.** The blue whale expels water through its blowhole.

_____ **2.** The blue whale can hold its breath for more than 1 hour as it glides under water.

_____ **3.** The blue whale feeds daily on trillions of tiny shrimplike animals called krill.

_____ **4.** Although large, the blue whale is not the largest animal that inhabits our earth.

_____ **5.** A human adult could crawl on hands and knees through the largest blood vessels of a blue whale.

Multiple-Choice

_____ **6.** In paragraph 1, "a spout as tall and straight as a telephone pole fountaining upward from the blowhole of a blue whale" refers to:
  a. ice.
  b. saltwater.
  c. fresh air.
  d. stale air that has condensed into water vapor.

_____ **7.** The "living mountain" mentioned in paragraph 2 refers to:
  a. the dinosaur.
  b. 8,000 pounds of krill.
  c. the blue whale.
  d. a grown elephant.

_____ **8.** After diving for food, the blue whale surfaces and:
  a. expels stale air through its blowhole, and then dives quickly again.
  b. expels stale air, rests long enough to take four breaths of fresh air, and then dives again.

    c. expels stale air, rests on the surface for 30 minutes, and then dives again.

    d. none of the above

9. Which of the following problems of day-to-day survival does the blue whale share with all other animals?

    a. how to extract energy (food) from the environment

    b. how to distribute materials to all the cells in the body

    c. how to balance the internal environment with the changes in the external environment

    d. all of the above

10. Because the blue whale is a warm-blooded animal and has a relatively high metabolic rate, it must:

    a. rid itself of organic wastes.

    b. expel stale air through its blowhole.

    c. consume and burn 1 million kilocalories a day in order to stay warm and active in the icy ocean.

    d. take four deep breaths of fresh air before diving again for food.

S E L E C T I O N **2.3**

Biology
(continued)

Vocabulary in Context

Directions: Items 11–20 test your ability to determine a word's meaning by using context clues. *Context clues* are words in a sentence that allow readers to deduce (reason out) the meaning of an unfamiliar word in the sentence. They also help readers determine the meaning an author intends when a word has more than one meaning. Each item below consists of a sentence from the selection, with the vocabulary word *italicized*. It is followed by another sentence that uses the same word in the same way. Use context clues to deduce the meaning of the *italicized* word. Be sure the meaning you choose makes sense in *both* sentences. Write each answer in the space provided. *Note:* Chapter 2 presents the skill of using context clues.

11. An *intrepid* visitor to the perpetually frozen Antarctic could stand at the coastline, raise binoculars, and witness a dramatic sight just a few hundred meters offshore.

Columbus was an *intrepid* explorer who set sail for the unknown New World.

intrepid (ĭn trĕp′ ĭd) means:

    a. extremely cold

    b. fun-loving

    c. fearless; bold

    d. weary; fatigued

12. An intrepid visitor to the *perpetually* frozen Antarctic could stand at the coast-line, raise binoculars, and witness a dramatic sight just a few hundred meters offshore.

The earth moves *perpetually* around the sun.

perpetually (pər pĕch′ ōō əl lē) means:
   a. continuing forever without interruption
   b. partially
   c. erratically; unpredictably
   d. once a month

13. An intrepid visitor to the perpetually frozen Antarctic could stand at the coast-line, raise binoculars, and witness a dramatic sight just a few hundred meters offshore: a spout as tall and as straight as a telephone pole fountaining upward from the blowhole of a blue whale, then *condensing* into a massive cloud of water vapor in the frigid air.

When you turn on your car heater in the winter, water vapor may start *condensing* and running down the inside of the windows.

condensing (kən dĕns′ ĭng) means:
   a. turning into steam
   b. changing from a gas into a liquid
   c. becoming colder
   d. changing from a liquid into a solid

14. An intrepid visitor to the perpetually frozen Antarctic could stand at the coast-line, raise binoculars, and witness a dramatic sight just a few hundred meters offshore: a spout as tall and as straight as a telephone pole fountaining upward from the blowhole of a blue whale, then condensing into a massive cloud of water vapor in the *frigid* air.

Snowflakes began to fall from the gray, *frigid* sky.

frigid (frĭj′ ĭd) means:
   a. smoky
   b. dry
   c. starry
   d. extremely cold

15. The gigantic animal beneath the water jet would be *expelling* stale air from its 1-ton lungs after a dive in search of food.

Our college is *expelling* five students for cheating on an exam.

expelling (ĭk spĕl′ ĭng) means:
   a. maintaining
   b. breathing out

   c. forcing out or ejecting

   d. preventing

_____ **16.** *Leviathan* proportions aside, it is difficult to grasp the enormous problems that so large an organism must overcome simply to stay alive.

The deep-sea fishermen swore they had seen a *leviathan*—a shark so huge that it was larger than their boat.

leviathan (lə vī′ ə thən) means:

   a. something unusually large of its kind

   b. measuring device

   c. large shark

   d. huge ship

_____ **17.** For starters, a blue whale is a warm-blooded animal with a *relatively* high metabolic rate; to stay warm in an icy ocean environment, it must consume and burn 1 million kilocalories a day.

Our boss is usually very talkative, but he was *relatively* quiet at the staff meeting today.

relatively (rĕl′ ə tĭv lē) means:

   a. pertaining to family relationships

   b. pertaining to reality

   c. pertaining to a member of the family

   d. in comparison with something else

_____ **18.** For starters, a blue whale is a warm-blooded animal with a relatively high *metabolic* rate; to stay warm in an icy ocean environment, it must consume and burn 1 million kilocalories a day.

Exercise increases a person's *metabolic* rate.

metabolic (mĕt ə bŏl′ ĭk) means:

   a. pertaining to the speed at which an organism moves

   b. pertaining to bodily physical and chemical processes that maintain life

   c. pertaining to breathing and respiration

   d. pertaining to survival

_____ **19.** For this reason, the whale needs *elaborate* transport systems to deliver oxygen and nutrients and to carry away carbon dioxide and wastes.

The plans for the queen's coronation ceremony were so *elaborate* that it took a staff of 500 people to carry out the arrangements.

elaborate (ĭ lăb′ ər ĭt) means:

   a. time-consuming

   b. very complex

c. difficult to understand

d. simple

_____ **20.** Finally, the *galaxy* of living cells inside a whale must be coordinated and controlled by a brain, a nervous system, and chemical regulators (hormones) so that the organism can function as a single unit.

From the dazzling *galaxy* of toys in the toy department, my young nephew finally selected a remote-controlled car.

galaxy (găl′ ək sē) means:

a. stars in the universe

b. collection of numerous things

c. system

d. display

SELECTION **2.3**

Biology
(continued)

SELECTION 2.3

Reading Skills Application

Directions: Items 21–25 test your ability to *apply* certain reading skills. You may not be familiar with all the skills yet, so some items will serve as a preview. As you work through *Opening Doors,* you will practice and develop these skills. These are important skills, which is why they are included on the state-mandated basic skills tests that some students must take. Write each answer in the space provided.

_____ **21.** The meaning of *lumbered* as it is used in paragraph 2 is:

a. swam.

b. walked clumsily.

c. crawled quickly.

d. starved.

_____ **22.** Which of the following is the main idea of the second paragraph of this selection?

a. It is difficult to comprehend the immense proportions of the blue whale, the largest animal ever to inhabit our planet.

b. It weighs more than 25 elephants or 1,600 fans at a basketball game.

c. Its heart is the size of a beetle—a Volkswagen beetle.

d. This living mountain can still swim at speeds up to 48 km (30 mi) per hour.

_____ **23.** The primary reason the authors wrote this selection is to:

a. convince readers that blue whales are big.

b. inform readers about the size of the blue whale and the challenges its size poses for its survival.

c. encourage conservationists to protect blue whales.

d. prove that the blue whale faces unique survival problems not faced by other animals.

_____   **24.** The tone of this selection can best be described as:
  a. alarmed.
  b. passionate.
  c. humorous.
  d. unemotional.

_____   **25.** According to information in the selection:
  a. the blue whale has a tongue the size of a telephone pole.
  b. tiny, shrimplike krill are the smallest animals on earth.
  c. the blue whale has 54,500 kg of skin, bones, and organs.
  d. the muscles of the blue whale weigh 60 tons.

S E L E C T I O N **2.3**

Biology
(continued)

Respond in Writing

Directions: Refer to the selection as needed to answer the essay-type questions below. (Your instructor may direct you to work collaboratively with other students on one or more items. Each group member should be able to explain *all* of the group's answers.)

1. Describe any three comparisons the author uses to illustrate the enormous size of the blue whale.

First comparison:

_____

_____

_____

Second comparison:

_____

_____

_____

Third comparison:

_____

_____

_____

2. Because of its size, what are three special problems that blue whales must overcome to survive?

One problem:

_____

_____

_____

_____

Another problem:

_____

_____

_____

_____

A third problem:

_____

_____

_____

_____

3. Explain why the title of this selection is clever.

_____

_____

_____

_____

4. **Overall main idea.** What is the overall main idea the authors want the reader to understand about the survival of the blue whale? Answer this question in one sentence. Be sure to include *blue whale* and *survive* (or *survival*) in your overall main idea sentence.

_____

_____

_____

_____

SELECTION 2.3

CHAPTER 3

Approaching College Assignments: Reading Textbooks and Following Directions

In this chapter, you will learn the answers to these questions:

- What is an effective way to read and study a college textbook?

- What is the SQ3R study system?

- How can I prepare to read an assignment?

- How can I guide my reading by asking questions?

- How can I review material by rehearsing?

- What are the keys to following directions on college assignments and tests?

SKILLS

College Textbooks: Methods for Reading and Studying Effectively

The SQ3R Study System

The Three-Step Process for Reading and Studying Textbooks

- Step 1: Prepare to Read
- Step 2: Ask and Answer Questions to Enhance Your Reading
- Step 3: Review by Rehearsing the Answers to Your Questions

Following Directions in Textbooks and on Tests

- Guidelines for Following Directions

CREATING YOUR SUMMARY

Developing Chapter Review Cards

READINGS

Selection 3.1 "African Americans: The Struggle for Equality"
from *The American Democracy*
by Thomas E. Patterson (Government)

Selection 3.2 "Parenthood: Now, Later, ... Never?"
from *Human Development*
by Diane E. Papalia, Sally Wendkos Olds, and Ruth Feldman
(Human Development)

Selection 3.3 "Art in the Service of Religion"
from *Living with Art*
by Rita Gilbert (Art Appreciation)

Nothing's fun until you're good at it.

Amy Chua

If you need a helping hand, look at the end of your sleeve.

Proverb

The book that can be read without any trouble was probably written without any trouble also.

Oscar Wilde

Education bridges the gap between the ears.

Unknown

COLLEGE TEXTBOOKS: METHODS FOR READING AND STUDYING EFFECTIVELY

When should you start studying for final exams? The answer is, "At the beginning of the semester." From the first day of classes, you should read and study your textbook assignments as if you were preparing for the final exam. If you read and study your assignments effectively the first time, you won't have to start over and reread them when it is time for a unit test, a major exam, or even a final exam.

Reading your textbooks requires more than casually looking at the pages. Reading and studying take time and effort. Moreover, you must make reading and studying textbook material an active process, not a passive one.

It is important to have a process for reading and studying college textbooks effectively.

How can you understand and remember what you read in your textbooks? This chapter presents two effective methods for reading textbook assignments that ultimately will save you time: the **SQ3R Study System** and the **Three-Step Process for Reading and Studying Textbooks.** Both these approaches are based on studying effectively the first time, so that when it is time to prepare for a test by reviewing, you will not have to spend additional hours rereading.

THE SQ3R STUDY SYSTEM

The SQ3R study system is a widely advocated textbook study system developed by Francis P. Robinson in 1946. The steps in the SQ3R method—**Survey, Question, Read, Recite,** and **Review**—offer a simple, systematic approach to studying textbook material. This time-tested method of asking and answering questions as you read and study a textbook chapter can enhance your reading comprehension and retention of what you read.

Survey	Get an overview before you begin reading a chapter. Look at headings and subheadings, charts, tables, photographs, and words in special print. Read the preface and chapter summary.
Question	Ask questions based on your preview during the Survey step. Turn chapter headings into questions. Create at least one question for each subsection or section in the chapter. Read any questions the author includes in the chapter.
Read	Read each section with your questions in mind. Read actively and search for answers to the questions you developed in the Question step. Reading with a purpose is essential to comprehension and retention.
Recite	After reading each section, stop, recite your questions, and try to answer them aloud from memory. If you cannot answer a question, go back to the section and reread. Don't go on to the next section until you can recite the answer from memory.
Review	After you have completed reading the chapter using the Question, Read, and Recite steps, review all your questions, answers, and other material from the chapter to transfer the information into your long-term memory.

There are many variations on Robinson's study system, such as the SQ4R system (**Survey, Question, Read, Recite, 'Rite** [that is, Write], and **Review**) and the PQ3R system (**Preview, Question, Read, Recite,** and **Review**).

THE THREE-STEP PROCESS FOR READING AND STUDYING TEXTBOOKS

This method for reading and studying textbooks combines all the features and techniques in the SQ3R study system into three steps:

Step 1: Prepare to read.

Step 2: Ask and answer questions to enhance your reading.

Step 3: Review by rehearsing the answer to your questions.

This study-reading process, like SQ3R, will ultimately save you time because you will be studying effectively the first time and will not have to spend additional hours rereading when you prepare for tests.

Step 1: Prepare to Read

preparing to read

Previewing the material, assessing your prior knowledge, and planning your reading and studying time.

Before you begin to read a textbook assignment, spend a few minutes preparing to read. **Preparing to read** involves previewing the chapter, assessing your prior knowledge, and planning your reading and study time.

Preview the Selection

previewing

Examining material to determine its topic and organization before actually reading it.

Previewing means examining material to determine its topic and organization before actually reading it. This gives you a general idea of what an entire assignment will be about and how the material is organized. This not only helps you comprehend what you read but also helps improve your concentration, motivation, and interest in what you are about to read. (That is why each reading selection in *Opening Doors* is preceded by the activity called "Prepare Yourself to Read.") Previewing is also known as "surveying" (as in the SQ3R method).

To preview a chapter assignment:

- **First, read the chapter title.**   This should tell you the overall topic of the chapter.
- **Next, read the chapter introduction.**   A chapter introduction (if there is one) usually presents some of the important points in the chapter, or it may give background information you will need.
- **Read the heading and subheadings of each section.**   Turn through the chapter to read the headings and subheadings. These tell you the topics that are included, and they provide an outline of the chapter information.
- **Read words in *italics*, bold print, or color.**   Notice words that appear in special print (italics or bold print) or in color; these are important terms you will be expected to understand and remember.
- **Look over any graphs and visual aids.**   Look at pictures, illustrations, charts, diagrams, and graphs in the chapter. These give you visual representations of the written material or supplement it.

Comprehension-Monitoring Questions for Previewing

What topics does the author seem to be emphasizing? How are the topics organized?

- **Read questions that accompany a chapter or appear in a study guide.**   They alert you to important information you should watch for as you read.
- **Finally, read the chapter summary.**   A chapter summary contains in brief form many of the important ideas of the chapter. A chapter summary, like a chapter introduction, is especially useful. Take advantage of it.

As you preview, ask yourself questions about the chapter you are preparing to read. Ask yourself, "What topics does the author seem to be emphasizing?" and "How are the topics organized?"

SUMMARY OF THE THREE-STEP PROCESS FOR READING AND STUDYING TEXTBOOKS

Step 1: Prepare to Read

Preview the selection to see what it contains and how it is organized.

- Read the title.
- Read the introduction.
- Read headings and subheadings in each section.
- Read words in italics or bold print.
- Look over graphs and visual aids.
- Read any questions that are included in the chapter or a study guide.
- Read the summary.

Assess your prior knowledge. Ask yourself, "What do I already know about the topic?" and "How familiar am I with this topic?"

Plan your reading and study time. Ask yourself, "How long will it take me to read this assignment?" and "Do I need to divide the assignment into smaller units?"

Step 2: Ask and Answer Questions to Enhance Your Reading

Guide your reading by asking and answering questions.

- Turn chapter headings into questions.
- Create questions based on what the paragraphs or sections appear to be about.
- If the author has included questions, use them.
- Use questions in a study guide, if there is one.
- Use questions given by the instructor.

Read actively.

- Look for answers to your questions.

Record the answers to your questions.

- Write the answers on notebook paper or in the margins of the textbook.
- Create notes for the material.
- Emphasize the answers by highlighting or underlining them.

Step 3: Review by Rehearsing the Answers to Your Questions

Review the material and transfer it into long-term memory by rehearsing.

- Recite (say aloud) the answers to your questions, and then review any you missed.
- Rewrite the important points from memory, and then fill in any missing information.

Assess Your Prior Knowledge

assessing your prior knowledge

Determining what you already know about a topic.

As you learned in Chapter 2, when you lack background knowledge in a subject—and this is often the case when you are reading college textbooks—you may have to take additional steps to comprehend the material. **Assessing your prior knowledge,** that is, determining what you already know about the topic, enables you to decide whether you need help with the assignment and need to allow additional time. To assess your prior knowledge, ask yourself, "What do I already know about this topic?" By introducing you to the chapter topics, previewing allows you to predict whether you will be dealing with unfamiliar material.

Comprehension-Monitoring Questions for Assessing Your Prior Knowledge

What do I already know about this topic? How familiar am I with this topic?

If the material is new to you, you may need to take extra steps to deal with the assignment successfully. While you are previewing, while you are reading, or after you finish reading, you may discover that you do not understand the material adequately and need more background knowledge. If so, it is your responsibility to fill in missing background information by taking some or all of these steps:

- Reading other, perhaps easier, textbooks on the same subject (other college textbooks or more general study aids, such as an outline of American history or a book with a title such as *Accounting Made Easy*).
- Consulting an encyclopedia, dictionary, or other reference book, or going online to get information.
- Talking with someone who is knowledgeable about the subject.

These steps require effort, and obviously there are no shortcuts. But going the extra mile to gain necessary background information is part of being a responsible, mature learner and student. As a bonus, you may discover that it is exciting and satisfying to understand new or difficult material through your own efforts. Taking responsibility for your own learning makes you feel good about yourself as a student. (Remember that a *student* is someone who *studies.*)

Plan Your Reading and Study Time

Comprehension-Monitoring Questions for Planning Your Study Time

How long will it take me to read and study this assignment? Do I need to divide the assignment into smaller units?

Previewing an assignment enables you to decide whether you can read all of it in one study session or need to divide it into smaller parts.

If you need more than one study session, divide the assignment into shorter segments and read them at times when you can concentrate best. For example, you could divide a 24-page chapter in half and read it over two days. Or you could divide this long assignment into three 8-page segments and read them during three 1-hour study sessions on the same day, perhaps at 1, 5, and 8 P.M. In any case, plan your study-reading session and follow your plan. Then reward yourself after you complete your studying!

Step 2: Ask and Answer Questions to Enhance Your Reading

The second step in reading and studying a college textbook assignment is enhancing your reading by asking and answering questions. To read and study effectively, you need to read and understand each paragraph or section. This means that you must determine what is important to learn and remember in each section. To put it another way, you must read for a specific purpose. This increases your interest and concentration, and it enables you to monitor (evaluate) your comprehension while you are reading. One of the best ways to learn the material is to ask and answer questions as you read.

Ask Questions as You Read

Creating one or more questions for each section of a reading assignment will guide you to the important information and help you remember it. When you seek answers to questions, you are reading selectively and purposefully.

Turning chapter headings and subheadings into questions is the easiest way to read purposefully. For example, if a section in a history textbook has a heading "The War in Iraq," you might want to ask, "Why did the war begin?" You may also want to ask, "When did it begin?"

When a section has no heading, you can still create a question based on what that section appears to be about. If you see a term or phrase in bold print, italics, or color, you might create a question about it. You can also create questions about names of people, places, events, and so on. Of course, you will be able to refine your questions later, when you read the material more carefully.

In addition to creating your own questions as you read, you may find that the author has included questions at the end of a chapter, at the beginning, throughout the chapter (perhaps in the margins), or in a study guide. If a chapter contains questions, read them before you read the chapter, and then keep them in mind as you read. When you have finished reading the chapter, you should be able to answer them. In fact, you will probably be asked some of them on a test.

Finally, your instructor may give you questions to guide your reading. Of course, you should be able to answer these questions by the time you finish reading and studying the chapter.

Chapter questions, regardless of the source, enable you to monitor your comprehension: Are you understanding the important information the author and your instructor expect you to know? Identifying important information lets you begin preparing for tests from the day you first read the assignment.

Answer Questions When You Come to the End of Each Section

As you read each paragraph or section, look for answers to your questions. Then, after you have finished reading that section, record the answers by writing them down. A word of warning: Do not try to record answers until you have *finished* reading a section. Constantly switching between reading and writing disrupts your comprehension and greatly slows you down.

There are several effective ways to record your answers. One is to write answers on notebook paper or in the margins of your textbook. Another way is to make review cards. With either technique, be sure your answer makes it clear which question you are answering. In addition to writing out your answers, you may want to mark information in the textbook that answers your questions.

Comprehension-Monitoring Question for Asking and Answering Questions as You Read

Am I understanding the important information the author and my instructor expect me to know?

What if you cannot locate or formulate an answer to one of your questions? In that case, there are several things you can do:

- Read ahead to see if the answer becomes apparent.
- If the question involves an important term you need to know, look the term up in the glossary or in a dictionary.
- Go back and reread a paragraph or a section.
- Do some extra reading, ask a classmate, or ask your instructor about it.
- If you still cannot answer all of your questions after you have read an assignment, note which questions remain unanswered. Put a question mark in the margin, or make a list of the unanswered questions. One way or another, be sure to find the answers.

As you can see, actively seeking answers to questions encourages you to concentrate and focus on *understanding* as you read. Reading for a purpose—to answer specific questions—can help you remember more and ultimately score higher on tests.

Step 3: Review by Rehearsing the Answers to Your Questions

Experienced college students know that to remember what they read in their textbooks and the answers they wrote to questions, they need to take certain steps to make it happen. They take these steps immediately after reading a section or a chapter, while the material is still in short-term memory—still fresh in their minds. They know that forgetting occurs rapidly and that they need to rehearse material immediately in order to remember it, to transfer it into long-term (permanent) memory. (Rehearsal and memory are discussed in Chapter 11.) The shocking fact is that unless you take special action immediately after you finish reading a textbook assignment, you will forget at least half of what you read.

Finally, you should rehearse important points in a chapter by reading your questions and *reciting* the answers. Simply rereading your answers is not good enough; you should say them *aloud*. The rule is this: "If you can't say it, you don't know it."

If you still need more practice with the material, or need to prepare for a test, continue to rehearse important points by *reciting or rewriting the material from memory.* When you give yourself a "practice test" in either of these ways, you transfer the material into long-term memory. When you check your answers, make corrections and add any information to make your answers complete. Writing the information allows you to learn the correct spelling of important terms, names, and so forth. This is especially helpful if you will have an essay test.

Taking time to review and rehearse immediately after you finish reading not only helps you remember what you learned, it gives you a feeling of accomplishment, which in turn encourages you to continue learning. One success builds on another.

To recapitulate, the three-step process is: (1) prepare to read by previewing, assessing your prior knowledge, and planning your study time; (2) ask and answer questions to enhance your reading; (3) review by rehearsing the answers to your questions. This process enables you to learn more from your assignments, and it provides the foundation for effective test preparation.

Comprehension-Monitoring Question for Reviewing by Rehearsing Your Answers

Can I recite answers to questions about the material and write the answers from memory?

Remember that preparing for a test begins with reading *each* textbook assignment effectively. Specific techniques for preparing for tests are discussed in Chapters 10 and 11. They include annotating textbooks by writing marginal study notes, outlining, mapping, writing summaries, creating review cards, and developing test review sheets. Part of doing well on any test, of course, is following the directions. The next section focuses on this important skill.

FOLLOWING DIRECTIONS IN TEXTBOOKS AND ON TESTS

An important part of success in college is following written directions. It can help you do your assignments correctly, carry out procedures in classes and labs (such as computer labs and science labs), and earn high grades on tests. Most people are not as good at following directions as they think they are.

You have learned from experience that problems can arise from misunderstanding directions or failing to follow them. Perhaps you have answered an entire set of test questions instead of the specific number stated in the directions ("Answer any *two* of the following five essay questions"). Or you may have had points deducted on a paper because you did not follow the directions about the format ("Double-space your paper and number the pages"). When you do not follow directions, you can waste time and lower your grade.

Guidelines for Following Directions

There are a few simple things to remember about following written directions:

- **Read the entire set of directions carefully before starting *any* of the steps.** Slow down and pay attention to every word. Even though most students *know* they should do this, they make the mistake of jumping in without doing it. Resist this temptation and read *all* of the directions!
- **Make sure you understand all the words in the directions.**   Although directions may use words you hear or see often, you may not know precisely what each word means. For example, on an essay test, you might be asked to compare two poems or contrast two pieces of music. Do you know the difference between *compare* and *contrast*? Unless you do, you cannot answer the question correctly. Other typical words in test questions include *enumerate, justify, explain,* and *illustrate.* Each has a specific meaning. General direction words include *above, below, consecutive, preceding, succeeding, former,* and *latter.* In addition, directions in college textbooks and assignments often include many specialized terms. For example, the directions for a biology lab experiment might instruct you to "stain a tissue sample on a slide." The words *stain, tissue,* and *slide* have specific meanings in biology.
- **Circle signals that announce steps in directions and underline key words.** Not every step in a set of directions will have a signal word, of course, but steps are frequently introduced by bullets (• • •), letters and numbers (*a, b, c,* or 1, 2, 3, etc.), and words such as *first, second, third, next, then, finally,* and *last* to indicate the sequence or order of the steps.

Mark directions *before* you begin following them, since you must understand what you are to do *before* you try to do it. This means finding and numbering steps if they are not already numbered. Be aware that a single sentence sometimes contains more than one step. (For example, "Type your log in, password, and press the Enter key" contains three.) When you are busy working on a test or an assignment, it is easy to become distracted and do the steps in the wrong order or leave a step out. Even though the steps may not be numbered or include signal words, you are still responsible for finding each step. Especially on tests, then, you should number each step and mark key words in directions.

Example: Directions for a Test

The first box below shows a set of directions for a unit test in a psychology course. Read these directions carefully. Marking the test directions as shown in the second box below would help you follow them accurately.

SAMPLE OF DIRECTIONS FOR UNIT TEST: PSYCHOLOGICAL DISORDERS

Directions:

Part I—Content Questions   (2 points each) Answer the 25 multiple-choice questions using the machine-scorable answer sheet provided. (You must use a number two pencil on this answer sheet.) Complete this part of the test before you begin Part II.

Part II—Discussion Questions   (25 points each) Answer two of the four discussion questions, using notebook paper. (You may use pen or pencil for this portion of the test.) The answer to each discussion question should be 3–5 paragraphs in length.

SAMPLE OF MARKED DIRECTIONS FOR UNIT TEST: PSYCHOLOGICAL DISORDERS

Directions:

50 points   ①

Part I—Content Questions   (2 points each) Answer the 25 multiple-choice questions using the machine-scorable answer sheet provided. (You must use a number two pencil on this answer sheet.) Complete this part of the test before you begin Part II.

50 points   ②

Part II—Discussion Questions   (25 points each) Answer two of the four discussion questions, using notebook paper. (You may use pen or pencil for this portion of the test.) The answer to each discussion question should be 3–5 paragraphs in length.

DEVELOPING CHAPTER REVIEW CARDS

Review cards, or *summary cards,* are an excellent study tool. They are a way to select, organize, and review the most important information in a textbook chapter. Creating review cards helps you organize information in a meaningful way and transfer it into long-term memory as you prepare for tests (see Part Three). The review card activities in this book give you structured practice in creating these valuable study tools. Once you have learned how to make review cards, you can create them for textbook material in your other courses.

Now complete the nine review cards for Chapter 3 by answering the questions or following the directions on each card. When you have completed them, you will have summarized important information about (1) preparing to read, (2) previewing a textbook chapter, (3) assessing your prior knowledge, (4) guiding your reading, (5) answering questions as you read, (6) reviewing by rehearsing, (7) following directions in textbooks and on tests, (8) monitoring your comprehension as you read, and (9) using the SQ3R method. Print or write legibly. You will find it easier to complete the review cards if you remove these pages before filling them in.

The SQ3R Study System

Summarize the techniques for each step of the SQ3R Study System. (See page 146.)

Survey:

Question:

Read:

Recite:

Review:

Card 1   Chapter 3: Approaching College Assignments

The Three-Step Process for Reading and Studying: Step 1

What is the first step of the three step study-reading process? (See page 146.)

Step 1 Involves these three parts: (See pages 147–149.)

1.

2.

3.

Card 2   Chapter 3: Approaching College Assignments

Previewing a Textbook Chapter

Part of step 1 in the study-reading process is previewing a chapter. List seven things to do when previewing.

(See page 147.)

1.
2.
3.
4.
5.
6.
7.

Card 3   Chapter 3: Approaching College Assignments

Assessing Your Prior Knowledge

Assessing your prior knowledge is part of step 1 in the study-reading process. Define *prior knowledge*. (See page 149.)

List three things you can do if you need to increase your prior knowledge about a topic. (See page 149.)

1.

2.

3.

Card 4   Chapter 3: Approaching College Assignments

The Three-Step Process for Reading and Studying: Step 2

What is the second step of the three-step study-reading process? (See page 149.)

List at least four chapter features or other sources on which you can base questions as you read. (See page 150.)

1.

2.

3.

4.

Card 5   Chapter 3: Approaching College Assignments

Answering Questions As You Read

When should you record the answers to your questions about a passage? (See page 150.)

List three ways to record or mark your answers. (See page 150.)

1.

2.

3.

Describe four things you can do if any of your questions remain unanswered when you have finished a passage. (See page 151.)

1.

2.

3.

4.

Card 6   Chapter 3: Approaching College Assignments

The Three-Step Process for Reading and Studying: Step 3

What is the third step of the three-step study-reading process? (See page 151.)

When should you rehearse the answers to your questions about material in a reading assignment? (See page 151.)

List two effective ways to rehearse. (See page 151.)

1.

2.

Card 7   Chapter 3: Approaching College Assignments

Following Directions

List three things to remember about following written directions. (See page 152.)

1.

2.

3.

Card 8   Chapter 3: Approaching College Assignments

Monitoring Your Comprehension as You Read and Study College Textbooks

1.   What questions should you ask yourself while you are previewing a chapter? (See page 147.)

2.   What questions should you ask yourself to assess your prior knowledge? (See page 149.)

3.   What questions should you ask yourself while you are planning your study time? (See page 149.)

4.   What question should you ask yourself as you are asking and answering questions as you read? (See page 150.)

5.   What question should you ask yourself as you review a chapter by rehearsing your answers? (See page 151.)

Card 9   Chapter 3: Approaching College Assignments

African Americans: The Struggle for Equality

From *The American Democracy*
by Thomas E. Patterson

Prepare Yourself to Read

Directions: Do these exercises *before* you read Selection 3.1.

1. First, read and think about the title. What do you already know about African Americans' struggle for equality?

   _____

   _____

   _____

   _____

   _____

2. Next, complete your preview by reading the following:

   Introduction (in *italics*)

   Headings

   All of the first paragraph (paragraph 1)

   First sentence of each of the other paragraphs

   On the basis of your preview, what aspects of African Americans' struggle for equality does the selection seem to be about?

   _____

   _____

   _____

   _____

   _____

3. **Build your vocabulary as you read.** If you discover an unfamiliar word or key term as you read the selection, try to determine its meaning by using context clues.

Internet Resources

Read More about This Topic Online

Use a search engine, such as Google or Yahoo!, to expand your existing knowledge about this topic *before* you read the selection or to learn more about it *afterward*. Use search terms such as "civil rights movement" or "equality African Americans." If you are unfamiliar with conducting Internet searches, read pages 25–26 on Boolean searches. You can also use Wikipedia, the free online encyclopedia, at www.wikipedia.com. Keep in mind that when you visit any website, it is a good idea to evaluate the site and the information it contains. Ask yourself questions such as "Who sponsors this website?" and "Is the information it contains up to date?"

SELECTION 3.1: **AFRICAN AMERICANS: THE STRUGGLE FOR EQUALITY**

In the 21st century, African Americans have been appointed to key positions in the federal government. President George W. Bush selected General Colin Powell as Secretary of State. Powell, the first African American to hold that office, was succeeded by Condoleezza Rice, the first African American woman to serve as Secretary of State.

Of greatest historical significance was Barack Obama's election as the 44th President of the United States. The night of his election, November 4, 2008, he opened his victory speech with these words: "If there is anyone out there who still doubts that America is a place where all things are possible; who still wonders if the dream of our founders is alive in our time; who still questions the power of our democracy, tonight is your answer." President Obama appointed Eric Holder Attorney General of the United States, the first African American to hold that office. In another first, the Republican National Committee in 2009 chose former Maryland Lt. Governor Michael S. Steele as party chairman.

Historians and political scientists agree that African Americans have made great progress toward social and judicial equality since the Civil War, but recognize that this progress has not come without a struggle. This selection from a government textbook explains how Supreme Court decisions and the civil rights movement altered the concept of equality for African Americans.

1   *Equality* has always been the least fully developed of America's founding concepts. Not even Thomas Jefferson, who had a deep admiration for the "common man," believed that broad meaning could be given to the claim of the Declaration of Independence that "all men are created equal." To Jefferson, "equality" had a restricted, though significant, meaning: people are of equal moral worth and, as such, deserve equal treatment under the law. Even then, Jefferson made a distinction between free men and slaves, who were not entitled to legal equality.

2   The history of America shows that disadvantaged groups have rarely achieved a greater measure of justice without a struggle. Legal equality has rarely been bestowed by the more powerful upon the less powerful. Their gains have nearly always occurred through intense and sustained political movements, such as the civil rights movement of the 1960s, that have pressured established interests to relinquish or share their privileged status.

3   Of all America's problems, none has been as persistent as the white race's unwillingness to yield a fair share of society's benefits to members of the black race. The ancestors of most African Americans came to this country as slaves, after having been captured in Africa, shipped in chains across the Atlantic, and sold in open markets in Charleston and other seaports.

Creating Questions Exercises

Directions: For each paragraph:

- Create a question based on what the paragraph seems to be about. Ask *who, what, when, where, why,* or *how.*
- Write your question in the spaces provided.
- Write the answer to your question in the margin or highlight it in the text.

Doing this will help you understand and remember the material.

Creating Questions Exercise

Question about paragraph 1:

_____

_____

_____

Creating Questions Exercise

Question about paragraph 2:

_____

_____

4   It took a civil war to bring slavery to an end, but the battle did not end institutionalized racism. When Reconstruction ended in 1877 with the withdrawal of federal troops from the South, whites in the region regained power and gradually reestablished racial segregation by enacting laws that prohibited black citizens from using the same public facilities as whites. In *Plessy v. Ferguson* (1896), the Supreme Court endorsed these laws, ruling the "separate" facilities for the two races did not violate the Constitution as long as the facilities were "equal." "If one race be inferior to the other socially," the Court argued, "the Constitution of the United States cannot put them on the same plane." The *Plessy* decision became a justification for the separate and *unequal* treatment of African Americans. Black children, for example, were forced into separate schools that rarely had libraries and had few teachers; they were given worn-out books that had been used previously in white schools.

5   Black leaders challenged these discriminatory state and local policies through legal action, but not until the late 1930s did the Supreme Court begin to respond favorably to their demands. The Court began modestly by ruling that where no public facilities existed for African Americans, they must be allowed to use those reserved for whites.

The *Brown* Decision

6   Substantial judicial relief for African Americans was finally achieved in 1954 with *Brown v. Board of Education of Topeka,* arguably the most significant ruling in Supreme Court history. The case began when Linda Carol Brown, a black child in Topeka, Kansas, was denied admission to an all-white elementary school that she passed every day on her way to her all-black school, which was twelve blocks farther away. In its decision, the Court fully reversed its *Plessy* doctrine by declaring that racial segregation of public schools "generates [among black children] a feeling of inferiority as to their status in the community that may affect their hearts and minds in a way unlikely ever to be undone. . . . Separate educational facilities are inherently unequal."

7   As a 1954 Gallup poll indicated, a sizable majority of southern whites opposed the *Brown* decision, and billboards were erected along southern roadways that called for the impeachment of Chief Justice Earl Warren. In the so-called Southern Manifesto, southern congressmen urged their state governments to "resist forced integration by any lawful means." In 1957, rioting broke out when Governor Orval Faubus called out the Arkansas National Guard to block the entry of black children to the Little Rock public schools. To restore order and carry out the desegregation of the Little Rock schools, President Dwight D. Eisenhower used his power as the nation's commander-in-chief to place the Arkansas National Guard

Creating Questions Exercise

Question about paragraph 3:

_____

_____

_____

Creating Questions Exercise

Question about paragraph 4:

_____

_____

_____

Creating Questions Exercise

Question about paragraph 5:

_____

_____

_____

_____

Creating Questions Exercise

Question about paragraph 6:

_____

_____

_____

_____

Creating Questions Exercise

Question about paragraph 7:

_____

_____

_____

under federal control. For their part, northern whites were neither strongly for nor strongly against school desegregation. A Gallup poll revealed that only a slim majority of whites outside the South agreed with the *Brown* decision.

The Black Civil Rights Movement

8   After *Brown,* the struggle of African Americans for their rights became a political movement. Perhaps no single event turned national public opinion so dramatically against segregation as a 1963 march led by Dr. Martin Luther King Jr. in Birmingham, Alabama. An advocate of nonviolent protest, King had been leading peaceful demonstrations and marches for nearly eight years before that fateful day in Birmingham. As the nation watched in disbelief on television, police officers led by Birmingham's sheriff, Eugene "Bull" Connor, attacked King and his followers with dogs, cattle prods, and fire hoses.

9   The modern civil rights movement peaked with the triumphant March on Washington for Jobs and Freedom of August 2, 1963. Organized by Dr. King, and other civil rights leaders, it attracted 250,000 marchers, one of the largest gatherings in the history of the nation's capital. "I have a dream," the Reverend King told the gathering, "that my four little children will one day live in a nation where they will not be judged by the color of their skin but by the content of their character."

Creating Questions Exercise

Question about paragraph 8:

_____

_____

_____

Creating Questions Exercise

Question about paragraph 9:

_____

_____

_____

Two police dogs attack a black civil rights activist during the 1963 Birmingham demonstrations. Such images of hatred and violence shook many white Americans out of their complacency regarding race relations.

10   A year later, after a months-long fight in Congress that was marked by every parliamentary obstacle that racial conservatives could muster, the Civil Rights Act of 1964 was enacted. The legislation provided African Americans and other minorities with equal access to public facilities and prohibited job discrimination. Even then, southern states resorted to legal maneuvering and other delaying tactics to blunt the new law's impact. The state of Virginia, for example, established a commission to pay the legal expenses of white citizens who were brought to court for violation of the federal act. Nevertheless, momentum was on the side of racial equality. The murder of two civil rights workers during a voter registration drive in Selma, Alabama, helped sustain the momentum. President Lyndon Johnson, who had been a decisive force in the battle to pass the Civil Rights Act, called for new legislation that would end racial barriers to voting. Congress's answer was the 1965 Voting Rights Act.

The Aftermath of the Civil Rights Movement

11   Although the most significant progress in history toward the legal equality of all Americans occurred during the 1960s, Dr. King's dream of a color-blind society has remained elusive. Even the legal rights of African Americans do not, in practice, match the promise of the civil rights movement. Studies have found, for example, that African Americans accused of crime are more likely to be convicted and to receive stiffer sentences than are white Americans on trial for comparable offenses. Federal statistics from the National Office of Drug Control Policy and the U.S. Sentencing Commission revealed that in 1997 black Americans accounted for more than 75 percent of crack cocaine convictions but only about 35 percent of crack cocaine users. It is hardly surprising that many African Americans believe that the nation has two standards of justice, an inferior one for blacks and a higher one for whites.

12   One area in which African Americans have made substantial progress since the 1960s is the winning of election to public office. Although the percentage of black elected officials is still far below the proportion of African Americans in the population, it has risen sharply over recent decades. As of 2000, there were more than 20 black members of Congress and 400 black mayors—including the mayors of some of this country's largest cities.

Martin Luther King Jr. (1929–1968) is the only American of the 20th century to be honored with a national holiday. The civil rights leader was the pivotal figure in the movement to gain legal and political rights for black Americans. The son of a Baptist minister, King used rhetorical skills and nonviolent protest to sweep aside a century of governmental discrimination and to inspire other groups, including women and Hispanics, to assert their rights. Recipient of the Nobel Peace Prize in 1964 (the youngest person ever to receive that honor), King was assassinated in Memphis in 1968.

Creating Questions Exercise

Question about paragraph 10:

_____

_____

_____

Creating Questions Exercise

Question about paragraph 11:

_____

_____

_____

Creating Questions Exercise

Question about paragraph 12:

_____

_____

_____

Reading Selection Quiz

SELECTION 3.1

This quiz has several parts. Your instructor may assign some or all of them.

Comprehension

Directions: Items 1–10 test your understanding of the selection. They are the type of questions a content area instructor (such as a government professor) might ask on a test. You may refer to the selection as you answer the questions. Write your answer choice in the space provided.

_____ **1.** To Thomas Jefferson, equality meant that:
    a. all men and women are created equal.
    b. people are of equal moral worth and as such deserve equal treatment under the law, but only if they are free men.
    c. there should be no distinction between free men and slaves.
    d. there should be two standards of justice.

_____ **2.** When Civil War Reconstruction ended in 1877:
    a. whites in the South gradually reestablished racial segregation.
    b. slaves were sold in open markets in Charleston and other seaports.
    c. legal equality for African Americans was achieved.
    d. the Arkansas National Guard was placed under federal control.

_____ **3.** Significant judicial relief for African Americans was achieved with the:
    a. 1896 Supreme Court ruling *Plessy v. Ferguson.*
    b. 1954 Supreme Court ruling *Brown v. Board of Education of Topeka.*
    c. 1957 desegregation of Little Rock public schools.
    d. 1963 March on Washington led by Dr. Martin Luther King, Jr.

_____ **4.** The *Brown* decision ruled that:
    a. separate educational facilities for blacks and whites did not violate the Constitution.
    b. separate educational facilities for blacks and whites were inherently unequal.
    c. black children could be denied admission to all-white schools.
    d. racial segregation of public schools was acceptable as long as the facilities were "equal."

5. A 1954 Gallup poll revealed that:
   a. only a slim majority of northern whites supported school desegregation.
   b. southern whites supported the *Brown* decision.
   c. southern whites would "resist forced integration."
   d. many Americans felt that desegregation was unlawful.

6. The Civil Rights Act of 1964:
   a. launched an important civil rights movement in the United States.
   b. eliminated racial barriers to voting.
   c. limited the legal rights of African Americans.
   d. provided African Americans and other minorities with legal access to public facilities and prohibited job discrimination.

7. The March on Washington for Jobs and Freedom organized by Dr. Martin Luther King, Jr. took place in:
   a. 1954.
   b. 1963.
   c. 1964.
   d. 1965.

8. The Voting Rights Act of 1965:
   a. launched an important civil rights movement in the United States.
   b. eliminated racial barriers to voting.
   c. limited the legal rights of African Americans.
   d. provided African Americans and other minorities with legal access to public facilities and prohibited job discrimination.

9. Although there has been significant progress in legal equality for all Americans, studies have found that African Americans:
   a. believe that the nation has two standards of justice, one for blacks and one for other minorities.
   b. want more legislation to improve judicial equality.
   c. accused of crime are more likely to be convicted than are white Americans on trial for comparable offenses.
   d. believe that equality is not fully developed in America.

10. In recent decades, the percentage of black elected officials has:
   a. declined.
   b. equaled the proportion of African Americans in the population.
   c. risen sharply.
   d. increased only slightly.

Vocabulary in Context

Directions: Items 11–20 test your ability to determine a word's meaning by using context clues. *Context clues* are words in a sentence that allow readers to deduce (reason out) the meaning of an unfamiliar word in the sentence. They also help readers determine the meaning an author intends when a word has more than one meaning. Each item below consists of a sentence from the selection, with the vocabulary word *italicized*. It is followed by another sentence that uses the same word in the same way. Use context clues to deduce the meaning of the *italicized* word. Be sure the meaning you choose makes sense in *both* sentences. Write each answer in the space provided. *Note:* Chapter 2 presents the skill of using context clues.

11. Legal equality has rarely been *bestowed* by the more powerful upon the less powerful.

Responsibility for the management and care of our family's farm was *bestowed* to me by my grandfather and grandmother.

bestowed (bĭ stōd′) means:

 a. negotiated

 b. handed over

 c. taken

 d. sold

12. Their gains have nearly always occurred through intense and sustained political movements, such as the civil rights movement of the 1960s, that have pressured established interests to *relinquish* or share their privileged status.

When Michael moved away to attend college, he was happy to *relinquish* his bedroom to his youngest sister.

relinquish (rĭ lĭng′ kwĭsh) means:

 a. pressure

 b. share

 c. let go of

 d. reverse

13. Of all America's problems, none has been as *persistent* as the white race's unwillingness to yield a fair share of society's benefits to members of the black race.

Yolanda's *persistent* headaches finally forced her to see a specialist.

persistent (pər sĭs′ tənt) means:

 a. painful

 b. mysterious; confusing

 c. terrible

 d. continuing; lasting

_____ **14.** "If one race be inferior to the other socially," the Court argued, "the Constitution of the United States cannot put them on the same *plane.*"

In a perfect world, every child would begin elementary school on the same *plane.*

plane (plān) means:
a. level surface
b. level of development or existence
c. grade
d. place or destination

_____ **15.** The Supreme Court declared that "separate educational facilities are *inherently* unequal."

Many people claim that men and women are *inherently* opposite from each other.

inherently (ĭn hîr′ ənt lē) means:
a. unfairly; unjustly
b. slightly; partly
c. intellectually; mentally
d. essentially; intrinsically

_____ **16.** The modern civil rights movement *peaked* with the triumphant March on Washington for Jobs and Freedom of August 2, 1963.

As usual, the holiday shopping season *peaked* on Christmas Eve, December 24th, when last-minute-gift buyers flooded the shopping malls.

peaked (pēkt) means:
a. reached a maximum of development
b. improved
c. flooded; clogged
d. came to an end; dissolved

_____ **17.** A year later, after a months-long fight in Congress that was marked by every parliamentary obstacle that racial conservatives could muster, the Civil Rights Act of 1964 was *enacted.*

Before the Miranda ruling was *enacted,* a person could be arrested without being informed of his or her legal rights.

enacted (ĕn ăk′ təd) means:
a. acted out, as on a stage
b. abandoned; given up
c. made into law
d. overturned

_____ **18.** Although the most significant progress in history toward the legal equality of all Americans occurred during the 1960s, Dr. King's dream of a color-blind society has remained *elusive.*

Despite intensive research during the last decade, a cure for breast cancer has remained *elusive.*

elusive (ĭ loo′ sĭv) means:

a. difficult to grasp or attain

b. likely to be unsuccessful

c. impossible

d. unlikely to be controlled

_____ **19.** One area in which African Americans have made *substantial* progress since the 1960s is the winning of election to public office.

In 2000, 2001, and 2002, many investors lost *substantial* sums of money in the stock market.

substantial (səb stăn′ shəl) means:

a. solidly built; strong

b. considerable; large

c. possessing wealth; well-to-do

d. substandard; unimportant

_____ **20.** Although the percentage of black elected officials is still far below the proportion of African Americans in the population, it has risen sharply over recent *decades.*

Many people say the 1960s and 1970s were the most socially permissive *decades* in our country's history.

decades (dĕk′ ādz) means:

a. attitudes

b. developments

c. periods of ten years

d. times

Reading Skills Application

> *Directions:* Items 21–25 test your ability to *apply* certain reading skills. You may not be familiar with all the skills yet, so some items will serve as a preview. As you work through *Opening Doors,* you will practice and develop these skills. These are important skills, which is why they are included on the state-mandated basic skills tests that some students must take. Write each answer in the space provided.

_____ 21. The author's primary purpose for writing this selection is to:
    a. inform readers about slavery and other injustices suffered by African Americans.
    b. persuade people to become more involved in the American political process.
    c. explain how African Americans have made gains in legal equality during the last century.
    d. explain why most Americans did not support the civil rights movement during the 1960s.

_____ 22. Which of the following best expresses the main idea of paragraph 2?
    a. Legal equality has rarely been bestowed by the more powerful upon the less powerful.
    b. Their gains have nearly always occurred through political movements.
    c. Disadvantaged groups in America are now making some progress toward social equality.
    d. The history of America shows that disadvantaged groups have rarely achieved a greater measure of justice without a struggle that includes sustained, intense political movements.

_____ 23. The information in paragraph 11 is organized using which of the following patterns?
    a. sequence
    b. comparison-contrast
    c. definition
    d. list

_____ **24.** Which of the following statements represents an opinion rather than a fact?

    a. Substantial judicial relief for African Americans was finally achieved in 1954 with *Brown v. Board of Education of Topeka,* arguably the most significant ruling in Supreme Court history.

    b. In 1957, rioting broke out when Governor Orval Faubus called out the Arkansas National Guard to block the entry of black children to the Little Rock public schools.

    c. Organized by Dr. King and other civil rights leaders, the March on Washington attracted 250,000 marchers, one of the largest gatherings in the history of the nation's capital.

    d. A year after the March on Washington, the Civil Rights Act of 1964 was enacted.

_____ **25.** Which of these is a logical conclusion that can be inferred from the information in the selection?

    a. African Americans no longer need to struggle for equality.

    b. Equality has always been the least fully developed of America's founding concepts.

    c. It is likely that the percentage of African Americans elected to public office will increase.

    d. Many African Americans believe there is now one standard of justice for both whites and blacks.

SELECTION **3.1**

Government
(continued)

Respond in Writing

Directions: Refer to the selection as needed to answer the essay-type questions below. (Your instructor may direct you to work collaboratively with other students on one or more items. Each group member should be able to explain *all* of the group's answers.)

1. Dr. Martin Luther King, Jr. is certainly one of America's best-known advocates for judicial equality and civil rights. What other persons (past or present) can you name who have contributed to the civil rights or equal rights movement for any groups in America?

_____

_____

_____

_____

_____

_____

2. Complete the chronological list of the Supreme Court decisions, civil rights demonstrations, and congressional acts that were mentioned in this selection.

1896: _____

1954: _____

1963: _____

1964: _____

1965: _____

3. **Overall main idea.** What is the overall main idea the author wants the reader to understand about African Americans and their struggle for equality? Answer this question in one sentence. Be sure to include the words *African Americans* and *equality* in your overall main idea sentence.

_____

_____

_____

_____

_____

_____

_____

SELECTION **3.2**

Human Development

Parenthood: Now, Later, . . . Never?

From *Human Development*

by Diane E. Papalia, Sally Wendkos Olds, and Ruth Feldman

Prepare Yourself to Read

Directions: Do these exercises *before* you read Selection 3.2.

1. It has been said that "parenthood is the hardest job in the world if you do it right." Do you agree? Why or why not?

    _____

    _____

    _____

    _____

2. Next, complete your preview by reading the following:

    Introduction (in *italics*)

    First paragraph (paragraph 1)

    Headings for each section

    The first sentence of paragraphs 2–17

    Line graph and explanation beside it

    On the basis of your preview, what aspects of parenthood do you think will be discussed?

    _____

    _____

    _____

3. **Build your vocabulary as you read.** If you discover an unfamiliar word or key term as you read the selection, try to determine its meaning by using context clues.

Internet Resources

Read More about This Topic Online

Use a search engine, such as Google or Yahoo!, to expand your existing knowledge about this topic *before* you read the selection or to learn more about it *afterward*. Use search terms such as "successful parenting" or "transition to parenthood." If you are unfamiliar with conducting Internet searches, read pages 25–26 on Boolean searches. You can also use Wikipedia, the free online encyclopedia, at www.wikipedia.com. Keep in mind that when you visit any website, it is a good idea to evaluate the site and the information it contains. Ask yourself questions such as "Who sponsors this website?" and "Is the information it contains up to date?"

SELECTION 3.2: PARENTHOOD: NOW, LATER, . . . NEVER?

"Just wait until you have children of your own!" At one time or another in our lives, we have all heard those words from our parents. Becoming a parent and being a parent affect every area of a person's life. In a 2001 study, researchers at the University of Washington found that *"essentially, happy marriages make for happy parents."* They suggest that helping couples *"strengthen their marital friendship would help them weather the transition to parenthood"* (*http://www.apa.org/monitor/jan01/parenthood.html*). In this human development textbook selection, the authors present some new, interesting, and sometimes surprising research findings about parenthood in the 21st century.

1   Although the institution of the family is universal, the "traditional" family—a husband, a wife, and their biological children—is not. In many African, Asian, and Latin American cultures the extended-family household is the traditional form. In western industrialized countries, family size, composition, structure, and division of labor have changed dramatically. Most mothers now work for pay, in or outside the home, and a small but growing number of fathers are primary caregivers. More single women and cohabiting couples are having or adopting children and raising them. Millions of children live with gay or lesbian parents or with stepparents.

2   On the other hand, an increasing number of couples remain childless by choice. Some of these couples want to concentrate on careers or social causes. Some feel more comfortable with adults or think they would not make good parents. Some want to retain the intimacy of the honeymoon. Some enjoy an adult lifestyle, with freedom to travel or to make spur-of-the-moment decisions. Some women worry that pregnancy will make them less attractive and that parenthood will change their relationship with their spouse.

3   Some people may be discouraged by the financial burdens of parenthood and the difficulty of combining parenthood with employment. In 2000 the estimated expenditures to raise a child to age 18 in a middle-income two-parent, two-child family were $165,630. Better childcare and other support services might help couples make truly voluntary decisions.

Creating Questions Exercises

Directions: For each paragraph:

- Create a question based on what the paragraph seems to be about. Ask *who, what, when, where, why,* or *how.*
- Write your question in the spaces provided.
- Write the answer to your question in the margin or highlight it in the text.

Doing this will help you understand and remember the material.

Creating Questions Exercise

Question about paragraph 1:

_____

_____

Creating Questions Exercise

Question about paragraph 2:

_____

_____

Creating Questions Exercise

Question about paragraph 3:

_____

_____

Becoming Parents

4   At one time, a blessing offered to newlyweds in the Asian country of Nepal was, "May you have enough sons to cover the hillsides!" Today, Nepali couples are wished, "May you have a very bright son." While sons still are preferred over daughters, even boys are not wished for in such numbers as in the past.

5   In preindustrial farming societies, large families were a necessity: children helped with the family's work and would eventually care for aging parents. The death rate in childhood was high, and having many children made it more likely that some would reach maturity. Today, infant and child mortality rates have improved greatly, and, in industrial societies, large families are no longer an economic asset. In developing countries, too, where overpopulation and hunger are major problems, there is recognition of the need to limit family size and to space children further apart.

6   Not only do people typically have fewer children today, but they also start having them later in life, often because they spend their early adult years getting an education and establishing a career. In 2004, the median age of first-time mothers in the United States was 24.6, having risen consistently for three decades. Since the mid-1970s the percentage of women who give birth in their thirties and even after 40 has increased steadily, often thanks to fertility treatments. Meanwhile, birthrates for women in their late twenties, which had declined after 1990, were again on the rise. For the first time in almost thirty years, the total fertility rate in 2000 (a projected total of 2.1 births per woman) exceeded "replacement level," the number of births needed to offset deaths. The U.S. fertility rate is higher than in several other developed countries.

7   Economically, delaying childbirth may pay off for women who intend to work later on. Among women born between 1944 and 1954, the first cohort to combine child raising and employment on a large scale, those who gave birth between ages 20 and 27 tend to earn less than women who gave birth at later ages. Further research may show whether this holds true in later cohorts.

8   Babies of older mothers may benefit from their mothers' greater ease with parenthood. When 105 new mothers ages 16 to 38 were interviewed and observed with their infants, the older mothers reported more satisfaction with parenting and spent more time at it. They were more affectionate and sensitive to their babies and more effective in encouraging desired behavior. And, among a large, nationally representative sample, men who became fathers after their thirty-fifth birthdays spent more leisure time with their children, had higher expectations for the children's behavior, and were more nurturing than a comparison group who became fathers before age 35.

Creating Questions Exercise

Question about paragraph 4:

_____

_____

_____

Creating Questions Exercise

Question about paragraph 5:

_____

_____

_____

Creating Questions Exercise

Question about paragraph 6:

_____

_____

_____

Creating Questions Exercise

Question about paragraph 7:

_____

_____

_____

Creating Questions Exercise

Question about paragraph 8:

_____

_____

_____

SELECTION 3.2

Figure 1

Birthrates by Age of Mother, 1960 to 2000.

Martin, J., Park, M., and Sutton, P. (2002). Births: Preliminary data for 2001. *National Vital Statistics Reports 50*(10). Hyattsville, MD. National Center for Health Statistics.

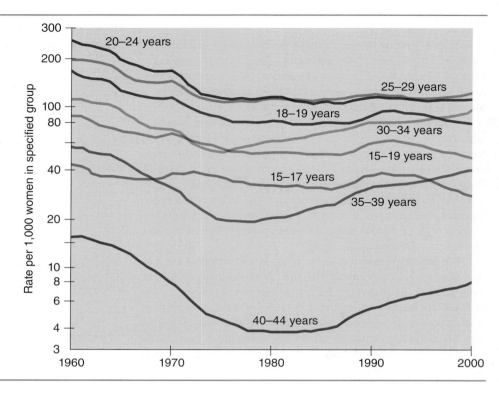

Couples today tend to have fewer children than in past generations, and to have them later in life. Infants may benefit from mature parents' ease with parenthood and willingness to invest more time in it.

On the other hand, looking far down the road, older parents are more likely to become a burden when their children reach middle age.

Parenthood as a Developmental Experience

9   A first baby marks a major transition in parents' lives. This totally dependent new person changes individuals and changes relationships. As children develop, parents do, too.

Men's and Women's Involvement in Parenthood

10   Both women and men often have mixed feelings about becoming parents. Along with excitement, they may feel anxiety about the responsibility of caring for a child and the commitment of time and energy it entails.

11   Fathers today are more involved in their children's lives, and even in childcare and housework, than ever before. Still, most are not nearly as involved as mothers are. In a study of parents of 4-year-olds in 10 European, Asian, and African countries and the United States, fathers averaged less than 1 hour a day in sole charge of their children during the work week, while U.S. mothers spent an average of nearly 11 hours each weekday caring for preschoolers—more than mothers in any of the other 10 countries.

12   Even working mothers are the primary caregivers in most families. This is especially true on weekdays, according to time diaries kept by a nationally representative sample of 2,400 intact U.S. families in 1997. However, the time fathers spend with children becomes more nearly equal to mothers' on weekends, and increases as children get older. Fathers spend considerably *more* time with children than mothers in television or video viewing, outdoor play, and coaching or teaching sports.

13   Some fathers do much more, sharing parenting equally with mothers. Such a choice challenges still-prominent social expectations that fathers are primarily breadwinners and mothers are primarily responsible for child raising. Equally sharing parents do not reverse roles; instead, both parents make job adjustments and career choices compatible with their parenting responsibilities.

14   In 2004, fathers were the primary caregivers for 11.4 percent of preschoolers with employed mothers. Studies show that fathers who are primary caregivers can be nearly as nurturing as mothers.

Creating Questions Exercise

Question about paragraph 9:

_____

_____

Creating Questions Exercise

Question about paragraph 10:

_____

_____

_____

Creating Questions Exercise

Question about paragraph 11:

_____

_____

_____

Creating Questions Exercise

Question about paragraph 12:

_____

_____

_____

Creating Questions Exercise

Question about paragraph 13:

_____

_____

_____

Creating Questions Exercise

Question about paragraph 14:

_____

_____

_____

SELECTION 3.2

15 Besides time spent in direct childcare, fatherhood may change men in other ways. Among 5,226 men ages 19 to 65, fathers living with their dependent children were less involved in outside social activities than those who had no children, but more likely to be engaged in school-related activities, church groups, and community service organizations. They tended to work more hours and were less likely to be unemployed. The most involved fathers were more satisfied with their lives and more involved in work, family, community, and socializing.

Creating Questions Exercise

Question about paragraph 15:

_____

_____

_____

How Parenthood Affects Marital Satisfaction

16 Marital satisfaction typically declines during the child-raising years. In a ten-year longitudinal study of predominantly white couples who married in their late twenties, both husbands and wives reported a sharp decline in satisfaction during the first four years, followed by a plateau and then another decline. Spouses who had children, especially those who became parents early in their marriage and those who had many children, showed a steeper decline. Although there was a high attrition rate—429 out of the original 522 couples divorced or separated during the course of the study or did not complete it—the presumably greater dissatisfaction of the couples who ultimately left the study did not seriously skew the findings while they were in it. The pattern of decline held true, though less strongly, even when this factor was controlled.

Creating Questions Exercise

Question about paragraph 16:

_____

_____

_____

17 Of course, this statistical pattern is an average; it is not necessarily true of all couples. One research team followed 128 middle- and working-class couples in their late twenties from the first pregnancy until the child's third birthday. Some marriages got stronger, while others deteriorated, especially in the eyes of the wives. In these marriages, the partners tended to be younger and less well educated, to earn less money, to have been married a shorter time, and to have lower self-esteem. The mothers who had the hardest time were those whose babies had difficult temperaments. Surprisingly, women who had planned their pregnancies were unhappier, possibly because they had expected life with a baby to be better than it turned out to be.

Creating Questions Exercise

Question about paragraph 17:

_____

_____

_____

18 Among young Israeli first-time parents, fathers who saw themselves as caring, nurturing, and protecting experienced less decline in marital satisfaction than other fathers and felt better about parenthood. Men who were less involved with their babies, and whose wives were more involved, tended to be more dissatisfied. The mothers who became most dissatisfied with their marriages were those who saw themselves as disorganized and unable to cope with the demands of motherhood.

Creating Questions Exercise

Question about paragraph 18:

_____

_____

_____

SELECTION **3.2**

Human Development

(continued)

SELECTION 3.2

Reading Selection Quiz

This quiz has several parts. Your instructor may assign some or all of them.

Comprehension

Directions: Items 1–10 test your understanding of the selection. They are the type of questions a content area instructor (such as a human development professor) might ask on a test. You may refer to the selection as you answer the questions. Write your answer choice in the space provided.

True or False

_____ **1.** Over the years, there have been few changes in family size, composition, structure, or division of labor in western industrialized countries.

_____ **2.** People today typically have fewer children and have them later in life.

_____ **3.** Older mothers tend to be more satisfied with their parenting and to spend more time on it.

_____ **4.** Having a baby changes the individual parents and their relationship.

_____ **5.** Both men and women often have mixed feelings about becoming parents.

Multiple-Choice

_____ **6.** During child-raising years, parents' marital satisfaction typically:
   a. declines.
   b. stays the same.
   c. increases.
   d. cannot be assessed.

_____ **7.** In most families, the primary caregivers are:
   a. the mothers.
   b. the fathers.
   c. both parents.
   d. relatives other than the parents.

_____ **8.** In marriages that deteriorated between pregnancy and the child's third birthday, the partners tended to:
   a. be younger and less well educated.
   b. earn less money.
   c. have been married a shorter time.
   d. all of the above

9. Parents who share equally in child raising:
   a. typically reverse their roles.
   b. make adjustments in their job and career choices.
   c. make no adjustments.
   d. tend to have higher divorce rates.

10. During the last three decades, the median age for first-time mothers in the United States has:
    a. consistently decreased.
    b. stayed the same.
    c. fluctuated up and down.
    d. consistently risen.

SELECTION **3.2**   *Vocabulary in Context*

Human Development
(continued)

> *Directions:* Items 11–20 test your ability to determine a word's meaning by using context clues. *Context clues* are words in a sentence that allow readers to deduce (reason out) the meaning of an unfamiliar word in the sentence. They also help readers determine the meaning an author intends when a word has more than one meaning. Each item below consists of a sentence from the selection, with the vocabulary word *italicized*. It is followed by another sentence that uses the same word in the same way. Use context clues to deduce the meaning of the *italicized* word. Be sure the meaning you choose makes sense in *both* sentences. Write each answer in the space provided. *Note:* Chapter 2 presents the skill of using context clues.

11. Although the institution of the family is *universal,* the "traditional" family—a husband, a wife, and their biological children—is not.

    Love is a *universal* emotion.

    universal (yōō nə vûr′ səl) means:
    a. knowledgeable about many subjects
    b. existing all over the world
    c. pertaining to the universe
    d. cosmic

12. More single women and *cohabiting* couples are having or adopting children and raising them.

    Many religious groups disapprove of *cohabiting* couples.

    cohabiting (kō hăb′ ĭt ĭng) means:
    a. legally married
    b. marrying late in life
    c. living together in a sexual relationship, especially when not legally married
    d. legally married and living in the same house

_____ **13.** In *preindustrial* farming societies, large families were a necessity; children helped with the family's work and would eventually care for aging parents.

In *preindustrial* times, many items that are now mass-produced by machines were produced singly, by hand.

preindustrial (prē ĭn dŭs′ trē əl) means:
- *a.* relating to a society whose industries do not yet produce manufactured goods on a large scale
- *b.* relating to a society in which all individuals are engaged in industry
- *c.* relating to a society in which all industry exists for profit
- *d.* relating to a society whose economic well-being rests only on the production of manufactured goods

_____ **14.** In a study of parents of 4-year-olds in 10 European, Asian, and African countries and the United States, fathers averaged less than 1 hour a day in *sole* charge of their children during the work week, while U.S. mothers spent an average of nearly 11 hours each weekday caring for preschoolers—more than mothers in any of the other 10 countries.

The child, the *sole* survivor of the plane crash, was adopted by her aunt and uncle.

sole (sōl) means:
- *a.* total, complete
- *b.* fortunate, lucky
- *c.* being religious in nature
- *d.* being the only one

_____ **15.** Even working mothers are the *primary* caregivers in most families.

College students report that for them the *primary* cause of stress is having too much to do and not enough time in which to do it.

primary (prī′ měr ē) means:
- *a.* highest paid
- *b.* main, principal
- *c.* dissatisfied
- *d.* temporary

_____ **16.** Such a choice challenges still-prominent social expectations that fathers are primarily *breadwinners* and mothers are primarily responsible for child raising.

In some families, wives are the *breadwinners* and husbands enjoy staying home caring for the children.

breadwinners (brĕd′ wĭn′ ərz) means:

a. those whose earnings are the main source of support for dependents

b. those who are the main source of meals for dependents

c. those who are lucky in gambling

d. those who have training as bakers

_____ **17.** In a ten-year longitudinal study of *predominantly* white couples who married in their late twenties, both husbands and wives reported a sharp decline in satisfaction during the first four years, followed by a plateau and then another decline.

His undergraduate grades are *predominantly* A's; he has only four B's on his entire transcript.

predominantly (prĭ dŏm′ ə nənt lē) means:

a. occasionally

b. a few

c. completely, totally

d. mainly, mostly

_____ **18.** In a ten-year longitudinal study of predominantly white couples who married in their late twenties, both husbands and wives reported a sharp decline in satisfaction during the first four years, followed by a *plateau* and then another decline.

Mortgage rates increased, reached a *plateau* during the summer, and then declined.

plateau (plă tō′) means:

a. an uneven level

b. a relatively stable level or period

c. a period of constant change

d. an unexplained change

_____ **19.** Although there was a high *attrition* rate—429 out of the original 522 couples divorced or separated during the course of the study or did not complete it—the presumably greater dissatisfaction of the couples who ultimately left the study did not seriously skew the findings while they were in it.

An unusually high number of retirements and resignations caused our employee *attrition* rate to be higher last year.

attrition (ə trĭsh′ ən) means:

a. frustration

b. dissatisfaction

c. reduction

d. achievement

_____ **20.** Although there was a high attrition rate—429 out of the original 522 couples divorced or separated during the course of the study or did not complete it— the presumably greater dissatisfaction of the couples who ultimately left the study did not seriously *skew* the findings while they were in it.

If there are patients in the study who do not take their medications consistently, it will *skew* the results and make the research meaningless.

skew (skyo͞o) means:

a. distort, influence unfairly

b. confirm, verify

c. improve

d. publish

SELECTION **3.2**

Human Development

(continued)

Reading Skills Application

Directions: Items 21–25 test your ability to *apply* certain reading skills. You may not be familiar with all the skills yet, so some items will serve as a preview. As you work through *Opening Doors,* you will practice and develop these skills. These are important skills, which is why they are included on the state-mandated basic skills tests that some students must take. Write each answer in the space provided.

_____ **21.** In paragraph 2, the authors use the term *spur-of-the-moment* to describe decisions made:

a. by adults only.

b. under extreme pressure.

c. hastily on impulse.

d. after careful consideration.

_____ **22.** In paragraph 5, a comparison is made between family size in:

a. preindustrial societies and industrial societies today.

b. preindustrial farming societies and developing countries today.

c. industrial societies and developing countries today.

d. preindustrial farming societies and industrial societies and developing countries today.

_____ **23.** Based on the information in the selection, it can be logically concluded that:

a. couples who enter into parenthood with a realistic understanding of its demands, challenges, and rewards are likely to find the experience more satisfying.

b. the greater the number of children, the more unhappy parents are likely to become.

SELECTION 3.2

    c. children born to younger, immature couples are likely to have no more problems than children born to older, more mature couples.

    d. couples who are unprepared for parenthood usually adjust fairly quickly once the baby is born.

_____ **24.** The author's would be most likely to agree with which of the following statements?

    a. Parenthood is a rewarding experience that ideally every couple should experience.

    b. Because parenthood causes changes in so many aspects of a couple's life, they should consider carefully whether they want to have children and, if so, when.

    c. There is nothing that can be done to prepare couples for the transition to parenthood.

    d. People who do not have children are self-centered.

_____ **25.** Which of the following represents an opinion rather than a fact?

    a. Babies of older mothers may benefit from their mothers' greater ease with parenthood.

    b. When 105 new mothers ages 16 to 38 were interviewed and observed with their infants, the older mothers reported more satisfaction with parenting and spent more time at it.

    c. They were more affectionate and sensitive to their babies and more effective in encouraging desired behavior.

    d. And, among a large, nationally representative sample, men who became fathers after their 35th birthdays spent more leisure time with their children, had higher expectations for the children's behavior, and were more nurturing than a comparison group who became fathers before age 35.

SELECTION **3.2**

Human Development

(continued)

Respond in Writing

Directions: Refer to the selection as needed to answer the essay-type questions below. (Your instructor may direct you to work collaboratively with other students on one or more items. Each group member should be able to explain *all* of the group's answers.)

1. According to the authors, which factors seem to be associated with making parenthood a successful and satisfying experience?

_____

_____

_____

_____

_____

_____

_____

_____

_____

_____

_____

_____

_____

_____

2. If couples wait until they are older, more mature, and better educated before becoming parents, what effects do you think this might have on their children? List at least three effects.

_____

_____

_____

_____

_____

_____

3. If most couples were older, more mature, and better educated when they become parents, what possible effects do you think this might have on society? List at least three effects.

_____

_____

_____

_____

_____

_____

_____

_____

4. **Overall main idea.** What is the overall main idea the authors want the reader to understand about parenthood? Answer this question in one sentence. Be sure to include the word *parenthood* in your overall main idea sentence.

_____

_____

_____

_____

_____

_____

_____

_____

SELECTION **3.3**

Art Appreciation

Art in the Service of Religion

From *Living with Art*
by Rita Gilbert

Prepare Yourself to Read

Directions: Do these exercises *before* you read Selection 3.3.

1. First, read and think about the title. What factors do you think architects must consider when they design churches, temples, or other places of religious worship?

    _____

    _____

    _____

2. Next, complete your preview by reading the following:

    Introduction (in *italics*)
    First paragraph (paragraph 1)
    First sentence of each paragraph
    Words in italics
    Picture and caption
    All of the last paragraph (paragraph 12)

    On the basis of your preview, how do you think architecture is used to serve religion?

    _____

    _____

    _____

    _____

    _____

3. **Build your vocabulary as you read.** If you discover an unfamiliar word or key term as you read the selection, try to determine its meaning by using context clues.

Internet Resources

Read More about This Topic Online

Use a search engine, such as Google or Yahoo!, to expand your existing knowledge about this topic *before* you read the selection or to learn more about it *afterward*. Use search terms such as "Parthenon" or "Great Stupa of Sanchi" or "Chartres Cathedral." If you are unfamiliar with conducting Internet searches, read pages 25–26 on Boolean searches. You can also use Wikipedia, the free online encyclopedia, at www.wikipedia.com. Keep in mind that when you visit any website, it is a good idea to evaluate the site and the information it contains. Ask yourself questions such as "Who sponsors this website?" and "Is the information it contains up to date?"

SELECTION 3.3: ART IN THE SERVICE OF RELIGION

Religious architecture (which is also referred to as "sacred architecture") is "concerned with the design and construction of places of worship and/or sacred spaces, such as churches, mosques, stupas, synagogues, and temples." Of all the structures created by humankind, they are among the most impressive and enduring. Because they were the most important building in any community, cultures devoted substantial money, manpower, and other resources to their creation, which often spanned several centuries. Before the advent of the modern skyscraper, sacred structures were the largest edifices in the world (http://en.wikipedia.org/wiki/Religious_architecture).

Think about the various religious structures you have seen, visited, or worshiped in. Have you ever considered how the architecture of a place of worship is related to the activities that occur there? In this selection from an art appreciation textbook, the author explains the relationship between three different religions and the architecture of some of their most famous places of worship.

1   Since earliest times art has served religion in two important ways. First, artists have erected the sacred temples where believers join to profess their faith and follow the observances faith requires. Second, art attempts to make specific and visible something that is, by its very nature, spiritual, providing images of the religious figures and events that make up the fabric of faith. In other words, art attempts to make concrete that which is abstract. In this section we shall explore how the theme of religious art has been adapted for different purposes, for different faiths, in different parts of the world.

2   A very large portion of the magnificent architecture we have was built in the service of religion. Naturally the architectural style of any religious structure reflects the culture in which it was built, but it is also dependent on the particular needs of a given religion. Three examples will show this.

3   On a high hill, the Acropolis, overlooking the city of Athens stands the shell of what many consider the most splendid building ever conceived: the Parthenon. The Parthenon was erected in the 5th century B.C. as a temple to the goddess Athena, patroness of the city, and at one time its core held a colossal statue of the goddess. However, the religion associated with the Parthenon was not confined to worship of a deity. In ancient Greece, veneration of the gods was closely allied to the political and social ideals of a city-state that celebrated its own greatness.

4   Rising proudly on its hill, visible from almost every corner of the city, and for miles around, the Parthenon functioned as a symbol of the citizens' aspirations. Its structure as a religious shrine seems unusual for us in that it turns outward, toward the city, rather than in upon itself. Worshipers were not meant to gather inside the building; actually, only priests could enter the inner chamber, or *cella,* where

Creating Questions Exercises

Directions: For each paragraph:

- Create a question based on what the paragraph seems to be about. Ask *who, what, when, where, why,* or *how.*
- Write your question in the spaces provided.
- Write the answer to your question in the margin or highlight it in the text.

Doing this will help you understand and remember the material.

Creating Questions Exercise

Question about paragraph 1:

_____

_____

Creating Questions Exercise

Question about paragraph 2:

_____

_____

Creating Questions Exercise

Question about paragraph 3:

_____

_____

SELECTION 3.3

the statue of Athena stood. Religious ceremonies on festal occasions focused on processions, which began down in the city, wound their way up the steep path on the west side of the Acropolis, and circled the Parthenon and other sacred buildings at the top.

5   Most of the Parthenon's architectural embellishment was intended for the appreciation of the worshipers outside. All four walls of the exterior were decorated with sculptures high up under the roof, and originally portions of the marble façade were painted a vivid blue and red. We shall concentrate on the theme of religion and on the Parthenon's purpose, which is both religious *and* political exaltation.

6   At about the same time the Parthenon was being constructed in Athens, but half a continent away, one of the world's great religions was developing and beginning to form its own architecture. Buddhism derives its principles from the teachings of Gautama Siddhartha, later known as the Buddha, who was born in India about 563 B.C. Although of noble birth, the Buddha renounced his princely status and life of ease. When he was about twenty-nine, he began a long period of wandering and meditation, seeking enlightenment. He began with the supposition that humans are predisposed to live out lives of suffering, to die, then to be reborn and repeat the pattern. Ultimately, he worked out a doctrine of moral behavior that he believed could break the painful cycle of life and death, and he attracted many followers.

7   Buddhism is predominantly a personal religion, and its observances depend less on communal worship than on individual contemplation. It places great emphasis on symbolism, much of it referring to episodes in the Buddha's life. Both of these aspects—the personal and the symbolic—are evident in one of Buddhism's finest early shrines, the Great Stupa at Sanchi, in India. Like the Parthenon, the Great Stupa turns more outward than inward, but its moundlike form is more sculptural, intended as a representation of the cosmos. At the very top is a three-part "umbrella," symbolizing the three major aspects of Buddhism—the Buddha, the Buddha's law, and the Monastic Order.

8   Buddhist shrines—the word *stupa* means "shrine"—often housed relics of the Buddha, and worship rituals called for circumambulation ("walking around") of the stupa. Thus, on the outside of the Great Stupa of Sanchi we see a railed pathway, where pilgrims could take the ritual clockwise walk following the Path of Life around the World Mountain. Elsewhere the stupa is embellished richly with carvings and sculpture evoking scenes from the Buddha's life. Every part of the stupa is geared to the pursuit of personal enlightenment and transcendence.

The Parthenon on the Acropolis. Athens, Greece. 447–432 B.C.

Creating Questions Exercise

Question about paragraph 4:

_____

_____

Creating Questions Exercise

Question about paragraph 5:

_____

_____

Creating Questions Exercise

Question about paragraph 6:

_____

_____

Creating Questions Exercise

Question about paragraph 7:

_____

_____

Creating Questions Exercise

Question about paragraph 8:

_____

_____

9   If the Buddhist temple is dedicated to private worship, then its extreme opposite can be found in the total encompassment of a community religious experience: the medieval Christian cathedral. And the supreme example of that ideal is the Cathedral of Notre Dame de Chartres, in France. Chartres Cathedral was built, rebuilt, and modified over a period of several hundred years, but the basic structure, which is in the Gothic style, was established in the 13th century. A cathedral—as opposed to a church—is the bishop's domain and therefore is always in a town or a city. This one fact is crucial to understanding the nature of Chartres and the role it played in the people's lives.

10   The cathedral towers magnificently over the surrounding city, much as the Parthenon does over Athens, but here the resemblance ends. Whereas the Parthenon is above and apart from the city, accessible only by a steep path, Chartres Cathedral is very much a living presence *within* the city. In the Middle Ages houses and shops clustered right up to its walls, and one side of the cathedral formed an edge of the busy marketplace. The cathedral functioned as a hub of all activities, both sacred and secular, within the town.

11   Medieval France had one dominant religion, and that was the Christianity of Rome. One could assume that almost every resident of the town of Chartres professed exactly the same faith, and so the church was an integral part of everyday life. Its bells tolled the hours of waking, starting work, praying, and retiring for the evening rest. Its feast days were the official holidays. Chartres Cathedral and its counterparts served the populace not only as a setting for religious worship but as meeting hall, museum, concert stage, and social gathering place. Within its walls business deals were arranged, goods were sold, friends met, young couples courted. Where else but inside the cathedral could the townsfolk hear splendid music? Where else would they see magnificent art?

The Great Stupa, Sanchi, India. Third century B.C. to first century A.D.

Creating Questions Exercise

Question about paragraph 9:

_____

_____

Creating Questions Exercise

Question about paragraph 10:

_____

_____

Creating Questions Exercise

Question about paragraph 11:

_____

_____

SELECTION 3.3

Chartres Cathedral,
France,
c. 1194–1260.

12   Three religious structures: the Parthenon, the Great Stupa, and
Chartres Cathedral. Each was built in the service of religion but for
each we can find another slightly different purpose. For the Parthenon the purpose is also *political;* for the Great Stupa there is the
purely *private* observance of religion; and for Chartres the *social* role
is as important as the religious.

Creating Questions Exercise

Question about paragraph 12:

_____

_____

Reading Selection Quiz

This quiz has several parts. Your instructor may assign some or all of them.

Comprehension

Directions: Items 1–10 test your understanding of the selection. They are the type of questions a content area instructor (such as an art appreciation professor) might ask on a test. You may refer to the selection as you answer the questions. Write your answer choice in the space provided.

True or False

_____ 1. Throughout history, art has served religion in three important ways.

_____ 2. The Parthenon was built as a temple to the Greek goddess Diana.

_____ 3. Greek citizens gathered inside the Parthenon to worship their gods.

_____ 4. Many consider the Parthenon the most splendid building ever constructed.

_____ 5. Buddhism was beginning to form its own architecture in India at approximately the same time as the Parthenon was being constructed in Greece.

_____ 6. "Circumambulation" is a Buddhist religious ritual that involves walking clockwise around a stupa, a Buddhist shrine.

Multiple-Choice

_____ 7. Which of the following does not describe early Buddhism?
  a. It was a personal religion.
  b. It required individual contemplation and a search for enlightenment.
  c. It required communal worship.
  d. It involved a ritual of walking around the shrine.

_____ 8. One of the finest Buddhist shrines, the Great Stupa of Sanchi in India, is characterized by all of the following except which?
  a. It contained a railed pathway.
  b. It resembled the cosmos with its moundlike form.
  c. It did not contain any carving or sculptures.
  d. It housed relics of the Buddha.

_____ **9.** In medieval France, the cathedral served as a:

    a. place of worship.

    b. concert stage and meeting hall.

    c. museum housing fine religious paintings and sculpture.

    d. all of the above

_____ **10.** Chartres Cathedral in France was built, rebuilt, and modified over a period of:

    a. 25 years.

    b. 50 years.

    c. 100 years.

    d. several hundred years.

SELECTION **3.3**

Art Appreciation
(continued)

Vocabulary in Context

Directions: Items 11–20 test your ability to determine a word's meaning by using context clues. *Context clues* are words in a sentence that allow readers to deduce (reason out) the meaning of an unfamiliar word in the sentence. They also help readers determine the meaning an author intends when a word has more than one meaning. Each item below consists of a sentence from the selection, with the vocabulary word *italicized*. It is followed by another sentence that uses the same word in the same way. Use context clues to deduce the meaning of the *italicized* word. Be sure the meaning you choose makes sense in *both* sentences. Write each answer in the space provided. *Note:* Chapter 2 presents the skill of using context clues.

_____ **11.** First, artists have erected the sacred temples where believers join to *profess* their faith and follow the observances faith requires.

Although the visiting scientists tried to *profess* loyalty to the host country, they were nevertheless deported as spies.

profess (prə fĕs′) means:

    a. discuss

    b. lie about

    c. deny

    d. declare

_____ **12.** In ancient Greece, *veneration* of the gods was closely allied to the political and social ideals of a city-state that celebrated its own greatness.

In Asian cultures older people, such as grandparents, are treated with great respect and *veneration*.

veneration (vĕn ə rā′ shən) means:

    a. reverence

    b. courtesy

    c. fondness

    d. patience

13. All four walls of the exterior were decorated with sculptures high up under the roof, and originally, portions of the marble *façade* were painted a vivid blue and red.

The architect updated the *façade* of the old hotel by adding a beautiful new brick exterior and elegant bronze doors.

façade (fə säd′) means:
   a. front of a building
   b. decorative trim
   c. columns; pillars
   d. steps or stairs

14. Although of noble birth, the Buddha *renounced* his princely status and life of ease.

When my brother became a Catholic priest, he *renounced* all of his worldly possessions and took a vow of poverty.

renounced (rĭ nounst′) means:
   a. ignored
   b. gave up, especially by formal announcement
   c. described in someone else's words
   d. collected; gathered together

15. He began with the *supposition* that humans are predisposed to live out lives of suffering, to die, then to be reborn and repeat the pattern.

Under the American judicial system, we begin with the *supposition* that a person is considered innocent until proven guilty.

supposition (sŭp ə zĭsh′ ən) means:
   a. scientific conclusion
   b. religious belief
   c. assumption
   d. hope

16. Like the Parthenon, the Great Stupa turns more outward than inward, but its moundlike form is more sculptural, intended as a representation of the *cosmos*.

Because human beings have always wondered how life began, every culture has its own explanation of the creation of the *cosmos*.

cosmos (kŏz′ mōs) means:
   a. city
   b. mountains and other significant geological features
   c. the universe regarded as an orderly, harmonious whole
   d. life after death

SELECTION 3.3

17. Buddhist shrines—the word "stupa" means "shrine"—often housed *relics* of the Buddha, and worship rituals called for circumambulation ("walking around") of the stupa.

The museum presented a splendid exhibit of Russian icons, altarpieces, and other religious *relics*.

relics (rĕl' ĭks) means:

a. objects of religious reverence

b. pieces of art

c. personal belongings

d. paintings

18. Elsewhere the stupa is *embellished* richly with carvings and sculpture evoking scenes from the Buddha's life.

The Sistine Chapel in Rome is *embellished* with magnificent frescoes by Michelangelo.

embellished (ĕm bĕl' ĭsht) means:

a. made colorful and bright

b. painted

c. made in a shape of a bell

d. adorned; made beautiful

19. Every part of the stupa is geared to the pursuit of personal enlightenment and *transcendence*.

The monk spent his days in solitude, meditation, and prayer as a way of seeking *transcendence*.

transcendence (trăn sĕn' dĕns) means:

a. suffering; punishment

b. existence beyond or independent of the material universe

c. a change from one physical place to another

d. public recognition

20. *Medieval* France had one dominant religion, and that was the Christianity of Rome.

Our favorite childhood stories were about *medieval* kings, queens, and castles.

medieval (mē dē ē' vəl) means:

a. pertaining to the Middle Ages, a 1,000-year period of European history between antiquity and the Renaissance

b. pertaining to the period of American history between the Civil War and the present

c. pertaining to a period in European history between the fourteenth and sixteenth centuries, a time of revived intellectual and artistic achievement

d. pertaining to a period in European history characterized by absence of artistic achievement

Reading Skills Application

Directions: Items 21–25 test your ability to *apply* certain reading skills. You may not be familiar with all the skills yet, so some items will serve as a preview. As you work through *Opening Doors,* you will practice and develop these skills. These are important skills, which is why they are included on the state-mandated basic skills tests that some students must take. Write each answer in the space provided.

_____ 21. According to this selection, which of the following is an accurate detail?

    a. The Acropolis stands high atop a hill known as the Parthenon.

    b. Chartres Cathedral was geared to the pursuit of personal enlightenment.

    c. The Christianity of Rome was the primary religion of medieval France.

    d. Worshipers at a Buddhist stupa follow a ritual of walking around the interior of the shrine.

_____ 22. Which of the following statements from this selection represents the main idea of paragraph 9?

    a. If the Buddhist temple is dedicated to private worship, then its extreme opposite can be found in the total encompassment of a community religious experience: the medieval Christian cathedral.

    b. A cathedral—as opposed to a church—is the bishop's domain and therefore is always in a town or a city.

    c. Chartres Cathedral was built, rebuilt, and modified over a period of several hundred years, but the basic structure, which is Gothic style, was established in the 13th century.

    d. The supreme example of that ideal is the Cathedral of Notre Dame de Chartres, in France.

_____ 23. What is the meaning of the word *pilgrims* in paragraph 8?

    a. religious devotees who journey to a shrine or sacred place

    b. those who travel to a new land seeking religious freedom

    c. priests and other religious leaders

    d. early settlers in what is now the United States

_____ 24. Which of the following describes the author's primary purpose for writing this selection?

    a. to explain and illustrate two ways art has served religion

    b. to present descriptions of three of the world's greatest religious structures

    c. to encourage readers to think about the architecture of religions

    d. to inspire readers to visit the Parthenon, the Great Stupa, and Chartres Cathedral

_____ **25.** Which of the following represents an inference that is based on the information in this selection?
  a. The architecture of any religious structure should encourage the private
      observance of religion.
  b. In order to design a religious structure, an architect must have a thorough
      understanding of the religion.
  c. The Parthenon is a more important religious structure than Chartres
      Cathedral.
  d. The Great Stupa of Sanchi is embellished richly with carvings and sculpture.

  _____

  _____

  _____

SELECTION **3.3**

Art Appreciation
(continued)

Respond in Writing

Directions: Refer to the selection as needed to answer the essay-type questions
below. (Your instructor may direct you to work collaboratively with other students on one or more items. Each group member should be able to explain *all* of
the group's answers.)

1. The Great Stupa of Sanchi was designed strictly for the private observance of
    religion by individuals. However, the Parthenon and Chartres Cathedral served
    other purposes besides private observance. In addition to religious worship,
    what *other purposes* did each of them serve?

    Parthenon:

    _____

    _____

    _____

    Chartres Cathedral:

    _____

    _____

    _____

    _____

    _____

2.   **Overall main idea.** What is the overall main idea the author wants the reader to understand about religious structures such as the Parthenon, the Great Stupa of Sanchi, and Chartres Cathedral? Answer this question in one sentence. Be sure to use the words *art* and *religion* in your overall main idea sentence.

_____

_____

_____

_____

_____

_____

_____

SELECTION 3.3

Comprehension

*Understanding College
Textbooks by Reading for Ideas*

Determining the Topic and the Stated Main Idea

In this chapter, you will learn the answers to these questions:

- Why is it important to determine the topic of a paragraph?

- How can I determine the topic of a paragraph?

- Why is the stated main idea of a paragraph important?

- How can I locate the stated main idea sentence of a paragraph?

SKILLS

The Topic of a Paragraph

- What Is the Topic of a Paragraph, and Why Is It Important?
- Determining and Expressing the Topic

The Stated Main Idea of a Paragraph

- What Is a Stated Main Idea, and Why Is It Important?
- Locating the Stated Main Idea Sentence
- How to Tell If You Have Identified the Stated Main Idea Sentence
- How to Avoid Two Common Errors in Locating a Stated Main Idea
- Stated Overall Main Ideas in Longer Passages

A Word about Standardized Reading Tests: Topics and Stated Main Ideas

CHECKPOINT: LOCATING THE STATED MAIN IDEA

CREATING YOUR SUMMARY

Developing Chapter Review Cards

TEST YOUR UNDERSTANDING: DETERMINING THE TOPIC AND THE STATED MAIN IDEA, PART 1

TEST YOUR UNDERSTANDING: DETERMINING THE TOPIC AND THE STATED MAIN IDEA, PART 2

READINGS

Selection 4.1   "A Warning to Students: Plagiarism, Term Papers and Web Research"
from *Using Information Technology: A Practical Introduction to Computers and Communications*
by *Brian K. Williams and Stacey C. Sawyer* (Information Technology)

Selection 4.2   "Classes without Walls: Distance Learning"
from *P.O.W.E.R. Learning and Your Life: Essentials of Student Success*
by *Robert S. Feldman* (Student Success)

Selection 4.3   "Muhammad"
from *The 100: A Ranking of the Most Influential Persons in History*
by *Michael K. Hart* (History)

Books are carriers of civilization. Without books, history is silent, literature dumb, science crippled, thought and speculation at a standstill.

Barbara Tuchman

Reading is to the mind like exercise is to the body.

Sir Richard Steele

A person who does not read good books has no advantage over a person who cannot read.

Mark Twain

Books had instant replay long before televised sports.

Bern Williams

THE TOPIC OF A PARAGRAPH

PERSONALIZED LEARNING

What Is the Topic of a Paragraph, and Why Is It Important?

Every paragraph is written about something, and that "something" is called the topic. A **topic** is a word, name, or phrase that tells what the author is writing about in a paragraph. Other names for the topic of a paragraph are the *subject* or *subject matter.* These are simply different terms for the topic. The important thing to understand is that every paragraph has a topic.

The topic is always expressed as a single word (for example, *procrastination*) or a name (for instance, *Barack Obama* or *the Rocky Mountains*) or as a phrase consisting of two or more words (for instance, *the increasing use of technology in education*). Each sentence in a paragraph relates in some way to the topic (explains it, tells more about it, gives examples of it, etc.). For this reason, the topic may be mentioned several times in a paragraph.

Determining the topic is the essential first step in understanding a passage that you are reading and studying. It focuses your attention and helps you understand complex paragraphs precisely. As you will learn later in this chapter, it is also a key to locating the stated main idea of a paragraph.

Determining and Expressing the Topic

You know from Chapter 2 that effective readers are active and interactive readers who ask questions as they read. When you read a paragraph, you can determine its topic by asking yourself, "Who or what is this paragraph about?" and then answering this question. Paragraphs, especially those in textbooks, contain various clues that will help you answer this question.

One or more of the following clues often make the topic of a textbook paragraph obvious. The topic is a word, name, or phrase that:

- Appears as a *heading* or *title*
- Appears in *special type* such as **bold print,** *italics,* or color
- Is *repeated* throughout the paragraph
- Appears at the beginning of the paragraph and is then referred to throughout the paragraph by *pronouns* (or other words)

topic

Word, name, or phrase that tells who or what the author is writing about.

The topic is also known as the *subject,* or the *subject matter.*

Comprehension-Monitoring Question for Determining the Topic

Who or what is this paragraph about?

Determining the topic is the essential first step in understanding a passage that you are reading and studying.

A paragraph does not usually contain all of these clues, but every paragraph has at least one of them. Let's look at each clue in more detail.

The Topic Is Often Used as the Heading or Title

Textbook authors typically use the topic of a section as the heading or title for that section. The following paragraph from a business communications textbook illustrates this clue (as well as some others). Read the paragraph and use its heading (and other clues) to determine its topic.

> ### Doing Business and Learning about a Culture through Its Language
>
> The best way to prepare yourself to do business with people from another culture is to learn something about their culture in advance by studying their language. If you plan to live in another country or do business there repeatedly, for example, make an attempt to learn the language of that country. The same holds true if you must work closely with a subculture that has its own language, such as Vietnamese-Americans or Hispanic-Americans. When traveling abroad you may end up doing business with foreigners in your own language, but you will show respect by having made the effort to learn their language. In addition, you will learn something about the culture and its customs in the process. If you do not have the time or opportunity to actually learn a new language, at least learn a few words and phrases.
>
> *Source:* Adapted from Courtland Bovée and John Thill, *Business Communication Today,* 3e, p. 570. Copyright © 1992 by The McGraw-Hill Companies, Inc. Reprinted with permission of The McGraw-Hill Companies, Inc.

Stop and Annotate

Go back to the textbook excerpt above. Underline or highlight the heading that indicates the topic.

Notice that in this excerpt, the heading *Doing Business and Learning about a Culture through Its Language* tells you its topic. This phrase describes everything that is discussed in the paragraph: It expresses the topic that all the sentences in the paragraph have in common. (Notice also that the words *business, language, culture,* and *learn* are repeated throughout the paragraph.)

Although the heading of a paragraph is often a clue to the topic, it may not always express the topic completely or accurately. To determine the topic, do not rely *only* on headings; you must also read the paragraph and ask yourself, "Who or what is this paragraph about?"

The Topic Often Appears in Special Print

A second clue to the topic of a paragraph is the use of special print (such as **bold** print, *italics,* or color) to emphasize a word, name, or phrase. The paragraph below is from a textbook on criminal justice. As you read it, watch for special print that indicates its topic.

> Depending on the nature and severity of the punishment, crimes are considered to be felonies, misdemeanors, or violations. **Felonies** are serious crimes that are subject to punishments of a year or more in prison to capital punishment. **Misdemeanors** are less serious than felonies and are subject to a maximum sentence of one year in jail or a fine. **Violations** are infractions of the law for which normally only a fine can be imposed. Fines can also be imposed for felonies and misdemeanors.
>
> *Source:* Adapted from Freda Adler, Gerhard O. W. Mueller, and William S. Laufer, *Criminal Justice: An Introduction,* 3e, p. 91. Copyright © 2003 by The McGraw-Hill Companies, Inc. Reprinted with permission of The McGraw-Hill Companies, Inc.

Stop and Annotate

Go back to the textbook excerpt above. Underline or highlight the words in bold print that indicate the topic.

Notice the three words in bold print: **felonies, misdemeanors,** and **violations.** These words, together, indicate the topic. The paragraph discusses *felonies, misdemeanors,* and *violations,* and the differences among these three types of crimes. Keep in mind that the topic can also appear in italics and that in many textbooks key words are printed in color. Special print, then, can often help you identify the topic.

The Topic Is Often Repeated throughout the Paragraph

A third clue to the topic is repetition of a word, name, or phrase throughout a paragraph. Read the paragraph below from a psychology textbook and use this clue to determine its topic.

> Claustrophobia. Acrophobia. Xenophobia. Although these sound like characters in a Greek tragedy, they are actually members of a class of psychological disorders known as phobias. Phobias are intense, irrational fears of specific objects or situations. For example, claustrophobia is a fear of enclosed places, acrophobia a fear of high places, and xenophobia a fear of strangers. Although the objective danger posed by an anxiety-producing stimulus is typically small or nonexistent, to the individual suffering from the phobia it represents great danger, and a full-blown panic attack may follow exposure to the stimulus.
>
> *Source:* Robert S. Feldman, *Understanding Psychology,* 6e, p. 479. Copyright © 2002 by The McGraw-Hill Companies, Inc. Reprinted with permission of The McGraw-Hill Companies, Inc.

Stop and Annotate

Go back to the textbook excerpt on the preceding page. Underline or highlight the repeated words that indicate the topic.

Notice that the word *phobias* or *phobia* appears three times in this paragraph, indicating that this is the topic. In addition, three specific types of phobias are given as examples.

The Topic Sometimes Appears Only Once, but Is Then Referred to by Pronouns or Other Words

A fourth clue to the topic of a paragraph is a word, name, or phrase that appears near the beginning of the paragraph and is then referred to throughout the paragraph by a pronoun (such as *he, she, it, they, his, her, its,* etc.) or other words. Here is a paragraph from a physics textbook. Use this clue to determine the topic of the paragraph.

> Before the age of 30, Isaac Newton had invented the mathematical methods of calculus, demonstrated that white light contained all the colors of the rainbow, and discovered the law of gravitation. Interestingly, this mathematical genius led a lonely and solitary life. His father died before he was born, and after his mother remarried, he was raised by an aged grandmother. In 1661, he was admitted to Cambridge University, where he worked for the next eight years, except for one year at home to escape the plague. During those years, he made his major discoveries, although none were published at that time. His genius was nonetheless recognized, and in 1669 he was appointed Lucasion Professor of Mathematics at Cambridge University, a position he retained until 1695. His major scientific work was completed prior to 1692, when he suffered a nervous breakdown. After his recovery, he determined to lead a more public life, and soon became the Master of the Mint in London. He was elected president of the Royal Society in 1703, and held that position until his death.
>
> *Source:* Adapted from Frederick Bueche, *Principles of Physics,* 5e, p. 70. Copyright © 1988 by The McGraw-Hill Companies, Inc. Reprinted with permission of The McGraw-Hill Companies, Inc.

Stop and Annotate

Go back to the textbook excerpt above. Underline or highlight the topic, pronouns, and other words that refer to the topic.

Notice that Newton's name appears only in the first sentence, but it is obvious from the words *this mathematical genius* and the pronouns *he* and *his* that the rest of the paragraph continues to discuss him. Therefore, *Isaac Newton* is the topic of this paragraph.

Be sure you understand that when authors present the topic at or near the beginning of a paragraph, they often refer to the topic by words other than pronouns. For instance, a paragraph might begin "Pneumonia is . . ." and then say "This disease is characterized by . . ." and "The condition worsens when . . ." and "The disorder is typically treated by . . ." The words *disease, condition,* and *disorder* refer to *pneumonia* and indicate that pneumonia is the topic of the paragraph. (In the preceding example, you saw *Isaac Newton* referred to as *this mathematical genius* as well as by pronouns.)

It is important to be precise when you identify the topic of a paragraph. If you choose a word or a phrase that is too general or too specific, it will not describe the topic accurately. A topic described in terms that are *too general,* or too broad, will go beyond what is discussed in the paragraph. A topic described in terms that are *too specific,* or too narrow, will fail to cover everything discussed in the paragraph. Suppose, for instance, that the topic of a paragraph is *causes of gang violence.* The word *gangs,* the word *violence,* or even the phrase *gang violence* would be too general to express this topic precisely. The paragraph could be about many different things that pertain to gangs or violence. On the other hand, the phrase *lack of parental supervision as a cause of gang violence* would be too specific, even though "lack of parental supervision" might be mentioned in the paragraph as one of the causes.

Keep in mind that it is often possible to express a topic correctly in more than one way. For example, the topic of a paragraph could be correctly expressed as *Winston Churchill's childhood, the childhood of Winston Churchill, Churchill's life as a child, Churchill's boyhood,* or *Churchill's youth,* since all these phrases mean the same thing. Keep in mind, too, that (as the examples show) the topic is *never* expressed as a complete sentence. You must always express the topic as a single word or as a phrase (a group of words).

Determining a topic precisely is the starting point in comprehending as you read. It is also a key to locating the main idea sentence in a paragraph, as you will see in the next section of this chapter.

EXERCISE 1

This paragraph comes from a career development textbook:

Kelly Driscoll, president and founder of Digitation, an e-portfolio service, describes what e-portfolios are and how they can be an advantage to you in your job search. Driscoll explains, "An e-portfolio is a collection of work, published online to document achievements, ideas, progress, performance, and activities. It can also showcase, publish, and compile your work to expand on a personal vision or life goal and create an archive of experiences." E-portfolios have several advantages. An electronic version of your credentials makes it possible to share them with a wider audience, regardless of location. E-portfolios are more practical than hard-copy versions of portfolios, usually binders, because your work can be better protected online and there is no need to transport the materials with you to interviews.

Source: Adapted from Donna J. Yena, *Career Directions: The Path to Your Ideal Career,* 5e, p. 115. Copyright © 2011 by The McGraw-Hill Companies, Inc. Reprinted with permission of The McGraw-Hill Companies, Inc.

Write a word, name, or phrase that tells the *topic:* _____

_____

Clue(s): _____

_____

_____

THE STATED MAIN IDEA OF A PARAGRAPH

What Is a Stated Main Idea, and Why Is It Important?

stated main idea

The sentence in a paragraph that contains both the topic and the author's most important point about this topic.

A stated main idea sentence is also known as the *topic sentence.*

Every paragraph has a main idea. A **stated main idea** is a sentence in a paragraph that contains both the topic and the author's most important point about this topic. There are other names for a stated main idea, such as the *topic sentence.*

Unlike the topic, which is always a single word, a name, or a phrase, the main idea is always expressed as a complete sentence. For that reason, you should never select a question from a paragraph as the stated main idea. Although the stated main idea is *never* written in the form of a question, it will often be the *answer* to a question presented at the beginning of a paragraph.

As you learned at the beginning of this chapter, the topic of a paragraph tells who or what the paragraph is about. In contrast, a stated main idea sentence goes further than the topic because it expresses the author's *most important point* about the topic. For example, the main idea sentence in a paragraph whose topic is *procrastination* might be "Procrastination is the major cause of stress for college students." This sentence includes the topic, *procrastination,* and tells the important point the author is making about *procrastination.* Because the word *main* means "most important," there can be only *one* main, or most important, idea in any paragraph. This is only logical: Two or three different sentences can't all be the most important sentence.

A main idea is called a *stated main idea* when the author presents it—*states* it as one of the sentences in the paragraph. An author can place the stated main idea sentence anywhere in the paragraph: at the beginning, end, or even in the middle. In this chapter, you will practice only with paragraphs that contain stated main ideas. Sometimes, however, an author does not state the main idea of a paragraph directly. In that case, the main idea is called an *implied main idea,* and the reader must create a sentence that states the author's main point. (Implied main ideas are discussed in Chapter 5.)

There are several reasons it is important to determine main ideas when you are studying:

- To increase your comprehension
- To enable you to mark textbooks effectively and take notes as you study
- To enable you to write summaries and outlines
- To help you identify and remember important material for tests

For these reasons, effective readers focus on main ideas.

Comprehension-Monitoring Question for Stated Main Idea

What is the most important point the author wants me to understand about the topic of this paragraph?

Locating the Stated Main Idea Sentence

Steps to Follow

Because a stated main idea is one of the sentences in the paragraph, your task is simply to determine *which* sentence it is. Often, it will be obvious. To identify the stated main idea sentence, find the sentence that contains both the topic and the most important point about it. In other words, to locate the stated main idea, follow these two steps:

- **Step 1:** After you have read the paragraph, determine the topic by asking yourself, "Who or what is the passage about?" and then answering this question. (Use the clues you learned earlier in this chapter for determining the topic.)
- **Step 2:** Locate the main idea sentence by asking yourself, "What is the most important point the author wants me to understand about the topic of this paragraph?" Then search the paragraph for the sentence that answers this question. That sentence is the stated main idea.

Here is a simple formula that gives the essential parts of any stated main idea sentence:

| The *topic* | + | Author's *most important point* about the topic | = | Main idea sentence |

Although authors can put a stated main idea sentence anywhere in a paragraph, they usually put it at the beginning. The next most common place is at the end. Of course, a stated main idea can also be placed elsewhere within the paragraph. Let's look at examples of each.

Where a Stated Main Idea Sentence May Appear in a Paragraph

Authors usually put their stated main idea sentence at the beginning of the paragraph. They put it first because it makes it easier for the reader to comprehend the most important point in the paragraph. Especially in textbooks, authors are likely to start a paragraph with the main idea.

The following excerpt from a textbook on career planning has the main idea stated at the beginning of the paragraph. The topic is *beginning a new job*. Read the paragraph and ask yourself, "What is the most important point the authors want me to understand about beginning a new job?" The sentence that answers this question, the first sentence, is the main idea.

> Beginning a new job is always exciting and sometimes intimidating. There is an invigorating feeling of a fresh start and a clean slate. You face new challenges and draw on a renewed sense of energy as you approach them. But you may also feel apprehensive about this new adventure. Will it actually turn out as well as you hope? You are entering a strange environment, and you must learn to work with new associates. If you were laid off or fired from your last job, you may feel particularly sensitive. "What if it happens again?" you ask yourself.
>
> *Source:* William Morin and James Cabrera, *Parting Company: How to Survive the Loss of a Job and Find Another.* San Diego, CA: Harcourt, Brace, 1982, p. 238. Reprinted with permission of Harcourt, Brace.

The first sentence in the excerpt is a general one that mentions two different types of feelings people have as they start a new job. Since the most important point the authors want you to understand is that people may have *both* types of feelings,

Stop and Annotate

Go back to the textbook excerpt on the preceding page. Underline or highlight the stated main idea sentence.

this sentence is the main idea of the paragraph: *Beginning a new job is always exciting and sometimes intimidating.* The rest of the paragraph presents specific details that support this sentence as the main idea: The first half of the paragraph explains why starting a new job is *exciting,* and the second half of the paragraph explains why it can be *intimidating.* In this paragraph, then, the first sentence states the main idea, and the rest of the sentences are details that tell more about it.

The author may place a stated main idea sentence at the end of a paragraph. Frequently, the last sentence of a paragraph is the stated main idea. Authors sometimes prefer to lead up to their main point, and so they place it at the end of the paragraph. They know it can help the reader if they first give an explanation, provide background information or present examples, and then state their main idea.

Read the following excerpt from a sociology textbook. The topic of this paragraph is *ethnocentrism.* As you read the paragraph, ask yourself, "What is the most important point the author wants me to understand about *ethnocentrism*?" The sentence that answers this question, the last sentence, is the stated main idea.

> It is tempting to evaluate the practices of other cultures on the basis of our own perspectives. For example, Westerners who think cattle are to be used for food might look down on India's Hindu religion and culture, which views the cow as sacred. Or people in one culture may dismiss as unthinkable the mate-selection or child-rearing practices of another culture. Sociologist William Graham Sumner (1906) coined the term **ethnocentrism** to refer to the tendency to assume that one's culture and way of life represent the norm or are superior to all others.
>
> *Source:* Adapted from Richard Schaefer, *Sociology,* 9e, p. 73. Copyright © 2005 by The McGraw-Hill Companies, Inc. Reprinted with permission of The McGraw-Hill Companies, Inc.

Stop and Annotate

Go back to the textbook excerpt above. Underline or highlight the stated main idea sentence.

In this paragraph, the first sentence is an introductory one. The second and third sentences give examples of how people in one culture might look down on or reject aspects of other cultures. The last sentence is the main idea because it states the author's most important point: that *ethnocentrism* is the term used to describe the tendency to assume that one's culture and way of life represent the norm or are superior to all others. Notice that this stated main idea sentence contains the topic and that the topic is in bold.

Authors sometimes put the stated main idea sentence within the paragraph. Sometimes the stated main idea sentence is neither the first nor the last sentence of a paragraph, but rather one of the other sentences in the paragraph. That is, the stated main idea appears within the paragraph. Sometimes authors begin a paragraph with an introductory comment or question designed to get the reader's attention, or with some background information. Then they present their main idea. The rest of the information then explains or tells more about the main idea, or gives examples. (Helpful hint: Whenever a paragraph begins with a question, expect the author to then answer that important question. Moreover, the answer is often the main idea of the paragraph.)

Here is a paragraph from a government textbook in which the second sentence is the main idea sentence. The topic is *television commercials and presidential campaigns.* As you read this paragraph, ask yourself, "What is the most important point the author wants me to understand about television commercials and presidential campaigns?"

> In addition to television interviews and debates, presidential campaigns include political advertising in the form of televised commercials. Television commercials are by far the most expensive part of presidential campaigns. Since 1976, political commercials on television have accounted for about half of the candidates' expenditures in the general election campaign. In 1992 Bush and Clinton each spent more than $30 million on advertising in the general election, and Perot spent even more. Perot relied heavily on "infomercials"—30-minute and hour-long commercials that emphasized substance over slogans.
>
> *Source:* Thomas E. Patterson, *The American Democracy,* 3e, p. 398. Copyright © 1996 by The McGraw-Hill Companies, Inc. Reprinted with permission of The McGraw-Hill Companies, Inc.

Stop and Annotate

Go back to the textbook excerpt above. Underline or highlight the stated main idea sentence.

The second sentence presents the author's most important point: *Television commercials are by far the most expensive part of presidential campaigns.* The first sentence introduces the use of televised commercials in presidential campaigns. Each of the other sentences presents facts or examples that illustrate how expensive television campaign commercials had become.

How to Tell If You Have Identified the Stated Main Idea Sentence

Stated Main Idea Checklist

How can you tell if you have *correctly* identified an author's stated main idea sentence in a paragraph? You have found it if the sentence has these five characteristics:

- The sentence contains the topic.
- The sentence states the *single* most important point about the topic.
- The sentence is general enough to cover all the information in the paragraph.
- The sentence makes complete sense by itself (in other words, a reader could understand it without having to read the rest of the paragraph).
- The other sentences introduce, explain, or tell more about the main idea sentence.

Here is an example of a sentence that could be a main idea sentence because it makes sense by itself: *Most historians consistently rank Abraham Lincoln among the five greatest U.S. presidents.* On the other hand, this sentence would not be meaningful by itself since the reader would not know who "him" refers to: *Most historians consistently rank him among the five greatest U.S. presidents.*

When you locate a stated main idea sentence in your textbooks, highlight or underline it. Be sure to mark the entire sentence. (Marking textbooks is discussed in Chapter 11.)

EXERCISE 2

This paragraph comes from a psychology textbook:

> To achieve your goals, you need to keep yourself on track and move forward. Self-discipline helps you do this. No matter how motivated you are, how many skills you have, and how self-confident you are, you will need self-discipline to achieve your goals. What is self-discipline? Self-discipline is the process of teaching yourself to do what is necessary to reach your goals, without becoming sidetracked by bad habits. Self-discipline can be hard, but it's worth it. It gives you a feeling of self-expectancy. It also gives you a feeling of control over your life.
>
> *Source:* Adapted from Denis Waitley, *Psychology of Success: Finding Meaning in Work and Life,* 5e, p. 211. Copyright © 2010 by The McGraw-Hill Companies, Inc. Reprinted with permission of The McGraw-Hill Companies, Inc.

Write a word, name, or phrase that tells the *topic:* _____

_____

Locate the *stated main idea* and write it here:

_____

_____

_____

How to Avoid Two Common Errors in Locating a Stated Main Idea

You have learned that a stated main idea sentence is most often the first or last sentence of a paragraph, and so you may be tempted to try to take a shortcut by reading only those sentences. This is an error you should avoid. You must read the entire paragraph to identify the main idea accurately. You will not be able to compare the sentences to determine which is the most important unless you read the entire paragraph. And you may miss a stated main idea sentence that occurs within the paragraph.

A second common error can occur when a paragraph is difficult. In this case, you may be tempted to select a sentence as the main idea simply because it contains familiar or interesting information, or because it seems to "sound important." These are not valid reasons for choosing a sentence as the stated main idea. To avoid this mistake, remind yourself that the stated main idea sentence must always answer the question "What is the *most important point* the author wants me to understand about the topic of this paragraph?"

Stated Overall Main Ideas in Longer Passages

Locating stated main ideas is a skill that can also be applied to passages longer than a single paragraph, such as sections of a textbook chapter, short reading selections, and essays. You will sometimes discover a sentence in a longer passage (usually an introductory or concluding sentence) that expresses the most important point or the overall message of the *entire passage*. This sentence is called the *overall main idea,* the *thesis statement,* or *thesis.* The chapter reading selections in *Opening Doors* include an exercise called Respond in Writing. As you may have noticed, the final item gives you practice in determining the overall main idea of the entire selection.

A WORD ABOUT STANDARDIZED READING TESTS: TOPICS AND STATED MAIN IDEAS

Many college students are required to take standardized reading tests as part of an overall assessment program, in a reading course, or as part of a state-mandated basic skills test. A standardized reading test typically consists of a series of passages, each of which is followed by multiple-choice reading skill application questions. The test is often a timed test; that is, students are permitted to work for only a specified amount of time. Included in Part Two of *Opening Doors* are tips that can help you earn higher scores on standardized reading tests. The tips below deal with determining topics and stated main ideas.

To begin with, you should be aware that students sometimes miss questions on reading tests because they do not realize what they are being asked. If the wording of an item is even slightly unfamiliar, they may not recognize that they are being asked to apply a reading comprehension skill they already know. Therefore, you should learn to recognize certain types of questions no matter how they are worded, just as you recognize your friends no matter what they are wearing.

You are being asked to identify the topic of a passage when the test question begins:

The best title for this selection is . . .

This passage discusses . . .

This passage focuses mainly on . . .

The topic of this passage is . . .

This passage is about . . .

This passage concerns . . .

The problem the author is discussing in this passage is . . .

The author is explaining the nature of . . .

To find the right answer, simply ask yourself, "Who or what is this passage about?" Then see which answer choice most closely matches your answer. Remember to use the four clues for determining topics: titles or headings, words emphasized in special print, repetition, and a mention of the topic that is then referred to by pronouns or other words.

You are being asked to identify the main idea when the question is worded:

The author's main point is that . . .

The central idea of this passage is that . . .

Which of the following best expresses the main idea of this paragraph?

Which of the following is the main idea of the last paragraph? (or some specified paragraph)

Which of the following best expresses the main idea of the entire passage?

The thesis of the passage is . . .

To find the right answer, ask yourself, "What is the most important point the author wants me to understand about the topic?" Next, search the paragraph or passage for a sentence that answers this question. Finally, read each of the choices and select the one that is the same as the sentence you selected or that *means* essentially the same thing even if the wording is different.

Directions: To determine the stated main idea, read each paragraph carefully and then ask yourself, "What is the most important point the author wants me to understand about the topic of this paragraph? (Notice that you are told the topic of each paragraph.) Then select the answer choice that expresses the main idea and write the letter in the space provided.

1. This paragraph comes from a United States government textbook:

One area in which African Americans have made substantial progress since the 1960s is elective office. Although the percentage of black elected officials is still far below the proportion of African Americans in the population, it has risen sharply over recent decades. There are now roughly 600 black mayors and more than 40 black members of Congress. The most stunning advance, of course, was the election of Barack Obama in 2008 as the first African American president.

Source: Adapted from Thomas E. Patterson, *The American Democracy,* Alternate Edition, 10e, p. 137. Copyright © 2011 by The McGraw-Hill Companies, Inc. Reprinted with permission of The McGraw-Hill Companies, Inc.

The topic of this paragraph is *African Americans in elective office.*

What is the stated main idea of this paragraph?
   a. The most stunning advance, of course, was the election of Barack Obama in 2008 as the first African American president.
   b. There are now roughly 600 black mayors and more than 40 black members of Congress.
   c. One area in which African Americans have made substantial progress since the 1960s is elective office.
   d. African Americans are still underrepresented in elective office.

2. This paragraph comes from a wellness textbook:

People often ask, "What makes a good marriage?" Is there a key trait that characterizes a successful marriage? Researchers have identified several patterns in "high-quality," or well-balanced, marriages. Some of these married people tend to focus their energies on joint activities. Their strongest wish is to spend time together, yet they also strike a balance between privacy and togetherness. Other couples focus their energies on being parents and on raising their children. Some dual-career couples, although they spend much of their energy on their individual careers, develop intimacy by sharing what is going on in their work.

Source: Adapted from Marvin R. Levy, Mark Dignan, and Janet H. Shirreffs, *Targeting Wellness: The Core,* p. 122. Copyright © 1992 by The McGraw-Hill Companies, Inc. Reprinted with permission of The McGraw-Hill Companies, Inc.

The topic of this paragraph is *high-quality marriages,* or *well-balanced marriages,* or *what makes a good marriage.*

_____ What is the stated main idea of this paragraph?

   a. What makes a good marriage?

   b. High-quality marriages happen when a couple's strongest wish is to spend time together.

   c. Some dual-career couples, although they spend much of their energy on their individual careers, develop intimacy by sharing what is going on in their work.

   d. Researchers have identified several patterns in "high-quality," or well-balanced, marriages.

3. This paragraph comes from a health textbook.

> Online dating sites like Match.com and eHarmony have become incredibly popular in recent years. This is especially true among young adults seeking an intimate partner or new friends. Connecting with people online has its advantages and its drawbacks. It allows people to communicate in a relaxed way, to try out different personas, and to share things they might not share with family or friends face-to-face. It's easier to put yourself out there without too much investment. You can get to know someone from the comfort of your own home, set your own pace, and start and end relationships at any time. With millions of singles using dating sites that let them describe exactly what they are seeking, the Internet can increase a person's chance of finding a good match. But there are drawbacks to meeting people online. Too often, participants misrepresent themselves, pretending to be very different—older or younger or even of a different sex—than they really are. Investing time and emotional resources in such relations can be painful. In rare cases, online romances become dangerous or even deadly.

Source: Adapted from Paul M. Insel and Walton T. Roth, *Connect Core Concepts in Health,* 12e, p. 108. Copyright © 2012 by The McGraw-Hill Companies, Inc. Reprinted with permission of The McGraw-Hill Companies, Inc.

The topic of this paragraph is *online dating sites.*

_____ What is the stated main idea of this paragraph?

   a. Online dating sites like Match.com and eHarmony have become incredibly popular in recent years.

   b. In rare cases, online romances become dangerous or even deadly.

   c. Too often, online dating participants misrepresent themselves, pretending to be very different—older or younger or even of a different sex—than they really are.

   d. Connecting with people online has its advantages and its drawbacks.

4. This paragraph comes from a business textbook:

Using a Business Course to Prepare for Your Career

The purpose of a college business course is to help you understand business so that you can use business principles throughout your life. You'll learn about production, marketing, finance, accounting, management, economics, and more. At the end of the course, you should have a much better idea about what careers would be best for you and what careers you would *not* enjoy. But what if you don't end up in business? You don't have to be in business to use business principles. You can use marketing principles to get a job and to sell your ideas to others. You can use your knowledge of financial planning to invest wisely in the stock market. Similarly, you'll be able to use management skills and general business knowledge wherever you go and whatever career you pursue— including government agencies, charities, and social causes.

Source: Adapted from William G. Nickels, James M. McHugh, and Susan M. McHugh, *Understanding Business,* 7e, p. 4. Copyright © 2005 by The McGraw-Hill Companies, Inc. Reprinted with permission of The McGraw-Hill Companies, Inc.

The topic of this paragraph is *using business principles.*

What is the stated main idea of this paragraph?

 a. You will learn about what careers would be best for you and what careers you would *not* enjoy if you take a course in business.

 b. You don't have to be in business to use business principles.

 c. Business courses will teach you about production, marketing, finance, accounting, management and economics.

 d. You can use your knowledge of financial planning to invest wisely in the stock market.

5. This paragraph comes from a student success textbook:

A person of good character has a core set of principles that most of us accept as constant and relatively noncontroversial. These principles include fairness, honesty, respect, responsibility, caring, trustworthiness, and citizenship. Recent surveys of business leaders indicate that dishonesty, lying, and lack of respect are top reasons for on-the-job difficulties. If an employer believes an employee lacks character, all of that person's positive qualities—from skill and experience to productivity and intelligence—are meaningless. Employers usually list honesty or good character as an essential personal quality, followed by the ability to relate to and get along with others. Clearly, good character is an essential personal quality for success in the workplace.

Source: Adapted from Sharon K. Ferrett, *Peak Performance: Success in College and Beyond,* 8e, p. 45. Copyright © 2010 by The McGraw-Hill Companies, Inc. Reprinted with permission of The McGraw-Hill Companies, Inc.

The topic of this paragraph is *having good character.*

What is the stated main idea of this paragraph?

_____
- *a.* A person of good character has a core set of principles that most of us accept as constant and relatively noncontroversial.
- *b.* If an employer believes an employee lacks character, all of that person's positive qualities—from skill and experience to productivity and intelligence—are meaningless.
- *c.* Employers usually list honesty or good character as an essential personal quality, followed by the ability to relate to and get along with others.
- *d.* Clearly, good character is an essential personal quality for success in the workplace.

DEVELOPING CHAPTER REVIEW CARDS

Review cards, or *summary cards,* are an excellent study tool. They are a way to select, organize, and review the most important information in a textbook chapter. Creating review cards helps you organize information in a meaningful way and transfer it into long-term memory as you prepare for tests (see Part Three). The review card activities in this book give you structured practice in creating these valuable study tools. Once you have learned how to make review cards, you can create them for textbook material in your other courses.

Now complete the seven review cards for Chapter 4 by answering the questions or following the directions on each card. When you have completed them, you will have summarized (1) what the topic of a paragraph is and (2) how to determine it; (3) what a stated main idea sentence is and (4) how to locate it; (5) where the stated main idea sentence of a paragraph may appear; (6) how to tell if you have identified a stated main idea sentence correctly; and (7) how to avoid two errors in identifying stated main idea sentences. Print or write legibly.

The Topic of a Paragraph

1. What is the topic of a paragraph? (See page 207.)

2. Why is determining the topic important? (See page 207.)

3. To determine the topic, what question should you ask yourself? (See page 207.)

Card 1   Chapter 4: Determining the Topic and the Stated Main Idea

---

Determining the Topic of a Paragraph

What are four clues that can help you determine the topic? (See page 207.)

1.

2.

3.

4.

Card 2   Chapter 4: Determining the Topic and the Stated Main Idea

The Stated Main Idea of a Paragraph

1.   What is a stated main idea sentence? (See page 212.)

2.   What are four reasons it is important to determine a stated main idea? (See page 212.)

Reason 1:

Reason 2:

Reason 3:

Reason 4:

Card 3   Chapter 4: Determining the Topic and the Stated Main Idea

Locating a Stated Main Idea Sentence

What are two steps to follow in locating a stated main idea sentence? (See pages 213–214.)

Step 1:

Step 2:

What is a formula for the essential parts of a stated main idea sentence? (See page 213.)

Formula:

Card 4   Chapter 4: Determining the Topic and the Stated Main Idea

Where a Stated Main Idea Sentence May Appear in a Paragraph

Where in a paragraph may the stated main idea sentence appear? List the three places. (See pages 213–214.)

1.

2.

3.

Card 5   Chapter 4: Determining the Topic and the Stated Main Idea

It must have the author's most important point about the topic

REVIEW CARDS

CHAPTER 4 Determining the Topic and the Stated Main Idea

Checking Your Identification of a Stated Main Idea Sentence

List five characteristics that will help you correctly identify a stated main idea sentence. (See page 215.)

1.

2.

3.

4.

5.

Card 6 Chapter 4: Determining the Topic and the Stated Main Idea

Avoiding Errors in Determining a Stated Main Idea Sentence

What are two common errors in determining a stated main idea sentence? Describe how each can be avoided. (See page 216.)

Error 1:

How to avoid it:

Error 2:

How to avoid it:

Card 7 Chapter 4: Determining the Topic and the Stated Main Idea

Directions: Read these paragraphs carefully and answer the questions that follow them. Write your answers in the spaces provided.

This paragraph comes from a human development textbook:

In most societies, marriage is considered the best way to ensure the orderly raising of children. It allows for a division of labor within a consuming and working unit as well. Ideally, it also offers intimacy, friendship, affection, sexual fulfillment, companionship, and an opportunity for emotional growth. In certain Eastern philosophical traditions, the harmonious union of a male and a female is considered essential to spiritual fulfillment and the survival of the species. Clearly, society views marriage as providing many benefits.

Source: Adapted from Diane E. Papalia, Sally Wendkos Olds, and Ruth Duskin Feldman, *Human Development,* 8e, p. 539. Copyright © 2001 by The McGraw-Hill Companies, Inc. Reprinted with permission of The McGraw-Hill Companies, Inc.

The main idea must have the topic of that paragraph

1. What is the topic of this paragraph?
   a. raising children
   b. challenges of marriage
   c. benefits of marriage
   d. traditions in Eastern societies

2. What is the stated main idea of this paragraph?
   a. In most societies, marriage is considered the best way to ensure orderly raising of children.
   b. Ideally, it also offers intimacy, friendship, affection, sexual fulfillment, companionship, and an opportunity for emotional growth.
   c. In certain Eastern philosophical traditions, the harmonious union of a male and a female is considered essential to spiritual fulfillment and the survival of the species.
   d. Clearly, society views marriage as providing many benefits.

This paragraph comes from a United States history textbook:

Asian American immigrants experienced two forms of downward mobility. First, highly educated Asian immigrants often found it difficult or impossible to land jobs in their professions. To American observers, Korean shopkeepers seemed examples of success, when in fact such owners often enough had been former professionals forced into the risky small-business world. Second, schools reported significant numbers of Asian American students who were failing. This "lost generation" were most often the children of families who entered the United States with little education and few job skills.

Source: Abridged from James Davidson et al., *Nation of Nations: A Narrative History of the American Republic, Volume II: Since 1865,* 6e, p. 960. Copyright © 2008 by The McGraw-Hill Companies, Inc. Reprinted with permission of The McGraw-Hill Companies, Inc.

3. What is the topic of this paragraph?
- *a.* American immigrants
- *b.* highly educated Asian immigrants
- *c.* the downward mobility of Asian Americans
- *d.* the "lost generation"

4. What is the stated main idea of this paragraph?
- *a.* Asian American immigrants experienced two forms of downward mobility.
- *b.* Highly educated Asian immigrants often found it difficult or impossible to land jobs in their professions.
- *c.* Schools reported significant numbers of Asian American students who were failing.
- *d.* This "lost generation" were most often the children of families who entered the United States with little education and few job skills.

This paragraph comes from a music appreciation textbook:

> During the 1980s and 1990s, women performers had a powerful impact on rock music. "Many new women rockers do a lot more than sing," observed one critic. "They play their own instruments, write their own songs, and they control their own careers." Their wide range of musical styles extended from pop and soul to funk, new wave, country rock, and heavy metal. Leading performers included Pat Benatar, Tina Turner, Madonna, Alanis Morissette, Sheryl Crow, Queen Latifah, Shania Twain, and Ani DiFranco.
>
> *Source:* Roger Kamien, *Music: An Appreciation,* 10e, p. 517. Copyright © 2011 by The McGraw-Hill Companies, Inc. Reprinted with permission of The McGraw-Hill Companies, Inc.

5. What is the topic of this paragraph?
- *a.* rock music
- *b.* music of the 1980s and 1990s
- *c.* women rock performers
- *d.* leading musical performers

6. What is the stated main idea of this paragraph?
- *a.* Leading performers included Pat Benatar, Tina Turner, Madonna, Alanis Morissette, Sheryl Crow, Queen Latifah, Shania Twain, and Ani DiFranco.
- *b.* Their wide range of musical styles extended from pop and soul to funk, new wave, country rock, and heavy metal.
- *c.* During the 1980s and 1990s, women performers had a powerful impact on rock music.
- *d.* Many new women rockers do a lot more than sing. They play their own instruments, write their own songs, and they control their own careers.

This paragraph comes from an information technology textbook:

> No matter how much students may be able to rationalize cheating in college, ignorance of the consequences is not an excuse. When a student tries to pass off someone else's term paper as their own, they are committing a form of cheating known as plagiarism. Most instructors announce the penalties for this type of cheating at the beginning of the course. They warn students that the penalty for cheating of this sort is usually a failing grade in the course and possible suspension or expulsion from school.
>
> *Source:* Adapted from Brian K. Williams and Stacey C. Sawyer, *Using Information Technology: A Practical Introduction to Computers and Communications,* 7e, p. 104. Copyright © 2007 by The McGraw-Hill Companies, Inc. Reprinted with permission of The McGraw-Hill Companies, Inc.

7. What is the topic of this paragraph?
   a. students who rationalize cheating in college
   b. a form of cheating known as plagiarism
   c. penalties for cheating in college
   d. passing off someone else's term paper as your own

8. What is the stated main idea of this paragraph?
   a. No matter how much students may be able to rationalize cheating in college, ignorance of the consequences is not an excuse.
   b. They warn students that the penalty for cheating of this sort is usually a failing grade in the course and possible suspension or expulsion from school.
   c. Most instructors announce the penalties for this type of cheating at the beginning of the course.
   d. When a student tries to pass off someone else's term paper as their own, they are committing a form of cheating known as plagiarism.

This paragraph comes from a mass communications textbook:

> Advertising is everywhere and, in general, it interferes with and alters our experience. For example, giant wall advertisements change the look of cities. Ads beamed by laser light onto night skies destroy evening stargazing. School learning aids provided by candy makers that ask students to "count the Tootsie Rolls" alter education. Many Internet users complain about the commercialization of the new medium and fear advertising will alter its open, freewheeling nature.
>
> *Source:* Adapted from Stanley Baran, *Mass Communication,* 3e, p. 390. Copyright © 2004 by The McGraw-Hill Companies, Inc. Reprinted with permission of The McGraw-Hill Companies, Inc.

9. What is the topic of this paragraph?
   a. advertising
   b. our everyday experiences
   c. Internet advertising
   d. benefits of advertising

10. What is the stated main idea of this paragraph?
   a. Many Internet users complain about the commercialization of the new medium and fear advertising will alter its open, freewheeling nature.
   b. Advertising is everywhere and, in general, it interferes with and alters our experience.
   c. Ads beamed by laser light onto night skies destroy evening stargazing.
   d. Giant wall advertisements change the look of cities.

Directions: Read these paragraphs carefully, and then write the topic and the main idea sentence for each paragraph in the spaces provided.

This paragraph comes from a psychology textbook:

Driven to Distraction?

If you've ever texted while driving, you're not alone. A recent survey conducted by the American Automobile Association Foundation for Traffic Safety found that nearly half of drivers aged 18 to 24 admit to texting while driving. The survey also found that the majority of these young drivers reported that they were aware that they were increasing their risk of having an accident. In fact, nearly 90% of these young drivers rated texting while driving as a "very serious threat" to safety. Researchers have conducted studies on distracted driving and are now able to confirm what intuition suggests is true. Clearly, the distraction caused by texting while driving is extremely dangerous.

Source: Adapted from Robert S. Feldman, *Essentials of Understanding Psychology,* 9e, p. 91. Copyright © 2011 by The McGraw-Hill Companies, Inc. Reprinted by permission of The McGraw-Hill Companies.

1. Write a word, name, or phrase that tells the topic:

_____

2. Locate the stated main idea sentence and write it here:

_____

_____

_____

This paragraph comes from an information technology textbook:

Electronic commerce, also known as **e-commerce**, is the buying and selling of goods on the Internet. Have you ever bought anything on the Internet? If you have not, there is a very good chance that you will within the next year or two. Shopping on the Internet is growing, and there seems to be no end in sight. Electronic commerce is growing rapidly because it provides incentives for both buyers and sellers. From the buyer's perspective, goods and services can be purchased at any time of day or night. Traditional commerce is typically limited to standard business hours when the seller is open. Additionally, buyers no longer have to physically travel to the seller's location. For example, busy parents with small children do not need to coordinate their separate schedules or to arrange for a babysitter whenever they want to visit the mall. From the seller's perspective, the costs associated with owning and operating a retail outlet can be eliminated. For example, a music store can operate entirely on the Web without an actual physical store and without a large sales staff. Another advantage is reduced inventory. Traditional stores maintain an inventory of goods in their stores and periodically replenish their inventory from warehouses. With e-commerce, there is no in-store inventory and products are shipped directly from warehouses.

Source: Adapted from Timothy J. O'Leary and Linda I. O'Leary, *Computing Essentials 2012: Making IT Work for You*, p. 45. Copyright © 2012 by The McGraw-Hill Companies, Inc. Reprinted with permission of The McGraw-Hill Companies, Inc.

3. Write a word, name, or phrase that tells the topic:

_____

4. Locate the stated main idea sentence and write it here:

_____

_____

_____

_____

This paragraph comes from an American government textbook:

Party Affiliation and Religious Denomination

In the United States there are significant differences in political party affiliation by religious denomination. Mormons and evangelical Protestant congregations, including Southern Baptists and Pentecostals, heavily favor the Republican Party. Mainline Protestants such as Episcopalians and Presbyterians are fairly evenly divided by party. High turnout among conservative evangelicals proved to be a powerful force for Republicans in recent elections. White evangelical Christians supported John McCain over Barack Obama in 2008 by three to one. Latino Protestants are overwhelmingly in the Democratic camp. Although Catholics have drifted away from the Democratic Party, a plurality still call themselves Democrats. While a majority of Catholics overall supported Obama over McCain, the reverse held true for white Catholics. Support for the Democratic Party is far stronger among both black and Latino Catholics. Smaller Christian congregations skew Republican, while Jews and members of minority religions continue a long tradition of support for Democrats. Among the growing number of those expressing no particular religious affiliation, Democrats outnumber Republicans.

Source: Adapted from Joseph Losco and Ralph Baker, *Am Gov, 2011,* p. 131. Copyright © 2011 by The McGraw-Hill Companies, Inc. Reprinted with permission of The McGraw-Hill Companies, Inc.

5. Write a word, name, or phrase that tells the topic:

_____

6. Locate the stated main idea sentence and write it here:

_____

_____

_____

_____

This paragraph comes from a student success textbook:

What Do You Want to Be Called?

How would you "label" yourself? White, Black, Hispanic, Asian, Native American, Pacific Islander. At some point in your life, you've probably had to check off your race or ethnicity on a form. But what if none of these categories truly reflects your personal identity or accommodates those of us (the majority) who have come from multiple backgrounds? Some people of Central and South American origin prefer to be called Hispanic; others prefer Latino. Many prefer to use their specific place or origin—Guatemalan, Mexican, Puerto Rican, Cuban, and so on. In the same way, some descendents of the first residents of the United States prefer American Indian, others prefer First Peoples, and others prefer Native American. Many prefer specific tribal names, such as Sioux, Navajo, Apache, or Wampanoag. Many people are from families of mixed racial or ethnic origins and do not want to be called by the name of any one group. "Blasian" is now used by many of Black and Asian descent. With regard to ethnicity, most people agree that all people have a right to be called what they want to be called and not have a group name imposed on them by someone else.

Source: Adapted from Sharon K. Ferrett, *Peak Performance: Success in College and Beyond,* 8e, p. 401. Copyright © 2010 by The McGraw-Hill Companies, Inc. Reprinted with permission of The McGraw-Hill Companies, Inc.

7. Write a word, name, or phrase that tells the topic:

_____

_____

_____

8. Locate the stated main idea sentence and write it here:

_____

_____

_____

_____

_____

This paragraph comes from an American government textbook:

Americans between the ages of eighteen and twenty-nine are much less attentive to traditional news sources than are members of any other generation. Only 22 percent watch television news daily, and just 16 percent read a newspaper every day. Fully a third of young people say that they do not pay attention to the news in any form. By contrast, nearly three-fifths of those sixty-five and above report reading a newspaper daily, and only 12 percent confess inattention to the news. To the extent that they get news from television, young people appear more interested in local news than in national stories available on network news programs or cable TV.

Source: Adapted from Joseph Losco and Ralph Baker, *Am Gov, 2011,* pp. 236–37. Copyright © 2011 by The McGraw-Hill Companies, Inc. Reprinted with permission of The McGraw-Hill Companies, Inc.

9. Write a word, name, or phrase that tells the topic:

_____

_____

10. Locate the stated main idea sentence and write it here:

_____

_____

_____

_____

_____

**Information
Technology**

SELECTION 4.1

A Warning to Students: Plagiarism, Term Papers and Web Research

From *Using Information Technology: A Practical Introduction to Computers and Communications*
by Brian K. Williams and Stacey C. Sawyer

Prepare Yourself to Read

Directions: Do these exercises *before* you read Selection 4.1.

1. First, read and think about the title. What do you already know about plagiarism?

_____

_____

_____

_____

2. Next, complete your preview by reading the following:

> Introduction (in *italics*)
> Headings
> Words in bold print
> Box in margin about "Types of Plagiarism"

Now that you have completed your preview, what does this selection seem to be about?

_____

_____

_____

3. **Build your vocabulary as you read.** If you discover an unfamiliar word or key term as you read the selection, try to determine its meaning by using context clues.

Read More about This Topic Online

Internet Resources

Use a search engine, such as Google or Yahoo!, to expand your existing knowledge about this topic *before* you read the selection or to learn more about it *afterward*. Use search terms such as "student plagiarism" or "cheating in college." If you are unfamiliar with conducting Internet searches, read pages 25–26 on Boolean searches. You can also use Wikipedia, the free online encyclopedia, at www.wikipedia.com. Keep in mind that when you visit any website, it is a good idea to evaluate the site and the information it contains. Ask yourself questions such as "Who sponsors this website?" and "Is the information it contains up to date?"

SELECTION 4.1: A WARNING TO STUDENTS: PLAGIARISM, TERM PAPERS AND WEB RESEARCH

In The Art of Public Speaking, *speech communications Professor Stephen Lucas writes:*

The term "plagiarism" comes from the Latin word plagiarus, *or kidnapper. To plagiarize means to present another person's language or ideas as your own. When you plagiarize, you give the impression that you have written or thought of something yourself when you have actually taken it from someone else. And, when it comes to plagiarism, no subject poses more confusion—or more temptation—than the Internet. Because it's so easy to copy information from the Web, many people are not aware of the need to cite sources (that is, to give credit to the author) when they use Internet materials in their research papers and speeches. To avoid plagiarism, you need to give credit to the authors of documents found on the Internet, just as you need to give credit to the authors of print books and articles. (41, 46)*

When you do research in the library or use the Web to prepare essays, term papers, or class presentations, it is your responsibility to avoid plagiarism. Plagiarism is a form of cheating just as inappropriate as cheating on a test. This selection from an information technology textbook presents a warning to students about plagiarism and explains how inappropriate use of materials found on the Web can lead to plagiarism and low-quality papers and presentations.

1   No matter how much students may be able to rationalize cheating in college, ignorance of the consequences is not an excuse. When students try to pass off someone else's term paper as their own, they are committing a form of cheating called **plagiarism,** and most instructors announce the penalties for this type of cheating at the beginning of the course. They warn students that the penalty for cheating of this sort is usually a failing grade in the course and possible suspension or expulsion from school.

2   Even so, probably every student becomes aware before long that the World Wide Web contains sites that offer term papers, either for free or for a price. Despite these warnings from their professors, some dishonest students may download papers and just change the author's name to their own. Others are more likely just to use the papers for ideas. Perhaps, as Ellen Laird suggests in an article on Internet plagiarism, "the fear of getting caught makes the online papers more a diversion than an invitation to widescale plagiarism."

How the Web Can Lead to Plagiarism

3   Numerous web sites offer term papers to students. There are two types of term paper web sites:

4   **Sites offering papers for free:** Such a site requires that users fill out a membership form and then provides at least one free student term paper. Good quality is not guaranteed, since free-paper mills often subsist on the submissions of poor students, whose contributions may be subliterate.

Annotation Practice Exercises

Directions: For each exercise below:

- Write the topic of the paragraph on the lines beside the paragraph.
- Underline or highlight the stated main idea of the paragraph.

Doing this will help you remember the topic and the stated main idea.

Practice Exercise

- Topic of paragraph 1:

  _____

  _____

- Underline or highlight the stated main idea of paragraph 1.

5   **Sites offering papers for sale:** Commercial Internet sites may charge $6 to $10 a page, which students may charge to their credit card. Expense is no guarantee of quality. Moreover, the term paper factory may turn around and make your $350 customized paper available to others—even fellow classmates working on the same assignment—for half the price.

How Instructors Catch Cheaters

6   How do instructors detect and defend against student plagiarism? There are several reasons professors are unlikely to be fooled by students who plagiarize the work of others. Often, professors tailor term paper assignments to work done in class. They also monitor students' progress through steps of an assignment, from preliminary outline to completion. And, professors are alert to papers that seem radically different from a student's past work.

7   Eugene Dwyer, a professor of art history at Kenyon College, requires that papers in his classes be submitted electronically, along with a list of World Wide Web site references. "This way I can click along as I read the paper. This format is more efficient than running around the college library, checking each footnote."

8   Just as the Internet is the source of cheating, it is also a tool for detecting cheaters. Search programs make it possible for instructors to locate texts containing identified strings of words from the millions of pages found on the World Wide Web. Thus, a professor can input passages from a student's paper into a search program that scans the Web for identical blocks of text. Indeed, some web sites favored by instructors build a database of papers over time so that students can't recycle work previously handed in by others. One system can lock on to a stolen phrase as short as eight words. It can also identify copied material even if it has been changed slightly from the original. More than 1,000 educational institutions have turned to Oakland, California-based Turnitin.com (*www.turnitin.com*), an online service that searches documents for unoriginality. Another program professors use is the Self-Plagiarism Detection Tool, or SplaT (*http://splat. cs.arizona.edu*).

How the Web Can Lead to Low-Quality Papers

9   William Rukeyser, coordinator for Learning in the Real World, a nonprofit information clearinghouse, points out another problem: The Web enables students "to cut and paste together reports or presentations that appear to have taken hours or days to write but have really been assembled in minutes with no actual mastery or understanding by the student."

Types of Plagiarism

Plagiarism, the act of presenting another person's language or ideas as one's own, can occur in several forms:

Global plagiarism: Stealing an essay, term paper, or speech from a single source and passing it off as your own.

Patchwork plagiarism: Stealing ideas or language from two or three sources and passing them off as your own.

Incremental plagiarism: Failing to give credit for particular parts of an essay, term paper, or speech that are borrowed from other people.

Source: Adapted from Stephen E. Lucas, *The Art of Public Speaking,* 9e, pp. 43–44. Copyright © 2007 by The McGraw-Hill Companies, Inc. Reprinted with permission of The McGraw-Hill Companies, Inc.

Practice Exercise

•   Topic of paragraph 6:

_____

_____

•   Underline or highlight the stated main idea of paragraph 6.

Practice Exercise

•   Topic of paragraph 8:

_____

_____

•   Underline or highlight the stated main idea of paragraph 8.

Online service Turnitin.com offers educators and students *Originality Checking* to ensure originality as well as use of proper citation. Turnitin.com's *Peer Review* feature organizes students to review each other's work and deliver clear, timely comments.

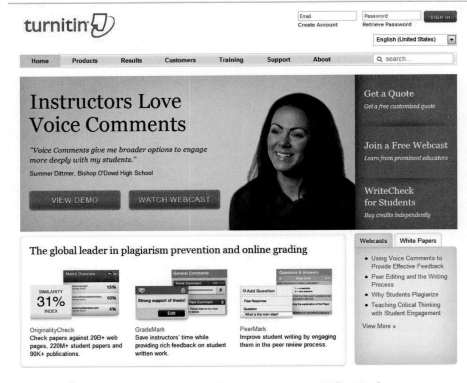

10 Philosophy professor David Rothenberg, of New Jersey Institute of Technology, reports that as a result of students doing more of their research on the Web, he has seen "a disturbing decline in both the quality of the writing and the originality of the thoughts expressed."

11 How does a professor spot an essay or a term paper that has relied too much on Web research? There are four clues that suggest that an essay or term paper has been based primarily on Web research. ***No books cited:*** The student's bibliography cites no books, just articles or references to web sites. Sadly, says Rothenberg, "One finds few references to careful, in-depth commentaries on the subject of the paper, the kind of analysis that requires a book, rather than an article, for its full development." ***Outdated material:*** "A lot of the material in the bibliography is strangely out of date," says Rothenberg. "A lot of stuff on the Web that is advertised as timely is actually at least a few years old." ***Unrelated pictures and graphs:*** Students may intersperse the text with a lot of impressive-looking pictures and graphs that actually bear little relation to the precise subject of the paper. Professor Rothenberg notes, "Cut and pasted from the vast realm of what's out there on the Web for the taking, they masquerade as original work." ***Superficial references:*** "Too much of what passes for information online these days is simply advertising for related information," points out Rothenberg. "Screen after screen shows you where you can find out more, how you can connect to this place or that." Other kinds of online information are detailed but often superficial. Professor Rothenburg writes, "Some sites include pages and pages of federal documents, corporate propaganda, and snippets of commentary written by people whose credibility is difficult to assess."

Sources: Adapted from Brian K. Williams and Stacey C. Sawyer, *Using Information Technology: A Practical Introduction to Computers and Communications,* 7e, p. 104. Copyright © 2007 by The McGraw-Hill Companies, Inc. Reprinted with permission of The McGraw-Hill Companies, Inc. Introduction adapted from Stephen E. Lucas, *The Art of Public Speaking,* 9e, pp. 41, 46. Copyright © 2007 by The McGraw-Hill Companies, Inc. Reprinted with permission of The McGraw-Hill Companies, Inc.

Ellen Laird, "Internet Plagiarism: We All Pay the Price," *The Chronicle of Higher Education,* June 13, 2001, p. B5. Eugene Dwyer, "Virtual Term Papers" [letter], *NewYork Times,* June 8, 1997, p. A20.

William L. Rukeyser, "How to Track Down Cyber-Cheaters" [letter], *New York Times,* June 14, 1997, sec. 6, p. 14.

David Rothenberg, "How the Web Destroys the Quality of Students' Research Papers," *The Chronicle of Higher Education,* August 15, 1997.

SELECTION **4.1**

**Information
Technology**
(continued)

Reading Selection Quiz

This quiz has several parts. Your instructor may assign some or all of them.

Comprehension

Directions: Items 1–10 test your understanding of the selection. They are the type of questions a content area instructor (such as an information technology professor) might ask on a test. You may refer to the selection as you answer the questions. Write your answer choice in the space provided.

True or False

_____ 1. Stealing an essay, term paper, or speech from a single source and passing it off as your own is called *incremental plagiarism.*

_____ 2. Professors can input passages from a student's paper into a search program that scans the Web for identical blocks of text.

_____ 3. Instructors can detect plagiarism when a student turns in an assignment that is radically different from past work.

_____ 4. Many instructors require students to submit their papers electronically along with a list of Web references so that they can easily check for patchwork or incremental plagiarism.

Multiple-Choice

_____ 5. Which of the following correctly describes plagiarism?
   a. stealing an essay, term paper, or speech from a single source and passing it off as your own
   b. giving the impression that you have written or thought of something yourself when you have actually taken it from someone else
   c. presenting another person's ideas or language as your own
   d. all of the above

_____ 6. Patchwork plagiarism is:
   a. failing to give credit for particular parts of an essay, term paper, or speech that are borrowed from other people.
   b. stealing an essay, term paper, or speech from a single source.
   c. stealing ideas or language from two or three sources and passing them off as your own.
   d. downloading impressive-looking pictures and graphs, and inserting them into an assignment.

_____ **7.** The phrase *to cite a source* means:
  a. to use a website to collect materials that will be used in an assignment.
  b. to locate information using the Internet.
  c. to give credit to the author.
  d. to research a topic using the Web.

_____ **8.** The online service Turnitin.com can be used by instructors to:
  a. search for websites that sell term papers to students.
  b. search a student's essay or term paper for unoriginality.
  c. locate all the works cited in a student's essay or term paper.
  d. assign a grade.

_____ **9.** A clue that can alert a professor that a student has relied too much on Web research is:
  a. superficial information.
  b. unrelated pictures and graphs.
  c. no books cited.
  d. all of the above

_____ **10.** A common problem with a great deal of the information found on the Web is that it:
  a. has been plagiarized.
  b. is outdated.
  c. is too complex to be used by students.
  d. is not original.

Selection **4.1**

Information Technology
(continued)

Vocabulary in Context

Directions: Items 11–20 test your ability to determine a word's meaning by using context clues. *Context clues* are words in a sentence that allow readers to deduce (reason out) the meaning of an unfamiliar word in that sentence. They also help readers to determine the meaning an author intends when a word has more than one meaning. Each item below consists of a sentence from the selection, with the vocabulary word *italicized*. It is followed by another sentence that uses the same word in the same way. Use context clues to deduce the meaning of the *italicized* word. Be sure the meaning you choose makes sense in *both* sentences. Write each answer in the space provided. *Note:* Chapter 2 presents the skill of using context clues.

_____ **11.** No matter how much students may be able to *rationalize* cheating in college, ignorance of the consequences is not an excuse.

Many people *rationalize* talking on their cell phones when driving by insisting that it does not distract them.

rationalize (răsh′ ə nəl īz) means:

a. get away with cheating in college

b. be unfamiliar with the penalties for incorrect behavior

c. invent self-satisfying but incorrect reasons for one's behavior

d. make excuses for violating established rules or procedures

12. And, professors are alert to papers that seem *radically* different from a student's past work.

Lynn's philosophy about how to educate her children differed *radically* from that of her parents.

radically (răd′ ĭk lē) means:

a. significantly improved

b. extremely unlike the usual or customary

c. wonderfully unique and interesting

d. not likely to be original or authentic

13. Often, professors *tailor* term paper assignments to work done in class.

When giving a speech in class, students should *tailor* their remarks to their audience of fellow students.

tailor (tā′ lər) means:

a. fit to a person's particular measurements or size

b. assign according to a person's special requirements

c. speak to particular audience

d. make, alter, or adapt for a particular purpose

14. The student's bibliography *cites* no books, just articles or references to websites.

In his essay on traveling abroad, James *cites* three articles he found that contained useful information about obtaining passports, visas, and discounted tickets.

cites (sītz) means:

a. refers to or quotes; gives credit to an author or speaker

b. accesses a website

c. obtains or discovers

d. does research on a subject for an essay, term paper, or speech

15. Other kinds of online information are detailed but often *superficial*.

After looking over her résumé, Norma's friend Nicole suggested a few *superficial* recommendations that did not really help her improve the document.

superficial (soo pər fĭsh′ əl) means:
a. difficult to understand; confusing
b. insignificant; trivial
c. optional; not required
d. important; substantial

_____ **16.** Some sites include pages and pages of federal documents, corporate propaganda, and snippets of commentary written by people whose *credibility* is difficult to assess.

We were comfortable with our baby-sitter's *credibility* because of the outstanding recommendations we received from her previous employers.

credibility (krēd′ ə bĭl′ ĭt ē) means:
a. interest in a subject
b. previous job experience
c. training; education
d. believability; trustworthiness

_____ **17.** Students may intersperse the text with a lot of impressive-looking pictures and graphs that actually bear little *relation* to the precise subject of the paper.

Scientific evidence shows a clear *relation* between smoking and lung disease.

relation (rĭ lā′ shən) means:
a. a precise method for connecting things together
b. the connection of people by blood or marriage
c. a way in which one person is connected to another
d. a logical or natural connection between two or more things

_____ **18.** Students may *intersperse* the text with a lot of impressive-looking pictures and graphs that actually bear little relation to the precise subject of the paper.

Most programs on television are difficult to enjoy because the networks *intersperse* them with too many commercials!

intersperse (ĭn′ tər spûrs′) means:
a. make something too lengthy
b. add things at intervals
c. spoil
d. add something to the end

_____ **19.** When students try to *pass off* someone else's term paper as their own, they are committing a form of cheating called plagiarism.

Our neighbor was arrested for trying to *pass off* counterfeit twenty-dollar bills at the shopping mall.

pass off (păs ôf′) means:

a. submit or present something fraudulently

b. steal money

c. hand in for a grade

d. commit plagiarism

_____ **20.** Some sites include pages and pages of federal documents, corporate propaganda, and snippets of commentary written by people whose credibility is difficult to *assess.*

Jake's résumé was so incomplete that it was impossible to *assess* his previous work experience.

assess (ə sĕs′) means:

a. determine the price of

b. evaluate

c. understand the meaning of

d. determine the size of

Selection **4.1**

Information Technology

(continued)

Reading Skills Application

Directions: Items 21–25 test your ability to *apply* certain reading skills. You may not be familiar with all the skills yet, so some items will serve as a preview. As you work through *Opening Doors,* you will practice and develop these skills. These are important skills, which is why they are included on the state-mandated basic skills tests that some students must take. Write each answer in the space provided.

_____ **21.** The information in paragraph 1 is organized using which of the following writing patterns?

a. sequence

b. comparison

c. definition

d. list

_____ **22.** As an example of how instructors help students avoid plagiarism, the authors mention:

a. not accepting papers that have been submitted electronically.

b. requiring students to complete their essays and other assignments in class.

c. monitoring students' progress through steps of an assignment, from preliminary outline to completion.

d. not allowing students to submit essays or term papers that have been based primarily on Web research.

_____ **23.** As used in paragraph 8 of this selection, *detecting* means:

    a. punishing

    b. reducing

    c. identifying

    d. researching

_____ **24.** Based on the information in the selection, it can be logically concluded that:

    a. the use of materials found on the Web is inappropriate for use in essays, term papers, and speeches.

    b. due to the growth of the Web, there is nothing that can be done about the problem of plagiarism among college students.

    c. instructors are likely to detect student plagiarism for a variety of reasons.

    d. it is usually impossible for instructors to prove that a student has submitted a term paper that has been purchased from a website.

_____ **25.** The authors' primary purpose for writing this selection is to:

    a. explain why students use the resources available on the Web without giving credit to authors.

    b. persuade students to avoid downloading Internet materials when doing research for essays, term papers, and speeches.

    c. inform students that the penalties for cheating can include failing course grades and possible suspension or expulsion from school.

    d. convince students that they must avoid all types of plagiarism.

SELECTION **4.1**

Information Technology

(continued)

Respond in Writing

Directions: Refer to the selection as needed to answer the essay-type questions below. (Your instructor may direct you to work collaboratively with other students on one or more items. Each group member should be able to explain *all* of the group's answers.)

1. In paragraphs 1–5 of this selection, the authors mention several things that students should do (and not do) in order to avoid plagiarism. List at least five of them below.

_____

_____

_____

_____

_____

_____

_____

_____

_____

_____

_____

2. In paragraph 11 of this selection, the authors explain how instructors can spot
    an essay or term paper that has relied too much on Web research, a problem
    that leads to low-quality papers. List and describe the four clues that would
    indicate to an instructor that a student's essay or term paper has been based
    primarily on Web research.

_____

_____

_____

_____

_____

_____

_____

_____

_____

_____

3. **Overall main idea.** What is the overall main idea the author wants the reader
    to understand about the plagiarism? Answer this question in one sentence. Be
    sure to include the word _plagiarism_ and the phrase _when doing research on
    the Web_ in your overall main idea sentence.

_____

_____

_____

_____

_____

_____

SELECTION **4.2**

Student Success

Classes without Walls: Distance Learning

From *P.O.W.E.R. Learning and Your Life: Essentials of Student Success*
by Robert S. Feldman

Prepare Yourself to Read

Directions: Do these exercises *before* you read Selection 4.2.

1. First, read and think about the title. What do you already know about *distance learning*?

_____

_____

_____

_____

2. Next, complete your preview by reading the following:

Introduction (in *italics*)

Headings

Words in bold print

Box with **TRY IT!** exercise

Now that you have completed your preview, what does this selection seem to be about?

_____

_____

_____

_____

3. **Build your vocabulary as you read.** If you discover an unfamiliar word or key term as you read the selection, try to determine its meaning by using context clues.

Internet Resources

Read More about This Topic Online

Use a search engine, such as Google or Yahoo!, to expand your existing knowledge about this topic *before* you read the selection or to learn more about it *afterward*. Use search terms such as "distance learning" or "online courses." If you are unfamiliar with conducting Internet searches, read pages 25–26 on Boolean searches. You can also use Wikipedia, the free online encyclopedia, at www.wikipedia.com. Keep in mind that when you visit any website, it is a good idea to evaluate the site and the information it contains. Ask yourself questions such as "Who sponsors this website?" and "Is the information it contains up to date?"

SELECTION 4.2: CLASSES WITHOUT WALLS: DISTANCE LEARNING

Distance learning is becoming increasingly popular. In this selection from a student success textbook, the author discusses this flexible option for completing college courses.

Although many new college students do not take a distance-learning course their first semester, it is very likely that they will take one or more (perhaps many!) distance-learning courses as they progress through college. According to the National Center for Education Statistics, in 2007–08, about 4.3 million undergraduate students, or 20 percent of all undergraduates, took at least one distance-learning course. Moreover, about 0.8 million, or 4 percent of all undergraduates, took their entire program through distance education (http://nces.ed.gov.fastfacts/display.asp?id=80; accessed 4/12/12). Because of the convenience and flexibility of distance-learning courses, it seems likely that their popularity will continue to grow.

1   Do you find that your schedule changes so much from one day to the next that it's hard to fit in a course that meets at a regularly scheduled time? Interested in an unusual course topic that your own college doesn't offer? Want to take a class during the summer, but your college doesn't have a summer program?

2   The solution to your problem may be to enroll in a distance-learning course. **Distance learning** is a form of education in which students participate via the Web or other kinds of technology. Although most distance-learning courses are taught via the Web, some use teleconferencing, fax, and/or express mail.

3   The key feature of distance-learning courses is the nature of interaction between instructor and students. Rather than meeting in a traditional classroom, where the instructors, you, and the other students are physically present, distance-learning classes are most often virtual. Although some schools use "Webcasts" of lectures with virtual discussion rooms or employ lectures on videotape or CDs, most students in distance-learning courses will never sit through a lecture or even participate in a real-time conversation with students in the class. They may never even know what their instructor or classmates look like or hear their voices.

4   If you take a distance-learning course, you may read lecture notes posted on the Web, search and browse Web sites, write papers, post replies to discussion topics on *a message board,* and take online quizzes and exams. You will see your instructor's and classmates' responses through comments they post on the Web. You may be expected to read a textbook entirely on your own.

5   You may already be familiar with the kinds of technologies used in distance-learning courses, because many traditional, face-to-face courses already contain elements of distance-learning courses. In **blended (or hybrid) courses,** instruction is a combination of the traditional face-to-face classroom interaction and a significant amount of online learning. Students in blended courses generally spend more time working alone or in collaboration with other students online.

Annotation Practice Exercises

Directions: For each exercise below:

- Write the topic of the paragraph on the lines beside the paragraph.
- Underline or highlight the stated main idea of the paragraph.

Doing this will help you remember the topic and the stated main idea.

Online courses are becoming increasingly popular, and more and more colleges are offering them.

6   In contrast to blended courses, all instruction takes place online in distance-learning classes. However, this kind of learning is not for everyone. Whether or not you are a good candidate for distance learning depends on your personal style of course-taking.

Complete the Try It! exercise on page 250 to see whether you are suited to learn at a distance.

7   Distance-learning classes have numerous advantages. One plus is that you can take a Web-based distance-learning course anywhere that you have access to the Web. You can be at home, at the office, or on vacation on the beach and still participate. Another plus is that distance-learning classes are more flexible than traditional classes. You can participate in a course any time of the day or night. You set your own schedule. This is particularly helpful for those with time-consuming family obligations. Distance-learning classes are self-paced, unlike most face-to-face classes. You may be able to spread out your work over the course of a week, or you may do the work in a concentrated manner on one day. With distance-learning classes you may have more contact with your instructor than you do with a traditional class. Even though you may not have face-to-face contact, you may have greater access to your instructor, via e-mail and the Web, than in traditional classes. You can leave a message for your instructor any time of the night or day. Most instructors of distance-learning classes respond in a timely way. Often, students find it easier to "speak up" in a distance-learning class. You can take time to think through your responses. You can re-read your responses to make sure you are communicating just what you wish to say. You don't have to worry about speaking in front of other people. For many people, distance learning is liberating. Because distance learning usually involves more writing than traditional courses, you can become a better writer. You receive more practice writing—and more feedback for it—than in traditional courses.

8   But there is a negative side. First, you are a prisoner of technology. If you lose access to a computer and the Web, you won't be able to participate in the class until the problem is fixed. Also, you won't have direct, face-to-face contact with your instructor or other students. Distance learning can be isolating, and students sometimes feel alone and lost in cyberspace. Keep in mind that you won't get immediate feedback. In a distance-learning class, it may be hours, sometimes days, before you receive feedback on what you have posted to a message board, depending on how well the pace of other students matches your own. Finally, distance-learning classes require significant discipline, personal responsibility, and time management skills. You won't have a set time to attend class as you do in traditional courses. Instead, you must carve out the time yourself. Although instructors provide a schedule of when things are due, you have to work out the timing of getting them done. In short, distance learning has some disadvantages that you should keep in mind.

Practice Exercise

• Topic of paragraph 6:

_____

_____

_____

• Underline or highlight the stated main idea of paragraph 6.

Practice Exercise

• Topic of paragraph 7:

_____

_____

_____

• Underline or highlight the stated main idea of paragraph 7.

Practice Exercise

• Topic of paragraph 8:

_____

_____

_____

• Underline or highlight the stated main idea of paragraph 8.

SELECTION 4.2

TRY IT!

Assess Your Course-Taking Style

Your preferred course-taking style—how you participate in classes, work with your classmates, interact with your instructors, and complete your assignments—may make you more or less suitable for distance learning. Read the following statements and indicate whether you agree or disagree with them to see if you have what it takes to be a distance learner.

		Agree	Disagree
1.	I need the stimulation of other students to learn well.		
2.	I need to see my instructor's face, expressions, and body language to interpret what is being said.		
3.	I participate a lot in class discussions.		
4.	I prefer to hear information presented orally rather than reading it in a book or article.		
5.	I'm not very good at keeping up with reading assignments.		
6.	I'm basically pretty easily distracted.		
7.	I'm not very well organized.		
8.	Keeping track of time and holding to schedules is NOT a strength for me.		
9.	I need a lot of "hand-holding" while I work on long assignments.		
10.	I need a close social network to share my feelings, ideas, and complaints with.		
11.	I'm not very good at writing.		
12.	Basically, I'm not very patient.		

The more you ***disagree*** with these statements, the more your course-taking style is suited to distance learning. Interpret your style according to this informal scale:

Disagreed with 10–12 statements = Excellent candidate for distance learning
Disagreed with 7–9 statements = Good candidate for distance learning
Agreed with 6–9 statements = Probably better off taking classes on campus
Agreed with 10–12 statements = Should avoid distance learning

9   Consequently, many students believe that distance-learning courses are more difficult than traditional classes. You must be focused and committed to keeping up with the course. You need to be prepared to work hard on your own for a substantial number of hours each week.

10   Despite these potential challenges to distance-learning courses, they are becoming increasingly popular. More and more colleges are offering them. Many companies encourage employees with crowded schedules to take distance learning as a way of providing continuing education.

Identifying Distance-Learning Course Possibilities

11   How do you find a distance-learning course? In some cases, your own college may offer courses on the Web and list them in your course catalog. In other cases, you'll have to find courses on your own.

12   What is the easiest, most efficient way to find these courses? The best place to look in order to identify distance-learning course possibilities is on the Web itself. By searching the Web, you can find distance-learning courses ranging from agronomy to zoology. Don't be deterred by the physical location of the institution that offers the course. It doesn't matter where the college is located, because for most distance-learning classes you'll never have to go to the campus itself.

13   But before you sign up for a potential course that you would like to count toward your degree, *make sure that your own college will give you credit for it.* Check with your adviser and registrar's office to be certain. You should also find out what the requirements of a course are before you actually sign up for it. Check the syllabus carefully and see how it meshes with your schedule. If it is a summer course and you are going to be away from your computer for a week, you may not be able to make up the work you miss.

Obtaining Access to Technology

14   Although you won't need to be a computer expert, you will need some minimal e-mail and Web skills to take a distance-learning course. If you don't have sufficient technological expertise, enhance your computer skills by taking a computer course or workshop before you actually sign up for the distance-learning course.

15   You'll also need access to a computer connected to the Internet. It doesn't have to be your own computer, but you will certainly need regular and convenient access to one. Make sure that the computer you plan to use has sufficient internal resources to quickly connect to the Internet; a very slow connection is frustrating. And be sure to make all your arrangements for computer access prior to the start of a course. It can take several weeks to set up an Internet service on a home computer if you don't have it already.

Practice Exercise

- Topic of paragraph 12:

_____

_____

_____

- Underline or highlight the stated main idea of paragraph 12.

Participating in a Distance Learning Course

16   How can you get the most out of a distance-learning course? Successfully participating in a distance-learning course requires several skills that are distinct from those needed for traditional classes. To be successful, you'll need to do the following:

- *Manage your time carefully.* You won't have the luxury of a regular schedule of class lectures, so you'll have to manage your time carefully. No one is going to remind you that you need to sit down to a computer and work. You will need every bit of self-discipline to be successful in a distance-learning course.
- *Check in frequently.* Instructors may make crucial changes in the course requirements. Make sure to check for any changes in due dates or class expectations.
- *Make copies of everything.* Don't assume everything will go well in cyberspace. Make a printed copy of everything you submit, or alternatively have a backup stored on another computer.
- *Have a technology backup plan.* Computers crash, your connection to the Internet may go down, or an e-mailed assignment may be mysteriously delayed or sent back to you. Don't wait until the last minute to work on and submit assignments, and have a plan in place if your primary computer isn't available.

Considering Your "Classroom" Performance

17   As with any class, you'll be receiving feedback from your instructor. But unlike many courses, in which almost all feedback comes from the instructor, much of the feedback in a distance-learning course may come from your fellow students. Consider what you can learn from their comments, while keeping in mind that they are, like you, students themselves.

18   At the same time you'll be receiving feedback, you will likely be providing feedback to your classmates. Consider the nature of the feedback you provide. Be sure that you use the basic principles of classroom civility.

19   Distance learning is not for everyone. If your preferred learning style involves extensive, face-to-face interaction with others, you may find your experience is less than satisfying. On the other hand, if you are at ease with computers and enjoy working on your own, you may find distance learning highly effective.

20   Most educational experts believe that distance learning will play an increasingly important role in higher education. Furthermore, because it offers an efficient way of educating people in far-flung locales, it is a natural means of promoting lifelong learning experiences. In short the first distance-learning class you take is likely not to be your last.

Source: Adapted from Robert S. Feldman, *P.O.W.E.R. Learning and Your Life: Essentials of Student Success,* pp. 169–74. Copyright © 2011 by The McGraw-Hill Companies, Inc. Reprinted with permission of The McGraw-Hill Companies, Inc.

Practice Exercise

- Topic of paragraph 16:

  _____

  _____

  _____

- Underline or highlight the stated main idea of paragraph 16.

Reading Selection Quiz

This quiz has several parts. Your instructor may assign some or all of them.

Comprehension

Directions: Items 1–10 test your understanding of the selection. They are the type of questions a content area instructor (such as a student success professor) might ask on a test. You may refer to the selection as you answer the questions. Write your answer choice in the space provided.

True or False

_____ **1.** According to the author, many students believe that distance-learning classes are more difficult than traditional courses.

_____ **2.** In blended courses, or hybrid courses, instruction is a combination of the traditional face-to-face classroom interaction and a significant amount of online learning.

_____ **3.** You need to have excellent Web skills and own a computer to be successful in a distance-learning class.

_____ **4.** Distance learning usually involves more writing than traditional courses.

_____ **5.** Many companies encourage employees with crowded schedules to take distance-learning courses as a way of providing continuing education.

Multiple-Choice

_____ **6.** The key feature of a distance-learning course is the:
　　a. amount of time and effort needed to complete the course.
　　b. ability to collaborate with other students enrolled in the course.
　　c. nature of interaction between the instructor and the students.
　　d. affordability of the course.

_____ **7.** Students find it easier to "speak up" in a distance-learning class because:
　　a. they don't have to worry about speaking in front of other people.
　　b. they can reread their responses to be sure they are communicating what they wish to say.
　　c. they can take time to think through their responses.
　　d. all of the above

_____ **8.** Before you sign up for a distance-learning course that you would like to count for your degree, you should:
　　a. make sure that your own college will give you credit for it.

    b. find out if your college offers a similar face-to-face course.

    c. compare the cost of the distance-learning course with the cost of a traditional course.

    d. all of the above

_____ **9.** Unlike traditional classes in which almost all of the feedback comes from your instructor, much of the feedback in distance-learning classes may come from:

    a. the Web.

    b. other instructors at the same college.

    c. a help desk.

    d. your fellow students.

_____ **10.** Distance-learning classes require:

    a. time management skills.

    b. significant discipline.

    c. personal responsibility.

    d. all of the above

SELECTION **4.2**

**Student
Success**

(continued)

Vocabulary in Context

Directions: Items 11–20 test your ability to determine a word's meaning by using context clues. *Context clues* are words in a sentence that allow readers to deduce (reason out) the meaning of an unfamiliar word in the sentence. They also help readers determine the meaning an author intends when a word has more than one meaning. Each item below consists of a sentence from the selection, with the vocabulary word *italicized*. It is followed by another sentence that uses the same word in the same way. Use context clues to deduce the meaning of the *italicized* word. Be sure the meaning you choose makes sense in *both* sentences. Write each answer in the space provided. *Note:* Chapter 2 presents the skill of using context clues.

_____ **11.** You may already be familiar with the kinds of technologies used in distance-learning courses, because many traditional, face-to-face courses already contain *elements* of distance-learning courses.

Inspiration, humor, and brevity are important *elements* of a successful speech.

elements (ĕl′ə mənts) means:

    a. unlimited amounts

    b. certain types

    c. essential parts

    d. specific examples

_____ **12.** You may be able to spread out your work over the course of a week, or you may do the work in a *concentrated* manner on one day.

Due to their *concentrated* efforts, the committee members completed their work in far less time than expected.

concentrated (kŏn′ sən trāt′əd) means:

a. gathered together

b. unusually fast

c. abbreviated

d. spread out over time

_____ **13.** Distance learning can be *isolating,* and students sometimes feel alone and lost in cyberspace.

After living in a large city, living in a small town can feel *isolating.*

isolating (ī′sə lā′tĭng) means:

a. confusing; unclear

b. removing

c. reducing

d. set apart or separated from others

_____ **14.** Don't be *deterred* by the physical location of the institution that offers the course.

Mark's anxiety about public speaking *deterred* him from volunteering to be on the program.

deterred (dĭ tûr′əd) means:

a. disappointed

b. confused by

c. prevented or discouraged by fear or doubt

d. allowed to proceed; to continue

_____ **15.** If you don't have sufficient technological *expertise,* enhance your computer skills by taking a computer course or workshop before you actually sign up for the distance-learning course.

Norman's impressive résumé reflects his abundant *expertise* in coaching, fitness training, and sports medicine.

expertise (ĕk′spûr tēz′) means:

a. technological training

b. educational support

c. experience with computers

d. skill or knowledge in a particular area

_____ **16.** Check the syllabus carefully and see how it *meshes* with your schedule.

A summer internship at a law firm *meshes* with my goal of exploring law as a career.

meshes (mĕsh′ əs) means:

a. fits together

b. develops

c. enhances

d. improves

_____ **17.** Be sure to make all your arrangements for computer access *prior* to the start
of a course.

Prior to using a person's name on an application as a reference, you should
ask the person's permission.

prior (prī′ ər) means:

a. submitting in advance

b. at the same time

c. instead of; substituting

d. before; preceding in time or order

_____ **18.** Successfully participating in a distance-learning course requires several skills
that are *distinct* from those needed for traditional courses.

Investigators discovered that on three *distinct* occasions, the suspect had been
seen near the house that was burglarized.

distinct (dĭs tĭngkt′) means:

a. different

b. significant; important

c. necessary; required

d. joyful; pleasing

_____ **19.** Be sure that you use the basic principles of classroom *civility*.

The judge found the witness in contempt of court when she failed to maintain
civility while answering the prosecutor's questions.

civility (sĭ vĭl′ ĭ tē) means:

a. obedience

b. communication

c. politeness; courtesy

d. truthfulness; sincerity

_____ **20.** Consider the *nature* of the feedback that you provide.

Rebecca's essay was moving and emotional because she included many specific details of a personal *nature*.

nature (nā′ chər) means:

a. amount or degree

b. effect

c. purpose

d. kind or sort

**Student
Success**

(continued)

SELECTION 4.2

Reading Skills Application

Directions: Items 21–25 test your ability to *apply* certain reading skills. You may not be familiar with all the skills yet, so some items will serve as a preview. As you work through *Opening Doors,* you will practice and develop these skills. These are important skills, which is why they are included on the state-mandated basic skills tests that some students must take. Write each answer in the space provided.

_____   **21.** Which of the following sentences best expresses the main idea of paragraph 19?
  a. If you are at ease with computers and enjoy working on your own, you may find distance learning highly effective.
  b. If your preferred learning style involves extensive, face-to-face interaction with others, you might find your experience with distance learning less than satisfying.
  c. Everyone should try at least one distance-learning class.
  d. Distance learning is not for everyone.

_____   **22.** As an example of how distance-learning classes are more flexible than face-to-face classes, the author mentions that you:
  a. will have more contact with your instructor than you do in a traditional class.
  b. don't have to worry about speaking up in class.
  c. can participate in a course any time of the day or night.
  d. will do less writing than in traditional courses.

_____   **23.** As used in paragraph 3 of this selection, *virtual* means:
  a. explained in a realistic manner
  b. organized in a flexible format
  c. presented in an exclusively electronic format
  d. arranged in a traditional way

_____   **24.** Based on the information in the selection, it can be logically concluded that:
  a. in the future, every college course will be available through distance learning.
  b. all students can be successful in distance-learning courses.
  c. instructors prefer teaching distance-learning classes rather than face-to-face classes.
  d. as more and more people become comfortable with technology, distance-learning classes will become commonplace.

_____   **25.** The author's primary purpose for writing this selection is to:
  a. persuade all students to take advantage of the convenience of distance-learning courses.
  b. inform students about the advantages and disadvantages of distance-learning courses and explain how to succeed in them.

    c. evaluate the effectiveness of distance-learning courses.

    d. explain to students why distance-learning courses are becoming popular.

Respond in Writing

Directions: Refer to the selection as needed to answer the essay-type questions below. (Your instructor may direct you to work collaboratively with other students on one or more items. Each group member should be able to explain *all* of the group's answers.)

1. The author mentions numerous advantages and several disadvantages of distance-learning classes. List at least five advantages and five disadvantages of distance-learning classes in the spaces below.

Advantages of Distance–Learning Classes

_____

_____

_____

_____

_____

_____

_____

_____

_____

_____

Disadvantages of Distance-Learning Classes

_____

_____

_____

_____

_____

_____

_____

_____

2. Although most educational experts believe that distance learning will play an increasingly important role in higher education, there may be some types of courses and some subject areas in which distance learning may not be suitable. Think of some college courses in which distance learning may not be appropriate or effective and explain why you believe this.

_____

_____

_____

_____

_____

_____

_____

3. **Overall main idea.** What is the overall main idea the author wants the reader to understand about distance-learning classes? Answer this question in one sentence. Be sure to include the phrase *distance-learning classes* in your overall main idea sentence.

_____

_____

_____

_____

_____

SELECTION **4.3**

History

Muhammad

From *The 100: A Ranking of the Most Influential Persons in History*
by Michael K. Hart

SELECTION 4.3

Prepare Yourself to Read

Directions: Do these exercises *before* you read Selection 4.3.

1. First, read and think about the title. What do you already know about Muhammad?

_____

_____

_____

2. Next, complete your preview by reading the following:

Introduction (in *italics*)

First paragraph (paragraph 1)

First sentence of each paragraph

Words in *italics*

Last paragraph (paragraph 9)

On the basis of your preview, what information about Muhammad does this selection seem to present?

_____

_____

_____

_____

3. **Build your vocabulary as you read.** If you discover an unfamiliar word or key term as you read the selection, try to determine its meaning by using context clues.

Internet Resources

Read More about This Topic Online

Use a search engine, such as Google or Yahoo!, to expand your existing knowledge about this topic *before* you read the selection or to learn more about it *afterward*. Use search terms such as "Muhammad" or "influence of prophet Muhammad." If you are unfamiliar with conducting Internet searches, read pages 25–26 on Boolean searches. You can also use Wikipedia, the free online encyclopedia, at www.wikipedia.com. Keep in mind that when you visit any website, it is a good idea to evaluate the site and the information it contains. Ask yourself questions such as "Who sponsors this website?" and "Is the information it contains up to date?"

SELECTION 4.3: MUHAMMAD

Of the billions of human beings who have populated the earth, which ones do you think have most influenced the world and the course of history? Historian Michael Hart attempts to answer this fascinating question in his book The 100: A Ranking of the Most Influential Persons in History. *He emphasizes that he was seeking to identify the "most influential" persons in history, not necessarily the "greatest." On his list of the top 100, the first 10 are (1) Muhammad, (2) Isaac Newton, (3) Jesus Christ, (4) Buddha, (5) Confucius, (6) St. Paul, (7) Ts'ai Lun, (8) Johannes Gutenberg, (9) Christopher Columbus, and (10) Albert Einstein. Perhaps you were surprised to see Muhammad listed first. In the selection below, Hart explains why he considers Muhammad to be the most influential person in history.*

This selection will be especially useful to you if you do not already know who Muhammad is. Every well-educated person should be familiar with the names and accomplishments of individuals who have significantly influenced the history and culture of the world.

Keep in mind that it does not matter whether or not you agree with Michael Hart that Muhammad is the most influential person in history. Hart does not expect everyone to agree with him. Your goal as a thoughtful reader should be to understand and consider the reasons Hart gives for his selection of Muhammad as the most influential person who has ever lived.

1   My choice of Muhammad to lead the list of the world's most influential persons may surprise some readers and may be questioned by others, but he was the only man in history who was supremely successful on both the religious and the secular level.

2   Of humble origins, Muhammad founded and promulgated one of the world's great religions, and became an immensely effective political leader. Today, fourteen centuries after his death, his influence is still powerful and pervasive.

3   The majority of the persons in this book had the advantage of being born and raised in centers of civilization, highly cultured and politically pivotal nations. Muhammad, however, was born in the year 570, in the city of Mecca, in southern Arabia, at that time a backward area of the world, far from the centers of trade, art, and learning. Orphaned at age six, he was reared in modest surroundings. Islamic tradition tells us that he was illiterate. His economic position improved when, at the age of twenty-five, he married a wealthy widow. Nevertheless, as he approached forty, there was little outward indication that he was a remarkable person.

4   Most Arabs at that time were pagans, who believed in many gods. There were, however, in Mecca, a small number of Jews and Christians; it was from them no doubt that Muhammad first learned of a single, omnipotent God who ruled the entire universe. When he was forty years old, Muhammad became convinced that this one true God (*Allah*) was speaking to him, and had chosen him to spread the true faith.

Annotation Practice Exercises

Directions: For each exercise below:

- Write the topic of the paragraph on the lines beside the paragraph.
- Underline or highlight the stated main idea sentence of the paragraph.

This will help you remember the topic and the stated main idea.

Practice Exercise

- Topic of paragraph 4:

_____

_____

_____

- Underline or highlight the stated main idea of paragraph 4.

5   For three years, Muhammad preached only to close friends and associates. Then, about 613, he began preaching in public. As he slowly gained converts, the Meccan authorities came to consider him a dangerous nuisance. In 622, fearing for his safety, Muhammad fled to Medina (a city some 200 miles north of Mecca), where he had been offered a position of considerable political power.

6   The flight, called the Hegira (hĕj′ ər ə, hǐ jī′ rə), was the turning point of the Prophet's life. In Mecca, he had had a few followers. In Medina, he had many more, and he soon acquired an influence that made him a virtual dictator. During the next few years, while Muhammad's following grew rapidly, a series of battles were fought between Medina and Mecca. This war ended in 630 with Muhammad's triumphant return to Mecca as conqueror. The remaining two and one-half years of his life witnessed the rapid conversion of the Arab tribes to the new religion. When Muhammad died, in 632, he was the effective ruler of all of southern Arabia.

7   How, then, is one to assess the overall impact of Muhammad on human history? Like all religions, Islam exerts an enormous influence upon the lives of its followers. It is for this reason that the founders of the world's great religions all figure prominently in this book. Since there are roughly 1.5 times as many Christians as Muslims in the world, it may initially seem strange that Muhammad has been ranked higher than Jesus. There are two principal reasons for that decision. First, Muhammad played a far more important role in the development of Islam than Jesus did in the development of Christianity. Although Jesus was responsible for the main ethical and moral precepts of Christianity (insofar as these differed from Judaism), St. Paul was the main developer of Christian theology, its principal proselytizer, and the author of a large portion of the New Testament.

8   Muhammad, however, was responsible for both the theology of Islam and its main ethical and moral principles. In addition, he played the key role in proselytizing the new faith, and in establishing the religious practices of Islam. Moreover, he is considered by Muslims to be Allah's vehicle for the Muslim holy scriptures, the *Koran* [Qu'ran]. It is a collection of certain of Muhammad's insights that he believed had been directly revealed to him by Allah. Most of these utterances were copied more or less faithfully during Muhammad's lifetime and were collected together in authoritative form not long after his death. The *Koran,* therefore, closely represents Muhammad's ideas and teachings and to a considerable extent his exact words. No such detailed compilation of the teachings of Christ has survived. Since the *Koran* is at least as important to Muslims as the Bible is to Christians, the influence of Muhammad through the medium of the *Koran* has been enormous. It is probable that the relative influence of Muhammad on Islam has been

Masjid al-Haram, Mecca, Saudi Arabia
The Masjid al-Haram is the largest mosque in the world. The mosque surrounds the Kaaba, which Muslims turn toward while offering daily prayer. Two pilgrimages, the *Hajj* and the *Umrah,* attract millions of Muslims to Mecca from all over the world.

SELECTION 4.3

Practice Exercise

•   Topic of paragraph 6:

_____

_____

_____

•   Underline or highlight the stated main idea of paragraph 6.

larger than the combined influence of Jesus Christ and St. Paul on Christianity. On the purely religious level, then, it seems likely that Muhammad has been as influential in human history as Jesus.

9   Furthermore, Muhammad (unlike Jesus) was a secular as well as a religious leader. In fact, as the driving force behind the Arab conquests, he may well rank as the most influential political leader of all time.

History

Reading Selection Quiz

> This quiz has several parts. Your instructor may assign some or all of them.

Comprehension

Directions: Items 1–10 test your understanding of the selection. They are the type of questions a content area instructor (such as a history professor) might ask on a test. You may refer to the selection as you answer the questions. Write your answer choice in the space provided.

True or False

_____   **1.** The author believes that everyone will agree with his choice of Muhammad as the most influential person in history.

_____   **2.** The author chose Muhammad solely because of Muhammad's success as a religious leader.

_____   **3.** Muhammad was born and raised in what was then called Arabia, a highly cultured and pivotal nation.

_____   **4.** According to the author, Muhammad learned about a single, all-powerful God from the small number of Christians and Jews living in Mecca.

Multiple-Choice

_____   **5.** Muhammad began preaching that Allah was the one true God when Muhammad was:
  a.   still in his teens.
  b.   26 years old.
  c.   30 years old.
  d.   40 years old.

_____   **6.** The Hegira was Muhammad's flight:
  a.   from Arabia.
  b.   from Medina to Mecca.
  c.   from Mecca to Medina.
  d.   to southern Arabia.

7. Since there are roughly 1.5 times as many Christians as Muslims, why does the author rank Muhammad higher than Jesus, the founder of Christianity?
   a. The author feels that Muhammad played a larger role in the development of Islam than Jesus did in the development of Christianity.
   b. The author is a Muslim.
   c. More books have been written about Muhammad than about Jesus.
   d. Muhammad, who died at age 62, lived longer than Jesus did.

8. The Koran is:
   a. the Bible translated into Arabic.
   b. another name for the Hegira.
   c. the Muslim holy scriptures.
   d. Muhammad's family name.

9. Of the statements below about Muhammad's life, which one is *not* true?
   a. He was orphaned at age 6.
   b. He preached to close friends for 3 years and then began preaching in public.
   c. He never married.
   d. He was a driving force behind Arab conquests.

10. The author maintains that Muhammad should top the list of the world's most influential persons because:
    a. Muhammad was responsible for the theology of Islam and its main principles.
    b. In Mecca, he became a virtual dictator.
    c. Muhammad was a great military leader.
    d. Muhammad was an influential religious leader and secular leader.

SELECTION **4.3**

History
(continued)

Vocabulary in Context

Directions: Items 11–20 test your ability to determine a word's meaning by using context clues. *Context clues* are words in a sentence that allow readers to deduce (reason out) the meaning of an unfamiliar word in the sentence. They also help readers determine the meaning an author intends when a word has more than one meaning. Each item below consists of a sentence from the selection, with the vocabulary word *italicized.* It is followed by another sentence that uses the same word in the same way. Use context clues to deduce the meaning of the *italicized* word. Be sure the meaning you choose makes sense in *both* sentences. Write each answer in the space provided. *Note:* Chapter 2 presents the skill of using context clues.

11. Of humble origins, Muhammad founded and *promulgated* one of the world's great religions, and became an immensely effective political leader.

    In the State of the Union speech, the president *promulgated* the new administration's policy on gun control.

promulgated (prōm′ əl gāt əd) means:
a. reversed or changed
b. made known or put into effect by public declaration
c. refused to reveal
d. denounced as untrue

_____ **12.** Today, fourteen centuries after his death, his influence is still powerful and *pervasive.*

The drug problem in the United States is difficult to deal with because the problem is so *pervasive.*

pervasive (pər vā′ sĭv) means:
a. important
b. widespread
c. decreasing or diminishing
d. popular

_____ **13.** The majority of the persons in this book had the advantage of being born and raised in centers of civilization, highly cultured or politically *pivotal* nations.

Supreme Court Justice Kennedy's opinion was the *pivotal* one that reversed the lower court's decision.

pivotal (pĭv′ ə təl) means:
a. causing rotation or spinning
b. pertaining to religion or theology
c. determining a direction or effect; crucial
d. going in two different directions

_____ **14.** Orphaned at age six, he was reared in *modest* surroundings.

Even after the Smiths won the lottery, they continued to live in a *modest* apartment and to take the subway to work.

modest (mŏd′ ĭst) means:
a. plain rather than showy
b. shy or reserved
c. luxurious
d. rural; pertaining to the country

_____ **15.** *Islamic* tradition tells us that Muhammad was illiterate.

Mosques are *Islamic* houses of worship.

Islamic (ĭs läm′ ĭc) means:
a. pertaining to the Christian religion based on the teachings of Jesus
b. pertaining to the Buddhist religion based on the teachings of Buddha
c. pertaining to the Muslim religion based on the teachings of Muhammad
d. pertaining to the Confucian religion based on the teachings of Confucius

SELECTION 4.3

_____   **16.** Furthermore, Muhammad (unlike Jesus) was a *secular* as well as a religious leader.

While some people view the use of stem cells as a religious issue, others view it as a purely *secular* issue.

secular (sĕk′ yə lər) means:

a. private
b. pertaining to worship
c. spiritual
d. not related to religion

_____   **17.** There were, however, in Mecca, a small number of Jews and Christians; it was from them no doubt that Muhammad first learned of a single, *omnipotent* God who ruled the entire universe.

Hitler's goal was to conquer all of Europe and Russia; he was a madman who thought he could be *omnipotent*.

omnipotent (ŏm nĭp′ ə tənt) means:

a. having unlimited power or authority
b. having limited power or authority
c. having authority given by the citizens of a country
d. having no power or authority

_____   **18.** As he slowly gained *converts,* the Meccan authorities came to consider him a dangerous nuisance.

The new political party in India rapidly gained *converts*.

converts (kŏn′ vûrts) means:

a. people who revert to previously held beliefs
b. people who adopt a new religion or new beliefs
c. people who cling to long-held beliefs
d. people who have no religious beliefs

_____   **19.** Although Jesus was responsible for the main ethical precepts of Christianity, St. Paul was the main developer of Christian *theology,* its principal proselytizer, and the author of a large portion of the New Testament.

Although my uncle is not a minister, he has continued to read ancient and modern Christian *theology* throughout his life.

theology (thē ŏl′ ə jē) means:

a. system or school of opinions about God and religious questions
b. study of beliefs throughout the world
c. study of ancient religious rituals
d. study of the lives of saints

_____ **20.** In addition, Muhammad played the key role in *proselytizing* the new faith, and in establishing the religious practices of Islam.

The evangelists went door to door *proselytizing,* telling anyone who was willing to listen about their religious beliefs.

proselytizing (prŏs′ ə lə tīz ĭng) means:

a. speaking loudly or shouting

b. deceiving with trickery

c. declaring false or untrue

d. attempting to convert people from one belief or faith to another

S ELECTION **4.3**

History
(continued)

Reading Skills Application

Directions: Items 21–25 test your ability to *apply* certain reading skills. You may not be familiar with all the skills yet, so some items will serve as a preview. As you work through *Opening Doors,* you will practice and develop these skills. These are important skills, which is why they are included on the state-mandated basic skills tests that some students must take. Write each answer in the space provided.

_____ **21.** Which of the following best expresses the author's argument in this selection?

a. My choice of Muhammad to lead the list of the world's most influential persons may surprise some readers and be questioned by others.

b. As the driving force behind the Arab conquests, Muhammad may well rank as the most influential political leader of all time.

c. When he was 40 years old, Muhammad became convinced that Allah had chosen him to spread the true faith.

d. Because he was supremely successful as a religious and a secular leader, Muhammad can be viewed as the most influential person in history.

_____ **22.** The meaning of *humble* in paragraph 2 is:

a. distinguished.

b. famous.

c. lowly.

d. comfortable.

_____ **23.** In this selection, the primary comparison and contrast the author presents is between:

a. Jesus and Muhammad.

b. Muhammad and his followers.

c. pagans and Christians.

d. secular and religious leaders.

S ELECTION 4.3

24. The author's tone in this selection can best be described as:

    a. persuasive.

    b. sympathetic.

    c. disapproving.

    d. sentimental.

25. Which of the following represents an opinion rather than a fact?

    a. Islamic tradition tells us that Muhammad was illiterate.

    b. This war ended in 630 with Muhammad's triumphant return to Mecca as conqueror.

    c. Most Arabs at that time were pagans who believed in many gods.

    d. On a purely religious level, then, it seems likely that Muhammad has been as influential in human history as Jesus.

SELECTION **4.3**

History
(continued)

Respond in Writing

Directions: Refer to the selection as needed to answer the essay-type questions below. (Your instructor may direct you to work collaboratively with other students on one or more items. Each group member should be able to explain *all* of the group's answers.)

1. List the three reasons the author chose Muhammad as the most influential person in history.

Reason 1: _____

_____

_____

Reason 2: _____

_____

_____

Reason 3: _____

_____

_____

2. Michael Hart, the author of *The 100: A Ranking of the Most Influential Persons in History,* selected 99 other important people for his book. List five names *you* would include in a list of the world's most influential people, and state your reasons for including them. Remember, these must be people who have influenced the *world,* not just you. They must be actual *people* who have lived or are currently living. They should be people who have had the *most* influence, regardless of whether their influence on the world was positive or negative. Choose people who are *not* in Hart's top 10, which are listed in the Introduction to Selection 4.3.

Person 1: _____

Reason: _____

_____

Person 2: _____

Reason: _____

_____

Person 3: _____

Reason: _____

_____

Person 4: _____

Reason: _____

_____

Person 5: _____

Reason: _____

3.   **Overall main idea.** What is the overall main idea the author wants the reader to understand about Muhammad? Answer this question in one sentence. Be sure that your overall main idea sentence includes the topic (*Muhammad*) and tells the overall most important point about him.

_____

_____

_____

_____

_____

SELECTION 4.3

CHAPTER 5

Formulating Implied Main Ideas

In this chapter, you will learn the answers to these questions:

- What is an implied main idea of a paragraph?

- Why is formulating implied main ideas important?

- How can I formulate implied main idea sentences?

- How can I know when a formulated main idea sentence is correct?

SKILLS

Implied Main Ideas in Paragraphs

- What Is an Implied Main Idea?

- Why Is Formulating Implied Main Ideas Important?

Formulating an Implied Main Idea

- Steps to Follow

- Three Formulas for Using Information
  in a Paragraph to Formulate the Main Idea

- Requirements for Correctly Formulated Main Idea Sentences

- Implied Overall Main Ideas in Longer Passages

A Word about Standardized Reading Tests: Implied Main Ideas

CHECKPOINT: FORMULATING IMPLIED MAIN IDEAS

CREATING YOUR SUMMARY

Developing Chapter Review Cards

TEST YOUR UNDERSTANDING: FORMULATING IMPLIED MAIN IDEAS, PART 1

TEST YOUR UNDERSTANDING: FORMULATING IMPLIED MAIN IDEAS, PART 2

READINGS

If you want to climb mountains, do not practice on molehills.

Unknown

The man who does not make any mistakes does
not usually make anything.

William Connor Magee

A lot of things are easy when you know how.

Proverb

IMPLIED MAIN IDEAS IN PARAGRAPHS

PERSONALIZED LEARNING

What Is an Implied Main Idea?

Every paragraph has a main idea, but not every paragraph includes a *stated* main idea sentence. When an author gives you the information needed to understand the main point without stating it directly as a single sentence, the main idea is *implied*. When an author implies the main idea, you, the reader, must use information in the paragraph to *infer* (reason out) the main idea and *formulate* (create) a sentence that expresses it. In other words, the **implied main idea** is a sentence formulated by the reader that expresses the author's main point about the topic.

implied main idea

A sentence formulated by the reader that expresses the author's main point about the topic.

An implied main idea is also known as an *unstated main idea*, an *indirectly stated main idea*, and a *formulated main idea*.

Sometimes you must infer that essential information needs to be added to an existing sentence to formulate the complete main idea. At other times, you must infer that information from two or more sentences in the paragraph has to be *combined* to formulate one complete main idea sentence. At still other times, you will have to formulate a *general* sentence that sums up the most important (but unstated) point the author is trying to illustrate or prove. That is, if a paragraph presents facts, descriptions, explanations, or examples that only *suggest* the main point the author wants you to understand, it is up to you to infer and formulate the main idea. When you grasp the main idea in these ways, you are *inferring* it.

Why Is Formulating Implied Main Ideas Important?

You limit your comprehension unless you understand main ideas; therefore, you must be able to identify the main idea when it is stated and formulate it when the author implies it. College instructors assume you read carefully enough to understand paragraphs with implied main ideas. They base test items on both implied main ideas and stated main ideas.

FORMULATING AN IMPLIED MAIN IDEA

Comprehension-Monitoring Question for Implied Main Idea

"What is the most important point the author wants me to *infer* about the topic of this paragraph?"

Steps to Follow

Of course, you will not know until you read a paragraph whether its main idea is stated or implied. Look first for a stated main idea sentence. If there is not one, formulate the implied main idea using the following steps:

- **Step 1:** After you have read the paragraph, *determine the topic* by asking yourself, "Who or what is this passage about?"

- **Step 2:** *Determine the main idea* by asking yourself, "What is the most important point the author wants me to *infer* about the topic of this paragraph?"
- **Step 3:** Use the information in the paragraph to *formulate a main idea sentence* that answers your question in step 2. The sentence you formulate will be the main idea of the paragraph.

Three Formulas for Using Information in a Paragraph to Formulate the Main Idea

Even when authors do not directly state a main idea as one sentence, they still provide the information you need in order to infer and formulate a main idea sentence yourself. Authors provide such information in three ways, and these three ways are the basis for three "formulas" for creating main idea sentences. Each of the three formulas and examples of its application is explained below.

As always, begin by reading the paragraph and determining its topic. Next, ask yourself, "What is the most important point the author wants me to infer about the topic of this paragraph?" Then use one of the three formulas explained below to help you create the formulated main idea sentence. The formula you need will depend on the type of information in the paragraph.

Formula 1: Add an Essential Word or Phrase to a Sentence That Almost States the Main Idea

Sometimes, an author expresses most of the main idea in one sentence of the paragraph, yet that sentence lacks some essential piece of information—one that you must insert to make the sentence a *complete* main idea sentence. To put it another way, a paragraph may contain a sentence that *almost* states the author's main idea, but you must add certain missing information to that sentence to make it express the main idea completely. You may have to add one word, several words, or a short phrase, depending on the situation. For instance, a sentence may need to have the topic of the paragraph inserted to make it express the complete main idea.

When a sentence in the paragraph almost states the main idea but lacks an essential word or phrase, use **formula 1** to create a complete main idea sentence:

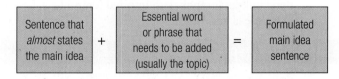

Here is an example of an implied main idea sentence formulated using formula 1. The paragraph is from a sociology textbook. Its topic is *ethnocentrism*. The last sentence almost states the authors' most important point—the definition of ethnocentrism—but it lacks the topic, the word *ethnocentrism*. A complete main idea sentence can be formulated by adding *ethnocentrism* (the topic) to the last sentence of the paragraph. This formulated main idea sentence expresses the most important point the authors want you to understand about ethnocentrism, its definition.

Each person is born into a particular society that has its own particular culture. At an early age, children begin to learn many aspects of this culture, such as language, standards of behavior, and beliefs. They also begin to learn many of the group's values concerning judgments of good and bad, proper and improper, and right and wrong. This learning continues into and throughout adulthood as people internalize, accept, and identify with their group's way of living. This feeling is called **ethnocentrism.** It is the basic inclination to judge other cultures in terms of the values and norms of one's own culture.

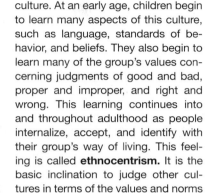

Formulated Main Idea Sentence

Source: Daniel Hebding and Leonard Glick, _Introduction to Sociology_, 4e, p. 62. Copyright © 1992 by The McGraw-Hill Companies, Inc. Reprinted with permission of The McGraw-Hill Companies, Inc.

Stop and Annotate

Go back to the textbook excerpt. Write the formulated main idea sentence in the space provided by adding essential information to the sentence that almost states the main idea.

The last sentence becomes a complete main idea sentence when the essential word _ethnocentrism_ is added: _Ethnocentrism is the basic inclination to judge other cultures in terms of the values and norms of one's own culture._

EXERCISE 1

This paragraph comes from an information technology textbook:

You have most likely heard of or used social networking Web sites such as Classmates.com, Facebook.com, and MySpace.com. But there are three other popular types of sites that help people communicate across the Web. Many individuals create personal Web sites, called **Web logs** or **blogs,** to keep in touch with friends and family. Blog postings are timestamped and arranged with the newest item first. Often, readers of these sites are allowed to comment. Some blogs are like online diaries with personal information; others focus on information about a hobby or theme, such as knitting, electronic devices, or good books. A **microblog** publishes short sentences that only take a few seconds to write, rather than long stories or posts like a traditional blog. Microblogs are designed to keep friends and other contacts up-to-date on your interests and activities. The most popular microblogging site, Twitter, enables you to add new content from your browser, instant messaging application, or even a mobile phone. A **wiki** is a Web site specifically designed to allow visitors to fill in missing information or correct inaccuracies. "Wiki" comes from the Hawaiian word for fast, which describes the simplicity of editing and publishing through wiki software. Wikis support collaborative writing in which there isn't a single expert author, but rather a community of interested people that builds knowledge over time. Creating blogs and wikis are examples of Web authoring.

Source: Adapted from Timothy J. O'Leary and Linda I. O'Leary, _Computing Essentials 2012: Making IT Work for You,_ p. 39. Copyright © 2012 by The McGraw-Hill Companies, Inc. Reprinted with permission of The McGraw-Hill Companies, Inc.

Write the *topic:* _____

Formulate the *implied main idea sentence* and write it here: _____

_____

_____

_____

Formula 2: Combine Two Sentences from the Paragraph into a Single Sentence

Sometimes two different sentences each give part of the main idea. The author assumes that you will understand that each contains part of the main idea and that the sentences, *together,* convey the main point. Both sentences contain important information; neither sentence by itself expresses the complete main idea. The author expects *you* to combine the two sentences to formulate one sentence that expresses the complete main idea. The two sentences may follow one another in the paragraph, or they may be separated. For example, the first sentence of the paragraph may present part of the main idea, and the last sentence may give the rest of it.

When two sentences in a paragraph each give part of the main idea, use **formula 2** to combine them into a single sentence that expresses the complete main idea:

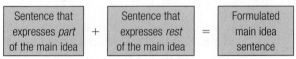

| Sentence that expresses *part* of the main idea | + | Sentence that expresses *rest* of the main idea | = | Formulated main idea sentence |

Here is an example of formula 2. The paragraph below is from a sociology textbook. Its topic is *tastes.* The main idea sentence can be formulated by combining its last two sentences into a single sentence. This formulated main idea sentence expresses the most important point the authors expect you to understand about tastes.

| Tastes—we all have them. You prefer certain styles of art, certain kinds of food and clothing, certain types of music, certain ways of decorating your room. The list could go on and on. *De gustibus non est disputandum,* the old Latin saying goes—there is no accounting for taste. Tastes just seem to spring from somewhere inside us, rather mysteriously. We can't really say why we prefer rock to Mozart, burgers to pâté, jeans to neatly pressed slacks. Tastes simply seem to be part of us, our individual selves. But tastes are also part of culture, which is a broader social phenomenon. | **Formulated Main Idea Sentence**

_____

_____

_____

_____

_____

_____

_____ |

Stop and Annotate

Go back to the preceding textbook excerpt. Write the formulated main idea sentence in the space provided by combining the two sentences in the paragraph that together express the complete main idea.

The last two sentences in the paragraph are the important ones: "Tastes simply seem to be part of us, our individual selves" and "But tastes are also part of culture, which is a broader social phenomenon." Neither sentence by itself expresses the complete main idea. The first sentence addresses tastes on a personal level; the other sentence addresses tastes as part of culture. You must combine these two sentences in order to formulate the complete main idea the authors intended: *Tastes simply seem to be part of us, our individual selves, but tastes are also part of culture, which is a broader social phenomenon.* (Of course, it would be equally correct to express this same main idea in other ways, such as *Although tastes simply seem to be part of our individual selves, tastes are also part of culture.*)

EXERCISE 2

This paragraph comes from a business textbook:

No country practices a pure form of communism, socialism, or capitalism, although most tend to favor one economic system over the others. Most nations operate as **mixed economies.** This means that they have some elements from more than one economic system. In socialist Sweden, most businesses are owned and operated by private individuals. In capitalist United States, the federal government owns and operates the postal service and the Tennessee Valley Authority, an electric utility. In Great Britain and Mexico, the governments are attempting to sell many state-run businesses to private individuals and companies. In once-communist Russia, Hungary, Poland, and other Eastern European nations, capitalist ideas have been implemented, including private ownership of businesses. Communist China allows citizens to invest in stocks and permits some private and foreign ownership of businesses.

Source: Adapted from O. C. Ferrell, Geoffrey A. Hirt, and Linda Ferrell, *Business in a Changing World,* p. 11. Copyright © 2011 by The McGraw-Hill Companies, Inc. Reprinted with permission of The McGraw-Hill Companies, Inc.

Write the *topic:* _____

Formulate the *implied main idea sentence* and write it here:

_____

_____

_____

Formula 3: Summarize Important Ideas into One Sentence or Write One Sentence That Gives a General Inference Based on the Details

For some paragraphs that have implied main ideas, you will have to either formulate a main idea sentence that *summarizes* the important information in the paragraph *or* formulate a sentence that gives a *general inference* based on the details. Which of these you do depends upon the type of information in the paragraph.

Sometimes parts of the main idea are in different sentences throughout the paragraph. They must be combined in order to express the complete main idea. When this is the case, you formulate a main idea sentence by *summarizing* this important information in one sentence. You will probably have to use some of your own words when you create this kind of formulated main idea sentence.

Sometimes a paragraph consists only of details. When this is the case, you formulate a main idea sentence by inferring the *general* point the author is illustrating or proving with the details, and then express this idea as a single sentence. This is not a matter of rewriting the details as one long sentence, but rather of writing a sentence that *sums up* the details the author presents. In other words, you have to create a general sentence that *summarizes* the details. When you write this formulated main idea sentence, you may also have to use some of your own words.

When a paragraph has important ideas in several sentences or the paragraph consists only of details, use **formula 3** to formulate a main idea sentence:

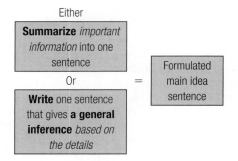

Here is an example of formulating an implied main idea using formula 3. The excerpt is from a special section in an algebra textbook that introduces interesting information to be used in solving problems. The topic is *pesticides*. The implied main idea must be formulated by making a general inference based on the details. As you read the paragraph, try to reason out (infer) the most important general point the authors are making about pesticides.

Unfortunately, pesticides often kill plants and animals other than the pests they are intended for. Pesticides also pollute water systems. Over time, some pests develop immunity to frequently used pesticides and, therefore, more and more pesticides must be used. Some pesticides, such as DDT and its relatives, can remain in the environment for many years beyond the time necessary to do their intended job. Some pesticides have been linked to cancer and other health problems in humans.

Formulated Main Idea Sentence

_____

_____

_____

_____

_____

_____

Source: Adapted from James Streeter, Donald Hutchison, and Louis Hoelzle, *Beginning Algebra,* 3e, p. 370. Copyright © 1993 by The McGraw-Hill Companies, Inc. Reprinted with permission of The McGraw-Hill Companies, Inc.

To formulate a main idea sentence for this paragraph, you must write a general inference that is based on the important information in *several* sentences. Examine the information, think about it, and ask yourself, "What is the most important general point the authors want me to understand about pesticides?" To answer that question, you will need to use some of your own words.

Although the phrase *dangerous effects* does not appear in this paragraph, it obviously describes dangerous effects of pesticides. It is up to you to reason out that the main idea should contain a general phrase such as *dangerous effects.* A correctly formulated main idea sentence would be *Pesticides can have dangerous, unintended effects on the environment, plants, animals, and human beings.* This formulated main idea sentence expresses the general point the authors want you to understand about pesticides.

The example above for the formulated main idea sentence is not the only possible correct formulation. An equally correct main idea sentence would be *Pesticides have several unintended, dangerous effects.* Still another possibility is *Certain unintended side effects of pesticides are dangerous.* There are other possibilities as well. What is important is not the exact wording but that the sentence express the authors' main point.

When formulating implied main ideas, remember to look at the type of information the author gives in the paragraph. The chart on page 282 summarizes what you must do to formulate the implied main idea once you determine what the author has given you to work with.

Stop and Annotate

Go back to the preceding textbook excerpt. Formulate a main idea sentence by making a general inference based on information from several sentences and write it in the space provided.

EXERCISE 3

This paragraph comes from a health textbook:

> What causes problem drinking? Why do some people develop problems with alcohol while others do not? These questions have no simple answers. Instead, a complex interaction of many factors is at work. These factors may be individual or may be psychological. A family history of alcoholism is a risk factor for the development of alcoholism. Family dysfunction in general, even without an alcoholic parent, increases the likelihood that children will grow up to have alcohol problems. However, most children who grow up in dysfunctional family environments do not develop problems with alcohol. Sociocultural factors also play an enormous role in how alcohol is used and misused. Some cultures have higher acceptance of alcohol use, more tolerant attitudes toward drinking and drunkenness, and/or higher levels of alcohol consumption than others do. Sociocultural factors also include economic factors, such as the availability and cost of alcohol, and the ease of access of alcohol, and these factors also play a role, as do laws governing drinking age and the sale of alcoholic beverages.
>
> *Source:* Adapted from Michael L. Teague, Sara L. C. Mackenzie, David M. Rosenthal, *Your Health Today,* p. 194. Copyright © 2011 by The McGraw-Hill Companies, Inc. Reprinted with permission of The McGraw-Hill Companies, Inc.

Write the *topic:* _____

_____

Formulate the *implied main idea sentence* and write it here: _____

_____

_____

_____

THREE WAYS TO FORMULATE IMPLIED MAIN IDEA SENTENCES

What the Author Gives You in the Paragraph	What You Must Do with the Information in Order to Formulate the Implied Main Idea
A sentence that *almost* states the main idea, but lacks some essential piece of information (usually the topic)	*Use formula 1:* *Add* the essential piece of information that is missing to that sentence. *How to apply the formula:* Use the sentence from the paragraph and simply add the essential piece of information to that sentence.
Two sentences in the paragraph, each of which presents part of the main idea	*Use formula 2:* *Combine* them into one sentence. *How to apply the formula:* You will probably have to add a word or two in order to connect the two sentences (usually words such as *and, but, or, although*). *or* You can write the main idea in your own words, as long as the meaning is the same.
Details only *or* parts of the main idea occurring in several sentences throughout the paragraph	*Use formula 3:* Write a *general sentence* that sums up the details or gives a general inference about the point the author is making. *How to apply the formula:* The sentence you write will contain several of your own words.

Requirements for Correctly Formulated Main Idea Sentences

When you formulate an implied main idea sentence (in other words, when you use one of the three formulas), there is a way to check to be sure that your

When the author does not state the main idea, the reader must *formulate* the author's main idea by piecing together important information.

sentence is correct. A correctly formulated implied main idea sentence meets these requirements:

- *A formulated main idea must be a complete sentence that includes the topic of the paragraph.*
- *A formulated main idea must express the author's most important general point about the topic.* In other words, if the formulated main idea sentence is placed at the beginning of the paragraph, the details explain, prove, or tell more about it.
- *A formulated main idea must make complete sense by itself (without the reader having to read the rest of the paragraph).* As you learned in Chapter 4, a stated main idea sentence must also be meaningful by itself (that is, even if the reader could not see the rest of the paragraph).

Remember that an implied main idea sentence can be expressed in various ways, as long as the sentence meets these three requirements. Keep in mind, however, that the formulated main idea sentence you write should express the author's most important point concisely. This means that there are many extraneous, or extra, words that you should *not* include in your formulated main idea sentence. For example, if the author's main idea is *Pesticides have several unintended dangerous effects,* you should write only that. You should *not* write a formulated main idea sentence with extraneous words such as the italicized ones shown here:

The author's main idea is that pesticides have several unintended dangerous effects.

The author says that pesticides have several unintended dangerous effects.

What the author wants us to understand is pesticides have several unintended dangerous effects.

The author is trying to say that pesticides have several unintended dangerous effects.

What the author means is that pesticides have several unintended dangerous effects.

When you formulate a main idea, it is enough merely to write the most important point the author wants readers to understand. In the examples above, for instance, you would use only the part of each sentence that is not in italics.

Implied Overall Main Ideas in Longer Passages

Of course, the ability to formulate implied main ideas is a skill that can be applied not only to paragraphs but also to longer passages, such as a section of a textbook chapter, a short reading selection, or an essay. In fact, you will often need to formulate the main idea of an entire passage in order to express its most important point, its overall message. These sentences are called the overall *main idea, thesis statement,* or *thesis.* Throughout this book, the chapter reading selections include a Respond in Writing item that will give you practice in determining, and often formulating, the overall main idea sentence of the entire selection.

A WORD ABOUT STANDARDIZED READING TESTS: IMPLIED MAIN IDEAS

Many college students are required to take standardized reading tests as part of an overall assessment program, in a reading course, or as part of a state-mandated basic skills test. A standardized reading test typically consists of a series of passages followed by multiple-choice reading skill application questions, to be completed within a specified time limit. Here is a tip about formulating implied main ideas that should help you score as high as possible on standardized tests:

Remember that test items about implied main ideas may be worded in several different ways. Depending on the test, the question stem may or may not indicate the main idea is implied. Possible wordings of the test question stems include:

The implied main idea is . . .
The author's main point is that . . .
The indirectly stated main idea is . . .
The principal idea of this passage is that . . .
Which of the following best expresses the main idea of the entire passage?
Which of the following best expresses the main idea of this paragraph? (or a specifically identified paragraph)

To answer test items such as these, first determine the topic of the passage. Then ask yourself, "What is the most important point the author wants me to understand about the topic?" If you cannot find a single sentence in the passage that answers this question, formulate a main idea sentence on scratch paper or in the margin next to the passage. Next, examine the answer choices, comparing each choice with your own formulation. Look for a choice that is similar *in meaning* to your own answer, but remember that the wording may be different. If none of the choices is at least somewhat similar to your formulation, you need to reread the passage and make another attempt at formulating the main idea.

CHECKPOINT
Formulating Implied Main Ideas

Directions: To determine the implied main idea, read each paragraph carefully and then ask yourself, "What is the most important point the author wants me to *infer* about the topic of this paragraph?" (Notice that you are told the topic of each paragraph.) Then select the answer choice that expresses the main idea and write the letter in the space provided.

1. This paragraph comes from a health textbook:

> Ink, hot stuff, mud, brew, joe, java, espresso, decaf. Coffee has many nicknames. And it is one of the most widely consumed beverages in the world. An estimated 400 billion cups of coffee are consumed worldwide every year. The coffee trade compares with wheat in global importance. Five million tons are produced annually in fifty countries. South American countries lead production, followed by Africa, Asia, and North and Central America. The larger producers ship most of their crop abroad to countries such as the United States and Europe. The United States consumes one-third of the world's coffee.

> *Source:* Adapted from Wayne Payne, Dale Hahn, and Ellen Mauer, *Understanding Your Health,* 8e, p. 251. Copyright © 2005 by The McGraw-Hill Companies, Inc. Reprinted with permission of The McGraw-Hill Companies, Inc.

The topic of this paragraph is *coffee.*

_____ What is the implied main idea of this paragraph?
- *a.* Coffee has many nicknames.
- *b.* The United States consumes one-third of the world's coffee.
- *c.* Coffee producers ship most of their crop abroad to places such as the United States and Europe.
- *d.* Coffee is one of the most widely consumed beverages in the world.

2. This paragraph comes from an economics textbook:

> **Inflation** is a rise in the general level of prices. When inflation occurs, each dollar of income will buy fewer goods and services than before. Inflation reduces the "purchasing power" of money. Inflation does not mean that *all* prices are rising. Even in periods of rapid inflation, some prices may be relatively constant and others may even fall. For example, although the United States experienced high rates of inflation during the 1970s and early 1980s, the prices of video recorders, digital watches, and personal computers declined.

> *Source:* Adapted from Campbell McConnell, Stanley Brue, and Sean Flynn, *Economics: Principles, Problems, and Policies,* 19e, p. 535. Copyright © 2012 by The McGraw-Hill Companies, Inc. Reprinted with permission of The McGraw-Hill Companies, Inc.

The topic of this paragraph is *inflation.*

_____ What is the implied main idea of this paragraph?

    a. During periods of inflation, prices constantly rise and fall.

    b. During the 1970s and early 1980s, the United States experienced high rates of inflation.

    c. Inflation is a rise in the general level of prices, which decreases the "purchasing power" of money.

    d. Consumers purchase fewer goods and services during periods of inflation.

3. This paragraph comes from a human development textbook:

> The institution of the family is universal. But the concept of the "traditional" family, that is, a husband, a wife, and their biological children, is not. In many African, Asian, and Latin American cultures the extended-family household is the traditional form. In western industrialized countries, family size, composition, structure, and division of labor have changed dramatically. Most mothers now work for pay, in or outside the home, and a small but growing number of fathers are primary caregivers. More single women and cohabiting couples are having or adopting children and raising them. Millions of children live with gay or lesbian parents or with stepparents.

Source: Adapted from Diane Papalia, Sally Wendkos Olds, and Ruth Duskin Feldman, *Human Development,* 9e, p. 512. Copyright © 2004 by The McGraw-Hill Companies, Inc. Reprinted with permission of The McGraw-Hill Companies, Inc.

The topic of this paragraph is *the concept of the "traditional" family.*

_____ What is the implied main idea of this paragraph?

    a. "Traditional" families consist of a husband, a wife, and their biological children.

    b. The concept of the "traditional" family, consisting of a husband, a wife, and their biological children, is not universal.

    c. In western industrialized countries, family size, composition, structure, and division of labor have changed dramatically.

    d. The concept of the family is universal.

4. This paragraph comes from a U.S. history textbook:

> For many decades, scholars believed that all early migrations into the Americas came from humans crossing an ancient land bridge over the Bering Strait into what is now Alaska, approximately 11,000 years ago. More recent archeological evidence, however, suggests that not all the early migrants came across the Bering Strait. Some migrants appear to have settled as far south as Chile and Peru

even before people began moving into North America by land. This suggests that these first South Americans may have come not by land but by sea, using boats. Other discoveries on other continents have made clear that migrants had traveled by water much earlier to populate Japan, Australia, and other areas of the Pacific. Those discoveries suggest that migrants were capable of making long ocean voyages—long enough perhaps to bring them to the American coasts.

Source: Adapted from Alan Brinkley, *American History: Connecting with the Past,* 14e, p. 3. Copyright © 2012 by The McGraw-Hill Companies, Inc. Reprinted with permission of The McGraw-Hill Companies, Inc.

The topic of this paragraph is *early migrations of humans to the Americas.*

What is the implied main idea of this paragraph?

_____
- *a.* Scholars once believed that all early migrations into the Americas came from humans crossing an ancient land bridge over the Bering Strait, but recent evidence suggests that early migrants may also have traveled to other continents by sea, using boats.
- *b.* Discoveries on other continents have made it clear that migrants traveled by water much earlier to populate Japan, Australia, and other areas of the Pacific.
- *c.* Scholars now believe that migrants settled as far south as Chile and Peru even before people began moving into North America by land.
- *d.* For many decades, scholars believed that all early migrations into the Americas came from humans crossing an ancient land bridge over the Bering Strait into what is now Alaska.

5. This paragraph comes from a health textbook:

Since 1995, more than 30 major population-based studies (involving 175,000 Americans) have been published on the association between physical activity and mental health. The overall conclusion is that exercise can help combat a variety of mental health problems. Even modest activity such as taking a daily walk can help reduce mental health problems. For example, studies found that regular physical activity protects against depression and the onset of major depressive disorder. It can also reduce symptoms of depression in otherwise healthy people. Other studies found that physical activity protects against anxiety and the onset of anxiety disorders (such as specific phobias, social phobia, generalized anxiety, and panic disorder). It also helps reduce symptoms in people affected with anxiety disorder. Physical activity can enhance feelings of well-being in some people, which may provide some protection against psychological distress. Physically active people are about 25–30% less likely to feel distressed than inactive people. Regardless of the age or health status of the people being studied, those who were active managed stress better than their inactive counterparts.

Source: Adapted from Paul Insel and Walton Roth, *Connect Core Concepts in Health,* 12e, p. 83. Copyright © 2012 by The McGraw-Hill Companies, Inc. Reprinted with permission of The McGraw-Hill Companies, Inc.

The topic of this paragraph is *physical activity (exercise)* and *mental health.*

_____   What is the implied main idea of this paragraph?

    a.   Studies found that regular physical activity protects against depression and can also reduce symptoms of depression in otherwise healthy people.

    b.   A large number of population-based studies support the overall conclusion that exercise—even modest activity—can help combat a variety of mental health problems.

    c.   Regardless of the age or health status of the people being studied, those who were active managed stress better than their inactive counterparts.

    d.   There is a strong connection between physical activity, such as walking, and mental health.

DEVELOPING CHAPTER REVIEW CARDS

Complete the five review cards for Chapter 5 by answering the questions or following the directions on each card. When you have completed them, you will have summarized important information about implied main ideas: (1) what they are and why they are important, (2) what steps and (3) what formulas to follow in formulating them, (4) how to check to see if your formulations are correct, and (5) how to formulate main ideas in longer passages. Print or write legibly.

Implied Main Ideas

1. What is an implied main idea? (See page 275.) *A Comple*

2. Why is formulating implied main ideas important? (See page 275.)

3. What question should you ask yourself in order to formulate the implied main idea of a paragraph? (See page 275.)

Card 1 Chapter 5: Formulating Implied Main Ideas

Steps to Follow in Formulating an Implied Main Idea Sentence

What are the three general steps to follow in formulating an implied main idea sentence? (See pages 275–76.)

Step 1:

Step 2:

Step 3:

Card 2   Chapter 5: Formulating Implied Main Ideas

Formulas for Creating Implied Main Idea Sentences

Write the three formulas for creating implied main idea sentences, and draw the formula boxes. (See pages 275–80.)

Formula 1:

Formula 2:

Formula 3:

Card 3   Chapter 5: Formulating Implied Main Ideas

Requirements for Correctly Formulated Main Idea Sentences

What are three requirements for a correctly formulated main idea sentence? (See page 283.)

Requirement 1:

Requirement 2:

Requirement 3:

Card 4   Chapter 5: Formulating Implied Main Ideas

Implied Overall Main Ideas in Longer Passages

1.   Give examples of types of longer reading passages that might have implied main ideas. (See page 284.)

2.   Why would a reader need to formulate the main idea of an entire passage? (See page 284.)

Card 5   Chapter 5: Formulating Implied Main Ideas

Directions: Read these paragraphs carefully and answer the questions that follow them. Write your answers in the spaces provided.

This paragraph comes from a health textbook:

For decades, people smoked whenever and wherever they wished. Smoking was glamorized in the movies, on television, and in print throughout most of the twentieth century. Famous athletes and movie stars were found in cigarette advertisements. Some ads even promoted the "health benefits" of smoking. Although a few people felt that smoking was dangerous, their voices had little effect on society's acceptance of tobacco use. Gradually, these attitudes began to change. As data from medical studies began to accumulate on the dangers of tobacco, antismoking advocates started to achieve some victories in society and in public policy.

Source: Adapted from Wayne A. Payne, Dale B. Hahn, and Ellen B. Mauer, *Understanding Your Health,* 8e, p. 327. Copyright © 2005 by The McGraw-Hill Companies, Inc. Reprinted with permission of The McGraw-Hill Companies, Inc.

1. What is the topic of this paragraph?
   a. the effects of smoking tobacco
   b. dangers of tobacco
   c. the glamorization of smoking in movies, on television, and in advertisements
   d. attitudes related to smoking

2. What is the implied main idea of this paragraph?
   a. Unfortunately, people have smoked whenever and wherever they wished.
   b. Although smoking was widely accepted in the past, there has been a gradual change in society's attitudes related to smoking.
   c. Data from medical studies clearly show the dangers of smoking.
   d. Although some people have always known that smoking was dangerous, their voices had little effect on society's acceptance of tobacco use.

This paragraph comes from a psychology textbook:

How to appropriately and effectively teach the increasing number of children who do not speak English is not always clear. Many educators maintain that *bilingual education* is best. With a bilingual approach, students learn some subjects in their native language while simultaneously learning English. Proponents of bilingualism believe that students must develop a sound footing in basic subject areas and that, initially at least, teaching those subjects in their native language is the only way to provide them with that foundation. In contrast, other educators insist that all instruction ought to be in English from the moment students, including those who speak no English at all, enroll in school. In

293

immersion programs, students are immediately plunged into English instruction in all subjects. The reasoning is that teaching students in a language other than English simply hinders nonnative English speakers' integration into society and ultimately does them a disservice.

Source: Adapted from Robert S. Feldman, *Essentials of Understanding Psychology,* 9e, pp. 255–56. Copyright © 2011 by The McGraw-Hill Companies, Inc. Reprinted with permission of The McGraw-Hill Companies, Inc.

_____ **3.** What is the topic of this paragraph?
  a. bilingual education
  b. teaching English using the immersion method
  c. teaching students in a language other than their own
  d. teaching children who do not speak English

_____ **4.** What is the implied main idea of this paragraph?
  a. Educating children who speak no English at all is a challenging task.
  b. There are various ways to teach children.
  c. Children learn best if they are taught certain subjects in their native language.
  d. Educators disagree about the best method for teaching children who do not speak English.

This paragraph comes from a U.S. history textbook:

The events of September 11, 2001, changed the United States profoundly. Not since the surprise attack by the Japanese on Pearl Harbor in 1941 had the nation experienced such a devastating attack on its homeland. Most directly the tragedy claimed approximately 3,000 lives. More than 20,000 residents living in lower Manhattan had to evacuate their homes. Officials estimated the cost to the New York City economy at over $83 billion.

Source: Adapted from James Davidson et al., *Nation of Nations: A Narrative History of the American Republic, Volume II: Since 1865,* 6e, p. 976. Copyright © 2008 by The McGraw-Hill Companies, Inc. Reprinted with permission of The McGraw-Hill Companies, Inc.

_____ **5.** What is the topic of this paragraph?
  a. the events of September 11, 2001
  b. the World Trade Center
  c. the New York City economy
  d. the effects of terrorism

_____ **6.** What is the implied main idea of this paragraph?
  a. More than 3,000 people lost their lives in the September 11, 2001, attack on the World Trade Center.
  b. The events of September 11, 2001, changed the United States profoundly because the nation had not experienced such a devastating attack on its homeland since the attack on Pearl Harbor in 1941.

c. The attack on the World Trade Center had a devastating effect on the New York City economy, estimated to be over $83 billion dollars.

d. More than 20,000 New York residents had to evacuate their homes.

This paragraph comes from a health textbook:

> How do you imagine your life in the future? Do you ever think about how your health allows you to participate in meaningful life activities—and what might happen if your health is compromised? Consider, for example, the numerous ways that your health affects your daily activities. Your health affects your ability to pursue an education or a career. It affects your opportunities to socialize with friends and family and the chance to travel—for business, relaxation, or adventure. Your health also affects your opportunity to meet and connect with new people and participation in hobbies and recreational activities. The opportunity to live independently and the ability to conceive or the opportunity to parent children is also affected by your health. Even your ability to enjoy a wide range of foods depends on your health.
>
> *Source:* Adapted from Wayne A. Payne, Dale B. Hahn, and Ellen B. Lucas, *Understanding Your Health,* 10e, pp. 1–2. Copyright © 2009 by The McGraw-Hill Companies, Inc. Reprinted with permission of The McGraw-Hill Companies, Inc.

7. What is the topic of this paragraph?
   a. planning for your future
   b. what might happen if your health is compromised
   c. maintaining a healthy lifestyle
   d. the importance of participating in meaningful life activities

8. What is the implied main idea of this paragraph?
   a. Maintaining a healthy lifestyle is important.
   b. Your health affects your ability to pursue an education or a career, and it affects your opportunities to socialize with friends and family.
   c. If your health is compromised, it might prevent you from participating in meaningful life activities.
   d. If you maintain your health, you will retain the opportunity to live independently and the ability to conceive and parent children.

This paragraph comes from a biology textbook:

> **Body Systems**
>
> The digestive system provides nutrients, and the excretory system rids the body of metabolic wastes. The respiratory system supplies oxygen but also eliminates carbon dioxide. The circulatory system carries nutrients and oxygen to and wastes from the cell so that tissue fluid composition remains constant. The immune system helps protect the body from disease. The nervous system directs

body movements, allowing the organism to manipulate the external environment, an important, life-sustaining function.

Source: Adapted from Sylvia Mader, *Inquiry into Life,* 4e, p. 3. Copyright © 1985 by The McGraw-Hill Companies, Inc. Reprinted with permission of The McGraw-Hill Companies, Inc.

9. What is the topic of this paragraph?
   a. the body's digestive and excretory systems
   b. life-sustaining activities
   c. systems of the body
   d. coping with the external environment

10. What is the implied main idea of this paragraph?
    a. The digestive system provides nutrients, and the excretory system rids the body of metabolic wastes.
    b. There are many different systems in the body.
    c. Each system of the body has specialized functions.
    d. The body systems allow the organism to manipulate the external environment.

Directions: Read these paragraphs carefully and then write the topic and a formulated main idea sentence for each paragraph in the spaces provided.

This paragraph comes from a health textbook:

Need a way to beat your stress? Look no further than your own back yard, local park, or nearby hiking trail. Mounting evidence shows that people who get outdoors—or just get to look out a window once in a while—experience an almost instant, if short-term, reduction in stress. Scientists are investigating "natural stress reduction" as an easy and inexpensive booster to cognitive and behavioral approaches to stress management. High-tech replications of nature won't do, though—it has to be the real thing. In a 2008 study at the University of Washington, participants were set up in two similar office environments with one difference. Some of the offices were equipped with plasma TV screens that displayed videos of a relaxing outdoor setting. The other offices were equipped with windows overlooking an actual outdoor setting. The volunteers were asked to perform a series of stress-inducing work tasks, and then their heart rates were measured. The volunteers with window views recovered from their stress significantly more quickly than the volunteers who viewed a natural scene on TV. The study supported the idea that exposure to nature can reduce stress. It also demonstrated that facsimiles of nature have little or no effect on stress.

Source: Adapted from Paul Insel and Walton Roth, *Connect Core Concepts in Health,* 12e, p. 56. Copyright © 2012 by The McGraw-Hill Companies, Inc. Reprinted with permission of The McGraw-Hill Companies, Inc.

1. Write a word, name, or phrase that tells the topic:

_____

2. Formulate a main idea sentence and write it here:

_____

_____

_____

This paragraph comes from a student success textbook:

Do you assume that tests have the power to define you as a person? If so, and you do badly on a test, you may be tempted to believe that you've received some fundamental information about yourself from your instructor, information that says you're a failure in some significant way. This is a dangerous—and wrongheaded—assumption. If you do badly on a test, it doesn't mean you're a bad person. Or stupid. Or that you don't belong in college. If you don't do well on a test, you're the same person you were before you took the test—no better, no worse. You just did badly on the test. Tests are tools. They are indirect and imperfect measures of what we know. Someone with a great deal of knowledge can do poorly on a test. Another person may know considerably less and still do better on the test simply because he or she may have learned some test-taking skills along the way. In short, tests are not a measure of your value as an individual. They are only a measure of how well you studied, how much you studied, and your test-taking skills.

Source: Adapted from Robert S. Feldman, *P.O.W.E.R. Learning and Your Life: Essentials of Student Success,* pp. 77–78. Copyright © 2011 by The McGraw-Hill Companies, Inc. Reprinted with permission of The McGraw-Hill Companies, Inc.

3. Write a word, name, or phrase that tells the topic:

_____

4. Formulate a main idea sentence and write it here:

_____

_____

_____

_____

This paragraph comes from a physical fitness and wellness textbook:

Human biology, or **heredity,** is a factor over which we have little control. Experts estimate that heredity accounts for 16 percent of all health problems, including early death. Heredity influences each of the parts of health-related physical fitness, including our tendencies to build muscle and to deposit body fat. Each of us reaps different benefits from the same healthy lifestyles, based on our hereditary tendencies. Even more important is that predispositions to diseases are inherited. For example, some early deaths are a result of untreatable hereditary conditions (e.g., congenital heart defects). Obviously, some inherited conditions like diabetes are manageable with proper medical supervision and appropriate lifestyles. Each of us can limit the effects of heredity by being aware of our personal family history. We can also make efforts to manage those factors over which we do have control.

Source: Adapted from Charles Corbin, Gregory Welk, William Corbin, and Karen Welk, *Concepts of Physical Fitness: Active Lifestyles for Wellness,* 15e, p. 9. Copyright © 2009 by The McGraw-Hill Companies, Inc. Reprinted with permission of The McGraw-Hill Companies, Inc.

5. Write a word, name, or phrase that tells the topic:

_____

6. Formulate a main idea sentence and write it here:

_____

_____

_____

_____

This paragraph comes from a health textbook:

What Causes Type 2 Diabetes?

Three major factors involved in the development of Type 2 diabetes are age, obesity, and a family history of diabetes. Physical inactivity and lifestyle are also major factors in the development of the disease. Excess body fat reduces cell sensitivity to insulin, and it is a major risk factor for Type 2 diabetes. Ethnic background also plays a major role. Thirteen percent of African Americans have diabetes, and African Americans and people of Hispanic background are 55 percent more likely than non-Hispanic whites to develop Type 2 diabetes. Over 20 percent of Hispanics over age 65 have diabetes. Native Americans also have a higher than average incidence of diabetes. American Indians and Alaska Natives are more than twice as likely to have diabetes as non-Hispanic whites.

Source: Adapted from Paul Insel and Walton Roth, *Core Concepts in Health,* 9e, p. 241. Copyright © 2002 by The McGraw-Hill Companies, Inc. Reprinted with permission of The McGraw-Hill Companies, Inc.

7. Write a word, name, or phrase that tells the topic:

_____

8. Formulate a main idea sentence and write it here:

_____

_____

This paragraph comes from a wellness textbook:

Although most marriages are based on romantic love, few couples sustain that romance as the years go by. Romantic love often develops into a less intense, less all-consuming type of love known as companionate love. A companionate love relationship is steadier than romantic love and is based on trust, sharing, affection, and togetherness. Maintaining the love in a marriage requires considerable effort and commitment. Married partners who succeed in communicating, giving physical warmth, and sharing interests and responsibilities are more likely to develop and sustain companionate love.

Source: Adapted from Marvin Levy, Mark Dignan, and Janet Shirreffs, *Targeting Wellness: The Core,* p. 123. Copyright © 1992 by The McGraw-Hill Companies, Inc. Reprinted with permission of The McGraw-Hill Companies, Inc.

9. Write a word, name, or phrase that tells the topic:

_____

10. Formulate a main idea sentence and write it here:

_____

_____

_____

_____

_____

SELECTION **5.1**

Personal Finance

SELECTION 5.1

Identity Theft: You Are at Risk
Information Synthesized from Internet Sources
by Janet Elder

Prepare Yourself to Read

Directions: Do these exercises *before* you read Selection 5.1.

1. First, read and think about the title. What do you already know about identity theft?

   _____

   _____

   _____

2. Next, complete your preview by reading the following:

   Introduction (in *italics*)

   Headings

   The first two paragraphs (paragraphs 1 and 2)

   First sentence of each of the other paragraphs

   Now that you have previewed the selection, tell what identity theft is, and write one or two ways you could reduce your risk of becoming an identity theft victim.

   _____

   _____

   _____

   _____

3. **Build your vocabulary as you read.** If you discover an unfamiliar word or key term as you read the selection, try to determine its meaning by using context clues.

Internet Resources

Read More about This Topic Online

Use a search engine, such as Google or Yahoo!, to expand your existing knowledge about this topic *before* you read the selection or to learn more about it *afterward*. If you are unfamiliar with conducting Internet searches, read pages 25–26 on Boolean searches. You can also use Wikipedia, the free online encyclopedia, at www .wikipedia.com. Keep in mind that when you visit any website, it is a good idea to evaluate the site and the information it contains. Ask yourself questions such as "Who sponsors this website?" and "Is the information it contains up to date?"

SELECTION 5.1: IDENTITY THEFT: YOU ARE AT RISK

Chances are that if you yourself have not been a victim of identity theft, you know someone who has, and you know the devastating effects this crime can have. College students, in particular, can be easy targets for identity thieves.

For more than a decade, identity theft has been consumers' most frequent complaint to the U.S. Federal Trade Commission. In 2010, the FTC received 250,854 identity theft complaints, or in other words, about 20 percent of all the complaints it received. Florida logged the most complaints, followed closely by Arizona and California.

Today, companies and government agencies are collecting more and more personal data from citizens and consumers. Despite precautions, databases are sometimes breached. The result is that globally, identity theft is a growing problem.

Two-thirds of identity theft victims do not know the source of the crime, and although not every identity theft can be prevented, consumers can take obvious precautions. The following selection explains the crime, the techniques these thieves use, and some ways to reduce your risk of becoming an identity theft victim.

The Crime of Identity Theft

1   Don't think it can't happen to you. Your credit card bill arrives with charges for items you never purchased. You pay your bills on time and always have. Suddenly, though, creditors start hounding you for payment of past-due bills, but you never ordered any of the goods or services they're demanding payment for. The grocery store and drugstore where you've always shopped are now refusing to accept your checks because of your bad credit history. Perhaps you even receive a summons to show up in court for a traffic ticket you never paid—and, in fact, which you never received. Guess what: You're now among the hundreds of thousands of people each year who become victims of identity theft.

2   In this fast-growing crime, perpetrators steal or gather data on individuals. The data that these criminals steal include Social Security numbers, driver's license numbers, dates of birth, bank account numbers, and credit card numbers, as well as credit cards and ATM cards. They use several methods of acquiring these. Once they have enough information, the thieves impersonate the victim. They spend as much money as possible as quickly as possible, charging the purchases to the victim. Then they do the same thing all over again, using someone else's identity and credit.

Forms of Identity Theft

3   There are two forms of this theft. The first type is "account takeover" theft, in which the thief uses existing credit information to make purchases. The criminal may use an actual credit card or

---

Annotation Practice Exercises

Directions: For each exercise below:

- Write the topic of the paragraph on the lines provided.

- Formulate the implied main idea of the paragraph and write it on the lines provided.

This will help you remember the topic and the main idea. Remember that you cannot use any sentence exactly as it appears in the paragraph.

Practice Exercise

- Topic of paragraph 2:

_____

_____

- Formulate the implied main idea of paragraph 2:

_____

_____

_____

_____

_____

_____

may simply charge purchases by phone or online using the credit card number and expiration date. The victim discovers the "theft" when the monthly account statement arrives. The second type of identity theft is "application fraud" (or "true name fraud"). Using the victim's information, the thief opens new accounts in the victim's name. The thief has the monthly statements sent to a different address, so considerable time may elapse before the victim realizes what has happened.

4   If there is any good news, it is this: in general, credit and banking fraud victims are liable for no more than the first $50 of loss. Many times, the victim will not have to pay for any of the loss.

5   The bad news is that victims are left with a time-consuming, frustrating mess to clear up. Because their credit has been wrecked, they may be denied credit and loans. They may have difficulty leasing an apartment, or even getting a job. Unfortunately, victims get little help from authorities as they try to untangle the problem.

Thieves' Information Sources

6   How do thieves obtain the information that enables them to "steal" someone else's identity? The easiest way is by stealing the person's wallet. For thieves, it's like one-stop shopping, since wallets usually contain credit cards, a driver's license, and other pieces of information, such as the person's Social Security number.

7   There are many other techniques thieves use. These include:

- Stealing documents from unlocked mailboxes and breaking into locked ones. Thieves look especially for boxes of checks, new credit cards, bank statements, tax documents, insurance statements, and credit card statements.

- Searching through trash receptacles ("dumpster diving") for unshredded documents with identifying Social Security numbers, unused pre-approved credit card applications, loan applications, and so forth.

- Using personnel files or customer files in the workplace to improperly access names, Social Security numbers, and other data.

- Obtaining people's credit reports fraudulently by impersonating an employer, a landlord, or a loan officer at a financial institution.

- "Shoulder surfing" at phone booths and ATMs to obtain people's PIN numbers (personal identification numbers).

- Going to Internet sites that provide identifying information and public records.

Practice Exercise
• Topic of paragraph 3:
_____
_____
• Formulate the implied main idea of paragraph 3:
_____
_____
_____
_____
_____
_____

Practice Exercise
• Topic of paragraph 6:
_____
_____
_____
_____
_____
• Formulate the implied main idea of paragraph 6:
_____
_____
_____
_____
_____

How to Reduce the Risk of Identity Theft

Check Your Credit Report

8   The single best protection is to check your credit report at least once a year. If a thief has stolen your identity, you will become aware of it much sooner. You should order credit reports from the three credit reporting agencies: Equifax (800) 525-6285 or www.equifax.com, Experian (888) 397-3742 or www.experian.com, and TransUnion (800) 680-7289 or www.transunion.com. There is a charge for each report.

Minimize Access to Your Personal Information

9   No one would carelessly leave money lying around in plain sight. It would be an open invitation to anyone who wanted to steal it. Unfortunately, most people are not as careful about their personal information, although they should be. You should protect your personal information with as much diligence as you protect your money.

10   In your wallet, carry only what you need. Carry only one or two credit cards and leave the rest at home. You should also cancel credit cards that you rarely use. Memorize your Social Security number. Leave the card at home unless you must have it with you for a specific reason. Do not carry any card in your wallet that has your Social Security number (SSN) on it.

11   Know where your wallet or purse is at all times. Keep it in a safe place at work or, if you are a student, at school. In restaurants, airports, and other public places, such as school campuses, be careful about not leaving a wallet in an unattended book bag or purse. When you are eating, visiting, or waiting for someone, don't hang your book bag or purse on the back of the chair or stow it beneath your chair.

12   If mail is delivered to your home, install a lockable mailbox. Better yet, rent a box at a post office or commercial mailbox service and have your mail sent there. Use the post office box number rather than your home address printed on your checks. If you do not have a lockable home mailbox or rent a box, have checks you order mailed to your bank, and then pick them up there.

13   For maximum safety when you mail envelopes with checks in them, use the drop boxes inside the post office. Do not leave them in your mailbox for the mail carrier to pick up. Nor should you leave them in open "outgoing mail" baskets at work.

14   Remove your name from marketing lists. To minimize nationwide marketers having your name and address, sign up for the Direct Marketing Association's Mail Preference Service (P.O. Box 643, Carmel, NY 10512 or www.dmaconsumers.org/offmailinglist.html) and Telephone Preference Service (P.O. Box 155, Carmel, NY 10512). If your state has a "do not call" list, sign up for it as well. Use an unlisted phone number.

Practice Exercise

- Topic of paragraph 8:

  _____

  _____

- Formulate the implied main idea of paragraph 8:

  _____

  _____

  _____

  _____

  _____

  _____

  _____

Protect Credit Cards, Passwords, PINs, and Receipts

15   You should know how to contact companies in the event your wallet and credit cards are stolen. Record the account numbers, expiration dates, and telephone contact information or photocopy the front and backsides of your credit cards. Store this information in a safe place. You need to be prepared to act quickly if your credit cards are ever stolen.

16   Unless you initiated contact, do not give out personal information over the phone, by mail, or over the Internet. Do not submit personal information to websites. Do not do business with companies online unless they provide transaction security protection. Beware, too, of phone scams in which the caller announces you have won a free trip or some other prize, and that all they need in order to verify that you are the winner is for you to give your Social Security number and a credit card number and its expiration date.

17   When you are given a credit card receipt, be sure to take it with you. If you are in a store, put the receipt in your wallet and not in the sack. Don't throw credit card receipts in the trash without first tearing them up or shredding them.

18   Shred pay stubs or file them in a safe place. They can reveal a great deal of personal data.

19   Identity thieves know that many people use their birthdate, mother's maiden name, or the last four digits of their Social Security number as PIN numbers. Thieves can easily obtain this information, so don't use any of it. You should also avoid using your middle name, consecutive numbers, or other easy-to-remember sequences since these are also obvious choices. Instead, choose a combination of numbers and letters, and preferably at least six in total. For computer passwords, use a combination of 6–8 numbers and uppercase and lowercase letters.

20   It goes without saying that carrying your passwords and PIN numbers in your wallet is asking for trouble. Memorize them. Don't reveal them to others.

21   "Shoulder surfers" may stand nearby ATMs and pay telephones. They may even use binoculars or a video camera. For this reason, you should shield your hand when you punch in PIN numbers at ATMs or calling card numbers at payphones.

Handle Information Responsibly

22   Social Security numbers are the key to credit and bank accounts. Consequently, they are prime targets of identity thieves. Guard yours carefully, and release it only when absolutely necessary.

23   Look through monthly statements that you receive for credit card transactions, phone usage, and bank transactions. File them, along with canceled checks (if your bank returns them), in a safe place.

24   Cut up old or unused credit cards and dispose of unwanted pre-approved credit card applications. College students in particular often receive numerous credit card offers, including pre-approved ones. Unwanted ones should be destroyed by tearing them into pieces or shredding them. (Office supply stores sell shredders at an affordable price. Cross-cut shredders are the best choice.) Many college students activate several or all of the pre-approved applications. Because they have so many cards, they not only get in over their heads in debt, they often do not realize it when a card is missing. With an actual card, an identity thief can do considerable damage in a short amount of time.

25   Although these measures require time and effort, they are much simpler than the time and effort required to try to undo the damage caused by identity theft. It takes years to build good credit. It can take even longer to restore it after it has been wrecked by an identity thief.

Further Information

26   If you would like more information about identity theft or privacy protection, there are several websites you can consult. The Privacy Rights Clearinghouse is a nonprofit consumer advocacy organization. At its website, www.privacyrights.org, you can take an "Identity Theft IQ Test" to see how at risk you are of becoming a victim of identity theft. The www.calpirg.org website, another nonprofit consumer advocacy website, also provides a wealth of information and links. In addition, the Identity Theft Resource Center, www.idtheftcenter.org, offers many resource guides for victims. The Federal Trade Commission (FTC) sponsors a tollfree Identity Theft Hotline (1-877-IDTHEFT; 438-4338), or you can visit the ID Theft website at www.consumer.gov/idtheft.

Source: Based on information from CALPIRG [California Public Interest Research Group] (Los Angeles, CA) and the Privacy Rights Clearinghouse (San Diego, CA).

Reading Selection Quiz

The quiz has several parts. Your instructor may assign some or all of them.

Comprehension

Directions: Use the information in the selection to answer each item below. You may refer to the selection as you answer the questions. Write each answer in the space provided.

_____ 1. One sign that you may have become the victim of identity theft is:
- *a.*   your monthly credit card statement arrives a few days later than usual.
- *b.*   a grocery store asks for your identification when you write a check.
- *c.*   you receive a traffic ticket.
- *d.*   creditors begin demanding payment for purchases you have not made.

_____ 2. It takes longer to detect application fraud theft because the thief:
- *a.*   opens a new account in the victim's name but has the bills sent to a different address.
- *b.*   keeps changing the name on the victim's credit card account.
- *c.*   makes purchases only by phone or online.
- *d.*   uses existing credit information to make purchases.

_____ 3. Until identity theft victims are able to resolve the problem, they may:
- *a.*   find it difficult to lease an apartment.
- *b.*   not be able to obtain credit or get a loan.
- *c.*   have difficulty getting a job.
- *d.*   all of the above

_____ 4. Stealing a wallet is the easiest way for identity thieves to obtain the information they need in order to steal someone else's identity because:
- *a.*   so many people are careless with their wallets.
- *b.*   it is easy to pickpocket a wallet.
- *c.*   people usually carry so much personal information in their wallets.
- *d.*   wallets are small, easy to conceal, and easy for thieves to dispose of.

_____ 5. Which of the following is the least safe place to have mail sent?
- *a.*   a regular home mailbox
- *b.*   a lockable home mailbox
- *c.*   a post office box
- *d.*   a box at a commercial mailbox service

_____ 6. An example of a safer choice for a computer password would be:
- *a.*   numbers that represent a person's birthdate.
- *b.*   a set of six sequential numbers.

     c.   a six-digit number and lowercase and uppercase letter combination.

     d.   the year a person was born.

7. Credit card receipts should be:

     a.   left on the counter.

     b.   carried in your wallet rather than in the sack.

     c.   thrown in the trash.

     d.   given to the salesclerk to throw away.

8. The one most effective way to protect yourself against identity theft is to:

     a.   shred monthly account statements and canceled checks.

     b.   check your three credit reports at least once a year.

     c.   remove your name from marketing lists.

     d.   photocopy the fronts and backs of all of your credit cards, and keep the copy in a safe place.

9. Identity thieves are especially interested in obtaining other people's Social Security numbers because SSNs are:

     a.   the key to credit and bank accounts.

     b.   prime targets.

     c.   easy to steal.

     d.   difficult to trace.

10. One phone scam identity thieves use is to:

     a.   pretend they are bank officers calling to verify account information.

     b.   call the victim's house to see if anyone is home, and if not, to rob the house.

     c.   pose as a representative of a credit card company and tell people they must select new PIN numbers.

     d.   tell people they have won a prize, but must reveal personal data to confirm that they are the winner.

S E L E C T I O N **5.1**

Personal Finance

(continued)

Vocabulary in Context

Directions: For each item below, use context clues to deduce the meaning of the *italicized* word. Be sure the answer you choose makes sense in both sentences. Write each answer in the space provided.

11. Suddenly, though, creditors start *hounding* you for payment of past-due bills, but you never ordered any of the goods or services they're demanding payment for.

Mrs. Ditherwater finally stopped taking her six-year-old twins with her to the grocery store because they were always *hounding* her to buy them cookies, candy, and toys.

hounding (haund′ ĭng) means:

a. begging desperately

b. asking politely

c. harassing persistently

d. pouting childishly

_____ **12.** Perhaps you even receive a *summons* to show up in court for a traffic ticket you never paid—and, in fact, which you never received.

If a person ignores a *summons,* he or she can be arrested for failure to appear in court.

summons (sŭm′ənz) means:

a. citation to appear in court

b. jury verdict of guilty

c. unresolved legal dispute

d. judge's final ruling

_____ **13.** The second type of identity theft is "application *fraud*" (or "true name *fraud*").

The company was convicted of *fraud* for reporting that its previous year's earnings were several millions of dollars higher than they actually were.

fraud (frôd) means:

a. lying in order to get out of an uncomfortable, embarrassing situation

b. misrepresenting the truth in order to trick someone into giving up something of value

c. pretending to be superior when that is not actually the case

d. refusing to cooperate with authorities

_____ **14.** The thief has the monthly statements sent to a different address, so considerable time may *elapse* before the victim realizes what has happened.

The more time that is allowed to *elapse* before a child is reported missing, the less likely it is that the child can be found and safely returned home.

elapse (ĭ lăps′) means:

a. hurry by

b. pass or go by

c. stay the same

d. evaporate instantly

_____ **15.** If there is any good news, it is this: in general, credit and banking fraud victims are *liable* for no more than the first $50 of loss.

Since the movers dented my refrigerator, their company was *liable* for the damage and paid to have it repaired.

liable (lī′ ə bəl) means:

a. punished

b. excused or exempted from

c. fined

d. obligated by law

_____ **16.** One technique identity thieves use is obtaining people's credit reports fraudulently by *impersonating* an employer, a landlord, or a loan officer at a financial institution.

The imposter, who was dressed in an official uniform and directing traffic at a busy intersection, was arrested for *impersonating* a police officer.

impersonating (ĭm pûr′ sə nāt ĭng) means:

a. pretending to be a relative of someone

b. using a false name

c. pretending to be someone you are not

d. acting as if you know a person when you do not know them

_____ **17.** When you are eating, visiting, or waiting for someone, don't hang your book bag or purse on the back of your chair or *stow* it beneath your chair.

For safety, airline passengers are required to *stow* carry-on luggage beneath the seat or in the overhead storage compartment.

stow (stō) means:

a. to place carelessly

b. to lock up for safekeeping

c. to put someplace until future use

d. to dispose of in an orderly fashion

_____ **18.** Better yet, rent a box at a post office or *commercial* mailbox service and have your mail sent there.

Professional truck drivers, bus drivers, and limousine drivers are required to have *commercial* driver's licenses for their work.

commercial (kə mər′ shəl) means:

a. pertaining to advertisements

b. pertaining to transportation

c. pertaining to mail delivery

d. pertaining to business

_____ **19.** Remove your name from *marketing* lists.

The dealership held a training session to familiarize its sales force with *marketing* material for its new models of cars.

marketing (mär′ kĭt ĭng) means:

a. related to the purchasing of new and used items

b. related to promoting, selling, and distributing a product or service *c.*   related to telephone sales

    d.   related to employee training and development

20. Beware, too, of phone *scams* in which the caller announces you have won a free trip or some other prize, and that all they need in order to verify that you are the winner is for you to give your Social Security number and a credit card number and its expiration date.

Elderly people are often the victim of insurance *scams* and other deceptions designed to trick them out of their money.

scams (skămz) means:

    a.   fraudulent operations intended to cheat others

    b.   cruel practical jokes

    c.   false, nonexistent charities created to seek donations

    d.   a hoax designed to fool older people

S E L E C T I O N **5.1**

Personal Finance

(continued)

Reading Skills Application

Directions: These items test your ability to *apply* certain reading skills. You may not have studied all of the skills yet, so some items will serve as a preview. Write each answer in the space provided.

21. The author's purpose for including the section "How to Reduce the Risk of Identity Theft" is to:

    a.   persuade readers not to become victims of identity theft.

    b.   inform readers about identity theft scams.

    c.   instruct readers how to lessen their likelihood of becoming identity theft victims.

    d.   convince identity thieves to stop ruining other people's lives.

22. Based on the information in the selection, it can be logically concluded that:

    a.   avoiding identity theft requires ongoing diligence and effort.

    b.   it is simple to avoid identity theft.

    c.   the main problem identity theft victims face is paying off unfair credit charges.

    d.   some identity theft victims can clear up the problem very quickly.

23. The author uses the term "dumpster diving" to refer to:

    a.   thieves' technique of searching through trash receptacles for documents that might enable them to steal someone else's identity.

    b.   the process of placing documents with personal information at the bottom of dumpsters so that they are less likely to be found by thieves.

    c.   shredding all personal information documents and putting them in dumpsters.

    d.   companies' getting rid of outdated customer files by placing them in dumpsters.

_____ **24.** Which of the following statements represents an opinion rather than a fact?

  a. Many times, the victim will not have to pay for any of the loss.

  b. The bad news is that victims are left with a time-consuming, frustrating mess to clear up.

  c. Because their credit has been wrecked, they may be denied credit and loans.

  d. They may have difficulty leasing an apartment, or even getting a job.

_____ **25.** The author would most likely agree with which of the following statements?

  a. Authorities should do more to help identity theft victims resolve the complicated problems they face.

  b. The Social Security system should be done away with since SSNs give identity thieves access to too much information.

  c. The crime of identity theft is likely to decrease in coming years.

  d. There is really nothing anyone can do to avoid identity theft.

SELECTION **5.1**

Personal Finance
(continued)

Respond in Writing

Directions: Refer to the selection as needed to answer the essay-type questions below. (Your instructor may direct you to work collaboratively with other students on one or more items. Each group member should be able to explain *all* of the group's answers.)

1. List at least four things you could do or change right away that would lessen your risk of becoming an identity theft victim.

_____

_____

_____

_____

_____

_____

2. If you were to become the victim of identity theft, describe *in order* the first three things you would do to begin to resolve the problem.

_____

_____

_____

_____

_____

_____

3. Do you think account takeover or application fraud identity theft would be harder to deal with as a victim? Tell which type and explain your reasoning.

_____

_____

_____

_____

_____

_____

4. **Overall main idea.** What is the overall main idea the authors want the reader to understand about identity theft? Answer this question in one sentence. Be sure to include the topic *identity theft* in your overall main idea sentence.

_____

_____

_____

_____

_____

_____

_____

_____

_____

_____

SELECTION 5.2

Psychology

Violence in Television and Video Games: Does the Media's Message Matter?

From *Essentials of Understanding Psychology*
by Robert S. Feldman

Prepare Yourself to Read

Directions: Do these exercises *before* you read Selection 5.1.

1. First, read and think about the title. What do you know about the effect of media (television and video game) violence on people who are exposed to it constantly?

   _____

   _____

2. Next, complete your preview by reading the following:

   > Introduction (in *italics*)
   >
   > First sentence of paragraphs 1–7
   >
   > Look at the photo and read the caption
   >
   > All of the last paragraph

   Now that you have previewed the selection, what point do you think the author is making about media violence?

   _____

   _____

   _____

   _____

   _____

3. **Build your vocabulary as you read.** If you discover an unfamiliar word or key term as you read the selection, try to determine its meaning by using context clues.

Read More about This Topic Online

Internet Resources

Use a search engine, such as Google or Yahoo!, to expand your existing knowledge about this topic *before* you read the selection or to learn more about it *afterward*. If you are unfamiliar with conducting Internet searches, read pages 25–26 on Boolean searches. You can also use Wikipedia, the free online encyclopedia, at www.wikipedia.com. Keep in mind that when you visit any website, it is a good idea to evaluate the site and the information it contains. Ask yourself questions such as "Who sponsors this website?" and "Is the information it contains up to date?"

SELECTION 5.2: VIOLENCE IN TELEVISION AND VIDEO GAMES: DOES THE MEDIA'S MESSAGE MATTER?

Do you play video games or computer games? If so, you are among millions of other Americans. Although people of all ages play them, the average U.S. video gamer is at least 30 years old and has been playing for more than a dozen years. More than 20 percent play games online, and iPad and smart phones make games available any time and anywhere (http://en.wikipedia.org/wiki/Gamer; accessed 3/23/12). In May 2010, the Bruin Business Review *reported that a good 40 percent of gamers are female. With regard to teens, Obe Hostetter (www.game-research.com) noted, "On average, they spend 1.5 hours per day playing video games. By the time they enter the workforce, they will have played 10,000 hours of computer or video games."*

Violent games—such as Call of Duty 4, Grand Theft Auto, Halo 3, *and* Assassin's Creed—*often grab the headlines. However, only about 15 percent of video games are rated "mature," and no one genre of games dominates sales (http://bruinbusinessreview.com/video-computer-game-demographics-industry-profile; accessed 3/23/12). Still, public concern lingers that violent media can have an effect on youth violence.*

And what about violent television shows? The average American has the TV turned on nearly 8 hours a day and actually watches it for 4 of those hours. What effect do you think prolonged, excessive exposure to media violence might have? Read the following excerpt from a psychology textbook to learn more about this issue.

1   In an episode of HBO's "The Sopranos," fictional mobster Tony Soprano murdered one of his associates. To make identification of the victim's body difficult, Soprano, along with one of his henchmen, dismembered the body and dumped the body parts.

2   A few months later, two real-life half brothers in Riverside, California, strangled their mother and then cut her head and hands from her body. Victor Bautista, 20, and Matthew Montejo, 15, who were caught by police after a security guard noticed that the bundle they were attempting to throw in a dumpster had a foot sticking out of it, told police that the plan to dismember their mother was inspired by "The Sopranos" episode.

Annotation Practice Exercises

Directions: For each exercise below:

- Write the topic of the paragraph on the lines provided.
- Formulate the implied main idea of the paragraph and write it on the lines provided.

This will help you remember the topic and the main idea. Remember that you cannot use any sentence exactly as it appears in the paragraph.

3   Like other "media copycat" killings, the brothers' cold-blooded brutality raises a critical issue: Does observing violent and antisocial acts in the media lead viewers to behave in similar ways? Because research on modeling shows that people frequently learn and imitate the aggression that they observe, this question is among the most important being addressed by psychologists.

4   Certainly, the amount of violence in the mass media is enormous. By the time of elementary school graduation, the average child in the United States will have viewed more than 8,000 murders. They will have viewed more than 800,000 violent acts on network television. Adult television shows also contain significant violence, with cable television leading the way with such shows as "When Animals Attack" and "World's Scariest Police Shootouts."

5   Most experts agree that watching high levels of media violence makes viewers more susceptible to acting aggressively, and recent research supports this claim. For example, a recent survey of serious and violent young male offenders incarcerated in Florida showed that one-fourth of them had attempted to commit a media-inspired copycat crime. A significant proportion of those teenage offenders noted that they paid close attention to the media.

6   Violent video games have also been linked with actual aggression. In one of a series of studies by psychologist Craig Anderson and colleagues, for example, college students who frequently played violent video games, such as *Postal* or *Doom,* were more likely to have been involved in delinquent behavior and aggression. Frequent players also had lower academic achievement.

Practice Exercise

- Topic of paragraph 3:

  _____

  _____

  _____

- Formulate the implied main idea of paragraph 3:

  _____

  _____

  _____

  _____

SELECTION 5.2

Does violence in television shows like *The Sopranos* lead to real-life violence? Most research suggests that watching high levels of violence makes viewers more susceptible to acting aggressively.

7   Several aspects of media violence may contribute to real-life aggressive behavior. For one thing, experiencing violent media content seems to lower inhibitions against carrying out aggression—watching television portrayals of violence or using violence to win a video game makes aggression seem a legitimate response to particular situations. Exposure to media violence also may distort our understanding of the meaning of others' behavior, predisposing us to view even nonaggressive acts by others as aggressive. Finally, a continuous diet of aggression may leave us desensitized to violence, and what previously would have repelled us now produces little emotional response. Our sense of the pain and suffering brought about by aggression may be diminished.

8   What about real-life exposure to actual violence? Does it also lead to increases in aggression? The answer is yes. Exposure to actual firearm violence (being shot or being shot at) doubles the probability that an adolescent will commit serious violence over the next two years.

9   Whether the violence is real or fictionalized, then, observing violent behavior leads to increases in aggressive behavior.

Practice Exercise

•   Topic of paragraph 8:

_____

_____

_____

•   Formulate the implied main idea of paragraph 8:

_____

_____

_____

_____

_____

_____

_____

Reading Selection Quiz

This quiz has several parts. Your instructor may assign some or all of them.

Comprehension

Directions: Use the information in the selection to answer each item below. You may refer to the selection as you answer the questions. Write each answer in the space provided.

True or False

1. By the time U.S. children complete elementary school, they will have seen more than 80,000 murders on network television shows.

2. With regard to adult television shows, cable television has more violent programming than network television.

3. An episode of *The Sopranos* was based on an actual murder committed by Victor Bautista and Matthew Montejo.

4. Experiencing media violence raises people's inhibitions against carrying out aggression.

5. Exposure to media violence can cause people to mistakenly interpret other people's nonaggressive acts as aggressive ones.

6. Research indicates that frequent video game players have approximately the same level of academic achievement as students who are not frequent video game players.

Multiple-Choice

7. Researchers found that media violence:
   a. causes no change in subjects' levels of aggressive behavior.
   b. always causes aggressive behavior.
   c. decreases aggressive behavior.
   d. may contribute to real-life aggressive behavior.

8. People continually exposed to media violence:
   a. become less sensitive to the pain that aggression causes other people.
   b. become more sensitive to the pain that aggression causes other people.
   c. experience no change in their response to the pain that aggression causes other people.
   d. none of the above

9. It is likely that violent young males who are in prison:

   a.   experienced less exposure to media violence than the general public.

   b.   were influenced by the large amount of media violence to which they were exposed.

   c.   are less violent than other inmates.

   d.   committed more serious crimes than other inmates.

10. College students who frequently play violent video games:

   a.   have lower academic achievement.

   b.   are more likely to be involved in delinquent behavior.

   c.   are more likely to be involved in aggression.

   d.   all of the above

SELECTION **5.2**

Psychology

(continued)

Vocabulary in Context

Directions: For each item below, use context clues to deduce the meaning of the *italicized* word. Be sure the answer you choose makes sense in both sentences. Write each answer in the space provided.

11. In an episode of HBO's "The Sopranos," *fictional* mobster Tony Soprano murdered one of his associates.

Harry Potter, Darth Vader, James Bond, Batman, and Forrest Gump are well-known *fictional* characters.

fictional (fĭk′ shən əl) means:

   a.   extremely dangerous; unusually violent

   b.   not real; created from imagination

   c.   wanted by the police or other law enforcement agencies

   d.   high-ranking and well-respected

12. Victor Bautista, 20, and Matthew Montejo, 15, who were caught by police after a security guard noticed that the bundle they were attempting to throw in a dumpster had a foot sticking out of it, told police that the plan to *dismember* their mother was inspired by "The Sopranos" episode.

Part of the ancient cult's ritual was to *dismember* an animal and offer it as a sacrifice to the gods.

dismember (dĭs mĕm′ bər) means:

   a.   to cut off the limbs (arms or legs)

   b.   to remove from membership

   c.   to forget

   d.   to show disrespect for

13. Most experts agree that watching high levels of media violence makes viewers more *susceptible* to acting aggressively, and recent research supports this claim.

Many parents are *susceptible* to their children's whining, and they end up giving them whatever they want.

susceptible (sə sĕp′ tə bəl) means:
a. easily influenced or affected by
b. annoyed by; irritated
c. made to feel guilty
d. unresponsive

14. For example, a recent survey of serious and violent young male offenders *incarcerated* in Florida showed that one-fourth of them had attempted to commit a media-inspired copycat crime.

According to the U.S. Justice Department's Bureau of Justice Statistics, in 2002 and for the first time in this nation's history, the number of people *incarcerated* passed the 2 million mark: 1 in 142 U.S. residents was in prison.

incarcerated (ĭn kär′ sə rat′ əd) means:
a. living in poverty
b. wanted by the police
c. put into jail
d. arrested

15. For one thing, experiencing violent media content seems to lower *inhibitions* against carrying out aggression—watching television portrayals of violence or using violence to win a video game makes aggression seem a legitimate response to particular situations.

Because drinking alcohol reduces people's *inhibitions,* they do things they would not do if they were completely sober.

inhibitions (ĭn hə bĭsh′ ənz) means:
a. energy levels
b. improper actions
c. sudden, violent disruptions
d. restraints of desires or impulses

16. For one thing, experiencing violent media content seems to lower inhibitions against carrying out aggression—watching television *portrayals* of violence or using violence to win a video game makes aggression seem a legitimate response to particular situations.

The actor has received awards for his convincing *portrayals* of president George Washington and writer Mark Twain.

portrayals (pôr trā′ əlz) means:
a. portraits painted by professional artists
b. realistic representations or images
c. reruns of televised programs
d. planned absences

17. For one thing, experiencing violent media content seems to lower inhibitions against carrying out aggression—watching television portrayals of violence or using violence to win a video game makes aggression seem a *legitimate* response to particular situations.

Scientists at the international conference hope to come up with several *legitimate* solutions to the problem of global warming.

legitimate (lə jĭt′ ə mĭt) means:
a. creative
b. inexpensive
c. reasonable
d. simple

18. *Exposure* to media violence also may distort our understanding of the meaning of others' behavior.

Visiting New York was my first *exposure* to a large city.

exposure (ĭk spō′ zhər) means:
a. appearance in the mass media
b. a repeated event
c. act of revealing something publicly
d. experiencing or being subjected to something

19. Exposure to media violence may also distort our understanding of the meaning of others' behavior, *predisposing* us to view even nonaggressive acts by others as aggressive.

Some students have unsuccessful experiences in elementary school, *predisposing* them to expect that it will always be that way.

predisposing (prə dĭ spōz′ ĭng) means:
a. resulting in correct or appropriate behavior
b. influencing toward a particular attitude
c. causing one to feel optimistic
d. producing stress or anxiety

_____ **20.** Finally, a continuous diet of aggression may leave us *desensitized* to violence, and what previously would have repelled us now produces little emotional response.

During World War II, guards in Nazi concentration camps carried out unspeakable acts because they became *desensitized* to human misery and suffering.

desensitized (dē sĕn′ sĭ tīzd) means:

a. emotionally insensitive or unresponsive

b. enthusiastic about

c. agitated or upset by

d. eager to talk about

Reading Skills Application

Directions: These items test your ability to *apply* certain reading skills. You may not have studied all of the skills yet, so some items will serve as a preview. Write each answer in the space provided.

_____ **21.** In paragraph 5, the author uses the term *media-inspired copycat crime* to describe crimes:

a. portrayed by make-believe characters in violent television shows.

b. depicted by animated characters in violent video games.

c. patterned after violent crimes shown on television and in video games.

d. carried out by users as part of a violent video game they are playing.

_____ **22.** The author includes information about research studies by psychologist Craig Anderson and colleagues to provide evidence about the negative effects of:

a. watching too much television.

b. engaging in delinquent behavior.

c. lowering inhibitions.

d. playing violent video games.

_____ **23.** Based on the information in the selection, it can be logically concluded that:

a. children who are exposed to little or no media violence are less likely to behave in aggressive or violent ways.

b. most children are naturally aggressive or even violent.

c. children will commit fewer crimes during the next 10 years.

d. television and video games have little effect on children.

_____ **24.** The author would be most likely to agree with which of the following statements?

a. Since they are already in prison, inmates should be permitted to watch violent television programs and play violent video games.

b. The level and amount of violence in television programs and video games should be reduced.

    c. There is nothing that can be done about the problem of excessive media violence.

    d. People who commit copycat crimes should not be held responsible since they were influenced by media violence.

25. Which of the following represents an opinion rather than a fact?

    a. Certainly, the amount of violence in the mass media is enormous.

    b. By the time of elementary school graduation, the average child in the United States will have viewed more than 8,000 murders.

    c. They will have viewed more than 800,000 violent acts on network television.

    d. none of the above

SELECTION **5.2**

Psychology
(continued)

Respond in Writing

Directions: Refer to the selection as needed to answer the essay-type questions below. (Your instructor may direct you to work collaboratively with other students on one or more items. Each group member should be able to explain *all* of the group's answers.)

1. In your opinion, why do you think people find computer and video games so appealing? Why do you think violent television shows are so popular?

_____

_____

_____

_____

2. Young children have difficulty separating fantasy from the real world. In video games, the gamer takes part in the violence and even gets rewards (such as points) for doing so. In many games, the only solution is violence; the gamer can't choose a nonviolent solution and stay alive (continue to play). Authorities say that watching violent television shows and playing violent video games causes the most harm before the age of nine. In light of this information, should children be prohibited from these activities? Why or why not?

_____

_____

_____

_____

3. Millions of Americans begin playing these games at an early age and then continue to play them throughout their adult life. In video games, approximately three-fourths of the perpetrators of violence go unpunished. In other words, the characters who commit violent crimes suffer no consequences. What are the implications of this for our society as a whole?

_____

_____

_____

_____

_____

4. If parents allow their children access to violent television and video games and those children commit copycat crimes, what responsibility do the parents bear? Should they be held responsible for their children's actions? Why or why not? If parents should be held responsible, what punishment should they be given? When the source of a copycat crime is an extremely violent television show or video game, what responsibility should be borne by the companies who produced them?

_____

_____

_____

_____

_____

_____

_____

_____

5. Are there *advantages* to playing computer and video games? List at least two.

_____

_____

_____

_____

_____

_____

6. **Overall main idea.** What is the overall main idea the author wants you to understand about exposure to violent television shows, violent video games, and real-life violence? Answer this question in one sentence. Be sure that your overall main idea sentence contains the topic (*exposure to violent television shows, violent video games, and real-life violence*) and tells the overall most important point about it.

_____

_____

_____

_____

_____

_____

SELECTION **5.3**

Sociology

Demography, the Study of Population

From *Sociology: An Introduction*
by Richard J. Gelles and Ann Levine

Prepare Yourself to Read

Directions: Do these exercises *before* you read Selection 5.2.

1. First, read and think about the title. What do you already know about demography?

   _____

   _____

   _____

2. Next, complete your preview by reading the following:
   Introduction (in *italics*)
   Headings
   All of the first paragraph (paragraph 1)
   First sentence of each of the other paragraphs
   The table and the two graphs

   On the basis of your preview, what does the selection now seem to be about?

   _____

   _____

   _____

   _____

   _____

3. **Build your vocabulary as you read.** If you discover an unfamiliar word or key term as you read the selection, try to determine its meaning by using context clues.

Internet Resources

Read More about This Topic Online

Use a search engine, such as Google or Yahoo!, to expand your existing knowledge about this topic *before* you read the selection or to learn more about it *afterward*. If you are unfamiliar with conducting Internet searches, read pages 25–26 on Boolean searches. You can also use Wikipedia, the free online encyclopedia, at www .wikipedia.com. Keep in mind that when you visit any website, it is a good idea to evaluate the site and the information it contains. Ask yourself questions such as "Who sponsors this website?" and "Is the information it contains up to date?"

SELECTION 5.3

SELECTION 5.3: DEMOGRAPHY, THE STUDY OF POPULATION

By 2011, the world's population had climbed to past 7 billion. Experts estimate that worldwide, 370,000 babies are born daily. In 1900, the world's population stood at 2 billion. Between 1900 and 1999—only 100 years—the human population tripled. There is great concern that humans are quickly consuming natural resources and are ruining the environment and the planet. And nearly half of the babies born will be born into poverty. If the overall rate of population growth in the developing countries remains stable, their populations will double in only 40 years.

There were 100 million people in the United States in 1915. Currently, our population is estimated at 314 million, making the United States the world's third most populous country. The U.S. population is expected to reach 400 million by 2046. The state of California alone is expected to increase its population by 18 million by the year 2025, raising its population to 50 million. That means that California will be adding one resident every 45 seconds—the biggest population explosion in the nation's history. The other most populous states also face significant population increases. (Those states, in order, are Texas, New York, Florida, Pennsylvania, Illinois, Ohio, Michigan, New Jersey, and North Carolina.) Also, the U.S. population is getting older and more Hispanic. The problems raised by population growth and by the rapid increases in certain segments of the population—problems such as health care, poverty, education, traffic, streets and road repair, housing, utilities, city services, and pollution, to name a few—will affect all of us.

The goal of the United States Census in the year 2010 was to count every person in this country; without reliable figures, it is difficult to plan for the future. It is easy to see why the work of demographers is so important. The selection below, from a sociology textbook, explains what demography is and the population changes that occurred as Western nations shifted from being agricultural nations to industrialized nations.

Demography: The Study of Population

1   The scientific study of population is known as *demography*. The word comes from the Greek for "measuring people." But counting heads is only a small part of what demographers do. They also attempt to calculate the growth rate of a population and to assess the impact of such things as the marriage rate and life expectancy, the sex ratio (the proportion of males to females), and the age structure (the proportions of young, middle-aged, and older people) on human behavior and the structure of society. They are interested in the distribution of population and in movements of people (migration). Put another way, demographers study the effects of such numbers on social trends.

2   Demographers use a number of standard measures in translating a locality's raw totals—births, deaths, the number of those moving in and out—into general statistics that allow them to identify trends. The *birthrate* is the number of births per 1,000 people in a given year. Suppose there were 900 births in a city of 50,000 in a specific year. Demographers calculate the birthrate for the city by dividing the

Annotation Practice Exercises

Directions: For each exercise below:

- Write the topic of the paragraph on the lines provided.

- Formulate the implied main idea of the paragraph and write it on the lines provided.

This will help you remember the topic and the main idea.

number of births (900) by the population (50,000) and multiplying the result (0.018) by 1,000 to get 18. The birthrate in developed countries is 1.6; in less developed countries (excluding China) it is 4.0. The death rate is the number of deaths per 1,000 people in a given year. (The death rate is calculated in the same way as the birthrate.) The fertility rate is the number of live births per 1,000 women of the world. As mentioned earlier, population and population growth rates are highest in developing nations and lower in Western nations. These rates are also complicated by mass movements of refugees to and from certain countries. By 1994 the population of refugees was over 23 million, up from about 10 million refugees worldwide in 1983. Mass movements of people into and out of Afghanistan, Somalia, Bosnia, and Mozambique have contributed to this sharp increase. Famine and political upheaval are usually behind these mass exoduses. (See Table 1 and Figure 1.) *Life expectancy* is the potential life span of the average member in any given population.

The Demographic Transition

3   The term *demographic transition* refers to a pattern of major population changes that accompanied the transformation of Western nations from agricultural into industrial societies. The demographic transition occurred in three stages. (See Figure 2.)

4   In *Stage I,* birthrates were high, but death rates were also high. As a result, the population growth rate was low. Thus in eighteenth-century Europe, birthrates were high, but many infants did not survive childhood and many adults did not reach old age. High infant mortality, epidemics, famines, and wars kept the population growth rate low.

In the United States, demographers analyze data gathered by the U.S. Census Bureau.

Practice Exercise

- Topic of paragraph 4:

  _____

- Formulate the implied main idea of paragraph 4:

  _____

  _____

  _____

  _____

  _____

		World	More Developed Countries	Less Developed Countries
Population		6,986,951,000	1,241,580,000	5,745,371,000
Births per	Year	139,558,000	14,070,000	125,488,000
	Day	382,351	38,548	343,803
	Minute	266	27	239
Deaths per	Year	56,611,000	12,201,000	44,410,000
	Day	155,099	33,427	121,671
	Minute	108	23	84
Natural increase (births-deaths) per	Year	82,947,000	1,869,000	81,078,000
	Day	227,252	5,121	222,132
	Minute	158	4	154
Infant deaths per	Year	6,078,000	77,000	6,001,000
	Day	16,652	211	16,441
	Minute	12	0.1	11

TABLE 1
POPULATION CLOCK, 2011

Source: Population Reference Bureau, *2011 World Population Data Sheet.* http://www.prb.org/pdf11/2011population-data-sheet_eng.pdf, accessed 3/28/12.

Figure 1
World Population Growth
Through most of human history, the population was more or less stable. In modern times, how-ever, world popula-tion has skyrocketed.

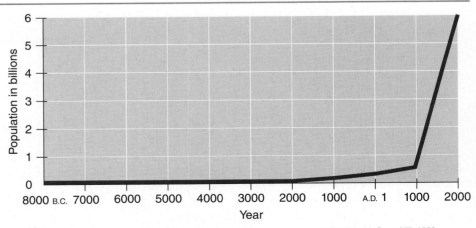

Source: From Richard J. Gelles and Ann Levine, *Sociology: An Introduction,* 6th ed. Boston: McGraw-Hill, 1999, pp. 594–597. Permission granted by Richard J. Gelles and Ann Levine. Data from John R. Weeks, *Population,* 5th ed., Belmont, CA: Wadsworth, 1992, p. 30.

**Figure 2
Demographic Tran-
sition in Western
Nations**
In Stage I, birthrates
and death rates were
both high, population
growth (the purple line)
was slow. In Stage II,
death rates declined
faster than birthrates,
so population growth
continued to climb.
Only when birthrates
and death rates are
both low, in Stage III,
does population
growth slow down.

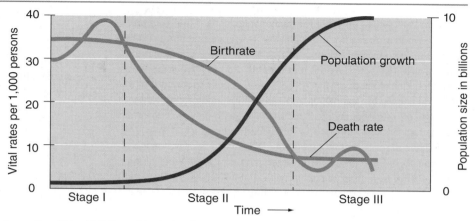

Source: From Richard J. Gelles and Ann Levine, *Sociology: An Introduction,* 6th ed. Boston: McGraw-Hill, 1999,
pp. 594–597. Permission granted by Richard J. Gelles and Ann Levine. Data from John R. Weeks, *Population,* 5th ed.,
Belmont, CA: Wadsworth, 1992, p. 76.

5   In *Stage II,* which began in Europe in the late eighteenth century,
birthrates remained high, but death rates began to fall. Why? Improvements in agricultural technology, the spread of new and hardier
crops (such as the potato), and increased food production. Improvements in transportation facilitated food distribution: people were
no longer dependent on local supplies or devastated by local crop
failures. Better nutrition meant that people were more able to resist
and survive disease. During the nineteenth century, improvements in
public health and sanitation (cleaner water, better sewage disposal,
pasteurized milk) and advances in modern medicine contributed further to the decline in death rates. Many more women survived into
their childbearing years. The population growth rate soared. (*Note:*
The eighteenth-century population explosion was due to lower death
rates rather than to higher birthrates.)

6   In *Stage III,* which began in the mid-nineteenth century in Western nations, birthrates started to fall. Stage III is associated with
industrial development. In agricultural societies, children are an economic asset: the more hands, the better. In urban, industrial societies, however, children become an "economic burden." They are
financially dependent on their parents for an extended period. Large
families mean crowded living quarters, additional household expenses, and a lower family standard of living. Four additional factors

Practice Exercise

•   Topic of paragraph 5:

_____

•   Formulate the implied main idea of
    paragraph 5:

_____

_____

_____

_____

_____

_____

that contributed to falling birthrates in the West in the twentieth century were the decline in infant mortality (which meant that a couple did not have to produce five or six children to ensure that three or four would live), government-sponsored Social Security programs in the 1930s and 1940s (which meant that parents did not have to depend on their children to support them in old age), access to modern birth control devices in the late 1950s and early 1960s, and postponement of the age of marriage. By the 1960s families with only two or three children had become the norm. Today birthrates in most Western nations have stabilized at replacement levels, while death rates have continued to decline. (Half of the Americans now alive would have been dead if the death rate had remained at 1900 levels.) Thus the balance between birthrates and death rates has been restored; as in Stage I the population growth rate is low.

Practice Exercise

- Topic of paragraph 6:

  _____

- Formulate the implied main idea of paragraph 6:

  _____

  _____

  _____

  _____

  _____

  _____

Source: Richard J. Gelles and Ann Levine, *Sociology: An Introduction*, 6th ed. Boston: McGraw-Hill, 1999, pp. 594–97. Permission granted by Richard J. Gelles and Ann Levine.

SELECTION **5.3**

Sociology
(continued)

Reading Selection Quiz

This quiz has several parts. Your instructor may assign some or all of them.

Comprehension

Directions: Use the information in the selection to answer each item below. You may refer to the selection as you answer the questions. Write each answer in the space provided.

True or False

_____ **1.** The scientific study of population trends is known as the *fertility* rate.

_____ **2.** *Life expectancy* is the potential life span of the average member in any given population.

_____ **3.** Population growth rates are highest in Western nations and lower in developing nations.

_____ **4.** According to the Population Reference Bureau, in 2011 there were 382,351 births each day worldwide.

Multiple-Choice

_____ **5.** Demographers:
   a. are interested in the distribution of population and in movements of people.
   b. assess the impact of such things as life expectancy and the marriage rate.
   c. count people and calculate the growth rate of a population.
   d. all of the above

_____ **6.** In a given year, the birthrate in less developed countries (excluding China) is:
   a. 18 per 1,000 people.
   b. 4.0 per 1,000 people.
   c. 1.6 per 1,000 people.
   d. 0.018 per 1,000 people.

_____ **7.** Population growth is slowed when:
   a. birthrates are high.
   b. death rates are low.
   c. both birthrates and death rates are low.
   d. birthrates are high and death rates are low.

SELECTION 5.3

8. World population skyrocketed in about:
   a.   2000 B.C.
   b.   1000 B.C.
   c.   A.D. 1000.
   d.   A.D. 2000.

9. During Stage III of the demographic transition in Western nations, birthrates declined because:
   a.   infant mortality increased.
   b.   access to modern birth control devices became available in the late 1950s and early 1960s.
   c.   fewer people postponed marriage.
   d.   couples began having children earlier.

10. In 2011 there were 27 births per minute in more developed countries, while in less developed countries the number of births per minute was:
    a.   239.
    b.   266.
    c.   108.
    d.   154.

SELECTION **5.3**

Sociology
(continued)

Vocabulary in Context

Directions: For each item below, use context clues to deduce the meaning of the *italicized* word. Be sure the answer you choose makes sense in both sentences. Write each answer in the space provided.

11. They also attempt to calculate the growth rate of a population and to assess the impact of such things as the marriage rate and life *expectancy.*

    Insurance rates are based on life *expectancy:* the younger the person, the lower the rate.

    expectancy (ĭk spĕk′ tən sē) means:
    a.   length
    b.   a known quantity or amount
    c.   an expected amount calculated on the basis of statistical data
    d.   a quantity or amount that cannot be determined or estimated

12. They are interested in the *distribution* of population and in movements of people (migration).

    The *distribution* of saguaro cactus is limited to the southwestern part of the United States and northern Mexico.

distribution (dĭ strĭ byōō′ shən) means:

a.   disappearance; extinction

b.   planting

c.   geographic occurrence or range

d.   destruction

_____   **13.** Demographers use a number of *standard* measures in translating a locality's raw totals—births, deaths, the number of those moving in and out—into general statistics that allow them to identify trends.

Nutritionists have established the *standard* amount of fats, carbohydrates, and protein adults need in their diet.

standard (stăn′ dərd) means:

a.   acknowledged measure

b.   imprecise

c.   incomplete

d.   ambiguous

_____   **14.** Demographers use a number of standard measures in translating a *locality's* raw totals—births, deaths, the number of those moving in and out—into general statistics that allow them to identify trends.

Because the population in our suburb is increasing, there are many new businesses moving into our *locality*.

locality (lō käl′ ĭ tē) means:

a.   voting precinct

b.   school district

c.   state

d.   a particular place

_____   **15.** *Mass* movements of people into and out of Afghanistan, Somalia, Bosnia, and Mozambique have contributed to this sharp increase.

Most large cities have subway systems, bus systems, or other forms of *mass* transit.

mass (măs) means:

a.   pertaining to religion

b.   related to a large number of people

c.   pertaining to citizens of a country

d.   related to high speed

16. Famine and political *upheaval* are usually behind these mass exoduses.

The earthquake caused a complete *upheaval* of life in the peaceful mountain village.

upheaval (üp hē′ vəl) means:

a. improvement

b. elevation

c. sudden, violent disruption

d. gradual change

17. Famine and political upheaval are usually behind these mass *exoduses.*

Historians report that seeking refuge from war, religious persecution, and epidemics are three major reasons for *exoduses.*

exoduses (ēk′ sə dəs əz) means:

a. trips or journeys

b. departures of large numbers of people

c. refusals to leave

d. planned absences

18. High infant *mortality,* epidemics, famines, and wars kept the population growth rate low.

Child *mortality* is higher in poor countries because health care for children is so inadequate.

mortality (môr tăl′ ĭ tē) means:

a. correct behavior

b. heart attacks

c. death rate

d. protection

19. Improvements in transportation *facilitated* food distribution: people were no longer dependent on local supplies or devastated by local crop failures.

The new, computerized traffic signals *facilitated* the smooth flow of traffic during rush hour.

facilitated (fə sĭl′ ĭ tāt ĕd) means:

a. made easier

b. slowed down

c. directed

d. authorized

_____ **20.** Today birthrates in most Western nations have *stabilized* at replacement levels, while death rates have continued to decline.

Once the victim's erratic breathing and heart rate were *stabilized,* the paramedics rushed her to the emergency room for treatment.

stabilized (stā′ bə līzd) means:

a. resuscitated

b. decreased

c. stopped

d. became steady or made stable

Reading Skills Application

Directions: These items test your ability to *apply* certain reading skills. You may not have studied all of the skills yet, so some items will serve as a preview. Write each answer in the space provided.

_____ **21.** In paragraph 1, *counting heads* means:

a. people who are demographers and mathematicians.

b. determining the number of people in a population.

c. the work that statisticians do.

d. measuring the size of people's heads.

_____ **22.** Which of the following statements from paragraph 2 expresses the main idea of the paragraph?

a. Demographers use a number of standard measures in translating a locality's raw totals—births, deaths, the numbers of those moving in and out—into general statistics that allow them to identify trends.

b. The birthrate is the number of births per 1,000 people in a given year.

c. The death rate is the number of deaths per 1,000 people in a given year.

d. These rates are also complicated by mass movements of refugees to and from certain countries.

_____ **23.** The authors organize the information in paragraphs 3–6 using which of the following patterns?

a. list

b. problem-solution

c. sequence

d. comparison

_____ **24.** Which of the following statements from paragraph 5 represents an opinion rather than a fact?

a. The population growth rate soared.

b. Improvements in transportation facilitated food distribution.

    c. Better nutrition meant that people were more able to resist and survive disease.

    d. During the nineteenth century, improvements in public health and sanitation and advances in modern science contributed further to the decline in death rates.

25. From information in the selection, it can be inferred that the size of a population is influenced by:

    a. the ratio between the birthrate and the death rate.

    b. the birthrate only.

    c. the death rate only.

    d. neither the birthrate nor the death rate.

SELECTION **5.3**

Sociology

(continued)

Respond in Writing

Directions: Refer to the selection as needed to answer the essay-type questions below. (Your instructor may direct you to work collaboratively with other students on one or more items. Each group member should be able to explain *all* of the group's answers.)

1. The world's population growth is not expected to slow down for the next 50 years. What are the implications of this for you and your family (or your future family)?

_____

_____

_____

_____

_____

2. In China, the government enforces a policy that restricts most couples to having only one child. Given the overpopulation problem the world is facing, do you think all countries should limit the number of children couples are allowed to have? Explain why or why not.

_____

_____

_____

_____

_____

_____

3. If the number of children couples could have were restricted by law, should couples be allowed to have an additional child if they can pay the government a special fee? Why or why not?

    _____

    _____

    _____

    _____

    _____

    _____

4. Are there any *advantages* to having so many more people in the world today? Try to think of at least two.

    _____

    _____

    _____

    _____

    _____

    _____

    _____

    _____

5. If there were a birth control pill for men, do you think the worldwide birthrate would decline? Explain why or why not.

    _____

    _____

    _____

    _____

    _____

SELECTION 5.3

6. Use the information from the table in the selection to complete this summary table of population change per minute in 2011:

WORLD POPULATION CLOCK, 2011 PER MINUTE		
	World	**More Developed Countries**	**Less Developed Countries**
Births			
Deaths			
Natural increase			
Infant deaths			

7. Based on your table above, what conclusion can you draw about where world population is increasing most rapidly?

_____

_____

_____

8. **Overall main idea.** What is the overall main idea the authors want the reader to understand about demography? Answer this question in one sentence. Be sure that your overall main idea sentence includes the topic (*demography*) and tells the overall most important point about it.

_____

_____

_____

_____

_____

_____

CHAPTER **6**

Identifying
Supporting Details

In this chapter, you will learn the answers to these questions:

- What are supporting details in a paragraph?

- Why is it useful to understand supporting details?

- How can I identify supporting details in paragraphs?

- How can I list supporting details clearly?

- What are major and minor details, and what is the difference between them?

SKILLS

Supporting Details in Paragraphs

- What Are Supporting Details?

- Why Are Supporting Details Important?

Identifying and Listing Supporting Details

Major and Minor Details, and How to Tell the Difference

A Word about Standardized Reading Tests: Supporting Details

CHECKPOINT: IDENTIFYING SUPPORTING DETAILS

CREATING YOUR SUMMARY

Developing Chapter Review Cards

TEST YOUR UNDERSTANDING: IDENTIFYING SUPPORTING DETAILS, PART 1

TEST YOUR UNDERSTANDING: IDENTIFYING SUPPORTING DETAILS, PART 2

READINGS

Selection 6.1   "Shaping Your Health: The Millennial Generation and Early Adulthood"
from *Understanding Your Health*
by *Wayne A. Payne, Dale B. Hahn, and Ellen B. Lucas* (Health)

Selection 6.2   "Quacks and Quackery"
from *Concepts of Fitness and Wellness*
by *Charles Corbin, Greg Welk, William Corbin, and Karen Welk* (Health)

Selection 6.3   "What Can Be Done to Help Third World Countries?"
from *A Beginner's Guide to the World Economy*
by *Randy Charles Epping* (Economics)

Men who wish to know about the world must learn about it in its particular details.

Heraclitus

Beware the man who won't be bothered with details.

William Feather, Sr.

Success is the sum of details.

Harry Firestone

It ain't braggin' if you can back it up.

Dizzy Dean

SUPPORTING DETAILS IN PARAGRAPHS

PERSONALIZED LEARNING

supporting details

Additional information in the paragraph that helps you understand the main idea completely.

Supporting details are also known as *support* or *details*.

What Are Supporting Details?

A paragraph consists of more than a topic and a main idea. When there is a stated main idea, all of the other sentences present supporting details. In fact, in most paragraphs, most of the sentences present supporting details. The topic and the main idea are essential to understanding the paragraph, but the **supporting details** provide additional information that helps you understand the main idea *completely*. In other words, supporting details explain, illustrate, or prove the main idea of a paragraph.

Supporting details typically consist of:

- Examples
- Descriptions
- Characteristics
- Steps
- Places
- Names
- Dates
- Statistics
- Reasons
- Results
- Other information explaining, illustrating, or proving the main idea

Be careful not to confuse the main idea with the supporting details. Details pertain to the main idea, but they are not the same thing. The main idea expresses an important *general* point that is based on the supporting details or is explained by them.

Why Are Supporting Details Important?

As just noted, the supporting details have an important connection with the main idea. First, they help explain the main idea. Second, they often lead you to the stated main idea. Similarly, supporting details contain information that can help you formulate the main idea when it is implied. Third, they can help you grasp the

343

Supporting details
are important to in-
clude on study cards
because the details
explain, illustrate, or
prove main ideas.

organization of a paragraph. And if you understand *how* the supporting details are organized to explain, illustrate, or prove the main idea of the paragraph, that makes it easier to remember the material, take notes, and mark your textbooks effectively. As you will learn in Chapter 7, details are usually organized according to one of several common writing patterns. Specific types of supporting details that authors use to organize ideas into paragraphs include lists of characteristics, things, places, and so on (called a *list pattern*); items in a series or steps in a process (called a *sequence pattern*); similarities, differences, or both (called a *comparison-contrast pattern*); or reasons and results (called a *cause-effect pattern*). Lastly, listing the supporting details on paper after you finish reading can help you later when you study for a test. For example, you might list important details from a history textbook on chapter review cards. Instructors often ask test questions based on supporting details—examples, reasons, steps, names, dates, places, and other important information. Along with determining the topic and the main idea, then, identifying supporting details helps you become a more successful reader and student.

The following diagram shows the relationship between a main idea and its supporting details:

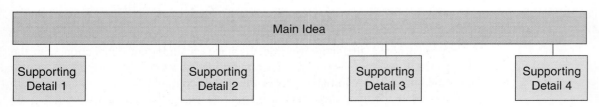

IDENTIFYING AND LISTING SUPPORTING DETAILS

Comprehension-Monitoring Question for Identifying Supporting Details

What additional information does the author provide to help me understand the main idea completely?

To identify a paragraph's supporting details, ask yourself, *"What additional information* does the author provide to help me understand the main idea completely?" One way to approach this is by turning the main idea sentence into a question by using the word *who, what, where, when, why,* or *how,* and then seeking the information that answers this question. For example, if the stated main idea is *In a corporation, the chief financial officer is responsible for four basic functions,* you could change it into the question *"What* are the four basic functions of a chief financial officer?" That question would lead you to the four details that describe the basic functions and, therefore, explain the main idea.

Often, supporting details are introduced by signal words such as *first, second, next, also, and, another, in addition,* and *moreover.* Watch for numbers (1, 2, 3) and letters (*a, b, c*) that signal lists of details. Watch for information introduced by the phrases *for example* and *to illustrate,* since examples are always details.

Here is an excerpt from a music appreciation textbook. Its topic is *the role of American colleges and universities in our musical culture.* The first sentence is the stated main idea: *American colleges and universities have played an unusually vital role in our musical culture.* Turn this main idea into the question *"What* role have American colleges and universities played in our musical culture?" After you have read the paragraph, identify the details that answer this question.

> American colleges and universities have played an unusually vital role in our musical culture. They have trained and employed many of our leading composers, performers, and scholars. Music courses have expanded the horizons and interests of countless students. And since the 1950s, many universities have sponsored performing groups specializing in contemporary music. In addition, they have housed most of the electronic music studios.
>
> *Source:* Adapted from Roger Kamien, *Music: An Appreciation,* 5e, p. 444. Copyright © 1992 by The McGraw-Hill Companies, Inc. Reprinted with permission of The McGraw-Hill Companies, Inc.

Listed below are the four details that answer the question *"What* role have American colleges and universities played in our musical culture?" As you can see, listing the supporting details below a question is an ideal format for study cards.

What role have American colleges and universities played in our musical culture?
1. They trained and employed many leading composers, performers, and scholars.
2. They expanded the horizons and interests of students through music courses.
3. Since the 1950s, they have sponsored performing groups specializing in contemporary music.
4. They have housed most of the electronic music studios.

The following diagram (which is one type of study map) shows the relationship between the main idea and the supporting details in this paragraph. (You will learn more about mapping in Chapter 10.) This is also a good format for study cards.

Main Idea
American colleges and universities have played an unusually vital role in our musical culture.

Supporting Detail 1	**Supporting Detail 2**	**Supporting Detail 3**	**Supporting Detail 4**
They trained and employed many leading composers, performers, and scholars.	They expanded the horizons and interests of students through music courses.	Since the 1950s, they have sponsored performing groups specializing in contemporary music.	They have housed most of the electronic music studios.

paraphrasing

Restating an author's material in your own words.

Stop and Annotate

Go back to the excerpt on page 345. Locate the four supporting details and number them with a small ①, ② ③, and ④. Underline or highlight the signal words *And* and *In addition* that helped you identify the last two details.

Notice that in the sample study card and map, the details are written out almost exactly as they appear in the paragraph. When *you* are listing details, however, you will want to use some of your own words and abbreviations in order to keep them brief. Restating an author's material in your own words is called **paraphrasing.** Notice also, in the original excerpt, the words *And* and *In addition* in the last two sentences. These words signal that two separate details are being given. However, notice that not every detail is introduced by a signal word.

In textbook paragraphs, you will find it helpful to go back and insert a *number* next to each detail in a paragraph. Numbering the details is helpful for at least three reasons. First, it helps you locate all the details. Second, it helps you remember how many details there were. Third, it prevents you from overmarking the paragraph by underlining or highlighting too much. (You will also find it helpful to number the details when you list them in your notes or on chapter review cards.)

In the next excerpt, the topic is *Richard Feynman* (fīn′ mən), an American physicist and writer. Feynman was a Nobel laureate who worked on the atomic bomb, and reinvented quantum mechanics (the mathematics describing atomic processes). He exposed the fatal error by NASA that caused the space shuttle *Challenger* to explode 73 seconds after launch in 1986, killing the entire crew. The first sentence of the paragraph is the stated main idea: *Mr. Feynman was one of the great characters of modern physics.* Change this main idea sentence into the question "*Why* was Feynman considered a character?" (As used here, the word *character* refers to an unusual or eccentric person.) Then read the paragraph to identify the details that answer this question.

> Richard Feynman was one of the great characters of modern physics. He was a jokester who figured out how to crack safes in Los Alamos offices while working on atomic bomb research in World War II. He was a computational genius, once beating early computers in a contest to track a rocket launch. He could demolish other physicists whose presentation contained an error or humiliate them by producing in minutes a complicated calculation that took them weeks or months.
>
> *Source:* Adapted from Tom Siegfried, "Exploring the Mind of a Genius," *Dallas Morning News,* October 25, 1992, sec. J, by permission of *Dallas Morning News.*

Listed below are the two details that answer the question "*Why* was Richard Feynman considered a character?" Again, notice how listing the supporting details below a question makes an easy-to-read study card.

Why was Richard Feynman considered a "character"?
1. He was a jokester.
2. He was a computational genius.

Stop and Annotate

Go back to the excerpt above. Locate the two supporting details and number them with a small ① and ②.

Notice how clearly the details stand out when they are listed on separate lines. Listing them this way makes it easy to see the information that explains why Feynman was considered a character. (The contest with the computer and his "demolishing" other physicists are minor details that give proof of his computational ability.) Did you notice that no signal words were used in this paragraph to identify the two supporting details? Instead, the author presents two details about Feynman that are quite different from each other: that he was a computational genius and, surprisingly, that he was also a jokester. The unusual combination of these two characteristics supports the author's main point that Feynman was a "character."

The next excerpt is from a classic book on writing. The excerpt contains a number of important details. The topic of this paragraph is *careless writing and ways readers get lost,* and its stated main idea is the second sentence: *If the reader is, lost, it's usually because the writer hasn't been careful enough.* Turn the main idea into the question "*How* do careless writers cause readers to get lost?" Now read the paragraph to find the details that answer this question.

It won't do to say that the reader is too dumb or too lazy to keep pace with the train of thought. If the reader is lost, it's usually because the writer hasn't been careful enough. The carelessness can take any number of forms. Perhaps a sentence is so excessively cluttered that the reader, hacking through the verbiage, simply doesn't know what it means. Perhaps a sentence has been so shoddily constructed that the reader could read it in several ways. Perhaps the writer has switched pronouns in mid-sentence, or has switched tenses, so the reader loses track of who is talking or when the action took place. Perhaps Sentence B is not a logical sequel to Sentence A—the writer, in whose head the connection is clear, has not bothered to provide the missing link. Perhaps the writer has used an important word incorrectly by not taking the trouble to look it up.

Source: Adapted from William K. Zinsser, *On Writing Well,* 5e, New York: Harper and Row, 1994, pp. 9, 12. Copyright © 1980 by William K. Zinsser. Used with permission.

Stop and Annotate

Go back to the excerpt above. Locate the five supporting details and number them with a small ①, ②, ③, ④, and ⑤. Underline or highlight the signal word *Perhaps* that helped you identify all five details.

Here is a list of the five details that answer the question "*How* do careless writers cause readers to get lost?"

How do careless writers cause readers to get lost?
1. Careless writers clutter sentences with too many words.
2. They write sentences that can be read in several ways.
3. They switch pronouns or tenses.
4. They don't supply links between sentences.
5. They use words incorrectly.

Notice that some of the details listed above have been paraphrased to make them briefer and easier to understand and remember. Notice also that no signal words were used in this paragraph. Instead, repeated use of the word *perhaps* signals each detail. Inserting small numbers next to the details makes them easy to locate, even though they are spread throughout the paragraph.

The next sample paragraph is from a health textbook. As the heading indicates, its topic is *water.* Its implied main idea is *Water serves many important functions in the body.* Turn this main idea into the question "*What* important functions does water serve in the body?" Then read the paragraph to find the details that answer this question.

> ### Water
> Water has no nutritional value, yet is a very important food component. It is used to transport nutrients to the cells and to remove cellular waste products. In addition, it acts as a medium for digestion, regulates body temperature, and helps cushion the vital organs. An inadequate water intake will restrict the function of all body systems. Finally, water and some of the chemicals it carries are responsible for bodily structure, since, on average, 60 percent of the body is water.
>
> *Source:* Adapted from Marvin Levy, Mark Dignan, and Janet Shirreffs, *Targeting Wellness: The Core*, p. 52. Copyright © 1992 by The McGraw-Hill Companies, Inc. Reprinted with permission of The McGraw-Hill Companies, Inc.

Stop and Annotate

Go back to the excerpt above. Locate the eight supporting details and number each with a small number. Underline or highlight the signal words *In addition* and *Finally,* which helped you identify two of the details.

Here is a list of the eight paraphrased details that answer the question "*What important functions does water serve in the body?*"

What important functions does water serve in the body?
1. an important food component
2. transports nutrients to cells
3. removes cellular waste
4. acts as a medium for digestion
5. regulates body temperature
6. helps cushion vital organs
7. inadequate intake restricts functions of all body systems
8. partly responsible for body structure because the body is 60 percent water

Remember that a single sentence can contain more than one detail. In this paragraph, there are five sentences, but eight details. The second sentence contains two details, and the third sentence contains three. There are two signals in the paragraph, *In addition* and *Finally.* (When you study, there are other ways to record details besides listing them. These techniques are called *annotation*, *outlining*, and *mapping*. They are presented in Chapter 10.)

EXERCISE 1

This paragraph comes from an American government textbook:

Until the presidency of Lyndon Johnson, all U.S. Supreme Court Justices had been Caucasians. In 1967, Johnson appointed the famous NAACP lawyer Thurgood Marshall to the bench. Thurgood Marshall's nomination was an acknowledgement that Marshall had been successful as an advocate in getting the Supreme Court to change civil rights policy. When Marshall retired from the bench in 1991, President George H. W. Bush filled

(Continued on next page)

the vacancy with another African American, albeit one with a far more conservative philosophy, Clarence Thomas. In 2009, President Barack Obama appointed Justice Sonia Sotomayor, who became the first Hispanic American to ever serve on the Supreme Court.

Source: Adapted from Joseph Losco and Ralph Baker, *Am Gov, 2011,* p. 370. Copyright © 2011 by The McGraw-Hill Companies, Inc. Reprinted with permission of The McGraw-Hill Companies, Inc.

Write the *main idea sentence:* _____

_____

List the three *supporting details*. Use a bullet for each detail and write each detail on a new line.

_____

_____

_____

MAJOR AND MINOR DETAILS, AND HOW TO TELL THE DIFFERENCE

major details

Details that directly support the main idea.

Major details are also known as *primary details.*

All the details in a paragraph ultimately support the main idea by explaining, illustrating, or proving it. In most of the examples presented earlier, all the details *directly* supported (explained) the main idea. Details that directly support the main idea are called **major details** (also known as *primary details*). However, some details support or explain *other details.* These are called **minor details** (also known as *secondary details*).

The following diagram shows the relationship between the main idea, major details, and minor details.

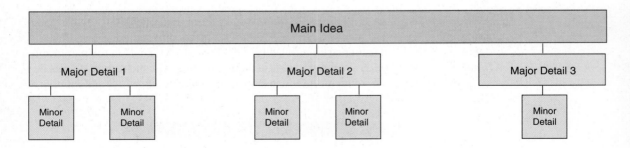

minor details

Details that support other details.

Minor details are also known as *secondary details.*

Here is a simple paragraph that has been created to illustrate major and minor details. Its topic is *uses of pepper.* Its stated main idea is the first sentence: *Throughout history, pepper has had many other uses besides as a way to season food.* There are three major details that explain those uses. The other sentences are minor details that explain the major details.

Throughout history, pepper has had many other uses besides as a way to season food. Pepper was also one of the first ways of preserving meat. During the Crusades, pepper was used to preserve sausages. Pepper is still used to preserve meat today. Pepper has also been used as a medicine. In medieval times, peppercorns were prescribed to cure aches and pains. Native Americans today use pepper to cure toothaches. Today, pepper is also used to control insects. For example, the French and Dutch use pepper to kill moths and to repel other insects.

The following diagram shows the relationship between the main idea and the major and minor details for this paragraph.

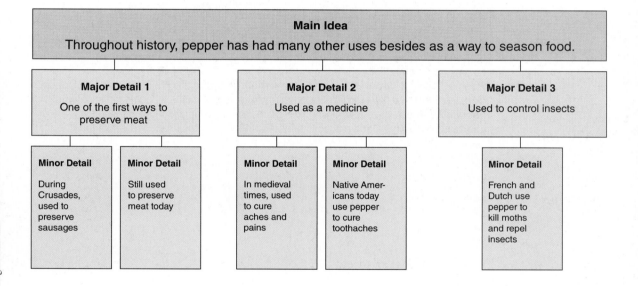

Stop and Annotate

Go back to the excerpt above. Locate the three major details and number them with a small ①, ②, and ③. Underline the signal word *also,* which helped you identify the last two major details.

Again, notice that only three details directly answer the main idea question "How has pepper been used in different ways throughout history besides as a way to season food?" Therefore, these three details are major details. The passage would make sense with only the main idea and those details. However, the author explains even more fully by giving examples of the three ways. Therefore, those details, which explain other details, are minor details.

Remember, to identify the supporting details of a paragraph, ask yourself, "What *additional information* does the author provide to help me understand the main idea completely?" Change the main idea into a question; then look for the major details that answer the question. Be aware that the author might also include minor details to further enhance your understanding. Don't spend too much time worrying about whether a detail is major or minor. The important thing is simply that you distinguish between the main idea and the details.

EXERCISE 2

This paragraph comes from an information technology textbook:

One of the fastest-growing uses of the Internet is **social networking,** or connecting individuals to one another. While many social networking sites support a wide range of activities, there are three broad categories. *Reuniting sites* are designed to connect people who have known one another but have lost touch. For example, you may reunite with an old high school friend that you have not seen for several years. You join a social network by connecting to a reuniting site and providing profile information such as your age, gender, name of high school, and so forth. Members are able to search the database to locate individuals. Many of the sites will even notify you whenever a new individual joins who matches some parts of your profile (such as a high school class). Two of the best-known reuniting sites are Classmates Online and Facebook. *Friend-of-a-friend sites* are designed to bring together two people who do not know one another but share a common friend. The theory is that if you share a common friend, then it is likely that you would become friends. For example, a network could be started by one of your acquaintances by providing profile information on him- or herself and a list of friends. You could visit your acquaintance's site to connect to a friend of your acquaintance. You could even join the list of friends provided at the site. Two well-known friend-of-a-friend sites are Friendster and MySpace. *Common interest sites* bring together individuals that share common interests or hobbies. You select a networking site based on a particular interest. For example, if you wanted to share images, you might join Flickr or YouTube. If you are looking for business contacts, you might join LinkedIn. If you wanted to locate or create a special interest group, you might join Meetup.

Source: Adapted from Timothy J. O'Leary and Linda I. O'Leary, *Computing Essentials 2012: Making IT Work for You,* p. 37. Copyright © 2012 by The McGraw-Hill Companies, Inc. Reprinted with permission of The McGraw-Hill Companies, Inc.

Write the *main idea sentence:* _____

List the three *major supporting details.* Use a bullet for each major detail and start each detail on a new line. List the *minor details* below the major details. Indent each minor detail. Use a dash, and start each one on a new line.

_____

_____

_____

_____

_____

_____

_____

_____

_____

_____

_____

_____

_____

_____

_____

_____

_____

A WORD ABOUT STANDARDIZED READING TESTS: SUPPORTING DETAILS

Many college students are required to take standardized reading tests as part of an overall assessment program, in a reading course, or as part of a state-mandated basic skills test. A standardized reading test typically consists of a series of passages followed by multiple-choice reading skill application questions to be completed within a specified time limit.

Standardized reading tests always include questions about supporting details. The purpose of such questions is to see if you can locate and comprehend specific information stated in a passage.

Test questions about supporting details often begin with phrases such as:
According to the passage . . .
According to the information in the passage . . .
The author states . . .
The author states that . . .

Questions may also refer to specific information in a passage, as in the following examples:
One function of water in the body is . . .
The museum mentioned in the passage is located in . . .
World War I began in the year . . .
The height of the tower was . . .

To answer an item about supporting details, read the question carefully to determine exactly what information you need (for instance, a place, a person's name, or a date). Then _skim_ the passage, looking for that information. When you come to the part of the passage that has what you are looking for, slow down and read it more carefully.

Don't overlook a correct answer simply because it is worded differently from the way the information appears in the passage. For instance, a passage might state that a child was rescued by a "police officer," but the correct answer choice might say "an officer of the law." Or a passage might specifically mention Bill Gates and Donald Trump, but the correct answer might be worded "two of America's wealthiest businessmen." Remember, you need to look for information in the answer choices that _means_ the _same thing_ as the information in the passage, even if the words themselves are different.

CHECKPOINT
Identifying Supporting Details

Directions: To identify major supporting details, read each paragraph carefully and then ask yourself, "What additional information does the author provide to help me understand the main idea completely?" Then select the answer choice that expresses a major supporting detail.

1. This paragraph comes from a biology textbook:

Primates

Primates are the highest order of mammals, and this group includes humans, together with the apes and monkeys. Primates are mammals with two distinct features. These distinct features allow them to live in an insect-eating, arboreal environment. Primates have grasping fingers and toes. Unlike the clawed feet of tree shrews and squirrels, primates have grasping hands and feet that let them grip limbs, hang from branches, seize food, and, in some primates, use tools. The first digit in many primates is opposable and at least some, if not all, of the digits have nails. Primates also have binocular vision. Unlike the eyes of tree shrews and squirrels, which sit on the side of the head so that the two fields of vision do not overlap, the eyes of primates are shifted forward to the front of the face. This produces overlapping binocular vision that lets the brain judge distance precisely, which is important to an animal moving through the trees.

Source: Adapted from George B. Johnson, *The Living World: Basic Concepts,* 4e, p. 486. Copyright © 2006 by The McGraw-Hill Companies, Inc. Reprinted with permission of The McGraw-Hill Companies, Inc.

Which of the following is a major supporting detail?
- *a.* Primates are the highest order of mammals, and this group includes humans, together with the apes and monkeys.
- *b.* Primates are mammals with two distinct features.
- *c.* These distinct features allow primates to live in an insect-eating, arboreal environment.
- *d.* Primates have binocular vision.

2. This paragraph comes from a music appreciation textbook:

The world of jazz has witnessed many changes since its beginnings at the turn of the twentieth century. Geographically, its center has shifted away from New Orleans to Chicago, Kansas City, and New York. Today, it is hard to speak of one single jazz center, since good jazz is heard worldwide, from Paris to Tokyo. Jazz has changed in function, too. For a long time, it was basically music for dancing; but since the 1940s, many newer jazz styles have been intended for listening. Now we are as likely to hear jazz in a concert hall or college classroom as in a bar or nightclub. The image of jazz has also changed. It was originally condemned for its emphasis on sexuality, but it has long since become respected as a major

American art form. In recent years, jazz has been sponsored by major American cultural institutions. Both Lincoln Center and Carnegie Hall in New York City have regular jazz series, and a Jazz Masterworks Orchestra has been founded at the Smithsonian National Museum of American History in Washington, D.C.

Source: Adapted from Roger Kamien, *Music: An Appreciation,* 10e, p. 465. Copyright © 2011 by The McGraw-Hill Companies, Inc. Reprinted with permission of The McGraw-Hill Companies, Inc.

_____ Which of the following is a major supporting detail?

a. The world of jazz has witnessed many changes since its beginnings at the turn of the twentieth century.

b. For a long time, jazz was basically music for dancing.

c. The image of jazz has changed.

d. Both Lincoln Center and Carnegie Hall in New York City have regular jazz series, and a Jazz Masterworks Orchestra has been founded at the Smithsonian National Museum of American History in Washington, D.C.

3. This paragraph comes from a marriage and family textbook:

There are several types of stress. First, there is physiological stress, which is the body's harmful reaction to whatever happens. There is evidence that stress causes physical reactions in our bodies, such as increased blood pressure or decreased immune response. Second, there is psychological stress, which involves appraising the threat, resulting in an emotional reaction. Finally, there is sociocultural stress, which is the disturbance of social systems in our lives. Examples of sociocultural stress might be war, neighborhood violence, unemployment, or poverty.

Source: Adapted from David H. Olson, John DeFrain, and Linda Skogrand, *Marriages and Families: Intimacy, Diversity, and Strengths,* 7e, p. 402. Copyright © 2011 by The McGraw-Hill Companies, Inc. Reprinted with permission of The McGraw-Hill Companies, Inc.

_____ Which of the following is a major supporting detail?

a. There is evidence that stress causes increased blood pressure or decreased immune response.

b. There are several types of stress.

c. Sociocultural stress is the disturbance of social systems in our lives.

d. Examples of sociocultural stress might be war, neighborhood violence, unemployment, or poverty.

4. This paragraph comes from a biology textbook:

The Flow of Energy

All living organisms require energy. They need it to carry out the activities of living—to build bodies, to do work, and to think thoughts. All of the energy used by most organisms comes from the sun. This energy is gradually used up as it flows in one direction through ecosystems. The easiest way to understand the flow of energy through the living world is to look at who uses it. The first stage of the flow of energy is its capture by green plants, algae, and some bacteria in photosynthesis. Then, plants serve as a source of life-driving energy for animals that eat them. Other animals may then eat the plant eaters. The flow of energy is a key factor in shaping ecosystems, affecting how many and what kind of animals live in a community.

Source: Adapted from George B. Johnson, *The Living World: Basic Concepts,* 4e, by p. 6. Copyright © 2006 by The McGraw-Hill Companies, Inc. Reprinted with permission of The McGraw-Hill Companies, Inc.

Which of the following is a major supporting detail?

  a. All living organisms need energy to carry out the activities of living.

  b. All of the energy used by most organisms comes from the sun.

  c. Energy from the sun, which is used by most organisms, is gradually used up as it flows in one direction through ecosystems.

  d. The first stage of the flow of energy is its capture by green plants, algae, and some bacteria in photosynthesis.

5. This paragraph comes from a marriage and family textbook:

   To stay out of bankruptcy, it is helpful to know why some people assume too much debt. Excessive debt for individuals and families may be due to several kinds of spending. Unwise *credit spending* can lead to serious overextension. *Crisis spending* is spending resulting from unexpected events in life such as unemployment, uninsured illness, and business income decline or failure. Personal finances can be thrown into turmoil as a result of crisis spending. *Careless* or *impulsive spending* includes overpaying for items that could be purchased for less, purchasing inferior merchandise that does not last, or buying things one does not really need. *Compulsive spending* occurs because some people simply can't say no to salespeople. Compulsive spending also occurs because people have an uncontrollable impulse to acquire material things.

Source: Adapted from David Olson, John DeFrain, and Linda Skogrand, *Marriages and Families: Intimacy, Diversity, and Strengths,* 7e, p. 243. Copyright © 2011 by The McGraw-Hill Companies, Inc. Reprinted with permission of The McGraw-Hill Companies, Inc.

Which of the following is a major supporting detail?

  a. Compulsive spending occurs because some people simply can't say no to salespeople.

  b. Personal finances can be thrown into turmoil as a result of crisis spending.

  c. Excessive debt for individuals and families may be due to several kinds of spending.

  d. To stay out of bankruptcy, it is helpful to know why some people assume too much debt.

DEVELOPING CHAPTER REVIEW CARDS

Complete the five review cards for Chapter 6 by answering the questions or following the directions on each card. When you have completed them, you will have summarized (1) what supporting details are, (2) why they are important, (3) how to find them in a paragraph, (4) how to list them, and (5) how to mark them. Print or write legibly. (*Note:* From this point on, page numbers no longer appear on the cards. You will find it more efficient to remove the Chapter Review Card pages before filling them in.)

What Supporting Details Are

Define supporting details.

Supporting details may consist of:

Card 1   Chapter 6: Identifying Supporting Details

Why Supporting Details Are Important

List four reasons supporting details are important.

1. **Reason 1:**

2. **Reason 2:**

3. **Reason 3:**

4. **Reason 4:**

Card 2   Chapter 6: Identifying Supporting Details

How to Find Supporting Details

To identify supporting details in a paragraph, what question should you ask yourself?

List some signal words that can introduce supporting details.

Besides signal words, what are two other ways authors indicate supporting details?

Is every supporting detail introduced by a signal of some sort?

Card 3   Chapter 6: Identifying Supporting Details

How to List Supporting Details

Define *paraphrasing.*

Why is paraphrasing useful when you are writing down supporting details?

When you write down supporting details, what should you do to make each supporting detail stand out clearly?

Card 4   Chapter 6: Identifying Supporting Details

How to Mark Supporting Details

How can you make supporting details easier to locate in a paragraph after you have read the paragraph?

List three rèasons this is a helpful technique.

Reason 1:

Reason 2:

Reason 3:

Card 5   Chapter 6: Identifying Supporting Details

Major and Minor Details

1. Define *major details*.

2. Define *minor details*.

Card 6   Chapter 6: Identifying Supporting Details

Directions: Read these paragraphs carefully and answer the questions that follow them. Write your answers in the spaces provided.

This paragraph comes from a psychology textbook:

Caffeine produces several reactions. One major behavioral effect is an increase in attentiveness. Another major behavioral effect is a decrease in reaction time. Caffeine can also bring about an improvement in mood, by mimicking the effects of a natural brain chemical, adenosine. Too much caffeine, however, can result in nervousness and insomnia. People can build up a biological dependence on the drug. Regular users who suddenly stop drinking coffee may experience headache or depression. Many people who drink large amounts of coffee on weekdays have headaches on weekends because of the sudden drop in the amount of caffeine they are consuming.

Source: Robert S. Feldman, *Essentials of Understanding Psychology,* 9e, pp. 151–52. Copyright © 2011 by The McGraw-Hill Companies, Inc. Reprinted with permission of The McGraw-Hill Companies, Inc.

_____ **1.** What is the main idea of this paragraph?
  a. Caffeine produces several reactions.
  b. The major behavioral effects of caffeine are an increase in attentiveness and a decrease in reaction time.
  c. There are several beneficial effects of caffeine.
  d. Many people who consume large amounts of coffee build up a biological dependence on the drug.

_____ **2.** Which of the following is a supporting detail mentioned in the paragraph?
  a. Caffeine produces several reactions.
  b. Regular users of caffeine often experience headaches and depression.
  c. Kicking the caffeine habit can be difficult.
  d. Caffeine can bring about an improvement in mood by mimicking the effects of a natural brain chemical, adenosine.

This paragraph comes from a United States government textbook:

Poverty in the United States

Although Americans are far better off economically than most of the world's peoples, poverty is a significant and persistent problem in the United States. The government defines the *poverty line* as the annual cost of a thrifty food budget for an urban family of four, multiplied by three to include the cost of housing, clothes, and other necessities. Families whose incomes fall below that line are officially considered poor. In 2005, the poverty line was set at an annual income of roughly $19,000 for a family of four. One in nine Americans—roughly thirty million people, including more than ten million children—lives below the poverty line. If they could all join hands, they would form a line stretching from New York to Los Angeles and back again.

Source: Adapted from Thomas E. Patterson, *The American Democracy,* 6e, p. 560. Copyright © 2006 by The McGraw-Hill Companies, Inc. Reprinted with permission of The McGraw-Hill Companies, Inc.

C

3. What is the main idea of this paragraph?
   a. One in nine Americans lives below the poverty line.
   b. The government defines the *poverty line* as the annual cost of a food budget for a family of four, multiplied by three to include the cost of clothes and other necessities.
   c. Although Americans are far better off economically than most of the world's peoples, poverty is a significant and persistent problem in the United States.
   d. There is no single solution to the problem of poverty in the United States.

4. Which of the following is a supporting detail mentioned in the paragraph?
   a. Roughly ten million people in the United States live below the poverty line.
   b. Poverty is a significant and persistent problem in the United States.
   c. There are more people in the United States living in poverty today than any time in our nation's history.
   d. In 2005, the poverty line was set at an annual income of roughly $19,000 for a family of four.

This paragraph comes from a management information systems textbook:

   The electronic nature of computers gives them several important attributes. First, computers are extremely fast at processing instructions, that is, at performing calculations and making logical comparisons. Second, computers are extremely accurate in their processing. Rarely does a computer make an electronic mistake that it does not catch itself. Almost all errors in computer data processing are caused by faulty programs prepared by humans. Third, computers are extremely reliable. Because they are primarily electronic and without moving parts, they seldom have failures.

Source: Adapted from George M. Scott, *Principles of Management Information Systems,* p. 14. Copyright © 1986 by The McGraw-Hill Companies, Inc. Reprinted with permission of The McGraw-Hill Companies, Inc.

5. What is the main idea of this paragraph?
   a. Computers make our lives easier in many ways.
   b. Computers seldom have failures because they are primarily electronic and do not have moving parts.
   c. The electronic nature of computers gives them several important attributes.
   d. Computers are efficient because they can correct their own electronic mistakes.

_____ **6.** Which of the following is a supporting detail mentioned in the paragraph?
   a. Computers enhance our lives in three ways.
   b. Computers are extremely accurate in their processing.
   c. The electronic nature of computers gives them several important attributes.
   d. Errors in computer data processing can be corrected electronically.

This paragraph comes from a psychology textbook:

   The brain stem is responsible for many basic functions. It takes in information from several senses through sensory regions for vision, hearing, taste, balance, and touch in the facial area. It controls involuntary activity of the tongue, the larynx, the eyes, and the facial muscles through specific motor neurons for these areas. It controls levels of sleep and arousal through the reticular formation, nestled within its central core, and it coordinates the motor neurons in the spinal cord that control such activities as walking, breathing, and the beating of our hearts.

Source: Adapted from Diane Papalia and Sally Olds, *Psychology,* p. 251. Copyright © 1988 by The McGraw-Hill Companies, Inc. Reprinted with permission of The McGraw-Hill Companies, Inc.

_____ **7.** What is the main idea of this paragraph?
   a. The brain stem is responsible for many basic functions.
   b. All body functions are controlled by the brain stem.
   c. The reticular formation, nestled within its central core, is the most important part of the brain stem.
   d. An injury to the brain stem can cause serious problems.

_____ **8.** Which of the following is *not* a supporting detail mentioned in the paragraph?
   a. The brain stem controls levels of sleep and arousal.
   b. The brain stem takes in information from several senses through sensory regions.
   c. The brain stem controls involuntary activity of the tongue, the larynx, the eyes, and the facial muscles.
   d. The brain stem is responsible for our speech and memory functions.

This paragraph comes from a health textbook:

   "Millennial generation" is the name given to today's young adults who were born between 1982 and 2000. There have been some initial research studies of the millennial generation's progress in mastering the developmental expectations for the transition from adolescence to early adulthood. These studies have found that, compared to earlier generations, the millennials are:
- more inclined to drop out of college for a period of time, and take longer to finish college even if they have not dropped out
- more likely to change colleges, and to change residence while at the same college

- more likely to return home to live after completing college, prompting the term "the boomerang phenomenon"
- more likely to share a residence with friends from college than to live alone or to return home
- more likely to take jobs in food services and retail sales that pay relatively low wages
- likely to leave a job rather than deal with job-related conflict, thus not experiencing advancement within the workplace
- more inclined to fill leisure time with technology-based media.
- less likely to have refined communications skills, due in large part to technology-based communication
- more likely to volunteer—not to pad their résumés, but for the well-being of others
- more likely to have a more diverse group of friends, in terms of both gender and race
- less likely to marry, less likely to marry at a younger age, and more likely to delay parenting until older

Source: Adapted from Wayne A. Payne, Dale B. Hahn, and Ellen B. Lucas, *Understanding Your Health,* 10e, p. 2. Copyright © 2009 by The McGraw-Hill Companies, Inc. Reprinted with permission of The McGraw-Hill Companies, Inc.

9. What is the main idea of this paragraph?
    a. Individuals who belong to the millennial generation are more likely to drop out of college for a period of time and to take longer to finish college even if they have not dropped out.
    b. Today's young adults who were born between 1982 and 2000 are called "millennials."
    c. Millennials are different from earlier generations.
    d. Studies have found that, compared to earlier generations, millennials have a difficult time making the transition from adolescence to adulthood.

10. Which of the following is *not* a supporting detail mentioned in the paragraph?
    a. Millennials are less likely to marry at a younger age.
    b. Millennials are more inclined to take longer to finish college.
    c. Millennials typically trust only their family members and parents.
    d. Millennials are more likely to have a more diverse group of friends.

Directions: Read these paragraphs carefully. Then write the main idea sentence and list the supporting details for each paragraph in the spaces provided.

This paragraph comes from a physical fitness and wellness textbook:

Effective Goals

If any lifestyle change is to be of value, it is important to determine—ahead of time—what you hope to accomplish. Learning to set goals is useful as a basis for self-planning. Effective goals have several important characteristics. The acronym SMART can help you remember several of these characteristics. Goals are objectives that you hope to accomplish as a result of lifestyle changes. They should be *specific (S)*. Many individuals make the mistake of setting vague goals, such as "be more active" or "eat less." These are really the reasons you want to set goals. A specific goal provides details such as limiting calories to a specific number each day. Goals should be *measurable (M)*. Assessments should be performed before establishing goals and again after a lifestyle change is made to see if the goals were met. Goals should also be *attainable (A)* and *realistic (R)*, neither too hard nor too easy. If the goal is too hard, failure is likely. Failure is discouraging. By setting a goal that is realistic and attainable, you have a greater chance of success. Finally, a goal should be *timely (T)*. Timely goals are especially relevant to you at the present time. If you set too many goals, you may not reach any of them. Choosing goals that are timely can help you decide on which goals you should focus your current efforts.

Source: Adapted from Charles Corbin, Gregory Welk, William Corbin, and Karen Welk, *Concepts of Physical Fitness: Active Lifestyles for Wellness,* 15e, p. 29. Copyright © 2009 by The McGraw-Hill Companies. Reprinted with permission of The McGraw-Hill Companies, Inc.

1. Write the main idea sentence:

_____

_____

2. List the major supporting details. Use a bullet for each detail and start each detail on a new line.

_____

_____

_____

_____

_____

This paragraph comes from a business textbook:

> The value of a college education can amount to much more than just a larger paycheck. Other benefits of a college education include increasing your ability to think critically and improving your ability to communicate your ideas to others. Improving your ability to use technology and preparing yourself to live in a diverse world are two more benefits. Knowing you've met your personal goals and earned a college degree also gives you the self-confidence to continue to strive to meet your future goals.
>
> *Source:* Adapted from William Nickels, James McHugh, and Susan McHugh, *Understanding Business,* 7e, p. 3. Copyright © 2005 by The McGraw-Hill Companies, Inc. Reprinted with permission of The McGraw-Hill Companies, Inc.

3. Write the main idea sentence:

_____

_____

4. List the five major supporting details. Use a bullet for each detail and start each detail on a new line.

_____

_____

_____

_____

_____

This paragraph comes from a career development textbook:

> In 2009, President Obama signed the American Recovery and Reinvestment Act, which called for the government to invest money in key initiatives to stimulate the economy by creating new jobs in new industries. One of these initiatives is a focus on the creation of green jobs, which are jobs that have a positive impact on the environment. These jobs are responsible for providing products or services that help lower prices or create greater efficiency so that consumers can spend less and rely on products over long periods of time. Jobs that build products or provide services that conserve energy or enable use of alternative energy sources are an example. These may include making buildings more energy efficient, or electric power renewable, or building energy-efficient vehicles. Green jobs require a wide range of skills from management, accounting, architectural, and marketing to more skilled trades such as construction and manufacturing.
>
> *Source:* Adapted from Donna Yena, *Career Directions: The Path to Your Ideal Career,* 5e, p. 5. Copyright © 2011 by The McGraw-Hill Companies, Inc. Reprinted with permission of The McGraw-Hill Companies, Inc.

5. Write the main idea sentence:

_____

_____

_____

6. List the major supporting details. Use a bullet for each detail and start each detail on a new line.

_____

_____

_____

_____

_____

_____

_____

This paragraph comes from a psychology textbook:

Consciousness

The nervous system in the human body is responsible for more than just monitoring our bodily functions. It is also responsible for *consciousness,* our awareness of the sensations, thoughts, and feelings we are experiencing at a given moment. Consciousness can take the form of extreme alertness, such as when we are taking a test or looking for a parking space on a crowded street. It can also take the form of reduced alertness, such as when we are daydreaming or driving a familiar route without having to think about what we are doing. Conscious activities are controlled by the **conscious mind,** the part of the brain that controls the mental processes of which we are aware. The conscious mind collects information from our environment, stores it in our memory, and helps us make logical decisions. The conscious mind is not the whole story, however. We also have a **subconscious mind,** the part of the brain that controls the mental processes of which we are not actively aware. The subconscious mind stores the emotions and sensations that we are not quite aware of, the feelings that are just under the surface. Our subconscious mind also helps us solve problems. Have you ever tried in vain to solve a difficult problem, only to have the solution pop into your head later when you were thinking about something else? This is the power of the subconscious mind. It came up with the solution while your conscious mind was busy with something else.

Source: Adapted from Denis Waitley, *Psychology of Success: Finding Meaning in Work and Life,* 5e, p. 211. Copyright © 2010 by The McGraw-Hill Companies, Inc. Reprinted with permission of The McGraw-Hill Companies, Inc.

7. List the minor supporting details that tell more about the *conscious mind.* Use a bullet for each detail and start each detail on a new line.

_____

_____

_____

_____

_____

8. List the minor supporting details that tell more about the *subconscious mind.* Use a bullet for each detail and start each detail on a new line.

_____

_____

_____

_____

_____

_____

This paragraph comes from a speech textbook:

Words and phrases have two kinds of meanings—denotative and connotative. *Denotative* meaning is precise, literal, and objective. It describes the object, person, place, idea, or event to which the word refers. One way to think of a word's denotative meaning is as its dictionary definition. For example, denotatively, the noun "school" means "a place, institution, or building where instruction is given." *Connotative* meaning is more variable, figurative, and subjective. The connotative meaning of the word "school" includes all the feelings, associations, and emotions that the word triggers in different people. For some people, "school" might connote personal growth, childhood friends, and a special teacher. For others, it might connote frustration, discipline, and boring homework assignments. Connotative meaning gives words their intensity and emotional power. It arouses in listeners feelings of anger, pity, love, fear, friendship, nostalgia, greed, guilt, and the like. Speakers, like poets, often use connotation to enrich their meaning.

Source: Adapted from Stephen E. Lucas, *The Art of Public Speaking,* 10e, p. 224. Copyright © 2009 by The McGraw-Hill Companies, Inc. Reprinted with permission of The McGraw-Hill Companies, Inc.

9. Write the main idea sentence:

_____

_____

_____

10. List the minor supporting details that tell more about *denotative and connotative meaning*. Use a bullet for each detail and start each detail on a new line.

Denotative meaning:

_____

_____

_____

_____

Connotative meaning:

_____

_____

_____

_____

_____

SELECTION **6.1**

Health

SELECTION 6.1

Shaping Your Health: The Millennial Generation and Early Adulthood

From *Understanding Your Health*
by Wayne A. Payne, Dale B. Hahn, and Ellen B. Lucas

Prepare Yourself to Read

Directions: Do these exercises *before* you read Selection 6.1.

1. First, read and think about the title. When you read or hear the term *millennial generation,* what comes to mind?

   _____

   _____

   _____

2. What term or phrase do you use to refer to *your* age group?

   _____

   _____

3. The phrase *generation gap* is widely used when discussing topics relating to parents and children. How would you define the meaning of this phrase?

   _____

   _____

   _____

   _____

4. Next, complete your preview by reading the following:

   > Introduction (in *italics*)
   > Headings
   > The visual aid in the margin near paragraph 6
   > Caption accompanying the cartoon

   Now that you have completed your preview, what does this selection seem to be about?

   _____

   _____

   _____

   _____

5. **Build your vocabulary as you read.** If you discover an unfamiliar word or key term as you read the selection, try to determine its meaning by using context clues.

371

Internet Resources

Read More about This Topic Online

Use a search engine, such as Google or Yahoo!, to expand your existing knowledge about this topic *before* you read the selection or to learn more about it *afterward*. If you are unfamiliar with conducting Internet searches, read pages 25–26 on Boolean searches. You can also use Wikipedia, the free online encyclopedia, at www .wikipedia.com. Keep in mind that when you visit any website, it is a good idea to evaluate the site and the information it contains. Ask yourself questions such as "Who sponsors this website?" and "Is the information it contains up to date?"

SELECTION 6.1: SHAPING YOUR HEALTH: THE MILLENNIAL GENERATION AND EARLY ADULTHOOD

This selection from the introductory chapter of a health and wellness textbook discusses the value of good health and how it affects the lives of young adults. The authors also describe the "millennial generation" of today's young adults and explain the growth and development tasks society expects to accomplish.

1   "Take care of your health, because you'll miss it when it's gone," younger people hear often from their elders. This simple and heartfelt advice is given in the belief that young people take their health for granted and assume that they will always maintain the state of health and wellness they now enjoy. Observation and experience should, however, remind all of us that youth is relatively brief, and health is always changing.

2   How do you imagine your life in the future? Do you ever think about how your health allows you to participate in meaningful life activities—and what might happen if your health is compromised? Consider, for example, the numerous ways that your health affects your daily activities. Your health affects your ability to pursue an education or a career. It affects your opportunities to socialize with friends and family and the chance to travel—for business, relaxation, or adventure. Your health also affects your opportunity to meet and connect with new people and to participate in hobbies and recreational activities. The opportunity to live independently and the ability to conceive or the opportunity to parent children is also affected by your health. Even your ability to enjoy a wide range of foods depends on your health.

3   As you will learn, quality of life is intertwined with activities such as these. This chapter will present a definition of health specifically related to accomplishing these important life tasks. But first, let's review the key growth and development tasks of early adulthood and a few familiar perceptions about health that are held by today's young adults.

The Millennial Generation

4   The generational period of *young adulthood* (ages 18–39) is often divided into sub-periods: early young adulthood, middle young adulthood, and later young adulthood. Many traditional-age college students are what we call "early young adults" (ages 18–29). Nontraditional-age college students are students of all other age groups—middle young adults, later young adults, as well as older individuals in middle or older adulthood and the occasional teenager and even preteenagers!

Annotation Practice Exercises

Directions: For each exercise below, write the topic and the main idea on the lines beside the paragraph. (You may need to formulate the main idea.) Then, identify the supporting details and list them *separately* on the lines provided.

Practice Exercise

• Topic of paragraph 2:

_____

_____

_____

• Main idea sentence of paragraph 2:

_____

_____

_____

• List the supporting details on separate lines:

_____

_____

_____

_____

_____

_____

_____

5   "Millennial generation" is the name given to today's early young adults, 18 to 29 years old. If you are a nontraditional-age college student (30 and older), you will have your own generational "name." (See the "Who Are You?" visual aid.) But if you are a traditional-age college student, you are placed in a larger group of persons born between 1982 and 2000 and referred to collectively by sociologists as "millennials." The term *millennials* was derived from the word *millennium,* meaning a span of 1,000 years. A new millennium, the 21ˢᵗ century, began on January 1, 2001.

6   There have been some initial research studies of the millennial generation's progress in mastering the developmental expectations for the transition from adolescence to early adulthood. These studies have found that, compared to earlier generations, the millennials are:

- more inclined to drop out of college for a period of time, and take longer to finish college even if they have not dropped out

- more likely to change colleges, and to change residence while at the same college

- more likely to return home to live after completing college, prompting the term "the boomerang phenomenon"

- more likely to share a residence with friends from college than to live alone or to return home

- more likely to take jobs in food services and retail sales that pay relatively low wages

- likely to leave a job rather than deal with job-related conflict, thus not experiencing advancement within the workplace

- more inclined to fill leisure time with technology-based media

- less likely to have refined communications skills, due in large part to technology-based communication

- more likely to volunteer—not to pad their résumés, but for the well-being of others

- more likely to have a more diverse group of friends, in terms of both gender and race

- less likely to marry, less likely to marry at a younger age, and more likely to delay parenting until older

Who Are You?

Generation 9/11
(2001– present)

The Millennial
Generation
(1982– 2000)

Gen X
(1961– 1981)

Baby Boomers
(1943 – 1960)

Silent Generation
(1925 – 1942)

7   Whether these generalizations about the millennial generation are compatible with our society's traditional developmental expectations will become clearer in the future. At this point, however, many experts believe that the millennials' growth and development are headed in a largely positive direction.

8   If you are a nontraditional-age college student (particularly if you were born before 1982), take an opportunity to look back to your early young adult years and assess, from the perspective of your current age, how you handled the developmental tasks just described. Also, speculate on how your soon-to-be-completed college education might have altered your initial progress through early young adulthood, if you had completed college at that younger age.

Developmental Tasks of Early Adulthood

9   Let's look at some predictable areas of growth and development that characterize the lives of early young adults and contribute to the shaping of one's health. Of course, society's expectations for the next generation of early young adults are always stated in the context of permissible "uniqueness," thus allowing you a fair measure of latitude so that you can do things "your way." Below are seven brief and general views of each early young adult developmental task. Note that the first five of these tasks are more immediate in their completion, while the last two are traditionally brought to fruition a bit later. As young adults make progress in these areas, this contributes to a sense of well-being and satisfaction in life, important factors that relate to good health.

Forming an Initial Adult Identity

10   As emerging adults, most young people want to present a personally satisfying initial adult identity as they transition from adolescence into early young adulthood. Internally they are constructing perceptions of themselves as the adults they wish to be; externally they are formulating the behavioral patterns that will project this identity to others. Completion of this first developmental task is necessary for early young adults to establish a foundation on which to nurture their identity during the later stages of adulthood. Good emotional health is important at this time.

Establishing Independence

11   Society anticipates that, by the time their college education is completed, younger adults should begin to establish their independence. They should be moving away from their earlier dependent relationships, particularly with their family and adolescent peer group. Travel, new relationships, military service, marriage, and, of course, college studies have been the traditional avenues for disengagement from the family.

"I'll have someone from my generation get in touch with someone from your generation."
Peter Steiner, *New Yorker*
(*cartoonbank.com*)

Practice Exercise

• Topic of paragraph 11:

_____

_____

Assuming Responsibility

12   Our society's third developmental expectation for traditional-age college students is that these early young adults will assume increasing levels of responsibility. Traditional-age students have a variety of opportunities, both on and off the college campus, to begin the process of becoming responsible for themselves and for other individuals, programs, and institutions. Central at this time is the need to assume increasing levels of responsibility for one's movement through the academic curriculum while they are attending college. Also, it is important at this time to assume increasing responsibility for one's own health and the health of others.

Broadening Social Skills

13   The fourth developmental task for early young adults is to broaden their range of appropriate and dependable social skills. Adulthood ordinarily involves "membership" in a variety of groups that range in size from a marital pair to a multiple-member community group or a multinational corporation. These memberships require the ability to function in many different social settings, with an array of people, and in many roles. Accomplishing this task particularly requires that early young adults refine their skills in communication, listening, and conflict management.

Nurturing Intimacy

14   The task of nurturing intimacy usually begins in early young adulthood and continues, in various forms, through much of the remainder of life. Persons of traditional college age can experience intimacy in a more mature sense, centered on deep and caring relationships, than was true during adolescence. Dating relationships, close and trusting friendships, and mentoring relationships are the situations in which mature intimacy will take root. From a developmental perspective, what matters is that we have quality relationships involving persons with whom we share our most deeply held thoughts, feelings, and aspirations as we attempt to validate our own unique approach to life. Young adults who are unwilling or unable to create intimacy can develop a sense of emotional isolation.

Obtaining Entry-Level Employment and Developing Parenting Skills

15   In addition to the five developmental tasks just addressed, two additional areas of growth and development seem applicable to early young adults, but may come into "focus" more gradually. They include obtaining entry-level employment within the field of one's academic preparation and the development of parenting skills.

- Main idea sentence of paragraph 11:

_____

_____

_____

_____

_____

- List the supporting details on separate lines:

_____

_____

_____

_____

_____

_____

16   For nearly seventy-five years (thanks in part to the GI Bill after World War II) the majority of students have pursued a college education in anticipation that graduation from college would open doors for them in particular professions or fields of employment. That is, their education would provide for them entry-level job opportunities. In many respects these forms of employment meet needs beyond those associated purely with money. Employment of this nature provides opportunities for graduates to build new skills that expand upon those learned in college. Employment also allows graduates to undertake new forms of responsibility beyond those available on campus, and to play a more diverse set of social roles, including that of colleague, supervisor, mentor, mentee, or partner. And today, more so than in the past, intimate relationships often have their origin in the workplace.

17   Parenting-related decisions and the development of parenting skills are important components of the young adulthood years. Decisions regarding parenting involve important questions regarding age for the onset of parenting, number of children, adoption, and the desired interval between subsequent children. It also involves decisions about the manner in which parenting will be undertaken and the role it will play relative to the overall aspirations of the parents involved. In today's complex society, young adults need to more clearly than ever understand the significant differences between reproduction and parenting. Consequently, we assign the development of parenting skills as a socially anticipated developmental task for young adults.

Practice Exercise

- Topic of paragraph 17:

_____

- Main idea sentence of paragraph 17:

_____

_____

_____

_____

_____

- List the supporting details on separate lines:

_____

_____

_____

_____

_____

_____

_____

_____

Source: Adapted from Wayne A. Payne, Dale B. Hahn, and Ellen B. Lucas, *Understanding Your Health,* 10e, pp. 1–4. Copyright © 2009 by The McGraw-Hill Companies, Inc. Reprinted with permission of The McGraw-Hill Companies, Inc.

SELECTION **6.1**

Health
(continued)

Reading Selection Quiz

This quiz has several parts. Your instructor may assign some or all of them.

Comprehension

Directions: Use the information in the selection to answer each item below. You may refer to the selection as you answer the questions. Write each answer in the space provided.

True or False

_____   **1.** Today's early young adults, 18 to 29 years old, are referred to collectively as the "millennial generation."

_____   **2.** Society anticipates that, by the time their college education is completed, younger adults should be moving away from their earlier dependent relationships, particularly with their family and adolescent peer group.

_____   **3.** According to the authors, millennials are more likely than older individuals to have a diverse group of friends, in terms of both gender and race.

_____   **4.** Studies have found that individuals in the millennial generation are more likely to marry and more likely to marry at a younger age.

Multiple-Choice

_____   **5.** Young people often do not take steps to maintain their health because they:
    a. fail to realize that they may miss it when it's gone.
    b. assume that they will always maintain the state of health and wellness that they currently enjoy.
    c. choose to participate in too many hobbies and social activities.
    d. all of the above

_____   **6.** If your health is compromised, you may be unable to:
    a. conceive or parent children.
    b. live independently.
    c. enjoy a wide range of foods.
    d. all of the above

_____   **7.** Individuals referred to as "baby boomers" were born between:
    a. 1982 and 2000.
    b. 1961 and 1981.
    c. 1943 and 1960.
    d. 1925 and 1942.

_____ **8.** Students who, for whatever reason, are pursuing a college degree at an age other than the 18–29-year-old student are referred to as:

    a. career-changing students.

    b. mature students.

    c. nontraditional students.

    d. baby boomers.

_____ **9.** As traditional-age college students move through the third developmental task of adulthood, they should assume increasing levels of responsibility for:

    a. their own health.

    b. their progress through the academic curriculum.

    c. the health of others.

    d. all of the above

_____ **10.** Early young adults can broaden their social skills by:

    a. nurturing personal relationships and intimacy.

    b. formulating a new adult identity.

    c. disengagement from their families.

    d. refining their skills in communication, listening, and conflict management.

SELECTION **6.1**

Health
(continued)

Vocabulary in Context

> *Directions:* For each item below, use context clues to deduce the meaning of the *italicized* word. Be sure the answer you choose makes sense in both sentences. Write each answer in the space provided.

_____ **11.** Do you ever think about how your health allows you to participate in meaningful life activities—and what might happen if your health is *compromised*?

The high-level security of the embassy building was *compromised* by several hidden listening devices.

compromised (kŏm′prə mīzd) means:

    a. maintained by regular exercise

    b. monitored

    c. exposed to danger; lessened

    d. increased

_____ **12.** As you will learn, quality of life is *intertwined* with activities such as these.

For the Mardi Gras celebration, Maxine *intertwined* lengths of purple, green, and gold beads into her long braids of hair.

intertwined (ĭn tər twīnd′) means:

    a. joined together by twisting

    b. improved the quality of

    c. enhanced by

    d. decorated with

13. As emerging adults, most young people want to present a personally satisfying initial adult identity as they *transition* from adolescence into early young adulthood.

Those released from prison often live in a halfway house while they *transition* back into society.

transition (trăn zĭsh′ ən) means:

    a. mature into adulthood

    b. develop a new identity

    c. grow older

    d. change from one state or stage to another

14. Internally they are constructing perceptions of themselves as the adults they wish to be; externally they are *formulating* the behavioral patterns that will project this identity to others.

During his first semester in college, James began *formulating* a strategy for repaying his student loan before he reached the age of thirty.

formulating (fôr′ myə lāt tĭng) means:

    a. suggesting

    b. creating

    c. repaying

    d. demonstrating

15. Travel, new relationships, military service, marriage, and, of course, college studies have been the traditional *avenues* for disengagement from the family.

As a sole proprietor, Natalie is always exploring new *avenues* for making her business more profitable.

avenues (ăv′ ə nōōs) means:

    a. requirements

    b. outcomes

    c. approaches

    d. locations

16. Travel, new relationships, military service, marriage, and, of course, college studies have been the traditional avenues for *disengagement* from the family.

Robert's *disengagement* from all his close friends was the result of his dropping out of high school.

disengagement (dĭs ĕn gāj′ mənt) means:

    a. detachment; separation

    b. accomplishments

    c. disappointment; unhappiness

    d. encouragement

_____ **17.** These memberships require the ability to function in many different social settings, with an *array* of people, and in many roles.

Mr. Henderson keeps an *array* of spare car parts on hand.

array (ə rā′) means:

    a. a type of skill or ability

    b. a specific group

    c. an arrangement or display

    d. an impressively large number of persons or objects

_____ **18.** It also involves decisions about the manner in which parenting will be undertaken and the role it will play relative to the overall *aspirations* of the parents involved.

Most teenagers today have *aspirations* of a high-paying career that they will enjoy.

aspirations (ăs pər ā′ shəns) means:

    a. types of decisions

    b. abilities

    c. strong desires or ambitions

    d. wishes

_____ **19.** Decisions regarding parenting involve important questions regarding age for the *onset* of parenting, number of children, adoption, and the desired interval between subsequent children.

At the *onset* of a cold, doctors recommend using lozenges to soothe your throat, drinking plenty of fluids, taking an over-the-counter cold medication, and getting some rest.

onset (ŏn′ sĕt) means:

    a. indication

    b. challenge

    c. beginning

    d. suggestion

_____ **20.** Decisions regarding parenting involve important questions regarding age for the onset of parenting, number of children, adoption, and the desired *interval* between subsequent children.

The *interval* between one full moon and the next is about 29.5 days.

interval (ĭn′ tər vəl) means:

    a. difference

    b. beginning of

    c. specific number

    d. period of time between two events

Reading Skills Application

Directions: These items test your ability to *apply* certain reading skills. You may not have studied all of the skills yet, so some items will serve as a preview. Write each answer in the space provided.

_____ 21. According to the authors, individuals from the millennial generation are more likely to:
   a.   change colleges and take longer to finish college.
   b.   believe that balancing home and work is important.
   c.   trust only their parents and family members.
   d.   all of the above

_____ 22. The information in paragraph 2 of this selection is organized according to which of the following patterns?
   a.   list
   b.   cause-effect
   c.   sequence
   d.   comparison

_____ 23. The authors' primary purpose for writing this selection is to:
   a.   inform readers about how making progress in the growth and development tasks of early adulthood can contribute to a sense of well-being and satisfaction in life.
   b.   convince readers to maintain the state of health and wellness that they currently enjoy.
   c.   persuade readers to formulate a unique adult identity.
   d.   convince readers that there will always be a significant difference between the generations.

_____ 24. In paragraph 16, the phrase *college would open doors for them* means:
   a.   admission to college would be provided to everyone who wants to attend.
   b.   their education would provide graduates with job security.
   c.   graduates would have more rapid career advancement.
   d.   their education would provide graduates with entry-level job opportunities.

_____ 25. In paragraph 6, the authors list several characteristics of millennials in order to:
   a.   show how millennials are different from earlier generations.
   b.   illustrate ways that their health can be compromised.
   c.   explain the difficulties they experience from adolescence to early adulthood.
   d.   all of the above

S ELECTION **6.1**

Health

(continued)

Respond in Writing

Directions: Refer to the selection as needed to answer the essay-type questions below. (Your instructor may direct you to work collaboratively with other students on one or more items. Each group member should be able to explain *all* of the group's answers.)

1. According to the generational categories presented in this selection, to which generation do you belong? Are you a Millennial, a Gen Xer, a Baby Boomer, or a member of the Silent Generation?

   _____

2. According to the information presented in paragraphs 4–8, which characteristics listed for your generation describe *you*? That is, which characteristics fit with the way you see yourself?

   _____

   _____

   _____

   _____

   _____

3. Which characteristics listed for your generation do *not* represent the way you see yourself? In other words, how would you say that you differ from the generalizations made about your generational group?

   _____

   _____

   _____

   _____

   _____

4. At this point in your life, what does being an adult mean to you? How would you explain this to your best friend?

   _____

   _____

   _____

5. Summarize the information about the seven *developmental tasks of early adulthood* presented in paragraphs 9–17. Complete the table on page 384 by paraphrasing the information presented for each developmental task. (The first one has been worked for you as an example.)

DEVELOPMENTAL TASKS OF EARLY ADULTHOOD

Task	Activities and Characteristics
Forming an Initial Adult Identity	Young people want to present a personally satisfying initial adult identity. They are constructing perceptions of themselves as the adults they wish to be, and they are formulating the behavioral patterns that will project this identity to others.

6. **Overall main idea.** What is the overall main idea the authors want the reader to understand about the developmental tasks of early adulthood? Answer this question in one sentence. Be sure to include the words "young adults" and the phrase "developmental tasks of early adulthood" in your overall main idea sentence.

_____

_____

_____

_____

_____

_____

Quacks and Quackery

From *Concepts of Fitness and Wellness*
by Charles Corbin, Greg Welk, William Corbin, and Karen Welk

Prepare Yourself to Read

Directions: Do these exercises *before* you read Selection 6.2.

1. First, read and think about the title. What knowledge do you have about quacks and quackery?

   _____

   _____

2. Why do you think it is important or useful for people to know something about quacks and quackery?

   _____

   _____

3. Next, complete your preview by reading the following:
   Introduction (in *italics*)
   First paragraph (paragraph 1)
   Section headings
   Last paragraph (paragraph 9)

   On the basis of your preview, what four aspects of quacks and quackery will be discussed?

   _____

   _____

4. **Build your vocabulary as you read.** If you discover an unfamiliar word or key term as you read the selection, try to determine its meaning by using context clues.

Read More about This Topic Online

Internet Resources

Use a search engine, such as Google or Yahoo!, to expand your existing knowledge about this topic *before* you read the selection or to learn more about it *afterward*. If you are unfamiliar with conducting Internet searches, read pages 25–26 on Boolean searches. You can also use Wikipedia, the free online encyclopedia, at www .wikipedia.com. Keep in mind that when you visit any website, it is a good idea to evaluate the site and the information it contains. Ask yourself questions such as "Who sponsors this website?" and "Is the information it contains up to date?"

SELECTION 6.2: QUACKS AND QUACKERY

Perhaps you have heard the phrase "Let the buyer beware." It has come to mean that it is the buyer's responsibility to inform him- or herself about what is being purchased. If a buyer is disappointed—or worse, cheated—it is the person's own fault. "Let the buyer beware" is a good motto if you are considering buying fitness, health, or wellness products or programs.

People have always searched for the fountain of youth and easy, quick, and miraculous routes to health and happiness. In current society, this search often focuses on fitness, nutrition, weight loss, or appearance. A variety of products are available that promise weight loss, improved health, or improved fitness with little or no effort. The sale of these products can typically be classified as either quackery or fraud, since most of them do not work. Advertisements for exercise that claim to "get you totally fit in 10 minutes" or that claim their program "will get you fit with little effort" are false. There is no "effortless" way to get the benefits from physical activity. Claims for exercise that will effortlessly reduce weight or produce significant health benefits are equally false.

Quacks, Quackery, and Fraud

1   The dictionary definition of quack is "a pretender of medical skill" or "one who talks pretentiously without sound knowledge of the subject discussed." These definitions imply that the promotion of quackery involves deliberate deception, but quacks often believe in what they promote. A consumer watchdog group called Quackwatch defines quackery more broadly as "anything involving overpromotion in the field of health." This definition encompasses questionable ideas as well as questionable products and services. The word fraud is reserved for situations in which deliberate deception is involved.

Warning Signs of Quackery and Fraud

2   Recognizing some common myths and understanding certain guidelines can help you be a more informed consumer of fitness, health, and wellness products. Quacks can be identified by their unscientific practices. Some of the ways to identify quacks, frauds, and rip-off artists are to look for these clues:

- They do not use the scientific method of controlled experimentation, which can be verified by other scientists.
- To a large extent, they use testimonials and anecdotes to support their claims rather than scientific methods. There is no such thing as a valid testimonial. Anecdotal evidence is no evidence at all.
- They have something to sell, and they advise you to buy something you would not otherwise have bought. They claim

Annotation Practice Exercises

Directions: For each paragraph indicated, in the spaces provided:

- Write the main idea sentence.
- List the supporting details on separate lines.

Doing this will help you remember main ideas and details.

Practice Exercise

- Main idea sentence of paragraph 1:

_____

_____

_____

_____

everyone can benefit from the product or service they are selling. There is no such thing as a simple, quick, easy, painless remedy for conditions for which medical science has not yet found a remedy.

- They promise quick, miraculous results. A perfect, no-risk treatment does not exist.
- Their claims cover a wide variety of conditions.
- They may offer a money-back guarantee. A guarantee is only as good as the company.
- They claim the treatment or product is approved by the Food and Drug Administration (FDA), but federal law does not permit mentioning the FDA to suggest marketing approval.
- They may claim the support of experts, but the experts are not identified.
- The ingredients in the product are not identified.
- They claim there is a conspiracy against them by "bureaucrats," "organized medicine," the FDA, the American Medical Association (AMA), and other groups. Never believe a doctor who claims the medical community is persecuting him or her or that the government is suppressing a wonderful discovery.
- Their credentials may be irrelevant to the area in which they claim expertise.
- They use scare tactics, such as "If you don't do this, you will die of a heart attack."
- They may appear to be a sympathetic friend who wants to share a new discovery with you.
- They misquote scientific research (or quote out of context) to mislead you; they also mix a little bit of truth with a lot of fiction.
- They cite research or quote from individuals or institutions with questionable reputations.
- They claim it is a new discovery (often originated in Europe). There is never a great medical breakthrough that debuts in an obscure magazine or tabloid.
- The person or organization named is similar to a famous person or credible institution (e.g., the Mayo diet had no connection with the Mayo Clinic).
- They often sell products through the mail, which does not allow you to examine the product personally.

3   Experts have a good education, have a good scientific base, and meet other professional criteria. Unlike quacks, experts base their work on the scientific method. Some characteristics of professional experts are an extended education, an established code of ethics, membership in well-known associations, involvement in the profession as an intern before obtaining credentials, and a commitment to perform an important social service. Some experts require a license. Examples of experts in the fitness, health, and wellness

- Supporting details:

_____

_____

_____

_____

_____

_____

_____

_____

_____

_____

_____

area are medical doctors, nurses, certified fitness leaders, physical educators, registered dietitians, physical therapists, and clinical psychologists.

How to Evaluate Credentials

4   In most cases, you can check if a person has the credentials to be considered an expert before obtaining services. The following list includes some things that can be done to determine a person's expertise.

- Determine the source of the person's education and the nature of the degree and/or certification.
- Check with the person's professional association or with a government board, licensing agency, or certifying agency to see if there are any complaints against the person; for example, you can check with the medical board in your state to check complaints against physicians.
- Check if the person has the credentials to provide the service you are seeking (e.g., a registered dietician is qualified to give nutrition advice but not medical advice).

Reducing Susceptibility to Quackery

5   You can reduce your susceptibility to quackery by being an informed consumer. First, know that the three key characteristics that predispose people to health-related quackery are a concern about appearance, health, or performance; a lack of adequate knowledge; and a desire for immediate results. Second, understanding the principles of exercise and nutrition will help you know when something sounds "too good to be true."

6   When evaluating health-related products or information, carefully consider the quality of your source. Common sources of misinformation are magazines, health food stores, and TV infomercials. These entities all have an economic incentive in promoting the purchase and use of exercise, diet, and weight loss products. Because of freedom of speech laws, it is legal to state opinions through these media. Note, however, that few companies make claims on product labels, since this is false advertising.

7   To avoid being a victim of quackery, follow these additional guidelines:

- Read the ad carefully, especially the small print.
- Do not send cash; use a check, money order, or credit card so you will have a receipt.
- Do not order from a company with only a post office box, unless you know the company.
- Do not let high-pressure sales tactics make you rush into a decision.

Practice Exercise

- Main idea sentence of paragraph 4:

_____

_____

_____

_____

- Supporting details:

_____

_____

_____

_____

_____

_____

Practice Exercise

- Main idea sentence of paragraph 5:

_____

_____

- Supporting details:

_____

_____

_____

_____

_____

_____

_____

_____

- When in doubt, check out the company through your Better Business Bureau (BBB).

8   Scientific research is a systematic search for truth. Occasionally, "quack" companies will mention that their product or program has been scientifically tested, but this does not necessarily mean that the results were positive. Even if a study did show positive results, the study may have been flawed. An article in a prominent scientific journal documented that results of studies, especially small studies that are not well controlled, are often found to be wrong or the effects are not as large as originally thought.

9   The media often highlight the results of novel or unusual findings, and this leads some people to conclude that experts simply "can't make up their minds." In actuality, scientists typically take a cautious approach with any new finding and wait for other studies to confirm the results. Beware of news reports that denounce established evidence based on a single study or "preliminary research." With accumulating evidence, even the most established beliefs may change. But it takes many confirming studies to provide the best evidence. Consider this before making quick consumer judgments.

Practice Exercise

- Main idea sentence of paragraph 8:

  _____

  _____

  _____

- Supporting details:

  _____

  _____

  _____

  _____

  _____

  _____

  _____

  _____

TV infomercials have one purpose: to sell. It is the consumer's responsibility to evaluate carefully any TV infomercial selling health-related products or programs.

Source: Adapted from Charles Corbin, Greg Welk, William Corbin, and Karen Welk, *Concepts of Fitness and Wellness*, 9e, pp. 474–75. Copyright © 2011 by The McGraw-Hill Companies, Inc. Reprinted with permission of The McGraw-Hill Companies, Inc.

Reading Selection Quiz

This quiz has several parts. Your instructor may assign some or all of them.

Comprehension

Directions: Use the information in the selection to answer each item below. You may refer to the selection as you answer the questions. Write each answer in the space provided.

True or False

_____ 1. All quacks deliberately deceive consumers with products they know are not effective.

_____ 2. There is no such thing as a valid testimonial.

_____ 3. The Mayo diet was created by the Mayo Clinic.

_____ 4. Health food stores are a common source of misinformation.

_____ 5. It is legal for quacks to give their opinions in their advertising, but not on product labels.

Multiple-Choice

_____ 6. To pay for a product that may be questionable, you should not use:
   a. cash.
   b. a money order.
   c. a check.
   d. a credit card.

_____ 7. Scientists who make a new finding usually:
   a. wait for other studies that confirm their results.
   b. denounce established evidence.
   c. contact the media immediately.
   d. base it on a small study.

_____ 8. Consumers are attracted to quacks because they:
   a. lack knowledge.
   b. want quick results.
   c. are concerned about their appearance, health, or performance.
   d. all of the above

_____ 9. Which of the following is *not* a characteristic of quacks?

  a.   They may claim their product is a new discovery from another country.

  b.   They sell products through stores, but not through the mail.

  c.   They promise excellent results with no risk.

  d.   They may not list product ingredients.

_____ 10. A quack's primary goal is to:

  a.   help people.

  b.   become famous.

  c.   use the scientific method.

  d.   make money.

Vocabulary in Context

Directions: For each item below, use context clues to deduce the meaning of the *italicized* word. Be sure the answer you choose makes sense in both sentences. Write each answer in the space provided.

_____ 11. The dictionary definition of quack is "a pretender of medical skill" or "one who talks *pretentiously* without sound knowledge of the subject discussed."

Whenever he had the opportunity, the professor spoke *pretentiously* about the awards he had won.

pretentiously (prĭ tĕn′ shəs lē) means:

  a.   hurriedly; at a fast pace

  b.   in a rude or unmannerly fashion

  c.   in a joking manner

  d.   claiming more importance than is deserved

_____ 12. The dictionary definition of quack is "a pretender of medical skill" or "one who talks pretentiously without *sound* knowledge of the subject discussed."

The detectives' *sound* investigation resulted in their solving the complicated case.

sound (sound) means:

  a.   distinctive; special

  b.   gained by hearing

  c.   thorough; complete

  d.   routine

_____   **13.** This definition *encompasses* questionable ideas as well as questionable products and services.

The realtor's service *encompasses* staging homes to make them attractive to buyers.

encompasses (ĕn kŭm′pəs əs) means:

a. includes

b. prohibits

c. overlooks

d. discourages

_____   **14.** They do not use the scientific method of controlled experimentation, which can be *verified* by other scientists.

My grandfather's military records *verified* that as a young soldier he was awarded the Bronze Star.

verified (vĕr′ə fīd) means:

a. claimed falsely

b. proved true

c. denied

d. ignored

_____   **15.** Never believe a doctor who claims the medical community is persecuting him or her or that the government is *suppressing* a wonderful discovery.

The automobile manufacturer is accused of *suppressing* information about a possible safety defect in its cars' brakes.

suppressing (sə prĕs′ ĭng) means:

a. advertising

b. claiming

c. announcing publicly

d. keeping from being revealed

_____   **16.** There is never a great medical breakthrough that *debuts* in an obscure magazine or tabloid.

A new television series about the Civil War *debuts* in the fall.

debuts (dā byōōz′) means:

a. is written about

b. is discussed

c. is made public for the first time

d. is surveyed

_____ **17.** You can reduce your *susceptibility* to quackery by being an informed consumer.

Her *susceptibility* to flattery has caused her to make many bad decisions.

susceptibility (sə sĕp′ tə bĭl′ ĭ tē) means:
- *a.* negative response
- *b.* tendency to be offended by
- *c.* anger at
- *d.* ability to be easily influenced

_____ **18.** These *entities* all have an economic incentive in promoting the purchase and use of exercise, diet, and weight loss products.

Under the law, persons and corporations are equivalent *entities*.

entities (ĕn′ tĭ tēz) means:
- *a.* things that exist as separate units
- *b.* things that are illegal
- *c.* businesses
- *d.* considerations

_____ **19.** Even if a study did show positive results, the study may have been *flawed*.

Flawed reasoning leads to an incorrect conclusion.

flawed (flôd) means:
- *a.* imperfect; defective
- *b.* thorough
- *c.* grounded in logic
- *d.* valid

_____ **20.** Beware of news reports that *denounce* established evidence based on a single study or "preliminary research."

Several senators said they would *denounce* the proposed tax increase as unfair to the middle class.

denounce (dĭ nouns′) means:
- *a.* condemn publicly
- *b.* sponsor
- *c.* consider thoughtfully
- *d.* accept

SELECTION 6.2

Reading Skills Application

> *Directions:* These items test your ability to *apply* certain reading skills. You may not have studied all of the skills yet, so some items will serve as a preview. Write each answer in the space provided.

_____   21. The purpose of paragraph 3 is to:
- *a.* instruct readers how to become an expert in a field.
- *b.* persuade readers that being an expert is overrated.
- *c.* inform readers about types of credentials experts are likely to have.
- *d.* persuade readers to get the credentials necessary to be considered an expert.

_____   22. The authors mention academic degrees, certificates, and licenses as examples of credentials that:
- *a.* quacks should have.
- *b.* no quack has.
- *c.* government employees will have.
- *d.* experts will have.

_____   23. Based on the information in the selection, it can be logically concluded that:
- *a.* not all quacks commit fraud.
- *b.* all quacks commit fraud.
- *c.* all people who commit fraud are quacks.
- *d.* all of the above

_____   24. What is the relationship of the two parts of the following sentence: "The media often highlight the results of novel or unusual findings, and this leads some people to conclude that experts simply 'can't make up their minds' "?
- *a.* comparison-contrast
- *b.* cause-effect
- *c.* concession
- *d.* summary

_____   25. The information in paragraph 2 is organized as a:
- *a.* sequence.
- *b.* list.
- *c.* definition.
- *d.* comparison-contrast.

SELECTION **6.2**

Health
(continued)

Respond in Writing

Directions: Refer to the selection as needed to answer the essay-type questions below. (Your instructor may direct you to work collaboratively with other students on one or more items. Each group member should be able to explain *all* of the group's answers.)

1. List at least three new things you learned about quacks and how to protect yourself against them.

   _____

   _____

   _____

   _____

   _____

   _____

   _____

   _____

   _____

2. Have you ever watched an infomercial or seen other advertising that "promised the moon"? If so, what products or services were being promoted? Have you or someone you know ever bought a quack beauty, fitness, or health product or service and later regretted it? If so, describe the experience.

   _____

   _____

   _____

   _____

   _____

   _____

   _____

   _____

   _____

SELECTION 6.2

3. Every year millions of consumers are cheated by quacks, disappointed with
    the products they ordered from them, or even harmed by the products. In your
    opinion, what are at least two things that could be done (by the government
    or through other sources) to educate the public about or protect them from
    quacks?

    _____

    _____

    _____

    _____

    _____

    _____

    _____

4. **Overall main idea.** What is the overall main idea the authors want the reader
    to understand about quacks and quackery? Answer this question in one sen-
    tence. Be sure that your overall main idea sentence includes the topic (*quacks
    and quackery*) and tells the most important point about it.

    _____

    _____

    _____

    _____

    _____

    _____

    _____

    _____

    _____

    _____

SELECTION **6.3**

Economics

What Can Be Done to Help Third World Countries?

From *A Beginner's Guide to the World Economy*
by Randy Charles Epping

Prepare Yourself to Read

Directions: Do these exercises *before* you read Selection 6.3.

1. First, read and think about the title. What knowledge do you have about the "world economy"? What approach do you think a "beginner's guide" might take?

    _____

    _____

2. Why do you think it is important or useful for the average person to know something about the world economy?

    _____

    _____

3. Next, complete your preview by reading the following:

    Introduction (in *italics*)
    First paragraph (paragraph 1)
    Section headings
    Last paragraph (paragraph 17)
    Diagrams

    On the basis of your preview, what three aspects of the Third World will be discussed?

    _____

    _____

4. **Build your vocabulary as you read.** If you discover an unfamiliar word or key term as you read the selection, try to determine its meaning by using context clues.

Internet Resources

Read More about This Topic Online

Use a search engine, such as Google or Yahoo!, to expand your existing knowledge about this topic *before* you read the selection or to learn more about it *afterward*. If you are unfamiliar with conducting Internet searches, read pages 25–26 on Boolean searches. You can also use Wikipedia, the free online encyclopedia, at www.wikipedia.com. Keep in mind that when you visit any website, it is a good idea to evaluate the site and the information it contains. Ask yourself questions such as "Who sponsors this website?" and "Is the information it contains up to date?"

SELECTION 6.3: WHAT CAN BE DONE TO HELP THIRD WORLD COUNTRIES?

According to http://world-poverty.org (accessed 3/8/12), "Absolute poverty involves people and their children having extreme difficulty in merely surviving. Such poverty at its worst can involve hunger amounting to starvation, often combined with inadequate shelter or housing and clothing. Absolute poverty has been common in more primitive societies, and is still common in many Third World countries in Africa, Asia and South America especially, where it can afflict the majority of the population."

A majority of the world's poorest countries today are in Asia, Africa, and South America, although conditions in the latter are improving somewhat. Extreme drought and famine in 2012 in East Africa will affect Somalia, Ethiopia, and Kenya severely. Asia's poverty problems are mainly due to overly dense populations. In Asia, poverty is concentrated in South Asian countries, such as India and Cambodia.

In Third World countries, education, adequate medicine, clean drinking water, transportation, and energy are major problems. Some of these countries are plagued with widespread AIDS, malaria, and cholera, with the latter two diseases fostered by poor, unsanitary water systems. Recently, food prices have been rising worldwide, which also worsens world poverty. Natural disasters such as droughts, tsunamis, earthquakes, and flooding add to the misery. These events result in the wide-scale loss of human life and crops, and often shelter, roads, and bridges as well. Disease usually follows natural disasters.

According to world-poverty.org, "Worldwide now, the poor are facing increased hardship. The present economic downturn also seems to have increased the abandonment and murders of children and elderly women in poorer countries."

What will be the ultimate fate of these and other Third World countries? How can the poorest of the poor countries survive? This selection will give you a basic understanding of the economic concept of "Third World," the roots of Third World poverty, and what can be done to improve the situation.

What Is the Third World?

1   The term *Third World* was based on the idea that the "first" and "second" worlds were made up of the free-market and centrally planned countries with advanced industrial economies. This developed world was seen to include most of the countries of Eastern and Western Europe as well as Australia, New Zealand, Japan, the United States, and Canada.

2   The developing and relatively poor countries that are said to make up the Third World can be divided into three groups: those developing rapidly, those developing moderately, and the poorest few whose economies are not developing at all.

3   At the top of the list of Third World nations are the rapidly developing countries called Newly Industrialized Countries (NICs). Most lists of NICs include Brazil, Argentina, Hong Kong, Israel, Singapore, South Africa, South Korea, Taiwan, and Thailand. These "lucky few" are seen to be on their way to joining the ranks of the advanced economies of the world.

Annotation Practice Exercises

Directions: For each paragraph indicated, in the spaces provided:

- Write the main idea sentence.
- List the supporting details on separate lines.

Doing this will help you remember main ideas and supporting details.

Practice Exercise

- Main idea sentence of paragraph 1:

_____

_____

_____

_____

_____

4   The bulk of the Third World consists of a large group of moderately developing economies that includes most of the countries in Africa, Asia, and Latin America. The most populous countries in this group are India, China, Indonesia, and Malaysia, which together comprise more than half of the world's population.

5   At the bottom of this list are the world's poorest countries, found mainly in sub-Saharan Africa, which have so few resources and so little money that it is virtually impossible for them to develop at all. In Somalia and Sudan, for example, there are essentially no natural resources on which to base economic growth. This group is sometimes called the "Fourth World."

6   Although the Third World comprises three quarters of the world's population and 90 percent of the world's population growth, it provides only 20 percent of the world's economic production. And even though the Third World holds much of the world's natural resources—including vast petroleum reserves in Latin America, Asia, and the Middle East—many raw materials from the Third World are shipped abroad for consumption in the world's wealthier and more developed countries.

What Are the Roots of Third World Poverty?

7   Economic and political misjudgment can be blamed for much of the Third World's poverty, but an important factor has also been the population explosion. This caused many developing countries to see their populations double in as little as twenty years. The growth was due mainly to lack of birth control, to improved medical care, and to declining mortality rates.

8   Extreme poverty in the Third World led many parents to create ever larger families, hoping that their children could work and increase family income. But the economic opportunities were often not available, and unemployed children and their parents ended up moving into already overcrowded Third World cities in a fruitless search for work.

9   By the end of the 1980s, most Third World nations found themselves in a vicious circle of poverty and overpopulation, with no hope in sight. The flood of poor families into major Third World cities put additional strains on the economic infrastructure. Growing urban areas like Bombay, São Paulo, and Shanghai became centers of glaring poverty and unemployment with extensive slums and squatter settlements ringing overgrown and polluted city centers.

10   Saddled with enormous debt payments, hyperinflation, surging populations, and mounting unemployment, many Third World countries in the late 1980s struggled just to keep their economies afloat. In many cases, with no money available for investment, even the infrastructure, such as roads and water systems, literally began to fall apart. The solution for many overburdened Third World governments

SELECTION 6.3

• Supporting details in paragraph 1:

_____

_____

_____

_____

_____

_____

_____

_____

Practice Exercise

• Main idea sentence of paragraph 7:

_____

_____

_____

_____

_____

• Supporting details in paragraph 7:

_____

_____

_____

_____

_____

_____

_____

_____

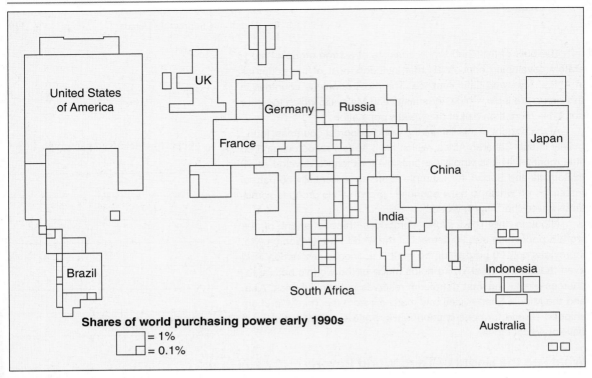

Purchasing power

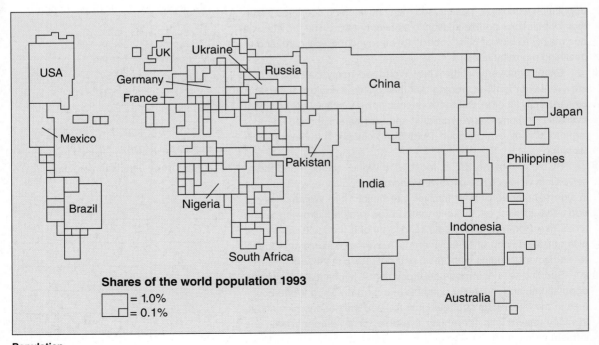

Population

Source: From *A Beginner's Guide to the World Economy,* by Randy Charles Epping, p. xix. Copyright © 1992 by Randy Charles Epping. Used by permission of Vintage Books, a division of Random House, Inc.

was to simply increase debt in order to keep money flowing. But rampant inflation often ends up eroding most of these efforts, creating an ever-widening gap between the Third World's poorest and richest nations.

11   While many economies in Latin America, Africa, and Asia stagnated, the economies of the elite developing countries of the Pacific Rim rose to levels that rivaled Japan's in the 1960s. The success of many Third World countries in growing their way out of poverty can be traced largely to effective economic policy. By efficiently producing and exporting manufactured goods, countries such as Taiwan and Korea earned enormous amounts of money that they have been able to reinvest in their growing economies.

What Can Be Done to Promote Third World Development?

12   Economic growth cannot possibly solve all the problems facing the billions of poor and undernourished people in the Third World, but because of rapid population growth, their problems would almost certainly get worse without it.

13   In order to provide the basic food, clothing, and shelter for their citizens, the underdeveloped Third World countries need to stimulate their stagnating economies caught in a vicious circle of low growth and declining export earnings. One of the first steps in encouraging development would be to reduce the Third World nations' debt and supply additional funds to revive their moribund economies. One such plan was formulated in the 1980s by U.S. Treasury Secretary Nicholas Brady, who called for the commercial banks to forgive part of the debt owed to them and to increase new lending. The basic goal of the Brady Plan was to encourage economic growth in the Third World.

14   The Brady Plan also called upon the world's major development banks and funds, such as the World Bank and the International Monetary Fund, to provide substantial "project loans" to rebuild the infrastructure in the Third World. In addition, continued bank lending in the form of "adjustment loans" would help with the payment of interest and principal on previous loans. Basically, the Brady Plan called for a net transfer of funds back to the developing countries.

15   Another way to promote Third World development is to increase development funds provided by regional development banks with the backing of the developed countries. The Inter-American Development Bank, for example, was set up to provide low-interest loans to developing countries in the Western Hemisphere. In this way, funds from wealthy countries can be channeled to less-developed nations in the form of "development loans."

16   Wealthy creditor governments also have the option of writing off their debt, accepting that it will never be repaid. France, for example, decided in the 1980s that most of its development loans to African

---

Practice Exercise

• Main idea sentence of paragraph 11:

_____

_____

_____

_____

_____

_____

_____

_____

• Supporting details in paragraph 11:

_____

_____

_____

_____

_____

_____

_____

_____

SELECTION 6.3

countries need not be repaid, in an effort to encourage further economic growth in the region.

17   In order to provide further assistance to Third World debtors, the world's wealthy countries can also work through specialized organizations such as the Lomé Convention, which channels development aid from the European Community to poor Third World countries, and the Paris Club, which helps governments of debtor nations "reschedule" or delay repayment of their loans until their economies are in better shape.

SELECTION **6.3**

Economics
(continued)

Reading Selection Quiz

This quiz has several parts. Your instructor may assign some or all of them.

Comprehension

Directions: Use the information in the selection to answer each item below. You may refer to the selection as you answer the questions. Write each answer in the space provided.

True or False

1. The *first* and *second worlds* are defined as the free-market countries and the centrally planned countries with advanced industrial economies.

2. The first and second worlds were considered to include most of the countries of Eastern and Western Europe, Australia, New Zealand, Japan, the United States, and Canada.

3. Some experts believe that the economic problems of Third World countries cannot be solved.

4. The Third World can be divided into three groups: countries with rapidly developing economies, countries with moderately developing economies, and countries whose economies are not developing at all.

5. The bulk of the Third World consists of a large group of moderately developing economies.

6. Economic growth cannot solve all the problems faced by billions of under-nourished people in the Third World.

Multiple-Choice

7. Newly Industrialized Countries (NICs) that seem to be on their way to joining the rank of advanced economies include:
   a. Somalia and Sudan.
   b. India, China, Indonesia, and Malaysia.
   c. South Africa, South Korea, Taiwan, and Thailand.
   d. all of the above

8. Third World poverty is caused by:
   a. economic and political misjudgment.
   b. enormous debt payments.
   c. overpopulation.
   d. all of the above

SELECTION **6.3**

_____ **9.** According to the author, Third World development will require that:

    a. Third World countries pay off their debts completely.

    b. commercial banks press hard for debt payment from Third World countries.

    c. wealthy countries discontinue making development loans to Third World countries.

    d. none of the above

_____ **10.** The author believes that wealthy creditor nations can aid Third World development by:

    a. agreeing to follow the Brady Plan.

    b. channeling funds in the form of development loans.

    c. writing off the debt owed by Third World countries.

    d. all of the above

SELECTION **6.3**

Economics
(continued)

Vocabulary in Context

Directions: For each item below, use context clues to deduce the meaning of the *italicized* word. Be sure the answer you choose makes sense in both sentences. Write each answer in the space provided.

_____ **11.** The term Third World was based on the idea that the "first" and "second" worlds were made up of the *free-market* and centrally planned countries with advanced industrial economies.

Currently, several countries are struggling to shift from a planned economy that the government controlled to a competitive *free-market* economy.

free market (frē mär′ kĭt) means:

    a. pertaining to a market in which everything is free

    b. pertaining to an economic system in which resources are allocated by corporations rather than by the government

    c. pertaining to a completely unregulated economy

    d. pertaining to an economic system in which the government is free to do whatever it pleases

_____ **12.** At the top of the list of Third World nations are the rapidly developing countries called Newly *Industrialized* Countries (NICs).

Advanced technology is characteristic of highly *industrialized* countries such as Japan and Germany.

industrialized (ĭn dŭs′ trē ə līzd) means:

    a. having highly developed industries that produce goods and services

    b. struggling

    c. controlled by industries

    d. busy or hardworking

_____ **13.** And even though the Third World holds much of the world's natural resources, many raw materials from the Third World are shipped abroad for *consumption* in the world's wealthier and more developed countries.

The level of energy *consumption* in the United States rose dramatically during the 20th century.

consumption (kən sŭmp′ shən) means:

a. use of consumer goods or services

b. spending

c. ingestion of food

d. debilitating illness

_____ **14.** The flood of poor families into major Third World cities put additional strains on the economic *infrastructure.*

The president pledged to improve two parts of the nation's *infrastructure:* public transportation and health care.

infrastructure (ĭn′ frə strŭk chər) means:

a. government buildings

b. hospitals

c. construction in rural areas

d. basic services and facilities needed by a society

_____ **15.** Saddled with enormous debt payments, *hyperinflation,* surging populations, and mounting unemployment, many Third World countries in the late 1980s struggled just to keep their economies afloat.

When Germany experienced *hyperinflation* in the 1920s, it took a wheelbarrow full of money to buy a single loaf of bread.

hyperinflation (hī pər ĭn flā′ shən) means:

a. decrease in inflation

b. rapid input of air

c. excessive rate of increase in consumer prices

d. rapid accumulation of debt

_____ **16.** Saddled with enormous debt payments, hyperinflation, *surging* populations, and mounting unemployment, many Third World countries in the late 1980s struggled just to keep their economies afloat.

When the storm hit, the *surging* sea water flooded the beaches and low-lying areas of the city.

surging (sûrj′ ĭng) means:

a. decreasing

b. angry

c. increasing suddenly

d. poor

_____ **17.** But *rampant* inflation often ends up eroding most of these efforts, creating an ever-widening gap between the Third World's poorest and richest nations.

In poverty-stricken areas of many large cities, crime is *rampant*.

rampant (răm′ pənt) means:
a. tolerated or accepted
b. decreasing
c. controlled
d. growing or spreading unchecked

_____ **18.** While many economies in Latin America, Africa, and Asia *stagnated,* the economies of the elite developing countries of the Pacific Rim rose to levels that rivaled Japan's in the 1960s.

The actor's career had *stagnated* for several years, but after he starred in a blockbuster movie, he received many offers for leading roles.

stagnated (stăg′ nā təd) means:
a. rotted
b. improved
c. smelled bad
d. failed to change or develop

_____ **19.** One of the first steps in encouraging development would be to reduce the Third World nations' debt and supply additional funds to revive their *moribund* economies.

The doctor summoned the family to the bedside of the *moribund* woman when she had only moments to live.

moribund (môr′ ə bŭnd) means:
a. abundant
b. dead
c. almost at the point of death
d. ill

_____ **20.** Wealthy *creditor* governments also have the option of writing off their debt, accepting that it will never be repaid.

Because the Newtons charged too many purchases on their credit cards and were unable to pay their debts, they were hounded by countless *creditor* calls and letters.

creditor (krĕd′ ĭ tər) means:
a. one to whom money is owed
b. one who deserves financial credit
c. one who is trustworthy
d. one who owes money

SELECTION **6.3**

Economics
(continued)

Reading Skills Application

Directions: These items test your ability to *apply* certain reading skills. You may not have studied all of the skills yet, so some items will serve as a preview. Write each answer in the space provided.

_____ **21.** As used in paragraph 8 of this selection, *fruitless* means:
    a.   half-hearted.
    b.   unrelated to fruit.
    c.   bearing no fruit.
    d.   yielding no productive results.

_____ **22.** Which of the following is the main idea of paragraph 5 of this selection?
    a.   At the bottom of this list are the world's poorest countries, found mainly in sub-Saharan Africa, which have so few resources and so little money that it is virtually impossible for them to develop at all.
    b.   The "Fourth World" is at the bottom of this list.
    c.   The "Fourth World" consists of the world's poorest countries.
    d.   In Somalia and Sudan, for example, there are essentially no natural resources on which to base economic growth.

_____ **23.** The information in paragraph 7 of this selection is organized according to which of the following patterns?
    a.   cause-effect
    b.   comparison-contrast
    c.   problem-solution
    d.   list

_____ **24.** Which of the following assumptions underlies the author's point of view that Third World countries should be helped economically?
    a.   Basic food, clothing, and shelter should be made available to all underdeveloped Third World countries.
    b.   Overpopulation is at the root of Third World countries' problems.
    c.   Wealthy countries should help Third World countries since the economies of all countries are to some extent linked.
    d.   Fixing the infrastructure of Third World countries would solve their economic problems.

_____ **25.** The author mentions the Lomé Convention and the Paris Club as examples of:
    a.   regional development banks backed by wealthy countries.
    b.   specialized organizations designed to help wealthy countries assist Third World countries with their economic problems.
    c.   organizations created by the World Bank and the International Monetary Fund.
    d.   agencies created by the Brady Plan to make "project loans" and "adjustment loans."

Respond in Writing

Directions: Refer to the selection as needed to answer the essay-type questions below. (Your instructor may direct you to work collaboratively with other students on one or more items. Each group member should be able to explain *all* of the group's answers.)

1. The author presents three essential questions that he expects you to be able to answer after you have read this selection. In the spaces below, write a complete answer to each question.

    What is the Third World? Now that you have read the selection, define this term in your own words.

    _____

    _____

    _____

    _____

    _____

    What are the roots (causes, origins) of Third World poverty?

    _____

    _____

    _____

    _____

    _____

    What can be done to promote Third World development?

    _____

    _____

    _____

    _____

    _____

2. Could the United States ever become a Third World country? In other words, are there circumstances that could cause a "first" or "second" world country to become a Third World country? Explain your answer.

     _____

     _____

     _____

     _____

     _____

3. Third World countries fall into three categories (newly industrialized coun- tries, moderately developed countries, and the world's poorest countries— "fourth world" countries). What would a Third World country have to do to become a "first" or "second" world country? Is there anything a "fourth world" country could do to improve its situation?

     _____

     _____

     _____

     _____

     _____

4. Which two countries have the greatest purchasing power? (Use the diagrams on page 400 to answer this question.)

     _____

5. **Overall main idea.** What is the overall main idea the author wants the reader to understand about the Third World and its economy? Answer this question in one sentence. Be sure that your overall main idea sentence includes the phrases *the Third World* and *economic growth.*

     _____

     _____

     _____

     _____

     _____

Recognizing Authors' Writing Patterns

In this chapter, you will learn the answers to these questions:

- What is meant by authors' writing patterns?

- Why is it helpful to be aware of writing patterns?

- How can I recognize list, sequence, definition, comparison-contrast, cause-effect, and spatial order patterns when I read?

- What are other common writing patterns and how can I recognize each?

- What are some common relationships within and between sentences?

SKILLS

Patterns of Writing
- What Are Authors' Writing Patterns?
- Why Is Recognizing Writing Patterns Important?

Recognizing Authors' Writing Patterns
- List Pattern • Sequence Pattern • Definition Pattern
- Comparison-Contrast Pattern • Cause-Effect Pattern • Spatial Order Pattern
- Avoid Seeing Everything as a List

CHECKPOINT: BASIC WRITING PATTERNS

Other Writing Patterns
- Addition Pattern • Generalization and Example Pattern
- Statement and Clarification Pattern • Summary/Conclusion Pattern • Mixed Pattern

CHECKPOINT: OTHER WRITING PATTERNS

Relationships within and between Sentences
- Clarification Pattern • Example Pattern • Addition Pattern
- Sequence Pattern • Comparison Pattern • Contrast Pattern
- Cause-Effect Pattern • Problem-Solution Pattern • Spatial Order Pattern
- Summary/Conclusion Pattern • Concession Pattern

A Word about Standardized Reading Tests: Authors' Writing Patterns

CHECKPOINT: RELATIONSHIPS WITHIN AND BETWEEN SENTENCES

CREATING YOUR SUMMARY

Developing Chapter Review Cards

TEST YOUR UNDERSTANDING: RECOGNIZING AUTHORS' WRITING PATTERNS, PART 1
TEST YOUR UNDERSTANDING: RECOGNIZING AUTHORS' WRITING PATTERNS, PART 2

READINGS

Selection 7.1   **"E-Commerce? It's E-Normous!"**
from *Understanding Business*
by William Nickels, James McHugh, and Susan McHugh (Business)

Selection 7.2   **"The Development of Rock Music and Rock in American Society"**
from *Music: An Appreciation*
by Roger Kamien (Music Appreciation)

Selection 7.3   **"Reactions to Impending Death"**
from *Essentials of Psychology*
by Dennis Coon (Psychology)

412

Good order is the foundation of all things.

Edmund Burke

If you don't know where you're going, you may end up somewhere else.

Yogi Berra

You can have it all. You just can't have it all at once.

Unknown

The limits of my language mean the limits of my world.

Ludwig Wittgenstein

PATTERNS OF WRITING

PERSONALIZED LEARNING

In this chapter, you will learn another skill to help you improve your reading comprehension: recognizing authors' patterns of writing. **Writing patterns** are authors' ways of organizing information they present. Writing patterns are also called *organizational patterns, patterns of development, rhetorical patterns,* and *thinking patterns.*

writing patterns

Ways authors organize the information they present.

Writing patterns are also known as *organizational patterns, patterns of development, rhetorical patterns,* and *thinking patterns.*

What Are Authors' Writing Patterns?

All of us use certain patterns to organize our thoughts in ways that seem logical to us. When people write, they use these same patterns to organize information in ways that seem logical to them. If you can identify the pattern a writer is using and think along with the author as you read, you will find it easier to comprehend what he or she is saying. Recognizing the pattern can also help you predict where the author is going.

The specific pattern an author uses depends on the relationship among the ideas he or she wants to emphasize. In this chapter, you will be introduced to several writing patterns commonly used by textbook authors:

- List
- Sequence
- Definition
- Comparison-contrast
- Cause-effect
- Spatial order

Toward the end of this chapter, you will also be introduced to some additional patterns. It is important to understand that, as mentioned above, the patterns authors use are the same thinking patterns you use every day. The box on page 414 gives examples of how college students use familiar patterns to organize the information in comments they make. You use these patterns yourself when you speak or write, but you still may not be aware of them when you read. This chapter will show you how

EXAMPLES OF THINKING PATTERNS IN EVERYDAY COMMENTS

- "I'm taking four courses this semester: art, psychology, reading, and math." **(list)**
- "The university has several different colleges: the college of fine arts, which includes music, dance, drama, and painting; the college of social sciences, which includes history, psychology, sociology, and anthropology; and the business college, which includes marketing, finance, accounting, and international business." **(division/classification)**
- "I have a psychology paper due on Monday, a math quiz on Wednesday, a vocabulary quiz in reading on Thursday morning, and an art test Thursday afternoon!" **(sequence)**
- "To write a research paper, you must first determine your topic, then gather information, write a draft, and finally, edit it to produce a correct, polished paper." **(process)**
- "To me, success means always giving your best effort, even if the results aren't perfect." **(definition)**
- "The baccalaureate, or bachelor's, degree is awarded to students who successfully complete a college or university's undergraduate course of study; for example, a student might earn a Bachelor of Arts degree or a Bachelor of Science degree." **(definition with example)**
- "Psychology focuses on the behavior of the individual, but sociology focuses on human behavior in groups." **(comparison-contrast)**
- "When I stick to my study schedule, I learn more, do better on tests, and feel less stress." **(cause-effect)**
- "The Student Center is just south of the library, between the fine arts building and the science complex." **(spatial order)**

to do that. Throughout the chapter, variations and other names for the patterns are given in parentheses; for example, division/classification (a type of list), time order/process (a type of sequence), and definition with example (a type of definition).

Why Is Recognizing Writing Patterns Important?

Recognizing authors' writing patterns has several advantages:

- **Improved comprehension.**   You will comprehend more because you will be able to follow the writer's ideas more accurately and more efficiently.
- **More accurate predictions.**   As soon as you identify a pattern, you can make predictions about what is likely to come next in a paragraph. As you learned in Chapter 2, effective readers are active readers who make logical predictions.
- **Easier memorization.**   You can memorize and recall information more efficiently if you understand the way it is organized.

List pattern.
Three sources of
information.

- **Improvement in your writing.**   Using these patterns yourself will enable you to write clearer, better-organized paragraphs. You can write better answers on essay tests when you use appropriate patterns to organize the information. Using these patterns when you prepare a presentation or a speech will help you organize your ideas logically, and this will make it easier for your listeners to follow your train of thought.

RECOGNIZING AUTHORS' WRITING PATTERNS

Comprehension-Monitoring Question for Recognizing Authors' Writing Patterns

Which pattern did the author use to organize the main idea and the supporting details?

Six common writing patterns are described below, accompanied by a textbook excerpt to illustrate each. Every writing pattern has certain signal words and phrases that are associated with it and convey to the reader which pattern is being used. The signals and clue words for each pattern are explained after each sample excerpt. They are summarized in the box on pages 431–33. Often, the main idea sentence contains clue words that signal which pattern is being used. As you read, ask yourself, "Which pattern did the author use to organize the main idea and supporting details?"

List Pattern

As its name indicates, the **list pattern** (sometimes called a *listing pattern*) presents a list of items in no specific order. The order of the items is not important. If the items were presented in a different order or rearranged, it would not matter.

Clue words that typically signal a list pattern are *and, also, another, moreover, in addition,* and words such as *first, second, third, fourth, last,* and *finally.* Watch for words or numbers in the main idea that announce *categories (two types, five ways, several kinds).* Sometimes bullets (•) or asterisks (*) are used to set off individual items in a list. Their purpose is to ensure that you notice each item. Sometimes authors use numbers (1, 2, 3) or letters (*a, b, c*) to set off individual items in a list even though their order is not important. Their purpose is to ensure that you notice each item and the total number of items. Your task is to identify *all* the items in the list, even when not all of them (or perhaps any of them) are "signaled."

Here is a paragraph from an economics textbook. The topic is *the financing of corporate activity.* The first sentence states the main idea: *Generally speaking, corporations finance their activity in three different ways.* The authors have listed three details that help you understand more about this main idea. Notice that these details are in no special order. As you read this paragraph, ask yourself, "What are the *three different ways* that corporations finance their activity?"

> Generally speaking, corporations finance their activity in three different ways. First, a very large portion of a corporation's activities is financed internally out of undistributed corporate profits. Second, as do individuals or unincorporated businesses, corporations may borrow from financial institutions. For example, a small corporation planning to build a new plant may obtain the needed funds from a commercial bank, a savings and loan association, or an insurance company. Third, unique to corporations, they can issue common stocks and bonds.
>
> *Source:* From Campbell McConnell and Stanley Brue, *Economics: Principles, Problems, and Policies,* 15e, p. 89. Copyright © 2002 by The McGraw-Hill Companies, Inc. Reprinted with permission of The McGraw-Hill Companies, Inc.

Stop and Annotate

Go back to the textbook excerpt above. Underline or highlight the words that signal the items in the list. Then number each supporting detail. Mark the words in the main idea sentence that signal a list, too.

The phrase *three different ways* and the clue words *first, second,* and *third* signal a list of three major supporting details: three ways of financing corporate activities. The order in which they are listed is not important. What is important is that there are three different ways, and what those three ways are. Notice that a minor supporting detail signaled by the phrase "for example" follows the second major detail. This sentence merely gives examples of financial institutions, a term mentioned in the second major detail. (Major and minor details are defined and explained on pages 350–51.)

The next excerpt is from a health and fitness textbook. It illustrates the listing pattern in a very obvious way: the items are numbered. The topic of the paragraph is *signs of alcoholism,* and its implied main idea (which must be formulated by the reader) is *The diagnosis of alcoholism is often imprecise and difficult for nonprofessionals to make, but there are certain changes in behavior that can warn of possible alcoholism.* On the basis of the topic and the main idea, what do you predict will be listed?

Signs of Alcoholism

The diagnosis of alcoholism is not something that can be precise, and it is often difficult for nonprofessionals to make. The disease carries such a stigma that the alcoholic, friends, and family often postpone seeking treatment. Meanwhile, it is not unusual for the alcoholic to deny the problem and rationalize continued drinking. Certain signs in a person's behavior that warn of possible alcoholism include :

1. Surreptitious, secretive drinking
2. Morning drinking (unless that behavior is not unusual in the person's peer group)
3. Repeated, conscious attempts at abstinence
4. Blatant, indiscriminate use of alcohol
5. Changing beverages in an attempt to control drinking
6. Having five or more drinks daily
7. Having two or more blackouts while drinking

Source: Adapted from Marvin Levy, Mark Dignan, and Janet Shirreffs, *Targeting Wellness: The Core.* Copyright © 1992 by The McGraw-Hill Companies, Inc. Reprinted with permission of The McGraw-Hill Companies, Inc.

Stop and Annotate

Go back to the textbook excerpt above. Underline or highlight the clues that signal a list.

division/ classification pattern

Groups or categories of items that are named, and the parts in each group are explained. (This is a variation of the list pattern.)

The list of warning signs of possible alcoholism is indicated by a colon (:), set off from the text, and announced by the phrase *Certain signs in a person's behavior that warn of possible alcoholism include.* The topic *signs of alcoholism* in the heading and the words *certain signs in a person's behavior* in the main idea sentence help readers predict that a list will be given. The authors list seven supporting details (signs) and number these details even though they are not in any particular order. The numbers are there to make sure readers note each detail and understand that, indeed, there are *several* signs in a person's behavior—not just one or two—that can warn of possible alcoholism. (Numbering items in a list is referred to as *enumeration.*)

A variation of the list pattern is the division or classification pattern. In the **division** or **classification pattern,** items are divided into groups or categories that are named, and the parts in each group are explained. In the main idea sentence, watch for clue words such as *two categories, four kinds, three types, five elements, six classes, three kinds,* and so forth. The paragraph below, from a nutrition textbook, uses the division or classification pattern.

Lipids

Lipids (mostly fats and oils) can be separated into two basic types—saturated fat and unsaturated fat—based on the chemical structure of their dominant fatty acids. *Saturated fats* are rich in saturated fatty acids. These fatty acids do not contain carbon-carbon double bonds. *Unsaturated fats* are rich in unsaturated fatty acids. These fatty acids contain one or more carbon-carbon double bonds. The presence of carbon-carbon double bonds determines whether the lipid is solid or liquid at room temperature. Plant oils tend to contain many unsaturated fatty acids—this makes them liquid. Animal fats are often rich in saturated fatty acids—this makes them solid.

Source: Adapted from Gordon Wardlaw and Anne Smith, *Contemporary Nutrition,* 6e, p. 7. Copyright © 2006 by The McGraw-Hill Companies, Inc. Reprinted with permission of The McGraw-Hill Companies, Inc.

Stop and Annotate

Go back to the textbook excerpt on page 417. Underline or highlight the clues that signal the division or classification form of the list pattern.

sequence pattern

A list of items presented in a specific order because the order is important.

The sequence pattern is also known as *time order, chronological order, a process,* or a *series.*

process

A series of actions or changes that bring about a result. (This is a variation of the sequence pattern.)

In the first sentence of the paragraph (the stated main idea sentence), the phrase *two basic types* alerts you that a classification will follow. The two classifications are the two types of fats: saturated and unsaturated. The authors italicize the terms, and they explain the two types and give the types of oils and fats (plant and animal) that belong in each category. Notice that it would not make any difference if the authors had presented the two categories in the reverse order because order is not important. What is important are the two types of fats and the distinguishing characteristics of each type.

Sequence Pattern

The **sequence pattern** presents a list of items *in a specific order* because the order is important. The sequence pattern is a type of list, but it differs from a simple list because the order of the items is significant. A very common type of sequence is the occurrence of events in time, and therefore a sequence pattern is often called *time order* or *chronological order.* The sequence pattern is also known as a **process** or a *series.* Sets of directions are examples of sequences you encounter daily.

Clue words that signal a sequence pattern include *first, second, third, then, next,* and *finally.* Dates and phrases that refer to time, such as *during the twenty-first century* or *in the last decade,* may also signal sequences. Watch also for enumeration (1, 2, 3, etc.), letters (*a, b, c,* etc.), and signal words such as *sequence, steps, stages, phases, progression, process,* and *series.* When numbers are used in a sequence, they indicate the order, and not just how many items there are.

Sequence pattern. Seasons follow a predictable sequence.

Following is an excerpt in which authors use a sequence pattern to show the order in which certain events occur. It is from the same health and fitness textbook, but this time the topic is *the alcohol continuum.* (A "continuum" is what it sounds like: a gradual progression from one stage to the next.) Read the paragraph and notice the list of details and the order in which they are given.

The Alcohol Continuum

Alcoholism is a progressive disease that develops as a series of stages through which any drinker may pass. At one end of the spectrum is occasional and moderate social drinking with family or friends on special occasions. At the other end is long-term, frequent, uncontrollable drinking with severe physical, psychological, and social complications. The full continuum can be summarized as follows :

1. **Occasional drinker** drinks in small quantities only on special occasions.
2. **Light drinker** drinks regularly in small and nonintoxicating quantities.
3. **Social drinker** drinks regularly in moderate and nonintoxicating quantities.
4. **Problem drinker** drinks to intoxication with no pattern to episodes, gets drunk without intending to or realizing it.
5. **Binge drinker** drinks heavily in recurrent episodes, often brought on by disturbances in work, home, or social life.
6. **Excessive drinker** experiences frequent episodes of uncontrollable drinking affecting work, family, and social relationships.
7. **Chronic alcoholic** is in serious trouble from long-term, frequent, and uncontrollable drinking; experiences physical complications including organic dysfunction, tolerance, and dependence; and develops severe work, home, and social problems.

Source: From Marvin Levy, Mark Dignan, and Janet Shirreffs, *Targeting Wellness: The Core.* Copyright © 1992 by The McGraw-Hill Companies, Inc. Reprinted with permission of The McGraw-Hill Companies, Inc.

Stop and Annotate

Go back to the textbook excerpt above. Underline or highlight the clues that signal a sequence.

The details in this paragraph are numbered, announced by a colon, and listed after the phrase *can be summarized as follows.* But there are additional sequence pattern clues: the words *progressive, continuum, series of stages,* and *spectrum.* In this paragraph, the order of the details is obviously important. You would be expected to learn them in this order.

Now read this music textbook excerpt, in which the author also uses the sequence pattern. Notice the dates that are associated with important events in the Beatles' career.

The Beatles

The Beatles—the singer-guitarists Paul McCartney, John Lennon, and George Harrison, and the drummer Ringo Starr—have been the most influential performing group in the history of rock. Their music, hairstyle, dress, and lifestyle were imitated all over the world, resulting in a phenomenon known as Beatlemania. All four Beatles were born during the early 1940s in Liverpool, England, and devoted themselves to rock in their teens. Lennon and McCartney, the main songwriters of the group, began working together in 1956 and were joined by Harrison about two years later. In 1962 Ringo Starr became their new drummer. The group gained experience by performing in Hamburg, Germany, and in Liverpool, a port to which sailors brought the latest American rock, rhythm-and-blues, and country-and-western records. In 1961, the Beatles made their first record, and by 1963 they were England's top rock group. In 1964, they triumphed in the United States, breaking attendance records everywhere and dominating the record market. Audiences often became hysterical, and the police had to protect the Beatles from their fans. Beatle dolls, wigs, sweatshirts, and jackets flooded the market. Along with a steady flow of successful records, the Beatles made several hit movies: *A Hard Day's Night, Help!* and *Yellow Submarine.*

Source: Adapted from Roger Kamien, *Music: An Appreciation,* 16e, p. 518. Copyright © 2011 by The McGraw-Hill Companies, Inc. Reprinted with permission of The McGraw-Hill Companies, Inc.

Stop and Annotate

Go back to the textbook excerpt above. Underline or highlight the clues that signal a sequence.

The details in this paragraph support the author's main idea: *The Beatles have been the most influential performing group in the history of rock.* The details are given in chronological order: the order in which they occurred. The dates throughout the paragraph tell when each important event occurred. In addition, the phrases *were born during the early 1940s* and *devoted themselves to rock* indicate the sequence of events in the Beatles' history.

Here is a passage from a business textbook that uses the process pattern, a form of the sequence pattern. As defined earlier, a process is a series of actions or changes that lead to a specific result, such as the process of obtaining a driver's license or the process of digestion. This paragraph presents seven steps managers can use in order to make sound decisions.

Planning and all the other management functions require decision making. Decision making is choosing among two or more alternatives, which sounds easier than it is. In fact, decision making is the heart of all the management functions. The rational decision-making process is a series of steps managers often follow to make logical, intelligent, and well-founded decisions. Think of the steps as the seven Ds of decision making:

1. Define the situation.
2. Describe and collect needed information.
3. Develop alternatives.
4. Develop agreement among those involved.
5. Decide which alternative is best.
6. Do what is indicated (begin implementation).
7. Determine whether the decision was a good one, and follow up.

Source: From William Nickels, James McHugh, and Susan McHugh, *Understanding Business,* 9e, pp. 185–86. Copyright © 2010 by The McGraw-Hill Companies, Inc. Reprinted with permission of The McGraw-Hill Companies, Inc.

Stop and Annotate

Go back to the textbook excerpt above. Underline or highlight the clues that signal the process form of the sequence pattern.

The details of the paragraph support the implied main idea: *Planning and all other management functions require decision making, and the seven Ds of decision making are the steps managers often follow to make good decisions.* The details present in order the specific steps of the process. Notice that the authors use the words *process, series of steps,* and *steps.* Furthermore, they number the steps in the process because the steps must be done in that order. These clue words and signals are characteristic of any sequence pattern, including processes.

Definition Pattern

The **definition pattern** presents the meaning of an important term that is discussed throughout the passage. The definition itself is the main idea. The details in the rest of the paragraph discuss or illustrate the term that is being defined.

Definitions are easy to identify because the terms being defined often appear in **bold print,** *italics,* or color. Moreover, they are typically introduced by signal words such as *the term, refers to, is called, is defined as, means,* and so forth. Even the simple verb *is* can be a signal to the reader that a definition is being given.

Sometimes an author uses a synonym (a word or a phrase with a similar meaning) in order to define a term. The synonym will be signaled by words such as *or, in other words,* or *that is.* Take, for example, this sentence:

> Many women encounter what is termed a *glass ceiling,* or barrier of subtle discrimination, that keeps them from the top positions in business.

The term that is being defined (glass ceiling) appears in italics. Notice that the word *or* introduces a phrase that is set off by commas and that defines the term: a barrier of subtle discrimination. The term *glass ceiling* is a metaphor, a type of figurative language introduced in Chapter 2. The term, of course, does not refer to a real ceiling made of glass but, rather, the invisible barrier of discrimination that many women encounter in the workplace.

Definitions can also be signaled by punctuation marks. All the examples below define the term *anorexia nervosa.* Notice how the different punctuation marks in each of the examples indicate the definition.

- **Commas (,)**
  Anorexia nervosa, an eating disorder that can lead to starvation, occurs most often in teenage girls.
  Teenage girls are the most common victims of anorexia nervosa, an eating disorder that can lead to starvation.
- **Parentheses ( )**
  Anorexia nervosa (an eating disorder that can lead to starvation) occurs most often in teenage girls.
- **Brackets [ ]**
  Anorexia nervosa [an eating disorder than can lead to starvation] occurs most often in teenage girls.
- **Dashes (—)**
  Anorexia nervosa—an eating disorder that can lead to starvation—occurs most often in teenage girls.
- **Colons (:)**
  An illness affecting primarily teenage girls is anorexia nervosa: an eating disorder that can lead to starvation.

Below is a psychology textbook excerpt in which the author presents a definition as the stated main idea in the second sentence and then goes on to explain it more fully by giving an example. The term the author is defining is the *foot-in-the-door principle.*

Foot-in-the-Door Principle

People who sell door-to-door have long recognized that once they "get a foot in the door," a sale is almost a sure thing. To state the **foot-in-the-door principle** more formally, a person who agrees to a small request is later more likely to comply with a larger demand. Evidence suggests, for instance, that if someone asked you to put a large sign in your front yard to support the police department you might refuse. If, however, you had first agreed to put a small sign in your window, you would later be much more likely to allow the big sign to be placed in your yard.

Source: From Dennis Coon, *Essentials of Psychology: Exploration and Application,* 5e. © 1991 Wadsworth, a part of Cengage Learning, Inc. Reproduced by permission. www.cengage.com/permissions.

Stop and Annotate

Go back to the textbook excerpt above. Underline or highlight the clues that signal a definition and example.

In this paragraph, the author gives the definition of the foot-in-the-door principle in the main idea sentence: *a person who agrees to a small request is later more likely to comply with a larger demand.* To announce to the reader that the foot-in-the-door effect is being defined precisely, the author uses the phrase *To state the foot-in-the-door principle more formally.* Did you notice that the definition is set off by a comma, and that the important term appears both in the heading and in bold print within the paragraph? To help readers understand the meaning of the foot-in-the-door principle, the author includes a specific example. In the third sentence, he says *for instance,* and then gives the example of a small sign placed in a window and then a large one placed in the yard.

Here is a business textbook paragraph in which the authors define two forms of *sexual harassment* in the workplace. Notice that the entire paragraph defines sexual harassment.

Another sensitive issue concerning primarily women in the workplace is **sexual harassment.** As defined by the Equal Employment Opportunity Commission, sexual harassment takes two forms : the obvious request for sexual favors with an implicit reward or punishment related to work, and the more subtle creation of a sexist environment in which employees are made to feel uncomfortable by off-color jokes, lewd remarks, and posturing.

Source: David Rachman, Michael Mescon, Courtland Bovée, and John Thill, *Business Today,* p. 110. Copyright © 1993. Reprinted by permission of Courtland Bovée and John Thill.

Stop and Annotate

Go back to the textbook excerpt above. Underline or highlight the clues that signal a definition.

In this paragraph, the phrases *as defined by* and *takes two forms* signal to the reader that there are two distinct definitions of sexual harassment in the workplace. Notice that a colon (:) announces the two definitions. Notice also that although the term *sexual harassment* appears in the first sentence, it is actually defined in the following sentence.

EXERCISE 1

This paragraph comes from an information technology textbook:

Many of you probably can't remember a world without computers, but for some of us, computers were virtually unknown when we were born and have rapidly come of age during our lifetime. Although there are many predecessors to what we think of as the modern computer, the computer age did not really begin until the first computer was made available to the public in 1951. The modern age of computers thus spans slightly more than fifty years (so far), which is typically broken down into five generations. Each generation has been marked by a significant advance in technology. During the first generation (1951–57), computers were built with vacuum tubes. Vacuum tubes were electronic tubes that were made of glass and were about the size of light bulbs. The second generation (1958–63) began with the first computers built with transistors. These are small devices that transfer signals across a resistor. Because transistors are much smaller, use less power, and create less heat than vacuum tubes, the new computers were faster, smaller, and more reliable than first-generation machines. During the third generation of the modern computer age (1964–69), computer manufacturers began replacing transistors with integrated circuits. An integrated circuit is a complete electronic circuit on a small chip made of silicon. These computers were more reliable and compact than computers made with transistors, and they cost less to manufacture. Many key advances were made during the fourth generation (1970–90), the most significant being the microprocessor, which is a specialized chip developed for computer memory and logic. Use of a single chip to create a smaller, "personal" computer revolutionized the computer industry. Our fifth generation (1991–2012 and beyond) has been referred to as the "Connected Generation" because of the industry's massive effort to increase connectivity of computers. The rapidly expanding Internet, World Wide Web, and intranets have created an information superhighway that has enabled both computer professionals and home computer users to communicate with others across the globe.

Source: Adapted from Timothy J. O'Leary and Linda I. O'Leary, *Computing Essentials 2012: Making IT Work for You,* p. 340. Copyright © 2012 by The McGraw-Hill Companies, Inc. Reprinted with permission of The McGraw-Hill Companies, Inc.

Write the *main idea sentence:* _____

_____

_____

_____

Which *writing pattern* did the authors use to organize the main idea and the supporting details?

_____

Write some of the *clues* that caused you to choose this pattern:

_____

Comparison-Contrast Pattern

Often writers want to emphasize comparisons and contrasts. A *comparison* shows how two or more things are similar or alike. A *contrast* points out the differences between them. The **comparison-contrast pattern** presents similarities (comparisons) between two or more things, differences (contrasts) between two or more things, or both. The comparison-contrast pattern is also known as *ideas in opposition*.

To signal comparisons, authors use the words *similarly, likewise, both, same,* and *also*. To signal contrasts, authors use clues such as *on the other hand, in contrast, however, while, whereas, although, nevertheless, different, unlike,* and *some . . . while others*. Contrasts are also signaled by words that have opposite meanings, such as *advantages* and *disadvantages, strengths* and *weaknesses, plusses* and *minuses*, or *assets* and *liabilities*.

In the following excerpt from an art appreciation textbook, the author presents important information about the advantages and disadvantages of the very slow rate at which oil paint dries. Read the paragraph to determine what the author says about the positive and negative aspects of this characteristic.

---

comparison-contrast pattern

Similarities (comparisons) between two or more things are presented, differences (contrasts) between two or more things are presented, or both similarities and differences are presented.

The comparison-contrast pattern is also known as *ideas in opposition*.

> The outstanding characteristic of oil paint is that it dries very slowly. This creates both advantages and disadvantages for the artist. On the plus side, it means that colors can be blended very subtly, layers of paint can be applied on top of other layers with little danger of separating or cracking, and the artist can rework sections of the painting almost indefinitely. This same asset becomes a liability when the artist is pressed for time—perhaps when an exhibition has been scheduled. Oil paint dries so very slowly that it may be weeks or months before the painting has truly "set."
>
> *Source:* From Rita Gilbert, *Living with Art,* 7e, pp. 169, 171. Copyright © 2005 by The McGraw-Hill Companies, Inc. Reprinted with permission of The McGraw-Hill Companies, Inc.

Comparison-contrast pattern. The size of these two dogs presents a startling contrast. How are these two animals alike? How are they different?

In this paragraph, *advantages, disadvantages, on the plus side, asset,* and *liability* are clues or signals that the author is presenting both the positive and the negative aspects of the slow rate at which oil paint dries.

Here is another paragraph from the same art appreciation textbook, which also uses the comparison-contrast pattern. It presents similarities and differences between a Buddhist shrine and a medieval Christian cathedral.

Stop and Annotate

Go back to the previous textbook excerpt. Underline or highlight the clues that signal a comparison-contrast pattern.

Buddhist shrines—the word stupa means "shrine"—often housed relics of the Buddha, and worship rituals called for circumambulation ("walking around") of the stupa. Thus, on the outside of the Great Stupa of Sanchi, in India, we see a railed pathway, where pilgrims could take the ritual clockwise walk following the Path of Life around the World Mountain. Elsewhere the stupa is embellished richly with carvings and sculpture evoking scenes from the Buddha's life. Every part of the stupa is geared to the pursuit of personal enlightenment and transcendence. But if the Buddhist temple is dedicated to private worship, then its extreme opposite can be found in the total encompassment of a community religious experience: the medieval Christian cathedral. And the supreme example of that ideal is the Cathedral of Notre Dame de Chartres, in France. Chartres Cathedral was built, rebuilt, and modified over a period of several hundred years, but the basic structure, which is in the Gothic style, was established in the thirteenth century. A cathedral is the bishop's domain and therefore is always in a town or a city. This one fact is crucial to understanding the nature of Chartres and the communal role it played in the people's lives.

Source: Adapted from Rita Gilbert, *Living with Art,* 3e, pp. 64–65. Copyright © 1992 by The McGraw-Hill Companies, Inc. Reprinted with permission of The McGraw-Hill Companies, Inc.

Stop and Annotate

Go back to the textbook excerpt above. Underline or highlight the clues that signal a comparison-contrast pattern.

In the middle of this passage, the author signals the major difference she is presenting between the Great Stupa of Sanchi and Chartres Cathedral by the words *extreme opposite.* She wants you to understand that these two structures were built to serve different religious purposes. More specifically, she wants the reader to understand that Buddhist stupas were designed for *personal enlightenment* and *private worship,* whereas Christian cathedrals were designed for a *community religious experience.* In this passage, the words *personal* and *private* are used in contrast to *community.*

When information is presented in the comparison-contrast pattern, take notes by creating a chart of the information. A chart makes it easy to see similarities and differences. The chart on page 426 lists the similarities and differences between the Great Stupa of Sanchi and Chartres Cathedral.

When you list the differences, use one column for each item. Be sure to write the contrasting information on the same lines. For example, the first line contrasts the religions, the second the location of the building, the third the buildings' shapes, and so on. Organizing comparison-contrast information in chart form makes it easier to memorize.

	Great Stupa of Sanchi & Chartres Cathedral
Similarities:	• Places of worship
	• Large and elaborate stone structures
(Comparisons)	• Centuries old
	• Embellished with carvings and sculpture
	• Designed for specific religious purposes

	Great Stupa of Sanchi	Chartres Cathedral
	• Buddhist	• Christian
Differences:	• Sanchi, India	• Chartres, France
	• Round structure	• Cruciform structure (cross-shaped)
(Contrasts)	• Domed roof (symbol of World Mountain)	• Gothic style
	• Housed relics of Buddha	
	• Circumambulation	
	• Geared to private worship	• Geared to community religious experience
	• Geared to the pursuit of personal enlightenment	• Played a communal role in people's lives

Cause-Effect Pattern

cause-effect pattern

Reasons (causes) and results (effects) of events or conditions are presented.

The **cause-effect pattern** presents *reasons* (causes) and *results* (effects) of events or conditions. Authors often use these words to indicate a cause: *because, the reasons, causes, is due to,* and *is caused by.* These words are often used to indicate an effect: *therefore, consequently, thus, as a consequence, led to, the results, as a result, the effect was,* and *resulted in.*

The following health textbook excerpt uses the cause-effect pattern. Its topic is *lung cancer and the way an individual smokes.* The verb *affects* and the phrase *depending on* signal to the reader that the cause-effect pattern is being used. The first sentence of this paragraph is its stated main idea.

> The way an individual smokes affects the chances of developing lung cancer. The risk increases depending on how many cigarettes are smoked each day, how deeply the smoker inhales, and how much tar and nicotine are contained in the cigarettes. People who started smoking early in their lives are also at greater risk than those who have only smoked for a few years.
>
> *Source:* Adapted from Marvin Levy, Mark Dignan, and Janet Shirreffs, *Targeting Wellness: The Core,* p. 261. Copyright © 1992 by The McGraw-Hill Companies, Inc. Reprinted with permission of The McGraw-Hill Companies, Inc.

Stop and Annotate

Go back to the textbook excerpt above. Underline or highlight the clues that signal a cause-effect pattern. Number the causes with a small ①, ②, ③, and ④. to make each cause stand out clearly.

In this paragraph, the authors present four supporting details that are *causes* that contribute to one *effect,* the smoker's increased risk of lung cancer: (1) how many cigarettes are smoked daily, (2) how deeply the smoker inhales, (3) the amount of tar and nicotine in the cigarettes, and (4) the age at which a person starts smoking. (Notice that three causes are mentioned in a single sentence.)

Arranging information presented in a cause-effect pattern by mapping is also an ideal format for study notes or review cards. (Mapping is an informal way of organizing main ideas and supporting details by using boxes, circles, lines, arrows, and so on. Guidelines for mapping are presented in Chapter 10.) The study map below presents information from the excerpt on page 426. It shows the four causes that increase a smoker's chances of developing lung cancer.

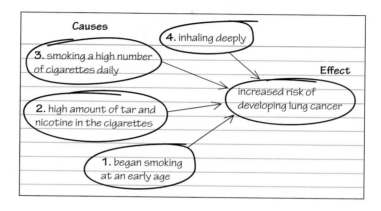

Here is a physics textbook excerpt that uses the cause-effect pattern. It explains *why* many people enjoy physics.

Many People Enjoy Physics. Why?

There are several reasons physicists and many of those who study physics find it enjoyable. First, it is a joy to find out how the world behaves. Knowledge of the laws of nature allows us to look on the world with a fuller appreciation of its beauty and wonder. Second, we all enjoy discovering something new. Scientists take great satisfaction in exposing a facet of nature that was previously not seen or perhaps not understood. Imagine how Columbus must have felt when he sighted America. Scientists share a similar excitement when their work results in the discovery of a new aspect of nature. Fortunately, it seems that the more we discover about nature, the more there is to discover. The excitement of discovery drives science forward. Third, most of us enjoy the successful completion of a demanding task. That is why people of all ages work puzzles. Each question or problem in science is a new puzzle to be solved. We enjoy the satisfaction of success. Fourth, science benefits humanity. A substantial fraction of those who embark on scientific work do so because they wish to contribute to the progress of civilization. Call it idealistic, perhaps, but ask yourself what medical tools we would have today without the work of countless scientists in physics, chemistry, biology, and the related sciences. Our present civilization is heavily indebted not only to those in science but also to those in the general populace who know enough about science to support its progress.

Source: From Frederick J. Bueche, *Principles of Physics,* 5e, p. 3. Copyright © 1988 by The McGraw-Hill Companies, Inc. Reprinted with permission of The McGraw-Hill Companies, Inc.

Cause-effect pattern.

Cause: bowling a ball

Effect: a strike

Stop and Annotate

Go back to the previous textbook excerpt. Underline or highlight the clues that signal a cause-effect pattern.

In the stated main idea sentence (the first sentence), this author uses the clue words *several reasons.* Then he uses *first, second, third,* and *fourth* to announce the four reasons that explain his main idea: *There are several reasons physicists and many of those who study physics find it enjoyable.* Even the word *Why?* in the title tells readers to expect a list of reasons (causes).

In the business textbook excerpt below, the authors present several effects (results) of employee assistance programs. This paragraph does not contain signal words such as *results* or *effects.* Instead, the authors assume that the reader will understand the relationship between these programs and their results. The phrase *Such programs have been reported to reduce* implies that employee assistance programs have certain effects. Read the paragraph and notice the four effects the authors present.

> A number of companies have also instituted **employee assistance programs** (EAPs) for employees with personal problems, especially drug or alcohol dependence. Such programs have been reported (on the average) to reduce absenteeism by 66 percent, to reduce health-care costs by 86 percent, to reduce sickness benefits by 33 percent, and to reduce work-related accidents by 65 percent. Participation in EAPs is voluntary and confidential. Employees are given in-house counseling or are referred to outside therapists or treatment programs.
>
> *Source:* From David Rachman, Michael Mescon, Courtland Bovée, and John Thill, *Business Today,* pp. 283–84. Copyright © 1993. Reprinted with permission of Courtland Bovée and John Thill.

Stop and Annotate

Go back to the textbook excerpt above. Underline or highlight the phrase that signals a cause-effect pattern. Number the effects with a small ①, ②, ③, and ④ to make each effect stand out clearly.

In a single sentence, these authors present four beneficial *effects* of employee assistance programs: reductions in (1) absenteeism, (2) costs of health care, (3) costs of sickness benefits, and (4) work-related accidents. (Notice that all four effects are given in a single sentence.)

Here is another informal study map that presents the information from the preceding excerpt. The study card shows the four positive effects of an employee assistance program.

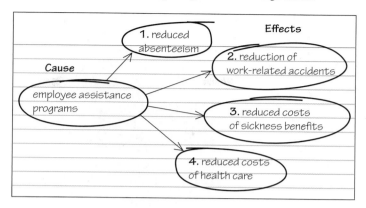

Spatial Order Pattern

The location or layout of something or someplace is described.

A spatial order pattern is also known as a *place order pattern.*

Stop and Annotate

In the excerpt, underline or highlight the words that signal the spatial order pattern.

The **spatial order pattern,** also known as *place order,* describes the location or layout of something or someplace. For example, authors would use this pattern to describe the location of troops in an important battle, the elements of a painting, the location of a country, or the floor plan of a medieval church. To do this, they use clue words such as *beside, near, adjacent to, next to, close to, below, beneath, above, over, opposite, facing, to the right or left, north, south, east, west, within, outside of,* and so forth. Also watch for clues such as *site, location, is located, is situated, placed, positioned,* and other such words.

The following passage describes the location of the state of Kansas. As you read it, watch for clues that indicate a spatial order pattern.

> Kansas is situated at the geographic center of the United States. It is halfway between the East and West coasts. It is bounded by four states: Nebraska to the north, Oklahoma to the south, Missouri to the east, and Colorado on the west.

Did you notice the words *situated at* in the first sentence, the stated main idea? The other sentences contains additional place words: *halfway between, East,* and *West* in the second sentence, and *north, south, east,* and *west* in the last sentence.

Now read this art history textbook's description of a famous painting that hangs in the Galleria degli Uffizi in Florence, Italy.

> *Madonna Enthroned,* painted by the 13th-century Italian master Cimabue, depicts Mary, mother of Christ, with her son. Mary sits tranquilly on her throne, her hand a classic gesture indicating the Christ child on her lap, who is the hope of the earth's salvation. On both sides of her are figures of angels, heavenly beings who assist humankind in its quest for Paradise. Again, all these wear halos symbolizing their holiness. Yet again, the Virgin, being the most important figure in this painting, dominates the composition, is the largest, and holds the most serenely frontal posture.

Source: Adapted from Mark Getlein, *Gilbert's Living with Art,* 7e, p. 54. Copyright © 2005 by The McGraw-Hill Companies, Inc. Reprinted with permission of The McGraw-Hill Companies, Inc.

Stop and Annotate

Go back to the previous textbook excerpt. Underline or highlight the words that signal the spatial order pattern.

The author describes the position of Mary in the painting: she sits *on her throne.* She is holding her child *on her lap,* and angels appear *on both sides* of her. Mary has a *frontal posture,* meaning that she faces directly out at the viewer. The author presents the picture with words.

In this chapter so far, you have learned about six common paragraph patterns textbook authors use: list, sequence, definition, comparison-contrast, cause-effect, and spatial order. The box on pages 431–33 summarizes the signals and clue words for each of these patterns.

EXERCISE 2

This paragraph comes from a human development textbook:

> Why do marriages fail and result in divorce? Looking back on their marriages, 130 divorced U.S. women who had been married an average of eight years showed remarkable agreement on the reasons for the failure of their marriages. The most frequently cited reasons were incompatibility and lack of emotional support. For more recently divorced, presumably younger women, this included lack of career support. Spousal abuse was cited third, suggesting that intimate partner violence may be more frequent than is generally realized.
>
> *Source*: Adapted from Diane E. Papalia, Sally Wendkos Olds, and Ruth Duskin Feldman, *Human Development*, 11e, p. 474. Copyright © 2009 by The McGraw-Hill Companies, Inc. Reprinted with permission of The McGraw-Hill Companies, Inc.

Write the *main idea sentence:* _____

_____

_____

Which *writing pattern* did the authors use to organize the main idea and the supporting details?

_____

Write some of the *clues* that caused you to choose this pattern:

_____

_____

SUMMARY OF PARAGRAPH PATTERN SIGNALS AND CLUE WORDS

1. List Pattern (Division/Classification)

and	*a, b, c . . .*
also	bullets (•)
another	asterisks (*)
moreover	words that announce lists
in addition	(such as *categories, kinds, types, ways, examples,*
first, second, third	*classes, groups, parts, elements, features,*
finally	*characteristics*, etc.)
1, 2, 3 . . .	

(Continued on next page)

(Continued from previous page)

2. Sequence Pattern (Time Order/Process)

first, second, third	*series*
now, then, next, finally	*stages*
dates	*when*
1, 2, 3 . . .	*before, during, after*
a, b, c . . .	*at last*
steps	*process, spectrum, continuum*
phases	*hierarchy*
progression	instructions and directions
words that refer to time	

3. Definition Pattern (Definition with Example)

words in bold print	*in other words*
words in italics	*that is* (also abbreviated as *i.e.,* for *id est,* Latin for "that is")
words in color	
is defined as	*by this we mean*
means	*or* (preceding a synonym)
refers to, is referred to as	punctuation that sets off a definition
the term	or synonym , : ( ) [ ] —
is called	examples that illustrate the definition or meaning of a term
in other words	
is, is known as	

4. Comparison-Contrast Pattern

<u>Comparisons:</u>	<u>Contrasts:</u>
similarly	*in contrast*
likewise	*however*
both	*on the other hand*
same	*whereas*
also	*while*
resembles	*although*
parallels	*nevertheless*
in the same manner	*instead (of)*
in the same way	*different*
words that compare (adjectives	*unlike*
that describe comparisons, such	*conversely*
as *safer, slower, lighter,*	*rather than*
more valuable, less toxic, etc.)	*as opposed to*
	some . . . others
	opposite words

5. Cause-Effect Pattern

Causes:	Effects:	Both the cause and the effect:
the reason(s)	*the result(s)*	• *(effect) is due to (cause)*
the cause(s)	*the effect(s)*	• *(effect) resulted from (cause)*
because	*the outcome*	• *(effect) was caused by (cause)*
is due to (cause)	*the final product*	• *(cause) led to (effect)*
was caused by (cause)	*therefore*	• *(cause) results in (effect)*
(cause) led to	*thus*	
resulted from (cause)	*consequently*	Some questions that indicate cause-effect:
since	*as a consequence*	• *What causes* (effect)*? (Answer will be the cause.)*
	hence	
	on that account	• *Why does* (effect) *occur? (Answer will be the cause.)*
	resulted in, results in (effect)	
	(effect) was caused by	• *What is the reason for* (effect)*? (Answer will be the cause.)*
	(effect) is due to	
	led to (effect)	• *How can* (effect) *be explained? (Answer will be the cause.)*
	(effect) resulted from	
		• *What does* (cause) *lead to? (Answer will be the effect.)*

6. Spatial Order Pattern (Place Order)

over, above	*north, south, east, west*
below, beneath	*right, left*
beside	*situated*
near, close to	*positioned*
adjacent to	*located*
opposite	*placed*
facing	*site*

Avoid Seeing Everything as a List

When you are first learning to identify authors' writing patterns, you may mistakenly view every paragraph as having a list pattern, since the same clue words can signal more than one pattern. For example, you may have noticed that some of the cause-effect clue words in the excerpt on physics (page 427) are the same clue words that could signal a sequence or a simple list. The passage about physics, however, uses the clue words *first, second, third,* and *fourth* to present a list of *reasons* (causes). Because these reasons demonstrate the cause-effect relationship that the author wants to emphasize, this paragraph should be viewed as having a cause-effect pattern, and not a list pattern.

Whenever you encounter what at first glance appears to be a list, ask yourself, "A list of *what?*" Your answer should help you realize if the author is using one of the other common patterns instead. For instance,

- If your answer is "a list of *events in a particular order,*" then the paragraph has a *sequence* pattern.
- If your answer is "a list of *similarities* or *differences,*" the paragraph has a *comparison-contrast* pattern.
- If your answer is "a list of *causes, reasons,* or *results,*" then the paragraph has a *cause-effect* pattern.

View a paragraph as having a list pattern only when you are certain that no other pattern can be used to describe the way the supporting details are organized.

Directions: To determine the author's writing pattern, read each paragraph carefully and then ask yourself, "Which pattern did the author use to organize the main idea and the supporting details?" Then select your answer choice and write the letter in the space provided.

1. This paragraph comes from a personal finance textbook:

> The lifework you select is a key to your financial well-being and personal satisfaction. For your lifework you may select a *job,* which is an employment position obtained mainly to earn money. Many people work in one or more jobs during their lives without considering their interests or opportunities for advancement. Alternatively, you may select a *career.* A career requires a commitment to a profession that requires continued training and offers a clearer path for occupational growth, potential salary increases, and on-the-job satisfaction.

> *Source:* Adapted from Jack R. Kapoor, Les R. Dlabay, and Robert J. Hughes, *Personal Finance,* 10e, p. 42. Copyright © 2012 by The McGraw-Hill Companies, Inc. Reprinted with permission of The McGraw-Hill Companies, Inc.

_____ Which writing pattern did the authors use to organize the main idea and the supporting details?

    a. list

    b. spatial

    c. comparison-contrast

    d. sequence

2. This paragraph comes from a business textbook:

> The basic courtesy rules of face-to-face communication also apply to e-mail exchanges. Practice good "netiquette" when you create e-mail messages. First, you should introduce yourself at the beginning of your first e-mail message. Next, you should let your recipients know how you got their names and e-mail addresses. Following these two important items, you can proceed with a clear but succinct message. Finally, include a concluding message or a request for some action from the recipient, and close the e-mail with your signature.

> *Source:* Adapted from William G. Nickels, James M. McHugh, and Susan M. McHugh, *Understanding Business,* 9e, p. 6. Copyright © 2010 by The McGraw-Hill Companies, Inc. Reprinted with permission of The McGraw-Hill Companies, Inc.

_____ Which writing pattern did the authors use to organize the main idea and the supporting details?

   a. list

   b. sequence

   c. comparison-contrast

   d. definition

3. This paragraph comes from a health textbook:

> Health professionals have several suggestions for reducing caffeine consumption. Consider keeping a log of where, when, how much, and with whom you consume coffee, tea, or caffeinated soda. To avoid withdrawal symptoms such as headaches, don't quit cold turkey. Instead, reduce your consumption slowly, by one cup or can per day. If you are a coffee drinker, gradually switch from regular to decaffeinated coffee by mixing them before brewing. Increase the decaffeinated proportion each day. Choose a premium decaf to reward yourself and to keep your coffee routine enjoyable. Another suggestion is to substitute decaffeinated tea for your regular caffeinated tea, and replace caffeinated soda with a caffeine-free drink. Try drinking from smaller cups or glasses instead of large mugs or tumblers. Avoid the huge "car cups" and the enormous beverage containers available from convenience stores and fast-food chains. Change your daily routine by taking a walk instead of your usual coffee break. Use more low-fat milk in your coffee or tea to reduce the amount of caffeinated beverage you consume while increasing your calcium consumption. Remember that noncaffeinated beverages are readily available; simply plan ahead.
>
> *Source:* Adapted from Wayne A. Payne, Dale B. Hahn, and Ellen B. Mauer, *Understanding Your Health,* 8e, p. 253. Copyright © 2005 by The McGraw-Hill Companies, Inc. Reprinted with permission of The McGraw-Hill Companies, Inc.

_____ Which writing pattern did the authors use to organize the main idea and the supporting details?

   a. definition

   b. sequence

   c. comparison-contrast

   d. list

4. This paragraph comes from a physical fitness and wellness textbook:

Physical fitness is associated with a person's ability to resist **hypokinetic diseases or conditions.** *Hypo-* means "under" or "too little," and *-kinetic* means "movement" or "activity." Thus, *hypokinetic* means "too little activity." A hypo-kinetic disease or condition is one associated with lack of physical activity or too little regular exercise. Examples include heart disease, low back pain, adult-onset diabetes, and obesity.

Source: Adapted from Charles B. Corbin, Gregory Welk, William R. Corbin, and Karen A. Welk, *Concepts of Physical Fitness: Active Lifestyles for Wellness,* 15e, pp. 6–7. Copyright © 2009 by The McGraw-Hill Companies, Inc. Reprinted with permission of The McGraw-Hill Companies, Inc.

_____   Which writing pattern did the authors use to organize the main idea and the supporting details?

    a. list

    b. definition

    c. spatial

    d. sequence

5. This paragraph comes from a wellness textbook:

How can people be sure they are marrying people with whom they are truly compatible? One way is by taking plenty of time to get to know the other person. Researchers have found that couples seem to go through three stages in this process. First, each person tries to measure his or her good and bad qualities against those of the other person. People tend to be drawn to others who seem to have about the same assets and liabilities they themselves possess. Second, people look for compatible beliefs, attitudes, and interests to support the initial attraction. It is not until the third stage that people reveal to each other how they handle responsibility, react to disappointment, and cope with a wide variety of situations. The key to compatibility is for the couple to be sure that they have arrived at this last stage before they think seriously about marriage.

Source: Marvin R. Levy, Mark Dignan, and Janet H. Shirreffs, *Targeting Wellness: The Core,* p. 123. Copyright © 1992 by The McGraw-Hill Companies, Inc. Reprinted with permission of The McGraw-Hill Companies, Inc.

_____   Which writing pattern did the authors use to organize the main idea and the supporting details?

    a. sequence

    b. definition

    c. comparison-contrast

    d. list

OTHER WRITING PATTERNS

Besides the six patterns you have just learned, there are other patterns textbook writers and nonfiction writers commonly use. And like the patterns you've already been introduced to, these patterns have clue words and phrases that signal each of them, and those clues often appear in the main idea sentence. You know that as you read any paragraph, you should ask yourself, "Which pattern did the author use to organize the main idea and supporting details?"

Addition Pattern

addition pattern

The author simply adds information or elaborates by presenting more details.

In the **addition pattern,** the author simply adds information or elaborates by presenting more details. The signal words and phrases are the same as those for a list: *also, moreover, in addition, besides, further, furthermore,* and *finally.*

Now read this sample passage about what to wear to a formal job interview. Its main idea is the last sentence: *You will increase your odds of being hired if you know how to dress for a formal job interview.*

Stop and Annotate

Underline or highlight the words *also* and *furthermore* that announce additional details are being given.

> If you are called back for a formal job interview, what should you wear? For both men and women, a simple, well-tailored, well-fitting, dark or neutral-colored suit is the right choice. Interviewers also notice applicants' shoes, so make sure yours are in good shape, clean, and polished. Their style should be basic, one that does not draw attention to itself. Furthermore, you should leave flashy accessories and jewelry at home. Men should opt for a classic, conservative tie; women, a simple scarf or necklace. You will increase your odds of being hired if you know how to dress for a formal job interview.

Generalization and Example Pattern

generalization and example pattern

An important concept or general principle, followed by one or more specific examples.

This pattern is similar to the definition with example pattern. Instead of a definition, however, the **generalization and example pattern** presents an important concept or general principle, followed by one or more specific examples. A *generalization* is a statement, idea, or principle that applies broadly to most people, things, or situations. As you would expect, examples in this pattern are introduced by the clue words and phrases *for example, for instance, to illustrate,* and *such as.*

The following passage illustrates the generalization and example pattern. The topic is cultural attitudes about making claims about one's accomplishments or abilities. It presents a generalization about intercultural communication (*Different cultures have different attitudes about the appropriateness of making claims about one's accomplishments or abilities*), followed by several specific examples of what certain cultures perceive as appropriate.

> Different cultures have different attitudes about the appropriateness of making claims about one's accomplishments or abilities. In a job interview, for instance, Americans and Kuwaitis consider it completely acceptable to make a point of their expertise. However, in Asian countries, such as China and Thailand, politeness dictates that job applicants be self-deprecating about their abilities. A highly renowned Asian scientist might say about his life's work, "I have a small amount of experience in that area."
>
> *Source:* Based on L. Beamer and I. Varner, *Intercultural Communication in the Global Workplace,* 4e, pp. 33–34. Copyright © 2008 by The McGraw-Hill Companies, Inc. Reprinted with permission of The McGraw-Hill Companies, Inc.

Stop and Annotate

Go back to the sample passage above. Underline or highlight the words *for instance* that introduce the examples.

In this paragraph, the author gives a generalization in the first sentence, the main idea. It is followed by specific examples of how appropriate Americans, Kuwaitis, and Asians think it is to put forth their accomplishments and abilities in a job interview. The words *for instance* announce the examples.

Statement and Clarification Pattern

statement and clarification pattern

A general statement, followed by explanatory information that makes the statement clearer or easier to understand.

This pattern is similar to the generalization and example pattern. Instead of a generalization, however, the **statement and clarification pattern** presents a general statement (the main idea), followed by explanatory information that makes the statement clearer or easier to understand. Watch for clue words and phrases such as *in other words, that is, to be more precise, clearly, obviously, as a matter of fact,* and *of course*.

The following passage illustrates the statement and clarification pattern. The topic is diabetes. It presents a general statement, the main idea, *According to Science Daily (www.sciencedaily.com,12/05/08), "A third of Americans with diabetes do not know that they have it, . . . millions more have prediabetic conditions and are unaware that they are at risk."* The author then provides further explanation about the information in that statement.

Stop and Annotate

Underline or highlight *To be more precise, In other words,* and *of course* that appear in the clarifying statement.

> It is particularly important that people who have certain characteristics be tested for diabetes, a costly medical condition that can damage organs throughout the body long before symptoms appear. To be more precise, people who are overweight, have a family history of the disease, or have high blood pressure should seek testing. A third of Americans with diabetes do not know that they have it (www.sciencedaily.com, 12/05/08). In other words, there are 6.2 million undiagnosed diabetic Americans. Millions more have prediabetic conditions and are unaware that they are at risk. And, of course, with obesity on the rise, diabetes is occurring in children and adults at much younger ages than in the past.

To clarify the first sentence further, the author explains exactly how many Americans are unaware they have diabetes and the risk they face (it is occurring earlier in people and can do great damage long before symptoms appear). The author uses *To be more precise* to clarify what the "characteristics" are; *In other words,* to explain exactly how many million Americans; and *of course* in explaining the link between obesity and the earlier onset of diabetes.

Summary/Conclusion Pattern

summary/conclusion pattern

The author summarizes a preceding section or presents an important conclusion.

At the end of a section, an author may include a paragraph with the **summary/ conclusion pattern** that summarizes a preceding section or presents an important conclusion. The summary statement or conclusion is the main idea. Watch for clue words and phrases such as *in summary, to sum up, in brief, in short, the point is, thus, therefore,* and *consequently.*

The following passage is organized using the summary/conclusion pattern. The topic is *technology* or, more specifically, *the dark side of technology* (its negative aspects). The author presents a general conclusion, the main idea that sums up the main ideas made in paragraphs that preceded this one.

> As we have seen, technology can be used to commit crimes, such as financial fraud and the dissemination of pornography. It can be used to violate people's privacy, spread false information and rumors, and ruin people's reputations and lives. It can be a tool for disrupting communications, and for manipulating data and people. It can be used by terrorists toward destructive ends. The point is, technology, for all of the advantages it offers, also has a dark side.

Stop and Annotate

Go back to the sample passage. Underline or highlight *The point is* that announces the author's summary/conclusion statement (main idea).

The opening words (*As we have seen*) indicate that the author is recapping points made in earlier paragraphs. The phrase *The point is* announces that this is the author's important conclusion. It is also the main idea of the paragraph.

SUMMARY OF OTHER WRITING PATTERN CLUE WORDS

1. Addition Pattern

also	moreover
in addition	besides
further	furthermore
finally	

2. Generalization and Example Pattern

for example	to illustrate
for instance	such as

3. Statement and Clarification Pattern

in other words	that is
to be more precise	clearly
obviously	as a matter of fact
of course	evidently

4. Summary/Conclusion Pattern

in summary	in short
to sum up	the point is
in brief	therefore
thus	consequently

Mixed Pattern

Each textbook excerpt presented so far in this chapter has illustrated one particular writing pattern, but authors frequently use two or more of the patterns in the *same* paragraph or a longer passage. A combination of two or more writing patterns in the same paragraph or passage is called a **mixed pattern.**

Below is an example of a *mixed pattern in a single paragraph.* This excerpt, from a health and fitness textbook, uses both the definition pattern and the cause-effect pattern. It presents a definition of passive smoking, as well as the effects of passive smoking.

Passive Smoking and the Rights of Nonsmokers

Reports from the U.S. surgeon general's office suggest that tobacco smoke in enclosed indoor areas is an important air pollution problem. This has led to the controversy about **passive smoking**—the breathing in of air polluted by the second hand tobacco smoke of others. Carbon monoxide levels of sidestream smoke (smoke from the burning end of a cigarette) reach a dangerously high level. True, the smoke can be greatly diluted in freely circulating air, but the 1 to 5 percent carbon monoxide levels attained in smoke-filled rooms can cause health problems in people with chronic bronchitis, other lung disease, or cardiovascular disease. As a result, nicotine also builds up in the blood of nonsmokers exposed to cigarette smoke hour after hour. It has been estimated that passive smoking can give nonsmokers the equivalent in carbon monoxide and nicotine of one to ten cigarettes per day.

Source: Adapted from Marvin Levy, Mark Dignan, and Janet Shirreffs, *Targeting Wellness: The Core,* pp. 262–63. Copyright © 1992 by The McGraw-Hill Companies, Inc. Reprinted with permission of The McGraw-Hill Companies, Inc.

Stop and Annotate

Go back to the textbook excerpt above. Underline or highlight the clues that signal the definition pattern and the cause-effect pattern.

In this paragraph, the bold print and the dash (**passive smoking**—) are clues that the authors are defining a term. The clue words that signal cause-effect are *cause* and *As a result.* Therefore, this paragraph can be described as a mixed pattern because it includes both a definition *and* a cause-effect relationship.

Here is an excerpt from an American government textbook that is an example of a *mixed pattern in a longer passage.* It consists of four paragraphs in which the author uses three patterns. The overall topic of the passage is *regionalism.* In the first paragraph, the author presents a *definition* of regionalism (the tendency of people in a particular geographic area to defend their interests against those of people in other geographic areas). In the second paragraph, the author uses the *comparison-contrast* pattern to emphasize differences between two regions of the United States, the "Sunbelt" and the "Frostbelt." In the third paragraph, the author uses the *cause-effect* pattern to explain the conflict over federal aid that resulted from a shift of economic influence to the Sunbelt. In the fourth paragraph, the author again uses a *cause-effect* pattern to explain a shift of political influence (an increased number of seats in Congress) from the northeastern and midwestern (Frostbelt) to the southern and western states (Sunbelt). (Although the passage includes several references to time—*past two decades, in the first half of the 1980s,* etc.—the author is not emphasizing a sequence relationship.)

Regionalism

An important characteristic of intergovernmental politics is **regionalism,** the tendency of people in a particular geographic area to defend their interests against those of people in other geographic areas. One central regional issue is the competition between Sunbelt and Frostbelt for federal moneys.

The so-called **Sunbelt** region (the states of the South and Southwest) experienced significant increases in population and economic development during the 1970s and 1980s. During that same time, the Northeastern and Midwestern states of the so-called **Frostbelt** saw both their population and their economic growth lag behind that of the nation at large. In the first half of the 1980s, the North Central region actually lost more jobs than it gained. Southwestern oil states such as Texas and Oklahoma were also hit hard in the middle 1980s by the collapse of the oil boom. Nevertheless, the Sunbelt grew in economic influence relative to the rest of the nation.

This shift of economic influence from the Frostbelt to the Sunbelt has led to a sharp conflict between these regions in seeking greater amounts of federal aid. Frostbelt leaders have charged that their region pays more income taxes into the federal treasury than comes back in the form of grants-in-aid, and they subsequently have pressured Congress to rewrite funding formulas so that they will be more favorable to the Frostbelt. Faced with this challenge, Sunbelt leaders also began to lobby Washington for their version of how federal aid ought to be distributed.

The rise of the South and the West is seen not only in economic influence but in political influence as well. The reapportionment of congressional seats after the 1990 census resulted in a dramatic shift of congressional seats from the Northeast and Midwest to fast-growing Southern and Western states such as Florida and California.

Source: Adapted from John J. Harrigan, *Politics and the American Future,* 3e, New York: McGraw-Hill, pp. 72–73. Copyright © 1992 by John J. Harrigan. Reprinted by permission of the author.

Stop and Annotate

Underline or highlight the clues that signal the three patterns used in this passage.

Here is another excerpt, from a business textbook, that illustrates the use of a mixed pattern in a longer passage. In this excerpt, which discusses *crisis management,* the authors have used four patterns: *definition, cause-effect, comparison-contrast,* and *sequence.* As you read this excerpt, look for clue words that indicate which pattern is being used in each paragraph. Write the patterns in the margin beside each paragraph.

Crisis Management

The most important goal of any business is to survive. But any number of problems may arise, some threatening the very existence of the company. An ugly fight for control of a company, a product failure, breakdowns in an organization's routine operations (as a result of fire, for example)—any surprising event may develop into a serious and crippling crisis. **Crisis management,** the handling of such unusual and serious problems, goes a long way toward determining the company's future. For example, Johnson & Johnson is widely thought to have done a good job of coping with the two Tylenol poisoning scares, moving quickly to remove capsules from the shelves and to publicize the problem. As a result, the effects of the first scare had been almost completely overcome by the time the second hit.

In contrast, H.J. Heinz handled a crisis so badly that the future of its Canadian subsidiary of StarKist Foods was in doubt. StarKist was accused of shipping a million cans of "rancid and decomposing" tuna, which were first rejected by Canadian inspectors but later passed by a high government official. Under the prodding of Canadian news media, the prime minister finally had the tainted tuna seized. All along, Heinz and StarKist maintained a stony silence over "Tunagate," and their mishandling of the crisis cost plenty: The company that once controlled half of the Canadian tuna market watched its revenues fall 90 percent.

Companies that experience a crisis for which they are ill prepared seem to make a series of mistakes. First, warnings about possible problems are ignored at one or several management levels. Then the crisis hits. Under pressure, the company does the worst thing it could do: It denies the severity of the problem or it denies its own role in the problem. Finally, when the company is forced to face reality, it takes hasty, poorly conceived action.

A better way does exist. Management experts caution that the first 24 hours of a crisis are critical. The first move is to explain the problem—both to the public and to the company's employees. Immediately after, the offending product is removed from store shelves. Finally, the offending action is stopped, or the source of the problem (whatever it is) is brought under control to the extent possible.

Source: From *Business Today* by David Rachman, Michael Mescon, Courtland Bovée, and John Thill, pp. 169–70. Copyright © 1993. Reprinted by permission of Courtland Bovée and John Thill.

Stop and Annotate

Underline or highlight the clues that signal the four patterns used in this mixed pattern.

CHECKPOINT
Other Writing Patterns

Directions: To determine the author's writing pattern, read each paragraph carefully and then ask yourself, "What pattern did the author use to organize the main idea and the supporting details?" Then select your answer choice and write it in the space provided.

1. This paragraph comes from a geography text:

> The 20th century was the warmest century of the past 600 years. The world's average surface temperature rose about 0.6°C (a bit over 1°F) in the 20th century, and the 1990s were the hottest decade of the century. As a matter of fact, winter temperatures in the Arctic have risen about 4°C (7°F) since the 1950s.
>
> *Source:* Adapted from Arthur Getis, Judith Getis, and Jerome Fellmann, *Introduction to Geography,* 13e, p. 114. Copyright © 2011 by The McGraw-Hill Companies, Inc. Reprinted with permission of The McGraw-Hill Companies, Inc.

_____   Which pattern did the authors use to organize the main idea and the supporting details?

  a. addition
  b. generalization and example
  c. summary/conclusion
  d. statement and clarification

2. This paragraph comes from a learning skills text:

> As you now know, creating concept maps forces you to rethink material in your notes in a new style—particularly important if you used traditional outlining while taking notes. Creating them helps you tie together the material for a given class session. You can use them to build a master concept map later, when you're studying the material for a final exam. In short, creating concept maps can help you in a variety of ways.
>
> *Source:* Adapted from Robert Feldman, *P.O.W.E.R. Learning,* 5e, p. 108. Copyright © 2011 by The McGraw-Hill Companies, Inc. Reprinted with permission of The McGraw-Hill Companies, Inc.

_____   Which writing pattern did the author use to organize the main idea and the supporting details?

  a. addition
  b. generalization and example
  c. statement and clarification
  d. summary/conclusion

3. This paragraph comes from a financial planning text:

> Financial advisers suggest that you have an emergency fund. That is, you should have money you can obtain quickly in case of immediate need. The amount of money to be put away in an emergency fund varies from person to person. However, most financial planners agree that an amount equal to three to nine months' living expenses is reasonable.

Source: Adapted from Jack Kapoor, Les Dlabay, and Robert Hughes, *Personal Finance,* 10e, p. 426. Copyright © 2012 by The McGraw-Hill Companies, Inc. Reprinted with permission of The McGraw-Hill Companies, Inc.

_____   Which writing pattern did the authors use to organize the main idea and the supporting details?

   a.   addition
   b.   generalization and example
   c.   statement and clarification
   d.   summary/conclusion

4. This paragraph comes from an art appreciation text:

> Did you know that orange results from mixing red and yellow? Also, green is created by mixing yellow and blue. Moreover, violet occurs when red and blue are mixed.

Source: Adapted from Otto Ocvirk, Robert Stinson, Philip Wigg, Robert Bone, and David Clayton, *Art Fundamentals,* 9e, p. 152. Copyright © 2007 by The McGraw-Hill Companies, Inc. Reprinted with permission of The McGraw-Hill Companies, Inc.

_____   Which writing pattern did the authors use to organize the main idea and the supporting details?

   a.   addition
   b.   generalization and example
   c.   statement and clarification
   d.   summary/conclusion

5. This paragraph comes from a psychology text:

Amphetamines such as Dexedrine and Benzedrine, popularly known as speed, are strong stimulants. In small quantities, amphetamines—which stimulate the central nervous system—bring about a sense of energy and alertness, talkativeness, heightened confidence, and a mood "high." They increase concentration and reduce fatigue. Amphetamines also cause a loss of appetite, increased anxiety, and irritability. When taken over long periods of time, amphetamines can cause feelings of being persecuted by others, as well as a general sense of suspiciousness. People taking amphetamines may lose interest in sex. If taken in too large a quantity, amphetamines overstimulate the central nervous system to such an extent that convulsions and death can occur.

Source: Robert Feldman, *Essentials of Understanding Psychology,* 9e, pp. 152–53. Copyright © 2011 by The McGraw-Hill Companies, Inc. Reprinted with permission of The McGraw-Hill Companies, Inc.

_____   Which writing pattern did the author use to organize the main idea and the supporting details?

    a.   addition

    b.   statement and clarification

    c.   summary/conclusion

    d.   mixed

RELATIONSHIPS WITHIN AND BETWEEN SENTENCES

transition words

Words and phrases that show relationships among ideas in sentences, paragraphs, and longer selections.

Authors also use many of the same clue words to indicate the relationship between information in a single sentence, or to show the connection between information in two consecutive sentences. Because you use these same transition words every day of your life, you may not be consciously aware of them. Although there seem to be many types of relationships described in this section, you will be pleased to discover that you are already familiar with them and that they are simply common sense. Words and phrases that show relationships among ideas are called **transition words.**

On a standardized reading test or state-mandated basic skills test, you may be asked about the relationship of ideas in two parts of the *same* sentence or between two *different* sentences. Such questions are usually worded, "What is the relationship between . . ." or "Identify the relationship between . . ." You will be asked to identify the way in which two ideas relate to each other, or in other words, how the ideas are connected to each other. Watch for clue words and transition words that can help you determine the connection. If there are two sentences, the transition word often appears at the beginning of the second sentence, such as the word *therefore* in *It takes time to review for a test. Therefore, you should start early.* Sometimes, though, you may have to supply the transition word. For example, in the sentence *It takes time to review for a test; start early,* you would mentally supply the word *so: It takes time to review for a test, so start early.*

Now read about various types of relationships and the transition words authors use to signal them. Two examples are given for each type. The first example illustrates the relationship in the context of a *single* sentence; the second illustrates the relationship in the context of *two or more* sentences. You have already met sequence, comparison-contrast, cause-effect, and spatial order as paragraph patterns. In this section, you will see them illustrated in single-sentence relationships as well.

1. Clarification Pattern

Authors use certain words to indicate that they are trying to make information in a sentence clearer or easier to understand. These include *in other words, clearly, it is obvious, that is, as a matter of fact, evidently,* and *of course.* Often a general or potentially confusing statement is followed by a clarification.

Examples:

- The most common form of marriage is monogamy, *that is,* a marriage consisting of one husband and one wife.
- A form of marriage that has been widely practiced throughout the world is polygamy. *In other words,* marriage that consists of one husband and several wives is widespread throughout the world.

2. Example Pattern

Authors use examples, specific incidences, or illustrations to help explain other, more general information in a sentence or paragraph. For this reason, the relationship is also referred to as "generalization and example." (The second example, below, illustrates this.) To introduce examples, authors use *for example, to illustrate, such as, are examples of,* and *for instance.*

Examples:

- Dogs, cats, lions, and bears are *examples* of carnivores, flesh-eating animals.
- Some animals are herbivores. Cows, goats, giraffes, and elephants, *for instance,* belong to this category of plant-eating animals.

3. Addition Pattern

To signal that information is being added, authors use the same clue words that they do for lists, that is, *and, also, further, in addition, equally, besides, next, moreover, furthermore,* and *finally.* This pattern or relationship is also referred to as *elaboration.*

Examples:

- Computer science is a popular major; business is *also* popular, *and* so is psychology.
- Driving a hybrid car is one way to reduce fuel costs. *Another* is to carpool or use public transportation. *Finally,* there are motorcycles, bicycling, *and* even walking.

4. Sequence Pattern

Authors sequence information in a specific order because the order is important. Events may be given in the order in which they occurred or in order of importance. Clue words are those that refer to time, such as *during the last century, next year, in the 1990s, at the start of the Middle Ages,* and specific dates, words such as *first, second, then, next, last, before, after, at that time, during, formerly, now, soon, while, presently, when, later, followed by;* and words such as *sequence, process, steps, procedure, ranking, series, and progression.* Authors may also use numbers, letters, or bullets when sequencing or ranking items. Narratives follow a sequence pattern since they tell a story.

Examples:

- In higher education, an associate's degree is *followed by* a bachelor's degree, *then* a master's degree, and *finally,* a doctorate.
- The Richter scale is used to *rank* the effects of earthquakes that occur near the earth's surface. Earthquakes with a *magnitude of 0, 1, or 2* are not felt at all; at *level 3,* some people feel it. At *levels 4 and 5,* windows rattle and break. At *magnitudes of 6 through 8,* there is increasingly severe damage to structures. *Finally,* at *9,* the *highest magnitude,* there is total destruction.

A special type of sequence is *climactic order.* When writers want to end a paragraph with the high point, the climax, they deliberately arrange the information from least to most important (or to a *conclusion*). (Logical conclusions are discussed, along with inductive and deductive reasoning, in Chapter 9.) Literary writers often use the climactic pattern because it is a way to build suspense. Nonfiction writers use it to emphasize their most important point, as well as to provide readers with information needed to understand that point or the reasoning to be convinced of it. There are no clue words for this pattern, but watch for increasing importance or intensity.

Examples:

- The proposed city budget will lead our community into financial difficulty, increasing debt, total bankruptcy!
- The proposed city budget is based on inaccurate numbers. It is based on unrealistic estimates of future costs. It can only lead to increasing, unsustainable debt. In short, it will plunge the city into bankruptcy!

5. Comparison Pattern

Comparisons show similarities or likenesses. Clue words are *as, like, similarly, likewise, same, similar,* and *in the same manner.* Also watch for comparative forms of words, such as *lesser, greater, highest,* and so on.

Examples:

- Reading, *like* writing, is a form of the thinking process.
- Paintings reflect an artist's culture and values. *Similarly,* musical compositions reflect a composer's culture and values.

6. Contrast Pattern

Contrasts focus on differences or opposites. Clue words include pairs of words that have opposite meanings (such as *rich* and *poor*), and words such as *in contrast, but, although, however, yet, nevertheless, on the contrary, on the one hand,* and *on the other hand.*

Examples:

- *Although* only a small percentage of pregnant women choose home birth, the number is increasing.
- It was assumed that with the increased use of computers, the amount of paper used in business would decrease. *However,* that has not proved to be the case.

7. Cause-Effect Pattern

Authors use *because, due to, since,* and *causes* to indicate reasons, and *thus, therefore, as a result, consequently, result, outcome, lead to, resulted in,* and *hence* to indicate results.

Examples:

- *Because* of Hurricane Katrina, millions of people were displaced from their homes.
- The number of years of school a person completes is correlated with the amount of money that person will make during a lifetime. *Therefore,* it is an advantage to complete as many years of school as possible.

8. Problem-Solution Pattern

The problem-solution pattern is actually just a variation of the cause-effect pattern that authors use when they present a problem and its solutions. They typically include the factors that led to the problem (causes) and explain the significance of the problem so that readers understand why the problem is important. Solutions or recommendations for solving the problem may be tied to each of the specific causes. (The *solution* itself may be a sequence pattern, in which the author spells out a certain procedure or steps that must be followed to remedy a situation.) Watch for words such as *problem* (the *cause* of the difficulty), the *significance* (the *effects* of the problem; why it matters), and *solutions*.

Examples:

- To address the *problem* of homelessness, the city must join with local organizations and churches to develop comprehensive, cost-effective *solutions*.
- A major *problem* in our country is drivers running red lights. The *consequences* include increased insurance premiums for all of us, but more importantly injury and death. Besides maiming or killing themselves, these reckless drivers hurt or kill thousands of innocent victims each year. What can be done? Possible *solutions* include installing traffic cameras at all high-risk intersections, imposing more stringent fines for violators, and suspending driving privileges of repeat offenders.

9. Spatial Order Pattern

Authors use *above, beyond, within, near, facing, next to, north, south, to the right, site, location,* and so forth to describe the placement or location of one or more things. (A variation of this pattern is the *description pattern*. For example, in a film history textbook, the author might describe Judy Garland's costume as Dorothy in *The Wizard of Oz* or certain lighting that was used in a famous movie scene.)

Examples:

- The floor plan of many Christian churches *forms the shape of* a cross: the large, open area called the nave intersects with the transept, a *lengthwise* section *perpendicular to* it.
- The *site of* central Chicago is on a lake plain. More important, it is *situated* astride the Great Lakes–Mississippi waterways, and *near* the *western margin* of the manufacturing belt, the *northern boundary* of the Corn Belt, and the *southeastern reaches* of a major dairy region.

10. Summary/Conclusion Pattern

Some paragraphs simply review the important points presented earlier. The author condenses or consolidates them in a sentence or paragraph at the end of a longer paragraph or selection. Sometimes the author draws an overall conclusion based on those major points, as well. To signal a summary or conclusion, authors use *in summary, in conclusion, in brief, thus, therefore, to summarize, to sum up, in short,* and *the point is.*

Examples:

- The *point is,* movement is a characteristic of all living things.

- Water helps digestion and circulation. It helps regulate body temperature and flushes toxins from the body. It also cushions the internal organs. *In short,* water serves a variety of important functions in the body.

11. Concession Pattern

In the concession relationship, one sentence admits or acknowledges something that goes against the writer's position, but that the writer considers less important than the point in the other sentence. To signal concession, authors use *granted, although, even though, at least, nevertheless, despite [the fact that], while it may be true, admittedly, at any rate, be that as it may, regardless, albeit,* and *notwithstanding.*

Examples:

- Losing weight is not easy. *Be that as it may,* maintaining the proper weight is essential for optimum health.
- The proposed salary cuts will help the company through the recession. *Nevertheless,* the reductions are not popular with employees.

A WORD ABOUT STANDARDIZED READING TESTS: AUTHORS' WRITING PATTERNS

Many college students are required to take standardized reading tests as part of an overall assessment program, in a reading course, or as part of a state-mandated basic skills test. A standardized reading test typically consists of a series of passages followed by multiple-choice reading skill application questions, to be completed within a specified time limit.

Questions about the organization of material in a passage may be worded several ways. Sometimes you are asked to identify the *type* of pattern; sometimes you are asked about specific *information* that has been listed, presented in a sequence, defined, compared or contrasted, or discussed in terms of causes and effects.

Here are some examples of typical wording of questions about authors' writing patterns:

Which of the following organizational patterns does the author use to present information in the passage?

In this passage the author presents . . . (*a comparison, a sequence of events,* etc.)

How is the information in the selection organized?

In this passage, what is compared with . . . ?

According to this passage, what are effects of . . . ?

This passage explains (*two, three, four*) similarities between . . .

Which of the following is an effect of . . . ?

Paragraph 3 contrasts childhood aggression with . . .

The second step in the process of carbon filtration is . . .

To answer questions about organization, watch for clue words that signal each pattern. When you find clue words in a passage, *circle them* so that you can clearly see relationships among the ideas presented. You will also find it helpful to *number items* in lists and sequences, and label causes and effects and similarities and differences so that you do not overlook any of them. Remember, too, that words in a stated main idea sentence often suggest the pattern (for example, words such as *ways, factors, causes, reasons, series, stages, differences, similarities,* etc.).

Directions: To determine the relationship between and within sentences, read each paragraph carefully and then ask yourself, "What is the relationship between the sentences?" or "What is the relationship between the parts of the sentence?" Then select your answer choice and write it in the space provided.

This paragraph is from a psychology textbook:

> [1]Stress is a normal part of life—and not necessarily a completely bad part. [2]For example, without stress, we might not be sufficiently motivated to complete the activities we need to accomplish. [3]However, it is also clear that too much stress can take a toll on physical and psychological health.
>
> *Source:* Robert Feldman, *Essentials of Understanding Psychology,* 9e, p. 420. Copyright © 2011 by The McGraw-Hill Companies, Inc. Reprinted with permission of The McGraw-Hill Companies, Inc.

1. What is the relationship between sentence 1 and sentence 2? In other words, how is sentence 2 related to sentence 1?

  a. contrast

  b. conclusion

  c. addition

  d. example

2. What is the relationship between sentence 2 and sentence 3? In other words, how is sentence 3 related to sentence 2?

  a. contrast

  b. conclusion

  c. addition

  d. example

This paragraph is from the same psychology textbook:

> [1]Lack of communication between medical care providers and patients can be a major obstacle to good medical care. [2]Such communication failures occur for several reasons. [3]One is that physicians make assumptions about what patients prefer, or they push a particular treatment that they prefer without consulting patients. [4]Furthermore, the relatively high prestige of physicians may intimidate patients. [5]Patients may also be reluctant to volunteer information that might cast them in a bad light, and physicians may have difficulties encouraging their patients to provide information. [6]In many cases, physicians dominate an interview with questions of a technical nature, whereas patients attempt to communicate a personal sense of their illness and the impact it is having on their lives.
>
> *Source:* Robert Feldman, *Essentials of Understanding Psychology,* 9e, p. 433. Copyright © 2011 by The McGraw-Hill Companies, Inc. Reprinted with permission of The McGraw-Hill Companies, Inc.

_____ **3.** What is the relationship between sentence 3 and sentence 4?

    a. contrast

    b. cause-effect

    c. summary/conclusion

    d. addition

_____ **4.** What is the relationship of the ideas within sentence 6?

    a. contrast

    b. conclusion

    c. addition

    d. example

This paragraph is from a U.S. government textbook:

> [1]At the birth of American radio broadcasting in the early 1920s, local stations practiced a kind of "narrowcasting" that was often oriented toward ethnic and religious minorities. [2]It was frequently in foreign languages. [3]Originally, the people who listened to radio had to build their own sets from simple kits and listen with headphones.
>
> *Source:* Joseph Losco and Ralph Baker, *Am Gov,* p. 216. Copyright © 2009 by The McGraw-Hill Companies, Inc. Reprinted with permission of The McGraw-Hill Companies, Inc.

_____ **5.** What is the relationship between sentence 2 and sentence 3?

    a. contrast

    b. conclusion

    c. addition

    d. example

This is another paragraph from the psychology textbook:

> Consider, ____1____, students with low self-esteem who are studying for a test. Because of their low self-esteem, they expect to do poorly on the test. In turn, this raises their anxiety level, making it increasingly difficult to study and perhaps even leading them not to work as hard. ____2____ these attitudes, the ultimate outcome is that they do, in fact, perform badly on the test. Ultimately, the failure reinforces their low self-esteem, and the cycle is perpetuated. ____3____, low self-esteem can lead to a cycle of failure that is self-destructive.
>
> *Source:* Robert Feldman, *Essentials of Understanding Psychology,* 9e, p. 393. Copyright © 2011 by The McGraw-Hill Companies, Inc. Reprinted with permission of The McGraw-Hill Companies, Inc.

6. The missing word or words in space 1 is:
  a. in short
  b. as a result of
  c. nevertheless
  d. for example

7. The missing word or words in space 2 is:
  a. In short
  b. Because of
  c. Nevertheless
  d. For example

8. The missing word or words in space 3 is:
  a. In short
  b. As a result of
  c. Nevertheless
  d. For example

This sample passage is about eyewitnesses to crimes:

> Eyewitnesses can provide useful information despite the fact that their memories can be influenced by the specific wording of questions posed to them by police officers or attorneys.

9. The relationship between the first part of the sentence and the second part is:
  a. contrast
  b. concession
  c. spatial
  d. example

This sample passage is about the Old West:

> During the mid-nineteenth century, the major route west was the 2,000-mile Oregon Trail, which stretched from Independence, Missouri, across the Great Plains and through the South Pass of the Rocky Mountains.

10. What is the relationship of the ideas within this sentence?
  a. comparison
  b. cause-effect
  c. spatial
  d. example

DEVELOPING CHAPTER REVIEW CARDS

Complete the seven review cards for Chapter 7, following the directions on each card. When you have completed them, you will have summarized (1) names and definitions of several writing patterns, (2) advantages of recognizing authors' patterns as you read, and (3) clues that signal writing patterns. Print or write legibly.

Authors' Writing Patterns
Name and describe six writing patterns commonly used by authors.
1. Pattern:
Description:
2. Pattern:
Description:
3. Pattern:
Description:
4. Pattern:
Description:
5. Pattern:
Description:
6. Pattern:
Description:
Card 1 Chapter 7: Recognizing Authors' Writing Patterns

Advantages of Identifying Writing Patterns

What are four advantages of identifying writing patterns as you read?

1.

2.

3.

4.

To recognize an author's writing pattern, what question should you ask yourself?

Card 2   Chapter 7: Recognizing Authors' Writing Patterns

Clues to Writing Patterns: Signal Words

List several clues or signal words that identify each of the six writing patterns described in this chapter.

1.   **List:**

2.   **Sequence:**

3.   **Definition:**

4.   **Comparison-contrast:**

5.   **Cause-effect:**

6.   **Spatial Order:**

Card 3   Chapter 7: Recognizing Authors' Writing Patterns

Other Paragraph Patterns

Tell the purpose of each pattern, and then list some transition words that signal it.

1. **Addition pattern:**

2. **Generalization and example pattern:**

3. **Statement and clarification pattern:**

4. **Summary/conclusion pattern:**

Card 4   Chapter 7: Recognizing Authors' Writing Patterns

Transition Words That Signal the Relationship of Ideas within Sentences and between Sentences

1. What is the definition of *transition* words?

2. What is the **clarification pattern** and what are some transition words that signal it?

3. What is the **example pattern** and what are some transition words that signal it?

4. What is the **addition pattern** and what are some transition words that signal it?

5. What is the **sequence pattern** and what are some transition words that signal it?

Card 5   Chapter 7: Recognizing Authors' Writing Patterns

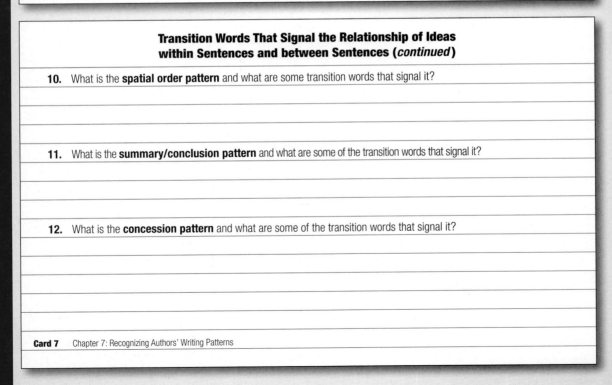

Transition Words That Signal the Relationship of Ideas within Sentences and between Sentences (*continued*)

6. What is the **comparison pattern** and what are some transition words that signal it?

7. What is the **contrast pattern** and what are some transition words that signal it?

8. What is the **cause-effect pattern** and what are some transition words that signal it?

9. What is the **problem-solution pattern** and what are some transition words that signal it?

Card 6 Chapter 7: Recognizing Authors' Writing Patterns

Transition Words That Signal the Relationship of Ideas within Sentences and between Sentences (*continued*)

10. What is the **spatial order pattern** and what are some transition words that signal it?

11. What is the **summary/conclusion pattern** and what are some of the transition words that signal it?

12. What is the **concession pattern** and what are some of the transition words that signal it?

Card 7 Chapter 7: Recognizing Authors' Writing Patterns

TEST YOUR UNDERSTANDING
Recognizing Authors' Writing Patterns, Part 1

Directions: Read these paragraphs carefully and answer the questions that follow them. Write your answers in the spaces provided.

This paragraph comes from a psychology textbook:

> Few people would feel embarrassed by a sprained ankle or broken arm. In contrast, sexual difficulties are often a source of concern and self-consciousness. And such difficulties are surprisingly common, with 43 percent of women and 31 percent of men experiencing problems associated with sexual performance.
>
> *Source:* Adapted from Robert Feldman, *Understanding Psychology,* 8e, p. 391. Copyright © 2008 by The McGraw-Hill Companies, Inc. Reprinted with permission of The McGraw-Hill Companies, Inc.

_____ **1.** Which writing pattern is used to organize the supporting details?
a. list
b. sequence
c. definition
d. comparison-contrast

This paragraph comes from a U.S. government textbook:

> Some refer to the movement between government service and interest group employment as a **revolving door.** The door swings in both directions. Not only do retiring lawmakers and staffers join firms that lobbied them when they were in government, but government agencies often recruit specialists from fields that they regulate. Critics believe this practice raises ethical concerns, especially when a person leaves a federal government position to join an interest group he or she once helped regulate. Representative Billy Tauzin (R-LA), for example, left the House of Representatives in 2004 to become the president of the Pharmaceutical Research and Manufacturers Association shortly after writing the Medicare Drug Benefit law that is widely seen as protecting the interests of drug companies he now represents.
>
> *Source:* Abridged from Joseph Losco and Ralph Baker, *Am Gov,* pp. 185–86. Copyright © 2011 by The McGraw-Hill Companies, Inc. Reprinted with permission of The McGraw-Hill Companies, Inc.

_____ **2.** Which writing pattern is used to organize the supporting details?
a. list
b. sequence
c. definition with example
d. classification

This paragraph comes from a criminology textbook:

> To gather evidence from a large crime scene, searchers typically use the zone/quadrant search pattern in which the area is divided into four large quadrants. If

the area to be searched is particularly large, each of the quadrants can be subdi-vided into four smaller quadrants.

Source: Adapted from Charles Swanson, Neil Chamelin, Leonard Territo, and Robert Taylor, *Criminal Investigation,* 9e, p. 78. Copyright © 2008 by The McGraw-Hill Companies, Inc. Reprinted with permission of The McGraw-Hill Companies, Inc.

3. Which writing pattern is used to organize the supporting details?
   a. definition with example
   b. spatial
   c. comparison-contrast
   d. cause-effect

This paragraph comes from an information technology textbook:

   When setting up a new microcomputer system, install your peripherals first—first your printer, then your backup drive, then your scanner, and so on. Test each one separately by restarting the computer. Then install the next peripheral. After this, install your applications software, again testing each program separately.

Source: Adapted from Brian Williams and Stacey Sawyer, *Using Information Technology,* 7e, p. 125. Copyright © 2007 by The McGraw-Hill Companies, Inc. Reprinted with permission of The McGraw-Hill Companies, Inc.

4. Which writing pattern is used to organize the supporting details?
   a. list
   b. sequence
   c. definition
   d. cause-effect

The remaining six paragraphs come from a psychology textbook:

   Methamphetamine is a white, crystalline drug that U.S. police now say is the most dangerous street drug. "Meth" is highly addictive and relatively cheap, and it produces a strong, lingering high. It has made addicts of people across the social spectrum, ranging from soccer moms to urban professionals to poverty-stricken inner-city residents. After becoming addicted, users take it more and more frequently and in increasing doses. Long-term use of the drug can lead to brain damage.

Source: Robert Feldman, *Essentials of Understanding Psychology,* 9e, p. 153. Copyright © 2011 by The McGraw-Hill Companies, Inc. Reprinted with permission of The McGraw-Hill Companies, Inc.

5. Which writing pattern is used to organize the supporting details?
   a. classification
   b. sequence
   c. definition
   d. comparison-contrast

Several warning signs indicate when a teenager's problems may be severe enough to warrant concern about the possibility of a suicide attempt. They include the following:

- school problems, such as missing classes, truancy, and a sudden change in grades
- frequent incidents of self-destructive behavior, such as careless accidents
- loss of appetite or excessive eating
- withdrawal from friends and peers
- sleeping problems
- signs of depression, tearfulness, or overt indications of psychological difficulties such as hallucinations
- a preoccupation with death, an afterlife, or what would happen "if I died"
- putting his or her affairs in order, such as giving away prized possessions or making arrangements for the care of a pet
- an explicit announcement of thoughts of suicide

Source: Robert Feldman, *Essentials of Understanding Psychology,* 9e, p. 359. Copyright © 2011 by The McGraw-Hill Companies, Inc. Reprinted with permission of The McGraw-Hill Companies, Inc.

6. Which writing pattern is used to organize the supporting details?
   a. list
   b. sequence
   c. definition
   d. comparison-contrast

The view many patients hold that physicians are "all-knowing" can result in serious communication problems. Many patients do not understand their treatments yet fail to ask their physicians for clearer explanations of a prescribed course of action. Consequently, about half of all patients are unable to report accurately how long they are to continue taking a medication prescribed for them, and about a quarter do not even know the purpose of the drug. In fact, some patients are not even sure as they are about to be rolled into the operating room, why they are having surgery.

Source: Robert Feldman, *Essentials of Understanding Psychology,* 9e, p. 433. Copyright © 2011 by The McGraw-Hill Companies, Inc. Reprinted with permission of The McGraw-Hill Companies, Inc.

7. Which writing pattern is used to organize the supporting details?
   a. list
   b. sequence
   c. definition
   d. cause-effect

We also have other, more direct, and potentially more positive ways of coping with stress. The first is *emotion-focused coping*. In emotion-focused coping, people try to manage their emotions in the face of stress by seeking to change the way they feel about or perceive a problem. Examples of emotion-focused coping include strategies such as accepting sympathy from others and looking at the bright side of a situation. The second is *problem-focused coping.* Problem-focused coping attempts to modify the stressful problem or source of stress. Problem-focused strategies lead to changes in behavior or to the development of a plan of action to deal with stress. Starting a study group to improve poor classroom performance is an example of problem-focused coping. In addition, one might take a time-out from stress by creating positive events. For example, taking a day off from caring for a relative with a serious, chronic illness to go a health club or spa can bring significant relief from stress.

Source: Robert Feldman, *Essentials of Understanding Psychology,* 9e, p. 420. Copyright © 2011 by The McGraw-Hill Companies, Inc. Reprinted with permission of The McGraw-Hill Companies, Inc.

8. Which writing pattern is used to organize the supporting details?
 a. list
 b. sequence
 c. spatial
 d. cause-effect

The spread of AIDS is particularly pronounced among women, who now account for almost half the cases worldwide. The annual number of AIDS cases increased 15 percent among women, compared with 1 percent among men, between 1999 and 2003. Younger women and women of color are particularly vulnerable. For instance, the rate of AIDS diagnosis was around 25 times higher for African American women than for white women, and four times higher for Hispanic women.

Source: Robert Feldman, *Understanding Psychology,* 8e, p. 390. Copyright © 2008 by The McGraw-Hill Companies, Inc. Reprinted with permission of The McGraw-Hill Companies, Inc.

9. Which writing pattern is used to organize the supporting details?
 a. list
 b. sequence
 c. definition
 d. comparison-contrast

More than 1.5 million people in the United States are regular methamphetamine users. Because it can be made from nonprescription cold pills, retailers such as Wal-Mart and Target have removed these medications from their shelves. As a result, illicit labs devoted to the manufacture of methamphetamine have sprung up in many locations around the United States.

Source: Robert Feldman, *Essentials of Understanding Psychology,* 9e, p. 153. Copyright © 2011 by The McGraw-Hill Companies, Inc. Reprinted with permission of The McGraw-Hill Companies, Inc.

10. Which writing pattern is used to organize the supporting details?
 a. list
 b. sequence
 c. spatial
 d. cause-effect

TEST YOUR UNDERSTANDING
Recognizing Authors' Writing Patterns, Part 2

Directions: Read these paragraphs carefully and then write the main idea sentence and the writing pattern for each paragraph in the spaces provided.

This paragraph comes from an American government textbook:

> Since its debut as a political medium in the 1996 presidential elections, the Internet has become an increasingly important part of political campaigns. In 1996, the presidential candidates created fairly simple home pages containing their profiles, positions on issues, campaign strategies, slogans, and email addresses. By 2000, the World Wide Web had become a major campaign tool for identifying potential supporters. In 2004, the campaign for Democratic contender Howard Dean used the Internet to raise millions of dollars, and the Kerry campaign later used the technology to overcome the early financial advantage President Bush enjoyed. The funds raised by the presidential candidates in 2008 dwarfed the figures from 2004. In 2008, presidential candidates used the Internet to create virtual town meetings and to share ideas and coordinate campaign events with bloggers—average citizens who create online diaries and forums for the posting of opinions and viewpoints.

Source: Adapted from Joseph Losco and Ralph Baker, *Am Gov, 2011,* p. 246. Copyright © 2011 by The McGraw-Hill Companies, Inc. Reprinted with permission of The McGraw-Hill Companies, Inc.

1. Write the main idea sentence: _____

_____

_____

2. Which writing pattern did the authors use to organize the main idea and the supporting details? _____

_____

This paragraph comes from a human development textbook:

> In pre-industrial farming societies, large families were a necessity. Children helped with the family's work and would eventually care for aging parents. The death rate in childhood was high, and having many children made it more likely that some would reach maturity. Today, infant and child mortality rates have improved greatly, and, in industrial societies, large families are no longer an economic asset. In developing countries, too, where overpopulation and hunger are major problems, there is recognition of the need to limit family size and to space children further apart. Not only do people typically have fewer children today, but they also start having them later in life, often because they spend their early adult years getting an education and establishing a career. Today

the median age of first-time mothers in the United States is 24.6, having risen consistently for three decades.

3. Write the main idea sentence: _____

_____

_____

_____

4. Which writing pattern did the authors use to organize the main idea and the supporting details? _____

_____

This paragraph comes from a student success textbook:

Each of us has preferred ways of learning, approaches that work best for us either in the classroom or on the job. And our success is not just dependent on how well we learn, but how we learn. A *learning style* reflects a person's preferred manner of acquiring, using and thinking about knowledge. We don't have just one learning style, but a variety of styles. Some involve our preferences regarding the way information is presented to us, some relate to how we think and learn most readily, and some relate to how our personality traits affect our performance. An awareness of your learning styles will help you in college by allowing you to study and learn course materials more effectively. On the job, knowing your learning styles will help you master new skills and techniques, ensuring you can keep up with changing office practices or an evolving industry.

5. Write the main idea sentence: _____

_____

_____

6. Which writing pattern did the author use to organize the main idea and the supporting details? _____

_____

This paragraph comes from a personal finance textbook:

> Career counselors stress the importance of personal traits adaptable to most work situations. While some of these traits can be acquired in school, others require experiences in other situations. The traits that cause people to be successful in the workplace include:
>
> - An ability to work well with others in a variety of settings.
> - A desire to do tasks better than they have to be done.
> - An interest in reading a wide variety of materials.
> - A willingness to cope with conflict and adapt to change.
> - An awareness of accounting, finance, and marketing fundamentals.
> - A knowledge of technology and computer software such as word processing and spreadsheet programs.
> - An ability to solve problems creatively in team settings.
> - A knowledge of research techniques and library resources.
> - Well-developed written and oral communication skills.
> - An understanding of both their own motivations and the motivations of others.
>
> These traits give people flexibility, and as a consequence, they have the ability to move from one organization to another and to successfully change career fields.
>
> *Source:* Adapted from Jack R. Kapoor, Les R. Dlabay, and Robert J. Hughes, *Personal Finance,* 5e, p. 32. Copyright © 2001 by The McGraw-Hill Companies, Inc. Reprinted with permission of The McGraw-Hill Companies, Inc.

7. Write the main idea sentence: _____

_____

_____

_____

8. Which writing pattern did the authors use to organize the main idea and the supporting details? _____

_____

_____

This paragraph comes from a health textbook:

> There is no cure for type 2 diabetes, but it can be successfully managed. Treatment involves keeping blood sugar levels within safe limits through diet, exercise, and, if necessary, medication. Blood sugar levels can be monitored using a home test. Nearly 90 percent of people with type 2 diabetes are overweight when diagnosed, including 55 percent who are obese. An important step in treatment is to lose weight. Even a small amount of weight loss can be beneficial.

People with diabetes should eat regular meals with an emphasis on complex carbohydrates and ample dietary fiber. Regular exercise and a healthy diet are often sufficient to control type 2 diabetes.

Source: Adapted from Paul Insel and Walton Roth, *Core Concepts in Health,* 12e, p. 413. Copyright © 2012 by The McGraw-Hill Companies, Inc. Reprinted with permission of The McGraw-Hill Companies, Inc.

9. Write the main idea sentence: _____

_____

_____

_____

_____

10. Which writing pattern did the authors use to organize the main idea and the supporting details? _____

_____

_____

_____

SELECTION **7.1**

Business

SELECTION 7.1

E-Commerce? It's E-Normous!

From *Understanding Business*
by William Nickels, James McHugh, and Susan McHugh

Prepare Yourself to Read

Directions: Do these exercises *before* you read Selection 7.1.

1. First, read and think about the title. What do you know about e-commerce?

   _____

   _____

2. Next, complete your preview by reading the following:

   Introduction (in *italics*)
   Headings
   First paragraph (paragraph 1)
   Photo and caption
   Figure 1
   First sentence of paragraphs 1–11

   Now that you have previewed the selection, what point do you think the author is making about e-commerce?

   _____

   _____

   _____

   _____

   _____

   _____

3. **Build your vocabulary as you read.** If you discover an unfamiliar word or key term as you read the selection, try to determine its meaning by using context clues.

Read More about This Topic Online

Internet Resources

Use a search engine, such as Google or Yahoo!, to expand your existing knowledge about this topic *before* you read the selection or to learn more about it *afterward*. If you are unfamiliar with conducting Internet searches, read pages 25–26 on Boolean searches. You can also use Wikipedia, the free online encyclopedia, at www.wikipedia .com. Keep in mind that when you visit any website, it is a good idea to evaluate the site and the information it contains. Ask yourself questions such as "Who sponsors this website?" and "Is the information it contains up to date?"

SELECTION 7.1: E-COMMERCE? IT'S E-NORMOUS!

Do you do your banking online? Do you ever purchase airline tickets, book hotel reservations, or make other travel arrangements online? Are you among the millions of Americans who shop online? If so, have your experiences generally been positive ones?

In his article "Online Shoppers Wary of Online Shopping" (www.e-commerce-guide.com/solutions/customer_relations/article.php/3566676, accessed 11/28/2005), Tim Gray reports that "nearly 90 percent of those making online purchases, at least some of the time, become frustrated with the process." Hardly a surprise! He continues, "More than 80 percent of shoppers polled said they are unwilling to accept lower levels of customer service online than they would offline." Moreover, a third said they would move to a competitor's website if they experienced a problem with online shopping, banking, travel, or insurance websites. Clearly, e-commerce businesses face many challenges.

A 2011 ABC News poll found that 31 percent of Americans planned to do holiday shopping on the Internet. These shoppers tended to be younger (18–54), be better educated, and have higher incomes (http://abcnews.go.com/Business/story?id=86203&page=1-.UBfbtUL5Fho, accessed 8/1/12). Cyber Monday, the Monday after Thanksgiving, is the official kickoff day for online holiday shopping. On that day in 2011, an estimated 123 million Americans participated, many of them shopping from their smart phones and other mobile devices (forbes.com/sites/anthonydemarco/2011/11/28/millions-of-americans-ready-to-do-their-holiday-shopping-online-on-cyber-monday, accessed 8/1/12).

Read this business textbook selection to learn more about e-commerce, its appeal, and what will distinguish the e-commerce companies that succeed from those that don't.

The Growth of E-Commerce

1   The business environment is rapidly changing and businesses need to adjust to these changes. One of the more important changes of recent years is the growth of **e-commerce,** the buying and selling of goods over the Internet. There are two major types of e-commerce transactions: business-to-consumer (B2C) and business-to-business (B2B).

2   As important as the Internet has been in the consumer market, it has become even more important in the B2B market, which consists of selling goods and services from one business to another. For example, IBM sells consulting services to banks. B2B e-commerce is already at least five times as big as B2C e-commerce. While the potential of the B2C e-commerce market is measured in billions, B2B e-commerce is said to be measured in trillions of dollars.

3   The rise of Internet marketing came so fast and furious that it drew hundreds of competitors into the fray. Many of the new Internet companies failed. Companies such as Pets.com, CDnow, Internet Capital Group, Peapod, eToys, and Drkoop.com have failed entirely or seen their stock prices drop dramatically. Many B2B stocks experienced similar failures. There is no question that some Internet businesses will grow and prosper, but along the way there will continue to

Annotation Practice Exercises

Directions: For each exercise, use the spaces provided to write:

- Main idea sentence of the paragraph
- Authors' pattern for organizing the supporting details (writing pattern)

be lots of failures, just as there have been in traditional businesses. Traditional businesses will have to learn how to deal with the new competition from B2B and B2C firms.

4   There once were dozens of automobile companies. Almost all of them failed, and only a few large companies now dominate the auto industry. Just as a few companies now dominate the auto industry, success will come to those e-commerce businesses that offer quality products at good prices with great service. Many of those successful companies, such as Sears and General Electric, combined their traditional brick-and-mortar operations with new Internet sites that make them more competitive.

Using Technology to Be Responsive to Customers

5   Businesses succeed or fail largely because of the way they treat their customers. The businesses that are most responsive to customer wants and needs will succeed, and those that do not respond to customers will not be as successful. One way traditional retailers can respond to the Internet revolution is to use technology to become much more responsive to customers. For example, businesses mark goods with Universal Product Codes (bar codes)—those series of lines and numbers that you see on most consumer packaged goods. Bar codes can be used to tell retailers what product you bought, in what size and color, and at what price. A scanner at the checkout counter can read that information and put it into a database.

6   Businesses use databases, electronic storage files where information is kept, several ways. One use of databases is to store vast amounts of information about consumers. For example, a retailer may ask for your name, address, and telephone number so that it can put you on its mailing list. The information you give the retailer is added to the database. Because companies routinely trade database information, many retailers know what you buy and from whom you buy it. Using that information, companies can send you catalogs and other direct mail advertising that offers the kind of products you might want, as indicated by your past purchases. Another use of databases is that they enable stores to carry only the merchandise that the local population wants. Finally, they enable stores to carry less inventory saving them money.

The Competitive Environment

7   Competition among businesses has never been greater than it is today. Some companies have found a competitive edge by focusing on quality. The goal for many companies is zero defects—no mistakes in making the product. Some companies, such as Motorola in the United States and Toyota in Japan, have come close to meeting that standard. However, simply making a high-quality product is not enough

Practice Exercise

- Main idea sentence of paragraph 4:

  _____
  _____
  _____
  _____
  _____

- Writing pattern:

  _____
  _____
  _____
  _____

Practice Exercise

- Main idea sentence of paragraph 6:

  _____
  _____
  _____
  _____

- Writing pattern:

  _____
  _____
  _____

Figure 1 How Competition Has Changed Business

Traditional Businesses	World-Class Businesses
Customer satisfaction	Delighting the customer
Customer orientation	Customer and stakeholder orientation
Profit orientation	Profit and social orientation
Reactive ethics	Proactive ethics
Productive orientation	Quality and service orientation
Managerial focus	Customer focus

to allow a company to stay competitive in world markets. Companies now have to offer both high-quality products and outstanding service at competitive prices (value). That is why General Motors (GM) is building automobile plants in Argentina, Poland, China, and Thailand. The strategies of combining excellence with low-cost labor and minimizing distribution costs have resulted in larger markets and potential long-term growth for GM. Figure 1 shows how competition has changed businesses from the traditional model to a new, world-class model.

Competing by Exceeding Customer Expectations

8   Manufacturers and service organizations throughout the world have learned that today's customers are very demanding. Not only do they want good quality at low prices, but they want great service as well. In fact, some products in the 21st century will be designed to fascinate, bewitch, and delight customers, exceeding their expectations. Every manufacturing and service organization in the world should have a sign over its door telling its workers that the customer is king. Business is becoming customer-driven, not management-driven as in the past. This means that customers' wants and needs must come first.

9   Customer-driven organizations include Nordstrom department stores (they have a very generous return policy, for example) and Disney amusement park (the parks are kept clean and appeal to all ages). Moto Photo does its best to please customers with fast, friendly service. Such companies can successfully compete against Internet firms if they continue to offer better and friendlier service. Successful organizations must now listen more closely to customers to determine their wants and needs, then adjust the firm's products, policies, and practices to meet those demands.

Adjusting to the E-Commerce Era

10   One of the more significant changes occurring today is the movement toward doing business on the Internet. Many businesses

are finding the new competition overwhelming. That includes, for example, traditional bookstores that now have to compete with eBay and Amazon.com.

11   Who would have thought that garage sales would be done over the Internet? Or that cars or homes could be sold online? What is this e-commerce revolution and why is it happening now? That is, what are the advantages of e-commerce that other businesses have to accept and incorporate into their long-term strategies? Businesses are lured to e-commerce for a number of reasons, including, but not limited to:

- *Less investment in land, buildings and equipment.* E-commerce firms can usually sell things for less because they don't have to invest as much in buildings (bricks), and can reach people inexpensively over the Internet (clicks).

- *Low transaction costs.* The automation of customer service lowers costs, which may make it possible for a company to offer products at a lower price. Also, nationally there are no sales taxes (yet) on the Internet, so in some states things may be a little less expensive than in stores.

- *Large purchases per transaction.* Online stores like Amazon. com often make personalized recommendations to customers that increase their order size.

- *Integration of business processes.* The Internet offers companies the ability to make more information available to customers than ever before. For example, a computer company that tracks each unit through the manufacturing and shipping process can allow customers to see exactly where the order is at any time. This is what overnight package delivery company Federal Express did when it introduced online package tracking.

- *Larger catalogs.* Amazon.com offers a catalog of several million books on the Internet. Imagine fitting a paper catalog that size in your mailbox!

- *Flexibility.* Successful websites are not just glorified mail-order catalogs. The Internet offers companies the ability to configure products and build custom orders, to compare prices between multiple vendors easily, and to search large catalogs quickly.

- *Improved customer interactions.* Online tools allow businesses to interact with customers in ways unheard of before, and at almost instant speeds. For example, customers can receive automatic e-mails to confirm orders and to notify them when orders are shipped. Despite these many benefits, Internet-based companies have not captured the retail market as expected. Instead, traditional retail stores have adapted to the changing environment and have used the

Practice Exercise

- Main idea sentence of paragraph 11:

  _____

  _____

  _____

  _____

- Writing pattern:

  _____

  _____

Internet to supplement their traditional stores. The combination of e-commerce with traditional stores is called click-and-brick retailing, for obvious reasons. The top 20 online sellers are names that are quite familiar to most students. They include Dell, Sears, Best Buy, Office Depot, QVC, JCPenney, Staples, and Victoria's Secret. Four years after going online, Victoria's Secret sold about a third of its goods on the Internet.

12   Two companies have done quite well as Web-only firms: eBay and Amazon.com.

Webvan, like many other Internet firms, failed during the dot-com explosion in 2000–2002. It's not that the Internet does not provide an excellent opportunity to sell things. It does. But the cost of setting up distribution centers and delivery systems and satisfying customer concerns of not being able to see, touch, and examine products has proven too difficult for some businesses to overcome.

Reading Selection Quiz

This quiz has several parts. Your instructor may assign some or all of them.

Comprehension

Directions: Use the information in the selection to answer each item below. You may refer to the selection as you answer the questions. Write each answer in the space provided.

True or False

_____   **1.** E-commerce refers to the buying and selling of goods over the Internet.

_____   **2.** "B2B" refers to business-to-consumer e-commerce transactions.

_____   **3.** In order to become more competitive, many businesses that sell through stores are adding Internet sites.

_____   **4.** Since only a few companies dominate each industry, business today is less competitive than it has been in the past.

_____   **5.** "Zero defects" refers to no mistakes in marketing a product.

_____   **6.** Amazon.com and Pets.com are cited as two companies that have done quite well as Web-only firms.

Multiple-Choice

_____   **7.** In terms of sales, B2B e-commerce is:
  a.   at least 5 times less than B2C e-commerce.
  b.   approximately the same as B2C e-commerce.
  c.   slightly greater than B2C e-commerce.
  d.   at least 5 times greater than B2C e-commerce.

_____   **8.** Whether businesses succeed or fail will depend mostly on:
  a.   the types of products they sell.
  b.   whether they have websites.
  c.   how they treat their customers.
  d.   whether they use bar codes in their products.

_____   **9.** Which of the following is not mentioned as an example of what is likely to be included in a database?
  a.   customers' names, addresses, and telephone numbers
  b.   customers' past purchases
  c.   customers' jobs and income levels
  d.   companies from which customers have made past purchases

_____ **10.** Many e-commerce firms are able to offer lower prices because:

    a.   they do not have to invest as much money in land.

    b.   they do not have to invest as much money in buildings.

    c.   they have automated customer service.

    d.   all of the above

SELECTION **7.1**

Business
(continued)

Vocabulary in Context

Directions: For each item below, use context clues to deduce the meaning of the *italicized* word. Be sure the answer you choose makes sense in both sentences. Write each answer in the space provided.

_____ **11.** As important as the Internet has been in the *consumer* market, it has become even more important in the B2B market, which consists of selling goods and services from one business to another.

Companies spend billions of dollars on *consumer* research in order to determine products their customers want, how much they are willing to pay, and so forth.

consumer (kən soo′ mər) means:

    a.   pertaining to people who buy things in order to resell them

    b.   pertaining to people who buy things to use in producing or manufacturing other items

    c.   pertaining to people who prefer to save money rather than spend it

    d.   pertaining to people who acquire goods for the direct purpose of owning or using them

_____ **12.** The rise of Internet marketing came so fast and furious that it drew hundreds of competitors into the *fray.*

During the debate, the two political opponents began shouting at each other, and then their supporters joined the *fray.*

fray (frā) means:

    a.   heated contest or competition

    b.   search for new opportunities

    c.   orderly discussion

    d.   a series of websites

_____ **13.** There is no question that some Internet businesses will grow and *prosper,* but along the way there will continue to be lots of failures, just as there have been in traditional businesses.

Many immigrants come to this country with little or no money, but are able to *prosper* because of their talent and hard work.

prosper (prŏs′ pər) means:

    a.   to merge with other businesses

    b.   to remain the same

c.   to be successful; thrive

d.   to become well known

14. Almost all of them failed, and only a few large companies now *dominate* the auto industry.

A few major television networks used to *dominate* the airways, but with the rise of cable television, there are now hundreds of channels viewers can choose from.

dominate (dŏm′ ə nāt) means:

a.   to have a commanding, controlling position in

b.   to treat in a harsh, cruel manner

c.   to block or shut out

d.   to govern by using superior power or force

15. Bar codes can be used to tell *retailers* what product you bought, in what size and color, and at what price.

Sears, Roebuck & Company, now called Sears, was one of the first great *retailers* in the United States, and for millions of people, it was their main source for clothes, tools, equipment, home furnishings, and appliances.

retailers (rə′ tāl ərz) means:

a.   those who advertise in magazines and newspapers

b.   those who sell goods in small quantities directly to consumers

c.   those who manufacture goods

d.   those who take items in trade

16. Manufacturers and service organizations throughout the world have learned that today's customers are very *demanding*.

Perfectionists are highly *demanding* people who never seem satisfied, no matter how good something is or how well it has been done.

demanding (dĭ măn′ dĭng) means:

a.   requiring great strength and endurance

b.   irritating; annoying

c.   weighing down; burdensome

d.   making severe and uncompromising demands

17. That is, what are the advantages of e-commerce that other businesses have to accept and *incorporate* into their long-term strategies?

The college is considering ways to *incorporate* actual work experience into its career training courses.

incorporate (ĭn kôr′ pə rāt) means:

a.   to review

b.   to legally form a corporation

c.   to replace

d.   to unite something with something else already in existence

18. Successful websites are not just *glorified* mail-order catalogs.

Because of the *glorified* description of the house in the ad, we were very disappointed when we saw how small and rundown it was.

glorified (glôr′ ə fīd) means:
  a. made to seem more wonderful than is actually the case
  b. made to seem more expensive than is actually the case
  c. made to seem more religious than is actually the case
  d. made to seem more time-saving than is actually the case

19. The Internet offers companies the ability to *configure* products and build custom orders, to compare prices between multiple vendors easily, and to search large catalogs quickly.

By modifying the engine, tires, and other features, manufacturers can *configure* trucks for different types of purposes and terrains.

configure (kən fĭg′ yər) means:
  a. to change the appearance of
  b. to improve the value of
  c. to lower the cost of
  d. to design for specific uses

20. The Internet offers companies the ability to configure products and build custom orders, to compare prices between multiple *vendors* easily, and to search large catalogs quickly.

Bill Gates is a billionaire; his company, Microsoft, is one of the most successful software *vendors* in the world.

vendors (vĕn′ dərz) means:
  a. people and companies that shop on the Internet
  b. people and companies that buy things
  c. people and companies that sell things
  d. people and companies that advertise on the Internet

SELECTION **7.1**

Business
(continued)

Reading Skills Application

Directions: These items test your ability to *apply* certain reading skills. You may not have studied all of the skills yet, so some items will serve as a preview. Write each answer in the space provided.

21. In paragraph 4, the term "brick-and-mortar operations" is used to describe companies':
  a. actual stores.
  b. sales personnel.

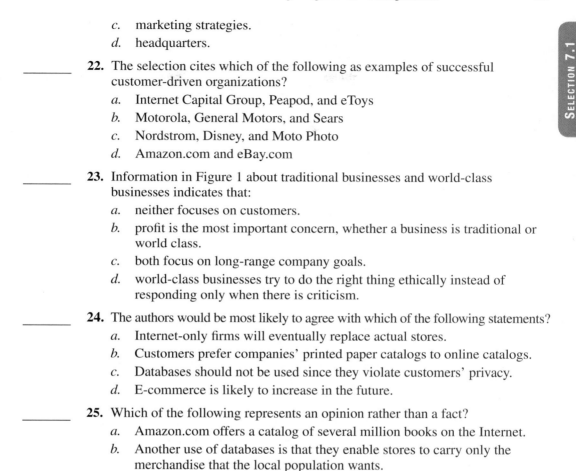

    c.   marketing strategies.

    d.   headquarters.

_____ **22.** The selection cites which of the following as examples of successful customer-driven organizations?

    a.   Internet Capital Group, Peapod, and eToys

    b.   Motorola, General Motors, and Sears

    c.   Nordstrom, Disney, and Moto Photo

    d.   Amazon.com and eBay.com

_____ **23.** Information in Figure 1 about traditional businesses and world-class businesses indicates that:

    a.   neither focuses on customers.

    b.   profit is the most important concern, whether a business is traditional or world class.

    c.   both focus on long-range company goals.

    d.   world-class businesses try to do the right thing ethically instead of responding only when there is criticism.

_____ **24.** The authors would be most likely to agree with which of the following statements?

    a.   Internet-only firms will eventually replace actual stores.

    b.   Customers prefer companies' printed paper catalogs to online catalogs.

    c.   Databases should not be used since they violate customers' privacy.

    d.   E-commerce is likely to increase in the future.

_____ **25.** Which of the following represents an opinion rather than a fact?

    a.   Amazon.com offers a catalog of several million books on the Internet.

    b.   Another use of databases is that they enable stores to carry only the merchandise that the local population wants.

    c.   Every manufacturing and service organization in the world should have a sign over its door telling its workers that the customer is king.

    d.   The Internet offers companies the ability to make more information available to customers than ever before.

Respond in Writing

Directions: Refer to the selection as needed to answer the essay-type questions below. (Your instructor may direct you to work collaboratively with other students on one or more items. Each group member should be able to explain *all* of the group's answers.)

1. Do you shop online? If so, what types of products have you ordered? Has your experience been a positive one? If you do not shop online, why not? If you have never purchased anything online, would you be likely to in the future? Why or why not?

_____

_____

_____

_____

2. List at least four reasons you think consumers might rather shop online than go to a store.

_____

_____

_____

_____

_____

_____

3. List at least four reasons you think consumers might rather shop at an actual store than to shop online.

_____

_____

_____

_____

_____

_____

4. Do you think the combination of stores ("bricks") and a website ("clicks") is the best option for most companies? Why or why not?

_____

_____

_____

_____

5. Based on the information in the selection, what types of things would a new e-commerce company need to do in order to become highly successful?

_____

_____

_____

_____

_____

_____

6. **Overall main idea.** What is the overall main idea the author wants you to understand about e-commerce? Answer this question in one sentence. Be sure that your overall main idea sentence includes the topic (*e-commerce*) and tells the overall most important point about it.

_____

_____

_____

_____

_____

_____

SELECTION **7.2**

Music Appreciation

The Development of Rock Music and Rock in American Society

From *Music: An Appreciation*

by Roger Kamien

Prepare Yourself to Read

Directions: Do these exercises *before* you read Selection 7.2.

1. First, read and think about the title. What do you already know about *rock music's* influence on American society?

   _____

   _____

   _____

2. Do you like rock music? If not, why not? If so, who are your favorite rock performers?

   _____

   _____

   _____

3. Many people disapprove of rock music for various reasons. List any reasons you are familiar with.

   _____

   _____

   _____

4. Next, complete your preview by reading the following:

   Introduction (in *italics*)

   Headings

   The visual aid in the margin near paragraph 5

   Captions accompanying the photos

   Now that you have completed your preview, what does this selection seem to be about and what decades are discussed?

   _____

   _____

   _____

5. **Build your vocabulary as you read.** If you discover an unfamiliar word or key term as you read the selection, try to determine its meaning by using context clues.

SELECTION 7.2

Internet Resources

Read More about This Topic Online

Use a search engine, such as Google or Yahoo!, to expand your existing knowledge about this topic *before* you read the selection or to learn more about it *afterward*. If you are unfamiliar with conducting Internet searches, read pages 25–26 on Boolean searches. You can also use Wikipedia, the free online encyclopedia, at www .wikipedia.com. Keep in mind that when you visit any website, it is a good idea to evaluate the site and the information it contains. Ask yourself questions such as "Who sponsors this website?" and "Is the information it contains up to date?"

SELECTION 7.2: THE DEVELOPMENT OF ROCK MUSIC AND ROCK IN AMERICAN SOCIETY

This selection is from a music appreciation textbook. Colleges offer courses such as music appreciation and art appreciation to give students a general introduction to the worlds of music and art, and students often say that these courses were among their favorite courses in college. In a music appreciation class, for example, students learn about (and listen to) all types of music, from ancient forms of music to classical music, sacred music, theatrical music, and opera to modern musical styles such as jazz, blues, popular music, and rock music. Students are also introduced to music from Africa, India, Japan, and China as well. Students are introduced to classical composers such as Mozart, Beethoven, Vivaldi, and Bach, and a range of musical styles such as the ragtime style of Scott Joplin, the New Orleans style of Louis Armstrong, and the bebop style of Charlie "Bird" Parker. In addition, students study the music of more contemporary performers, such as Chuck Berry, Jimi Hendrix, Elvis Presley, Bob Dylan, Bruce Springsteen, Madonna, Carlos Santana, Sheryl Crow, Alicia Keys, and Usher.

If you are a young college student, this selection about the development of rock music through the 1950s, 60s, 70s, 80s, and 90s may seem like a history or sociology lesson as much as a lesson in music appreciation, since it also presents background information about the political events and trends that occurred during these decades.

1   The mid-1950s saw the growth of a new kind of popular music that was first called *rock and roll* and then simply *rock*. Though it includes diverse styles, **rock** tends to be vocal music with a hard, driving beat, often featuring electric guitar accompaniment and heavily amplified sound. Early rock grew mainly out of *rhythm and blues,* a dance music of African Americans that fused *blues, jazz,* and *gospel* styles. Rock also drew on *country and western,* a folklike, guitar-based style associated with rural white Americans, and *pop music,* a smooth, highly polished style exemplified by such performers as Frank Sinatra and Perry Como. In little more than a decade, rock evolved from a simple, dance-oriented style to music that was highly varied in its tone colors, lyrics, musical forms, and electronic technology.

The Development of Rock

2   In the late 1940s, rhythm and blues became a dominant style among African Americans. Rhythm and blues (R & B) of the late 1950s differed from earlier blues in its more powerful beat and its use of the saxophone and electric guitar. Among the leading performers influenced by rhythm and blues were Little Richard, Chuck Berry, Bo Didley, and Fats Domino. Gospel-tinged vocal groups, such as The Drifters, and the soaring falsetto lead sounds of The Platters were also an important part of rhythm-and-blues style.

Annotation Practice Exercises

Directions: For each exercise, use the spaces provided to write:

- Main idea sentence of the paragraph
- Authors' pattern for organizing supporting details (writing pattern)

Practice Exercise

- Main idea sentence of paragraph 2:

_____

_____

_____

_____

_____

- Writing pattern:

_____

_____

3   During the 1950s many rhythm-and-blues hits were issued by white performers in versions ("covers") with less sexually explicit lyrics. Little Richard's *Tutti Fruiti* and *Long Tall Sally,* for example, were issued in "cover" versions by Pat Boone one month after the release of the originals.

4   One of the earliest important rock and roll groups was Bill Haley and His Comets, whose *Rock Around the Clock* is often identified as the first big hit of the new style. The song was recorded in 1954, but did not become a number-one hit until a year later, when it was prominently featured in *The Blackboard Jungle,* a provocative movie about teenage delinquency in a contemporary setting: a New York City high school. To many people, the new music seemed rebellious in its loudness, pounding beat, and sexual directness; and the image of youthful rebellion was also projected by Elvis Presley, who reigned as "king" of rock and roll.

5   During the 1960s, much of the rock music by black performers was called *soul,* a term that emphasized its emotionality, its gospel roots, and its relationship to the black community. Soul musicians included James Brown, Ray Charles, and Aretha Franklin. *Motown*—derived from "Motor Town USA," a nickname for Detroit, the city from which the style emerged—was a type of music that blended rhythm and blues with elements of popular music. Among its stars were Diana Ross and the Supremes and Stevie Wonder. With Motown, African American composers and performers entered the mainstream of popular music.

6   A new era of British influence began in 1964 with the American tour of the Beatles, an English rock group whose members probably have been the most influential performers in the history of rock. The Beatles—the singer-guitarists Paul McCartney, John Lennon, and George Harrison; and the drummer Ringo Starr (all born in the 1940s)—dominated the popular music scene in the United States, along with the Rolling Stones and other British groups. Under their influence, rock musicians of the middle and late 1960s explored a wider range of sources for sounds and musical ideas. They experimented with electronic effects, with "classical" and nonwestern instruments, and with unconventional scales, chord progressions, and rhythms.

7   Rock in the 1960s also absorbed elements of folk music and often had lyrics dealing with such contemporary issues as war and social injustice. This development was spurred by the success of the songwriter and singer Bob Dylan, whose *Blowin' in the Wind*—a song against racial bigotry—articulated the feelings of many young people.

CONTEMPORARY MUSIC STYLES

blues
jazz
gospel
rhythm and blues
country and western
pop music
rock and roll
soul
Motown
British rock
fusion
folk rock
jazz rock
psychedelic rock
acid rock
art rock
disco
country rock
reggae
funk
punk
new wave
heavy metal
rap
thrash
speed metal
death metal
gansta rap
grunge
alternative
techno
electronica

8   During the late 1960s, the popular music scene was enormously varied. The diversity of rock styles is reflected in the many terms that arose to describe the music of this period: *fusion, folk rock, jazz rock, psychedelic rock, acid rock,* and *art rock.* During this time technological advancements in recording techniques often added important features to the sound as well. Rock style grew more theatrical as many groups began to concentrate on visual aspects of their stage shows.

9   The 1970s saw the continuation of many styles from the 1960s, the revival of early rock and roll from the 1950s, and the rise of a dance music called *disco.* Many veteran performers of the 1960s continued to be active; but new stars also emerged, including the singer-songwriters Billy Joel and Bruce Springsteen, as well as the Mexican American Linda Ronstadt and the "disco queen" Donna Summer. For a while in the early 1970s, there was a nostalgic fascination with 1950s rock and roll and its pioneer performers. Record companies released many albums of re-packaged old hits—and the term "oldies" came into popular use. A blend of country music and rock called *country rock* became popular in the early 1970s. Country music itself moved into the musical mainstream as its stars (Johnny Cash, Dolly Parton, Willie Nelson, and others) won national popularity. Other musical styles of the 1970s included *reggae,* a music from Jamaica; *funk,* a rhythmically assertive development of black soul music; *punk,* a return to a primal form of rock; and *new wave,* a technically refined eclectic derivative of punk.

10   In the early 1980s, new wave bands from Britain such as the Police and The Clash were popular with American rock audiences. This "second British invasion" was comparable to the one that had been led by the Beatles during the early 1960s. Though their styles varied, many British bands of this period, such as New Order and The Cure, made extensive use of electronic technology—synthesizers and computers—and often featured outlandish-looking performers. The 1980s saw a renewed interest among teenagers in *heavy metal,* a type of basic rock characterized by pounding drums, heavily amplified bass, and unrestrained guitars played at peak volume. Heavy metal's lyrics, with their increasingly overt references to sex and violence, gave rise to concern about their possible effect on young people. Popular heavy metal bands of this period include Metallica, Iron Maiden, Mötley Crüe, and Guns 'n Roses.

11   Among young urban blacks, rap music developed. It began as a kind of rhythmically accented poetic recitation accompanied by a disc jockey who manipulated recordings on two turntables to create a collage of percussive and musical effects. First popularized in black neighborhoods of east coast American cities, with works like Sugarhill Gang's *Rapper's Delight* (1979), rap later depicted the anger

Aretha Franklin

Bob Dylan

Jimi Hendrix

The Beatles

SELECTION 7.2

During the 60s and 70s, rock stars became enormously successful as a result of royalties, movie contracts, and astronomical concert fees.

Practice Exercise

- Main idea sentence of paragraph 9:

  _____

  _____

  _____

  _____

  _____

  _____

- Writing pattern:

  _____

  _____

  _____

  _____

and frustration of urban youth. Through artists like Run-D.M.C. and the white group the Beastie Boys, rap appealed to a wider audience by the late 1980s.

12   Heavy metal and rap continued to grow in popularity throughout the 1980s and into the 1990s. Heavy metal broadened its audience appeal and was no longer the exclusive domain of white working-class adolescents. In the late 1980s and early 1990s, heavy metal spawned a variety of substyles such as *thrash, speed metal,* and *death metal.*

13   By 1990, rap had adopted stylistic features from other forms of popular music and had begun to attract new audiences. There was a successful rap show on cable television; early rap artists included De La Soul, Public Enemy, and Niggaz with Attitude (N.W.A.). By the end of the 1990s, rap and rap-flavored rhythm and blues moved into the mainstream and dominated the recording charts. Particularly influential were Dr. Dre, Tupac Shakur, Missy Elliot, and the Detroit rapper Marshall Mathers (Eminem). Recordings of the controversial *gangsta rap*—with its deliberately antisocial and sexually explicit lyrics—had enormous sales.

14   The brash, grinding guitar sounds and angry lyrics of despair of Seattle's *grunge* or *alternative* rock bands were embraced by many young people disenchanted with the polished sounds of mainstream rock of the early 1990s. Alternative bands such as Nirvana, Pearl Jam, Soundgarden, and Alice in Chains offered a great range of stylistic variety. They also exhibited a clear stylistic influence of 1970s punk and hard rock, as well as heavy metal.

15   At the end of the twentieth century, interesting trends included the emergence of Latino artists who incorporated pan-Latin influences in their music (Gloria Estefan and Ricky Martin), the appearance of crossover artists from the world of country music (Garth Brooks) and a renewed interest in music from the 1970s.

Rock in American Society

16   "Hey! That's our music; that was written for us!" shouted the fourteen-year-old Bob Dylan when he first heard Bill Haley's *Rock Around the Clock* in 1955. Like Dylan, millions of young people felt that rock belonged to them and that it expressed their search for identity and independence. Many leading rock performers and songwriters were themselves in their teens or early twenties. In contrast to rock, popular music before the 1950s had appealed about equally to people of all ages.

17   As a result of the "baby boom" after World War II, there were more American young people in the 1950s and 1960s than ever before, and they had more money to spend, because of a generally rising economy. American industry quickly responded to this vast youth

Practice Exercise

• Main idea sentence of paragraph 11:

_____

_____

_____

• Writing pattern:

_____

_____

_____

_____

Practice Exercise

• Main idea sentence of paragraph 16:

_____

_____

_____

_____

_____

• Writing pattern:

_____

_____

_____

market, and rock became a big business. Sales of electric guitars, phonographs, records, and transistor radios increased dramatically. Rock superstars struck it rich through record royalties, movie contracts, and astronomical concert fees. Rock performances took place everywhere: in auditoriums, gymnasiums, sports arenas, and baseball stadiums. A single concert by a leading group could gross hundreds of thousands of dollars and might be seen by an audience of up to 75,000 people. There even were rock festivals, like the three-day Woodstock Music and Art Fair in August 1969. At that event, over 300,000 people listened in the open fields to the music of Joan Baez, Janis Joplin, Jimi Hendrix, Jefferson Airplane, Santana, and many others.

18   Often rock performances were as much theatrical as musical events. From the earliest days of rock and roll, costumes and staging were essential to the show. For example, Elvis Presley's appearance was heightened by the tight-fitting sequined pants, a leather jacket, and gyrations that led to the nickname "Elvis the pelvis." In the late 1960s, Jimi Hendrix, Pete Townsend (of the Who), and other performers destroyed their instruments as part of their stage show. The image of "psychedelic rock" was heightened by flashing strobe lights that simulated the sensations of a drug experience. Rock performances of the 1970s became even more theatrical. Alice Cooper—a male vocalist—appeared onstage with a boa constrictor and performed acts of simulated violence. The members of a group called Kiss wore macho glitter costumes and makeup influenced by the kabuki theater of Japan. The act involved flames, smoke, and explosions. David Bowie, who, in one of his many stage personae (Aladdin Sane), wore women's clothing and dyed his hair bright orange, often said that his records were only "half there," because the visual aspect was missing. Some British new wave stars of the 1980s continued the tradition of David Bowie and were as famous for their outrageous appearance as for their music. Among the best-known was Boy George of the group Culture Club, whose androgynous looks, rouge, and mascara were meant to shock.

19   Rock songs often reflected the trends in American life. For example, many songs demonstrated an increased openness about sexuality. Lyrics tended to be more sexually explicit than those of the sentimental love songs of the 1930s and 1940s. In fact, the term *rock and roll* originally had an explicit sexual connotation. During the 1960s, rock performers often sang about a wide range of topics including the war in Vietnam, experiences associated with drugs, and the struggle for civil rights. Unlike pop vocalists of the 1930s and 1940s, many rock performers wrote their own songs. For many young people of the time, rock was part of a life style that seemed less inhibited and less materialistic than that of their parents. They quickly adopted the longer hair styles and casual dress popularized by rock stars.

Practice Exercise

- Main idea sentence of paragraph 17:

_____

_____

_____

_____

_____

- Writing pattern:

_____

_____

_____

The Woodstock music festival gained worldwide attention in 1969 when thousands of young music lovers descended on a farm in upstate New York to hear performances by rock's superstars.

SELECTION 7.2

20   During the 1970s, rock became integrated into the mainstream of American popular music. Although rock concerts still appealed primarily to the young, a wide variety of rock records were purchased by people of all ages. And rock songs of the 1970s were less likely to deal with social and political issues.

21   During the 1980s and 1990s, women performers had a powerful impact on rock. "Many new women rockers do a lot more than sing," observed one critic. "They play their own instruments, write their own songs, control their own careers." Their wide range of musical styles extended from pop and soul to funk, new wave, country rock, and heavy metal. Leading performers included Pat Benatar, Tina Turner, Madonna, Alanis Morissette, Sheryl Crow, Queen Latifah, Shania Twain, and Ani DiFranco.

22   In the 1990s, most major record companies involved with mainstream rock and pop played it safe by promoting established superstars. Among the most popular artists of the decade were Mariah Carey, Whitney Houston, Madonna, Celine Dion, Janet Jackson, and the group Boyz II Men.

Rock and Television (MTV)

23   The 1980s saw the development of MTV, a cable television network broadcasting rock videos. MTV gave a needed boost to the music industry and contributed to the popularity of many performers. An innovator in the use of rock video was Michael Jackson, whose documentary on the production of *Thriller* became one of the most widely sold prerecorded videocassettes ever made. Rock video adds a new dimension to the rock experience through the addition of a narrative and a wide variety of visual effects that are often fantastic and provocative.

Rock and Dancing

24   Since its beginning, rock music has accompanied a dizzying succession of dances, such as the twist, the frug, the monkey, the shake, and the mashed potato. In most rock dances of the 1960s, partners did not hold each other, as in earlier dances, but moved individually to the music's powerful beat.

25   Most rock dances were improvisational and did not require dancers to learn a series of complicated steps. Among the best-known rock dances was the twist, associated with a New York nightclub, the Peppermint Lounge, and popularized in 1961 through a television performance by the singer Chubby Checker. By the 1960s, many adults became influenced by the youth culture and danced to rock music at nightclubs called *discotheques.*

26   During the 1970s, thousands of discotheques—mostly featuring recorded music—mushroomed around the country. *Disco* became the

dominant dance music of the time. Many dances of the 1970s—such as the hustle and its variants—often required intricate steps and turns, a throwback to earlier times. These dances frequently required partners to remain in close contact with each other. Also popular were line dances, in which many dancers performed the same choreographed movements. The late 1970s and 1980s saw the development of break dancing, a combination of dancing and gymnastics, often to rap music. Through the 1990s, in alternative and punk clubs, slam dancing and the *mosh pit* were an integral part of the scene. Dancing at social events known as *raves* were often accompanied by *techno* and *electronica,* types of music that shared a musical heritage with disco and made prominent use of drum machines and computer sequencers.

Practice Exercise

- Main idea sentence of paragraph 26:

_____

_____

_____

_____

_____

- Writing pattern:

_____

_____

_____

SELECTION 7.2

S ELECTION **7.2**

**Music
Appreciation**

(continued)

Reading Selection Quiz

This quiz has several parts. Your instructor may assign some or all of them.

Comprehension

Directions: Use the information in the selection to answer each item below. You may refer to the selection as you answer the questions. Write each answer in the space provided.

True or False

_____ **1.** Rock and roll, a profoundly popular 20th-century idiom, is a fusion of many different styles.

_____ **2.** The members of the British rock group the Beatles were the singer-guitarists Paul McCartney, John Lennon, and Bob Dylan, and the drummer Ringo Starr.

_____ **3.** Rhythm and blues became a dominant music style among African Americans in the late 1940s.

Multiple-Choice

_____ **4.** The appeal of rock in the 1950s was:
  a. to people of all ages.
  b. limited to its own performers and songwriters.
  c. mainly to the younger generation.
  d. mainly to urban communities.

_____ **5.** The dominant dance music of the 1970s was:
  a. the twist.
  b. the mashed potato.
  c. break dancing.
  d. disco.

_____ **6.** Rock was an active force in the growth of the manufacturing and sale of:
  a. electric guitars.
  b. phonographs and records.
  c. transistor radios.
  d. all of the above

_____ **7.** The *Motown* sound emerged from which U.S. city?
  a. Detroit
  b. Nashville
  c. Los Angeles
  d. New Orleans

_____ 8. The author suggests that the most influential performers in the history of rock were:
    a. Little Richard, Chuck Berry, Bo Didley, and Fats Domino.
    b. Bill Haley and His Comets.
    c. James Brown, Ray Charles, Aretha Franklin, and Stevie Wonder.
    d. John Lennon, Paul McCartney, George Harrison, and Ringo Starr.

_____ 9. In the 1980s, the music industry received a needed boost from:
    a. the Woodstock Music and Art Fair.
    b. grunge and alternative rock bands.
    c. the development of MTV.
    d. the acceptance of rap music by mainstream audiences.

_____ 10. A notable characteristic of rock music has been:
    a. the image of youthful rebellion.
    b. the use of lyrics dealing with contemporary issues.
    c. sexual directness.
    d. all of the above

SELECTION **7.2**

Music Appreciation
(continued)

Vocabulary in Context

Directions: For each item below, use context clues to deduce the meaning of the *italicized* word. Be sure the answer you choose makes sense in both sentences. Write each answer in the space provided.

_____ 11. Rock also drew on country and western, a folklike, guitar-based style associated with rural white Americans, and pop music, a smooth, highly polished style *exemplified* by such performers as Frank Sinatra and Perry Como.

The group Kiss and the rock performers Alice Cooper, David Bowie, and Boy George *exemplified* the outrageous and often shocking behavior of rock stars of the 70s and 80s.

exemplified (ĭg zĕm′ plə fīd) means:
    a. performed
    b. invented
    c. known to be the cause of
    d. served as an example of

_____ 12. Rock in the 1960s also absorbed elements of folk music and often had lyrics dealing with such *contemporary* issues as war and social injustice.

The bed, sofa, table, and chair in the White House's Lincoln Bedroom are *contemporary* pieces because they all were made during the 19th century.

contemporary (kən tĕm′ pə rĕ rē) means:
    a. out of the ordinary or unusual
    b. having to do with a special time and place

    c.   happening at or belonging to the same period

    d.   modern

13. A new *era* of British influence began in 1964 with the American tour of the Beatles, an English rock group whose members probably have been the most influential performers in the history of rock.

The period of time of Queen Victoria's reign, from June 1837 to January 1901, is known as the Victorian *Era*.

era (îr′ ə, ĕr′ ə) means:

    a.   a current fashion or trend

    b.   a period of time counting from an important point in history

    c.   an influential person or group

    d.   a moment in time

14. They experimented with electronic effects, with "classical" and nonwestern instruments, and with *unconventional* scales, chord progressions, and rhythms.

Alexis did not get the job because her flamboyant dress and extreme hairstyle were too *unconventional*.

unconventional (ŭn kən vĕn′ shə nəl) means:

    a.   unacceptable

    b.   excessive

    c.   out of the ordinary

    d.   unbelievable

15. This development was spurred by the success of the songwriter and singer Bob Dylan, whose song *Blowin' in the Wind*—a song against racial bigotry—*articulated* the feelings of many young people.

The magazine article about poisonous snakes *articulated* the deep fear I have always had of these creatures!

articulated (är tĭk′ yə lä təd) means:

    a.   expressed in coherent verbal form; put into words

    b.   exaggerated; increased the size of

    c.   transformed; changed the meaning of

    d.   corrected; clarified

16. Heavy metal's lyrics, with their increasingly *overt* references to sex and violence, gave rise to concern about their possible effect on young people.

During her divorce proceedings, Sara stared at her soon-to-be ex-husband with *overt* hostility.

overt (ō vûrt′, ō′ vûrt) means:

    a.   extreme

    b.   inappropriate, improper

    c.   unusual

    d.   open and obvious; not hidden

_____   **17.** In the late 1980s and early 1990s, heavy metal *spawned* a variety of substyles such as thrash, speed metal, and death metal.

In the United States, racially discriminatory laws and racial violence aimed at African Americans *spawned* the Civil Rights Movement.

spawned (spônd) means:
a.   duplicated in a wide variety of ways; reproduced
b.   discovered
c.   caused something to be created; gave rise to
d.   transformed; changed

_____   **18.** At the end of the twentieth century, interesting trends included the emergence of Latino artists who *incorporated* pan-Latin influences in their music, the appearance of crossover artists from the world of country music, and a renewed interest in music from the 1970s.

Chris *incorporated* many interesting and relevant personal anecdotes in his presentation.

incorporated (ĭn kôr′ pə rā tĭd) means:
a.   combined; introduced as a part of the whole
b.   borrowed; duplicated
c.   formed into an organized legal unit
d.   described fully

_____   **19.** Most rock dances were *improvisational* and did not require dancers to learn a series of complicated steps.

The beautiful speech Richard gave at his brother's wedding was completely *improvisational*—no script, no notes, and no memorization!

improvisational (ĭm prŏv ĭ zā′ shən əl) means:
a.   simple; uncomplicated
b.   requiring much effort
c.   created from whatever materials are at hand
d.   invented or performed with little or no preparation

_____   **20.** Through the 1990s, in alternative and punk clubs, slam dancing and the mosh pit were an *integral* part of the scene.

For people who love to cook, eat, and entertain, the kitchen is an *integral* part of a house.

integral (ĭn′ tĭ grəl, ĭn tĕg′ rəl) means:
a.   innovative
b.   essential or necessary for completeness
c.   difficult to understand; complex
d.   typical; ordinary

SELECTION 7.2

Reading Skills Application

Directions: These items test your ability to *apply* certain reading skills. You may not have studied all of the skills yet, so some items will serve as a preview. Write each answer in the space provided.

_____ **21.** What is the definition of the term *rock* as it is used in paragraph 1?

    a.   electronic guitar music with a powerful beat

    b.   vocal music with a hard, driving beat, often featuring electric guitar accompaniment and heavily amplified sound

    c.   music with electronic effects, often with nonwestern and "classical" instruments

    d.   music characterized by pounding drums and unrestrained guitars played at peak volume

_____ **22.** Which of the following best expresses the main idea of paragraph 19?

    a.   Rock songs often reflected the trends in American life.

    b.   Young people quickly adopted the longer hair styles and casual dress popularized by rock stars.

    c.   Rock songs tended to be more sexually explicit than those of the sentimental love songs of the 1930s and 1940s.

    d.   Rock performers often sang about the war in Vietnam, experiences associated with drugs, and the struggle for human rights.

_____ **23.** The author organizes the information in paragraphs 2–15 using which of the following patterns?

    a.   list

    b.   comparison-contrast

    c.   sequence

    d.   definition

_____ **24.** Which of the following statements from the selection represents an opinion rather than a fact?

    a.   Female rock performers included Pat Benatar, Tina Turner, Madonna, Alanis Morissette, Sheryl Crow, Queen Latifah, Shania Twain, and Ani DiFranco.

    b.   During the 1980s and 1990s, women performers had a powerful impact on rock.

    c.   The range of musical styles performed by female rockers extended from pop and soul to funk, new wave, country rock, and heavy metal.

    d.   Female rockers played their own instruments and wrote their own songs.

_____ **25.** Two trends in rock music at the end of the 20th century were:

    a.   the use of elements of folk music and lyrics dealing with war and social injustice.

    b.   the influence of British rockers and nonwestern music.

    c. the emergence of Latino artists who incorporated pan-Latin influences in their music and crossover artists from the world of country music.

    d. the use of lyrics about lifestyles that were less inhibited and less materialistic.

SELECTION **7.2**

Music Appreciation

(continued)

Respond in Writing

Directions: Refer to the selection as needed to answer the essay-type questions below. (Your instructor may direct you to work collaboratively with other students on one or more items. Each group member should be able to explain *all* of the group's answers.)

1. This selection discusses several ways that rock music differed from the music of the 1920s, 1930s, and 1940s and also describes other ways that rock music was different from other types of music. List several characteristics that made rock music unique.

_____

_____

_____

_____

_____

_____

_____

_____

_____

_____

_____

_____

_____

2. College professors often ask students to prepare brief presentations on textbook material and to share these presentations in class. Preparing a presentation gives students practice in summarizing and organizing material, as well as practice in public speaking. Assume you have been asked to give a short presentation on "Musical Styles, Artists, Songs, and Dances from the 1950s through the 1990s." To prepare for this presentation, complete the chart below by summarizing the information on pages 483–89. (Note how each row of this chart could be presented on a separate PowerPoint slide.)

SELECTION 7.2

	MUSICAL STYLES	ARTISTS, SONGS, AND DANCES
1950s		
1960s		
1970s		
1980s		
1990s		

3. This selection discusses many musical styles and dances that were popular in the 50s, 60s, 70s, 80s, and 90s, but does not list current ones. What musical styles and dances can you name that became popular since 2000 or ones that are popular *today*? Use your favorite search engine such as Google to Yahoo! to find the names of current musical styles and the names of artists associated with each style.

	MUSICAL STYLES	ARTISTS, SONGS, AND DANCES
2000 to present		

4. **Overall main idea.** What is the overall main idea the author wants the reader to understand about the development of rock music? Answer this question in one sentence. Be sure to include the topic (*rock music*) and the phrase "developed from" in your overall main idea sentence.

_____

_____

_____

_____

SELECTION **7.3**

Psychology

Reactions to Impending Death

From *Essentials of Psychology*
by Dennis Coon

Prepare Yourself to Read

Directions: Do these exercises *before* you read Selection 7.3.

1. First, read and think about the title. What do you already know about dying people's reactions to impending death?

   _____

   _____

   _____

   _____

2. Next, complete your preview by reading the following:
       Introduction (in *italics*)
       First paragraph (paragraph 1)
       Headings
       First sentence of each paragraph
       Words in **bold print** and *italics*
       Last paragraph (paragraph 16)

   On the basis of your preview, what does this selection seem to be about?

   _____

   _____

   _____

   _____

3. **Build your vocabulary as you read.** If you discover an unfamiliar word or key term as you read the selection, try to determine its meaning by using context clues.

Internet Resources

Read More about This Topic Online

Use a search engine, such as Google or Yahoo!, to expand your existing knowledge about this topic *before* you read the selection or to learn more about it *afterward*. If you are unfamiliar with conducting Internet searches, read pages 25–26 on Boolean searches. You can also use Wikipedia, the free online encyclopedia, at www.wikipedia.com. Keep in mind that when you visit any website, it is a good idea to evaluate the site and the information it contains. Ask yourself questions such as "Who sponsors this website?" and "Is the information it contains up to date?"

SELECTION **7.3**

SELECTION 7.3: **REACTIONS TO IMPENDING DEATH**

"It's not that I'm afraid to die; I just don't want to be there when it happens," Woody Allen once quipped. Although he was making a joke, his comment reflects our culture's squeamish attitude toward death. Kahlil Gibran, author of The Prophet, *had a very different view: "For life and death are one, even as the river and the sea are one."*

Because the topic of death makes many people in our society uncomfortable, it tends not to be discussed. Yet death is a reality, the natural, inevitable end of life, and not talking about it only makes death more difficult for those who are dying and for the survivors who will grieve for them. Fortunately, extensive, thorough, and thoughtful research on terminally ill patients' reactions to their impending deaths was done by Dr. Elisabeth Kübler-Ross. We now know that certain reactions are normal and predictable. Kübler-Ross's findings have proved extraordinarily helpful to the terminally ill, to those who love them, to others who provide them emotional support, and to those who provide their health care.

In this selection from a psychology textbook, the author presents Kübler-Ross's findings, as well as helpful information on hospices and bereavement. This selection will provide you with valuable insights that will benefit you in a variety of ways.

1   A direct account of emotional responses to death comes from the work of Elisabeth Kübler-Ross (1975). Kübler-Ross is a **thanatologist** (one who studies death) who spent hundreds of hours at the bedsides of the terminally ill. She found that dying persons tend to display several emotional reactions as they prepare for death. Five basic reactions are described here:

1. **Denial and isolation.** A typical first reaction to impending death is an attempt to deny its reality and to isolate oneself from information confirming that death is really going to occur. Initially the person may be sure that "It's all a mistake," that lab reports or X-rays have been mixed up, or that a physician is in error. This may proceed to attempts to ignore or avoid any reminder of the situation.

2. **Anger.** Many dying individuals feel anger and ask, "Why me?" As they face the ultimate threat of having everything they value stripped away, their anger can spill over into rage or envy toward those who will continue living. Even good friends may temporarily evoke anger because their health is envied.

3. **Bargaining.** In another common reaction the terminally ill bargain with themselves or with God. The dying person thinks, "Just let me live a little longer and I'll do anything to earn it." Individuals may bargain for time by trying to be "good" ("I'll never smoke again"), by righting past wrongs, or by praying that if they are granted more time they will dedicate themselves to their religion.

Annotation Practice Exercises

Directions: For each exercise, use the spaces provided to write:

*   Main idea sentence of the paragraph

*   Authors' pattern for organizing supporting details (writing pattern)

Practice Exercise

*   Main idea sentence of paragraph 1:

_____

_____

_____

*   Writing pattern:

_____

_____

_____

_____

_____

_____

4. **Depression.**   As death draws near and the person begins to recognize that it cannot be prevented, feelings of futility, exhaustion, and deep depression may set in. The person recognizes that he or she will be separated from friends, loved ones, and the familiar routines of life, and this causes a profound sadness.

5. **Acceptance.**   If death is not sudden, many people manage to come to terms with dying and accept it calmly. The person who accepts death is neither happy nor sad, but at peace with the inevitable. Acceptance usually signals that the struggle with death has been resolved. The need to talk about death ends, and silent companionship from others is frequently all that is desired.

2   Not all terminally ill persons display all these reactions, nor do they always occur in this order. Individual styles of dying vary greatly, according to emotional maturity, religious beliefs, age, education, the attitudes of relatives, and so forth. Generally, there does tend to be a movement from initial shock, denial, and anger toward eventual acceptance of the situation. However, some people who seem to have accepted death may die angry and raging against the inevitable. Conversely, the angry fighter may let go of the struggle and die peacefully. In general, one's approach to dying will mirror his or her style of living.

3   It is best not to think of Kübler-Ross's list as a fixed series of stages to go through in order. It is an even bigger mistake to assume that someone who does not show all the listed emotional reactions is somehow deviant or immature. Rather, the list describes typical and appropriate reactions to impending death. It is also interesting to note that many of the same reactions accompany any major loss, be it divorce, loss of a home due to fire, death of a pet, or loss of a job.

As cultural rituals, funerals encourage a release of emotion and provide a sense of closure for survivors, who must come to terms with the death of a loved one.

Question: How can I make use of this information?

4   First, it can help both the dying individual and survivors to recognize and cope with periods of depression, anger, denial, and bargaining. Second, it helps to realize that close friends or relatives of the dying person may feel many of the same emotions before or after the person's death because they, too, are facing a loss.

5   Perhaps the most important thing to recognize is that the dying person may have a need to share feelings with others and to discuss death openly. Too often, the dying person feels isolated and separated from others by the wall of silence erected by doctors, nurses, and family members. Adults tend to "freeze up" with a dying person, saying things such as, "I don't know how to deal with this."

6   Understanding what the dying person is going through may make it easier to offer support at this important time. A simple willingness to be with the person and to honestly share his or her feelings can help bring dignity, acceptance, and meaning to death. In many communities these goals have been aided by the hospice movement.

Practice Exercise

• Main idea sentence of paragraph 6:

_____

_____

_____

• Writing pattern:

_____

_____

_____

_____

SELECTION 7.3

Hospice

7   A **hospice** is basically a hospital for the terminally ill. The goal of the hospice movement is to improve the quality of life in the person's final days. Hospices typically offer support, guidance, and companionship from volunteers, other patients, staff, clergy, and counselors. Pleasant surroundings, an atmosphere of informality, and a sense of continued living help patients cope with their illnesses. Unlimited around-the-clock visits are permitted by relatives, friends, children, and even pets. Patients receive constant attention, play games, make day trips, have predinner cocktails if they choose, and enjoy entertainment. In short, life goes on for them.

8   At present most larger cities in the United States have hospices. They have been so successful that they are likely to be added to many more communities. At the same time, treatment for the terminally ill has dramatically improved in hospitals—largely as a result of pioneering efforts in the hospice movement.

Bereavement

9   After a friend or relative has died, a period of grief typically follows. Grief is a natural and normal reaction to death as survivors adjust to loss.

10   Grief tends to follow a predictable pattern. Grief usually begins with a period of **shock** or numbness. For a brief time the bereaved remain in a dazed state in which they may show little emotion. Most find it extremely difficult to accept the reality of their loss. This phase usually ends by the time of the funeral, which unleashes tears and bottled-up feelings of despair.

11   Initial shock is followed by sharp **pangs of grief.** These are episodes of painful yearning for the dead person and, sometimes, anguished outbursts of anger. During this period the wish to have the dead person back is intense. Often, mourners continue to think of the dead person as alive. They may hear his or her voice and see the deceased vividly in dreams. During this period, agitated distress alternates with silent despair, and suffering is acute.

12   The first powerful reactions of grief gradually give way to weeks or months of **apathy, dejection,** and **depression.** The person faces a new emotional landscape with a large gap that cannot be filled. Life seems to lose much of its meaning, and a sense of futility dominates the person's outlook. The mourner is usually able to resume work or other activities after 2 or 3 weeks. However, insomnia, loss of energy and appetite, and similar signs of depression may continue.

13   Little by little, the bereaved person accepts what cannot be changed and makes a new beginning. Pangs of grief may still occur, but they are less severe and less frequent. Memories of the dead person, though still painful, now include positive images and nostalgic pleasure. At this point, the person can be said to be moving toward **resolution.**

Practice Exercise

- Main idea sentence of paragraph 7:

  _____

  _____

  _____

  _____

- Writing pattern:

  _____

  _____

Practice Exercise

- Main idea sentence of paragraph 10:

  _____

  _____

  _____

  _____

- Writing pattern:

  _____

  _____

  _____

  _____

  _____

14   As was true of approaching death, individual reactions to grief vary considerably. In general, however, a month or two typically passes before the more intense stages of grief have run their course. As you can see, grief allows survivors to discharge their anguish and to prepare to go on living.

Question: Is it true that suppressing grief leads to more problems later?

15   It has long been assumed that suppressing grief may later lead to more severe and lasting depression. However, there is little evidence to support this idea. A lack of intense grief does not usually predict later problems. Bereaved persons should work through their grief at their own pace and in their own way—without worrying about whether they are grieving too much or too little. Some additional suggestions for coping with grief follow.

Coping with Grief
- Face the loss directly and do not isolate yourself.
- Discuss your feelings with relatives and friends.
- Do not block out your feelings with drugs or alcohol.
- Allow grief to progress naturally; neither hurry nor suppress it.

16   The subject of death brings us full circle in the cycle of life.

Source: From Dennis Coon, *Essentials of Psychology: Exploration and Application*, 5e, pp. 136–138. © 1991 Wadsworth, a part of Cengage Learning, Inc. Reproduced by permission. www.cengage.com/permissions.

SELECTION **7.3**

Psychology
(continued)

Reading Selection Quiz

This quiz has several parts. Your instructor may assign some or all of them.

Comprehension

Directions: Use the information in the selection to answer each item below. You may refer to the selection as you answer the questions. Write each answer in the space provided.

True or False

_____ **1.** Elisabeth Kübler-Ross found that every terminally ill patient displays five basic reactions to dying.

_____ **2.** Kübler-Ross's list of reactions represents a fixed series of stages.

_____ **3.** Many of the reactions outlined by Kübler-Ross also accompany major losses such as divorce, loss of a job, and loss of a home in a fire.

_____ **4.** The primary goal of the hospice movement is to provide advanced medical treatment for the dying person.

_____ **5.** The hospice movement has had no effect on the quality of care that terminally ill patients receive in hospitals.

_____ **6.** Patients in a hospice may have a predinner cocktail if they choose to.

Multiple-Choice

_____ **7.** A thanatologist is one who studies:
  a. hospital care.
  b. diseases.
  c. death.
  d. psychology.

_____ **8.** The author states that individual styles of dying are influenced by all the following factors *except* the:
  a. attitude of relatives.
  b. gender of the dying person.
  c. age of the dying person.
  d. emotional maturity of the dying person.

_____ **9.** Which of the following does *not* illustrate the value of Kübler-Ross's findings?
  a. We can assume that someone who does not exhibit all the emotional reactions described by Kübler-Ross is immature.
  b. The dying person who is familiar with Kübler-Ross's theory may be able to recognize, cope with, and discuss the various stages.

c.   As survivors, we can better understand and support the terminally ill person.

d.   Doctors and nurses may have a better understanding of the feelings of the terminally ill person.

_____ **10.** Hospice care is characterized by:

a.   restricted visits.

b.   a hospital-like environment.

c.   day trips, entertainment, and visits by the family (even pets), if the patient is able.

d.   care, guidance, and support by doctors and staff only.

Vocabulary in Context

Directions: For each item below, use context clues to deduce the meaning of the *italicized* word. Be sure the answer you choose makes sense in both sentences. Write each answer in the space provided.

_____ **11.** As death draws near and the person begins to recognize that it cannot be prevented, feelings of *futility,* exhaustion, and deep depression may set in.

When they saw how vast the forest fire was, the firefighters realized the *futility* of their efforts to put it out and simply tried instead to prevent it from spreading.

futility (fyo͞o tĭl′ ĭ tē) means:

a.   reasonableness; sensibleness

b.   uselessness; lack of useful results

c.   cheerfulness

d.   helpfulness

_____ **12.** Acceptance usually signals that the struggle with death has been *resolved.*

My parents always *resolved* their problems by discussing them.

resolved (rĭ zōlvd′) means:

a.   found a solution to; settled

b.   ignored; paid no attention to

c.   made known publicly

d.   kept secret

_____ **13.** It is an even bigger mistake to assume that someone who does not show all the listed emotional reactions is somehow *deviant* or immature.

Children who are abused often exhibit *deviant* behavior later in their lives.

deviant (dē′ vē ənt) means:

a.   kind; gentle

b.   illegal; against the law

    c.   difficult to diagnose

    d.   differing from accepted standards

14. Rather, the list describes typical and appropriate reactions to *impending* death.

We knew from the dark clouds that the *impending* storm could hit at any minute.

impending (ĭm pĕn′ dĭng) means:

    a.   about to take place

    b.   severe; harsh

    c.   delayed; later than expected

    d.   soothing

15. For a brief time the *bereaved* remain in a dazed state in which they may show little emotion.

The *bereaved* widow of the police officer received hundreds of letters expressing sympathy over the loss of her courageous husband.

bereaved (bĭ rēvd′) means:

    a.   peaceful; serene

    b.   young; childlike

    c.   suffering the loss of a loved one

    d.   suffering from a serious illness

16. This phase usually ends by the time of the funeral, which *unleashes* tears and bottled-up feelings of despair.

When a hurricane *unleashes* its fury, it can cause millions of dollars of damage.

unleashes (ŭn lēsh′ əz) means:

    a.   releases

    b.   controls

    c.   calms; soothes

    d.   prevents

17. Initial shock is followed by sharp *pangs* of grief.

We had not eaten since morning, and our hunger *pangs* increased when we smelled the delicious aroma coming from the campfire that night.

pangs (păngz) means:

    a.   strong desires

    b.   strong, sudden sensations

    c.   sad, despondent feelings

    d.   strong dislikes

_____ **18.** During this period, agitated distress alternates with silent despair, and suffering is *acute.*

Everyone in the search party felt *acute* relief when the missing child was found.

acute (ə kyo͞ot′) means:

a. intense

b. mild

c. moderate

d. not noticeable

_____ **19.** The first powerful reactions of grief gradually give way to weeks or months of apathy, *dejection,* and depression.

We could tell from their *dejection* that they had lost the final game of the baseball playoffs.

dejection (dĭ jĕkt′ shən) means:

a. agitation; nervousness

b. energy; liveliness

c. discouragement or low spirits

d. happiness; elation

_____ **20.** Life seems to lose much of its meaning, and a sense of futility *dominates* the person's outlook.

The rumor of the president's resignation *dominates* the media this week.

dominates (dŏm′ ə nāts) means:

a. controls or occupies

b. treats harshly

c. treats as unimportant

d. is excluded from

SELECTION **7.3**

Psychology

(continued)

Reading Skills Application

Directions: These items test your ability to *apply* certain reading skills. You may not have studied all of the skills yet, so some items will serve as a preview. Write each answer in the space provided.

_____ **21.** The main idea of paragraph 6 is best expressed by which of the following sentences from this selection?

a. A simple willingness to be with a dying person and to honestly share his feelings can help bring dignity, acceptance, and meaning to death.

b. In many communities, these goals have been aided by the hospice movement.

SELECTION 7.3

    c.   Understanding what the dying person is going through may make it easier for you to offer support at this important time.

    d.   The hospice movement was created to help terminally ill people die with dignity.

22. Which of the following is an accurate assessment of the author's credibility?

    a.   The author has little credibility because he presents only his personal experience.

    b.   The author has limited credibility because he presents only theories, not facts.

    c.   The author has credibility because he is a renowned thanatologist.

    d.   The author has credibility because he presents the results of research studies.

23. What is the meaning of *discharge* as it is used in paragraph 14?

    a.   to dismiss

    b.   to empty

    c.   to survive

    d.   to be relieved of

24. Which of the following does the author intend as his primary audience?

    a.   anyone who is going through bereavement

    b.   anyone who might at some point become terminally ill or deal with someone who is terminally ill

    c.   anyone who is in denial after being diagnosed with a terminal illness

    d.   anyone who works in a hospice

25. Which of the following assumptions underlies the author's main argument?

    a.   The process of grieving can be speeded up if a person understands the process.

    b.   Knowing the typical reactions to impending death allows those who deal with the terminally ill to assess whether they are going through the appropriate stages.

    c.   The more people understand about impending death, loss, and bereavement, the more likely they are to be able to cope and to help others.

    d.   All people eventually die, so it is important to reassure the terminally ill that they are not unique or alone in what they are feeling.

Respond in Writing

Directions: Refer to the selection as needed to answer the essay-type questions below. (Your instructor may direct you to work collaboratively with other students on one or more items. Each group member should be able to explain *all* of the group's answers.)

1. The thanatologist Elisabeth Kübler-Ross found five basic reactions to death (or any major loss). Give examples of how each of these reactions might manifest itself in a person's behavior. You may add examples of your own to any the author gives. (For instance, one possible behavior accompanying the first emotional reaction is avoiding calling to get results of medical tests.)

Emotional reaction	Possible behaviors accompanying the reaction
Denial and isolation	
Anger	
Bargaining	
Depression	
Acceptance	

2. What are at least two important ways a person could benefit from knowing about the five reactions Kübler-Ross describes?

_____

_____

_____

_____

_____

_____

_____

_____

_____

3. How does a hospice differ from a hospital? In your answer, use words that signal contrasts (see page 432 for these words).

_____

_____

_____

_____

_____

_____

_____

_____

_____

_____

_____

_____

4. With the exception of the "bargaining stage," there is a predictable pattern of grief, just as there is a predictable pattern of reactions to impending death. Review this comparison (presented at the end of the selection) and complete the table on page 511. (To get you started, the answers to be inserted opposite _Denial and isolation_ are "shock or numbness" and "difficulty accepting the reality of the loss." Write them on the first two lines provided.)

Reactions to death or loss	Reactions to grief
Denial and isolation	_____
	_____
Anger	_____
	_____
Bargaining	(No equivalent reaction)
Depression	_____
Acceptance	_____

5. Think of a situation in which you or someone you know experienced a significant loss (such as the loss of a valued job, divorce, loss of a home through fire or a natural disaster, or the death of a pet). Describe any of the reactions mentioned in the selection that you or the person who experienced the loss went through.

    _____

    _____

    _____

    _____

6. In his best-selling book *Tuesdays with Morrie,* the journalist Mitch Albom chronicles the final months of his favorite college professor's life. Morrie Schwartz, a sociology professor, was dying from amyotrophic lateral sclerosis (ALS), a terminal illness that gradually moves up the body, destroying the nerves and eventually rendering a person unable to move, swallow, or breathe. Morrie tells Mitch, "Death ends a life, not a relationship" and "Learn how to die and you learn how to live." Take one of these "lessons" of Morrie's and explain why you agree or disagree with it.

    _____

    _____

    _____

    _____

7. **Overall main idea.** What is the overall main idea the author wants the reader to understand about reactions to impending death? Answer this question in one sentence. Be sure that your overall main idea sentence includes the topic (*reactions to impending death*) and tells the overall most important point about it.

    _____

    _____

    _____

    _____

SELECTION 7.3

CHAPTER 8

Reading Critically

In this chapter, you will learn the answers to these questions:

- What is critical reading?

- How can I determine an author's purpose?

- How can I determine an author's intended audience?

- How can I determine an author's point of view or bias?

- How can I determine an author's tone and intended meaning?

SKILLS

What Is Critical Reading?

Critical Reading Skills

- Determining an Author's Purpose and Intended Audience
- Determining an Author's Point of View, Tone, and Intended Meaning

A Word about Standardized Reading Tests: Critical Reading

CHECKPOINT: READING CRITICALLY

CREATING YOUR SUMMARY

Developing Chapter Review Cards

TEST YOUR UNDERSTANDING: READING CRITICALLY, PART 1

TEST YOUR UNDERSTANDING: READING CRITICALLY, PART 2

READINGS

Selection 8.1   "Prologue"
from *The Illustrated Man*
by *Ray Bradbury* (Literature)

Selection 8.2   "Think Before You Speak: Public Speaking in a Multicultural World"
from *The Art of Public Speaking*
by *Stephen E. Lucas* (Speech Communication)

Selection 8.3   Two Excerpts
from *The Things They Carried*
by *Tim O'Brien* (Literature)

What we see depends mainly on what we look for.
John Lubbock

The end of reading is not more books, but more life.
Holbrook Jackson

Where all think alike, no one thinks very much.
Walter Lippmann

Once you have learned to ask questions—relevant and appropriate and substantial questions—you have learned how to learn and no one can keep you from learning whatever you want or need to know.
Neil Postman and Charles Weingartner

WHAT IS CRITICAL READING?

Going *beyond* basic comprehension to gain insights as you read is called **critical reading.** Whenever you read, of course, you should identify basic information: topic, main idea, and supporting details. However, to gain greater understanding, you will need to go beyond these basic elements.

Reading critically requires you to ask certain questions *after* you read a passage and think carefully about what you have read. It requires you to understand implied (suggested) and figurative (nonliteral) meanings in addition to literal (stated) meanings. As you will learn in Chapter 9, this also means taking time to reread and reconsider an author's message so that you can make careful evaluations and judgments about what you have read.

critical reading

Gaining insights and understanding that go beyond comprehending the topic, main idea, and supporting details. Critical reading is also referred to as *critical reasoning.*

CRITICAL READING SKILLS

These important critical reading skills are presented in this chapter:

- Determining an author's purpose (the author's reason for writing)
- Determining an author's intended audience (whom the author had in mind as his or her readers)
- Determining an author's point of view (the author's position on an issue)
- Determining an author's tone and intended meaning (a way an author reveals his or her attitude toward the topic)

Because these skills are *interrelated,* they are presented together in this chapter. As you will soon discover, an author's *purpose* causes him or her to present certain facts and opinions, and to use a certain *tone* to convey a *point of view* and an *intended meaning* to an *intended audience.*

515

Reading critically involves asking yourself certain questions *after* you read a passage and thinking carefully about what you have read.

Determining an Author's Purpose and Intended Audience

purpose

An author's reason for writing.

Authors write for specific purposes. An author's **purpose** is simply his or her reason for writing. The author's purpose may be to *inform,* to *instruct,* to *entertain,* or to *persuade* you to believe something or take a certain action. Most textbook authors write for the purpose of informing (giving information, explaining) or instructing (teaching readers how to do something). However, some authors, such as movie critics, newspaper editors, and political writers, write to give their opinion and to persuade readers to accept this opinion. Finally, other writers, such as humorists or certain newspaper columnists, write for the purpose of entertaining. They may entertain readers, for example, with humorous stories or with enjoyable descriptions.

Sometimes an author announces his or her purpose. For example, the author of a biology textbook might simply tell readers, "The purpose of this section is to define and explain the two types of cell division." At other times, the author may feel the purpose is obvious and assume you can infer it.

To determine an author's purpose, think about the words he or she has used. Authors often choose certain words precisely because those words can direct or influence the reader's thinking.

For example, when authors want to *inform* you of important information or *explain* something, they use phrases such as:

> The important point is . . .
> Be sure you know . . .
> It is important to understand . . .
> Remember that . . .

When authors want to *instruct,* or *teach* you how to do something, they use phrases such as:

> Follow these directions to . . .
> The steps below will enable you to . . .
> These instructions tell how to . . .
> This is the procedure for . . .

When authors want to *persuade* you to do something or *convince* you to believe something, they use phrases such as:

> The only intelligent choice, then, is . . .
> Any reasonable person will agree that . . .
> Only an uninformed person would believe that . . .
> Those who understand the issue will certainly agree . . .

When authors are writing to *entertain* or *amuse* readers, they use phrases such as:

> You'll never believe what happened to me when I . . .
> The funny thing about . . .
> And then the oddest thing happened . . .
> I'll never forget the day I . . .

Noticing certain words and phrases the author has used is one way to determine the author's purpose. Another way is to examine whether the author presents both sides of a controversial issue. Check to see whether important information has been left out: Authors frequently leave out information that does not support their point of view. Keep in mind that although an author may appear to be neutral on an issue, his or her real purpose may be to persuade you to support one side. It is important to understand an author's purpose to keep from being manipulated—unknowingly influenced—by the author.

Remember, then: To read critically, you must determine the author's purpose by asking yourself, "Why did the author write this?"

Authors also have specific audiences in mind when they write. An author's **intended audience** consists of the people the author has in mind as readers. The intended audience will be a particular individual, a specific group, or the general public. For instance, a psychologist writing a textbook may assume the audience will be students taking an introductory psychology course. The psychologist will have these students in mind while writing, and this will shape decisions about the material to include and the level of difficulty. "Who did the author intend to read this?" is a question you as a critical reader should always ask yourself.

Comprehension-Monitoring Question for Determining an Author's Purpose

Why did the author write this?

intended audience

People an author has in mind as his or her readers.

Sometimes an author will state who the intended audience is, but when you must determine an author's intended audience, examine these three things: (1) the topic being discussed (Is it of *technical* or of *general interest*?), (2) the level of language used (Is it *simple, sophisticated,* or *specialized*?), and (3) the purpose for writing (Is it to *instruct, inform, persuade,* or *entertain*?). These three things should help you answer the question "Who did the author intend to read this?"

The following paragraph is about using humor to deal with stress. After you read it, ask yourself, "Why did the author write this?" and "Who did the author intend to read this?"

It's true. You really can laugh your stress away. In fact, humor is one of the best stress busters around. You can't belly laugh and feel bad at the same time. So, if you're caught in a situation you can't escape or change (a traffic jam, a slow line at the bank, a long wait at the doctor's office, or a crying baby at the table next to you at a restaurant, for example), then humor may be the healthiest form of temporary stress release possible.

What is the author's purpose?

_____

_____

_____

Who is the author's intended audience?

_____

Stop and Annotate

Go back to the excerpt above. Determine the author's purpose and intended audience, and write your responses in the spaces provided.

In this paragraph, the author's purpose is simply to *inform* you that humor can be an effective way to temporarily reduce stress. You can see that the author uses simple language and short sentences. Notice that he uses informal language: *stress busters* and *belly laugh.* He also includes several everyday examples of potentially stressful situations. Because his topic requires no special prior knowledge and his approach is uncomplicated, you can assume that the author's intended audience is *the general public.* Practically anyone could understand and benefit from the information he presents.

Now read this passage from a business communication textbook to determine the authors' purpose and the audience they had in mind.

Think about the people you know. Which of them would you call successful communicators? What do these people have in common? Chances are, the individuals on your list share five qualities:

- **Perception.** They are able to predict how their message will be received. They anticipate your

What is the authors' purpose?

_____

_____

reaction and shape the message accordingly. They read your response correctly and constantly adjust to correct any misunderstanding.

- **Precision.** They include specific definitions and helpful examples. They create a "meeting of the minds." When they finish expressing themselves, you share the same mental picture.

- **Credibility.** They are believable. You have faith in the substance of their message. You trust their information and their intentions.

- **Control.** They shape your response. Depending on their purpose, they can make you laugh or cry, calm down, change your mind, or take action.

- **Congeniality.** They maintain friendly, pleasant relations with the audience. Regardless of whether you agree with them, good communicators command your respect and goodwill. You are willing to work with them again, despite your differences.

Source: Adapted from Courtland Bovée and John Thill, *Business Communication Today,* 4e, p. 44. Copyright © 1995 by The McGraw-Hill Companies, Inc. Reprinted with permission of The McGraw-Hill Companies, Inc.

_____

_____

_____

_____

_____

Stop and Annotate

Go back to the preceding excerpt. Determine the authors' purpose and intended audience, and write your responses in the spaces provided.

In this excerpt, the authors' purpose is also to *inform*. They list specific elements that characterize good communicators and describe how these people interact with others. The authors' intended audience is a particular group of people: *students in a business communications course* or *adults who want to know about characteristics of effective communication.*

The following passage is from a health textbook whose purpose and audience are easy to determine. The authors use simple, factual language to describe the Heimlich maneuver, the procedure to use when someone is choking.

The Heimlich Maneuver

If a person who seems to be choking on food or a foreign object can speak, do not interfere with that individual's attempt to cough up the object. If the person is unable to speak, it is appropriate to provide emergency care by using the Heimlich maneuver. Stand behind the victim and place both arms around his or her waist. Grasp one fist with the other hand and place the thumb side of the fist against the victim's abdomen, slightly above the navel and below the rib cage. Press your fist into the victim's abdomen with a quick inward and upward thrust. Repeat this procedure until the object is dislodged. The Heimlich maneuver should not be used with infants under one year of age.

What is the authors' purpose?

_____

_____

_____

Who is the authors' intended audience?

_____

_____

_____

_____

Source: Marvin R. Levy, Mark Dignan, and Janet H. Shirreffs, *Targeting Wellness: The Core,* pp. 284–85. Copyright © 1992 by The McGraw-Hill Companies, Inc. Reprinted with permission of The McGraw-Hill Companies, Inc.

Stop and Annotate

Go back to the excerpt above. Determine the authors' purpose and intended audience, and write your responses in the spaces provided.

The purpose of the passage is to *instruct*. The paragraph describes the steps for performing the Heimlich maneuver. The intended audience is *students in a health course* or *people who are interested in learning how to perform the Heimlich maneuver.*

Here is a short paragraph from an article titled "The Time Message." After you have read it, ask yourself, "Why did the author write this?" and "Who did the author intend to read this?"

Stop and Annotate

Go back to the excerpt above. Determine the author's purpose and intended audience, and write your responses in the spaces provided.

Time is dangerous. If you don't control it, it will control you! If you don't make it work for you, it will work against you. You must become the master of time, not the servant. In other words, as a college student, time management will be your number-one problem.

What is the author's purpose?

_____

_____

Who is the author's intended audience?

_____

Source: E. N. Chapman, "The Time Message," in Frank Christ, Ed., *SR/SE Resource Book,* Chicago: SRA, 1969, p. 3.

Although the author informs you about the importance of controlling time, his primary purpose is to *persuade* you to deal with this potentially "dangerous" problem. The author also used an exclamation point in the second sentence to emphasize the importance of dealing with time so that you are not controlled by it. The author's intended audience is clearly stated in the last sentence of the paragraph: the *college student,* especially one who has not yet mastered time management.

Here is a paragraph written for a completely different purpose. It is from the best-selling memoir *Having Our Say: The Delany Sisters' First 100 Years.* In this excerpt, 103-year-old Bessie Delany describes her nearly fatal bout with typhoid fever when she was 15 years old.

When I got out of the hospital, I looked like death. They had cut off my hair, real short, and I weighed next to nothing. I could not get enough to eat. Mama was so worried that she fixed a small basket of fruit each morning for me to carry with me all day, so I could eat whenever I wanted. For a long time I was on crutches, and I was not expected to recover fully. They used to say that typhoid fever left its mark on people. Well, nothing has shown up yet, so I guess I'm in the clear!

What is the authors' purpose?

_____

_____

Who is the authors' intended audience?

_____

Source: From Sarah Delany, Elizabeth Delany with Amy Hill Hearth, *Having Our Say: The Delany Sisters' First 100 Years,* Kodansha America, Inc., 1993, p. 83. Reprinted by permission of Kodansha America, Inc.

Stop and Annotate

Go back to the excerpt above. Determine the authors' purpose and intended audience, and write your responses in the spaces provided.

As the humor in the last sentence suggests, the purpose of this paragraph is to *entertain* you. At 103 years of age, Bessie Delany "guesses" she's "in the clear" and no longer needs to worry about any aftereffects from typhoid fever in childhood. The intended audience is *the general public,* who would enjoy reading about a centenarian's recollection of her childhood.

Remember, part of critical reading involves asking yourself these two questions in order to determine the author's purpose and intended audience: "Why did the author write this?" and "Who did the author intend to read this?"

EXERCISE 1

This paragraph comes from a health textbook:

Is it possible for individuals to make a difference in climate change? Yes. In fact, some believe we have moved past the time when we can depend on experts to solve environmental problems such as climate change. Instead, a broader understanding of environmental issues by the general public is needed, along with a willingness to make different choices in everyday life. Of course, government at every level is needed to lead the way, but there are hundreds of actions each of us can and should take to

(Continued on next page)

reduce our impact on the environment and therefore not contribute to global warming. Here are just a few:

- Drive less. Walk, bike, and take public transportation more.
- Use less energy. Use less heat, hot water, and air conditioning, and turn off lights and electronic devices, including power strips, when not in use.
- Buy energy-efficient products, from cars to appliances to compact fluorescent light bulbs.
- Eat responsibly. Buy locally grown foods to reduce the amount of fuel needed to transport food, as well as air pollution and greenhouse gas emissions. Eating organically keeps petroleum-based pesticides and chemicals out of the food chain and water supply.
- Measure your personal carbon footprint with an online calculator, and learn what you can do to reduce it.

Source: Adapted from Paul M. Insel and Walton T. Roth, *Connect Core Concepts in Health,* 12e, p. 16. Copyright © 2012 by The McGraw-Hill Companies, Inc. Reprinted with permission of The McGraw-Hill Companies, Inc.

Write the *main idea sentence:* _____

_____

_____

What is the *authors' primary purpose?*

_____

_____

Who is the *authors' intended audience?*

_____

Determining an Author's Point of View, Tone, and Intended Meaning

point of view

An author's position (opinion) on an issue.

Point of view is also known as the *author's argument* or the *author's bias.*

author's bias

The side of an issue an author favors; an author's preference for one side of an issue over the other.

Point of view refers to an author's position on an issue. In other words, an author's point of view is his or her opinion about that topic. It is the position he or she hopes to convince you to accept or believe. An author's point of view is also known as the *author's argument* or the *author's bias.*

Even authors who are experts in their fields do not agree on every topic and issue. Therefore, it is important that you determine what each author's point of view is. For example, one author's point of view might be "Gun control is necessary if we are to have a safe society." The point of view of an author with the opposite bias would be "Gun control would only make society less safe." A neutral point of view would be "Gun control has both advantages and disadvantages."

Notice the use of the word *bias* in the preceding paragraph. In everyday conversation, people often use *bias* to mean *prejudice:* They mean that a biased person has taken a position without thinking it through and without examining the evidence. In this context, the word *bias* has a negative connotation. However, with regard to written material, an **author's bias** simply represents his or her *preference* for one side of an issue over the other—his or her point of view. (For example, one writer might have a bias for year-round school, while another writer has the opposite bias.) There is nothing wrong with an author having a bias; after all, most thoughtful writers weigh the evidence carefully, and then adopt the point of view that makes the most sense to them. When you read, try to determine whether the author has a bias. In some cases, a bias may cause an author to slant the facts and not be objective.

Sometimes the author states his or her bias or point of view directly. For example, an author might state that he or she has a bias against home schooling. At other times, authors expect you to recognize their bias, on the basis of the information they include (or leave out) and the way they present the information. Consider the following paragraph, in which the author clearly expresses a bias about using a cell phone while driving.

There should be a law against using a cell phone when driving. In spite of what drivers say, they become distracted reaching for the phone, dialing, answering, and texting. The conversation itself can also take their attention away from the road. Suppose a driver gets upset or angry with the caller. In that case, is the driver's full concentration really on the road? Drivers who are busy with their cell phones are involved in more accidents than drivers who do not use cell phones. They cause more accidents that kill and injure not only themselves, but other innocent, unsuspecting drivers. The bumper sticker has it right: "Hang up and drive!"

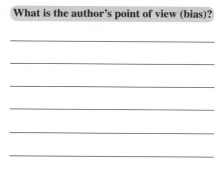

What is the author's point of view (bias)?

_____

_____

_____

_____

_____

_____

Stop and Annotate

Go back to the excerpt above. Determine the author's point of view (bias), and write your response in the spaces provided.

Clearly, this author has a bias against people using cell phones while driving. This author's point of view is that using cell phones when driving is dangerous and should be forbidden by law. (Incidentally, the author's purpose here is to persuade anyone who uses a cell phone when driving to stop doing so and to persuade everyone to support laws against using cell phones when driving. The author's intended audience is the general public, but especially anyone who uses a cell phone when driving.)

By the way, you should be aware of your *own* biases whenever you are reading about a controversial issue. If you have a strong bias on a subject and an author has the opposite bias, you can be tempted to reject the author's point of view without giving it serious consideration. (For example, readers who favor being

Comprehension-Monitoring Question for Determining an Author's Point of View

What is the author's position on this issue?

able to use cell phones while driving might immediately close their minds after reading the first sentence of the sample paragraph above.) Do not let your own bias cause you to automatically reject an author's point of view because it differs from your own.

To determine the author's point of view, critical readers ask, "What is the author's position on this issue?" Look for words that reveal the author's point of view:

Supporting this new policy is *essential* because . . .

The proposed legislation *will benefit* all the citizens of Dallas County because . . .

It is *not in the best interest* of the country to . . .

Voters *should oppose* the state lottery because . . .

tone

Manner of writing (choice of words and style) that reveals an author's attitude toward a topic.

An author's **tone** is a manner of writing that reveals or reflects his or her attitude toward a topic, just as tone of voice reveals a speaker's attitude. When someone is speaking, you can generally tell by the tone whether he or she is serious, sarcastic, sympathetic, enthusiastic, and so forth. To convey a tone, a speaker relies on pitch, volume, and inflection, along with choice of words. For example, if someone says, "I made a C on my biology test," you would need to know the speaker's tone to know whether he or she was excited, relieved, or disappointed.

Authors use tone just as speakers do. Authors, however, must rely on style of writing and choice of words to convey their tone. They select words and writing styles that fit their purposes for writing (to inform, instruct, persuade, or entertain) and their point of view (for example, in favor of or opposed to something). In other words, they use a certain tone (informal, serious, sincere, humorous, etc.) to help convey their intended meaning. You can determine an author's tone by carefully examining his or her choice of words and style of writing. To determine an author's tone, ask yourself, "What do the author's choice of words and style of writing reveal about his or her attitude toward the topic?"

As just noted, choice of words—or *word choice*—is one way authors convey their tone. For example, when describing a politician who did not tell the truth, one writer might use the word *lied* to convey a critical, disapproving, or bitter tone; another author might choose the word *exaggerated* instead to convey a tolerant or even an amused tone. Compare the following two sentences; they contain the same message (taxpayers' money will be used to help the unemployed), but the word choice makes their tone very different:

Comprehension-Monitoring Question for Determining an Author's Tone

What do the author's choice of words and style of writing reveal about his or her attitude toward the topic?

- Once again, the American taxpayers have to foot the bill for those who are too lazy or unmotivated to work.
- Once again, American taxpayers are showing their compassion by helping those who are unable to find employment.

Note the disapproving tone conveyed by the word choice in the first sentence (*foot the bill* and *too lazy or unmotivated to work*). A more positive, compassionate tone is conveyed by the choice of words in the second sentence (*showing their generosity by helping* and *unable to find employment*).

Now consider how an author's *writing style* also conveys a tone. Compare the sentences below. They contain the same message (computer science majors should consider a career in video game design), but the writing style makes their tone quite different:

- Since there will be a significant increase in employment opportunities in the field of video game design, computer science majors would be wise to investigate this fast-growing area.
- Video game design is becoming a real career option, so all you gamers and computer science majors should check it out!

These two sentences present essentially the same information, but the first sentence has a more formal, factual tone. It is the type of sentence you might find in a career brochure or a computer science textbook. In the second sentence, however, the use of the phrase *real career option* and the expression *check it out!* convey an informal and enthusiastic tone. This kind of sentence might appear in a computer magazine or in an advertisement for this type of training.

Although an author's tone is often obvious, there may be times when it is less clear and requires careful thought. If you misunderstand an author's tone, you may misinterpret his or her entire message. For example, if you read a short story and you miss the author's ironic or sarcastic tone, you will mistakenly think his or her meaning is the opposite of what it actually is. When authors use **irony,** they create a deliberate contrast between their apparent meaning and their intended meaning: Their words say one thing but mean the opposite. That is, the words are intended to express something different from their literal meaning. You use irony every day in conversation. For example, you might say, "Well, *that* test was easy!" but your ironic tone makes it clear how difficult the test actually was. Another form of irony occurs when there is incongruity between what might be expected and what actually occurs. For example, it would be ironic if you won a new car in a contest on the same day that you bought a new one. Students sometimes confuse irony with sarcasm. **Sarcasm** is a remark, often ironic, that is intended to convey contempt or ridicule. Sarcasm is always meant to hurt; irony is not intended to be hurtful.

If you overlook irony or sarcasm, you may think authors are being serious when they are actually joking; that they are calm when, in fact, they are angry; or that they favor something when, in reality, they oppose it. An author's **intended meaning** is what an author wants readers to understand even when his or her words seem to be saying something different. Identifying the author's tone correctly enables you to grasp the author's intended meaning, even when the words appear on the surface to be saying something different. Critical readers ask themselves, "What is the author's *real* meaning?"

For many students, especially those for whom English is a second language, it can be challenging to detect sarcasm in written material and therefore understand the author's intended meaning. When you are reading, you can concentrate so much on following what the author is saying that you forget to think about how sensible it is and whether the author really expects you to take the words literally. It is often helpful to step back and think about whether the author is being sarcastic. If so, his or her true message will be the opposite of what the words appear to be saying. For

irony

A deliberate contrast between an author's apparent meaning and his or her intended meaning.

sarcasm

A remark, often ironic, that is intended to convey contempt or ridicule.

intended meaning

What an author wants readers to understand even when his or her words seem to be saying something different.

Comprehension-Monitoring Question for Determining an Author's Intended Meaning

"What is the author's *real* meaning?"

example, suppose you read this letter from a high school principal to a newspaper editor about students who cheat in school:

> As a high school principal, I strongly believe that there shouldn't be any penalties for students who are caught cheating. After all, everyone does it. Besides, cheating in school will help prepare these same students to cheat their employers later on, to cheat on their spouses when they marry, and to cheat on their income taxes. In fact, we could help students even more if we offered a course on how to cheat.

What is the author's intended meaning?

_____

_____

_____

What is the author's tone?

_____

Stop and Annotate

Go back to the excerpt above. Determine the author's intended meaning and tone, and write your responses in the spaces provided.

The fact that you feel surprised, shocked, or confused at what the writer is saying should alert you to the fact that he or she is being sarcastic. Does the writer, a high school principal, really mean that it is fine for students to cheat in school? No, of course not. To make his point, the writer sarcastically says the *opposite* of what he or she actually means. Sometimes an author is deliberately ridiculous, so absurd, in fact, that the absurdity makes it clear that he or she does not mean at all what the words seem to be saying. In the preceding example, the author's intended meaning is that students who are caught cheating in school *should* be punished. Otherwise, those who cheat in school without any consequences will turn out to be dishonorable adults who continue to cheat in a variety of ways and think that there is nothing wrong with it. Would it really make sense that a school principal, the writer of the letter, would advocate cheating? Of course not. However, if you are not reading critically and you fail to notice the writer's sarcasm and intended meaning, you might come away puzzled or mistakenly believing that the principal who wrote the letter thinks it is all right for students to cheat.

There are additional clues that can help you detect sarcasm in written material. First, pay attention when authors use words that seem inappropriate for what they are describing, such as an obvious exaggeration or understatement. For example, an author might exaggerate by saying that if the city's baseball team ever won a single game, the entire city would hold a week-long celebration. Or in describing a bitter legal case over property rights that has gone on for years, the writer might deliberately understate and describe it as "that unfriendly little property dispute." A second way to detect sarcasm is to think about how a passage would sound if the author *spoke* the words rather than wrote them. You may even want to read the passage aloud yourself and listen to your tone of voice. Can you hear any sarcasm in it?

As noted earlier, irony involves using words that seem straightforward but that actually contain a different, hidden meaning. For example, in the year 2000, just before the Academy Awards, there were many complaints that the program the preceding year had lasted entirely too long—four hours. In spite of this, the 2000 Academy Awards lasted even longer—four and a half hours! The emcee, comedian Billy Crystal, made an ironic comment when he said he didn't understand why anyone was complaining because "the 2000 Academy Awards ceremony was the shortest one of the millennium." His comment was ironic because technically he was right—and very funny—since that evening's ceremony was the first and *only* ceremony in this millennium. Therefore, regardless of how long the ceremony was, it was automatically the "shortest one of the millennium."

Another form of irony occurs when there is incongruity or difference between what is expected and what actually occurs. For example, it would be ironic if you took a trip to surprise a friend in another city, and your friend was not there because he was making a trip to pay a surprise visit to you in your city! The cartoon below is another example of this form of irony.

Satire is a type of writing in which the author sometimes uses sarcasm or irony for a specific purpose. To be precise, **satire** is a style of writing in which the author uses sarcasm, irony, or ridicule to attack or expose human foolishness, corruption, or stupidity. When authors are being satirical (using satire), they expect readers to pick up on it and understand their real message. Many famous writers have used satire to expose weaknesses in human society and morals. When you read a selection, ask

satire

A style of writing in which the author uses sarcasm, irony, or ridicule to attack or expose human foolishness, corruption, or stupidity.

This cartoon illustrates situational irony since it is the *mosquito* that is being bitten.

THE FAR SIDE®   BY GARY LARSON

© 1993 FarWorks, Inc. All Rights Reserved/Dist. by Creators Syndicate

The Far Side® by Gary Larson

"Wow. ... That's ironic. I think something bit me."

yourself if the writer is trying to expose some problem by making fun of it. Here is an example of a passage in which the author uses satire to expose a politician's corrupt nature:

Would our distinguished state senator ever accept bribes from large corporations in exchange for his vote on important issues? Certainly not! He was never convicted when those charges were brought against him in the past. Is he a corrupt man who would accept illegal campaign contributions? Absolutely not. When it was revealed that he had accepted several questionable donations, he eventually returned all of them. Would the noble senator ever fail to report income on his tax form? Ridiculous. Although he has refused to release any of his tax returns, he obviously has nothing to hide. Would this fine man ever accept luxury trips or other expensive gifts from lobbyists? Definitely not. Even though he could not afford all of them on his salary, he shouldn't have to explain how he paid for those expensive golf and ski vacations or how he is able to afford a second home in the country. After all, he's told us he hasn't done anything wrong, and as we all know, the senator is an honorable man.	**What is the author's intended meaning?** _____ _____ _____ **What is the author's tone?** _____ _____

You can almost hear the writer's voice drip with sarcasm. To show how "honorable" the senator is, the writer reveals that the senator:

- Has previously had charges brought against him of selling his votes for bribes.
- Returned certain campaign contributions once it was revealed to the public that they might be illegal.
- Refuses to make his income tax returns available to the public.
- Refuses to explain how he can afford certain numerous, very expensive luxuries on his salary.

By mentioning one questionable matter after another that the senator has been involved in or accused of, and pretending to discount them, the writer reveals the senator's dishonest nature. The writer refers to the senator as "distinguished," "noble," and "honorable," although the sarcasm makes it clear that the writer believes the

Stop and Annotate

Go back to the preceding excerpt. Determine the author's intended meaning and tone, and write your responses in the spaces provided.

senator is none of these. In response to accusations about the senator's behavior, the writer vigorously declares, "Certainly not," "Absolutely not," "Ridiculous," and "Definitely not." Again, though, these overly strong denials make it clear the writer thinks the senator is guilty of the charges. A reader who fails to recognize that the writer is satirizing the senator will completely misunderstand the writer's intended meaning: The senator is corrupt.

It is not so important that you be able to distinguish among sarcasm, irony, and satire. What is important is that you pick up on clues that authors use to signal that their intended meaning is different from what their words *appear* to be saying.

To understand an author's intended meaning, you must understand the author's tone. Ask yourself the questions critical readers ask: "What do the author's choice of words and style of writing reveal about his or her attitude toward the topic?" and "What is the author's *real* meaning?"

WORDS THAT DESCRIBE TONE

Many words can be used to describe tone. You already know lots of them, such as *happy, sad,* and *angry,* but you may not realize how many there are. Here is a list of several. (Incidentally, these are valuable words to have in your own vocabulary.) To make it easier for you to learn the words, they are grouped into general categories.

Words That Describe a *Neutral* Tone

(typically used in textbooks, reference material, sets of directions, instructional manuals, most newspaper and magazine articles, and other factual, objective material that is presented in a straightforward manner)

unemotional	involving little or no emotion or feeling
dispassionate	devoid or unaffected by passion, emotion, or bias
indifferent	appearing to have no preference or concern

Words That Describe a *Serious* Tone

(typically used in important formal announcements and obituaries, for example)

solemn	deeply earnest, serious, and sober
serious	grave, earnest, not trifling or joking; deeply interested or involved
reserved	marked by self-restraint and reticence

Words That Describe an *Emotional* Tone

(typically found in personal articles, political writing, and some persuasive writing, such as editorials)

compassionate	showing kindness, mercy, or compassion; sympathetic
concerned	caring deeply about a person or an issue
impassioned	characterized by passion or zeal
nostalgic	feeling bittersweet longing for things, persons, or situations in the past
sentimental	based on emotion rather than reason

(Continued on next page)

remorseful	feeling regret
self-pitying	feeling sorry for oneself
urgent	calling for immediate attention; instantly important
defiant	intentionally contemptuous; resisting authority or force

Words That Describe a *Critical, Disapproving* Tone

(typically found in movie and book reviews, editorials, some magazine articles)

critical	inclined to criticize or find fault
disapproving	passing unfavorable judgment upon; condemning
pessimistic	expecting the worst; having a negative attitude or gloomy outlook
intolerant	not allowing a difference of opinion or sentiment
indignant	angered by something unjust, mean, or unworthy; irate

Words That Describe a *Humorous, Sarcastic, Ironic,* or *Satiric* Tone

(can appear in writing of many sorts, including literature and social criticism and some newspaper and magazine columns and articles)

lighthearted	not being burdened by trouble, worry, or care; happy and carefree
irreverent	disrespectful; critical of what is generally accepted or respected; showing a lack of reverence
cynical	scornful of the motives, virtue, or integrity of others; expressing scorn and bitter mockery
scornful	treating someone or something as despicable or unworthy; showing utter contempt
contemptuous	showing open disrespect or haughty disdain
mocking	treating with scorn or contempt
malicious	intended to cause harm or suffering; having wicked or mischievous intentions or motives
ironic	humorously sarcastic or mocking
sarcastic	characterized by the desire to show scorn or contempt
bitter	characterized by sharpness, severity, or cruelty
skeptical	reluctant to believe; doubting or questioning everything
disbelieving	not believing; refusing to believe

Words That Describe a *Supportive* Tone

(found in writing of many types, such as certain textbooks, inspirational writing, some magazine articles, and personal correspondence)

encouraging	showing support
supportive	showing support or assistance
enthusiastic	showing excitement
optimistic	expecting the best; having a positive outlook
approving	expressing approval or agreement
positive	being in favor of; supportive; optimistic
sympathetic	inclined to sympathy; showing pity
tolerant	showing respect for the rights or opinions or practices of others

Some *Other* Words That Can Describe Tone

authoritative	speaking in a definite and confident manner
ambivalent	having opposite feelings or attitudes at the same time
conciliatory	willing to give in on some matters
cautious	careful; not wanting to take chances; wary
arrogant	giving oneself an undue degree of importance; haughty
grim	gloomy; dismal; forbidding
humble	marked by meekness or modesty; not arrogant or prideful
apologetic	self-deprecating; humble; offering or expressing an apology or excuse

In the following passage from a study skills textbook, the authors' purpose is to define concentration and explain why it is a complex process. After you read this paragraph, ask yourself, "What is the authors' position on this issue?" and "What do the authors' choice of words and style of writing reveal about their attitude toward the topic?"

Psychologically defined, concentration is the process of centering one's attention over a period of time. In practical application, however, concentration is not as simple to cope with as the definition may imply. For this reason, it is important to keep the following points in mind:

- Your attention span varies.
- Your attention span is short.
- When you truly concentrate, you are paying attention to only one thing at a time.
- Distractors to concentration can be both physical and psychological.
- Emotions are the most powerful psychological distractors.

What is the authors' point of view (bias)?

_____

_____

_____

What is the authors' tone?

_____

_____

Source: Adapted from William Farquar, John Krumboltz, and Gilbert Wrenn, "Controlling Your Concentration," in Frank Christ, Ed., *SR/SE Resource Book*, Chicago: SRA, 1969, p. 119.

Stop and Annotate

Go back to the previous excerpt. Determine the authors' point of view (bias) and tone, and write your responses in the spaces provided.

In this paragraph, the authors' tone is *unemotional and straightforward* rather than emotional and persuasive. Their point of view is that *concentration is not as simple a process as it might seem.* Since this is factual material presented in a straightforward manner, the authors' intended meaning is exactly what it appears to be.

Remember, part of reading critically involves asking yourself, "What is the author's position on this issue?" "What do the author's choice of words and style of writing reveal about his or her attitude toward the topic?" and "What is the author's *intended* meaning?"

It is obvious from the two examples above that an author's tone is related to his or her purpose for writing and his or her point of view: Being aware of the author's tone will help you determine that purpose and point of view. The first chart on page 533 shows the *interrelationship* among author's purpose, tone, point of view, intended meaning, and intended audience.

EXERCISE 2

This paragraph comes from a communications textbook:

The Importance of a Sense of Humor

Recognizing the humor in daily situations and occasionally being able to laugh at yourself will make you feel better not only about others but also, more importantly, about yourself. In addition, others will enjoy being associated with you, plus your ability to perform physically and to recover from injuries and illnesses will probably be enhanced. For example, any student-athlete who has experienced a career-threatening injury can attest that a positive outlook and a sense of humor were key ingredients in relation to the speed and extent of recovery. Develop your sense of humor. Learn to laugh at yourself. It's good for you!

Source: Adapted from Ronald Adler and Jeanne Elmhorst, *Communicating at Work,* 5e. Copyright © 1996 by The McGraw-Hill Companies, Inc. Reprinted with permission of The McGraw-Hill Companies, Inc.

Write the *main idea sentence*: _____

_____

_____

What is the *authors' point of view*?

_____

_____

What is the *authors' tone*?

_____

What is the *authors' primary purpose*?

_____

HOW THE CRITICAL READING SKILLS ARE INTERRELATED

The author's purpose causes him or her to use a certain tone to convey a point of view to an intended audience.

- *The author decides on a **purpose** (reason) for writing:*

    to inform   to instruct   to persuade   to entertain

    - *To accomplish this purpose, the author uses an appropriate **tone,** such as:*

serious	formal	sincere	enthusiastic
disapproving	sympathetic	informal	humorous
ironic	lighthearted	ambivalent	encouraging

        - *To convey his or her main idea or **point of view** (position on an issue):*

            expresses *support* for an issue or *opposition* to an issue

            - *To an **intended audience:***

                the general public   a specific group   a particular person

The chart below illustrates the application of critical reading skills to a make-believe movie critic's review of an imaginary movie. It is also designed to show that critical reading skills are related and that they can be applied to reading tasks that you encounter daily.

EXAMPLE OF CRITICAL READING APPLIED TO A MOVIE CRITIC'S REVIEW

Here is an imaginary critic's review of *Cyberpunk,* a new science fiction movie:

Another movie from Extreme Studios has just been released, *Cyberpunk.* Is it worth seeing? That depends: Do you enjoy violence? Do you like vulgar language? Do you appreciate painfully loud sound effects? What about watching unknown actors embarrass themselves? Or sitting for three hours and ten minutes without a break? If so, and you've got $8.50 to burn, then *Cyberpunk* is the movie you must see!

Critical Reading Questions	Answers
What is the author's purpose?	To persuade readers to skip this movie
Who is the author's intended audience?	The moviegoing public
What is the author's point of view?	*Cyberpunk* is a terrible movie.*
What is the author's tone?	Sarcastic
What is the author's intended meaning?	Don't waste your money or your time on this movie. (*Not* "This is a movie you must see.")

*Notice that this is also the author's main idea or argument.

A WORD ABOUT STANDARDIZED READING TESTS: CRITICAL READING

Many college students are required to take standardized reading tests as part of an overall assessment program, in a reading course, or as part of a state-mandated basic skills test. A standardized reading test typically consists of a series of passages followed by multiple-choice reading skill application questions, to be completed within a specified time limit.

Here are some examples of the typical wording of critical reading questions on tests:

Questions about the *author's purpose:*

> The author's purpose for writing this passage is to . . .
>
> The reason the author wrote this passage is to . . .
>
> It is likely that the author wrote this in order to . . .
>
> The reason the author wrote this selection is primarily to . . .
>
> The author wrote this passage because . . .

Questions about the *author's intended audience:*

> The author intended this passage to be read by . . .
>
> The author's intended audience is . . .
>
> The author expects this passage to be read by . . .

Questions about the *author's point of view:*

> The passage suggests that the author's point of view is . . .
>
> The author's opinion about . . . is . . .
>
> It is clear that the author believes that . . .
>
> The passage suggests that the author's opinion about . . . is . . .

Questions about the *author's tone:*

> The tone of this passage is . . .
>
> The tone of this passage can be described as . . .
>
> Which of the following words best describes the tone of this passage?

Questions about the *author's intended meaning:*

> The author wants the reader to understand that . . .
>
> The author's use of sarcasm suggests that . . .
>
> The author's meaning is . . .
>
> The author's use of irony indicates . . .
>
> In this passage, the author intended the reader to understand that . . .
>
> Although the author states that . . . , she means that . . .
>
> Although the author appears to be supporting . . . , he actually wants the reader to . . .

Directions: Read each paragraph critically and then answer the questions about the author's purpose or point of view. Write your answers in the spaces provided.

1. This paragraph comes from a business communication textbook:

Can I Use Blogging on the Job?

Creating Web logs, or **blogging,** is an increasingly popular way of communicating on the Web. Millions of bloggers post thoughts, images, and links in journal-like entries made available through the Internet and in such languages as Arabic, Chinese, English, French, German, Italian, Japanese, Portuguese, Korean, and Spanish. Blogging is so popular, some businesses are turning to it to aid in recruiting employees, and CEOs are posting their own blogs in an effort to speak directly to customers and associates. A few people have managed to turn blogging into a career. But blogging in a professional setting is different than blogging in a personal one. For instance, many bloggers feel free to share deeply personal information about themselves or unflattering opinions about people in their lives or the companies they work for. To do so in a business situation might be considered inappropriate. In fact, some employees have been disciplined or fired for doing just that, such as programmer Mark Jen, whose complaints about the health care benefits and free food policy of his employer, Google, got him fired. Remember that if companies own and pay for computer resources, they may be entitled to access e-mail and blogs created by employees on their systems. In addition, blogs may be cached just like Web pages, meaning that years after the fact someone may be able to access an otherwise nonexistent blog. An employee who uses blogging on the job must remain professional.

Source: Adapted from Kitty O. Locker and Stephen Kaczmarek, *Business Communication: Building Critical Skills,* 5e, p. 239. Copyright © 2011 by The McGraw-Hill Companies, Inc. Reprinted with permission of The McGraw-Hill Companies, Inc.

_____   What is the authors' purpose in this paragraph?

    a. to inform readers that blogging has become an increasingly popular way of communicating on the Web

    b. to convince readers that using blogging on the job is inappropriate

    c. to persuade readers to remain professional if they use blogging on the job

    d. to instruct readers in how to use blogging effectively

2. This paragraph comes from a psychology textbook:

Tackling Procrastination

One of the biggest plusses of time management is that it helps you overcome procrastination. **Procrastination** is the habit of putting off tasks until the last minute. Procrastination can have minor consequences, such as having to pay a late fine for an overdue library book, or major consequences such as failing a course or losing a job. It's normal to procrastinate from time to time. When procrastination becomes a habit, however, it can erode your self-determination and self-expectancy. The more you procrastinate, the harder it is to stop. Moreover, procrastination has an enormous effect on one's success in college. Consider the key difference between A students and C students. Is it intelligence? Knowledge? Study skills? According to researchers, the real difference between A students and B or C students is that A students get started early. They buy their books on time, come to class prepared, and get started quickly on assignments. They don't procrastinate.

Source: Adapted from Denis Waitley, *Psychology of Success: Finding Meaning in Work and Life,* 5e, pp. 302–3. Copyright © 2010 by The McGraw-Hill Companies, Inc. Reprinted with permission of The McGraw-Hill Companies, Inc.

_____   What is the author's point of view in this paragraph?
   a.   It is relatively easy to resist putting off tasks until the last minute.
   b.   Students who buy their books on time, come to class prepared, and get started quickly on assignments will succeed in college.
   c.   It is normal to procrastinate.
   d.   Everyone, but especially college students, should avoid developing a habit of procrastinating.

3. This paragraph comes from an information technology textbook:

Cell phone apps or **cell phone applications** are add-on features to a cell phone that allow users to perform a variety of tasks not typically associated with cell phone use. Cell phone apps have been widely used for years. Traditional applications include address books, to-do lists, alarms, and message lists. With the introduction of smart-phones and wireless connections to the Internet, cell phone capabilities have exploded. Now, any number of specialized applications are available, and the breadth and scope of available specialized applications is ever expanding. There are over 10,000 apps just for Apple's iPhone alone. Some of the most widely used cell phone apps are text messaging, Internet browsing, and connecting to social networks.

Source: Adapted from Timothy J. O'Leary and Linda I. O'Leary, *Computing Essentials 2012: Making IT Work for You,* p. 114. Copyright © 2012 by The McGraw-Hill Companies, Inc. Reprinted with permission of The McGraw-Hill Companies, Inc.

_____　　What is the authors' purpose in this paragraph?

　　　a.　to inform readers about the expanding use of cell phone apps

　　　b.　to convince readers that cell phone apps are becoming more affordable

　　　c.　to explain to readers why cell phone apps have become a necessity

　　　d.　to instruct readers in how to use cell phone apps effectively

4. This paragraph comes from a United States government textbook:

> When Americans go to the polls on election day, they are electing more than a president. They are also picking a secretary of state, the director of the FBI, and hundreds of other federal executives. Each of these is a presidential appointee, and each of these is an extension of the president's authority. Although the president cannot be in a hundred places at once, the president's appointees collectively can be. Not surprisingly, presidents typically appoint party loyalists who are committed to the administration's goals.

Source: Adapted from Thomas E. Patterson, *The American Democracy, Alternate Edition,* 10e, p. 337. Copyright © 2011 by The McGraw-Hill Companies, Inc. Reprinted with permission of The McGraw-Hill Companies, Inc.

_____　　What is the author's point of view in this paragraph?

　　　a.　The secretary of state and the director of the FBI should not be appointed by the president.

　　　b.　There are too many federal executives appointed each year by the president.

　　　c.　Presidential appointees extend the president's authority because appointees typically support the administration's policy goals.

　　　d.　Presidents always select appointees from their own political party.

5. This paragraph comes from a psychology textbook:

> Do you have a shopping habit? Many people overspend because they engage in impulse buying and recreational shopping. *Impulse buying* means spending money because you see something and suddenly want it, not because you planned to buy it beforehand. Grocery stores make impulse buying easy by placing appealing items, such as candy and magazines, right next to checkout stands. Even online retailers such as amazon.com cash in on impulse buying by making personalized suggestions for products that shoppers might like to add to their carts. *Recreational shopping* means using shopping, especially in malls, as a form of entertainment. Recreational shopping is common in our society; in fact, people now spend more time in malls than anywhere else except home, work, and school. The easiest way to avoid recreational shopping is simply to stop using shopping as a hobby. Plan outings that are low-cost or free, such as hiking,

playing sports, or making dinner at a friend's house. Avoid malls, which are specially designed to engage you in an endless loop of shopping. Avoid impulse buying and recreational shopping by reminding yourself again and again to shop only for things that you really need and have planned to buy. Do you really need that fireproof wallet or electronic spatula? Before you buy, ask yourself questions such as:

- Do I really need this item?
- Is there something else I need more?
- Have I allowed for this item in my budget?
- Do I own something similar already?
- Can I borrow a similar item instead?
- Is this the best time to buy?
- Am I buying this in an attempt to satisfy a psychological need?

Stopping to ask yourself these questions before you buy can help you limit your spending and become more self-aware. You can also become more self-aware by thinking about your past spending mistakes.

Source: Adapted from Denis Waitley, *Psychology of Success: Finding Meaning in Work and Life,* 5e, p. 319. Copyright © 2010 by The McGraw-Hill Companies, Inc. Reprinted with permission of The McGraw-Hill Companies, Inc.

What is the author's purpose in this paragraph?
   a.   to explain to readers the reasons why so many people overspend
   b.   to persuade readers to avoid impulse buying and recreational shopping by questioning their reason to buy before they make a purchase
   c.   to inform readers about what it means to become more self-aware
   d.   to convince readers that impulse buying and recreational shopping can lead to serious debt problems, including bankruptcy

DEVELOPING CHAPTER REVIEW CARDS

Complete the five review cards for Chapter 8 by answering the questions or following the directions on each card. When you have completed them, you will have summarized (1) what critical reading is, (2) author's purpose, (3) author's intended audience, (4) author's point of view, and (5) author's tone and intended meaning. Print or write legibly.

Critical Reading

Define *critical reading*.

List and define the skills of critical reading.

1.

2.

3.

4.

Card 1   Chapter 8: Reading Critically

Author's Purpose

Define *author's purpose.*

List four common purposes for writing.

1.

2.

3.

4.

What are two ways to determine an author's purpose?

1.

2.

To determine an author's purpose, what question should you ask yourself?

Card 2   Chapter 8: Reading Critically

Author's Intended Audience

Define *intended audience.*

To determine an author's intended audience, what question should you ask yourself?

What are three things you can examine in order to determine the author's intended audience?

1.

2.

3.

Card 3   Chapter 8: Reading Critically

Author's Point of View

Define *point of view*.

Give some examples of words that reveal an author's point of view.

Define *author's bias*.

To determine an author's point of view, what question should you ask yourself?

Card 4   Chapter 8: Reading Critically

Author's Tone and Intended Meaning

Define *tone*.

What are two things you can examine in order to determine an author's tone?

   1.

   2.

To determine an author's tone, what question should you ask yourself?

Define *intended meaning*.

To determine an author's intended meaning, what question should you ask yourself?

Card 5   Chapter 8: Reading Critically

Directions: Read these paragraphs carefully and answer the questions that follow them. Write your answers in the spaces provided.

This paragraph comes from a health textbook:

> Is your happiness within your control? Are people born naturally happy or sad? One important key to psychological health is the way you think about and interpret events in your life. For example, if you say "hello" to someone and don't get a response, do you begin to wonder if that person is angry with you? Or do you surmise that he or she didn't hear you or perhaps was distracted? Research shows that having a positive interpretation of life's events, particularly how you cope with adversity, can make a significant difference in terms of your health, academic and work performance, as well as how long you will live. Do you see the glass half empty, as pessimists do, or half full, as optimists do? Does it matter? Again, studies overwhelmingly contend that your perspective makes a tremendous difference in your psychological health. Compared to pessimists, optimists tend to contract fewer infectious diseases, have better health habits, possess stronger immune systems, be more successful in their careers, and perform better in sports, music and academics.
>
> *Source:* Adapted from Wayne A. Payne, Dale B. Hahn, and Ellen B. Lucas, *Understanding Your Health,* 10e, pp. 43–44. Copyright © 2009 by The McGraw-Hill Companies, Inc. Reprinted with permission of The McGraw-Hill Companies, Inc.

1. What is the authors' purpose in this paragraph?
   a. to teach readers how to have a more positive outlook on life
   b. to inform readers about the psychological and physical benefits of an optimistic perspective on life
   c. to instruct readers in how to cope with adversity
   d. to illustrate for readers the major differences between pessimists and optimists

2. What is the authors' point of view in this paragraph?
   a. People are born naturally optimistic or pessimistic.
   b. Pessimists are not able to control their own happiness.
   c. Interpreting life's events in a positive way and maintaining an optimistic perspective can have a positive effect on many aspects of your life.
   d. People who perform better in sports, music, and academics, and are successful in their careers are usually optimists.

This paragraph comes from a psychology textbook:

The SQ3R Study Method

Use of the SQ3R learning system entails the following specific steps. The first step is to *survey* the material by reading the headings, figure captions, recaps, providing yourself with an overview of the major points of the chapter. The next step—the "Q"—is to *question*. Formulate questions about the material, either aloud or in writing, prior to actually reading a section of text. *Read* carefully and, even more importantly, read actively and critically. While you are reading, answer the questions that you have asked yourself. Critically evaluate material by considering the implications of what you are reading, thinking about possible exceptions and contradictions, and examining underlying assumptions. The *recite* step involves describing and explaining to yourself (or to a friend) the material you have just read and answering the questions you have posed earlier. Recite aloud; the recitation process helps to identify your degree of understanding of the material you have just read. Finally, *review* the material, looking it over, re-reading any summaries, and answering any review questions that are included at the end of a section.

Source: Adapted from Robert S. Feldman, *Essentials of Understanding Psychology,* 9e, pp. xxxix–xl. Copyright © 2011 by The McGraw-Hill Companies, Inc. Reprinted with permission of The McGraw-Hill Companies, Inc.

3. What is the author's purpose in this paragraph?
   a. to convince readers that reading is a five-step process
   b. to inform readers about effective study strategies
   c. to instruct readers in how to use the SQ3R study method
   d. to explain to readers why studying college textbook material is challenging

4. Who is the author's intended audience in this paragraph?
   a. students who are unable to comprehend what they are reading
   b. students who want to be more effective when they are reading and studying
   c. students who have difficulties managing their study time
   d. students who want to improve their concentration

This paragraph comes from an information technology textbook:

No matter how much students may be able to rationalize cheating in college, ignorance of the consequences is not an excuse. When a student tries to pass off someone else's term paper as their own, they are committing a form of cheating known as plagiarism. Most instructors announce the penalties for this type of cheating at the beginning of the course. They warn students that the penalty for cheating of this sort is usually a failing grade in the course and possible suspension or expulsion from school.

Source: Adapted from Brian K. Williams and Stacey C. Sawyer, *Using Information Technology: A Practical Introduction to Computers and Communications,* 7e, p. 104. Copyright © 2007 by The McGraw-Hill Companies, Inc. Reprinted with permission of The McGraw-Hill Companies, Inc.

5. What is the authors' purpose in this paragraph?

   a. to inform readers about the problem of cheating in college

   b. to explain the reasons why college students are tempted to cheat

   c. to inform students about the penalties for plagiarism in college

   d. to persuade college students to avoid plagiarism

6. What is the authors' point of view in this paragraph?

   a. College students' ignorance about plagiarism is not an excuse.

   b. College instructors should not have to warn students about the penalties for cheating.

   c. Students who rationalize cheating in college should be suspended.

   d. There are many reasons why college students commit plagiarism.

This paragraph comes from psychology textbook:

> A number of theories for why we forget have been suggested. According to the *theory of motivated forgetting,* we forget material we need to forget. In other words, we repress certain uncomfortable memories. *Decay theory* holds that certain memories decay or fade with the passage of time if we do not use the information. *Interference theory* holds that we forget information because other information interferes with or confounds our memory. *Proactive interference* describes a situation where the material we learned first interferes with the ability to remember new material. *Retroactive interference* refers to a situation where information learned later interferes with our remembering previously learned material.
>
> *Source:* Adapted from Diane Papalia and Sally Olds, *Psychology,* p. 122. Copyright © 1988 by The McGraw-Hill Companies, Inc. Reprinted with permission of The McGraw-Hill Companies, Inc.

7. What is the authors' purpose in this paragraph?

   a. to teach readers ways they can improve their ability to remember material

   b. to illustrate for readers the theory of forgetting

   c. to instruct readers in how to avoid interference when memorizing new material

   d. to inform readers about the different theories for why we forget things

8. What is the authors' tone in this paragraph?

   a. urgent

   b. indifferent

   c. unemotional

   d. concerned

This paragraph comes from a health textbook:

> How do you imagine your life in the future? Do you ever think about how your health allows you to participate in meaningful life activities—and what might happen if your health is compromised? Consider, for example, the numerous ways that your health affects your daily activities. Your health affects your ability to pursue an education or a career. It affects your opportunities to socialize with friends and family and the chance to travel—for business, relaxation, or adventure. Your health also affects your opportunity to meet and connect with new people and participation in hobbies and recreational activities. The opportunity to live independently and the ability to conceive or the opportunity to parent children is also affected by your health. Even your ability to enjoy a wide range of foods depends on your health.
>
> *Source:* Adapted from Wayne A. Payne, Dale B. Hahn, and Ellen B. Lucas, *Understanding Your Health,* 10e, pp. 1–2. Copyright © 2009 by The McGraw-Hill Companies, Inc. Reprinted with permission of The McGraw-Hill Companies, Inc.

9. What is the authors' purpose in this paragraph?

   a. to inform readers about the activities that promote a healthy lifestyle

   b. to explain the reasons why diet and exercise are important to your health

   c. to teach readers how to avoid compromising their health

   d. to convince readers that there are numerous reasons for maintaining your health

10. What is the authors' point of view in this paragraph?

    a. Your health affects your ability to pursue an education or a career, and it affects your opportunities to socialize with friends and family.

    b. Maintaining your health will allow you to continue to participate in a variety of meaningful life activities.

    c. If you maintain your health, you will retain the opportunity to live independently.

    d. It is challenging to maintain a healthy lifestyle.

Directions: Read each paragraph critically and then answer the questions about the author's purpose, point of view, intended audience, or tone. Write your answers in the spaces provided.

This paragraph comes from a business textbook:

When you think of business, you probably think of a huge corporation such as General Electric, Procter & Gamble, or Sony. This is understandable, since a large portion of your consumer dollars go to such corporations. In fact, corporations account for the majority of all U.S. sales and income. A **corporation** is a legal entity, created by the state, whose assets and liabilities are separate from its owners. As a legal entity, a corporation has many of the rights, duties, and powers of a person. For example, a corporation has the right to receive, own, and transfer property. Corporations can enter into contracts with individuals or with other legal entities. In addition, corporations can sue and be sued in court.

Source: Adapted from O. C. Ferrell, Geoffrey Hirt, and Linda Ferrell, *Business in a Changing World,* 8e, p. 129. Copyright © 2011 by The McGraw-Hill Companies, Inc. Reprinted with permission of The McGraw-Hill Companies, Inc.

1. What is the authors' purpose in this paragraph?

2. What is the authors' tone in this paragraph?

This paragraph comes from a speech textbook:

Weddings are celebrated in many ways, depending on religious, ethnic, and family traditions. Many of these traditions call for brief speeches of tribute at the rehearsal dinner and the wedding reception. The remarks may be delivered by members of the wedding party, parents, grandparents, siblings, and friends. Here are some guidelines.

- Focus on the couple. Instead of dwelling on your own experiences and emotions, talk mostly about the wedding couple and their love and future happiness.
- Be brief, but not too brief. If you speak for only 15 seconds, saying that the honorees are wonderful people whom everyone likes, you are not giving them the respect that they deserve. Say something specific and heartfelt, but keep your remarks under three minutes.
- Don't say anything that could embarrass anyone in the room. You've seen the movies in which a wedding celebration is marred when the best man reveals humiliating details about the groom or says something that is insulting to the bride. Such behavior is not limited to the movies. In real life, people make

547

major blunders. Never mention ex-boyfriends or ex-girlfriends. Never tease about past misdeeds, goofy habits, or unfortunate shortcomings. For this occasion, focus entirely on the positive.

- Consider using an appropriate poem or quotation. Anthologies and the Internet are full of apt quotations, such as this one by an ancient Chinese philosopher Lao Tzu: "To love someone deeply gives you strength. Being loved by someone deeply gives you courage."
- End with a toast. It's customary, and the perfect way to complete your speech.

Source: Adapted from Hamilton Gregory, *Public Speaking for College and Career,* 9e, p. 381. Copyright © 2012 by The McGraw-Hill Companies, Inc. Reprinted with permission of The McGraw-Hill Companies, Inc.

3. What is the author's purpose in this paragraph?

_____

_____

4. Who is the author's intended audience in this paragraph?

_____

_____

This paragraph comes from a psychology textbook:

Limiting credit card spending can be difficult when we are bombarded with seductive advertisements. The lure of advertising is strong. It's hard to ignore advertising, which has a powerful psychological effect. Advertisements don't just convey information. They also try to convince us that material objects can fulfill our psychological needs. Ads for alarm systems, for example, prey on our need for security by shocking us with alarming crime statistics and scenes of break-ins. Ads for makeup, perfume, and cologne tap into our needs for belonging and esteem, promising that these products will transform us into irresistible sex objects. Some advertisements also try to make us feel bad about ourselves if we don't already have or plan to buy the latest must-have. Some ads for luxury cars, for example, suggest that we are bad parents if we don't buy an $80,000 car with the latest safety features. How can you resist advertising's lure? The next time you read an ad or see a commercial, ask yourself what need the advertisers are trying to arouse. The more you become aware of advertising tactics, the less they will sway your purchasing decisions.

Source: Adapted from Denis Waitley, *Psychology of Success: Finding Meaning in Work and Life,* 5e, p. 315. Copyright © 2010 by The McGraw-Hill Companies, Inc. Reprinted with permission of The McGraw-Hill Companies, Inc.

5. What is the author's purpose in this paragraph?

_____

_____

_____

6. Who is the author's intended audience?

_____

This paragraph comes from a sociology textbook:

> How do students first learn about sociology? Perhaps they take a sociology course in high school. Others may study sociology at a community college, where 40 percent of all college students in the United States are enrolled. Indeed, many future sociology majors first develop their sociological imaginations at a community college. As a student at Princeton University, Michelle Obama majored in sociology. She used that degree as a stepping-stone to Harvard law school. But an undergraduate degree in sociology doesn't just serve as excellent preparation for future graduate work in sociology. It also provides a strong liberal arts background for entry-level positions in business, social services, foundations, community organizations, not-for-profit groups, law enforcement, and many government jobs. A number of fields—among them marketing, public relations, and broadcasting—now require investigative skills and an understanding of diverse groups found in today's multiethnic and multinational environment. Moreover, a sociology degree requires accomplishment in oral and written communication, interpersonal skills, problem solving, and critical thinking—all job-related skills that may give sociology majors an advantage over those who pursue more technical degrees.
>
> _Source:_ Adapted from Richard T. Schaefer, _Sociology: A Brief Introduction,_ 9e, p. 21. Copyright © 2011 by The McGraw-Hill Companies, Inc. Reprinted with permission of The McGraw-Hill Companies, Inc.

7. What is the author's point of view in this paragraph?

_____

_____

8. What is the author's tone in this paragraph?

_____

This paragraph comes from a speech textbook:

> PowerPoint has dozens of fonts to choose from, but they all fall into one or another of two basic categories—serif or sans-serif. Serif fonts have little tails on each letter, like the type in this sentence. Sans-serif fonts do not have tails, like the type in this sentence. Examples of serif fonts are Times New Roman, Bookman Old Style, and Book Antiqua. Examples of sans-serif fonts are Arial, Tahoma, and Verdana. Serif fonts are easier to read in large patches of text, while sans-serif fonts are better for headings and short bursts of text. Most multimedia experts recommend sans-serif fonts for titles and headings on PowerPoint slides. And some experts say sans-serif should be used for *all* text in PowerPoint. When choosing fonts for PowerPoint slides, keep the following guidelines in mind:
>
> - Choose fonts that are clear and easy to read.
> - Avoid using ALL CAPS because they are difficult to read.
> - Don't use more than two fonts on a single slide—one for the title or major heading and another for subtitles or other text.
> - Use the same fonts on all your slides.
>
> *Source:* Adapted from Stephen E. Lucas, *The Art of Public Speaking,* 10e, pp. 288–89. Copyright © 2009 by The McGraw-Hill Companies, Inc. Reprinted with permission of The McGraw-Hill Companies, Inc.

9. What is the author's purpose in this paragraph?

_____

_____

_____

10. Who is the author's intended audience?

_____

SELECTION **8.1**

Literature

SELECTION 8.1

Prologue

From *The Illustrated Man*
by Ray Bradbury

Prepare Yourself to Read

Directions: Do these exercises *before* you read Selection 8.1.

1. First, read and think about the title. What do you expect the story to be about?

   _____

   _____

   _____

2. Next, complete your preview by reading the following:

   First paragraph (paragraph 1)

   First and last sentence of the remaining paragraphs

   Now that you have previewed the selection, tell what you think the selection will be about.

   _____

   _____

   _____

   _____

   _____

3. **Build your vocabulary as you read.** If you discover an unfamiliar word or key term as you read the selection, try to determine its meaning by using context clues.

Read More about This Topic Online

Internet Resources

Use a search engine, such as Google or Yahoo!, to expand your existing knowledge about this topic *before* you read the selection or to learn more about it *afterward*. If you are unfamiliar with conducting Internet searches, read pages 25–26 on Boolean searches. You can also use Wikipedia, the free online encyclopedia, at www.wikipedia.com. Keep in mind that when you visit any website, it is a good idea to evaluate the site and the information it contains. Ask yourself questions such as "Who sponsors this website?" and "Is the information it contains up to date?"

SELECTION 8.1: PROLOGUE FROM *THE ILLUSTRATED MAN*

Ray Bradbury is the author of more than 500 published works that include short stories, novels, plays, essays, screenplays, television scripts, and poetry. The publication of The Martian Chronicles *in 1950 established him as a top science fiction writer. Other best-known works include* Fahrenheit 451, Something Wicked This Way Comes, *and* Dandelion Wine. *Bradbury's fans include science fiction, fantasy, horror, and mystery enthusiasts. He was the recipient of innumerable awards and honors. Born in 1920, Bradbury was self-taught after high school. He said, "Libraries raised me. . . . When I graduated from high school, it was during the Depression and we had no money. I couldn't go to college, so I went to the library three days a week for 10 years" (www.nytimes.com/2009/06/20/us/20ventura.html, accessed 6/6/12). He had the lifelong habit of writing every day. Bradbury, who lived in California, died on June 5, 2012, at the age of 91.*

A prologue is an introduction. The following excerpt is the prologue from one of Bradbury's famous works, The Illustrated Man. *It sets the stage for the stories that comprise the rest of the book. Although written more than half a century ago,* The Illustrated Man *continues to intrigue readers and win new fans for Bradbury.*

1   It was a warm afternoon in early September when I first met the Illustrated Man. Walking along an asphalt road, I was on the final leg of a two weeks' walking tour of Wisconsin. Late in the afternoon I stopped, ate some pork, beans, and a doughnut, and was preparing to stretch out and read when the Illustrated Man walked over the hill and stood for a moment against the sky.

2   I didn't know he was Illustrated then. I only knew that he was tall, once well muscled, but now, for some reason, going to fat. I recall that his arms were long, and the hands thick, but that his face was like a child's, set upon a massive body.

3   He seemed only to sense my presence, for he didn't look directly at me when he spoke his first words:

4   "Do you know where I can find a job?"

5   "I'm afraid not," I said.

6   "I haven't had a job that's lasted in forty years," he said.

7   Though it was a hot late afternoon, he wore his wool shirt buttoned tight about his neck. His sleeves were rolled and buttoned down over his thick wrists. Perspiration was streaming from his face, yet he made no move to open his shirt.

8   "Well," he said at last, "this is as good a place as any to spend the night. Do you mind company?"

9   "I have some extra food you'd be welcome to," I said.

10   He sat down heavily, grunting. "You'll be sorry you asked me to stay," he said. "Everyone always is. That's why I'm walking. Here it is, early September, the cream of the Labor Day carnival season. I should be making money hand over fist at any small town side show celebration, but here I am with no prospects."

11   He took off an immense shoe and peered at it closely. "I usually keep a job about ten days. Then something happens and they fire

Annotation Practice Exercises

Directions: For each of the exercises below, read critically to answer the questions. This will help you gain additional insights as you read.

Practice Exercise

In paragraph 8, what is the Illustrated Man's *intended meaning* when he says, "Do you mind company?"

_____

_____

_____

me. By now every carnival in America won't touch me with a ten-foot pole."

12   "What seems to be the trouble?" I asked.

13   For an answer, he unbuttoned his tight collar, slowly. With his eyes shut, he put a slow hand to the task of unbuttoning his shirt all the way down. He slipped his fingers in to feel his chest. "Funny," he said, eyes still shut. "You can't feel them but they're there. I always hope that someday I'll look and they'll be gone. I walk in the sun for hours on the hottest days, baking, and hope that my sweat'll wash them off, the sun'll cook them off, but at sundown they're still there." He turned his head slightly toward me and exposed his chest. "Are they still there now?"

14   After a long while I exhaled. "Yes," I said. "They're still there."

15   The Illustrations.

16   "Another reason I keep my collar buttoned up," he said, opening his eyes, "is the children. They follow me along country roads. Everyone wants to see the pictures, and yet nobody wants to see them."

17   He took his shirt off and wadded it in his hands. He was covered with Illustrations from the blue tattooed ring about his neck to his belt line.

18   "It keeps right on going," he said, guessing my thought. "All of me is Illustrated. Look." He opened his hand. On his palm was a rose, freshly cut, with drops of crystal water among the soft pink petals. I put my hand out to touch it, but it was only an Illustration.

19   As for the rest of him, I cannot say how long I sat and stared, for he was a riot of rockets and fountains and people, in such intricate detail and color that you could hear the voices murmuring small and muted, from the crowds that inhabited his body. When his flesh twitched, the tiny mouths flickered, the tiny green-and-gold eyes winked, the tiny pink hands gestured. There were yellow meadows and blue rivers and mountains and stars and suns and planets spread in a Milky Way across his chest. The people themselves were in twenty or more odd groups upon his arms, shoulders, back, sides, and wrists, as well as on the flat of his stomach. You found them in forests of hair, lurking among a constellation of freckles, or peering from armpit caverns, diamond eyes aglitter. Each seemed intent upon his own activity; each was a separate gallery portrait.

20   "Why, they're beautiful!" I said.

21   How can I explain about his Illustrations? If El Greco had painted miniatures in his prime, no bigger than your hand, infinitely detailed, with all his sulphurous color, elongation, and anatomy, perhaps he might have used this man's body for his art. The colors burned in three dimensions. They were windows looking in upon fiery reality. Here gathered on one wall, were all the finest scenes in the universe; the man was a walking treasure gallery. This wasn't the work of a cheap carnival tattoo man with three colors and whisky on his breath. This was the accomplishment of a living genius, vibrant, clear, and beautiful.

22   "Oh yes," said the Illustrated Man. "I'm so proud of my Illustrations that I'd like to burn them off. I've tried sandpaper, acid, a knife . . ."

23   The sun was setting. The moon was already up in the East.

24   "For, you see," said the Illustrated Man, "these Illustrations predict the future."

25   I said nothing.

26   "It's all right in sunlight," he went on. "I could keep a carnival day job. But at night—the pictures move. The pictures change."

27   I must have smiled. "How long have you been Illustrated?"

28   "In 1900, when I was twenty years old and working a carnival, I broke my leg. It laid me up; I had to do something to keep my hand in, so I decided to get tattooed."

29   "But who tattooed you? What happened to the artist?"

30   "She went back to the future," he said. "I mean it. She was an old woman in a little house in the middle of Wisconsin here somewhere not far from this place. A little old witch who looked a thousand years old one moment and twenty years old the next, but she said she could travel in time. I laughed. Now, I know better."

31   "How did you happen to meet her?"

32   He told me. He had seen her painted sign by the road: SKIN ILLUSTRATION! Illustration instead of tattoo! Artistic! So he had sat all night while her magic needles stung him wasp stings and delicate bee stings. By morning he looked like a man who had fallen into a twenty-color print press and been squeezed out, all bright and picturesque.

33   "I've hunted every summer for fifty years," he said, putting his hands out on the air. "When I find that witch I'm going to kill her."

34   The sun was gone. Now the first stars were shining and the moon had brightened the fields of grass and wheat. Still the Illustrated Man's pictures glowed like charcoals in the half light, like scattered rubies and emeralds, with Rouault colors and Picasso colors and the long, pressed-out El Greco bodies.

35   "So people fire me when my pictures move. They don't like it when violent things happen in my Illustrations. Each Illustration is a little story. If you watch them, in a few minutes they tell you a tale. In three hours of looking you could see eighteen or twenty stories acted right on my body, you could hear their voices and think their thoughts. It's all here, just waiting for you to look. But most of all, there's a special spot on my body." He bared his back. "See? There's no special design on my right shoulder blade, just a jumble."

36   "Yes."

37   "When I've been around a person long enough, that spot clouds over and fills in. If I'm with a woman, her picture comes there on my back, in an hour, and shows her whole life—how she'll live, how she'll die, what she'll look like when she's sixty. And if it's a man, an hour later his picture's here on my back. It shows him falling off a cliff, or dying under a train. So I'm fired again."

38   All the time he had been talking, his hands had wandered over the Illustrations, as if to adjust their frames, to brush away dust—the

Practice Exercise

What is the Illustrated Man's *tone* in paragraph 22?

_____

motions of a connoisseur, an art patron. Now he lay back, long and full in the moonlight. It was a warm night. There was no breeze and the air was stifling. We both had our shirts off.

39   "And you've never found the old woman?"

40   "Never."

41   "And you think she came from the future?"

42   "How else could she know these stories she painted on me?"

43   He shut his eyes tiredly. His voice grew fainter. "Sometimes at night I can feel them, the pictures, like ants, crawling on my skin. Then I know they're doing what they have to do. I never look at them anymore. I just try to rest. I don't sleep much. Don't you look at them either, I warn you. Turn the other way when you sleep."

44   I lay back a few feet from him. He didn't seem violent, and the pictures were beautiful. Otherwise I might have been tempted to get out and away from such babbling. But the Illustrations . . . I let my eyes fill up on them. Any person would go a little mad with such things upon his body.

45   The night was serene. I could hear the Illustrated Man's breathing in the moonlight. Crickets were stirring gently in the distant ravines. I lay with my body sidewise so I could watch the Illustrations. Perhaps half an hour passed. Whether the Illustrated Man slept I could not tell, but suddenly I heard him whisper, "They're moving, aren't they?"

46   I waited a minute.

47   Then I said, "Yes."

48   The pictures were moving, each in its turn, each for a brief minute or two. There in the moonlight, with the tiny tinkling thoughts and the distant sea voices, it seemed, each little drama was enacted. Whether it took an hour or three hours for the dramas to finish, it would be hard to say. I only know that I lay fascinated and did not move while the stars wheeled in the sky.

49   Eighteen Illustrations, eighteen tales. I counted them one by one.

50   Primarily my eyes focused upon a scene, a large house with two people in it. I saw a flight of vultures on a blazing flesh sky, I saw yellow lions, and I heard voices.

51   The first Illustration quivered and came to life.

Practice Exercise

What is the Illustrated Man's *point of view* about being "illustrated"?

_____

_____

_____

Practice Exercise

Who is the author's *intended audience*?

_____

_____

_____

Practice Exercise

What is the author's *purpose* in writing this?

_____

_____

Source: Ray Bradbury, *The Illustrated Man,* pp. 1–4. Copyright © 1951, by Ray Bradbury. New York: Doubleday, 1951. Reprinted with permission.

Reading Selection Quiz

This quiz has several parts. Your instructor may assign some or all of them.

Comprehension

Directions: Use the information in the selection to answer each item below. You may refer to the selection as you answer the questions. Write each answer in the space provided.

True or False

_____ **1.** The Illustrated Man is a small man with a large head.

_____ **2.** The story opens in early September in Wisconsin in 1950.

_____ **3.** There are eighteen illustrations on the Illustrated Man.

_____ **4.** If a person stayed around the Illustrated Man long enough, the person's picture appeared on the Illustrated Man's right shoulder blade and showed the person's future.

_____ **5.** That night, the other man in the Prologue watches the illustrations until he has seen all of them.

Multiple-Choice

_____ **6.** The Illustrated Man is called that because he:
  a. is covered with tattoos that look like fine drawings.
  b. is a tattoo artist.
  c. draws illustrations that he sells at carnivals.
  d. reads illustrated comic books.

_____ **7.** The Illustrated Man earns money by:
  a. being in carnival side shows.
  b. tattooing people who come to carnivals.
  c. painting.
  d. being a storyteller at carnivals.

_____ **8.** When the story opens, how old is the Illustrated Man?
  a. 20 years old
  b. 40 years old
  c. 60 years old
  d. 70 years old

_____ **9.** The Illustrated Man has been forced to leave jobs because:

a. he steals money from the carnivals' owners.

b. at night the pictures move and show the future, which often include violent events.

c. he goes back to the future.

d. the carnival season ends.

_____ **10.** The Illustrated Man says he does not sleep much at night because:

a. the weather is very hot and he sleeps outdoors.

b. he is worried about not finding work.

c. he is angry at the woman who put the illustrations on his skin.

d. he can feel the illustrations crawling on his skin.

SELECTION **8.1**

Literature
(continued)

Vocabulary in Context

Directions: For each item below, use context clues to deduce the meaning of the *italicized* word. Be sure the answer you choose makes sense in both sentences. Write each answer in the space provided.

_____ **11.** Perspiration was *streaming* from his face, yet he made no move to open his shirt.

She was so touched by the stranger's kindness that tears of gratitude were *streaming* down her cheeks.

streaming (strēm′ ĭng) means:

a. stinging

b. evaporating

c. clouding

d. flowing

_____ **12.** I should be making money hand over fist at any small town side show celebration, but here I am with no *prospects*.

Martin not only lost his job, but he has no *prospects*.

prospects (prŏs′ pĕkts) means:

a. job-related skills

b. financial bonuses and raises

c. expectations of financial success

d. savings

_____ **13.** As for the rest of him, I cannot say how long I sat and stared, for he was a riot of rockets and fountains and people, in such *intricate* detail and color that you could hear the voices murmuring small and muted, from the crowds that inhabited his body.

The pattern in the handwoven rug was extremely small and *intricate*.

intricate (ĭn′ trĭ kĭt) means:
a. elaborate; complex
b. colorful
c. careless; imprecise
d. uninteresting; boring

_____ **14.** As for the rest of him, I cannot say how long I sat and stared, for he was a riot of rockets and fountains and people, in such intricate detail and color that you could hear the voices murmuring small and *muted,* from the crowds that inhabited his body.

Before the funeral began, the guests talked among themselves in *muted* voices.

muted (myo͞ot′ əd) means:
a. loud
b. unpleasant in tone
c. silent
d. muffled in sound

_____ **15.** You found them in forests of hair, *lurking* among a constellation of freckles, or peering from armpit caverns, diamond eyes aglitter.

The mentally ill patient thought danger was *lurking* everywhere.

lurking (lûrk′ ĭng) means:
a. disappearing
b. existing, but barely observable
c. increasing, growing
d. fading; passing out of sight

_____ **16.** If El Greco had painted miniatures in his *prime,* no bigger than your hand, infinitely detailed, with all his sulphurous color, elongation, and anatomy, perhaps he might have used this man's body for his art.

During the *prime* of his life, the horse won every major race he was entered in.

prime (prīm) means:
a. period of greatest success
b. old age
c. earliest stage
d. difficult phase

_____ **17.** By morning he looked like a man who had fallen into a twenty-color print press and been squeezed out, all bright and *picturesque*.

Viewed from an airplane, the charming Swiss village was so *picturesque* that it looked like a postcard.

picturesque (pĭk′ chə rĕsk′) means:
a. unusually small in size
b. unfamiliar
c. odd and old-fashioned
d. visually attractive and producing a strong impression

_____ **18.** All the time he had been talking, his hands had wandered over the Illustrations, as if to adjust their frames, to brush away dust—the motions of a *connoisseur*, an art patron.

Professor Lloyd is such a *connoisseur* of music that he can distinguish between different recordings of the same symphony.

connoisseur (kŏn ə sûr′) means:
a. fan; enthusiast
b. critic; faultfinder
c. person with expert knowledge of the fine arts
d. creator

_____ **19.** Crickets were stirring gently in the distant *ravines*.

Ravines are formed when the earth's surface is worn away by running water.

ravines (rə vēnz′) means:
a. dry, sandy areas with no vegetation
b. woods; forests
c. deep, narrow gorges with steep sides
d. broad, flat-topped hills with steep sides

_____ **20.** The first Illustration *quivered* and came to life.

The lost child's lip *quivered,* and then she began to cry.

quivered (kwĭv′ ərd) means:
a. shook with slight, rapid movements
b. flashed; flickered
c. glowed brightly
d. jerked violently

Reading Skills Application

Directions: These items test your ability to *apply* certain reading skills. You may not have studied all of the skills yet, so some items will serve as a preview. Write each answer in the space provided.

_____ **21.** In paragraph 16, what is the relationship between the first sentence and the second sentence?

    a. comparison

    b. example

    c. cause-effect

    d. contrast

_____ **22.** The author mentions El Greco, Rouault, and Picasso to indicate that the Illustrated Man's illustrations were:

    a. based on old paintings.

    b. colorful.

    c. intricate.

    d. of high artistic quality.

_____ **23.** The Illustrated Man says that when he finds the woman who tattooed him, he is going to kill her. It can be inferred he feels this way because:

    a. the tattoos she put on him have ruined his life.

    b. she broke his leg when he was twenty.

    c. she has gone back to the future.

    d. he is frustrated at having searched for her for so many years.

_____ **24.** What is the meaning of the simile in paragraph 32: ". . . he looked like a man who had fallen into a twenty-color press and been squeezed out, all bright and picturesque"?

    a. He was a painter.

    b. He was covered with brightly colored tattoos.

    c. He had once worked as a printer.

    d. He still had colorful bruises from an earlier injury.

_____ **25.** In paragraph 10, what is the meaning of the word *cream* in the sentence "Here it is, early September, the *cream* of the Labor Day carnival season"?

    a. best part

    b. slowest part

    c. beginning

    d. end

SELECTION **8.1**

Literature
(continued)

SELECTION 8.1

Respond in Writing

Directions: Refer to the selection as needed to answer the essay-type questions below. (Your instructor may direct you to work collaboratively with other students on one or more items. Each group member should be able to explain *all* of the group's answers.)

1. If you could see your future, would you want to know it? Explain why or why not.

    _____

    _____

    _____

    _____

2. If you could have a single tattoo that revealed other people's future, would you choose to have it? Explain why or why not.

    _____

    _____

    _____

    _____

3. The Illustrated Man in the story is a living canvas. How do you think someone that heavily tattooed would be received today? Why do you think that?

    _____

    _____

    _____

    _____

4. In the United States, people of all ages and social groups now have tattoos. In your opinion, why have tattoos become so popular?

    _____

    _____

    _____

    _____

SELECTION 8.2

Speech Communication

Think Before You Speak: Public Speaking in a Multicultural World

From *The Art of Public Speaking*

by Stephen E. Lucas

Prepare Yourself to Read

Directions: Do these exercises *before* you read Selection 8.2.

1. First, read and think about the title. What do you already know about public speaking?

    _____

    _____

    _____

    _____

2. Next, complete your preview by reading the following:

    Introduction (in *italics*)

    Headings

    All of the first paragraph (paragraph 1)

    First sentence of each of the other paragraphs

    The last paragraph (paragraph 30)

    Now that you have previewed the selection, what aspects of public speaking does the selection seem to be about?

    _____

    _____

    _____

    _____

    _____

3. **Build your vocabulary as you read**. If you discover an unfamiliar word or key term as you read the selection, try to determine its meaning by using context clues.

Read More about This Topic Online

Internet Resources

Use a search engine, such as Google or Yahoo!, to expand your existing knowledge about this topic *before* you read the selection or to learn more about it *afterward*. If you are unfamiliar with conducting Internet searches, read pages 25–26 on Boolean searches. You can also use Wikipedia, the free online encyclopedia, at www .wikipedia.com. Keep in mind that when you visit any website, it is a good idea to evaluate the site and the information it contains. Ask yourself questions such as "Who sponsors this website?" and "Is the information it contains up to date?"

SELECTION 8.2: THINK BEFORE YOU SPEAK: PUBLIC SPEAKING IN A MULTICULTURAL WORLD

This selection from a speech communication textbook explains how cultural diversity in our society affects the way we should communicate. Adjusting your delivery to the diversity and multiculturalism of your audience will play a role in almost any speech you give. Many—perhaps most—of the audiences you address will include people of different cultural backgrounds. The need for effective public speaking can affect you as a college student, a businessperson, a traveler, or a member of a civic, social, or religious organization. This selection gives you pointers on how to effectively address a diverse, multicultural audience.

Cultural Diversity in the Modern World

1   The United States has always been a diverse society. In 1673, more than three centuries ago, a visitor to what is now New York City was astonished to find that 18 languages were spoken among the city's 8,000 inhabitants. By the middle of the nineteenth century, so many people from so many lands had come to the United States that novelist Herman Melville exclaimed, "You cannot spill a drop of American blood without spilling the blood of the whole world."

2   One can only imagine what Melville would say today! The United States has become the most diverse society on the face of the earth. For more than a century, most immigrants to the United States were Europeans—Irish, Germans, English, Scandinavians, Greeks, Poles, Italians, and others. Together with African-Americans, they made America the "melting pot" of the world. Today another great wave of immigration—mostly from Asia and Latin America—is transforming the United States into what one writer has called "the first universal nation," a multicultural society of unmatched diversity.

3   The diversity of life in the United States can be seen in cities and towns, schools and businesses, community groups and houses of worship all across the land. Consider the following:

- There are 215 nations in the world, and every one of them has someone living in the United States.
- New York City has over 170 distinct ethnic communities.
- Houston has two radio stations that broadcast in Chinese and a daily newspaper that prints in Chinese.
- Nearly 61 percent of the people of Miami were born outside the United States.
- More than 32 million people in the United States speak a language other than English at home.
- Asian Americans make up 45 percent of first-year students at the University of California, Berkeley.

4   These kinds of changes are not limited to the United States. We are living in an age of international multiculturalism. The Internet

Annotation Practice Exercises

Directions: For each of the exercises below, read critically to answer the questions. This will help you gain additional insights as you read.

SELECTION 8.2

allows for instant communication almost everywhere around the world. CNN is broadcast in more than 200 countries. International air travel has made national boundaries almost meaningless. The new global economy is redefining the nature of business and commerce. All nations, all people, all cultures are becoming part of a vast global village. For example:

- There are 60,000 transnational corporations around the world, and they account for more than a quarter of the world's economic output.
- Restaurants in coastal towns of Queensland, Australia, print their menus in both Japanese and English.
- McDonald's sells more hamburgers and French fries abroad than it does in the United States; Gillette makes 70 percent of its sales through exports.
- In Geneva, Switzerland, there are so many people from around the world that nearly 60 percent of the school population is non-Swiss.
- France has more Muslims than practicing Catholics; radio CHIN in Toronto, Canada, broadcasts in 32 languages.
- Four out of every five new jobs in the United States are generated as a direct result of international trade.

Cultural Diversity and Public Speaking

5   "That's all very interesting," you may be saying to yourself, "but what does it have to do with my speeches?" The answer is that diversity and multiculturalism are such basic facts of life that they can play a role in almost any speech you give. Consider the following situations:

- A business manager briefing employees of a multinational corporation.
- A lawyer presenting her closing argument to an ethnically mixed jury.
- A minister sermonizing to a culturally diverse congregation.
- An international student explaining the customs of his land to students at a U.S. university.
- A teacher addressing parents at a multiethnic urban school.

These are only a few of the countless speaking situations affected by the cultural diversity of modern life.

6   As experts in intercultural communication have long known, speech-making becomes more complex as cultural diversity increases. Part of the complexity stems from the differences in language from culture to culture. But language and thought are closely linked. So, too, are language and culture. Nothing separates one culture from another more than language. Not only do words change

Today, speakers
should be prepared
for the multicultural
audiences they are
likely to encounter.

from language to language, but so do ways of thinking and of seeing the world. Language and culture are so closely bound that we communicate the way we do because we are raised in a particular culture and learn its language, rules, and norms.

7   The meanings attached to gestures, facial expressions, and other nonverbal signals also vary from culture to culture. Even the gestures for such basic messages as "yes" and "no," "hello" and "goodbye" are culturally based. In the United States people nod their heads up and down to signal "yes" and shake them back and forth to signal "no." In Thailand the same actions have exactly the opposite meaning! To take another example, the North American "goodbye" wave is interpreted in many parts of Europe and South America as the motion for "no," while the Italian and Greek gesture for "goodbye" is the same as the U.S. signal for "come here."

8   Many stories have been told about the fate of public speakers who fail to take into account cultural differences between themselves and their audiences. Consider the following scenario:

9   The sales manager of a U.S. electronics firm is in Brazil to negotiate a large purchase of computers by a South American corporation. After three days of negotiations, the sales manager holds a gala reception for all the major executives to build goodwill between the companies.

10   As is the custom on such occasions, time is set aside during the reception for an exchange of toasts. When it is the sales manager's turn to speak, she praises the Brazilian firm for its

many achievements and talks eloquently of her respect for its president and other executives. The words are perfect, and the sales manager can see her audience smiling in approval.

11   And then—disaster. As the sales manager closes her speech, she raises her hand and flashes the classic U.S. "OK" sign to signal her pleasure at the progress of the negotiations. Instantly the festive mood is replaced with stony silence; smiles turn to icy stares. The sales manager has given her Brazilian audience a gesture with roughly the same meaning as an extended middle finger in the United States.

12   The next day the Brazilian firm announces it will buy its computers from another company.

13   As this scenario illustrates, public speakers can ill afford to overlook their listeners' cultural values and customs. This is true whether you are speaking at home or abroad, in Atlanta or Rio de Janeiro, in a college classroom or at a meeting of community volunteers. Because of the increasing diversity of modern life, many—perhaps most—of the audiences you address will include people of different cultural backgrounds.

14   With that in mind, let us turn now to the importance of avoiding ethnocentrism. Ethnocentrism, which is explained below, often blocks communication between speakers and listeners of different cultural, racial, and ethnic backgrounds.

Avoiding Ethnocentrism

15   *Ethnocentrism* is the belief that our own group or culture—whatever it may be—is superior to all other groups or cultures. Because of ethnocentrism, we identify with our group or culture and see its values, beliefs, and customs as "right" or "natural"—in comparison to the values, beliefs, and customs of other groups or cultures, which we tend to think of as "wrong" or "unnatural."

16   Ethnocentrism is part of every culture. If you were born and raised in the United States, you may find it strange that most people in India regard the cow as a sacred animal and forgo using it as a source for food. On the other hand, if you were born and raised in India, you might well be shocked at the use of cows in the United States for food, clothing, and other consumer goods. If you are Christian, you most likely think of Sunday as the "normal" day of worship. But if you are Jewish, you probably regard Saturday as the "correct" Sabbath. And if you are Muslim, you doubtless see both Saturday and Sunday as unusual times for worship. For you, Friday is the "right" day.

17   Ethnocentrism can play a positive role in creating group pride and loyalty. But it can also be a destructive force—especially when it leads to prejudice and hostility toward different racial, ethnic, or

Practice Exercise

What is the author's *purpose* in paragraphs 5–13?

_____

_____

_____

_____

_____

_____

_____

_____

_____

_____

SELECTION 8.2

cultural groups. To be an effective public speaker in a multicultural world, you need to keep in mind that all people have their special beliefs and customs.

18   Avoiding ethnocentrism does not mean you must agree with the values and practices of all groups and cultures. At times you might try to convince people of different cultures to change their traditional ways of doing things—as speakers from the United Nations seek to persuade farmers in Africa to adopt more productive methods of agriculture, as Muslim parents in the United States urge public school officials to accommodate Muslim customs for children who adhere to Islam, or as delegates from the United States and Japan attempt to influence the other country's trade policies.

19   If such speakers are to be successful, however, they must show respect for the cultures of the people they address. They cannot assume that their cultural assumptions and practices will be shared—or even understood—by all members of their audience. They need to adapt their message to the cultural values and expectations of their listeners.

20   When you work on your speeches, keep in mind the growing diversity of life in the modern world and be alert to how cultural factors might affect the way listeners respond to your speeches. For classroom speeches, you can use audience-analysis questionnaires to learn about the backgrounds and opinions of your classmates in regard to specific speech topics. For speeches outside the classroom, the person who invites you to speak can usually provide information about the audience.

21   Once you know about any cultural factors that might affect the audience's response to your speech, you can work on adapting the speech to make it as effective and appropriate as possible. As you prepare the speech, try to put yourself in the place of your listeners and to hear your message through their ears. If there is a language difference between you and your audience, avoid any words or phrases that might cause misunderstanding. When researching the speech, keep an eye out for examples, comparisons, and other supporting materials that will relate to a wide range of listeners. Also consider using visual aids in your speech. They can be especially helpful in bridging a gap in language or cultural background.

22   When delivering your speech, be alert to feedback that might indicate the audience is having trouble grasping your ideas. If you see puzzled expressions on the faces of your listeners, restate your point to make sure it is understood. With some audiences, you can encourage feedback by asking, "Am I making myself clear?" or "Did I explain this point fully enough?"

23   If you pose such questions, however, be aware that listeners from different cultures may respond quite differently. Most Arabs, North Americans, and Europeans will give you fairly direct feedback if you ask for it. Listeners from Asian and Caribbean countries, on the other hand, may not respond, out of concern that doing so will show disrespect for the speaker.

24   Finally, we should note the importance of avoiding ethnocentrism when *listening* to speeches. Speech audiences have a responsibility to listen courteously and attentively. When you listen to a speaker from a different cultural background, be on guard against the temptation to judge that speaker on the basis of his or her appearance or manner of delivery. Too often we form opinions about people by the way they look or speak rather than by listening closely to what they say. No matter what the cultural background of the speaker, you should listen to her or him as attentively as you would want your audience to listen to you.

Some Final Thoughts

25   The need for effective public speaking will almost certainly touch you sometime in your life. When it does, you want to be ready. But even if you never give another speech in your life, you still have much to gain from studying public speaking. A speech class will give you training in researching topics, organizing your ideas, and presenting yourself skillfully. This training is invaluable for every type of communication.

26   There are many similarities between public speaking and daily conversation. The three major goals of public speaking—to inform, to persuade, to entertain—are also the three major goals of everyday conversation. In conversation, almost without thinking about it, you employ a wide range of skills. You tell a story for maximum impact. You adapt to feedback from your listener. These are among the most important skills you will need for public speaking.

27   Public speaking is also different from conversation. First, public speaking is more highly structured than conversation. It usually imposes strict time limitations on the speaker, and it requires more detailed preparation than does ordinary conversation. Second, public speaking requires more formal language. Listeners react negatively to speeches loaded with slang, jargon, and bad grammar. Third, public speaking demands a different method of delivery. Effective speakers adjust their voices to the larger audience and work at avoiding distracting physical mannerisms and verbal habits.

Practice Exercise

What is the author's *purpose* in paragraphs 15–23?

_____

_____

_____

_____

_____

Practice Exercise

What is the author's *purpose* in paragraph 24?

_____

_____

_____

_____

_____

_____

SELECTION 8.2

28   One of the major concerns of students in any speech class is stage fright. Actually, most successful speakers are nervous before making a speech. A speech class will give you an opportunity to gain confidence and make your nervousness work for you rather than against you. You will take a big step toward overcoming stage fright if you think positively, prepare thoroughly, visualize yourself giving a successful speech, and think of your speech as communication rather than as performance in which you must do everything perfectly. Like other students over the years, you too can develop confidence in your speech-making abilities.

29   Besides building your confidence, a course in public speaking can help you develop your skills as a critical thinker. Critical thinking is the ability to perceive relationships among ideas. It can help you spot weaknesses in other people's reasoning and avoid them in your own. Critical thinking can make a difference in many areas of your life, from your schoolwork to your activities as a consumer to your responsibilities as a citizen.

30   Because of the growing diversity of modern life, many—perhaps most—of the audiences you address will include people of different cultural, racial, and ethnic backgrounds. When you work on your speeches, be alert to how such factors might affect the responses of your listeners and take steps to adapt your message accordingly. Above all, avoid the ethnocentric belief that your own culture or group—whatever it may be—is superior to every other culture or group. Also keep in mind the importance of avoiding ethnocentrism when listening to speeches. Accord every speaker the same courtesy and attentiveness you would want from your listeners.

Practice Exercise

Who is the author's *intended audience* for this selection?

_____

_____

_____

Practice Exercise

What is the author's *point of view* throughout this selection?

_____

_____

_____

_____

Practice Exercise

What is the author's *tone* throughout this selection?

_____

_____

_____

Source: Adapted from Stephen E. Lucas, *The Art of Public Speaking,* 8e, pp. 22–28. Copyright © 2004 by The McGraw-Hill Companies, Inc. Reprinted with permission of The McGraw-Hill Companies, Inc.

SELECTION **8.2**

Speech Communication
(continued)

Reading Selection Quiz

This quiz has several parts. Your instructor may assign some or all of them.

Comprehension

Directions: Use the information in the selection to answer each item below. You may refer to the selection as you answer the questions. Write each answer in the space provided.

_____ 1. How many people in the United States speak a language other than English at home?
    a. more than 32 million
    b. more than 170 million
    c. more than 215 million
    d. more than 320 million

_____ 2. If current trends in the United States continue:
    a. immigration from Latin America and Asia will decline.
    b. immigration from Europe will increase.
    c. people of European descent will become a minority of U.S. citizens by 2050.
    d. America will become the "melting pot" of the world.

_____ 3. International multiculturalism is on the rise as a result of:
    a. worldwide communication available via the Internet.
    b. the new global economy and the redefining of the nature of worldwide business and commerce.
    c. international air travel becoming more popular and more convenient.
    d. all of the above

_____ 4. Ethnocentrism is the belief that:
    a. our own group's culture is different from all other groups' cultures.
    b. our own group or culture is superior to all other groups or cultures.
    c. cultural diversity is at the center of every society.
    d. ethnic groups are the most important part of our cultural heritage.

_____ 5. Once you have learned about any cultural factors that might affect the audience's response to your speech, you should:
    a. work on adapting the speech to make it as effective and appropriate as possible.
    b. restate your point to make sure it is clear.
    c. agree with the values and practices of the audience.
    d. select a topic that will be understood by everyone in the audience.

_____ **6.** The goals of public speaking are:
   a. to build confidence and to conquer nervousness.
   b. to treat all audiences the same.
   c. to persuade, to inform, and to entertain.
   d. to create group pride and loyalty.

_____ **7.** One way that public speaking is different from everyday conversation is that you must:
   a. organize your ideas logically.
   b. use more formal language.
   c. tailor your message to your audience.
   d. adapt to feedback from your listeners.

_____ **8.** When giving a speech, you should remember that:
   a. your audience will very likely include people of different cultural backgrounds.
   b. audiences react well to informal communication and jargon.
   c. your audience will identify with only one particular group or culture.
   d. audiences expect you to maintain your composure.

_____ **9.** One way to help overcome nervousness when giving a speech is to:
   a. encourage feedback by asking, "Am I making myself clear?" or "Did I explain this point fully enough?"
   b. adapt your message to each person in the audience.
   c. think of your speech as communication rather than as a performance in which you must do everything perfectly.
   d. memorize as much of the speech as possible and rehearse the speech several times in private.

_____ **10.** To be successful, speakers must:
   a. adapt their message to the cultural values of their audience.
   b. show respect for the cultures of the people they address.
   c. not assume that their cultural practices will be understood by all members of their audience.
   d. all of the above

S E L E C T I O N **8.2**

**Speech
Communication**
(continued)

Vocabulary in Context

Directions: For each item below, use context clues to deduce the meaning of the *italicized* word. Be sure the answer you choose makes sense in both sentences. Write each answer in the space provided.

_____ 11. Today another great wave of immigration—mostly from Asia and Latin America—is *transforming* the United States into what one writer has called "the first universal nation," a multicultural society of unmatched diversity.

Computer technology is *transforming* American businesses into high-tech, networked work environments.

transforming (trăns fôrm′ ĭng) means:

a. modernizing; renovating

b. changing the nature of; converting

c. forming improved environments

d. limiting the nature of; stifling

_____ 12. There are 60,000 *transnational* corporations around the world, and they account for more than a quarter of the world's economic output.

Worldwide, the governments of free countries are working to deal with the *transnational* threats of terror networks.

transnational (trănz năsh′ ə nəl) means:

a. within the boundaries of a single country

b. reaching beyond the boundaries of states within the United States

c. reaching beyond national boundaries

d. reaching across the boundaries of oceans

_____ 13. All nations, all people, all cultures are becoming part of a *vast* global village.

Our thirteen-hour flight from Los Angeles to Sydney over the *vast* Pacific Ocean transported us from the North American continent to the Australian continent.

vast (văst) means:

a. having extensive variety; diverse

b. extremely long

c. complicated

d. very great in size or extent

_____ 14. Four of every five new jobs in the United States are *generated* as a direct result of international trade.

The worldwide demand for cell phones has *generated* a new kind of specialty retail store, where customers can buy, rent, or upgrade cell phones.

generated (jĕn′ ə rā təd) means:

a. brought into being; produced

b. forfeited; lost

c. ended; stopped

d. changed the shape of; transformed

15. As experts in *intercultural* communication have long known, speech-making becomes more complex as cultural diversity increases.

Robert and Madhu have a truly *intercultural* marriage; he was born and reared in Canada, and she lived the first nineteen years of her life in India.

intercultural (ĭn tər kŭl′ chər əl) means:

a. complex

b. representing different cultures

c. a bond between two cultures

d. difficult to communicate or comprehend

16. After three days of negotiations, the sales manager holds a gala reception for all the major executives to build *goodwill* between the companies.

Many of our city's restaurants and shops contribute financial support to youth athletic teams in order to promote *goodwill* with the community.

goodwill (gŏod wĭl′) means:

a. a financial relationship; a contract

b. a cheerful willingness to help the less fortunate

c. a good relationship, as between a business enterprise with its customers

d. a negotiation between two parties for profit

17. If you were born and raised in the United States, you may find it strange that most people in India regard the cow as a sacred animal and *forgo* using it as a source for food.

We ate so much during dinner that everyone at our table decided to *forgo* dessert.

forgo (fôr gō′) means:

a. to consume; eat

b. to choose not to do something

c. to feast on; devour

d. to give away or contribute something of value

18. They cannot *assume* that their cultural assumptions and practices will be shared—or even understood—by all members of their audience.

Most people *assume* that the price of most of the things we buy will rise each year.

assume (ə sōōm′) means:

a. to take responsibility for; adopt

b. to take for granted; suppose

c. to understand; comprehend

d. to think; ponder

19. They need to *adapt* their message to the cultural values and expectations of their listeners.

When a person moves from one city to another, it can often take several months to *adapt* to his or her new surroundings.

adapt (ə dăpt′) means:

a. to create

b. to match

c. to adjust

d. to change

20. In conversation, almost without thinking about it, you employ a wide *range* of skills.

We had difficulty finding an apartment that was within our price *range*.

range (rānj) means:

a. a collection of useful skills

b. amount required for ownership; price

c. suitable style; preference

d. an amount of variation; variation within limits

Selection **8.2**

Speech Communication
(continued)

Reading Skills Application

Directions: These items test your ability to *apply* certain reading skills. You may not have studied all of the skills yet, so some items will serve as a preview. Write each answer in the space provided.

21. The information in paragraph 16 is organized using which of the following patterns?

a. list

b. sequence

c. comparison-contrast

d. cause-effect

22. Which of the following represents a fact rather than an opinion?

a. The new global economy is redefining the nature of business and commerce.

b. All nations, all people, all cultures are becoming part of a vast global village.

c. Asian Americans make up 45 percent of first-year students at the University of California, Berkeley.

d. International air travel has made national boundaries almost meaningless.

_____ **23.** The author's purpose for including the story about the U.S. sales manager who spoke to a group of executives in Brazil is to:

    a. inform readers about the cultural values and customs of Brazil.

    b. instruct readers how to avoid ethnocentrism.

    c. convince readers that an inappropriate gesture or remark to an audience with different cultural backgrounds can have a disastrous effect.

    d. persuade readers not to take into account the cultural differences between themselves and their audiences.

_____ **24.** The author mentions the use of audience analysis questionnaires and contacting the person who has invited you to speak in order to:

    a. suggest ways that you can learn about your audience's backgrounds, opinions, and cultural differences.

    b. demonstrate the challenges of public speaking in today's world.

    c. prove that diversity and multiculturalism are basic facts of life.

    d. show that ethnocentrism is part of every culture.

_____ **25.** Which of the following best expresses the main idea of paragraph 2?

    a. Today a great wave of immigrants from Asia and Latin America is transforming the United States.

    b. For more than a century, most immigrants to the United States were Europeans.

    c. The United States is now the most diverse society in the world.

    d. African Americans and Europeans made America a "melting pot."

SELECTION **8.2**

**Speech
Communication**
(continued)

Respond in Writing

Directions: Refer to the selection as needed to answer the essay-type questions below. (Your instructor may direct you to work collaboratively with other students on one or more items. Each group member should be able to explain *all* of the group's answers.)

1. Describe at least three situations in which you have addressed a group of people who have had diverse, multicultural backgrounds. If you have not yet had this type of experience, describe at least three situations when you might have to address a diverse, multicultural group in the future.

_____

_____

_____

_____

2. List at least three ways that you can find out about your audience in order to prepare an appropriate speech.

_____

_____

_____

_____

_____

_____

3. **Overall main idea.** What is the overall main idea the author wants the reader to understand about public speaking in a multicultural world? Answer this question in one sentence. Be sure to include the topic (*public speaking in a multicultural world*) in your overall main idea sentence.

_____

_____

_____

_____

_____

SELECTION 8.2

Selection **8.3**

Literature

From *The Things They Carried*
by Tim O'Brien

Prepare Yourself to Read

Directions: Do these exercises *before* you read Selection 8.3.

1. First, read and think about the title. What do you already know about what soldiers carry with them when they go to war?

   _____

   _____

   _____

2. Next, complete your preview by skimming the selection. Each of the two sections is written as a single paragraph.

   Now that you have previewed the selection, list some of the things the author mentions that the soldiers carried with them to war.

   _____

   _____

   _____

   _____

   _____

   _____

3. **Build your vocabulary as you read**. If you discover an unfamiliar word or key term as you read the selection, try to determine its meaning by using context clues.

Read More about This Topic Online

Internet Resources

Use a search engine, such as Google or Yahoo!, to expand your existing knowledge about this topic *before* you read the selection or to learn more about it *afterward*. If you are unfamiliar with conducting Internet searches, read pages 25–26 on Boolean searches. You can also use Wikipedia, the free online encyclopedia, at www .wikipedia.com. Keep in mind that when you visit any website, it is a good idea to evaluate the site and the information it contains. Ask yourself questions such as "Who sponsors this website?" and "Is information it contains up to date?"

SELECTION 8.3

SELECTION 8.3: FROM *THE THINGS THEY CARRIED*

The Vietnam War (1954–1975) was a controversial, unpopular war in which the United States backed the non-Communist forces of South Vietnam against the Communist forces of North Vietnam (which was supported by China and the Soviet Union). As a young college graduate who had attended war protests and peace vigils, Tim O'Brien was drafted and sent to Vietnam. Although he despised war, he served in the infantry from 1969 to 1970. He survived his tour, received the Purple Heart for wounds he received, and then attended graduate school at Harvard. He worked, as a national affairs reporter for the Washington Post, *but left to pursue his own writing full-time.*

The Things They Carried tells the fictional story of Alpha Company, a platoon of young Americans sent to Vietnam. It includes the character Tim O'Brien since it was based on some of the writer's own experiences. The young soldiers feel fear, rage, loneliness, and isolation. They long for their "old lives," their families, girlfriends, and buddies. In Vietnam, they are each other's family.

Although The Things They Carried *is a work of fiction, it portrays war truthfully. It is considered an American classic, one that is widely read and taught in American high schools, universities, and reading groups. It is a Vietnam testament that is unparalleled as a study of men at war and the pervasive, life-changing, and enduring effects war has on those who survive it. O'Brien's work is particularly relevant because of U.S. involvement in Iraq, a war as unpopular as Vietnam.*

The excerpts contain military terms, such as "rations" (prepackaged meals) and "flak jackets" (bullet-proof jackets). There are also acronyms and abbreviations, such as "R&R" (rest and recreation), "SOP" (standard operating procedure), and "USO" (United Services Organization). There is also military jargon, such as "hump" (to carry an item), "fatigues" (clothing worn by military personnel for field duty), and "grunts" (slang for U.S. military infantrymen). You do not need to understand all of the terms, though, to understand the selection.

Because the two excerpts are each a single, long paragraph, the lines are numbered every five lines (rather than the paragraphs being numbered).

1   The things they carried were largely determined by necessity. Among the necessities or near-necessities were P-38 can openers, pocket knives, heat tabs, wristwatches, dog tags, mosquito repellent, chewing gum, candy, cigarettes, salt tablets, packets of Kool-
5 Aid, lighters, matches, sewing kits, Military Payment Certificates, C rations, and two or three canteens of water. Together, these items weighed between 15 and 20 pounds, depending upon a man's habits or rate of metabolism. Henry Dobbins, who was a big man, carried extra rations; he was especially fond of canned peaches in heavy

Annotation Practice Exercises

Directions: For each of the exercises below, read critically to answer the questions. This will help you gain additional insights as you read.

10 syrup over pound cake. Dave Jensen, who practiced field hygiene, carried a toothbrush, dental floss, and several hotel-sized bars of soap he'd stolen on R&R in Sydney, Australia. Ted Lavender, who was scared, carried tranquilizers until he was shot in the head out-side the village of Than Khe in mid-April. By necessity, and because
15 it was SOP, they all carried steel helmets that weighed 5 pounds including the liner and camouflage cover. They carried the standard fatigue jackets and trousers. Very few carried underwear. On their feet they carried jungle boots—2.1 pounds—and Dave Jensen car-ried three pairs of socks and a can of Dr. Scholl's foot powder as
20 a precaution against trench foot. Until he was shot, Ted Lavender carried 6 or 7 ounces of premium dope, which for him was a neces-sity. Norman Bowker carried a diary. Rat Kiley carried comic books. Kiowa, a devout Baptist, carried an illustrated New Testament that had been presented to him by his father, who taught Sunday school
25 in Oklahoma City, Oklahoma. As a hedge against bad times, how-ever, Kiowa also carried his grandmother's distrust of the white man, his grandfather's old hunting hatchet. Necessity dictated. Because the land was mined and booby-trapped, it was SOP for each man to carry a steel-centered, nylon-covered flak jacket, which weighed
30 6.7 pounds, but which on hot days seemed much heavier. Because you could die so quickly, each man carried at least one large com-press bandage, usually in the helmet band for easy access. Because the nights were cold, and because the monsoons were wet, each carried a green plastic poncho that could be used as a raincoat or
35 ground sheet or makeshift tent. With its quilted liner, the poncho weighed almost 2 pounds, but it was worth every ounce. In April, for instance, when Ted Lavender was shot, they used his poncho to wrap him up, then to carry him across the paddy, then to lift him into the chopper that took him away.

***

40 They carried USO stationery and pencils and pens. They carried Sterno, safety pins, trip flares, signal flares, spools of wire, razor blades, chewing tobacco, liberated joss sticks and statuettes of the smiling Buddha, candles, grease pencils, *The Stars and Stripes,* fin-gernail clippers, Psy Ops leaflets, bush hats, bolos, and much more.
45 Twice a week, when the resupply choppers came in, they carried hot chow in green marmite cans and large canvas bags filled with iced beer and soda pop. They carried plastic water containers, each with a 2-gallon capacity. Mitchell Sanders carried a set of starched tiger fatigues for special occasions. Henry Dobbins carried Black
50 Flag insecticide. Dave Jensen carried empty sandbags that could be filled at night for added protection. Lee Strunk carried tanning lotion. Some things they carried in common. Taking turns, they car-ried the big PRC-77 scrambler radio, which weighed 30 pounds with its battery. They shared the weight of memory. They took up
55 what others could no longer bear. Often, they carried each other,

---

Practice Exercise

What is the author's *purpose* in writing this?

_____
_____
_____
_____
_____
_____
_____
_____
_____
_____

Practice Exercise

Who is the author's *intended audience?*

_____
_____
_____
_____
_____

Practice Exercise

What is the author's/soldiers' *point of view* about their role in the war and the war itself?

_____
_____
_____
_____
_____
_____

SELECTION 8.3

the wounded or weak. They carried infections. They carried chess
sets, basketballs, Vietnamese-English dictionaries, insignia of rank,
Bronze Stars and Purple Hearts, plastic cards imprinted with the
Code of Conduct. They carried diseases, among them malaria and
60 dysentery. They carried lice and ringworm and leeches and paddy
algae and various rots and molds. They carried the land itself—Vietnam,
the place, the soil—a powdery orange-red dust that covered
their boots and fatigues and faces. They carried the sky. The whole
atmosphere, they carried it, the humidity, the monsoons, the stink
65 of fungus and decay, all of it, they carried gravity. They moved like
mules. By daylight they took sniper fire, at night they were mortared,
but it was not battle, it was just the endless march, village to village,
without purpose, nothing won or lost. They marched for the sake
of the march. They plodded along slowly, dumbly, leaning forward
70 against the heat, unthinking, all blood and bone, simple grunts, sol-
diering with their legs, toiling up the hills and down into the paddies
and across the rivers and up again and down, just humping, one step
and then the next and then another, but no volition, no will, because
it was automatic, it was anatomy, and the war was entirely a matter
75 of posture and carriage, the hump was everything, a kind of inertia, a
kind of emptiness, a dullness of desire and intellect and conscience
and hope and human sensibility. Their principles were in their feet.
Their calculations were biological. They had no sense of strategy or
mission. They searched the villages without knowing what to look
80 for, not caring, kicking over jars of rice, frisking children and old men,
blowing tunnels, sometimes setting fires and sometimes not, then
forming up and moving on to the next village, then other villages,
where it would always be the same. They carried their own lives. The
pressures were enormous. In the heat of early afternoon, they would
85 remove their helmets and flak jackets, walking bare, which was dangerous but which helped ease the strain. They would often discard
things along the route of march. Purely for comfort, they would throw
away rations, blow their Claymores and grenades, no matter, because by nightfall the resupply choppers would arrive with more of
90 the same, then a day or two later still more, fresh watermelons and
crates of ammunition and sunglasses and woolen sweaters—the
resources were stunning—sparklers for the Fourth of July, colored
eggs for Easter—it was the great American war chest—the fruits of
science, the smokestacks, the canneries, the arsenals at Hartford,
95 the Minnesota forests, the machine shops, the vast fields of corn and
wheat—they carried like freight trains; they carried it on their backs
and shoulders—and for all the ambiguities of Vietnam, all the mysteries and unknowns, there was at least the single abiding certainty that
they would never be at a loss for things to carry.

> **Practice Exercise**

What is the author's *tone* in the second excerpt?

_____

_____

_____

_____

_____

> **Practice Exercise**

What is the author's *intended meaning* when he says, "there was at least the single abiding certainty that they would never be at a loss for things to carry"?

_____

_____

_____

_____

Source: From Tim O'Brien, *The Things they Carried,* pp. 2–3, 14–16. Copyright © 1990 by Tim O'Brien. Reprinted by permission of Houghton Mifflin Harcourt Publishing Company and HarperCollins Publishers Ltd. All rights reserved.

" . . . it was just
the endless march,
village to village,
without purpose,
nothing won or lost."

SELECTION **8.3**

Literature
(continued)

Reading Selection Quiz

This quiz has several parts. Your instructor may assign some or all of them.

Comprehension

Directions: Use the information in the selection to answer each item below. You may refer to the selection as you answer the questions. Write each answer in the space provided.

True or False

_____ **1.** All of the items the soldiers carried were necessities.

_____ **2.** In Vietnam, the days could be hot and the nights cold.

_____ **3.** Some soldiers brought items they thought would help keep them safer or healthier.

_____ **4.** Kiowa was a Native American.

_____ **5.** Malaria and tuberculosis were two diseases soldiers contracted.

Multiple-Choice

_____ 6. Of these items that soldiers carried, which one was the heaviest?
   a. flak jacket
   b. steel helmet
   c. poncho
   d. jungle boots

_____ 7. Based on items that the soldiers carried, it can be concluded that:
   a. they thought there would be some time for recreation.
   b. the military sent new soldiers a list of items they should bring.
   c. all soldiers were required to bring the same things.
   d. soldiers were not permitted to bring any personal items.

_____ 8. Soldiers:
   a. did not receive replacements for items they discarded.
   b. were punished for being wasteful with items the military supplied.
   c. were not allowed to discard items.
   d. often discarded items they were tired of carrying.

_____ 9 Ted Lavender brought with him to Vietnam:
   a. three pairs of socks and foot powder.
   b. tranquilizers.
   c. an illustrated New Testament.
   d. dental floss.

_____ 10. The soldiers were resupplied:
   a. once a month.
   b. every two weeks.
   c. once a week.
   d. more than once a week.

SELECTION **8.3**
Literature
(continued)

Vocabulary in Context

Directions: For each item below, use context clues to deduce the meaning of the *italicized* word. Be sure the answer you choose makes sense in both sentences. Write each answer in the space provided.

_____ **11.** As a *hedge* against bad times, however, Kiowa also carried his grandmother's distrust of the white man, his grandfather's old hunting hatchet.

To protect their assets, some investors invest in gold as a *hedge* against inflation.

hedge (hĕj) means:

a. a row of shrubs that forms a boundary

b. noncommittal, vague statement

c. enclosure

d. protection by counterbalancing

_____ **12.** Necessity *dictated.*

The rain *dictated* a change in our plans: We went to a movie instead of going hiking.

dictated (dĭk′ tāt əd) means:

a. said out loud

b. canceled; undid

c. imposed; controlled

d. ended; stopped

_____ **13.** . . . each carried a green plastic poncho that could be used as a raincoat or groundsheet or *makeshift* tent.

Because my roommate and I lived in an apartment and didn't have much money, we used a curtain as a *makeshift* room divider.

makeshift (māk′ shĭft) means:

a. suitable as a temporary substitute when something else is not available

b. made from recycled material

c. inexpensive; economical

d. constructed in a hurry

_____ **14.** In April, for instance, when Ted Lavender was shot, they used his poncho to wrap him up, then to carry him across the *paddy,* then to lift him into the chopper that took him away.

In his *paddy,* the Chinese farmer worked barefooted in water up to his calves.

paddy (păd′ ē) means:

a. structure used for storage on a farm

b. boat that floats in shallow water

c. large farm owned by a group of people

d. flooded field where rice is grown

_____   **15.** They carried chess sets, basketballs, Vietnamese-English dictionaries, *insignia* of rank, Bronze Stars and Purple Hearts, plastic cards imprinted with the Code of Conduct.

The *insignia* on his uniform told us that he was the chief of police.

insignia (ĭn sĭg′ nē ə) means:

a. fabric braid or trim

b. badges or emblems of office or rank

c. marks; spots

d. stripes

_____   **16.** By daylight they took sniper fire, at night they were *mortared,* but it was not battle, it was just the endless march, village to village, without purpose, nothing won or lost.

The war-ravaged countryside was filled with holes where it had been *mortared.*

mortared (môr′ tərd) means:

a. covered with plaster

b. defended with military weapons

c. crushed

d. bombarded with explosive artillery shells

_____   **17.** They plodded along slowly, *dumbly,* learning forward against the heat, unthinking, all blood and bone . . .

You could have heard a pin drop: we were so stunned at what the tornado had done that we just stood there and stared *dumbly* at where our house had been.

dumbly (dŭm′ lē) means:

a. angrily refusing to speak

b. unintelligently

c. unintentionally

d. temporarily speechless

_____   **18.** They plodded along . . . one step and then the next and then another, but no *volition,* no will, because it was automatic . . .

No one persuaded Alonzo to become a police officer; he did it of his own *volition.*

volition (və lĭsh′ ən) means:

a. willpower

b. fear

c. conscious choice or decision

d. self-control

_____ 19. . . . and for all the *ambiguities* of Vietnam, all the mysteries and unknowns, there was at least the single abiding certainty that they would never be at a loss for things to carry.

The poem was so full of *ambiguities* that each of us had a different interpretation.

ambiguities (ăm bĭ gyo͞o′ĭ tēz) means:

a. errors; mistakes

b. documents written about various aspects of the same topic

c. uncertainties with regard to meaning

d. inspiring aspects

_____ 20. . . . and for all the ambiguities of Vietnam, all the mysteries and unknowns, there was at least the single abiding certainty that they would never *be at a loss* for things to carry.

When she hears her name called as the award winner, she's going to *be at a loss* for words!

be at a loss means:

a. lack; not have

b. be unable to locate a missing object

c. be puzzled

d. sell below cost

SELECTION **8.3**

Literature
(continued)

Reading Skills Application

Directions: These items test your ability to *apply* certain reading skills. You may not have studied all of the skills yet, so some items will serve as a preview. Write each answer in the space provided.

_____ 21. In the first excerpt, what is the relationship between the first sentence and the second sentence?

a. sequence

b. summary

c. example

d. contrast

_____ 22. In the second excerpt, a comparison is made between the soldiers and:

a. paddies.

b. snipers.

c. blood and bone.

d. mules.

SELECTION **8.3**

23. Based on information in the first half of the selection, which of these is a logical conclusion?

  a. Mitchell Sanders did not need to bring starched tiger fatigues for special occasions.

  b. Ted Lavender was a calm man who coped well with stress.

  c. Dave Jensen became a dentist after the war was over.

  d. Norman Bowker published a memoir based on the diary he kept during the war.

24. The author would be most likely to agree with which of the following statements?

  a. Young U.S. soldiers sent to the Vietnam War were all very similar to each other.

  b. To many U.S. soldiers, the Vietnam War was a senseless, meaningless war.

  c. U.S. soldiers came back from Vietnam physically and mentally stronger than they were when they went there.

  d. All young U.S. adults should be required to serve in the military.

25. Which of the following represents an opinion rather than a fact?

  a. The pressures were enormous.

  b. Because you could die so quickly, each man carried at least one large compress bandage, usually in the helmet band for easy access.

  c. They carried the standard fatigue jackets and trousers.

  d. They would often discard things along the route of march.

SELECTION **8.3**

Literature
(continued)

Respond in Writing

Directions: Refer to the selection as needed to answer the essay-type questions below. (Your instructor may direct you to work collaboratively with other students on one or more items. Each group member should be able to explain *all* of the group's answers.)

1. Of all the items you read about that the men took to war with them, what was the most surprising? Which items will you remember, and why?

_____

_____

_____

2. If you were suddenly sent to war, what items would you take with you, and why?

_____

_____

_____

_____

_____

_____

3. In the first section (lines 1–39), the narrator often mentions how much things weigh. (a) Why does he do that? (b) Besides actual items and equipment, what intangible things does the author say the soldiers "carried" with them? (c) Which do you think were heavier, the actual items or the intangible ones, and why?

_____

_____

_____

_____

_____

_____

_____

SELECTION 8.3

Thinking Critically

In this chapter, you will learn the answers to these questions:

- What is critical thinking?

- How can I distinguish between facts and opinions?

- How can I make inferences and draw logical conclusions?

- What is the difference between deductive and inductive reasoning?

- How can I evaluate an author's argument?

- What are propaganda devices?

SKILLS

What Is Critical Thinking, and Why Is It Important?

Critical Thinking Skills

- Why Readers Fail to Think Critically
- Distinguishing Facts from Opinions and Determining Whether Opinions Are Well-Supported
- Making Inferences and Drawing Logical Conclusions
- Distinguishing between Deductive and Inductive Reasoning
- Evaluating an Author's Argument
- Identifying Propaganda Devices

A Word about Standardized Reading Tests: Critical Thinking

CHECKPOINT: THINKING CRITICALLY

CREATING YOUR SUMMARY

Developing Chapter Review Cards

TEST YOUR UNDERSTANDING: THINKING CRITICALLY, PART 1

TEST YOUR UNDERSTANDING: THINKING CRITICALLY, PART 2

READINGS

Selection 9.1   "Poverty in America and Improving Social Welfare through Public Education"
    from *The American Democracy*
    by *Thomas E. Patterson* (Government)

Selection 9.2   "Your Financial Wellness"
    from *Connect Core Concepts in Health*
    by *Paul Insel and Walton Roth* (Health)

Selection 9.3   "Our Ecological Footprint: Do We Consume Too Much?"
    from *Environmental Science: A Study of Interrelationships*
    by *Eldon Enger and Bradley Smith* (Environmental Science)

People see only what they are prepared to see.

Ralph Waldo Emerson

It is not enough to have a good mind.
The main thing is to use it well.

René Descartes

There is one thing about which I am certain, and that
is that there is very little about which one can be certain.

M. Somerset Maugham

WHAT IS CRITICAL THINKING, AND WHY IS IT IMPORTANT?

PERSONALIZED LEARNING

critical thinking

Thinking in an organized way about material you have read in order to evaluate it accurately.

Critical thinking is also referred to as *critical reasoning* or *critical analysis*.

Critical thinking means thinking in an organized way about material that you have read in order to evaluate it accurately. Before you can think critically about the material, though, you must understand the main idea, supporting details, and pattern of organization. Only after you understand this basic information are you ready to think critically about it.

You may be wondering why it is necessary to think critically rather than just accept the author's information and leave it at that. After all, thinking critically about what you have read can, quite frankly, be hard work. However, the consequences of *not* thinking critically and of *not* evaluating ideas for yourself can be costly. Failing to think critically can result, for example, in your choosing a college major that does not really suit you, accepting a job that you are ill-suited for, signing a contract or credit agreement you do not fully understand, making the wrong decision as a member of a jury, being misled or defrauded by an individual or organization, supporting a cause that later turns out to be an embarrassment, and even marrying the wrong person! Most professors would agree that learning to think critically, along with learning how to learn, is one of the most important skills a college student can acquire.

Not only will thinking critically help you when you read, it will also help you when you write. This is because reading and writing are both forms of the thinking process. To improve the quality of your reading and writing, you must improve the quality of your *thinking*. Although thinking critically may seem difficult at times, it simply means applying certain thinking skills in a systematic way. Thinking critically when you read means consistently asking certain additional questions and applying logic when you read.

CRITICAL THINKING SKILLS

In order to think critically when you read, you must apply these three skills in a systematic, careful manner:

- Distinguishing facts from opinions, and determining how well supported the opinions are
- Making inferences and drawing logical conclusions
- Evaluating an author's argument accurately

Thinking critically involves thinking in an organized way about material you have read in order to evaluate it accurately.

In this chapter, each of these important skills will be explained and demonstrated. They can also be applied to things you hear, but our focus in this chapter is on applying them to material that you read.

Why Readers Fail to Think Critically

If critical thinking simply means applying thinking skills in a systematic, careful manner, why do people not do it more often when they read? Actually, besides mental laziness, there are at least five reasons:

1. **We let "experts" and "authorities" do our thinking for us.**   Rather than think through a complex issue, we accept the information or judgment of someone or something we perceive as an authority. This might be a parent or other relative; a college advisor; a doctor or therapist; or a minister, priest, or rabbi. We may accept the beliefs or positions of a political entity (such as a political party or the government itself) or the beliefs and rules of a religious or social institution without thinking critically about them. (This is not to say that all experts and authorities are wrong, only that you should think through what they have written or said, rather than accept their words without question.) For example, you might be tempted to accept the advice of a favorite uncle who is a highly successful real estate agent that you should also become a real estate agent—even though you may prefer to work by yourself at a computer rather than sell to the public.

2. **We want things to be different from the way they are.**   In other words, we deny reality and refuse to see what is really there. Denial is based on emotion, not reason. Perhaps a person you have just begun dating is attractive, yet has a serious drinking problem. But because you like dating someone who is so attractive, you ignore obvious facts and deny to yourself that the person is alcoholic. Or, for example, you are not making any systematic effort to save money each month, yet you are hoping that you will somehow have enough money by the time you graduate to pay for a new car and a trip to Europe.

3. **We mentally put things into one of two mutually exclusive categories.**   This means that we mistakenly view things as "either-or." Another way of putting this is "seeing everything as either black or white." Needless to say, very few things in life are simple enough to fall into one of only two categories. Thinking of everything in terms of good or bad, beautiful or ugly, fair or unfair, generous or selfish, conservative or liberal, immature or mature, and so forth, prevents us from thinking critically about issues.

4. **We view things too much in light of our culture and our experience.**   We are all ethnocentric, which can cause us to accept that whatever our own cultural group believes or does is the proper way. Whether it is encouraging large or small families, eating with a fork or chopsticks or one's fingers, or celebrating events and holidays in certain ways, we consider anything different from what we do to be odd or even wrong. Viewing things only in light of our culture and past experience prevents us from looking at new ideas and considering them objectively. With regard to personal experience, for example, someone who had a happy experience being a stepchild would have a very different view of stepparents from someone who had an unhappy experience as a stepchild.

5. **We stereotype and label.**   The world can be overwhelming and confusing. One way we try to make sense of it is to put things and people into categories. While this is helpful, it also has some negative effects. It prevents us from seeing situations and individuals as unique because we assume things about them that may not be true. For example, on the first day of the semester, suppose you notice a classmate who is very physically fit and is wearing a baseball cap. You might be inclined to make an automatic judgment (stereotype) about him and what he is like as a person: that he is a "jock" (or even a "dumb jock"). Consequently, you decide he is not worth taking the time to get to know. Perhaps he is a straight-A student who has a full academic scholarship and whose goal is to become a dentist. You will never know unless you think critically enough to question your assumptions and the stereotypes you hold.

Which of these reasons prevent you from thinking critically when you read? (Think critically about this! You may find it helpful to mark the items in the preceding list that pertain to you.) Becoming aware of these tendencies in yourself is essential in order for you to think critically. Let's look now at three critical thinking skills.

Distinguishing Facts from Opinions and Determining Whether Opinions Are Well-Supported

Many students mistakenly believe that anything that appears in print, especially in textbooks, must be a fact. Although most college textbooks do consist primarily of facts, textbooks typically include many useful and valuable opinions as well.

What is the difference between a fact and an opinion? A **fact** is something that can be proved to exist or to have happened. An example would be: *In 1620 the Pilgrims landed in what is now Plymouth, Massachusetts.* In addition, a fact can be something that is generally assumed to exist or to have happened. An example would be: *Thousands of years ago, early people migrated from Asia to the North American continent*

fact

Something that can be proved to exist or to have happened.

by walking from Siberia to Alaska across the frozen Bering Strait. The process of proving that something is a fact (that it is true) is called *verification.* Verification requires experimentation and research or direct experience and observation.

An **opinion,** on the other hand, is a judgment or belief that cannot be proved or disproved. When information in a statement cannot be proved to be either factual or false, it represents an opinion. It is important to realize, however, that not all opinions are equally valuable. Although opinions cannot be proved, they are valuable when they are supported by valid reasons and plausible evidence. Therefore, well-supported opinions are useful because they are based on facts or on the ideas of knowledgeable people. Opinions in textbooks typically represent this type of valuable opinion: They are the well-reasoned beliefs of the author or other experts. Scientific theories are also examples of expert opinions. (If a theory could be proved, then it would no longer be a theory, of course. It would become a fact.) Needless to say, poorly supported or unsupported opinions are not useful.

Students sometimes mistake incorrect information for an opinion because they assume if something is not a fact, it must automatically be an opinion. However, information can be one of three things: It can be a fact (it is correct information); it can be an opinion (it represents someone's belief); or it can be a *false statement* (it is simply incorrect information). *January follows February* and *Water freezes at 212°F* are examples of false statements. Since they can be *proved incorrect,* they are not opinions.

How can you tell when you are reading an opinion? Because opinions represent judgments, beliefs, or interpretations, authors often use certain words or phrases to indicate that they are presenting an opinion. These words and phrases signal an opinion:

perhaps	a possible explanation is
apparently	one theory is that
presumably	it seems likely
one possibility is	this suggests
one interpretation is	in our view
in our opinion	in the opinion of

In addition, words that indicate value judgments can signal opinions. They include descriptive words such as:

better	interesting
more	outdated
less	beautiful
safer	wealthy
most	incompetent
greatest	successful
worst	irresponsible
best	dangerous
excellent	fascinating
harmful	effective

---

opinion

Something that cannot be proved or disproved; a judgment or a belief.

These words signal opinions because people often disagree about what is "successful," "fascinating," and so on. For example, in the sentence *Adults must have a college degree in order to be successful,* the word *successful* could mean successful financially, personally, socially, or in all these ways. Because there are different interpretations of what *successful* means, it would be impossible to prove a statement like this (although it could be supported with certain facts about college graduates). Consequently, the statement expresses an opinion. (Even though it may be a widely held opinion, it is still an opinion.) As you read, then, watch for value judgments that can be interpreted in different ways by different people.

Comprehension-Monitoring Question for Thinking Critically to Evaluate Whether Statements Are Facts or Opinions

Can the information the author presents be proved, or does it represent a judgment?

Critical readers ask themselves, "Can the information the author presents be proved, or does it represent a judgment?" When an author includes opinions, it is important for you to evaluate them, because not all opinions are valid or useful. An opinion is of little value if it is poorly supported (the author does not give good reasons for it). A well-supported opinion, on the other hand, can be as important and as useful as a fact. To repeat: Even though opinions cannot be proved, they are valuable when supported by facts and other well-reasoned opinions; poorly supported opinions are of little value, even if the author writes persuasively. For example, consider the following two sets of support for the statement *Anna Garcia has excellent qualifications for serving as governor.* (This statement is an opinion, of course, because of the use of the word *excellent.*) Note how both facts and opinions are used to support the statement. Also, note the important difference between the quality of the two sets of facts and opinions given as support for the statement.

Opinion: Anna Garcia has excellent qualifications for serving as governor.

Well-reasoned support:
She has a law degree from Harvard. (*fact*)
She was chief legal counsel of a *Fortune* 500 company for six years. (*fact*)
She served 12 years as a state senator. (*fact*)
She is extremely ethical. (*opinion*)
She is strongly committed to family values. (*opinion*)
She is an effective problem-solver. (*opinion*)

Poor support:
Her father served as an ambassador. (*fact*)
Her brother is a millionaire. (*fact*)
She has been married to the same man for 20 years. (*fact*)
She has smart, beautiful children. (*opinion*)
She is attractive. (*opinion*)
She comes across well on TV. (*opinion*)

A critical reader would be much more likely to accept the opinion that "Anna Garcia has excellent qualifications for serving as governor" if it were supported with good reasons (the first set of support) rather than with poor reasons (the second set). Support is convincing when it consists of relevant facts and well-reasoned opinions. Don't discount a statement simply because it is an opinion or is supported with other opinions. They may all be valuable, pertinent opinions.

The flowchart below summarizes the process for determining whether statements are facts, false statements, or opinions (which will be well-supported and valuable or unsupported or poorly supported, and of no value).

DETERMINING WHETHER A STATEMENT REPRESENTS A FACT, A FALSE STATEMENT, OR AN OPINION

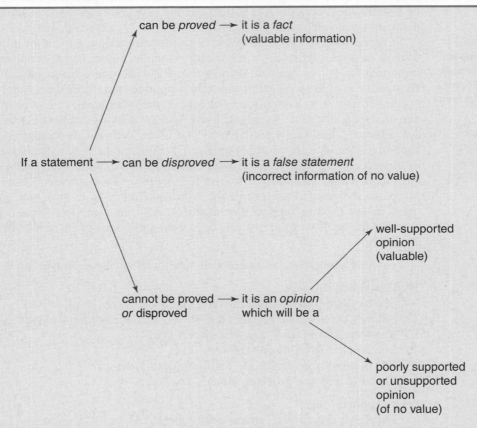

To distinguish between facts and opinions, ask yourself these questions in this order:

1. *Can the information in the statement be proved?*
   If so, it is a fact (correct information).

2. *Can the information in the statement be disproved?*
   If so, it is a false statement (incorrect information).

3. *Is the information in the statement something that cannot be proved* or *disproved?*
   If so, it is an opinion.

When the statement is an opinion, ask yourself these additional questions:

- *Is the opinion well-supported?* (That is, is it based on valid reasons and plausible evidence?)
  If so, it is a valuable opinion.

- *Is the opinion poorly supported or unsupported?*
  If so, it is of little or no value.

Following are two excerpts from *The Autobiography of Malcolm X* (Selection 1.3, "Saved"). The first contains *facts* that can be verified about the prison in which Malcolm X served time.

> The Norfolk Prison Colony's library was in the school building. A variety of classes was taught there by instructors who came from such places as Harvard and Boston universities. The weekly debates between inmate teams were also held in the school building.

List the facts in this excerpt.

_____

_____

_____

_____

_____

_____

Source: From Malcolm X and Alex Haley, *The Autobiography of Malcolm X*, p. 173. Copyright © 1964 by Alex Haley and Malcolm X. Copyright © 1965 by Alex Haley and Betty Shabazz. Used by permission of Random House, Inc.

Stop and Annotate

Go back to the excerpt above. In the space provided, list on separate lines the facts contained in the excerpt.

Notice that the information in this passage can be verified by objective proof: the location of the prison library, some of the universities the instructors came from, and that weekly debates were held in the school building.

In the next passage, Malcolm X states his *opinions* about the new vistas that reading opened to him:

> Reading had changed forever the course of my life. The ability to read awoke inside me some long dormant craving to be mentally alive.

List the opinions in this excerpt.

_____

_____

_____

_____

_____

_____

Source: From Malcolm X and Alex Haley, *The Autobiography of Malcolm X*, p. 179. Copyright © 1964 by Alex Haley and Malcolm X. Copyright © 1965 by Alex Haley and Betty Shabazz. Used by permission of Random House, Inc.

Stop and Annotate

Go back to the excerpt above. In the space provided, list on separate lines the opinions contained in the excerpt.

Malcolm X's opinions are that reading changed the course of his life forever and that it awoke in him a craving to be mentally alive. These statements reflect Malcolm X's judgment about reading; they cannot be proved or disproved.

The next excerpt, from an American government textbook, discusses how historians and political scientists rank the first 39 presidents of the United States. It includes four lists that summarize the results of several surveys. As this passage shows, experts often agree in their opinions. When such agreement exists, the opinions are especially valuable.

Scholars Rank the Presidents

Several surveys have asked American historians and political scientists to rank the presidents from best to worst. Although some presidential reputations rise or fall with the passage of time, there has been remarkable consistency in whom the scholars rank as the best and worst presidents. The consistency of these results suggests that scholars use some unspoken criteria when assessing the presidents. At least four criteria stand out: the effectiveness of presidential policy, the president's vision of the office, the president's handling of crises, and the president's personality.

In three surveys conducted in the 1980s, scholars were asked to rank the presidents. The results below show only those presidents who clearly and consistently ranked near the top or bottom. The surveys included all presidents except Reagan (who was still in office and thus could not be assessed dispassionately), George H. W. Bush, Bill Clinton, George W. Bush, and Barack Obama (who had not yet served at the time these surveys were conducted); and William Harrison and James Garfield (whose terms were too short to be realistically assessed).

What is the opinion of these historians and political scientists as to which presidents have been the greatest?

_____

_____

_____

_____

_____

_____

Greatest presidents
(in top five on all three surveys)
- Abraham Lincoln
- George Washington
- Franklin Delano Roosevelt
- Thomas Jefferson
- Theodore Roosevelt

Near-greats

(in top ten on all three surveys)

- Woodrow Wilson
- Andrew Jackson
- Harry S. Truman

Near-failures

(in bottom ten on all three surveys)

- Calvin Coolidge
- Millard Fillmore
- Andrew Johnson
- John Tyler
- Franklin Pierce

Failures

(in bottom five in all three surveys)

- James Buchanan
- U.S. Grant
- Warren G. Harding
- Richard M. Nixon

Source: John J. Harrigan, *Politics and the American Future,* 3e, New York: McGraw-Hill, pp. 282–83. Copyright © 1992 by John J. Harrigan. Reprinted by permission of the author. Data in table from: 1982 poll of forty-nine scholars in *Chicago Tribune Magazine,* January 10, 1982, pp. 8–13, 15, 18; poll of forty-one scholars by David L. Porter in 1981, reprinted in Robert K. Murray and Tim H. Blessing, "The Presidential Performance Study: A Progress Report," *Journal of American History* 70, No. 3 (December 1983: 535–55).

Stop and Annotate

Go back to the preceding excerpt. In the space provided, list the presidents who have been the greatest, in the opinion of the scholars surveyed.

As you can see from the information in the selection, five presidents have been judged, in the opinion of all the scholars surveyed, to be the greatest: Abraham Lincoln, George Washington, Franklin Delano Roosevelt, Thomas Jefferson, and Theodore Roosevelt.

Here are two additional points to remember about facts and opinions: First, although some paragraphs contain only facts or only opinions, a paragraph may contain *both* facts and opinions (it may even present both facts and opinions in the same sentence). Second, it may seem difficult at times to distinguish opinions from facts because authors sometimes present opinions in ways that make them seem like facts. For example, a writer might introduce an opinion by stating, "The fact is . . ." (For example, "The fact is, Hawaii's weather makes it the perfect place for your winter vacation." This statement is really an opinion about winter vacations and Hawaii's weather.) Stating that something is a fact, however, does not make it a fact. (Hawaii certainly isn't the perfect place for your winter vacation if you want to go snow skiing.)

Ideally, of course, an author would always express an opinion in a way that makes it clear that it *is* an opinion. ("In this writer's opinion, Hawaii's weather makes it the perfect place for your winter vacation.") But authors do not always do this, so it is your job to *think critically* as you read, being alert for opinions. When you identify an opinion, continue reading to determine whether the opinion is well-supported. Although you should not accept an opinion unless it is well-supported, you should be open to accepting opinions that *are* well-supported.

This paragraph comes from a business textbook:

So You Want to Be a Manager

What kind of manager do you want to be? Experts suggest that the need for managers will increase by millions of jobs by 2016. But the requirements for these management jobs will become more demanding with every passing year. However, if you like a challenge and you have the right kind of personality, management remains an exciting and viable field. In fact, the Bureau of Labor Statistics predicts that management positions in public relations, marketing and advertising will rise 12% overall between 2006 and 2016. Salaries for managerial positions remain strong overall. Pay can vary significantly depending on your level of experience, the firm where you work, and the region of the country where you live. Nationwide average income for chief executives is $151,370; for human resource managers, $99,810; for administrative managers, $76,370. In short, if you want to be a manager, there will be a wealth of opportunities in almost every field.

Source: Adapted from O. C. Ferrell, Geoffrey A. Hirt, and Linda Ferrell, *Business in a Changing World,* p. 201. Copyright © 2011 by The McGraw-Hill Companies, Inc. Reprinted with permission of The McGraw-Hill Companies, Inc.

Identify each of these statements from the excerpt as either a *fact* or an *opinion*. Write your answer in the space provided.

1. The requirements for these management jobs will become more demanding with

    every passing year. _____

2. If you like a challenge and you have the right kind of personality, management re-

    mains an exciting and viable field. _____

3. The Bureau of Labor Statistics predicts that management positions in public relations, marketing and advertising will rise 12% overall between 2006 and 2016.

    _____

    _____

4. Salaries for managerial positions remain strong overall.

    _____

5. Pay can vary significantly depending on your level of experience, the firm where you work, and the region of the country where you live.

    _____

6. Nationwide average income for chief executives is $151,370; for human resource managers, $99,810; for administrative managers, $76,370.

    _____

7. If you want to be a manager, there will be a wealth of opportunities in almost every

    field. _____

8. Experts suggest that the need for managers will increase by millions of jobs by 2016. _____

Making Inferences and Drawing Logical Conclusions

Thinking critically as you read entails understanding not only what the author states directly but also what the author *suggests.* In other words, it is your responsibility as a critical reader to make inferences and draw conclusions about what you have read. An **inference** is a logical conclusion based on what an author has stated. A **conclusion** is a decision that is reached after thoughtful consideration of information the author presents. The information that is given will lead you to the conclusion that should be drawn. Needless to say, any inferences or conclusions you draw will be affected by your experience, your prior knowledge (or lack of it), and your own biases.

Making inferences is not new to you; you make inferences continually in your daily life. You draw conclusions based on descriptions, facts, opinions, experiences, and observations. Assume, for example, that a classmate arrives late. She seems frustrated and upset, and her hands are covered with grease and grime. It would be logical to infer that she has had a flat tire or some other car trouble and she had to fix the problem herself. Your inference would be based on your observations. Similarly, you make inferences every day about things you read. For instance, suppose that your roommate leaves you a note saying, "Hope you didn't need your iPod this afternoon. I wanted to listen to music while I worked out." You would infer that your roommate has borrowed—and is using—your iPod. This is your roommate's *intended meaning* ("I borrowed your iPod, and I'm using it"), even though this information does not appear in the message. Making logical inferences helps you understand an author's intended meaning, just as the author's tone can (Chapter 8).

In fact, jokes and cartoons (including editorial and political cartoons) are funny only if the listener or reader makes the correct inference. (Interpreting political

inference

A logical conclusion based on what an author has stated.

conclusion

A decision that is reached after thoughtful consideration of information the author presents.

Source: Chan Lowe. © Tribune Media Services, Inc. All rights reserved. Reprinted with permission.

cartoons is presented in Chapter 10.) Take, for example, the editorial cartoon on page 603. It comes from *BusinessWeek* magazine. What inferences does the cartoonist expect readers to make about the fuel efficiency and size of the SUV (sport utility vehicle)? What inference could be made about the cartoonist's (and the publication's) position regarding SUVs?

You have already had countless opportunities to make inferences earlier in this book. The skill in Chapter 5, "Formulating Implied Main Ideas," involves making inferences. You learned that when authors *suggest* a main idea but do not state it directly, they are *implying* it. When readers comprehend an implied main idea, they are *inferring* it (making an inference about it). The writer implies the main idea; the reader infers it. Some of the critical reading skills in Chapter 8 involve making inferences. You learned, for example, that an author's tone helps you infer his or her intended meaning. You learned that after determining the author's purpose, you can conclude who the intended audience is.

Critical thinking routinely involves making inferences and drawing logical conclusions, although there are times when an author simply states his or her conclusion. When the author does state the conclusion, it typically appears at the end of the passage, and it is often the main idea of a paragraph or the overall main idea of the selection. Authors use phrases such as these to announce a conclusion: *in conclusion, consequently, thus,* and *therefore.* Stated conclusions are important, so pay careful attention to them.

When the author states the conclusion, you do not need to infer it: The author has done the work for you. However, when there is a conclusion to be drawn—that is, when the author does not state it—it is up to you to infer it.

An inference goes beyond what the author states but must always be *based on* what is stated in the passage. Remember that you cannot use as an inference anything already *stated* in the paragraph. For example, if the author says, "The *Titanic* sank because it hit an iceberg," you cannot give as an inference "The *Titanic* sank because it hit an iceberg": This has been directly stated. This is logical: If the author has already stated it, there is no reason for you to infer it. Nor are you making an inference if you merely paraphrase (restate) information that is presented in the paragraph. For example, you cannot give as an inference "An iceberg caused the *Titanic* to sink," because it is merely a paraphrase of information given by the author. You could, however, make this inference: "The water in which the *Titanic* sank was extremely cold." This is a logical inference since the author states that there were icebergs in the water, which suggests that the water was extremely cold.

When you read, you should ask yourself, "What logical inference (conclusion) can I make, based on what the author has stated?" To draw a conclusion, you must deduce (reason out) the author's meaning. That is, you must use the "evidence" and facts the author presents to arrive at the conclusion or inference the author wants you to make. You must make a connection between what an author says and what the author wants you to conclude. For example, a writer might describe the benefits of regular exercise but not state directly that you should exercise. By presenting certain facts, the writer expects you to make the inference (draw the conclusion) that you should exercise regularly.

You can understand more about how to make logical inferences by studying examples of correct inferences. An excerpt from a business communications textbook

Comprehension-Monitoring Question for Making Inferences

What logical inference (conclusion) can I make, based on what the author has stated?

Down at the factory in Waterbury, Vermont, they were known as "the boys." They are Ben Cohen and Jerry Greenfield, arguably America's most famous purveyors of ice cream and certainly two of America's most colorful entrepreneurs. They've been friends since seventh grade and business partners since 1978 when they opened their first scoop shop, using techniques gleaned from a $5 correspondence course on how to make ice cream. In 2000, they sold their firm, Ben & Jerry's Homemade, to Unilever, which aspires to carry on certain values. It has become a billion-dollar enterprise and a leading retailer of super-premium ice cream.

Ben and Jerry have strong personalities and strong opinions. They believed that work should be fun, or else it wasn't worth doing. They also believed in helping the unfortunate, protecting the environment, and treating people fairly. They wanted their company to be a happy, humanitarian place where everybody felt good about coming to work and producing a top-notch product.

Actions also telegraphed Ben & Jerry's commitment to an egalitarian work environment: the open office arrangement, the bright colors, the pictures of cows and fields hanging on warehouse walls, the employee committees, the casual clothes, the first-name relationships, the compressed pay scale that kept executive salaries in balance with lower-level compensation, the free health club memberships for everyone, the on-site day-care facility. And the free ice cream. Three pints a day per person. Now that's communication at its best!

> **What logical conclusions can you make about the employees at Ben & Jerry's Homemade?**

Source: Adapted from Courtland Bovée and John Thill, "Communication Close-Up at Ben & Jerry's Homemade," _Business Communication Today,_ 4e. Upper Saddle River, NJ: Prentice-Hall, 1995, pp. 26–28. Reprinted with permission of Prentice-Hall.

about the early days of a well-known ice cream company, Ben & Jerry's Home-made, appears on page 605. After reading the excerpt, you can draw logical inferences about how employees felt about working at Ben & Jerry's. Read it now.

Because the owners of Ben & Jerry's Homemade provided their employees with a fair, supportive, informal, and comfortable work environment, it is logical to conclude that:

> Employees were happy to work there.
>
> They appreciated the company's philosophy.
>
> They did not feel a high level of stress.
>
> They were likely to remain employees of Ben & Jerry's.

The following details from the passage are the ones on which these inferences are based:

> Employees called Ben and Jerry "the boys."
>
> Ben and Jerry believed that work should be fun.
>
> Ben and Jerry were interested in protecting the environment.
>
> They believed in treating people fairly.
>
> They wanted their company to be a happy, humanitarian place.
>
> They had an open office arrangement.
>
> They used bright colors.
>
> There were pictures on warehouse walls.
>
> Employees wore casual clothes.
>
> First names were used.
>
> There was a compressed pay scale.
>
> There was a free health club.
>
> There was an on-site day-care facility.
>
> Employees received free ice cream daily.

Stop and Annotate

Go back to the preceding excerpt. In the space provided, write the logical conclusions that can be made about the employees at Ben & Jerry's Homemade.

You could draw other logical conclusions from these details as well. For example, you could conclude that companies can be humane and humanitarian yet still be extremely profitable, that the public appreciates a high-quality product and is willing to pay for it, or even that you would like to work at Ben & Jerry's.

Here is another textbook excerpt in which conclusions must be inferred by reading and thinking critically. The passage is from a health textbook, and its topic is *passive smoking*.

Passive Smoking

Reports from the U.S. surgeon general's office suggest that tobacco smoke in enclosed indoor areas is an important air pollution problem. This has led to the controversy about **passive smoking**—the breathing in of air polluted by the secondhand tobacco smoke of others. Carbon monoxide levels of sidestream smoke (smoke from the burning end of a cigarette) reach a dangerously high level. True, the smoke can be greatly diluted in freely circulating air, but the 1 to 5 percent carbon monoxide levels attained in smoke-filled rooms can be sufficient to harm the health of people with chronic bronchitis, other lung disease, or cardiovascular disease.

> **What logical conclusions can you make about nonsmokers and smokers?**
>
> _____
>
> _____
>
> _____
>
> _____
>
> _____
>
> _____

Source: Marvin R. Levy, Mark Dignan, and Janet H. Shirreffs, *Targeting Wellness: The Core,* pp. 262–63. Copyright © 1992 by The McGraw-Hill Companies, Inc. Reprinted with permission of The McGraw-Hill Companies, Inc.

Stop and Annotate

Go back to the excerpt above. In the space provided, write the logical conclusions that can be made about both nonsmokers and smokers.

The authors want the reader to conclude that nonsmokers, especially those with certain health conditions, should avoid enclosed indoor areas in which there is cigarette smoke. Smokers should also conclude that they ought to refrain from smoking around others in an enclosed area. These are conclusions the authors want the reader to infer, even though they do not state them. These inferences are based on the statements that "carbon monoxide levels of sidestream smoke reach dangerously high levels" and that these levels "can be sufficient to harm the health of people with chronic bronchitis, other lung disease, or cardiovascular disease."

When you read, remember to ask yourself, "What logical conclusion can I draw, based on what the author has stated?"

The chart on page 608 illustrates the application of critical thinking skills to a review of an imaginary movie. (This is the same movie review that appeared in Chapter 8, "Reading Critically.") It is designed to show that critical thinking skills are related and that they are applicable to reading tasks that you encounter daily.

EXERCISE 2

This paragraph comes from a geography textbook:

International English

Worldwide, English has no rivals. Along with French, it is one of the two working languages of the United Nations. Two-thirds of all scientific papers are published in it, making it the first language of scientific discourse. In addition to being the accepted language of international air traffic control, English is the sole or joint language of more

(Continued on next page)

nations and territories than any other tongue. "English as a second language" is indicated with near-universal or mandatory English instruction in public schools. In Continental Europe, more than 80% of secondary school students study it as a second language and more than one-third of European Union residents can easily converse in it.

Source: Adapted from Arthur Getis, Judith Getis, and Fellmann, *Introduction to Geography,* 10e, p. 241. Copyright © 2006 by The McGraw-Hill Companies, Inc. Reprinted with permission of The McGraw-Hill Companies, Inc.

Based on the information in this passage, write a *logical conclusion* that could be made about *learning English if it is not a person's first language:*

_____

_____

_____

Distinguishing between Deductive and Inductive Reasoning

deductive reasoning

A process of reasoning in which a general principle is applied to a specific situation.

No discussion of critical thinking would be complete without explaining the difference between deductive reasoning and inductive reasoning. **Deductive reasoning** refers to reasoning that involves taking a generalization and seeing how it applies to a specific situation. It is often called "reasoning from the general to the specific." This is the type of reasoning that is used when a judge applies a general law to a specific legal case. It is the kind of reasoning you use when you apply a general value, such as honesty, to a particular situation ("I need to find the owner of this billfold and return it").

EXAMPLE OF CRITICAL THINKING APPLIED TO MOVIE CRITIC'S REVIEW

Here is a critic's imaginary review of *Cyberpunk,* a new science fiction movie:

Another movie from Extreme Studios has just been released: *Cyberpunk.* Is it worth seeing? That depends: Do you enjoy violence? Do you like vulgar language? Do you appreciate painfully loud sound effects? What about watching unknown actors embarrass themselves? Or sitting for three hours and ten minutes without a break? If so, and you've got $8.50 to burn, then *Cyberpunk* is a movie you must see!

Critical Reading Questions	Answers
What is the author's purpose?	To persuade readers to skip this movie
Who is the author's intended audience?	The moviegoing public
What is the author's point of view?	*Cyberpunk* is a terrible movie.*
What is the author's tone?	Sarcastic
What is the author's intended meaning?	Don't waste your money or your time on this movie.
Does the author include facts, opinions, or both?	Both
What logical inference (conclusion) does the author expect you to make?	This movie isn't worth seeing.

*Notice that this is also the author's main idea or argument.

inductive reasoning

A process of reasoning in which a general principle is developed from a set of specific instances.

The opposite of deductive reasoning is **inductive reasoning,** drawing a general conclusion that is based on specific details or facts. It is also called "reasoning from the specific to the general." You use inductive reasoning when you read a paragraph that consists only of details and you reason out the general point the author is making (the implied main idea).

Students sometimes get deductive and inductive reasoning mixed up. Here is a memory peg that may help you avoid this problem:

- With *de*ductive reasoning, you are going *down* or *away* from something larger and more general to smaller, more specific things (deduct = take away).
- With *in*ductive reasoning, the smaller parts or specific details lead *in* to the larger generalization (induct = lead into).

Evaluating an Author's Argument

You now know that critical thinking includes the skills of distinguishing between facts and opinions and making logical inferences. Now you will learn how to use these two skills (along with the critical reading skills you learned in Chapter 8) to *evaluate* material you read. The steps below describe the process for evaluating an author's argument.

Step 1: Identify the Issue

Critical Thinking Question for Identifying the Issue

What controversial topic is this passage about?

The first step, of course, is to identify the issue. An *issue* is simply a controversial topic. In other words, an issue is a topic that people have differing opinions about. To identify the issue, ask yourself, "What controversial topic is this passage about?" Examples of issues are *whether there should be regulation of pornographic websites, whether government-subsidized health care should be provided for all Americans,* and *whether U.S. corporations should outsource jobs to workers in foreign countries.*

Step 2: Determine the Author's Argument

author's argument

The author's position on an issue.

The author's argument is also known as the author's *point of view.*

Critical Thinking Question for Determining the Author's Argument

What is the author's position on the issue?

The second step is to determine the author's argument. An **author's argument** is the author's position on an issue. That is, an author's argument is his or her opinion on an issue. (An author's argument is simply an overall main idea that is an opinion.) The author's argument is what the author believes and wants to persuade the reader to believe or do. You may also hear an author's argument referred to as his or her *point of view.*

An author's argument is not the same as an argument that is verbal disagreement or dispute. The author's purpose in a written argument is to persuade the reader to believe or do something by "arguing" (presenting) a case for it. An author "argues" for it in the same way an attorney "argues" his or her client's side of a case during a trial. For example, an author might argue that *All college students should be required to take at least one computer science course.* To persuade the reader to accept (believe) his or her argument, the author typically presents support or evidence that backs it up. An author does this in the same way that an attorney presents evidence to support his or her case. To determine the author's argument, ask yourself, "What is the author's position on this issue?"

Part of understanding an author's argument is recognizing the **author's bias** in favor of one side of an issue. For example, if the author's argument is *All college students should be required to take at least one computer science course,* then the author's bias is that he or she *favors* computer literacy for college students. If an author's argument is *Our government should not impose any restrictions on gun ownership,* then the author's bias is that he or she *opposes* gun control.

Authors who have a bias in favor of one side of a controversial issue support that side: They are *for* it. For example, the term *pro-environmental* would describe an author who favors legislation to protect the environment. Authors who have an opposing bias take the opposite position: They are *against* it. For example, the term *anti-environmental* would describe an author who opposes efforts or legislation to protect the environment. As you can see, the prefixes *pro-* and *anti-* can be helpful in describing an author's bias on an issue.

How can you tell whether an author has a bias when the author does not directly state his or her position? The best way is to examine the support the author gives. Ask yourself, "Does the author present support and information about both sides of the issue?" If not, ask yourself, "Which side of the issue does the author present support for?" This will reveal the author's bias.

By the way, part of thinking critically involves asking yourself whether *you* have a bias about an issue. If you do, make an extra effort to be open-minded and objective when you evaluate an author's argument. Otherwise, you may reject the author's argument without seriously considering it or without considering it objectively.

Of course, there will be times when an author chooses not to take a position on an issue. That is, the author remains *neutral* on an issue. The author does not take a position because his or her purpose is to present *both* sides of the issue objectively. The author presents relevant support for both sides of an issue so that readers can make their own informed decision about the matter. Most of the time, however, authors *do* have a point of view.

Step 3: Identify the Assumptions on Which the Author Bases His or Her Argument

When authors present an argument, they typically base it on certain assumptions. An **author's assumption** is something that he or she takes for granted, or assumes to be true. The author does not state directly but accepts as true, without offering any proof. To identify an author's assumptions, ask yourself, "What does the author take for granted?" To illustrate, suppose an author's argument is *Society must do more to protect children from abuse.* To make this argument, the author would have to have made these assumptions:

- Children are worth protecting.
- Children are not being protected adequately at present.
- Children are not able to protect themselves.
- There are things society can and should do to protect children.

author's bias

The side of an issue an author favors; an author's preference for one side of the issue over the other.

Critical Thinking Question for Determining the Author's Bias

Which side of the issue does the author support?

author's assumption

Something the author takes for granted without proof.

Critical Thinking Question for Identifying the Author's Assumptions

What does the author take for granted?

These are all valid assumptions because they are reasonable and logical. Sometimes, though, an author bases an argument on illogical, unreasonable, or even incorrect assumptions. Incorrect assumptions weaken an argument. For example, an author's argument might be *The minimum age for obtaining a driver's license should be 20.* In this case, the author's assumptions might be:

- Teenagers are irresponsible.
- If people are older when they begin driving, they will be better drivers.

It is incorrect to assume that all teenagers are irresponsible, or that if people are older when they begin driving, they will automatically be better drivers.

When you read an author's argument, think critically about assumptions the author makes to be sure they are not incorrect, so that you are not manipulated by the author. Let's say that an author's argument is *We should hire Margaret Jones as our city manager because only a woman cares enough about the city's historic district to preserve it.* Two of the assumptions this argument is based on are:

- A man would not care about the city's historic district.
- A man is not capable of saving the city's historic district.

The author also assumes that saving the city's historic district is the sole or most important issue upon which the selection of the city manager should be based. These are illogical and incorrect assumptions, of course. Readers who do not question the author's assumptions might be manipulated into believing the author's faulty argument.

Step 4: Identify the Types of Support the Author Presents

Examine the supporting details to see if the author gives facts, examples, case studies, research results, or expert opinions. Is the author himself or herself an expert? Does he or she cite personal experience or observations, make comparisons, or give reasons or evidence? Ask yourself, "What types of support does the author present?"

Step 5: Decide Whether the Support Is Relevant

Support is *relevant* when it pertains directly to the argument. In other words, the support is meaningful and appropriate. Ask yourself, "Does the support pertain directly to the argument?" For example, the author might argue that *All states should lower the blood alcohol level used to determine if drivers are legally drunk.* Statistics that show a decrease in traffic accidents and deaths in the states that have a lower blood alcohol level would be relevant support. Sometimes, however, an author will try to persuade readers by using irrelevant support. If the author mentions that many drivers damage their own vehicles after drinking a large amount of alcohol, it would not be relevant support.

Step 6: Determine Whether the Author's Argument Is Objective and Complete

The term *objective* means that an argument is based on facts and evidence instead of on the author's feelings or unsupported opinions. Suppose the author who

Critical Thinking Questions for Evaluating Whether an Author's Argument Is Objective and Complete

Is the argument based on facts and other appropriate evidence?

Did the author leave out information that might weaken or disprove the argument?

is arguing that *All states should lower the blood alcohol level used to determine if drivers are legally drunk* knows someone who was injured by a drunk driver and is angry because the driver was not penalized. As support for his argument, the author talks about how angry drunk drivers make him. This would not be objective support; it would be *subjective* support (personal or emotional). Ask yourself, "Is the author's argument based on facts and other appropriate evidence?" An author's support should be objective, not merely personal or emotional.

The term *complete* means that an author has not left out information simply because it might weaken or even disprove his or her argument. Suppose an author's argument is *Our city would benefit from a new sports arena.* The author mentions that a new arena would boost the city's image and increase civic pride, but does not mention that a special bond would have to be passed by voters in order to pay for the arena, or that the new arena would cause major traffic congestion whenever sports events were held. Particularly when an author has a bias, he or she may deliberately leave out important information that would weaken the argument. When evaluating the completeness of an author's argument, ask yourself, "Did the author leave out information that might weaken or disprove the argument?" To be fully convincing, an author should *present and overcome* opposing points.

Step 7: Evaluate the Overall Validity and Credibility of the Author's Argument

The term *valid* means that an argument is correctly reasoned and its conclusions follow logically from the information, evidence, or reasons that are presented. You must evaluate the author's logic, the quality of his or her thinking. To evaluate the validity of an author's argument, ask yourself, "Is the author's argument logical?" You should not accept an author's argument if it is not valid. Before you can determine whether an argument is valid, you must consider your answers to the questions mentioned in the previous steps:

- "What does the author take for granted?"
- "What type of support does the author present?"
- "Does the support pertain directly to the argument?"
- "Is the argument objective and complete?"

Critical Thinking Question for Evaluating Whether an Author's Argument Is Valid and Credible

Is the author's argument logical and believable?

Finally, you must evaluate the credibility of the author's argument. The term *credibility* refers to how believable an author's argument is. To be believable, the argument must be based on logic or relevant evidence. You must once again consider the author's assumptions, the types and relevance of the support, objectivity, completeness, and validity to determine the believability of the argument. To evaluate the credibility of an author's argument, ask yourself, "Is the argument believable?" An argument that has credibility is a convincing one. Just as you should reject any argument that lacks validity and credibility, you should be open to accepting one that is valid and credible.

Let's look at an example of how an author's argument could be evaluated critically. Consider the argument *All college students should be required to take at least one computer science course.* To evaluate its credibility, you would first examine the assumptions the author has made. For example, he or she obviously assumes that it is valuable to know about computers, that computers will continue to be important in people's personal and professional lives, and so on. The types of support the author gives might include facts and research findings about the growing use of computers, several examples of ways college students could benefit from computer skills, and his or her personal experience with computers. As a reader, you would then have to decide whether the support is relevant (directly supports the argument), whether it is complete (whether information that might support the other side of the issue was omitted), whether it is objective (based on facts and other appropriate evidence), and whether it is valid (logical). Consideration of these elements enables you to evaluate whether or not the author's argument has validity and credibility.

Now look at two short selections that both address the issue of legalizing drugs that are currently illegal. As you read, think about which side presents the better argument. (Before you begin reading, think about whether *you* already have a bias on this issue.)

Pro-legalization: Weighing the Costs of Drug Use

For over 100 years this society has made the use of certain drugs illegal and has penalized illegal drug use. But during that time the use of marijuana, heroin and other opiates, and cocaine has become an epidemic. Most recently, Americans have spent billions of dollars on arresting and imprisoning sellers and importers of crack cocaine, with almost no effect on the supply or street price of the drug.

The societal costs of illegal drugs are immense. They include the costs of law enforcement, criminal proceedings against those arrested, and jails and prisons. They also include the spread of deadly diseases such as AIDS and hepatitis through the use of shared needles; the cost to society of raising "crack babies," children poisoned by drugs even before birth; and the cost of raising a generation of young people who see illegal drug

Evaluating an Author's Argument

Issue: *"What controversial topic is this passage about?"*

_____

Authors' argument: *"What is the authors' position on the issue?"*

_____

Authors' assumptions: *"What do the authors take for granted?"*

_____
_____
_____

selling and violence as their only escape from poverty and desperation. Finally, the societal costs include the emotional cost of the violence that no one can now escape.

Legalizing drug use in this country would eliminate many of these costs. Billions of dollars would be saved. This money could be spent on treatment of addicts, job training, and education programs to help many disadvantaged young people assume valuable roles in society. The government could make drug use legal for adults but impose severe penalties on anyone who sells drugs to young people. Drug sales could be heavily taxed, thus deterring drug purchases and giving society the benefit of tax revenues that could be used for drug treatment and education.

Type of support: *"What type of support do the authors present?"*

_____

_____

_____

_____

Relevance of support: *"Does the support pertain directly to the argument?"*

_____

_____

Objectivity and completeness: *"Is the argument based on facts and other appropriate evidence?"* and *"Did the authors leave out information that might weaken or disprove the argument?"*

_____

_____

_____

_____

Validity and credibility: *"Is the argument logical and believable?"*

_____

_____

_____

_____

_____

_____

Anti-legalization: Providing a Positive Role Model

Certain drugs are illegal because they are dangerous and deadly and provide no societal value. To make their possession or use legal would send a message to young people that using drugs is acceptable and that drugs are not treacherous or life-destroying.

Making drugs illegal has not increased the number of drug users or sellers, just as making alcohol legal after Prohibition did not reduce the number of people who drank. Recent law enforcement efforts have indeed made a difference. Over the past few years, as law enforcement efforts have sent more and more people to jail, the number of young people who use illegal drugs has steadily declined. Furthermore, education about the ill effects of drug use has begun to deter people from buying and using illegal drugs.

Recently, the incidence of drug-related deaths and violence has begun to level off even in the areas of the most hard-core drug use. This is proof that strict law enforcement is working. This country has begun to turn the corner on this drug epidemic.

Evaluating an Author's Argument

Issue: *"What controversial topic is this passage about?"*

_____

_____

_____

Authors' argument: *"What is the authors' position on the issue?"*

_____

_____

Authors' assumptions: *"What do the authors take for granted?"*

_____

_____

_____

Type of support: *"What type of support do the authors present?"*

_____

_____

_____

_____

Relevance of support: *"Does the support pertain directly to the argument?"*

_____

_____

_____

Objectivity and completeness: *"Is the argument based on facts and other appropriate evidence?"* and *"Did the authors leave out information that might weaken or disprove the argument?"*

_____

_____

_____

_____

Validity and credibility: *"Is the argument logical and believable?"*

_____

_____

_____

_____

_____

_____

_____

_____

_____

_____

Source: Richard Schlaad and Peter Shannon, "Legalizing Drugs," in Marvin R. Levy, Mark Dignan, and Janet H. Shirreffs, *Targeting Wellness: The Core*, p. 235. Copyright © 1992 by The McGraw-Hill Companies, Inc. Reprinted with permission of The McGraw-Hill Companies, Inc.

Stop and Annotate

Go back to the two preceding selections. In the spaces provided, answer the two sets of critical thinking questions for evaluating an author's argument.

Of the two selections, the pro-legalization argument (the first argument) is stronger. The authors give five distinct "costs" of illegal drugs and then explain how legalizing drugs (and the revenue from taxing them) could be directed at treating the problem. Further, the authors make it clear that there could still be strong penalties for any adults who sell drugs to young people. The anti-legalization argument is very general and is less convincing. Of course, the issue of drug legalization is a complex one, and this is not to say that these two short passages address all the issues. Still, of the two selections, the stronger argument was made in the pro-legalization selection.

Identifying Propaganda Devices

**Comprehension-
Monitoring Question
for Thinking
Critically to Identify
Propaganda Devices**

Has the author tried to unfairly influence me to accept his or her point of view?

To persuade a reader to believe their arguments, authors sometimes resort to **propaganda devices,** techniques designed to unfairly influence the reader to accept their point of view. They try to manipulate the reader by presenting "support" that is inadequate, misleading, or flawed. You are more likely to encounter propaganda in editorials, political pieces, advertisements, and certain other types of writing than in textbooks, of course. Still, you must think critically to detect whether authors are using propaganda devices. If you are not alert to these devices, you can be taken in by them.

Although speakers often use these same techniques, our focus is on authors' use of them. In either case, and as the explanations show, each propaganda device is based on either emotion or flawed reasoning. To think critically and detect propaganda devices, ask yourself, "Has the author tried to unfairly influence me to accept his or her point of view?"

Here are brief descriptions and examples of several common propaganda devices. After each group of three, try the short application exercise.

1. **Appeal to emotion.**   Rather than provide support based on reason, the author appeals to readers' emotions, such as appeals to fear, sympathy, vanity, guilt, and hatred.

    Examples

    "If you don't know how to use a computer, you might as well give up any hope of having a good career."

    "Adopt a pet today. There's nothing more heartbreaking than a sad, lonely kitten or puppy in need of a loving home."

    "Discriminating buyers insist on a Lexus."

2. **Appeal to tradition.**   The author tells readers they should do or believe something because it has always been done or believed in the past, or that by doing as the author says, they can create a new tradition.

    Example

    "In this state, we've always voted for conservative candidates."

3. **Bandwagon.**   The author says readers should believe something because "everyone else" believes it, or in other words, readers should "get on the bandwagon." This strategy appeals to people's desire to be part of the crowd and not feel different or left out.

    Example

    "We all want to be in great shape nowadays, so join the millions of Americans who have bought the home Exer-Gym. Everyone agrees that it's the only piece of exercise equipment you'll ever need, that it's the world's best, and that it's the most enjoyable way to get in shape. Join the Exer-Gym crowd now!"

Exercise: Label each statement a, b, or c according to the propaganda device it exemplifies.

a. appeal to emotion

b. appeal to tradition

c. bandwagon

_____
_____
_____

- Don't be left out of the fun! Book a SeaView cruise today!
- Dixie-Belle Lemonade: A Proud Southern Tradition
- Voting is your civic duty, a right, a privilege. If you don't vote, shame on you!

4. **Appeal to authority.**   The author tries to influence readers to accept his or her argument or point of view by citing some authority who believes it.

Example

"Professor Dorf believes there was once life on Mars. If he believes it, it must be right. He is well-educated and has written a book about extraterrestrial life."

5. **Testimonial.**   This is similar to the appeal to authority. In this case, the author presents a famous person's endorsement of an idea or product to influence readers to believe it. Often, the person endorsing the product has no special knowledge about it or experience with it, so the testimonial is not worth much. Testimonial is also called *endorsement.*

Example

"Brad Pitt knows that Nike athletic products are the best money can buy!"

6. **Straw man.**   The author misrepresents what an opponent believes, and then attacks that misrepresented belief rather than the opponent's actual belief.

Example

"Our college cafeteria has awful food. Obviously, the cafeteria's manager doesn't care at all about students' preferences or their health. The college administration needs to replace the current manager with someone who actually cares about cafeteria customers."

Exercise: Label each statement a, b, or c according to the propaganda device it exemplifies.

a. appeal to authority

b. testimonial

c. straw man

_____

_____

_____

- "Got Milk?" (American Dairy Association's ad campaign featuring photos of celebrities holding a glass of milk and wearing a milk "moustache")
- The governor says he won't sign the proposed anti-gang legislation. Why would he want to leave citizens at the mercy of criminals?
- Three out of four dentists who recommend mouthwash recommend Rinse-O-Dent to their patients.

7. **Either-or.**   The author puts everything into one of two mutually exclusive categories and acts as if there are no other possibilities besides those two categories.

Example

"Either install a Blammo Home Security System or pay the consequences."

8. **False analogy.**   The author makes a comparison that is either inaccurate or inappropriate.

Example

"Taking a shower with Spring Burst soap is like a refreshing romp in the surf."

9. **Circular reasoning.**   The author merely restates the argument or conclusion rather than providing any real support. This is also called *begging the question.*

Example

"Vote for Bob Griggs for senator. He's the best person for the job because there is no one else who's better!"

Exercise: Label each statement a, b, or c according to the propaganda device it exemplifies.

a.   either-or

b.   false analogy

c.   circular reasoning

_____   • These transactions must be ethical because if they weren't, there would be a law against them.

_____   • It's clear that many professional athletes are just overgrown, spoiled children.

_____   • Cultured people appreciate opera; uncultured people don't.

10. **Transfer.**   The author transfers the good or bad qualities of one person or thing to another in order to influence readers' perception of it.

Example

"Mother Teresa would have supported the legislation we are proposing to help the country's homeless."

11. **Sweeping generalization.**   The author presents a broad, general statement that goes far beyond the evidence. (*Stereotyping* is one form of sweeping generalization.)

Example

"All women are bad drivers."

12. **Hasty generalization.**   The author jumps to a conclusion that is based on insufficient proof or evidence.

Example

"Sudzo made my clothes spotless and bright again. It'll work on all of your laundry, too!"

Exercise: Label each statement a, b, or c according to the propaganda device it exemplifies.

a. transfer

b. sweeping generalization

c. hasty generalization

_____ • If General Robert E. Lee were alive today, he would have made the same decision that General Jones made last week.

_____ • The homeless are lazy, unmotivated people who would rather ask for a hand-out than work for a living.

_____ • My brother was a Boy Scout, and he loved it. Any boy would find that becoming a Boy Scout is one of the best decisions he could ever make!

13. Plain folks.   The author presents himself or herself as someone who is just like the readers, someone they can relate to.

Example

"For the rich, there's therapy. For the rest of us, there's bass. The Cariolus reel is built with care and precision by people who, just like you, would go crazy if they couldn't fish." (Shimano fishing reels advertisement)

14. Ad hominem.   The author attacks the person rather than the views or ideas the person presents.

Example

"My opponent once lied about serving in the military when he was a young man. Why should you believe him now when he says he will reduce taxes if you elect him? He's a liar, and every campaign promise he makes is just another lie."

15. Red herring.   The author presents an irrelevant issue to draw readers' attention away from the real issue. The name comes from a trick used to throw hunting dogs off the scent of the track: a person trying to escape would drag a red herring (a strong-smelling fish) across his tracks.

Example

"This issue isn't about bailing out companies whose management made irresponsible decisions; it's about saving people's jobs."

Exercise: Label each statement a, b, or c according to the propaganda device it exemplifies.

a. plain folks

b. ad hominem

c. red herring

_____ • Professor Linden says cheating is wrong, but his opinion doesn't count because he's just parroting the administration's point of view.

_____ • Why should we hardworking, middle-class folks have to carry the tax burden in this country?

_____

- The proposed Community Center is popular with citizens, but two older buildings would have to be bulldozed to create the space for it. We can't go around razing buildings willy-nilly all over the city.

16. Post hoc.   The author implies that because one event happened before another, it caused the second event.

Example

"I read *The Keys to Success,* and a week later I was offered a job!"

17. Hypostatization.   The author treats an abstract concept as if it were a concrete reality.

Example

"Technology is stripping us of our privacy and controlling our lives.

18. Non sequitur.   The author links two ideas or events that are not related; one does not logically follow from the other.

Example

"Kiki's favorite color is orange. She plans to become a flight attendant."

Exercise: Label each statement a, b, or c according to the propaganda device it exemplifies.

a.   post hoc

b.   hypostatization

c.   non sequitur

_____
_____

- Although it may not seem like it, the universe is always watching out for us.
- The picture on my TV got fuzzy, so I went over and smacked it. It fixed the problem: the picture cleared up.

_____

- Marie lives uptown. She must be wealthy.

PROPAGANDA TECHNIQUES EXERCISE

Directions: Here is a list of the propaganda devices that have been presented. Decide which one is used in each statement below. Appeal to emotion is used three times in the exercise, but the other propaganda devices are used only once. An example has been worked for you.

ad hominem	either-or	post hoc
appeal to authority	false analogy	red herring
appeal to emotion	hasty generalization	straw man
appeal to tradition	hypostatization	sweeping generalization
bandwagon	non sequitur	testimonial
circular reasoning	plain folks	transfer

Example

Insist on Best Brand Turkeys—because you don't want to be embarrassed on Thanksgiving Day.

appeal to emotion (fear)

1. Christmas just wouldn't be Christmas without Creamy Smooth Eggnog! It's been America's number one choice for more than 50 years.

2. Each year more than one million Americans trust Nationwide Realty to sell their homes. Shouldn't you?

3. Parents are justified in doing whatever it takes to keep themselves informed about their child if they think their child is doing something wrong. Dr. Laura says it's OK for parents to search their teenagers' rooms, read their diaries, and even make them take drug tests.

4. I've been a radio talk show host for 15 years now, and I've never found an arthritis pain reliever more effective than Salvo.

5. If Congress had passed that bill, we'd all be better off today.

6. The victims of the devastating tornado need more than your pity. They need you to roll up your sleeve and donate blood.

7. The governor opposes legislation that mandates safety locks on guns. Obviously, he has no problem with innocent children being killed by playing with guns.

8. You can either buy a Health Trip exercise bicycle or continue to be overweight and out of shape.

9. Having a career in real estate is like being able to print money!

10. Install a Gold Star Home Alarm today! After all, no one wants to become a crime statistic.

_____

11. America will have better-educated citizens when fewer students drop out of school.

_____

12. Princess Diana would have donated her time and energy to this worthy cause.

_____

13. The plan for the new freeway may not be perfect, but keep in mind the City Council disagreed even more about the new library.

_____

14. Today's youth are self-centered and irresponsible.

_____

15. Government needs to be corralled and restrained.

_____

16. Blue Label Beer—the workingman's brew!

_____

17. Senator Bledsoe is opposed to campaign funding reform. He's just the type of person who would solicit illegal contributions! I'll bet that during the last decade he's taken in hundreds of thousands of dollars illegally.

_____

18. If you like being near the beach, you'll love living in Hawaii.

_____

19. Why shouldn't you have the best? Pamper yourself with a getaway weekend at Windcliff Resort and Spa.

_____

20. Mattie is vegetarian. She works at the bank.

_____

A WORD ABOUT STANDARDIZED READING TESTS: CRITICAL THINKING

Many college students are required to take standardized reading tests as part of an overall assessment program, in a reading course, or as part of a state-mandated basic skills test. A standardized reading test typically consists of a series of passages followed by multiple-choice reading skill application questions, to be completed within a specified time limit.

Here are some examples of typical wording of questions about critical thinking:

● Questions about _fact and opinion_ may be worded:

Which of the following statements expresses an opinion rather than a fact?

Which of the following sentences from the passage represents a fact?

Which of the following sentences from the passage represents an opinion?

(Continued on next page)

(Continued from previous page)

In dealing with questions about fact and opinion, watch for words (such as *perhaps, apparently, it seems,* or *this suggests*) that signal opinions. Watch also for judgmental words (such as *best, worst,* or *beautiful*), which also indicate opinions. In dealing with questions about inferences and logical conclusions, remember that an inference must be logical and must be based on information in the passage.

- Questions about *inferences and logical conclusions* may be worded:

  Which of the following conclusions could be made about . . . ?

  On the basis of information in this passage, the reader could conclude . . .

  It can be inferred from the passage that . . .

  The passage implies that . . .

- Questions about the *author's argument* may be worded:

  In this selection, the author argues that . . .

  The author's position on this issue is . . .

  The author's point of view is . . .

  The passage suggests that the author believes . . .

- Questions about the *author's credibility* may be worded:

  The author has credibility because . . .

  The author establishes his credibility by . . . (by presenting data, giving examples, etc.)

  The author's argument is believable because . . .

  The author is believable because . . .

- Questions about the *author's assumptions* may be worded:

  The author bases his (or her) argument on which of the following assumptions?

  Which of the following assumptions underlies the author's argument?

  The author's argument is based on which of the following assumptions?

- Questions about *types of support* the author presents may be worded:

  The author presents which of the following types of support?

  The author includes all of the following types of support except . . .

- Questions about *author's bias* may be worded:

  In this passage, the author shows bias against . . .

  Which of the following statements most likely contains a biased attitude expressed in this passage?

CHECKPOINT
Thinking Critically

Directions: Think critically as you read these paragraphs and then answer the questions that follow them. Write your answers in the spaces provided.

1. This paragraph comes from a business textbook:

Since you've signed up for this business course, we're guessing you already know the value of a college education. But just to give you some numerical backup, you should know that the gap between the earnings of high school graduates and college graduates, which is growing every year, now ranges from 60 to 70 percent. Holders of bachelor's degrees will make an average of $51,000 per year as opposed to just $31,500 for high school graduates. Thus, what you invest in a college education is likely to pay you back many times. A college degree can make a huge salary difference by the end of a 30-year career: more than half a million dollars. That doesn't mean that there aren't good careers available to non–college graduates. It just means that those with a college education are more likely to have higher earnings over their lifetime.

Source: Adapted from William G. Nickels, James M. McHugh, and Susan M. McHugh, *Understanding Business,* 7e, p. 3. Copyright © 2005 by The McGraw-Hill Companies, Inc. Reprinted with permission of The McGraw-Hill Companies, Inc.

_____ Which of the following statements from the paragraph represents a fact rather than an opinion?

    a. Holders of bachelor's degrees will make an average of $51,000 per year.

    b. High school graduates will make an average of $31,500 per year.

    c. What you invest in a college education is likely to pay you back many times.

    d. The gap between the earnings of high school graduates and college graduates is growing every year.

2. This paragraph comes from a U.S. government textbook:

One area in which African Americans have made substantial progress since the 1960s is elective office. Although the percentage of black elected officials is still far below the proportion of African Americans in the population, it has risen sharply over recent decades. There are now roughly 500 black mayors and more than 40 black members of Congress. The most stunning advance, of course, is the election of Barack Obama in 2008 as the first African-American president.

Source: Adapted from Thomas E. Patterson, *The American Democracy,* Alternate Edition, 10e, pp. 137–39. Copyright © 2011 by The McGraw-Hill Companies, Inc. Reprinted with permission of The McGraw-Hill Companies, Inc.

_____   Which of the following statements is a logical conclusion that can be inferred from the information in the paragraph?

- *a.* The percentage of black elected officials is still far below the proportion of African Americans in the population.
- *b.* It is likely that the percentage of African Americans elected to public office will increase.
- *c.* There are now many black mayors and black members of Congress.
- *d.* Full equality has been achieved in America.

3. This paragraph comes from a biology textbook:

What Is Cancer?

Cancer is a growth disorder of cells. It starts when an apparently normal cell begins to grow in an uncontrolled way, spreading out to other parts of the body. The result is a cluster of cells, called a *tumor,* that constantly expands in size. Benign tumors are completely enclosed by normal tissue and are said to be encapsulated. These tumors do not spread to other parts of the body and are therefore noninvasive. Malignant tumors are invasive and not encapsulated. Because they are not enclosed by normal tissue, cells are able to break away from the tumor and spread to other areas of the body. Cells that leave the tumor and spread throughout the body, forming new tumors at distant sites, are called *metastases.* Cancer is perhaps the most devastating and deadly disease. Of the children born in 1985, one-third will contract cancer at some time during their lives; one-fourth of the male children and one-third of the female children will someday die of cancer. Most of us have had family or friends affected by the disease.

Source: Adapted from George B. Johnson, *The Living World: Basic Concepts,* 4e, p. 150. Copyright © 2006 by The McGraw-Hill Companies, Inc. Reprinted with permission of The McGraw-Hill Companies, Inc.

_____   Which of the following statements from the paragraph represents an opinion rather than a fact?

- *a.* Benign tumors are completely enclosed by normal tissue and are said to be encapsulated.
- *b.* Cancer cells that leave the tumor and spread throughout the body, forming new tumors at distant sites, are called metastases.
- *c.* Malignant tumors are invasive and not encapsulated.
- *d.* Cancer is perhaps the most devastating and deadly disease.

4. This paragraph comes from a health textbook:

Are people the way they are as a result of their genetic endowment or because of experiences they have had? The answer isn't black and white. Who we are as individuals is the result of a complex, ongoing interaction among our genetic inheritance, our lifestyle choices, and environmental factors of many kinds. Environmental factors include everything from our prenatal environment, to our family and community, to our ethnic or cultural group, to our society and the world at large. What we can say definitively about genetic inheritance is that it plays a key role in establishing some of the outside parameters of what you can be and do in your life. You can think of genetic inheritance as your blueprint, or starting point. The blueprint is filled in and actualized over the course of your entire life.

Source: Adapted from Michael L. Teague, Sara L. C. Mackenzie, and David M. Rosenthal, *Your Health Today,* p. 20. Copyright © 2011 by The McGraw-Hill Companies, Inc. Reprinted with permission of The McGraw-Hill Companies, Inc.

Which of the following statements is a logical conclusion that can be inferred from the information in the paragraph?
   a. Your genetic inheritance is your blueprint for what you can be and do in your life.
   b. You are the way you are as a result of your genetic endowment.
   c. You have control over some factors that shape you, but you do not have control over all of them.
   d. Your blueprint is filled in over the course of your entire life.

5. This paragraph comes from a U.S. history textbook:

The Founding of Jamestown

Only a few months after receiving its charter from King James I, the London Company launched a colonizing expedition headed for Virginia—a party of 144 men aboard three ships. Only 104 men survived the journey from England. They reached the American coast in the spring of 1607, sailed into the Chesapeake Bay and up a river they named James, and established their colony on a peninsula extending from the river's northern bank. They called it Jamestown. The colonists had chosen their site poorly. In an effort to avoid the mistakes of Roanoke (whose residents were assumed to have been killed by Indians), they selected what they thought to be an easily defended location—an inland setting that they believed would offer them security. The site was low and swampy, and hot and humid in the summer. In addition, the site was subject to outbreaks of malaria. It was surrounded by thick woods, which were difficult to clear for cultivation. And it lay within the territories of powerful local Indians, a confederation led by the imperial chief Powhatan. The result could hardly have been more disastrous.

Source: Adapted from Alan Brinkley, *American History: Connecting with the Past,* 14e, p. 37. Copyright © 2012 by The McGraw-Hill Companies, Inc. Reprinted with permission of The McGraw-Hill Companies, Inc.

_____   Which of the following statements from the paragraph represents an opinion rather than a fact?

    a. They reached the American coast in the spring of 1607, sailed into the Chesapeake Bay and up a river they named James, and established their colony on a peninsula extending from the river's northern bank.

    b. The site was low and swampy, and hot and humid in the summer.

    c. The result could hardly have been more disastrous.

    d. Only 104 men survived the journey from England.

DEVELOPING CHAPTER REVIEW CARDS

Complete the eight review cards for Chapter 9 by answering the questions or following the directions on each card. When you have completed them, you will have summarized (1) what critical thinking is, (2) distinguishing facts from opinions, (3) making logical inferences and drawing logical conclusions, (4) deductive and inductive reasoning, (5) the steps in evaluating an author's argument, (6) the definition of author's argument, author's bias, and author's assumptions, (7) critical thinking questions to ask yourself, and (8) propaganda devices. Print or write legibly.

Critical Thinking

Define *critical thinking*.

List the skills of critical thinking.

    1.

    2.

    3.

Card 1   Chapter 9: Thinking Critically

Distinguishing Facts and Opinions

What is a *fact*?

What is an *opinion*?

List several clue words and phrases that typically signal an opinion.

To distinguish facts from opinions, what question should you ask yourself?

What makes an opinion valuable?

Card 2   Chapter 9: Thinking Critically

Making Inferences and Drawing Logical Conclusions

What is an *inference*?

What is a *conclusion*?

When reading, what question should you ask yourself about making an inference?

Card 3   Chapter 9: Thinking Critically

Deductive and Inductive Reasoning

Define *deductive reasoning*.

Define *inductive reasoning*.

Card 4   Chapter 9: Thinking Critically

Steps in Evaluating an Author's Argument

List the seven steps you must take to evaluate an author's argument.

1.

2.

3.

4.

5.

6.

7.

Card 5   Chapter 9: Thinking Critically

Author's Argument, Bias, and Assumptions

Define *author's argument*.

Define *author's bias*.

Define *author's assumption*.

Card 6   Chapter 9: Thinking Critically

Critical Thinking Questions for Evaluating an Author's Argument

What questions should you ask yourself in order to complete the seven steps for evaluating an author's argument?

1.

2.

3.

4.

5.

6.

7.

Card 7   Chapter 9: Thinking Critically

Identifying Propaganda Devices

What are propaganda devices?

List 18 types of propaganda devices.

Card 8   Chapter 9: Thinking Critically

Directions: Read these paragraphs carefully and answer the questions that follow them. Write your answers in the spaces provided.

This paragraph comes from an economics textbook:

Paying for energy in its various forms, from electricity to heat to gasoline, plays a larger part in the budget of poor families than well-to-do families. This is because energy is largely used for essentials. For families in the lowest ten percent of households, energy costs account for a full third of household expenditures. For households in the top ten percent, it absorbs only five percent of household expenses. Indeed, paying for energy presents a significant challenge for poor families.

Source: Adapted from Robert Heilbroner and Lester Thurow, *Five Economic Challenges,* Englewood Cliffs, NJ: Prentice-Hall, 1981, p. 171. Reprinted with permission of Prentice-Hall.

1. What logical conclusion can be drawn about the cost of energy?
  a. Energy costs play a large part in family budgets.
  b. Energy costs are increasing steadily.
  c. A rise in gasoline prices affects rich families less than it affects poor families.
  d. We must develop alternate sources of energy.

2. Which of the following statements expresses an opinion rather than a fact?
  a. For families in the lowest ten percent of households, energy costs account for a full third of household expenditures.
  b. For households in the top ten percent, energy absorbs only five percent of household expenses.
  c. Paying for energy in its various forms, from electricity to heat to gasoline, plays a larger part in the budget of poor families than well-to-do families.
  d. Indeed, paying for energy presents a significant challenge for poor families.

This paragraph comes from a music appreciation textbook:

During the 1980s and 1990s, women performers had a powerful impact on rock music. "Many new women rockers do a lot more than sing," observed one critic. "They play their own instruments, write their own songs, and they control their own careers." Their range of musical styles extended from pop and soul to funk, new wave, country rock, and heavy metal. Leading performers included Pat Benatar, Tina Turner, Madonna, Alanis Morissette, Sheryl Crow, Queen Latifah, Shania Twain, and Ani DiFranco.

Source: Roger Kamien, *Music: An Appreciation,* 10e, p. 517. Copyright © 2011 by The McGraw-Hill Companies, Inc. Reprinted with permission of The McGraw-Hill Companies, Inc.

3. Which of the following statements expresses an opinion rather than a fact?
   a. Women rockers play their own instruments and write their own songs.
   b. The range of musical styles of female rockers extended from pop and soul to funk, new wave, country rock, and heavy metal.
   c. Female rock performers included Pat Benatar, Tina Turner, Madonna, Alanis Morissette, Sheryl Crow, Queen Latifah, Shania Twain, and Ani DiFranco.
   d. During the 1980s and 1990s, women performers had a powerful impact on rock music.

This excerpt is from an environmental science textbook:

> On August 29, 2005, Hurricane Katrina came ashore on the U.S. Gulf Coast between Mobile, Alabama, and New Orleans, Louisiana. It was an enormous and frightening hurricane that ultimately caused tremendous property damage as well as the loss of many human lives. Hurricane Katrina was just one of the 26 named storms that hit the Americas in the worst Atlantic hurricane season in history. A few hours after the hurricane made landfall, the combination of the storm surge and the torrential rain falling inland overwhelmed levees that were supposed to protect New Orleans. Up to 80 percent of the city flooded. Close to 1,000 people died in Louisiana alone, with most of those deaths occurring in New Orleans. Mandatory evacuation orders were issued for New Orleans' 500,000 residents in the days that followed the storm.
>
> The devastation caused by Hurricane Katrina starkly illustrated the way in which environmental destruction can cause hardships for people. Twenty-eight percent of New Orleans residents lived below the poverty line. Information about the hurricane and about evacuation options was harder for the city's poorer residents to access. Compounding the problem, a large number of these poorer households did not own cars. Without a car, a driver's license, or a credit card, even a timely evacuation order can be extremely hard to obey. As Hurricane Katrina battered the city, many residents were essentially left behind, forced to flee to crowded and unsanitary temporary shelters like the New Orleans Superdome.
>
> *Source:* Adapted from Eldon D. Enger and Bradley F. Smith, *Environmental Science: A Study of Interrelationships,* 12e, p. 24. Copyright © 2010 by The McGraw-Hill Companies, Inc. Reprinted with permission of The McGraw-Hill Companies, Inc.

4. Which of the following statements expresses an opinion rather than a fact?
   a. On August 29, 2005, Hurricane Katrina came ashore on the U.S. Gulf Coast between Mobile, Alabama, and New Orleans, Louisiana.
   b. Mandatory evacuation orders were issued for New Orleans' 500,000 residents in the days that followed the storm.
   c. It was an enormous and frightening hurricane that ultimately caused tremendous property damage as well as the loss of many human lives.
   d. Twenty-eight percent of New Orleans residents lived below the poverty line.

5. Which of the following statements is a fact?

   a. The devastation caused by Hurricane Katrina was shocking, and starkly illustrated the way in which environmental destruction can cause hardships for people.

   b. It was an enormous and frightening hurricane that ultimately caused tremendous property damage as well as the loss of many human lives.

   c. Without a car, a driver's license, or a credit card, even a timely evacuation order can be extremely hard to obey.

   d. Mandatory evacuation orders were issued for New Orleans' 500,000 residents in the days that followed the storm.

6. Based on the information in the passage, which of the following is an inference that can be made about residents of New Orleans?

   a. In the days following the storm, residents were issued mandatory evacuation orders.

   b. Twenty-eight percent of New Orleans residents lived below the poverty line.

   c. Many poorer residents were unable to obey the evacuation order.

   d. Many residents throughout the city elected to remain in their homes and hoped that the levees would protect the city from flooding.

7. Which of the following is a logical conclusion that can be drawn about Hurricane Katrina?

   a. Hurricane Katrina was not predicted.

   b. Hurricane Katrina was particularly hard on poorer citizens.

   c. Mandatory evacuation orders should have been issued after Hurricane Katrina hit.

   d. Hurricane Katrina was the largest and most destructive tropical storm in recorded history.

This excerpt is from a government textbook:

One of the most sensitive and controversial issues regarding gay and lesbian rights has been the legalization of same-sex marriages. The issue gained heightened attention in 1993 when the Supreme Court of Hawaii ruled that denying marriage licenses to gay couples might violate the equal protection clause of their state constitution. Other states then began to worry that under the "full faith and credit clause" of the United States Constitution, they might be forced to accept the legality of same-sex marriages performed in Hawaii—or any other state that chose to legalize same-sex marriage. Opponents advocated state laws banning same-sex marriages, and a number of states enacted such laws. In 1996, Congress passed the Defense of Marriage Act, which prohibits federal recognition of gay and lesbian couples and allows state governments to ignore same-sex marriages performed in other states.

The issue ignited again in 1999 when the Supreme Court of Vermont ruled that gay couples are entitled to the same benefits of marriage as heterosexual couples. The next year, the Vermont legislature passed a statute permitting homosexual couples to form civil unions. The law entitled these couples to receive the same state benefits as married couples, including insurance benefits and inheritance rights. More public attention followed in 2004, when cities such as San Francisco began performing same-sex marriages. Media images of gay and lesbian couples waiting in line to be married spurred opponents to react by initiating referenda banning same-sex marriages. On the day George W. Bush was reelected to the presidency in 2004, ballot initiatives banning same-sex marriages passed easily in eleven states. Two years later, voters in seven states passed ballot measures amending their state constitutions to recognize marriage only between a man and woman. Then in 2008, voters in Arizona, California, and Florida approved bans on same-sex marriage.

Source: Joseph Losco and Ralph Baker, *Am Gov,* p. 114. Copyright © 2011 by The McGraw-Hill Companies, Inc. Reprinted with permission of The McGraw-Hill Companies, Inc.

8. Which of the following statements expresses an opinion rather than a fact?
   a. In 1996, Congress passed the Defense of Marriage Act.
   b. One of the most sensitive and controversial issues regarding gay and lesbian rights has been the legalization of same-sex marriages.
   c. Then in 2008, voters in Arizona, California, and Florida approved bans on same-sex marriage.
   d. In 2000, the Vermont legislature passed a statute permitting homosexual couples to form civil unions.

9. Based on the information in the passage, which of the following is an inference that can be made about civil unions?
   a. The Vermont legislature passed a statute permitting homosexual couples to form civil unions.
   b. Civil unions in Vermont entitle homosexual couples to receive the same benefits as married couples.
   c. A civil union entitles a couple to the same benefits as a married couple, but it is not a legal marriage.
   d. Civil unions are permitted in most states.

10. Which of the following is a logical conclusion that can be drawn about the issue of legalizing same-sex marriages?
    a. The issue began in 1993 when the Supreme Court of Hawaii denied marriage licenses to gay couples.
    b. It is likely that the legalization of same-sex marriages will continue to be a controversial issue.
    c. The same-sex marriage issue is causing voters in many states to worry that they might be forced to accept civil unions.
    d. Each state must decide whether to legalize same-sex marriages.

Directions: Read these paragraphs carefully and answer the questions that follow them. Write your answers in the spaces provided.

This paragraph comes from a music appreciation textbook:

During the last two centuries, more music has been written for the piano than for any other solo instrument. The piano is exceptionally versatile. A pianist can play many notes at once, including both a melody and its accompaniment. The piano commands a wide range of pitches. Its eighty-eight keys span more than seven octaves. The dynamic range is broad, from a faint whisper to a powerful fortissimo. The piano has exceptional and dynamic flexibility. The Italians named it *pianoforte* (meaning *soft-loud*).

Source: Adapted from Roger Kamien, *Music: An Appreciation,* 10e, p. 25. Copyright © 2011 by The McGraw-Hill Companies, Inc. Reprinted with permission of The McGraw-Hill Companies, Inc.

1. Locate two sentences in the paragraph that represent facts and write them here:

_____

_____

_____

2. Locate two sentences in the paragraph that represent opinions and write them here:

_____

_____

_____

_____

This paragraph comes from an information technology textbook:

Webmasters develop and maintain Web sites and resources. The job may include backup of the company Web site, updating resources, or development of new resources. Webmasters are often involved in the design and development of the Web site. Some Webmasters monitor traffic on the site and take steps to encourage users to visit the site. Webmasters also may work with marketing personnel to increase site traffic and may be involved in development of Web promotions. Employers look for candidates with a bachelor's degree in computer science or information systems and knowledge of common programming languages and Web development software. Knowledge of HTML is considered essential. Those with experience using Web authoring software and programs like Adobe Illustrator and Adobe Flash are often preferred. Good communication and organizational skills are vital to this position. Webmasters can expect to earn an annual salary of $49,500 to $82,500. This position is relatively new in many corporations and tends to have fluid responsibilities. With technological advances and increasing corporate emphasis on Web presence, experience in this field could lead to managerial opportunities.

Source: Adapted from Timothy J. O'Leary and Linda I. O'Leary, *Computing Essentials 2012: Making IT Work for You,* p. 53. Copyright © 2012 by The McGraw-Hill Companies, Inc. Reprinted with permission of The McGraw-Hill Companies, Inc.

3. Two college graduates are candidates for the same webmaster position. Their credentials are the same, but only one has experience using Web authoring software. Based on information in the passage, write a logical inference that can be made about *which candidate is more likely to get the, job.*

_____

_____

_____

_____

4. Based on information in the passage, what can logically be concluded about *the preparation needed to become a successful webmaster*?

_____

_____

_____

_____

_____

This paragraph comes from a U.S. history textbook:

Postwar Computer Technology

The first significant computer of the 1950s was the Universal Automatic Computer, or UNIVAC. It was developed initially for the U.S. Bureau of Census by the Remington Rand Company. The UNIVAC was the first computer to be able to handle both alphabetical and numerical information. It used tape storage and could perform calculations and other functions much faster than its predecessor, the ENIAC, developed in 1946 by the same researchers at the University of Pennsylvania who were responsible for the UNIVAC. Searching for a larger market than the U.S. Bureau of the Census for their very expensive new device, Remington Rand arranged to use a UNIVAC to predict the results of the 1952 election for CBS television news. It would, the developers at Remington Rand believed, produce valuable publicity for the machine. Analyzing early voting results, the UNIVAC accurately predicted an enormous landslide victory for Eisenhower over Stevenson. Most Americans had never heard of a computer before that night, and the UNIVAC's television debut increased public awareness of computer technology.

Source: Adapted from Alan Brinkley, *American History: Connecting with the Past,* 14e, p. 784. Copyright © 2012 by The McGraw-Hill Companies, Inc. Reprinted with permission of The McGraw-Hill Companies, Inc.

5. Locate two sentences in the paragraph that represent facts and write them here:

_____

_____

_____

_____

6. Locate two sentences in the paragraph that represent opinions and write them here:

_____

_____

_____

_____

This paragraph comes from an economics textbook:

A **monopoly** exists when a single firm is the sole producer of a product for which there are no close substitutes. Examples of pure monopoly are relatively rare, but there are many examples of less pure forms. In most cities, government-owned or government-regulated public utilities—natural gas and electric companies, the water company, the cable TV company, and the local telephone company—are all monopolies, or virtually so. There are also many "near monopolies" in which a single firm has the bulk of sales in a specific market. Intel, for example, produces 80 percent of the central microprocessors used in personal computers. First Data Corporation, via its Western Union subsidiary, accounts for 80 percent of the market for money order transfers. Wham-O, through its Frisbee brand, sells 90 percent of plastic throwing discs. The DeBeers diamond syndicate effectively controls 55 percent of the world's supply of rough-cut diamonds. Some monopolies are geographic in nature. For example, a small town may be served by only one airline or railroad. In a small, isolated community, the local barber shop, dry cleaner, or grocery store may approximate a monopoly.

Source: Adapted from Campbell R. McConnell, Stanley L. Brue, and Sean M. Flynn, *Economics: Principles, Problems, and Policies,* 19e, p. 195. Copyright © 2012 by The McGraw-Hill Companies, Inc. Reprinted with permission of The McGraw-Hill Companies, Inc.

7. Based on the information in this passage, write a logical conclusion about *firms that are "near monopolies."*

_____

_____

_____

_____

8. Based on information in the passage, what can logically be inferred about *the type of monopoly that might be most likely to draw competitors: pure monopolies, "near monopolies," or geographic monopolies?*

_____

_____

_____

This paragraph comes from a biology textbook:

Apes

Apes evolved from their anthropoid ancestors. The apes living today consist of the gorilla (genus *Gorilla*), chimpanzee (*Pan*), gibbon (*Hylobates*), and orangutan (*Pongo*). Apes have larger brains than monkeys, and they lack tails. With the exception of the gibbon, apes are larger than any monkey. Apes exhibit the most adaptable behavior of any mammal except human beings. Once widespread in Asia and Africa, there are fewer apes today. No apes ever occurred in North or South America.

Source: Adapted from George B. Johnson, *The Living World: Basic Concepts,* 4e, p. 488. Copyright © 2006 by The McGraw-Hill Companies, Inc. Reprinted with permission of The McGraw-Hill Companies, Inc.

9. Locate two sentences in the paragraph that represent facts and write them here:

_____

_____

10. Locate any sentences in the paragraph that represent opinions and write them here:

_____

_____

_____

_____

SELECTION **9.1**

Government

Poverty in America and Improving Social Welfare through Public Education

From *The American Democracy*
by Thomas E. Patterson

Prepare Yourself to Read

Directions: Do these exercises *before* you read Selection 9.1.

1. First, read and think about the title. What comes to mind when you think about the term *social welfare*?

   _____

   _____

   _____

2. Next, complete your preview by reading the following:

   Introduction (in *italics*)

   All of the first paragraph (paragraph 1)

   Headings

   Terms in **bold** print

   Now that you have completed your preview, what does this selection seem to be about?

   _____

   _____

   _____

   _____

3. **Build your vocabulary as you read.** If you discover an unfamiliar word or key term as you read the selection, try to determine its meaning by using context clues.

Internet Resources

Read More about This Topic Online

Use a search engine, such as Google or Yahoo!, to expand your existing knowledge about this topic *before* you read the selection or to learn more about it *afterward.* If you are unfamiliar with conducting Internet searches, read pages 25–26 on Boolean searches. You can also use Wikipedia, the free online encyclopedia, at www .wikipedia.com. Keep in mind that when you visit any website, it is a good idea to evaluate the site and the information it contains. Ask yourself questions such as "Who sponsors this website?" and "Is the information it contains up to date?"

SELECTION 9.1: POVERTY IN AMERICA AND IMPROVING SOCIAL WELFARE THROUGH PUBLIC EDUCATION

In 2012, the poverty line for a family of four was $23,000 (total yearly income). At the end of 2011, 49 million Americans (16 percent) were living below the poverty line. Moreover, it is estimated that nearly 60 percent of Americans will spend at least one year below the poverty line. How is it that the wealthiest country in the world has so many of its citizens living in poverty? What should be done to improve the economic condition of millions of American families, and why are there such strong disagreements about ways to remedy this situation? This selection from a U.S. government textbook examines the problem of poverty in our nation and describes how our public education system was created to provide "equality of opportunity" and, ultimately, to improve the welfare of its citizens.

Social Welfare Policy

1   In the broadest sense, social welfare policy includes any effort by government to improve social conditions. In a narrower sense, however, social welfare policy refers to those efforts by government to help individuals meet basic human needs, including food, clothing and shelter.

The Poor: Who and How Many?

2   Americans' social welfare needs are substantial. Although Americans are far better off economically than most of the world's peoples, poverty is a significant and persistent problem in the United States. The government defines the **poverty line** as the annual cost of a thrifty food budget for an urban family of four, multiplied by three to include the cost of housing, clothes, and other necessities. Families whose incomes fall below that line are officially considered poor. In 2005, the poverty line was set at an annual income of roughly $19,000 for a family of four. One in nine Americans—roughly thirty million people, including more than ten million children—lives below the poverty line. If they could all join hands, they would form a line stretching from New York to Los Angeles and back again.

3   America's poor include individuals of all ages, races, religions, and regions, but poverty is concentrated among certain groups. Children are one of the largest groups of poor Americans. One in every five children lives in poverty. Most poor children live in single-parent families, usually with the mother. In fact, a high proportion of Americans residing in families headed by divorced, separated, or unmarried women live below the poverty line. *(See Figure 1.)* These families are at a disadvantage because most women earn less than men for comparable work, especially in nonprofessional fields. Women without higher education or special skills often cannot find jobs that pay significantly more than

Annotation Practice Exercises

Directions: For each of the exercises below, think critically to answer the questions. This will help you gain additional insights as you read.

Practice Exercise

Does the author present a statement of *fact* or *opinion* in the first sentence of paragraph 2?

_____

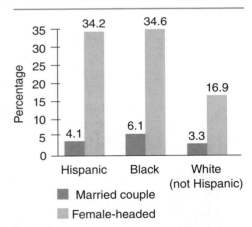

Figure 1
Percentage of Families Living in Poverty, by Family Composition and Race/Ethnicity
Poverty is far more prevalent among female-headed households and African American and Hispanic households.
Source: U.S. Bureau of the Census, 2004.

the child-care expenses they incur if they work outside the home. Single-parent, female-headed families are roughly five times as likely as two-income families to fall below the poverty line, a situation re-ferred to as "the feminization of poverty."

4   Poverty is also widespread among minority-group members. Compared with whites, significantly more African Americans and Hispanics live below the poverty line.

5   Poverty is also geographically concentrated. Although poverty is often portrayed as an urban problem, it is somewhat more preva-lent in rural areas. About one in seven rural residents—compared with one in nine urban residents—lives in a family with income below the poverty line. The urban figure is misleading, however, in that the poverty rate is very high in some inner-city areas. Suburbs are the safe haven from poverty. Because suburbanites are far removed from it, many of them have no sense of the impoverished condition of what Michael Harrington called "the other America."

6   The "invisibility" of poverty in America is evident in polls show-ing that most Americans greatly underestimate the number of poor in their country. Certainly nothing in the daily lives of many Ameri-cans or in what they see on television would lead them to think that poverty rates are uncommonly high. Yet the United States has the highest level of poverty among the advanced industrialized nations, and its rate of child poverty is roughly twice the average rate of the others. *(See Figure 2.)*

Practice Exercise

Does the author present a statement of *fact* or *opinion* in the first sentence of paragraph 5?

_____

Practice Exercise

What logical *conclusion* does the author want you to draw about the number of Americans living in poverty?

_____

_____

_____

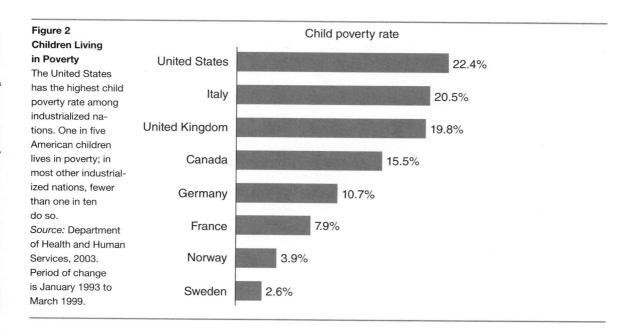

Figure 2
Children Living in Poverty
The United States has the highest child poverty rate among industrialized na-tions. One in five American children lives in poverty; in most other industrial-ized nations, fewer than one in ten do so.
Source: Department of Health and Human Services, 2003. Period of change is January 1993 to March 1999.

Child poverty rate

United States	22.4%
Italy	20.5%
United Kingdom	19.8%
Canada	15.5%
Germany	10.7%
France	7.9%
Norway	3.9%
Sweden	2.6%

Living in Poverty: By Choice or Chance?

7   Many Americans hold to the idea that poverty is largely a matter of choice—that most low-income Americans are unwilling to make the effort to hold a responsible job and get ahead in life. In his book *Losing Ground,* Charles Murray argues that America has a permanent underclass of unproductive citizens who prefer to live on welfare and whose children receive little educational encouragement at home and grow up to be copies of their parents. There are, indeed, many such people in America. They number in the millions. They are the toughest challenge for policymakers because almost nothing about their lives equips them to escape from poverty and its attendant ills.

8   Yet most poor Americans are in their situations as a result of circumstance rather than choice. A ten-year study of American families by a University of Michigan research team found that most of the poor are poor only for a while and that they are poor for temporary reasons such as the loss of a job or desertion by the father. When the U.S. economy goes into a tailspin, the impact devastates many families. The U.S. Department of Labor reported that three million jobs were lost in the manufacturing sector alone during the recessionary period that began in 2000.

9   It is also true that a full-time job does not guarantee that a family will rise above the poverty line. A family of four with one employed adult who works forty hours a week at seven dollars an hour (roughly the minimum wage level) has an annual income of about $14,500, which is well below the poverty line. Millions of Americans—mostly household workers, service workers, unskilled laborers, and farm workers—are in this position. The U.S. Bureau of Labor Statistics estimates that roughly 7 percent of full-time workers do not earn enough to lift their family above the poverty line.

Education as Equality of Opportunity: The American Way

10   Economic security has a higher priority in European democracies than in the United States. European democracies have instituted programs such as government-paid health care for all citizens, compensation for all unemployed workers, and retirement benefits for all elderly citizens. The United States provides these benefits only to some citizens in each category. For example, not all elderly Americans are entitled to social security benefits. If they paid social security taxes for a long enough period when they were employed, they (and their spouses) receive benefits. Otherwise they do not, even if they are in dire economic need.

Practice Exercise

What *controversial topic* does the author present in paragraph 7?

_____

_____

_____

Practice Exercise

Does the author present a statement of *fact* or *opinion* in the last sentence of paragraph 9?

_____

Practice Exercise

Does the author present *facts, opinions,* or both in paragraph 10?

_____

11   Such policy differences between Europe and the United States stem from cultural and historical differences. Democracy developed in Europe in reaction to centuries of aristocratic rule, which brought the issue of economic privilege to the forefront. When strong labor and socialist parties then emerged as a result of industrialization, European democracies initiated sweeping social welfare programs that brought about greater economic equality. In contrast, American democracy emerged out of a tradition of limited government that emphasized personal freedom. Equality was a lesser issue, and class consciousness was weak. No major labor or socialist party emerged in America during industrialization to represent the working class, and there was no persistent and strong demand for welfare policies that would bring about a widespread sharing of wealth.

12   Americans look upon jobs and the personal income that comes from work as the proper basis of economic security. Rather than giving welfare payments to the poor, Americans prefer that the poor be given training and education so that they can learn to help themselves. This attitude is consistent with Americans' preference for **equality of opportunity,** the belief that individuals should have an equal chance to succeed on their own. The concept embodies *equality* in its emphasis on giving everyone a fair chance to get ahead. Yet equality of opportunity also embodies *liberty* because it allows people to succeed or fail on their own as a result of what they do with their opportunities. The expectation is that people will end up differently—some will be rich, some poor. It is sometimes said that equality of opportunity offers individuals an equal chance to become unequal.

13   In practice, equality of opportunity works itself out primarily in the private sector, where Americans compete for jobs, promotions, and other advantages. However, a few public policies have the purpose of enhancing equality of opportunity. The most significant of these policies is public education.

Public Education: Enhancing Equality of Opportunity

14   During the first hundred years of our nation's existence, the concept of a free education for all children was a controversial and divisive issue. Wealthy interests feared that an educated public would challenge their power. The proponents of a more equal society wanted to use education as a means of enabling ordinary people to get ahead. This second view won out. Public schools sprang up in nearly every community and were open free of charge to all children who could attend.

15   Today, the United States invests more heavily in public education at all levels than does any other country. The curriculum in American schools is also relatively standardized. Unlike those countries

---

Practice Exercise

What logical *conclusion* does the author want you to draw about the concept of "equality of opportunity" and economic success or security?

_____

_____

_____

_____

_____

Practice Exercise

What *controversial topic* does the author present in paragraph 14?

_____

_____

_____

that divide children even at the grade school level into different tracks that lead ultimately to different occupations, the United States aims to educate all children in essentially the same way. Of course, public education is not a uniform experience for American children. The quality of education depends significantly on the wealth of the community in which a child resides.

16   Nevertheless, the United States through its public schools educates a broad segment of the population. Arguably, no country in the world has made an equivalent effort to give children, whatever their parents' background, an equal opportunity in life through education. Per pupil spending on public elementary and secondary schools is roughly twice as high in the United States as it is in Western Europe. America's commitment to broad-based education extends to college. The United States is far and away the world leader in terms of the proportion of adults receiving a college education.

17   The nation's education system preserves both the myth and the reality of the American dream. The belief that success can be had by anyone who works for it could not be sustained if the education system were tailored for a privileged few. And educational attainment is related to personal success, at least as measured by annual incomes. In fact, annual incomes of college graduates consistently exceed the incomes of those with only a high school diploma.

18   In part because the public schools play such a large role in creating an equal-opportunity society, they have been heavily criticized in recent years. Violence in public elementary and secondary schools is a major parental concern. So too is student performance on standardized tests. American students are not even in the top ten internationally in terms of their test scores in science or math.

19   Disgruntled parents have demanded changes in public schools, and these demands have led some communities to allow parents to choose the public school their children will attend. Under this policy, the schools compete for students, and those that attract the most students are rewarded with the largest budgets. A majority of Americans favor such a policy. Advocates of this policy contend that it compels school administrators and teachers to do a better job and gives students the option of rejecting a school that is performing poorly. Opponents of the policy say that it creates a few well-funded schools and a lot of poorly funded ones, yielding no net gain in educational quality. Critics also claim that the policy discriminates against poor and minority-group children, whose parents are less likely to be in a position to steer them toward the better schools.

20   An even more contentious issue than school choice is the voucher system issue. The voucher system allows parents to use tax dollars to send their children to private or parochial schools instead of public schools. The recipient school receives a voucher redeemable from the government, and the student receives a corresponding

What *controversial topic* does the author present in paragraph 19?

_____

_____

_____

reduction in his or her tuition. Advocates claim that vouchers force failing schools to improve their instructional programs. Opponents argue that vouchers weaken the public schools by siphoning off both revenue and students. They also note that vouchers are of little value to students from poor families because they cover only part of the cost of attending a private or parochial school. (*See Figure 3.*)

21   The issue of school choice reflects the tensions inherent in the concept of equal opportunity. On one hand, competition between schools expands the number of alternatives available to students. On the other hand, not all students have a realistic opportunity to choose among the alternatives.

Practice Exercise

What *controversial topic* does the author present in paragraph 20?

_____

_____

_____

SELECTION 9.1

Figure 3
Opinions on School Vouchers
Americans are divided in their opinions on school vouchers.
Source: Lowell C. Rose and Alec M. Gallup, *The 35th Annual Phi Delta Kappa/ Gallup Poll of the Public's Attitudes Toward the Public Schools. Phi Delta Kappan*, September, 2003, pp. 29, 56. Reprinted by permission of Phi Delta Kappa International, Inc.

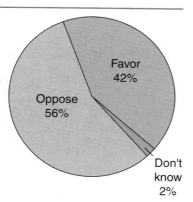

Favor
42%

Oppose
56%

Don't
know
2%

Reading Selection Quiz

This quiz has several parts. Your instructor may assign some or all of them.

Comprehension

Directions: Use the information in the selection to answer each item below. You may refer to the selection as you answer the questions. Write each answer in the space provided.

1. In a specific sense, social welfare policy refers to the efforts of our government to:
   a. improve the conditions in our society.
   b. help people meet basic human needs, including shelter, clothing, and food.
   c. eliminate poverty.
   d. provide Americans with equal opportunities.

2. In 2005, the poverty line annual income for a family of four was set at about:
   a. $9,000.
   b. $12,000.
   c. $19,000.
   d. $24,000.

3. Which of the following is an *incorrect* statement about poverty in America today?
   a. One in every five children lives in poverty.
   b. Single-parent, female-headed families are more likely to fall below the poverty line than two-income families.
   c. More whites than Hispanics and African Americans live below the poverty line.
   d. Poverty is somewhat more prevalent in rural areas than in urban areas.

4. According to the information presented in the bar graph and accompanying caption in Figure 1, poverty is:
   a. more prevalent in married-couple households.
   b. the most urgent problem facing the United States.
   c. more prevalent in female-headed households.
   d. likely to affect all minority-group families.

5. According to information in Figure 2, the child poverty rate in the United States is:
   a. more than 50 percent.
   b. about 22 percent.

    c. 7 percent.

    d. less than 3 percent.

6. The American concept of *equality of opportunity* is the belief that:

    a. all people are basically the same.

    b. everyone in the United States deserves economic equality.

    c. individuals should have an equal chance to succeed on their own.

    d. no one in the United States should live in poverty.

7. An example of evidence that supports the United States' commitment to providing public education for the purpose of enhancing equality of opportunity would be:

    a. The United States invests more heavily in public education at all levels than does any other country.

    b. The public education system in the United States is tailored for children and young adults, regardless of their parents' background.

    c. Per pupil spending on public elementary and secondary schools is roughly twice as high in the United States as it is in Western Europe.

    d. all of the above

8. Today a majority of Americans support:

    a. a voucher system.

    b. public school choice.

    c. standardized tests.

    d. a tracking system.

9. Opponents of the voucher system claim that the system:

    a. weakens public schools by reducing revenues and the number of students.

    b. reduces the number of alternatives available to students.

    c. forces failing schools to change their instructional programs.

    d. creates a few well-funded schools and many poorly funded ones.

10. It can be inferred that public education in the United States:

    a. can help lift people out of poverty.

    b. benefits a broad segment of the population.

    c. enhances equality of opportunity.

    d. all of the above

Vocabulary in Context

Directions: For each item below, use context clues to deduce the meaning of the *italicized* word. Be sure the answer you choose makes sense in both sentences. Write each answer in the space provided.

_____ **11.** Americans' social welfare needs are *substantial.*

When Joe began college, he was surprised to discover that each of his courses required a *substantial* amount of reading and writing.

substantial (səb stăn′ shəl) means:

   a. having substance; material

   b. related to poverty

   c. solidly built; strong

   d. large in amount or degree

_____ **12.** Although Americans are far better off economically than most of the world's peoples, poverty is a significant and *persistent* problem in the United States.

Throughout her childhood, Carmen was annoyed by *persistent* rumors about her parents' wreckless lifestyle.

persistent (pər sĭs′ tənt) means:

   a. existing for a long time; continuing

   b. important; significant

   c. cruel; unkind

   d. bothered; troubled

_____ **13.** These families are at a disadvantage because most women earn less than men for *comparable* work, especially in nonprofessional fields.

The cost of living in Boston is *comparable* to the cost of living in Chicago; both cities are expensive places to live.

comparable (kŏm′ pər ə bəl) means:

   a. different; opposite

   b. difficult; challenging

   c. similar; equivalent

   d. expensive; costly

_____ **14.** Although poverty is often portrayed as an urban problem, it is somewhat more *prevalent* in rural areas.

Today, violence is *prevalent* in movies and on network television.

prevalent (prĕv′ ə lənt) means:

   a. concentrated in urban and rural areas

   b. widely or commonly occurring or existing

c.   gradually increasing

d.   accepted

15. In his book *Losing Ground,* Charles Murray *argues* that America has a permanent underclass of unproductive citizens who prefer to live on welfare and whose children receive little educational encouragement at home and grow up to be copies of their parents.

Our father routinely *argues* that without a good education, it will be difficult for us to obtain satisfying jobs and earn substantial incomes.

argues (är′ gyōōz) means:

a.   quarrels constantly; disputes

b.   pesters; nags

c.   attempts to prove by reasoning; claims

d.   explains in writing

16. If they paid social security taxes for a long enough period when they were employed, they (and their spouses) receive benefits. Otherwise they do not, even if they are in *dire* economic need.

Following the disastrous super storm Sandy, residents found themselves in *dire* need of basic necessities such as water, food, clothing, and shelter.

dire (dīr) means:

a.   urgent; desperate

b.   expensive; difficult to obtain

c.   basic; essential

d.   deserving; entitled

17. The *proponents* of a more equal society wanted to use education as a means of enabling ordinary people to get ahead.

Recycling *proponents* want everyone to get into the habit of properly recycling all bottles, glass, paper, and plastic containers.

proponents (prə pō′ nənts) means:

a.   officials; authorities

b.   opponents; detractors

c.   supporters; advocates

d.   manufacturers; producers

18. Of course, public education is not a *uniform* experience for American children.

All McDonalds cheeseburgers have a *uniform* taste and appearance because they are made with the same ingredients and in the exact same way.

uniform (yo͞o′ nə fôrm) means:

  a.   always the same; unvarying

  b.   similar in color and texture

  c.   satisfying; fulfilling

  d.   successful; productive

19. *Advocates* of this policy contend that it compels school administrators and teachers to do a better job and gives students the option of rejecting a school that is performing poorly.

Fitness *advocates* remind us to maintain a healthy diet and exercise regularly.

advocates (ăd′ və kĭts) means:

  a.   those who argue against a cause; opponents

  b.   those who argue for a cause; supporters

  c.   those who reject an idea

  d.   those who debate an issue

20. An even more *contentious* issue than school choice is the voucher system issue.

Human cloning, stem cell research, alternative medicine, and abortion are examples of *contentious* topics.

contentious (kən tĕn′ shəs) means:

  a.   controversial

  b.   important

  c.   confusing

  d.   difficult

S E L E C T I O N **9.1**   *Reading Skills Application*

Government
(continued)

Directions: These items test your ability to *apply* certain reading skills. You may not have studied all of the skills yet, so some items will serve as a preview. Write each answer in the space provided.

21. Which of the following sentences expresses the main idea of the second paragraph of this selection?

  a.   If all the people living in poverty in the United States could join hands, they would form a line stretching from New York City to Los Angeles and back again.

  b.   The United States will never be able to eliminate poverty completely.

  c.   Americans' social welfare needs are substantial, and poverty is a significant and persistent problem in our nation.

  d.   The poverty line is the annual cost of basic human needs for a family of four.

_____ **22.** Which writing pattern did the author use to organize the main idea and supporting details in paragraph 8?

    a.   list

    b.   comparison-contrast

    c.   sequence

    d.   cause-effect

_____ **23.** Which of the following best describes the author's purpose for writing this selection?

    a.   to persuade readers that poverty is largely a matter of choice and to inform readers about ways to alleviate it

    b.   to explain the nature of the problem of poverty in the United States and to illustrate how public education policy is designed to improve social welfare

    c.   to instruct readers how to combat social inequity in the United States and how to reduce the number of children living in poverty

    d.   to inform readers about the educational opportunities that exist in the United States today

_____ **24.** Our nation has the highest child poverty rate among the advanced industrialized nations, but two countries that have child poverty rates almost as high as the United States are:

    a.   France and Germany.

    b.   Italy and the United Kingdom.

    c.   Sweden and Norway.

    d.   China and Japan.

_____ **25.** Which of the following expresses an opinion rather than a fact?

    a.   All individuals should have an equal chance to succeed on their own.

    b.   If individuals paid social security for a long enough period when they were employed, they (and their spouses) receive benefits.

    c.   Spending on public schools is roughly twice as high in the United States as it is in Europe.

    d.   America's poor include individuals of all ages, races, religions, and regions.

SELECTION **9.1**

Government

(continued)

Respond in Writing

Directions: Refer to the selection as needed to answer the essay-type questions below. (Your instructor may direct you to work collaboratively with other students on one or more items. Each group member should be able to explain *all* of the group's answers.)

1. The author explains that our system of public education was designed to benefit individuals in many ways. List at least four of these ways.

    _____

    _____

    _____

    _____

    _____

    _____

    _____

    _____

2. In paragraph 19, the author presents what both the advocates and the opponents have to say about the issue of public school choice, the policy that allows parents to choose the public school their children will attend. What is your position on this issue? Explain why you support or oppose public school choice.

    _____

    _____

    _____

    _____

    _____

3. In paragraph 20, the author presents what both the supporters and detractors have to say about the issue of school vouchers, the policy that allows parents to use tax dollars to send their children to private or parochial schools instead of public schools. What is your position on this issue? Explain why you support or oppose the voucher system.

    _____

    _____

    _____

    _____

    _____

4. **Overall main idea.** What is the overall main idea the author wants the reader to understand about the relationship between poverty and public education? Answer this question in one sentence. Be sure to include the words *poverty* and *public education* in your overall main idea sentence.

_____

_____

_____

_____

_____

Your Financial Wellness

From *Connect Core Concepts in Health*
by Paul Insel and Walton Roth

Prepare Yourself to Read

Directions: Do these exercises *before* you read Selection 9.2.

1. First, read and think about the title. What comes to mind when you read the phrase *financial wellness*?

   _____

   _____

   _____

   _____

2. Next, complete your preview by reading the following:

   Introduction (in *italics*)

   Headings

   Words in **bold** print

   Now that you have completed your preview, what does this selection seem to be about?

   _____

   _____

   _____

   _____

3. **Build your vocabulary as you read.** If you discover an unfamiliar word or key term as you read the selection, try to determine its meaning by using context clues.

Read More about This Topic Online

Internet Resources

Use a search engine, such as Google or Yahoo!, to expand your existing knowledge about this topic *before* you read the selection or to learn more about it *afterward*. Use search terms such as "financial wellness" or "managing your money." If you are unfamiliar with conducting Internet searches, read pages 25–26 on Boolean searches. You can also use Wikipedia, the free online encyclopedia, at www.wikipedia.com. Keep in mind that when you visit any website, it is a good idea to evaluate the site and the information it contains. Ask yourself questions such as "Who sponsors this website?" and "Is the information it contains up to date?"

SELECTION 9.2: **YOUR FINANCIAL WELLNESS**

Wellness is a term that is often used to refer to a person's health, fitness, and lifestyle activities. And there are, indeed, many dimensions of wellness: physical wellness, emotional wellness, intellectual wellness, interpersonal wellness, spiritual wellness, and environmental wellness. But have you ever considered assessing your financial wellness? In this selection from a health textbook, the authors explain the basic elements of financial wellness and discuss how you can become financially "healthy."

1   With the news full of stories of home mortgage foreclosures, credit card debt, and personal bankruptcies, it has become painfully clear that many Americans do not know how to manage their finances. Are such stressful experiences inevitable in today's world? Not at all. You can avoid them—and gain financial peace of mind—by developing the skills that contribute to financial wellness.

2   What exactly is financial wellness? Basically, it means having a healthy relationship with money. It involves such skills as knowing how to manage your money, using self-discipline to live within your means, using credit cards wisely, staying out of debt, meeting your financial obligations, having a long-range financial plan, and saving. It also includes managing your emotional relationship with money and being in charge of your financial decisions. If you haven't developed these skills yet, now is the time to start.

Learn to Budget

3   Although the word "budget" may conjure up thoughts of deprivation, a budget is really just a way of tracking where your money goes and making sure you're spending it on the things that are most important to you. Basic budgeting worksheets are available online, but you can also just use a notebook with lined paper. On one page, list your monthly income by source (for example, job, stipend, or parental aid), and on another, list your expenditures. If you're not sure where you spend your money, track your expenditures for a few weeks or a month. Then organize them into categories, such as housing (rent, utilities), food (groceries, eating out), transportation (car, insurance, parking, public transportation), entertainment

Annotation Practice Exercises

Directions: For each of the exercises below, think critically to answer the questions. This will help you gain additional insights as you read.

Practice Exercise

Do the authors present a statement of *fact* or *opinion* in the last sentence of paragraph 2?

The best way to avoid credit card debt is to have just one card, to use it only when necessary, and to pay off the entire balance every month.

(movies, music, cable TV, parties), services (cell phone, Internet service provider), personal care (haircuts, cosmetics), clothes, books and school supplies, health, credit card/loan payments, and miscellaneous. These are suggestions—use categories that reflect the way you actually spend your money. Knowing where your money goes is the first step in gaining control of it.

4   Now total your income and expenditures. Are you taking in more than you spend, or are you spending more than you're taking in? Are you spending your money where you want to spend it, or are you surprised by your spending patterns? Use what you find out to set guidelines and goals for yourself. If your expenditures exceed your income, identify where you can begin to make some cuts. If morning lattes are adding up, consider making coffee at home. If you have both a cell phone and a land line, consider whether you can give one up. If you're spending money on movies and restaurants, consider less expensive options like having a game night with friends or organizing a potluck.

5   Be realistic about what you can cut, but also realize that you may have to adjust your mind-set about what you can afford. Once you have a balance between income and expenses, don't stop. Try to have a little bit left over each month for an emergency fund or savings. You may be surprised by how much peace of mind you can gain by living within your means.

Be Wary of Credit Cards

6   College students are prime targets for credit card companies, and most undergraduates have at least one card. A 2009 report found that college students use credit cards to live beyond their means, not just for convenience. According to the report, half of all students have four or more cards, and the average outstanding balance on undergraduate credit cards was $3,173. Seniors graduated with an average credit card debt of $4,100; nearly 20% of seniors carried balances of more than $7,000. The report also found that 82% of college students carried balances on their credit cards and thus incurred finance charges each month.

7   The best way to avoid credit card debt is to have just one card, to use it only when necessary, and to pay off the entire balance every month. Make sure you understand terms like APR (annual percentage rate—the interest you're charged on your balance), credit limit (the maximum amount you can borrow at any one time), minimum monthly payment (the smallest payment your creditor will accept each month), grace period (the number of days you have to pay your bill before interest, late fees, or other penalties are charged), and over-the-limit fees (the amount you'll be charged if your payment is

Practice Exercise

Does the author present a statement of *fact* or *opinion* in the first sentence of paragraph 5?

Practice Exercise

What logical *conclusion* can you draw about what college students should do if they have accumulated high outstanding balances on their credit cards?

Practice Exercise

Does the author present a statement of *fact* or *opinion* in the first sentence of paragraph 7?

late or you go over your credit limit). Read the fine print on your statement! Banks make most of their money from fees.

Get Out of Debt

8   If you do have credit card debt, stop using your cards and start paying them off. If you can't pay the whole balance, try to at least pay more than the minimum payment each month. Most people are surprised by how long it will take to pay off a loan by making only the minimum payments. For example, to pay off a credit card balance of $2,000 at 10% interest with monthly payments of $20 would take 203 months—17 years! By carrying a balance and incurring finance charges, you are also paying back much more than your initial loan—money you could be putting to other uses.

9   Some experts recommend choosing one card—the one with the largest balance or the highest interest—and paying off as much as you can every month. Others recommend paying off one or two cards with smaller balances to give yourself a sense of accomplishment and motivation to continue. Whatever your choice, if you have credit card debt, make it a priority to pay it off as soon as you can.

Start Saving

10   The same miracle of compound interest that locks you into years of credit card debt can work to your benefit if you start saving early. An online compound interest calculator can be found by visiting http://www.moneychimp.com/calculator/compound_interest_calculator.htm.

11   Experts recommend "paying yourself first" every month. That is, putting some money into savings before you start paying your bills, depending on what your budget allows. You may want to save for a large purchase, like a car or a vacation, or you may even be looking ahead into retirement. If you work for a company with a 401(k) retirement plan, contribute as much as you can every pay period. Some companies match contributions up to a certain amount, so be sure you contribute at least that amount.

Become Financially Literate

12   Modern life requires **financial literacy.** This means understanding everything from basics like balancing a checkbook to more sophisticated endeavors like developing a long-term financial plan. Unfortunately, a majority of Americans have not received any kind of education in financial skills. Even before the economic meltdown that began in 2008, the U.S. government had established the Financial Literacy and Education Commission (www.MyMoney.gov) to help Americans understand the concept of financial literacy and learn how to save, invest, and manage their money better. The consensus is that developing lifelong financial skills should begin in early adulthood, during the college years, if not earlier.

Practice Exercise

What logical *conclusion* can you draw about what college students with a new credit card should do?

_____

_____

_____

_____

_____

_____

_____

Practice Exercise

Does the author present a statement of *fact* or *opinion* in the first sentence of paragraph 10?

_____

Practice Exercise

What logical *conclusion* can you draw about the "financial literacy" of most Americans?

_____

_____

_____

_____

13   If you want to improve your financial literacy, a good way to start is to take a course in personal finance or financial management skills. There are also many magazines that focus on money management, and of course a wealth of information can be found online. Make it a priority to achieve financial wellness, and start now. Money may not buy you love, but having control over your money can buy you a lot of peace of mind.

SELECTION 9.2

Source: Adapted from Paul Insel and Walton Roth, *Connect Core Concepts in Health,* 12e, pp. 4–5. Copyright © 2012 by The McGraw-Hill Companies, Inc. Reprinted with permission of The McGraw-Hill Companies, Inc.
Additional sources: Federal Deposit Insurance Corporation. 2009. "Money Smart: A Financial Education Program" (http://www.fdic.gov/consumers/ consumer/moneysmart/young.html; retrieved 10/21/10); Plymouth State University. 2009. "Financial Wellness" (http://www.plymouth.edu/finaid/ wellness/index.html; retrieved 10/21/10); Sallie Mae. 2009. "How Undergraduate Students Use Credit Cards: Sallie Mae's National Study of Usage Rates and Trends," 2009 (http://www.salliemae.com/NR/rdonlyres/0BD600F1-9377-46EA-AB1F-6061FC63246/10744SLMCreditCardUsageStudy 41309FINAL2pdf; retrieved 10/21/10); U.S. Financial Literacy and Education Commission. 2009. "Do You Want to Learn How to Save, Manage, and Invest Your Money Better?" (http://www.mymoney.gov; retrieved 10/21/10).

Reading Selection Quiz

This quiz has several parts. Your instructor may assign some or all of them.

Comprehension

Directions: Use the information in the selection to answer each item below. You may refer to the selection as you answer the questions. Write each answer in the space provided.

True or False

_____ **1.** According to the authors, a budget is really just a way of tracking where your money goes and making sure you're spending it on the things that are most important to you.

_____ **2.** The annual percentage rate (APR) is the interest rate you are charged on your credit card balance.

_____ **3.** Your credit card's *grace period* tells you how long it will take you to pay off your loan by making only the minimum payments.

_____ **4.** If you work for a company with a 401(k) retirement plan that matches contributions up to a certain amount, you should contribute at least that amount.

_____ **5.** A 2009 report found that 82% of college students carried balances on their credit cards and thus incurred finance charges each month.

Multiple-Choice

_____ **6.** If your budget indicates that your expenditures are exceeding your income, you should:
   a.   make sure you are spending your money where you want to spend it.
   b.   identify where you can begin to make some cuts.
   c.   have just one credit card and use it only when necessary.
   d.   pay your credit card bill before interest, late fees, or other penalties are charged.

_____ **7.** When your budget has helped you achieve a balance between your income and your expenses, the authors suggest your next step should be to:
   a.   track your expenditures for a few weeks or a month.
   b.   be sure to make the minimum monthly payment on each of your credit cards.
   c.   develop a long-term financial plan.
   d.   try to set aside a small amount each month for savings or for emergencies.

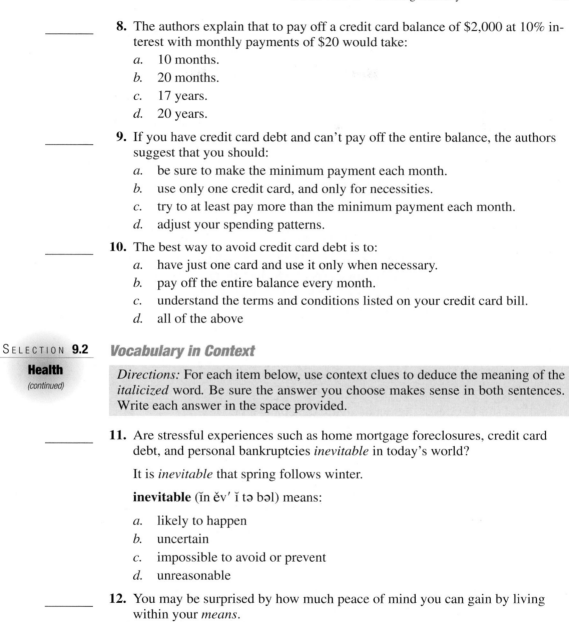

8. The authors explain that to pay off a credit card balance of $2,000 at 10% interest with monthly payments of $20 would take:

  a.   10 months.

  b.   20 months.

  c.   17 years.

  d.   20 years.

9. If you have credit card debt and can't pay off the entire balance, the authors suggest that you should:

  a.   be sure to make the minimum payment each month.

  b.   use only one credit card, and only for necessities.

  c.   try to at least pay more than the minimum payment each month.

  d.   adjust your spending patterns.

10. The best way to avoid credit card debt is to:

  a.   have just one card and use it only when necessary.

  b.   pay off the entire balance every month.

  c.   understand the terms and conditions listed on your credit card bill.

  d.   all of the above

SELECTION **9.2**

Health

(continued)

Vocabulary in Context

Directions: For each item below, use context clues to deduce the meaning of the *italicized* word. Be sure the answer you choose makes sense in both sentences. Write each answer in the space provided.

11. Are stressful experiences such as home mortgage foreclosures, credit card debt, and personal bankruptcies *inevitable* in today's world?

It is *inevitable* that spring follows winter.

inevitable (ĭn ĕv′ ĭ tə bəl) means:

  a.   likely to happen

  b.   uncertain

  c.   impossible to avoid or prevent

  d.   unreasonable

12. You may be surprised by how much peace of mind you can gain by living within your *means.*

Because Carol lives within her *means,* she can afford to help her grandchildren with their school tuition.

means (mēns) means:

  a.   money or other wealth you have

  b.   lifestyle you are accustomed to

     c. money spent on luxuries

     d. money obtained on credit

13. Although the word "budget" may *conjure* up thoughts of deprivation, a budget is really just a way of tracking where your money goes and making sure you're spending it on the things that are most important to you.

For most Americans, Las Vegas *conjures* up an image of money, glitz, gambling, and fast living.

conjure (kŏn′ jər) means:

     a. to call or summon

     b. to confuse or make unclear

     c. to wish for

     d. to call or bring to mind

14. Although the word "budget" may conjure up thoughts of *deprivation,* a budget is really just a way of tracking where your money goes and making sure you're spending it on the things that are most important to you.

Phillip's sleep *deprivation* was caused by working from eight o'clock in the morning until midnight, six days a week.

deprivation (dĕp′ rə vā′ shən) means:

     a. a removal of privileges

     b. a reduction

     c. the act of giving something up

     d. exhaustion

15. If your *expenditures* exceed your income, identify where you can begin to make some cuts.

Credit card *expenditures* for recreation, eating out, and other non-necessities can lead to unwanted and costly debt.

expenditures (ĭk spĕn′ də chərs) means:

     a. excesses

     b. amounts of money spent

     c. debts

     d. budgeted amounts

16. Be *wary* of credit cards.

Most parents teach their children to be *wary* of strangers.

wary (wâr′ ē) means:

     a. on guard; watchful

     b. using good judgment; smart

c. overused; excessive

d. causing trouble; dangerous

17. College students are *prime* targets for credit card companies, and most undergraduates have at least one card.

The bank robbery investigation was abandoned when the investigators failed to come up with any *prime* suspects.

prime (prīm) means:

a. excellent in quality or value

b. first in time or sequence; original

c. to make ready; to prepare

d. highest in degree; first in rank

18. This means understanding everything from basics like balancing a checkbook to more sophisticated *endeavors* like developing a long-term financial plan.

Mark is careful to set aside time for the two *endeavors* that are most important to him: spending time with his family and doing volunteer work.

endeavors (ĕn dĕv′ ərs) means:

a. complicated projects

b. actions which have monetary value

c. purposeful activities

d. tasks requiring large amounts of time and energy

19. The *consensus* is that developing lifelong financial skills should begin in early adulthood, during the college years, if not earlier.

The committee immediately reached *consensus* that Sonia should be the chairperson.

consensus (kən sĕn′ səs) means:

a. general or widespread agreement

b. recommendations from experts

c. voting results

d. a conclusion

20. According to the report, half of all students have four or more cards, and the average *outstanding* balance on undergraduate credit cards was $3,173.

The bill for the wedding dress has been paid, but there is an *outstanding* charge for the alterations.

outstanding (out′ stăn′ dĭng) means:

a. unpaid amount

b. greater in value

SELECTION 9.2

c.   difficult to correct; challenging

d.   not settled or resolved

Reading Skills Application

Directions: These items test your ability to *apply* certain reading skills. You may not have studied all of the skills yet, so some items will serve as a preview. Write each answer in the space provided.

_____   **21.** As used in paragraph 6 of this selection, *incurred* means:

a.   carried.

b.   avoided.

c.   acquired.

d.   borrowed.

_____   **22.** Which of the following sentences best expresses the main idea of paragraph 2?

a.   Financial wellness means managing your emotional relationship with money.

b.   Financial wellness involves using self-discipline to live within your means and using credit cards wisely.

c.   Financial wellness requires following a budget, staying out of debt, and having a long-range saving plan.

d.   Financial wellness results from developing a variety of specific skills that allow you to have a healthy relationship with money.

_____   **23.** The information in paragraph 2 is organized using which of the following writing patterns?

a.   list

b.   definition

c.   sequence

d.   comparison-contrast

_____   **24.** The authors would be likely to agree with which of the following statements?

a.   Credit cards should be used only for necessities such as food, transportation, services, clothing, and personal care.

b.   There is little that can be done about the problem of credit card debt among college students because they are prime targets for credit card companies.

c.   Too often, college students use credit cards to live beyond their means.

d.   Credit card debt and other stressful financial situations such as bankruptcies and mortgage foreclosures are inevitable in today's world.

_____ **25.** Which of the following expresses an opinion rather than a fact?

    a.   This means understanding everything from basics like balancing a checkbook to more sophisticated endeavors like a long-term financial plan.

    b.   Unfortunately, a majority of Americans have not received any kind of education in financial skills.

    c.   Even before the economic meltdown that began in 2008, the U.S. government had established the Financial Literacy and Education Commission to help Americans understand the concept of financial literacy and learn how to save, invest, and manage their money better.

    d.   The consensus is that developing lifelong financial skills should begin in early adulthood, during the college years, if not earlier.

SELECTION **9.2**

Health
(continued)

Respond in Writing

Directions: Refer to the selection as needed to answer the essay-type questions below. (Your instructor may direct you to work collaboratively with other students on one or more items. Each group member should be able to explain *all* of the group's answers.)

1. Create a "Top 10" list of strategies, techniques, or behaviors that you believe can help college students achieve the kind of financial wellness and "financial literacy" that the authors described. You may use some or all of the suggestions in the selection or include your own suggestions. (Item 1 on your list should be what you view as the *most* important contributor to financial wellness.)

1. _____

  _____

2. _____

  _____

3. _____

  _____

4. _____

  _____

5. _____

  _____

6. _____

  _____

7. _____

  _____

8. _____

_____

9. _____

_____

10. _____

_____

2. The authors state, "College students are prime targets for credit card companies." Explain why you think credit card companies target college students.

_____

_____

_____

_____

_____

_____

3. List two or more things that are getting in the way of your financial wellness
or contributing to your "financial illiteracy."

_____

_____

_____

_____

_____

4. **Overall main idea.** What is the overall main idea the authors want the reader
to understand about the concept of financial wellness? Answer this question in
one sentence. Be sure to include the words _financial wellness_ in your overall
main idea sentence.

_____

_____

_____

_____

SELECTION **9.3**

Environmental Science

Our Ecological Footprint: Do We Consume Too Much?

From *Environmental Science: A Study of Interrelationships*

by Eldon Enger and Bradley Smith

Prepare Yourself to Read

Directions: Do these exercises *before* you read Selection 9.3.

1. First, read and think about the title. What comes to mind when you read the phrase *ecological footprint*?

   _____

   _____

   _____

   _____

2. Next, complete your preview by reading the following:

   Introduction (in *italics*)

   Headings

   Words in **bold** print

   Now that you have completed your preview, what does this selection seem to be about?

   _____

   _____

   _____

   _____

3. **Build your vocabulary as you read.** If you discover an unfamiliar word or key term as you read the selection, try to determine its meaning by using context clues.

Internet Resources

Read More about This Topic Online

Use a search engine, such as Google or Yahoo!, to expand your existing knowledge about this topic *before* you read the selection or to learn more about it *afterward*. Use search terms such as "ecological footprint" or "sustainable development." If you are unfamiliar with conducting Internet searches, read pages 25–26 on Boolean searches. You can also use Wikipedia, the free online encyclopedia, at www .wikipedia.com. Keep in mind that when you visit any website, it is a good idea to evaluate the site and the information it contains. Ask yourself questions such as "Who sponsors this website?" and "Is the information it contains up to date?"

SELECTION 9.3: OUR ECOLOGICAL FOOTPRINT: DO WE CONSUME TOO MUCH?

This selection comes from an environmental science textbook. Environmental science *is a relatively new term for the study of interrelationships between humans and the natural world. Most of the concepts covered in environmental science courses today have previously been taught in ecology, conservation, biology, or geography courses. Environmental science is an applied science designed to help address and solve the challenges the world faces.*

Authors Enger and Smith explain, "Environmental science is a subject that fosters new ways of thinking. We present a balanced view of issues. It is not the purpose of our textbook to tell readers what to think. Rather our goal is to provide access to information needed to understand complex issues, some of them controversial, so that readers can comprehend the nature of environmental problems and formulate their own points of view."

In this selection, Professors Enger and Smith suggest that "human ingenuity," that is, human cleverness and inventiveness, has the potential to help us solve or avoid many of the environmental challenges of the future.

---

1   People of different cultures view their place in the world from different perspectives. Among the things that shape their views are religious understandings, economic pressures, geographic location, and fundamental knowledge of nature. Because of this diversity of backgrounds, different cultures put different values on the natural world and the individual organisms that compose it.

2   There are three common attitudes toward nature and the environment. The first is the development approach, which assumes that nature is for people to use for their own purposes. The second is the preservationist approach, which assumes that nature has value in itself and should be preserved intact. And the third is the conservational approach, which recognizes that we must use nature to meet human needs but encourages us to do so in a sustainable manner. Today, the conservationist approach is generally known as the "sustainable development" approach.

Your Ecological Footprint

3   The concept of an **ecological footprint** has been developed to help individuals measure their environmental impact on the Earth. One's ecological footprint is defined as "the area of the Earth's productive land and water required to supply the resources that an individual demands as well as to absorb the wastes that the individual produces." Websites exist that allow you to estimate your ecological footprint and to compare it to the footprint of others by answering a few questions about your lifestyle. Running through one of these exercises is a good way to gain a sense of personal responsibility for your own environmental impact. To learn more about ecological footprints, visit: http://www.earthday.org/footprint-calculator.

Annotation Practice Exercises

Directions: For each of the exercises below, think critically to answer the questions. This will help you gain additional insights as you read.

Do we in the Northern Hemisphere consume too much? Is our rate of consumption of food, energy, and water sustainable?

Do We Consume Too Much?

4   In 1994, when delegates from around the world gathered in Cairo, Egypt, for the International Conference on Population and Development, representatives from developing countries protested that a baby born in the United States will consume during its lifetime at least 20 times as much of the world's resources as an African or Indian baby. The problem for the Earth's environment, they argued, is overconsumption in the Northern Hemisphere, not just overpopulation in the Southern Hemisphere. Do we in the Northern Hemisphere consume too much?

5   North Americans, who make up only 5 percent of the world's population, consume 25 percent of the world's oil. They use more water and own more cars than anybody else. They waste more food than most people in sub-Saharan Africa eat. It has been estimated that if the rest of the world consumed at the rate at which people in the United States consume, we would need five more planet Earths to supply the resources.

6   Ever since he wrote a book called *The Population Bomb* in 1968, ecologist Paul Ehrlich has argued that the American lifestyle is driving the Earth's ecosystem to the brink of collapse. But others, including the economist Julian Simon, have argued that Ehrlich couldn't be more wrong. It is not resources that limit economic growth and lifestyles, Simon insisted, but human ingenuity—the ability to find or create solutions to the challenges we face.

7   In 1980 Ehrlich and Simon wagered money on their opposing worldviews. They picked something easily measurable—the value of metals—to put their claims to the test. Ehrlich predicted that world economic growth would make copper, chrome, nickel, tin, and tungsten scarcer and thus drive the prices up. Simon argued that human ingenuity is always capable of finding technological fixes for scarcity and that the price of metals would go down. By 1990, all five metals had decreased in value. Simon had won the bet. Ehrlich claimed that the decrease in price was the result of a global recession. But Simon argued that the metals decreased in price because superior materials such as plastics, fiber optics, and ceramics had been developed to replace them. The Ehrlich-Simon argument is actually an old one, and despite the outcome of their bet, it remains unsettled. What do you think? Will human ingenuity solve our future challenges regarding our consumption of food, energy, water, and wild nature?

Food

8   Two hundred years ago economist Thomas Malthus predicted that worldwide famine was inevitable as human population growth outpaced food production. In 1972, a group of scholars known as the Club of Rome predicted much the same thing for the last years of

Practice Exercise

Do the authors present statements of *fact* or *opinion* in paragraph 5?

_____

_____

Practice Exercise

What logical *conclusion* can be drawn about North Americans' rate of consumption of the world's resources?

_____

_____

_____

_____

_____

_____

_____

_____

_____

_____

_____

SELECTION 9.3

the twentieth century. Worldwide famine did not happen because—so far, at least—human ingenuity has outpaced human population growth.

9   Fertilizers, pesticides, and high-yield crops have more than doubled world food production in the past 40 years. The reason 850 million people go hungry today and 6 million children under the age of five die each year from hunger-related causes is not that there is not enough food in the world. It is social, economic, and political conditions that make it impossible for those who need the food to get it.

10   Norman Borlaug, who won the Nobel Peace Prize in 1970 for his role in developing high-yield crops, predicts that genetic engineering and other new technologies will keep food production ahead of population increases over the next 50 years. New technologies such as genetic engineering, however, are not free from controversies. The European Union requires labeling of all U.S. imported foods containing more than 0.9 percent materials from genetically modified organisms.

11   With global population set to peak at around 9 billion people by 2050, it remains unclear whether there will be enough food to go around. Even if it turns out that enough food can be produced for the world in the twenty-first century, whether everybody will get a fair share is much less certain.

Energy

12   If everybody on Earth consumed as much oil as the average American, the world's known reserves would be gone in about 40 years. Even at the current rates of consumption, known reserves will not last through the current century. Technological optimists, however, tell us not to worry. New technologies, they say, will avert a global energy crisis.

13   Already oil companies have developed cheaper and more efficient ways to find oil and extract it from the ground, possibly extending the supply to around the year 2100. In many regions of the world, natural gas is replacing oil as the primary source of domestic and industrial power. New coal gasification technologies also hold promise for cleaner and extended fossil fuel power. However, it is impossible to ignore the fact that there is a finite amount of fossil fuel on the planet. These fuels cannot be the world's primary power source forever.

14   The more foresighted energy companies are already looking ahead by investing in the technologies that will replace fossil fuels. In some countries, the winds of change have brought nuclear power back onto the table. In others, solar, wind, wave, and biomass technologies are already meeting increasing proportions of national energy needs. A great deal of optimism is placed on the development of fuel cell technologies. A fuel cell is essentially a

> **Practice Exercise**
>
> Do the authors present a statement of *fact* or *opinion* in the first sentence of paragraph 9?
>
> _____

refillable, hydrogen-powered battery that produces zero pollution. Since hydrogen is the most abundant element in the universe, there is no shortage of supply. The problem is that most of this hydrogen exists in unusable forms, already combined with other elements in more stable molecules. Separating the unstable hydrogen is not difficult, but the process takes energy itself. With ever-accelerating global demand, it remains unclear whether there will be enough clean energy supply to meet the world's needs in the years ahead.

Water

15   The world of the future may not need oil, but without water, humanity could not last more than a few days. Right now, humans use about 50 percent of the planet's accessible supply of renewable fresh water—the supply generated each year and available for human use. A simple doubling of agricultural production with no efficiency improvements would push that amount to about 85 percent. Unlike fossil fuels, which could eventually be replaced by other energy sources, there is no substitute for water.

16   Technologies such as desalination, which removes salt from seawater, can be used in rare circumstances. But removing salt from seawater takes a lot of energy and is expensive. In the Persian Gulf, one place that uses desalination, wealth makes it possible. It has been said that in the Persian Gulf, they turn "oil into water."

17   Some regions have already reached their water limits, with massive dams and aqueducts diverting almost every drop of water for human use. In the U.S. Southwest, the diversion is so complete that by the time the Colorado River reaches its mouth in the Sea of Cortez, it has no water in it. Much of Los Angeles' water comes from more than 300 kilometers (186 miles) away.

18   More than any other resource, water may limit consumerism during the next century. A few years ago, World Bank Vice President Ismail Serageldin predicted that, "In the next century, wars will be fought over water."

Wild Nature

19   Every day in the United States, somewhere from 1000 to 2000 hectares of farmland and natural areas are permanently lost to development. As more and more people around the world achieve modern standards of living, the land area converted to houses, shopping malls, roads, and industrial parks will continue to increase. Tropical rainforests will be cut and wild lands will become entombed under pavement. Mighty rivers like the Yangtze and Nile, already dammed and diverted, will become even more canal-like. As the 21st century progresses, more and more of us will live urbanized lives. The few pockets of wild nature that remain will be biologically

Practice Exercise

Do the authors present statements of *fact* or *opinion* in paragraph 15?

_____

_____

Practice Exercise

What logical *conclusion* can you draw about the use of desalination in the future?

_____

_____

_____

_____

_____

SELECTION 9.3

isolated from each other by development. We will increasingly live not in a natural world, but a world of our own making.

Using Human Ingenuity

20   A quick read of the headlines of any newspaper provides images of hunger, disease, poverty, and pollution. Challenges to our environment like these, however, are also opportunities. We cannot continue with business as usual because such a path is not sustainable. What does that mean? In short, we must all do things differently. For example, different farming practices will allow crops to be raised with fewer chemicals and less water. Buildings can be constructed with new, more sustainable methods. Transportation can be provided while using less energy. In other words, we must think differently. At the end of the day we all share the same air, water, and not-so-big planet. It's important that all of us make it last.

Practice Exercise

Do the authors present a statement of *fact* or *opinion* in the last sentence of paragraph 19?

_____

Reading Selection Quiz

This quiz has several parts. Your instructor may assign some or all of them.

Comprehension

Directions: Use the information in the selection to answer each item below. You may refer to the selection as you answer the questions. Write each answer in the space provided.

True or False

_____ **1.** An individual's ecological footprint is the area of the Earth's productive land and water required to supply the resources that an individual demands as well as to absorb the wastes that the individual produces.

_____ **2.** The reason so many people in the United States go hungry today is that human population growth has outpaced worldwide food production.

_____ **3.** North Americans make up only 5 percent of the world's population, but they consume 25 percent of the world's energy.

_____ **4.** It has been predicted that genetic engineering and other new technologies will keep food production ahead of population increases over the next 50 years.

_____ **5.** Currently, humans use 15 percent of the world's accessible supply of fresh water.

Multiple-Choice

_____ **6.** The attitude toward our environment that is known as the conservational approach:
  a. assumes that nature is for people to use for their own purposes.
  b. assumes that nature has value in itself and should be preserved intact.
  c. recognizes that we must use nature to meet human needs but encourages us to do so in a sustainable manner.
  d. requires us to conserve energy, water, and wild nature.

_____ **7.** By 2050, global population will peak at:
  a. 6 million.
  b. almost 850 million.
  c. around 9 billion.
  d. over 17 billion.

_____ **8.** The reason so many people throughout the world go hungry today is that:
  a. there is not enough food being produced globally.
  b. there is an insufficient water supply for agriculture in many areas of the world.

c.   social and economic conditions make it impossible for those who need food to get it.

d.   new crop technologies such as genetic engineering are too controversial.

_____ **9.** An example of a technology that may someday replace fossil fuels is:

a.   biomass technology.

b.   fuel cell technology.

c.   solar technology.

d.   all of the above

_____ **10.** The resource that may limit consumerism the most during the next century is:

a.   food.

b.   energy.

c.   water.

d.   technology.

SELECTION **9.3**

Environmental Science

(continued)

Vocabulary in Context

Directions: For each item below, use context clues to deduce the meaning of the *italicized* word. Be sure the answer you choose makes sense in both sentences. Write each answer in the space provided.

_____ **11.** The preservationist approach assumes that nature has value in itself and should be preserved *intact*.

We know the size and body style of many dinosaurs because their fossil remains have been discovered *intact*.

intact (ĭn tăkt′) means:

a.   untouched; left complete or perfect

b.   handled with care

c.   incomplete; not whole

d.   respected; having value

_____ **12.** Do we in the Northern Hemisphere *consume* too much?

A visit to any shopping mall makes it clear how much Americans *consume*.

consume (kən sōōm′) means:

a.   take in as food; eat or drink

b.   spend

c.   destroy totally; ravage

d.   purchase economic goods and services

_____ **13.** Ever since he wrote a book called *The Population Bomb* in 1968, ecologist Paul Ehrlich has argued that the American lifestyle is driving the Earth's ecosystem to the *brink* of collapse.

Eric felt he was on the *brink* of disaster when his wallet, credit cards, and checkbook were stolen the day before his rent and his tuition payment were due.

brink (brĭngk) means:

   a. edge or border of a steep place
   b. point at which something is likely to begin; verge
   c. highest point; top
   d. end; final

_____ **14.** Two hundred years ago economist Thomas Malthus predicted that worldwide *famine* was inevitable as human population growth outpaced food production.

Potato crop failures in Ireland between 1846 and 1851 led to a *famine* that caused a million people to starve to death and another 1.6 million to immigrate to America.

famine (făm′ ĭn) means:

   a. a severe food shortage
   b. an overcrowding
   c. a crop failure
   d. a rapid increase in a population

_____ **15.** A great deal of *optimism* is placed on the development of fuel cell technologies.

Even though her friends felt that Jane's new business was not going to succeed, Jane was full of *optimism*.

optimism (ŏp′ tə mĭz′ əm) means:

   a. suspicion; doubtfulness
   b. energy
   c. value; effort
   d. hopefulness; confidence

_____ **16.** New technologies, optimists say, will *avert* a global energy crisis.

The bus driver was able to *avert* an accident by slamming on the brakes and turning the bus sharply.

avert (ə vûrt′) means:

   a. produce
   b. cause
   c. prevent
   d. lessen

17. In many regions of the world, natural gas is replacing oil as the primary source of *domestic* and industrial power.

   Unlike most people, Charles enjoyed *domestic* chores such as doing the laundry, ironing, and cooking.

   domestic (do měs′ tĭk) means:

   a. essential
   b. efficient
   c. inexpensive
   d. household

18. However, it is impossible to ignore the fact that there is a *finite* amount of fossil fuel on the planet.

   Unfortunately, Janet's boss gave her only a *finite* number of choices: Accept the job transfer and to move to another state, resign, or be terminated.

   finite (fī′ nīt) means:

   a. decreasing
   b. related
   c. limited
   d. unacceptable

19. Some regions have already reached their water limits, with massive dams and aqueducts *diverting* almost every drop of water for human use.

   Immediately following the crash involving several cars on the Interstate, police officers began *diverting* traffic around the scene of the accident.

   diverting (dĭ vûr′ tĭng) means:

   a. providing enjoyment
   b. turning aside; changing direction
   c. preventing entry or access
   d. stopping completely

20. We cannot continue with business as usual because such a path is not *sustainable*.

   Bamboo can be used for building, food, and clothing, and since it is one of the fastest growing plants, it is considered one of the most inexpensive and *sustainable* resources in the world.

   sustainable (sə stā′ nə bəl) means:

   a. capable of economic growth
   b. capable of being used over and over
   c. capable of lasting far into the future
   d. capable of being continued without exhausting natural resources

Reading Skills Application

Directions: These items test your ability to *apply* certain reading skills. Write each answer in the space provided.

21. Which of the following expresses an opinion rather than a fact?
  a. Oil companies have developed cheaper and more efficient ways to find oil and extract it from the ground.
  b. There is a finite amount of fossil fuel on the planet.
  c. In many regions of the world, natural gas is replacing oil as the primary source of domestic and industrial power.
  d. New technologies will avert a global energy crisis.

22. The information in paragraph 3 is organized using which of the following writing patterns?
  a. list
  b. spatial
  c. sequence
  d. definition

23. As used in paragraph 16 of this selection, *desalination* means:
  a. using technology for genetic engineering.
  b. turning "oil into water."
  c. the process of removing salt from seawater.
  d. using aqueducts for diverting water for human use.

24. According to information in the selection, worldwide famine did not happen during the last 40 years of the 20th century because:
  a. fertilizers, pesticides, and high-yield crops have more than doubled world food production.
  b. global population did not increase significantly.
  c. worldwide economic and political conditions improved.
  d. the human population growth rate slowed.

25. What is the authors' primary purpose for writing this selection?
  a. to inform readers about environmental problems such as hunger, disease, poverty, and pollution
  b. to persuade North Americans to make changes in their lifestyle that will reduce their ecological footprint
  c. to present a variety of issues related to North Americans' consumption of food, energy, water, and wild nature
  d. to compare the problem of overconsumption in the Northern Hemisphere with overconsumption in the Southern Hemisphere

Respond in Writing

Directions: Refer to the selection as needed to answer the essay-type questions below. (Your instructor may direct you to work collaboratively with other students on one or more items. Each group member should be able to explain *all* of the group's answers.)

1. The authors invite readers to go to this website to find out more about their ecological footprint and to compare it to the footprint of others by answering a few questions about your lifestyle: http://www.earthday.org/Footprint/info. asp. Visit this website now in order to gain insights about your own impact on the environment, including learning what simple actions you can take in order to change your footprint. Then summarize what you learned about your own ecological footprint.

    _____

    _____

    _____

    _____

    _____

    _____

    _____

    _____

    _____

2. The authors mention several ways human ingenuity has helped solve or avoid environmental challenges such as worldwide shortages of food, energy, and water. List at least five of them:

    _____

    _____

    _____

    _____

    _____

    _____

_____

_____

_____

_____

_____

_____

3. Other than shortages of food, energy, and water, what worldwide social and economic challenges need to be solved or avoided using human ingenuity? List at least three other challenges.

_____

_____

_____

_____

_____

_____

4. In this chapter, you learned the steps to evaluating an author's argument. Answer the seven comprehension-monitoring questions below in order to evaluate the argument presented in this selection.

    What controversial subject is this selection about?

    _____

    _____

    _____

    What is the authors' position on this issue?

    _____

    _____

    _____

    _____

What do the authors take for granted?

_____

_____

_____

What type of support do the authors present?

_____

_____

_____

_____

_____

_____

Does the support pertain directly to the argument?

_____

_____

_____

_____

Is the argument based on facts and other appropriate evidence? Did the authors leave out information that might weaken or disprove the argument?

_____

_____

_____

_____

Is the argument logical and believable?

_____

_____

5. **Overall main idea.** What is the overall main idea the authors want the reader to understand about how much we consume—our ecological footprint—and the world's challenges to have sufficient food, water, and energy? Answer this question in one sentence.

_____

_____

_____

_____

PART 3

Systems for Studying Textbooks

Developing a System
That Works for You

CHAPTER 10

Selecting and Organizing Textbook Information

In this chapter, you will learn the answers to these questions:

- How can I select important textbook information?

- Why should I organize textbook information as I read?

- How can I use textbook features to make my studying more efficient?

- What are effective ways to mark textbooks?

- How can I take notes from textbooks by outlining, mapping, and summarizing?

- How can I interpret graphic material correctly?

SKILLS

Studying Better Rather Than Harder

Three Keys to Studying College Textbooks

- Key 1: Selectivity
- Key 2: Organization
- Key 3: Rehearsal

Using Textbook Features

- Prefaces • Tables of Contents • Part Openings • Chapter Outlines
- Chapter Objectives and Introductions • Boxes • Tables • Graphic Aids
- Vocabulary Aids • Study Questions and Activities • Chapter Summaries
- Appendixes • Bibliographies, Suggested Readings, and Webliographies
- Indexes • Additional Features • Supplements

Marking Textbooks: Underlining, Highlighting, and Annotating

Taking Notes from Textbooks: Outlining, Mapping, and Summarizing

- Taking Notes on a Laptop or Tablet Notebook
- Guidelines for Outlining
- Guidelines for the Cornell Method of Note-Taking
- Guidelines for Mapping
- Guidelines for Summarizing

Guidelines for Interpreting Graphs and Visual Aids

- Bar Graphs • Line Graphs • Pie Charts • Tables
- Photographs • Diagrams • Flowcharts • Maps • Cartoons

CREATING YOUR SUMMARY

Developing Chapter Review Cards

READING

Selection 10.1 "The Age of Globalization"
from *American History: A Survey*
by Alan Brinkley (History)

SKILLS

Good order is the foundation of all things.

Edmund Burke

Don't mistake motion for action.

Ernest Hemingway

Failure is a signal that you're moving in the wrong direction.

Oprah Winfrey

STUDYING BETTER RATHER THAN HARDER

Chapter 1 of this book emphasized that it can take considerable time to learn the information in your textbooks. Although experienced college students know this, new students sometimes do not. Beginning students often have unrealistic expectations about how much time it will take to read and study textbooks and prepare for tests. In fact, they are often shocked at how much time studying requires. They may mistakenly conclude they are the *only* ones who have to spend so much time.

Simply spending large amounts of time studying will not by itself guarantee success; what you *do* during your study times is equally important. The reality is this: Staring at a book is not the same as reading, and sitting at a desk is not the same as studying. Some students who claim they are studying are daydreaming instead. Other students really do invest many hours in studying, yet are disappointed in the results. Still other students are successful at studying, but feel discouraged because it seems to take them too much time. You yourself have undoubtedly had the experience of finishing an assignment, realizing that you did it the "hard way," and feeling frustrated because you know you worked harder and longer than you needed to. You are probably wondering, "Isn't there a better, more efficient way?"

The answer is yes, there *is* a better way to study. This chapter and the next one describe specific techniques for reading textbooks more efficiently and studying *better,* rather than harder or longer. Often, the difference between a successful student and a less successful one involves *applying these study skills in a systematic way.*

You may be familiar with some of these study techniques, or you may be learning them for the first time. In either case, mastering them will make you a more effective student. They will serve you well in all your courses and a variety of other learning situations. There will always be situations in college and in the workplace in which you must organize, learn, and remember information.

Keep in mind, however, that these study skills are not magic. They simply allow you to study better rather than harder. Being a successful student demands time, effort, skill, and dedication. You can become a better student each semester if you are willing to invest enough time and effort, and if you bring enough skill and dedication to the task.

689

Effective students learn to select, organize, and rehearse information as they read and study their college textbook assignments.

THREE KEYS TO STUDYING COLLEGE TEXTBOOKS

The strategies in this chapter and Chapter 11 are based on three *keys* to studying better: *selecting* essential information to study, *organizing* that information in a meaningful way, and *rehearsing* it in order to remember it. As you will see, the skills of selectivity, organization, and rehearsal are interrelated and interdependent.

Key 1: Selectivity

selectivity

Identifying main ideas and important supporting details. First of three essential study strategies.

Selectivity is the first essential key to understanding and remembering what you read. Too many students think that they can—in fact, must—learn and remember everything in their textbooks, but this mistaken idea leads only to frustration. Generally, *it is necessary to identify and remember only main ideas and major supporting details.* Therefore, you must be selective as you read and study.

Chapters 4 through 9 (Part Two, the "comprehension core") explained how to read selectively by focusing on main ideas and major supporting details. The techniques in the present chapter will further increase your ability to be selective: You will learn about textbook features, textbook marking, and taking textbook notes.

Key 2: Organization

organization

Arranging main ideas and supporting details in a meaningful way. Second of three essential study strategies.

Organization is the second key to learning and remembering what you read. The reason is simple: *Organized material is easier to learn, memorize, and recall than unorganized material.*

Chapter 7 explained how to see relationships between main ideas and supporting details by identifying authors' patterns of writing, a skill that makes learning and remembering easier. Using textbook features, along with your own textbook marking and note-taking, will help you to organize material more effectively.

Key 3: Rehearsal

rehearsal

Saying or writing material to transfer it into long-term memory. Third of three essential study strategies.

Rehearsal, a concept introduced in Chapter 3, is the third key to learning and remembering textbook material. Rehearsal involves saying aloud or writing down material you want to memorize. It is *not* merely rereading, nor is it a casual overview. Rehearsal is a way of reviewing material that puts the material into your memory. Particularly with complex material, it is necessary to *rehearse information to transfer it to long-term (permanent) memory.*

It is important to understand that comprehending and remembering are two separate tasks. The fact that you comprehend material does not necessarily mean that you will remember it. To *remember* material as well as understand it, you must take additional steps; that is, you must rehearse. Just as actors begin to memorize their lines long before a performance, you need to rehearse textbook material frequently, starting long before a test. (Rehearsal is discussed in detail in Chapter 11.)

Selectivity, organization, and rehearsal are the foundation for the study techniques in this chapter and Chapter 11. At this point, however, it will be useful to look back at the three-step process for reading and studying textbooks presented in Chapter 3, since we will now be adding specific study skills to that general approach. The three-step process is summarized in the box below.

SUMMARY OF THE THREE-STEP PROCESS FOR STUDYING COLLEGE TEXTBOOKS

Step 1: Prepare to Read

- Preview to see what the selection contains and how it is organized.
- Assess your prior knowledge.
- Plan your reading and study time.

Step 2: Ask and Answer Questions to Guide Your Reading

- Use questions to guide your reading.
- Read actively, looking for answers.
- Record the answers to your questions.

Step 3: Review by Rehearsing Your Answers

- Review the material by *rehearsing,* to transfer it to long-term memory.

USING TEXTBOOK FEATURES

textbook feature

Device used by an author to emphasize important material and show how it is organized.

To study better rather than harder, you must take advantage of textbook features to locate, select, and organize material you want to learn. A **textbook feature** is a device an author uses to emphasize important material or to show how material is organized. It is a way authors help readers get the most out of a textbook. Another term for *textbook feature* is *learning aid.*

There are many kinds of textbook features, and in this section you will look at some of the most important. Though no single college textbook is likely to include all of these features, most of your textbooks will have several of them.

Keep in mind that different authors may call the same feature by different names. For example, what one author may call a *chapter summary,* another may call a *chapter review, chapter highlights, key points, points to remember, a look back,* or *summing up.*

Be sure to take advantage of textbook features as you study; they are there to help you locate, select, and organize the material you must learn. The box below describes the most common textbook features.

STUDY TIPS FOR USING TEXTBOOK FEATURES

Prefaces

Read the preface to see what the book contains, how it is organized, and what its special features are.

Tables of Contents

Use the table of contents, particularly if no chapter outlines are given. Your chapter study notes should cover each item listed in the table of contents. Pay attention to the size and type style, which indicate major and minor headings.

Part Openings

Read part openings to help you understand the scope of what is contained in the section, how the section is organized, and how its chapters are interrelated.

Chapter Outlines

Pay attention to major topics in a chapter outline. Your notes should also include all subtopics. The author has done some of the selecting for you, so take advantage of it.

Chapter Objectives and Introductions

Use objectives and introductions to test yourself on the chapter material. Try to write out the answers from memory.

Boxes

Pay attention to boxed information. It helps you understand the text. Also, you may be tested on boxed material.

Tables

Pay attention to tables. They consolidate important information and help you understand relationships among ideas. Instructors may base test questions on them.

Graphic Aids

Watch for graphic aids. Figures, cartoons, and photographs may present or reinforce important information or may explain the text.

Vocabulary Aids

Write out the definition for each term included in a vocabulary aid. If your book includes a glossary, use it. It is your responsibility to learn the special vocabulary of each subject you study. Expect to be asked these terms on tests.

Study Questions and Activities

Take the time to answer study questions and work on exercises, especially if your instructor has not provided study questions. Think carefully about discussion topics. Items like these may appear on tests.

Chapter Summaries

Read the chapter summary both *before and after* you read the chapter itself. This will help you to read thoughtfully and to consolidate your learning.

Appendixes

Use appendixes for reference and as a source of additional information.

Bibliographies, Suggested Readings, and Webliographies

Use source lists when you are doing papers, reports, and other research assignments. You can also use supplementary readings to improve your understanding of the textbook.

Indexes

Use indexes to help you quickly locate specific material in textbooks.

Additional Features

Look for epigraphs (quotations), exhibits, and examples in the text. Don't neglect special reference material that may appear on the inside of the cover.

Supplements

Study guides, study guides with supplemental readings, workbooks, and software accompanying your textbooks usually prove to be good investments. Use supplements like these to direct and focus your study, to test yourself, and to evaluate your learning.

All these textbook features can help you use your study time effectively and efficiently. Students often remark that in college textbooks "everything seems important." They find it hard to get a sense of how the facts and concepts add up to a coherent whole. Taking advantage of textbook features as you read can enable you to identify the essential information in a chapter and to understand its organization. Remember that authors and publishers want to help you study and learn from your textbooks. For this reason, they put a great deal of time, effort, and thought into designing textbook features.

MARKING TEXTBOOKS: UNDERLINING, HIGHLIGHTING, AND ANNOTATING

underlining and highlighting

Techniques for marking topics, main ideas, and definitions.

annotation

Explanatory notes you write in the margins of a textbook to organize and remember information.

It has been estimated that as much as 80 percent of the material on college tests comes from textbooks. For this reason alone, you need to be able to underline, highlight, and annotate your textbooks effectively.

Underlining and **highlighting** are techniques for marking topics, main ideas, and important definitions in reading materials. **Annotation** refers to explanatory notes you write *in the margins of your textbook* to help you organize and remember important information. Annotating information (writing it down) also helps you concentrate. When you read a difficult textbook, you should concentrate on one paragraph at a time. Effective students mark their textbooks by either underlining or highlighting *and* annotating.

Here are some guidelines for *underlining and highlighting:*

- **First, avoid the most typical mistake in marking textbooks:** *overmarking* **(underlining or highlighting too much).**   Students often overmark because they try to underline or highlight *while* they are reading instead of *after* they have read the material. Underlining and highlighting a textbook is a selective process. You cannot know what is important in a paragraph or section until you have *finished* reading it. And as you know, the main idea sometimes does not appear until the end of a paragraph. You may not be able to understand some paragraphs until you have read an entire section. The rule, then, is this: *Read first, and underline only after you have identified the important ideas.* A word of caution: Underlining and highlighting are not substitutes for *thinking.* Marking a lot in a chapter does not mean you have read it carefully and found the important information. To avoid this mistake, follow these steps: Read and *think; then* underline or highlight *selectively.*

- **Second, know the kinds of things you** *should* **underline or highlight.**   As mentioned above, underline or highlight the *topic* of a paragraph and the *main idea* if it is stated. Often you will not need to underline every word of a main idea sentence to capture the idea it is expressing. Underline or highlight important terms and *definitions.*

- **Third, know the kinds of things you should** *not* **underline or highlight.**   Do *not* underline or highlight supporting details, since this results in overmarking. (As you will see below, annotation can be used effectively to indicate supporting details.)

Once you have underlined and highlighted topics, main ideas, and important terms and definitions, you should *annotate,* that is, write explanatory notes and symbols in the margins. If a textbook has narrow margins, use notebook paper or even stick-on notes for your annotations.

The box on page 695 shows how a passage from a human development textbook (about different forms of marriage) could be underlined and annotated. Notice how relatively little is underlined and how helpful the annotations would be in reviewing for a test on this material.

AN EXAMPLE OF UNDERLINING AND ANNOTATION

A lifestyle practice that apparently exists in all societies is marriage—a socially and/or religiously sanctioned union between a woman and a man with the expectation that they will perform the mutually supportive roles of wife and husband. After studying extensive cross-cultural data, anthropologist George P. Murdock (1949) concluded that reproduction, sexual relations, economic cooperation, and the socialization of offspring are functions of families throughout the world. We now recognize that Murdock overstated the matter, because in some societies, such as Israeli [?]Kibbutz communities, the family does not perform all four of these functions (Spiro, 1954; Gough, 1960). What Murdock describes are commonly encountered tendencies in family functioning in most cultures.

(def) marriage: socially and/or religiously sanctioned union of a woman and a man with the expectation they will play the mutually supportive roles of wife and husband

*4 tendencies in functions of families:
—reproduction
—sexual relations
—economic cooperation
—socialization of offspring

Societies differ in how they structure marriage relationships. Four patterns are found: ① monogamy, one husband and one wife; ② polygyny, one husband and two or more wives; ③ polyandry, two or more husbands and one wife; and ④ group marriage, two or more husbands and two or more wives. Although monogamy exists in all societies, Murdock discovered that other forms are not only allowed but preferred. Of 238 societies in his sample, only about one-fifth were strictly monogamous.

(def) Four patterns of marriage:
—monogamy: 1 husband/1 wife
—polygyny: 1 husband/2+ wives
—polyandry: 2+ husbands/1 wife
—group marriage: 2+ husbands/2+ wives

Polygyny has been widely practiced throughout the world. The Old Testament reports that both King David and King Solomon had several wives. In his cross-cultural sample of 238 societies, Murdock found that 193 (an overwhelming majority) permitted husbands to take several wives. In one-third of these polygynous societies, however, less than one-fifth of the married men had more than one wife. Usually only the rich men in a society can afford to support more than one family.

Polygyny: widely practiced
Old Testament kings with several wives:
—Solomon ⎤
—David   ⎦ ex.
—Murdock study: 193/238 societies permitted polygyny
—Usually only rich were polygynous

In contrast with polygyny, polyandry is rare among the world's societies. And in practice, polyandry has not usually allowed freedom of mate selection for women—it has often meant simply that younger brothers have sexual access to the wife of an older brother. For example, if a father is unable to afford wives for each of his sons, he may secure a wife for only his oldest son.

Polyandry: rare
—women not usually allowed to choose mates
—often simply means younger brothers have sexual access to wife of older brother

Source: James Vander Zanden, revised by Thomas Crandell and Corinne Crandell, *Human Development*, Updated 7e, p. 476. Copyright © 2003 by The McGraw-Hill Companies, Inc. Reprinted with permission of The McGraw-Hill Companies, Inc.

You may be wondering what types of annotations to make. First, you can list the topics of certain paragraphs in the margin. This can help you grasp the sequence of the author's ideas.

CLOSE TO HOME   JOHN McPHERSON

Source: CLOSE TO HOME © 2000 John McPherson. Reprinted with permission of UNIVERSAL PRESS SYNDICATE. All rights reserved.

Writing out an *important term* and a brief *definition* in the margin is also helpful. When your instructor uses these terms, you will recognize them and be able to record them more easily in your lecture notes. And, of course, you will remember the terms and definitions more clearly. Obviously, you will need to know them for tests.

Also, you may choose to list major *supporting details* in shortened form. Annotating is an effective, convenient, and concise way to organize details; also, jotting them in the margin helps you connect them with the main ideas they support.

Formulated main ideas are another helpful annotation. Write your formulated main idea sentence beside the paragraph.

Symbols and *abbreviations* are still another helpful annotation because they enable you to locate important material quickly and (if necessary) return to passages that need further study. Here are examples of abbreviations and symbols you can use:

def	*Definition.* Use *def* when an important term is defined.
?	*Question mark.* Use this when you do not understand something and need to study it further or get help with it.
1, 2, 3 . . .	*Numbers.* Use numbers when an author gives unnumbered items in a list or series.

*	*Asterisk.* Use an asterisk to mark important information.
ex	*Example.* Use *ex* to identify helpful examples.

TAKING NOTES FROM TEXTBOOKS: OUTLINING, MAPPING, AND SUMMARIZING

In addition to underlining, highlighting, and marginal annotations, *taking notes from textbooks* is an important study skill. Students who take notes and review them are four to five times more likely to recall important information during a test. In fact, you are much more likely to recall *any* idea that you have written out. Note-taking is your single greatest aid to successful test preparation later on. (Note-taking during a lecture is also your single greatest aid to concentration during class.) Three useful types of textbook note-taking are outlining, mapping, and summarizing.

Taking Notes on a Laptop or Tablet Notebook

Like many students, you may prefer to take lecture or textbook notes on a laptop or tablet notebook. The advantages include easy revision and reorganization, highlighting, spell check, the ability to easily integrate additional information, and the capability to print out, share, or post your notes. You can use Facebook or other social networking sites to ask questions, share notes and review sheets, and quiz study partners before a test. You can post your notes to a blog so that you can access them from anywhere you have Internet access.

If you prefer to take notes on a laptop or tablet notebook, you can use Microsoft Word™ or other word processing software. However, if you google "note-taking software," you can find software that suits your learning style more precisely. For example, some software is designed primarily for outlining, and some for creating concept maps. Note-taking software can include a search feature, freehand drawing tools, even a vocabulary feature to track key terms and definitions. Regardless of the software you use, create a separate file for each class session or textbook chapter. Also, back up your data regularly to another drive. And, of course, use common sense about any electronic equipment you bring to campus: Keep a close eye on it, and do not lend it to others.

Guidelines for Outlining

outlining

Formal way of organizing main ideas and supporting details to show relationships among them.

Outlining is a formal way of organizing main ideas and the supporting details that go with them. Even if you underline main ideas in your textbook and annotate the details in the margin, there may be times when it is helpful to outline a section or chapter. Outlines are especially useful for organizing complex material. Outlining is best done on separate paper rather than written in the textbook.

In addition to organizing complex material, outlining is useful when you need to condense a lengthy section or chapter. This gives you an overview that enables you to see how an entire section or chapter is organized. This makes the material easier to study and remember.

How do you create an outline? To outline a paragraph, write its main idea. Then, on separate, indented lines below the main idea, write the supporting details that go with it, like this:

I. Main idea sentence
  A. Supporting detail
  B. Supporting detail
  C. Supporting detail
  D. Supporting detail

For longer passages consisting of several paragraphs, continue your outline in the same way:

I. First main idea sentence
  A. Supporting detail for main idea I
  B. Supporting detail for main idea I
  C. Supporting detail for main idea I
  D. Supporting detail for main idea I

II. Second main idea sentence
  A. Supporting detail for main idea II
  B. Supporting detail for main idea II

III. Third main idea sentence
  A. Supporting detail for main idea III
  B. Supporting detail for main idea III
  C. Supporting detail for main idea III

The purpose of a study outline is to show how ideas are related. Making your outline look perfect is not as important as making sure that the relationships are clear to *you*. Main ideas should stand out, and it should be obvious which details go with each main idea. Roman numerals (I, II, III) are often used for main ideas, and uppercase letters (A, B, C, D) are used for supporting details. This notation helps you see how ideas are related. When the information you are writing is longer than a single line, indent the second line beneath the first word in the line above it. Do not go any farther to the left. The goal is to make the numbers and letters stand out clearly.

An outline can consist of phrases or sentences. However, when you have complex material, a sentence outline is better because it gives complete thoughts.

Use the same title for your outline as the one that appears in the original material. Do not entitle your outline "Outline." It will be obvious that it is an outline.

The box on page 699 shows a sentence outline of a passage from Selection 7.3. Notice also the identifying title: *Reactions to Impending Death.*

Guidelines for the Cornell Method of Note-Taking

The Cornell method is an organized note-taking format that includes a built-in review column. Sheets of loose-leaf notebook paper are marked ahead of time with a line to rule off a review column on the left side of the page. (See the examples on pages 700–701.) Record information on the main part of the page by outlining the

SAMPLE OUTLINE

Reactions to Impending Death

I. Elisabeth Kübler-Ross, a thanatologist, found in her research on the terminally ill that they tend to have certain basic emotional reactions as they prepare for death.

   A.   There are five types of reactions: denial and isolation, anger, bargaining, depression, and acceptance.

   B.   Different patients display different emotions.

   C.   Reactions may occur in various orders, although the general pattern is shock, denial, anger, and acceptance.

   D.   Several factors influence a person's type and sequence of emotional reactions.

   E.   Overall, a person's approach to dying reflects his or her approach to living.

   F.   These same emotions are characteristic of anyone who has experienced a major loss.

II. There are several uses of Kübler-Ross's research.

   A.   It can be used to help the dying cope with their emotions by enabling them to discuss these emotions.

   B.   It can be used to help survivors cope with the dying person's emotions as well as their own.

III. A hospice is a special hospital for the terminally ill.

   A.   A hospice can enhance a dying person's final days.

   B.   Life goes on more normally in this pleasant, informal environment.

   C.   There are many supportive people, including personnel and family members.

IV. Survivors normally go through a period of grieving or bereavement following an ill person's death.

   A.   Grief follows the pattern of shock or numbness; pangs of grief; apathy, dejection, and depression; and resolution.

   B.   Survivors' reactions vary, but survivors are usually able to discharge their anguish by grieving, and thus prepare to go on living.

   C.   Each person must grieve at his or her own pace and in his or her own way.

main ideas and supporting details. Read over your notes to make sure you will be able to understand them weeks from now. Write out words that are unclear and be sure you understand all your abbreviations. Add any words or information needed to clarify your notes, such as a detail, an example, or a definition. Underline, circle, or star key points. (To evaluate your current note-taking skills, complete the "Checklist for Good Note-Taking" on page 703.)

After you finish taking notes from a book or lecture, fill in the review column by writing clue words or questions. When you are ready to review, cover your notes so that only the review column shows. (See page 702.) Try to answer the review column questions by reciting the information aloud. If you cannot remember, uncover the material, look at the answer, re-cover it, and try it again until you can recite it successfully. (An example of the information in Selection 7.3, "Reactions to Impending Death," in Cornell method format is provided on page 701.)

The Cornell method of note-taking.

(Rule Review Column off ahead of time.)

Date/Course	Topic of Notes
Reduce to clues to Recite from when Reviewing	Record information in outline form. (At a minimum, put topics on separate lines and indent details on separate lines beneath the points they go with.)
After class, fill in this column with either clue words or questions to help you recite the material in your notes.	Write notes in your own words. Use abbreviations and sketches. To review, cover the portion of your notes to the right of the line. Try to recite information in this part out loud, from memory. If you need help, uncover the material, look at the answer, re-cover it, and try it again until you can recite it successfully from memory. *If you can't say it from memory, you don't know it!*

↑
Review Column   ↑
Note-Taking Area

Review Column	Record Section
↓	↓
Nov. 14-PSY/1301	Reactions to Impending Death

What are 5 general reactions of dying persons?	1. Thanatologist Elisabeth Kübler-Ross found terminally-ill patients have certain reactions as they prepare for death: • denial and isolation ("test results are wrong!") • anger (at God, at those who are healthy, etc.) • bargaining ("If you let me live, I'll be a better person.") • depression • acceptance (uses time left as well as possible)
Is there one specific sequence of reactions?	—not everyone has all 5 reactions or has them in that order
Uses of findings?	—helps both the dying and the survivors understand and cope with their reactions
What is a hospice?	2. Hospice = hospital for the terminally ill that seeks to improve the quality of life their final days: • supportive staff, clergy, counselors • pleasant surroundings • round-the-clock visits from everyone, including pets • constant attention, flexible rules
What is bereavement?	3. Bereavement = natural, normal period of grief after a death
What are the stages of grief?	Grief follows predictable pattern: • shock or numbness (dazed; ends by time of funeral) • pangs of grief (painful yearning for person; suffering acute; may think person is still alive, see them in dreams) • apathy, dejection and depression (lasts weeks or months; person feels futility, but resumes activities) • resolution (acceptance; memories now include positive images and nostalgic pleasure)
Purpose of grief?	—Allows survivors to discharge anguish and prepare to go on living
Does suppressing grief lead to problems later on?	—Suppressing grief does not lead to depression later on; lack of intense grief does not predict problems later on; each person must grieve in his or her own way and at own pace.

↑	↑
Fill in questions after writing information in the Record Section. Cover Record Section so you can test yourself aloud.	**Record information here in an organized fashion.**

Because of its built-in "Review Column," the Cornell method is an effective way to take notes. The review column is especially helpful when studying for tests.

CREATING A REVIEW SHEET USING THE CORNELL NOTE-TAKING METHOD

- Take notes on loose-leaf notebook paper in the Cornell method. Remove your notes and spread them out on a desk or tabletop so that only the review column of each page is visible.
- Overlap the review columns to create a continuous review column for the material you want to review.
- Use this built-in review aid when you review for tests. Prepare by reciting the answers to questions you have written in the review column.
- As you answer each question in the review column, lift up the page to check whether your answer is complete and correct.
- When you can say the information from memory—without looking at it—you *know* it.

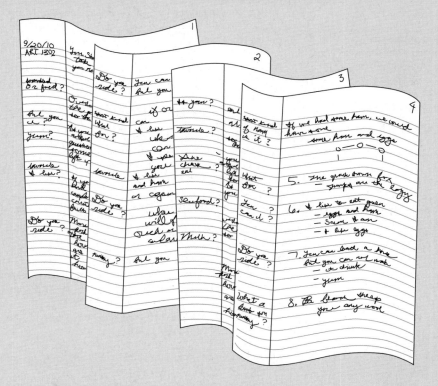

Sample of notes in the Cornell method overlapped with only review columns showing.

CHECKLIST FOR GOOD NOTE-TAKING

Here are guidelines for evaluating notes you take from classroom lectures or from your textbooks. Check **yes** or **no** for each question.

Which of the following do you currently do when you take notes?

Yes No

_____ _____ 1. Use standard-sized loose-leaf notebook paper rather than a spiral notebook?

_____ _____ 2. Rule off your paper ahead of time so that you can use the Cornell method for clear, organized notes?

_____ _____ 3. Always label your notes with the name of the course and the date (for lecture notes) or the chapter and pages (for material from your text)?

_____ _____ 4. Write the title or general topic of the notes at the top of the page?

_____ _____ 5. Wait until a point shapes up before you write it down?

_____ _____ 6. Write each major point on a separate line and skip a line or two before writing another major point?

_____ _____ 7. Set off details and examples by indenting them beneath the main point they go with?

_____ _____ 8. Add quick sketches or diagrams whenever they can help illustrate a point or aid recall later on?

_____ _____ 9. Invent your own abbreviations to save time?

_____ _____ 10. Strive for brief yet complete notes?

_____ _____ 11. Edit your notes for readability, clarity, and completeness as soon as possible after you take them, and then review your notes within 24 hours?

_____ _____ 12. Review again within a week to strengthen your recall later on?

Circle items to which you answered **no.** Consider ways to change or improve your note-taking skills by following the strategy listed in the items you circled.

Guidelines for Mapping

mapping

Informal way of organizing main ideas and supporting details by using boxes, circles, lines, arrows, etc.

Another form of textbook note-taking is mapping. **Mapping** is an informal way of organizing main ideas and supporting details by using boxes, circles, lines, arrows, and the like. The idea is to show information in a way that clarifies relationships among ideas. Like outlining, mapping is done on separate paper rather than in the margins of the textbook.

One simple type of map consists of the topic or main idea in a circle or box in the middle of the sheet of paper, with supporting details radiating out from it. Another type of map has the main idea in a box at the top of the paper, with supporting ideas in smaller boxes below it and connected to it by arrows or leader lines. If the information is sequential (for instance, significant events in World War I), a map can take the form of a flowchart. Samples of these kinds of maps are shown on page 704.

TYPES OF MAPS

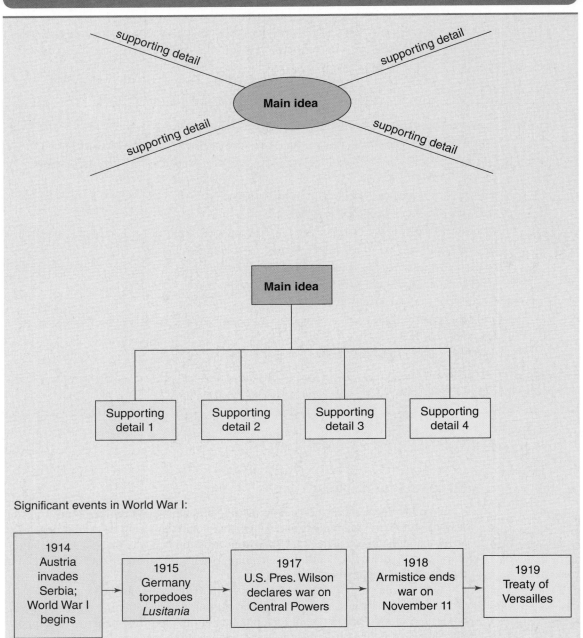

Significant events in World War I:

There is no one right way to make maps since they are personal records of information. However, research on study maps (which are also called *concept maps, learning maps,* and *idea maps*) indicates that using color helps many students remember the material. It also seems to help if key words are written in bold capital letters and if simple sketches are included. Finally, when you make a map, you may find that turning the page sideways gives you more room.

A study map for the passage on reactions of dying patients is shown below. It condenses all the important information onto a single page. A complete study map such as this requires considerable thought and effort.

Since outlines and study maps both show relationships among important ideas in a passage, how can you decide which to use? Your decision will depend on how familiar you are with each technique and how the passage itself is written. Keep in mind that mapping is an informal study technique, whereas outlining can be formal or informal. When you are asked to prepare a formal outline in a college course, do not assume that you can substitute a study map.

SAMPLE STUDY MAP

Reactions to Impending Death

Hospice =
special hospital for
the terminally-ill
• informal
• pleasant
• visitors/pets
• supportive
  personnel

Additional support for terminally ill

Kubler-Ross's findings on
terminally-ill patients'
**Reactions to Impending
Death**

Typical reactions

Reactions
• Denial and Isolation
• Anger #!?*!
• Bargaining
• Depression
• Acceptance

Value of findings
• Helps the dying cope
• Helps survivors cope

*Survivors discharge anguish
and prepare to go on living*

Bereavement =
period of grieving
• shock; numbness
• pangs of grief
• apathy; dejection
• depression
• resolution

Reactions don't always occur in this order.

Not every dying person has every reaction.

Same reactions people have to any major loss.

People should grieve at their own pace and in their own way.
Suppressing grief or lack of intense grief does NOT lead to problems later on.

Guidelines for Summarizing

A third technique of textbook note-taking is summarizing. A **summary** is a way of condensing into one paragraph all the main ideas an author has presented in a longer selection (such as an essay or article) or a section of a chapter. When you have correctly identified the main ideas in a passage, you have identified the information necessary to prepare your summary.

Summarizing is an effective way to check your comprehension. It also helps you transfer the material into your long-term memory. It is particularly beneficial if you will be answering essay questions because it allows you to rehearse answers you may have to write on the test.

Here are things to keep in mind when you write a summary:

- **Include all the main ideas.**   Include *all* the main ideas the author presents in the section. Include a supporting detail (such as the definition of an important term) *only* if a main idea cannot be understood without it.
- **Do not add anything.**   Do *not* add anything beyond the author's ideas, such as information from other sources or your own opinions.
- **Keep the original sequence.**   Present ideas in the *same* order the author does. In other words, keep the same sequence in which the author presents the information.
- **Reword as necessary, providing connections.**   Paraphrase the main ideas and supply clear connections that show the relationship among these ideas.
- **Give your summary a title.**   Use the *same* title that the original material has. Do not title your summary "Summary."

The box below shows a sample summary of the passage about the reactions of terminally ill people.

SAMPLE SUMMARY

Reactions to Impending Death

Elisabeth Kübler-Ross is a thanatologist whose research with terminally ill patients revealed that they tend to display several emotional reactions as they prepare for death. The five basic responses she found were *(1) denial and isolation, (2) anger, (3) bargaining, (4) depression,* and *(5) acceptance.* Different patients display different emotions. These may occur in various orders, although the general pattern is shock, denial, anger, and acceptance. Several factors influence a person's types and sequence of emotions. Overall, the individual's approach to dying reflects his or her approach to living. Emotions displayed by a dying person are the typical, appropriate ones that accompany any major loss. This information can be used to help dying persons and survivors cope with their emotional reactions. Most important, knowledge of these emotions can enable others to be supportive of dying people and help them discuss death and their feelings. The hospice, a hospital for the terminally ill, can enhance a dying person's last days. The ill person is offered emotional support and guidance from family as well as from other people. Life goes on more nearly as normal in this informal, pleasant environment. A period of bereavement (grieving) by survivors normally follows the death of the ill person. Grief also follows a pattern: *shock or numbness; pangs of grief; apathy, dejection, and depression;* and *resolution.* Survivors' reactions vary, but survivors are usually able to discharge their anguish by grieving, and thus they prepare to go on living. Each person must grieve at his or her own pace and in his or her own way.

SUMMARIZING EXERCISE

Directions: Read the following passage, and then summarize it on other paper. Your summary will be better if you write a rough draft first. Be sure to follow the guidelines on page 706 for writing a correct summary.

Plagiarism

Plagiarism refers to using and passing off someone else's ideas or writings as your own. Taking credit for someone else's work is a form of academic dishonesty, of cheating. Ignorance of plagiarism is not an excuse, and in college, stealing someone else's words or ideas can result in severe penalties.

If you "borrow" from a writer or Web source without crediting the source, you are likely to get caught. College professors can easily check student papers for plagiarism: They simply run electronic files of papers, or suspicious sections of them, through one of several Web-based programs that compares the content to material already on the Web.

Buying a term paper on the Web is even more foolish than plagiarizing: You may be buying a poor-quality paper that has already been sold to countless students. Moreover, professors can quickly identify it as a purchased paper. Is buying a paper worth possible expulsion from college?

To avoid plagiarism, *always credit the source of material that is not your own original work*, whether the material comes from books, the Web, magazines, newspapers, other publications, or an interview. *If you do not know the source, do not use the material.*

What else can you do to avoid plagiarizing? First, do not cut and paste into your papers information you find on websites. Second, use quotation marks whenever you quote directly. Even if you are paraphrasing, you must make it clear that the ideas are someone else's ("According to the biologist John Doe, director of Save the Environment, . . ."), and you must cite the source. Third, cite the source for facts that are not commonly known ("The average number of alcoholic drinks per week correlates with college students' GPA, with A students consuming four drinks, and D or F students consuming ten."). However, you do not need to give the source for commonly known facts ("At sea level, water boils at 212° F and freezes at 32° F.").

The format for source citations is very specific. If you are not sure about the correct form for various types of citations, seek help. Consult your instructor or your college's tutoring center or library. You can also go online and type "source citations" in Google or another search engine.

Plagiarism is a serious offense. Avoid it.

GUIDELINES FOR INTERPRETING GRAPHS AND VISUAL AIDS

visual literacy

The ability to "read" (interpret) images, graphs, diagrams, and other visual representations.

Every day, you see thousands of images and symbols in print and on screen in both school-related materials and other areas of your life. For this reason, **visual literacy,** the ability to "read" (interpret) images, graphs, diagrams, and other visual representations, is a critical skill in today's world. Popular newspapers and magazines, the Web, and textbooks and educational resources are filled with graphs and visual aids.

Authors use graphs and visual aids for many reasons. First, they can be used to simplify, clarify, illustrate, and summarize information. Second, they can show how things relate to and compare with each other. Third, they can be used to emphasize important points and reveal trends and patterns. Finally, they make the material more memorable, especially for visual learners.

Graphs consist of diagrams and pictorial devices that show relationships between sets of numbers (quantitative relationships). They consist of bar graphs, pie charts, line graphs, and tables.

As the name indicates, **visual aids** are instructional aids that present information visually rather than in words alone. In textbooks, they include illustrations such as photographs, diagrams, maps, flowcharts, timelines, and cartoons. (In regard to a presentation, they could include such things as a poster, a PowerPoint presentation, a video clip, an object, or a scale model.)

Graphs and visual aids present explanations of concepts and relationships in ways that are often more concise and easier to understand than words alone. Sometimes they accompany a written explanation in the text. Sometimes, however, they present *additional* material that isn't given elsewhere: They provide information that goes beyond the written explanation; for example, they are used to present support or proof. You must be able to read, interpret, and understand them. You must be able to determine how they fit with the written material in the chapter.

As you preview a reading assignment, note graphs and visual aids. When you actually read the assignment, don't skip over or rush past graphs and visual aids. Rather, stop and examine each one when the author *first* mentions it (for example, "See Figure 1-3" or "As Table 7.4 shows, . . ."). Authors refer to them at the point they believe the information will help readers most. Shift back and forth between the written explanation and the graph or visual aid as needed. For example, if you are reading about the four chambers of the heart in a biology text, refer to the labeled illustration each time a new chamber is described.

graphs

Diagrams and pictorial devices that show relationships between sets of numbers (quantitative relationships).

visual aids

Instructional aids that present information visually rather than in words alone.

Graphs

Although graphs contain important information, they can seem confusing unless you know how to interpret them. Read the steps for interpreting graphs (bar graphs, pie charts, line graphs, and tables). After you read about each type of graph, study the example, and then try the sample exercise by following these steps:

- Read the *title* and any *explanation* that accompanies the graphic aid. The title tells you what aspect of the writer's topic is being clarified or illustrated.
- Check the *source* of the information presented in the graphic aid to see if it seems current and reliable.
- Read all the *headings* in a table and all the *labels* that appear in a chart or a graph (such as those on the bottom and side of a graph) to determine what is being presented or measured. For example, the side of a bar graph may be labeled "Annual Income in Thousands of Dollars" and the bottom may be labeled "Level of Education."
- Examine the *units of measurement* in a graphic aid (for example, decades, percents, thousands of dollars, per hour, kilograms, per capita, or milliseconds).

- Study the graph. Try to understand how the graph clarifies, exemplifies, or proves the written explanation. Note any extremes, that is, any highs and lows in the data. See if there is a *trend,* a steady, overall increase or decrease. Look for patterns or trends in the data that allow you to draw a general conclusion.
- Finally, use the information provided collectively by the title and explanation, source, headings and labels, and units of measurement to determine the *important points or conclusions* the author is conveying.

Here are explanations and examples of four commonly used graphic aids: bar graphs, line graphs, pie charts, and tables. With bar graphs, line graphs, and tables, look for trends. Along with each sample graphic aid is a summary of its important elements as well as the conclusions that can be drawn from the graph.

Bar Graphs

A *bar graph* is a chart in which the length of parallel rectangular bars is used to indicate relative amounts of the items being compared. The bars in a bar graph may be vertical or horizontal. Examine the vertical bar graph below from a human development textbook.

Figure 14.3
Median age at first marriage for men and women ages 15 years and over: United States, 1970–2003.
Source: Fields, 2004, Figure 5

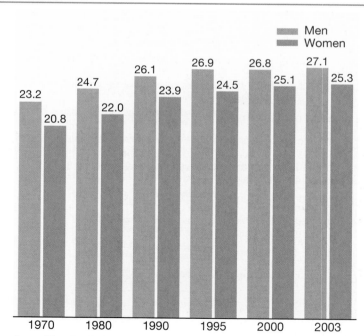

Source: Diane Papalia, Sally Olds, and Ruth Feldman, *Human Development,* 10e, p. 531. Copyright © 2007 by The McGraw-Hill Companies, Inc. Reprinted with permission of The McGraw-Hill Companies, Inc.

- *Title or explanation.* Median age at first marriage for men and women ages 15 years and over: United States, 1970–2003.
- *Source.* Fields, 2004, Figure 5.
- *Headings and labels.* Dates between 1970 and 2003; median years of age; men and women.
- *Units of measurement.* Age (in years), years (10-year increments from 1970 to 1990; 5-year increments from 1995 to 2000; 2003).
- *Important points or conclusions.* Both U.S. men and women married for the first time at later ages in 2003 than in 1970. For women the age at first marriage rose steadily, increasing by four and a half years between 1970 (20.8 years) and 2003 (25.3). For men the age at first marriage increased by approximately four years between 1970 (23.2 years) and 2003 (27.1). During the period between 1970 and 2003, men age 15 and over were consistently older at the time of their first marriage than women were at the time of their first marriage.

Exercise: Study the horizontal bar graph below from a business textbook and answer the questions based on the information in it.

Figure 4.1   Likelihood Teens and Adults May Engage in Online Activity
Source: Pew Internet and American Life Project, July, 2005.

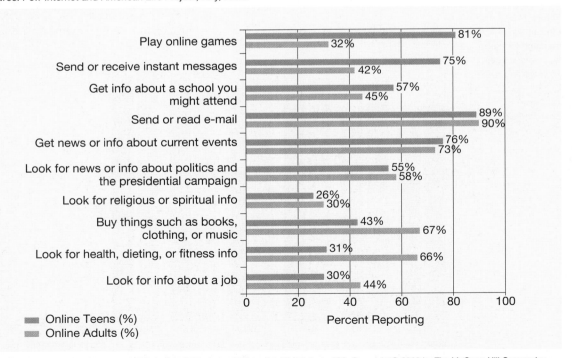

- *Title or explanation.* _____

  _____

- *Source.* _____

- *Headings and labels.* _____

  _____

- *Units of measurement.* _____

- *Important points or conclusions.* _____

  _____

  _____

  _____

  _____

  _____

Line Graphs

A *line graph* is a diagram whose points are connected to show a relationship between two or more variables. There may be one line or several lines, depending on what the author wishes to convey. The following example is also from a human development textbook.

Figure 17.2
United States population age 65 and over; 1900–2000 and 2010–2050, projected
Source: Federal Interagency Forum on Aging-Related Statistics, 2004. p. 2.

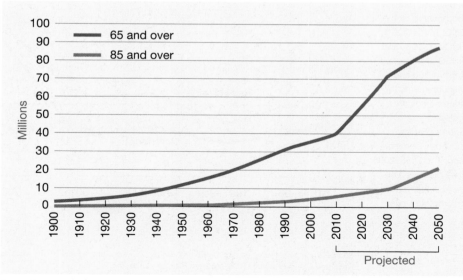

Source: Diane E. Papalla, Sally Wendkos Olds, and Ruth Feldman, *Human Development,* 10e, p. 628. Copyright © 2007 by The McGraw-Hill Companies, Inc. Reprinted with permission of The McGraw-Hill Companies, Inc.

- *Title or explanation.* United States population age 65 and over, 1900–2000 and 2010–2050, projected.
- *Source.* Federal Interagency Forum on Aging-Related Statistics, 2004, p. 2.
- *Headings and labels.* Number of people; year; 65 and over; 85 and over.
- *Units of measurement.* Numbers, in millions; years from 1900 to 2050, by decades.
- *Important points and conclusions.* Between 1900 and 2009, the number of U.S. adults age 65 and older increased from approximately 2 million to 40 million, and is projected to reach almost 90 million by 2050. A steep increase was projected beginning in 2010 when baby boomers began moving into this age group. By 1970, the number of Americans age 85 and older also began to climb steadily and is projected to increase to slightly more than 20 million by 2050.

Exercise: Study the line graph below from a political science textbook and answer the questions based on the information in it.

Figure 4.4
National Party Fund-Raising, 1995–2006
The figures include fund-raising by the DNC, RNC, DCCC, NRCC, DSCC, and NRSC. Soft-money fund-raising and disbursements to state parties are not included.
Source: Federal Elections Commission. The 2005–2006 data are based on projections from an incomplete cycle.

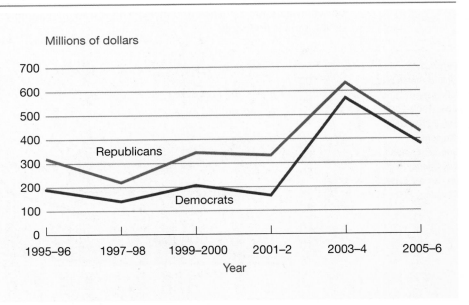

Source: Thomas E. Patterson, *We the People,* 7e, p. 278. Copyright © 2008 by The McGraw-Hill Companies, Inc. Reprinted with permission of The McGraw-Hill Companies, Inc.

- *Title or explanation.* _____

- *Source.* _____

- *Headings and labels.* _____

  _____

- *Units of measurement.* _____

- *Important points or conclusions.* _____

  _____

  _____

  _____

  _____

Pie Charts

A *pie chart* is a circle graph in which the sizes of the "slices" represent parts of the whole. Pie charts are a convenient way to show the relationship among component parts as well as the relationship of each part to the whole. The example is from a personal finance textbook.

Source: U.S. Bureau of the Census, Statistical Abstract of the United States, 2004–2005 (Washington, D.C.: U.S. Government Printing Office), p. 448 (www.census .gov).

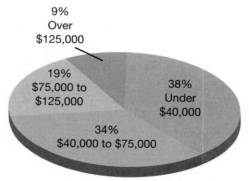

Household Income Levels for U.S. Families

Source: Jack Kapoor, Les Dlabay, and Robert Hughes, *Personal Finance,* 8e, p. 410. Copyright © 2007 by The McGraw-Hill Companies, Inc. Reprinted with permission of The McGraw-Hill Companies, Inc.

- *Title or explanation.* Household Income Levels for U.S. Families.
- *Source.* U.S. Bureau of the Census, Statistical Abstract of the United States, 2004–2005 (Washington, D.C.: U.S. Government Printing Office), p. 448 (www.census.gov).
- *Headings and labels.* Income ranges.
- *Units of measurement.* Percents.
- *Important points and conclusions.* The majority of U.S. households (72%) have incomes of less than $75,000; 38% have incomes under $40,000. Only the top 9% have incomes greater than $125,000.

Exercise: Study the pie chart below from a government textbook and answer the questions based on the information in it.

Source: OMB Watch

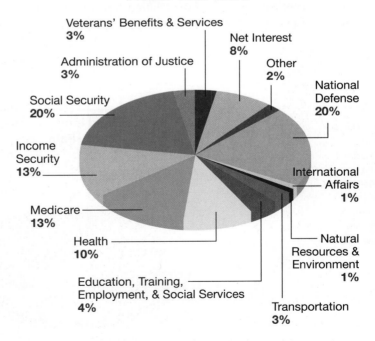

Total Federal Outlays Fiscal Year 2006

Source: John Losco and Ralph Baker, *Am Gov,* p. 349. Copyright © 2008 by The McGraw-Hill Companies, Inc. Reprinted with permission of The McGraw-Hill Companies, Inc.

- *Title or explanation.* _____
- *Source.* _____
  _____
- *Headings and labels.* _____
- *Units of measurement.* _____
- *Important points or conclusions.* _____
  _____
  _____
  _____
  _____
  _____

Tables

A *table* is a systematic listing of data in rows and columns. The following example is taken from a marketing textbook.

Exhibit 14-1
Leading retailers

Company	Sales ($ millions)	Profits ($ millions)	Employees
1. Wal-Mart	288,189	10,267	1,600,000
2. Home Depot	73,094	5,001	325,000
3. Kroger	56,434	(128)	290,000
4. Target	49,934	3,198	300,000
5. Costco	48,107	882	82,150
6. Albertson's	40,052	444	241,000
7. Walgreens	37,508	1,360	140,000
8. Lowe's	36,464	2,176	139,678
9. Sears	36,099	(507)	247,000
10. Safeway	35,823	560	191,000

Source: William Bearden, Thomas Ingram, and Raymond LaFarge, *Marketing: Principles and Perspectives,* 5e, p. 320. Copyright © 2007 by The McGraw-Hill Companies, Inc. Reprinted with permission of The McGraw-Hill Companies, Inc.

- *Title or explanation.* Leading Retailers.
- *Source.* None given; presumably, data compiled by textbook authors.
- *Headings or labels.* Company, Sales, Profits, Employees.
- *Units of measurement.* Dollars, in millions; numbers (for employees).
- *Important points and conclusions.* Leading retailers have annual sales between approximately $36 million and $300 million. Three of the top ten retailers are grocery chains; two are home improvement stores. The largest retailer (Wal-Mart) has nearly four times the sales and five times the number of employees as the next closest retailer, yet makes only twice as much in profits. Two of the top ten retailers (Kroger and Sears) have losses.

Exercise: Study the table below from a business textbook and answer the questions based on the information in it.

Table 15.1
The Life
Expectancy of
Paper Currency
Source: Federal Reserve Bank of New York (n.d.)

Denomination of Bill	Life Expectancy (Years)
$ 1	1.8
$ 5	1.3
$ 10	1.5
$ 20	2
$ 50	4.6
$100	7.4

Source: O. C. Ferrell, Geoffrey Hirt, and Linda Ferrell, *Business: A Changing World,* 6e, p. 126. Copyright © 2008 by The McGraw-Hill Companies, Inc. Reprinted with permission of The McGraw-Hill Companies, Inc.

- *Title or explanation.* _____
- *Source.* _____
- *Headings and labels.* _____
- *Units of measurement.* _____
- *Important points or conclusions.* _____

_____

_____

_____

Visual Aids

Visual aids consist of photographs, diagrams, maps, flowcharts, timelines, and cartoons that supplement or illustrate narrative information. As with graphs, stop and examine visual aids when the author first mentions them. Then return to your reading. Now read about each type of visual aid and how to interpret it. Study the example, and then try the sample exercise.

Photographs

Photographs are images recorded by a camera. Authors use them to bring information to life, make it concrete, and help you visualize it. (Think how much more helpful it would be to see a photograph of a coral reef rather than simply read a description of it.) Authors also use photos to show an example, such as a photo of a motherboard in a computer science book. Finally, they use photos to help readers relate to material on an emotional level, such as a history book photo of hundreds of hungry people standing in a breadline during the Great Depression; a picture of New York City on September 11, 2001; or a war-ravaged village in Africa.

When you see photographs in textbooks, examine them and read the accompanying caption. Ask yourself questions such as, What are the main elements (people, objects, activities) of the photograph? What does the photo illustrate or exemplify? What is its most important "message"? How does it fit with the written material? Is the date of the photograph given? The location at which it was taken?

The sample photograph is from an environmental science textbook. Perhaps you are aware that many major cities in China have a severe problem with pollution that hurts both its citizens and the environment at large. Even so, the photograph of Chinese citizens wearing masks, with industrial smokestacks in the background, dramatically depicts for viewers the severity of the problem.

Figure 19.9

Developing Concerns

If China's current "modernization" continues, the boom will be fueled by coal to the possible detriment of the planet as a whole.

Source: Eldon Enger and Bradley Smith, *Environmental Science,* 11e, p. 442. Copyright © 2008 by The McGraw-Hill Companies, Inc. Reprinted with permission of The McGraw-Hill Companies, Inc.

Exercise: Examine the art history textbook photograph below and answer the questions based on it.

**Figure 13.30
Frank O. Gehry,
architect.
Guggenheim
Museum Bilbao,
Bilbao, Spain, 1997.**

Source: Mark Getlein, *Living with Art,* 8e, p. 334. Copyright © 2008 by The McGraw-Hill Companies, Inc. Reprinted with permission of The McGraw-Hill Companies, Inc.

1. When and where was the photograph taken? _____

2. What is pictured in the photograph? _____

3. What point does the photograph illustrate about the architecture Frank Gehry

   designs? _____

   _____

   _____

Diagrams

Diagrams appear in nearly every type of textbook. *Diagrams* are sketches, drawings, or plans that show or explain how something works or show the relationship between the parts of a whole. The "something" might be an object (a microscope), a process (the life cycle of a lake), or an idea (a proposed solution to the problem of overflowing landfills). *Flowcharts,* like the one shown on page 719, are a specific type of diagram that shows a procedure or steps in a process.

When you study any diagram, ask yourself, What is the purpose of this diagram? Why is it included? What does it show? A good test preparation strategy is to photocopy any important diagram from your text. In a biology text, for example, it might be a diagram of a cell or the bones of the arm. Cover the labels and make one or more copies. Test yourself to see if you can correctly label the parts. You can also make diagrams or drawings of your own. Creating them is an excellent study strategy.

The purpose of the information technology textbook flowchart below is to show the five basic operations of a computer and the order in which they occur. For a test, you would need to know both the operations and their sequence. This flowchart,

Panel 1.6
Basic Operations of
a Computer

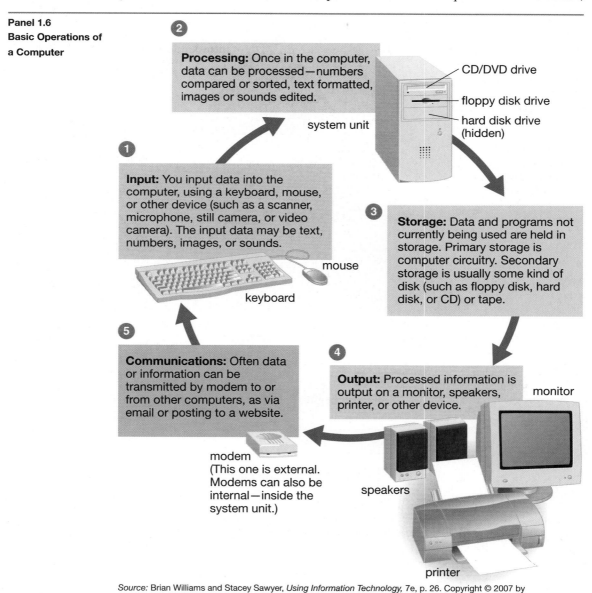

Source: Brian Williams and Stacey Sawyer, *Using Information Technology,* 7e, p. 26. Copyright © 2007 by The McGraw-Hill Companies, Inc. Reprinted with permission of The McGraw-Hill Companies, Inc.

with arrows, objects, and colors, is more effective and memorable than a paragraph alone with the same information.

Exercise: This diagram of the writing pyramid comes from a student success book. Study the diagram and answer the questions based on the information in it.

Figure 9.3
Writing Pyramid
Start at the top of the pyramid with your major topic, and move down to each subtopic and its main points. Provide support for your main points, including examples and statistics. End with a powerful conclusion that summarizes the paper.

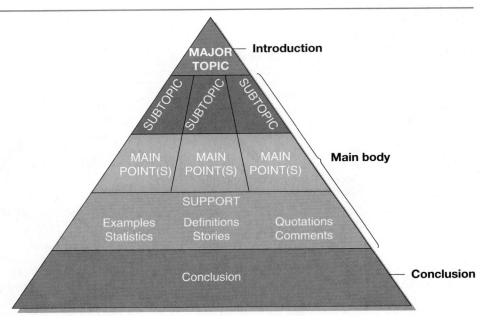

Source: Sharon Ferrett, *Peak Performance,* 6e, p. 293. Copyright © 2008 by The McGraw-Hill Companies, Inc. Reprinted with permission of The McGraw-Hill Companies, Inc.

1. Where should you begin when you write a paper? _____

_____

2. What are the three major parts of a paper? _____

_____

3. What elements comprise the main body of the paper? _____

_____

4. What types of things can be used for support? _____

_____

5. What comes at the end of the paper and what is its purpose? _____

_____

_____

_____

Maps

Maps are representations of regions or other information presented on a flat surface. At one time or another, everyone has used a *location map:* a road map, atlas, or even campus map. For any map, ask yourself, What is the purpose of this map? What important information does it show? What does the date of its creation suggest about the information it contains?

You will encounter maps in history, geography, archaeology, anthropology, astronomy, and many other courses. Some maps are designed to show the exact location of cities, states, countries, battlefields, mountain ranges, rivers, and other physical objects. Pay particular attention to each item's position relative to every other item. For example, a map might indicate that shorelines are being encroached upon by rising oceans as global warming melts polar ice caps. In maps such as these, note the following:

- *Title:* the subject matter of the map
- *Legend or key:* an explanatory table or list of symbols in the map and the use of color or shading (such as a star for capital cities, or various colors or shading to indicate different age categories)
- *Scale:* a ratio showing the relationship between the dimensions on the map and the object it represents, such as 1" = 100 miles; enables users to calculate the actual size of features represented on the map
- *Compass:* a symbol indicating the directions north, south, east, and west
- *Source:* the mapmaker; the person, agency, or group that created the map
- *Date:* when the map was created (for example, it might be ancient, from the 1800s, or recent)

The sample map on the next page is from an American history textbook. Its purpose is to show the distribution of Native Americans in the western United States before and after the establishment of government reservations. As you study the map, note the box in the upper right that indicates reservations are in blue. Also note the explanation of the other colors in the caption beneath the map. The most striking information in this map is how small the reservations are compared to the areas the tribes previously dominated. The distance scale at the bottom left of the map allows you to estimate the dimensions of the territories. No date is given as to when the map was created, probably because the information in it has not changed and is not likely to.

In addition to location maps, there are *thematic* or *special-purpose maps* that present factual or statistical information for a specific region (rather than showing

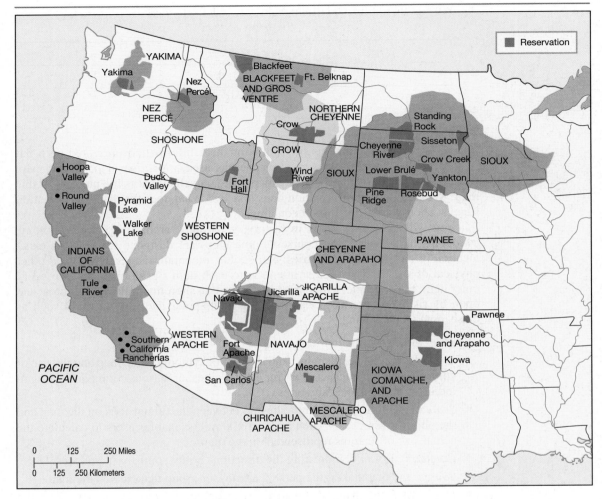

ABORIGINAL TERRITORIES AND MODERN RESERVATIONS OF WESTERN INDIAN TRIBES This map shows the rough distribution of the Native American population in the western United States before the establishment of reservations by the federal government in the nineteenth century. The large shaded regions in colors other than yellow represent the areas in which the various tribes were dominant a century and more ago. The blue shaded areas show the much smaller areas set aside for them as reservations after the Indian wars of the late nineteenth century.

Source: Alan Brinkley, *A Survey of American History,* 12e, p. 858. Copyright © 2007 by The McGraw-Hill Companies, Inc. Reprinted with permission of The McGraw-Hill Companies, Inc.

the location of physical objects). For example, a map might use different colors to show rates of car thefts in various parts of the United States during the last five years. In such maps, look for patterns and trends, in addition to the other aspects noted above. Remember that you can create maps of your own as study aids.

The thematic map below uses color to show the major crops in the South in 1860. The map makes it easy to see that cotton was the dominant crop, with tobacco second. Both cotton and tobacco had to be gathered by hand. How might that be related to the War Between the States?

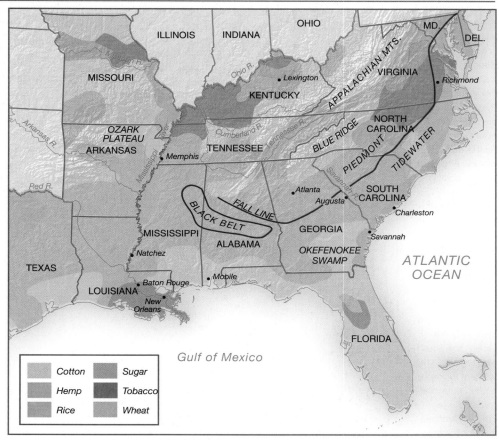

Cotton and Other Crops of the South *By 1860, the cotton kingdom extended across the Lower South into the Texas prairie and up the Mississippi River valley. Tobacco and hemp were the staple crops of the Upper South, where they competed with corn and wheat. Rice production was concentrated in the swampy coastal region of South Carolina and Georgia as well as the lower tip of Louisiana. The sugar district was in southern Louisiana.*

Source: James Davidson, Brian DeLay, Christine Heyman, Mark Lytle, and Michael Stoff, *Nation of Nations,* 6e, p. 352.
Copyright © 2008 by The McGraw-Hill Companies, Inc. Reprinted with permission of The McGraw-Hill Companies, Inc.

Exercise: Study the following American history textbook map and answer the questions based on the information in it.

IMMIGRANT GROUPS IN COLONIAL AMERICA, 1760 Even though the entire Atlantic seaboard of what is now the United States had become a series of British colonies by 1760, the population consisted of people from many nations. As this map reveals, English settlers dominated most of the regions of North America. But note the large area of German settlement in the western Chesapeake and Pennsylvania; the swath of Dutch settlement in New York and New Jersey; the Scotch-Irish regions in the western regions of the South; and the large areas in which Africans were becoming the majority of the population, even if subjugated by the white minority.

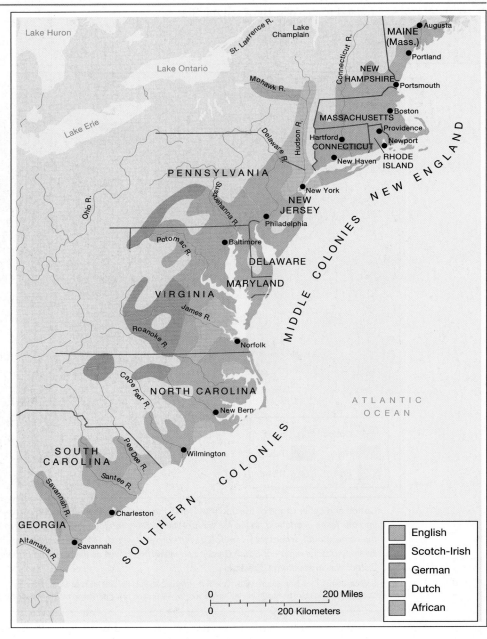

1. What were the major groups of colonies? _____

_____

2. Which immigrant group was predominant in colonial America in 1760? ___

_____

3. Which colony was farthest south? _____

4. Where did the Dutch immigrants settle? _____

_____

5. Why were Africans concentrated in the southern colonies? _____

_____

Some graphs and visual aids, including bar graphs, diagrams, and maps, contain *pictograms,* in which a picture or symbol represents numerical data or relationships. The symbols could be stick figures of people, bombs, dollar signs, flags, or bushels of grain, for example. The greater the number of symbols, the greater the proportional quantity represented. Pictograms, which are also called *pictographs,* make information more realistic, appealing, and memorable. For example, a bar graph that uses one cross to represent every 1,000 people killed by drunk drivers carries more emotional impact than a plain bar graph with numbers. The pictogram on page 726 shows federal government full-time civilian personnel employees in 1999, with each symbol representing 2,000 employees. The pictogram shows the various occupational categories of these government employees. What conclusions can you draw as to which sectors of government have the most employees? What might you conclude, for example, from the fact that "quality assurance, inspection, and grading" have a mere fraction of the number of employees in most other categories?

Cartoons

Cartoons are humorous drawings that may or may not include a caption. Textbook authors sometimes include them in textbooks to lighten things up, but more often to present a point of view or illustrate a point in a memorable way. (You learned about point of view in Chapter 8.) Your ability to understand a cartoon depends heavily on your prior knowledge. If a cartoon doesn't make sense to you, it is usually because you lack the information necessary for grasping it.

When you encounter a cartoon in a textbook or educational resource, ask yourself, Who or what do the cartoon characters or objects represent? What is going on in the cartoon? What is the suggested meaning? A newspaper cartoon that could easily have appeared in an information technology textbook or a sociology textbook appears on page 727.

Full-Time Civilian
Personnel
Employees of the
Federal Government

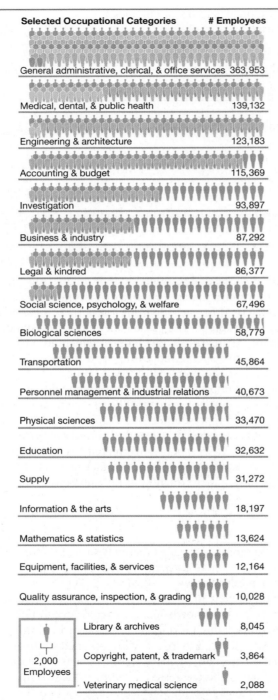

Selected Occupational Categories   # Employees

General administrative, clerical, & office services 363,953

Medical, dental, & public health   139,132

Engineering & architecture   123,183

Accounting & budget   115,369

Investigation   93,897

Business & industry   87,292

Legal & kindred   86,377

Social science, psychology, & welfare   67,496

Biological sciences   58,779

Transportation   45,864

Personnel management & industrial relations   40,673

Physical sciences   33,470

Education   32,632

Supply   31,272

Information & the arts   18,197

Mathematics & statistics   13,624

Equipment, facilities, & services   12,164

Quality assurance, inspection, & grading   10,028

Library & archives   8,045

Copyright, patent, & trademark   3,864

Veterinary medical science   2,088

2,000
Employees

Source: U.S. Office of Personnel Management, *Occupations of Federal White-Collar and Blue-Collar Workers,* Federal Civilian
Workforce Statistics, as of September 30, 1999 (Washington, D.C., U.S. Government Printing Office, 2000), Table W-2.

Here's the explanation: The baby has just texted his first word rather than say-ing it. The cartoonist is making a point about what an integral part of our lives tech-nology has become—and clearly, most children born in the United States today will grow up with it from the beginning of their lives.

Exercise: Now look at this cartoon and answer the questions on page 728.

What point is the cartoon making? In other words, what is the cartoonist's point of view about food prices today?

_____

_____

    Political cartoons reflect a publication's point of view on an issue, often by expressing disapproval of or poking fun at a public figure or current issue. They are also called *editorial cartoons* because they appear on newspapers' and magazines' editorial pages. They typically appear in government and history textbooks. Some of these cartoons contain caricatures, in which a person's distinctive features are exaggerated (such as Abraham Lincoln's long face or Barack Obama's ears). Cartoonists also use visual metaphors, such as an elephant for the Republican Party and a donkey for the Democratic Party, a "Wall St." street sign to represent the stock market, and Uncle Sam to represent the United States.

Exercise: Look at the following editorial cartoon. Can you interpret its meaning? Notice that it appeared during the summer of 2008.

'Recession? What recession?'

Source: John Sherffius © Creators Syndicate. By permission of John Sherffius and Creators Syndicate, Inc.

What point is the editorial cartoon making?

_____

_____

_____

_____

_____

_____

INTERPRETING GRAPHS AND VISUAL AIDS EXERCISE

Graphs

Directions: For each graph, or graphic aid, answer the questions that follow.

Figure 1
Average annual working hours of five nations
Source: Organization for Economic Cooperation and Development.

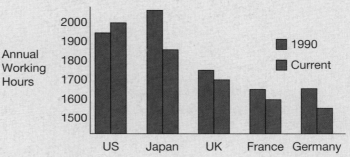

Source: Figure 1 from Charles Corbin, Gregory Welk, William Corbin, and Karen Welk, Concepts of Fitness and Wellness, 7e, p. 364. Copyright © 2008 by The McGraw-Hill Companies, Inc. Reprinted with permission of The McGraw-Hill Companies, Inc.

1. What type of graph is this? _____

2. What is the topic of this graph? _____

3. According to the graph, what was the trend in countries other than the U.S.? _____

_____

4. Which country had the steepest decline in average number of hours worked annually? _____

5. What important points or conclusions can be drawn about the average annual working hours of these five nations?

_____

_____

_____

_____

_____

_____

_____

_____

Table 3

Various sounds, their decibel levels, and the amount of exposure that results in hearing damage

Source: © 1998 Better Hearing Institute. Washington, DC. All rights reserved.

Sound	Decibel Level	Exposure Time Leading to Damage
Whispering	25 dB	
Library	30 dB	
Average home	50 dB	
Normal conversation	60 dB	
Washing machine	65 dB	
Car	70 dB	
Vacuum cleaner	70 dB	
Busy traffic	75 dB	
Alarm clock	80 dB	
Noisy restaurant	80 dB	
Average factory	85 dB	16 hours
Live rock music (moderately loud)	90 dB	8 hours
Screaming child	90 dB	8 hours
Subway train	100 dB	2 hours
Jackhammer	100 dB	2 hours
Loud song played through earphones	100 dB	30 minutes
Helicopter	105 dB	1 hour
Sandblasting	110 dB	30 minutes
Auto horn	120 dB	7.5 minutes
Live rock music (loud)	130 dB	3.75 minutes
Air raid siren	130 dB	3.75 minutes
THRESHOLD OF PAIN	140 dB	Immediate damage
Jet engine	140 dB	Immediate damage
Rocket launching	180 dB	Immediate damage

Source: Table 3 data from Better Hearing Institute, Washington, D.C., in Robert Feldman, *Understanding Psychology,* 8e, p. 116. Copyright © 2008 by The McGraw-Hill Companies, Inc. Reprinted with permission of The McGraw-Hill Companies, Inc.

6. What type of graphic aid is this? _____

7. What is the topic of this graphic aid? _____

_____

8. What are the three column headings? _____

9. Assuming they did not take precautions to protect their hearing, would an average factory worker or a helicopter pilot be more likely to experience job-related hearing damage? _____

_____

10. At what decibel level do sounds become painful to humans? _____

11. What important points or conclusions can be drawn about the decibel level of sounds and damage to hearing? _____

_____

_____

_____

Figure 15.3
Distribution's effect
on your food dollar

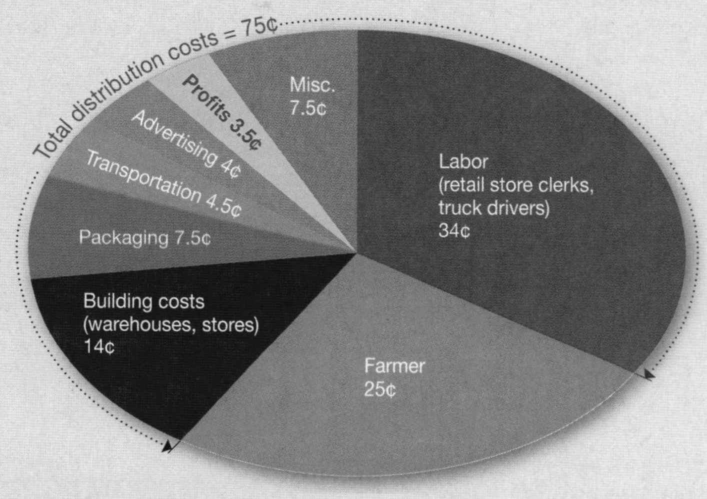

Total distribution costs = 75¢

Profits 3.5¢

Advertising 4¢

Transportation 4.5¢

Packaging 7.5¢

Building costs
(warehouses, stores)
14¢

Misc.
7.5¢

Labor
(retail store clerks,
truck drivers)
34¢

Farmer
25¢

Source: From William Nickels, James McHugh, and Susan McHugh, *Understanding Business,* 8e, p. 407. Copyright © 2008 by The McGraw-Hill Companies, Inc. Reprinted with permission of The McGraw-Hill Companies, Inc.

12. What type of graph is this? _____

13. What is the topic of this graph? _____

14. What category represents the greatest share of distribution costs? _____

15. What part of each food dollar represents profits? _____

16. What important points or conclusions can be drawn about the effect of distribution on the food dollar? _____

_____

_____

_____

**Figure 1
Trends in Sexu-
ally Transmitted
Infections Rates
in the United
States.**
Based on data
from the annual
CDC Sexuality
Transmitted Dis-
ease Surveillance
reports and
HIV/AIDS Surveil-
lance reports.

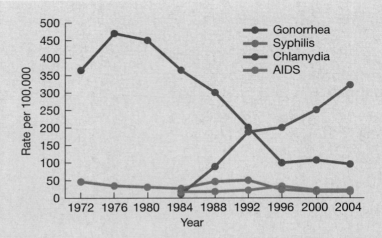

Source: Charles Corbin, Gregory Welk, William Corbin, and Karen Welk, *Concepts of Fitness and Wellness,* 7e, p. 428. Copyright © 2008 by The McGraw-Hill Companies, Inc. Reprinted with permission of The McGraw-Hill Companies, Inc.

17. What is the topic of this line graph? _____

_____

18. What is the unit of measure? _____

_____

19. What was the rate of chlamydia in 2004? _____

_____

20. What important points or conclusions can be drawn about trends in STI rates between 1972 and 2004? _____

_____

_____

_____

_____

Photograph

Street Scene from Manila, Capital of the Philippines

Source: Richard Schaefer, *Sociology: A Brief Introduction,* 7e, p. 216. Copyright © 2008 by The McGraw-Hill Companies, Inc. Reprinted with permission of The McGraw-Hill Companies, Inc.

Visual Aids

Directions: For each visual aid, answer the questions that follow.

1.   What is the topic of this photograph? _____

2.   What can be concluded about some U.S. corporations? _____

_____

3.   On what do you base your conclusion (in question 2, above)? _____

_____

**Figure 10.4
Comparison of
Library and Web**
The various parts
of the Web are
similar to the
components of a
traditional library.

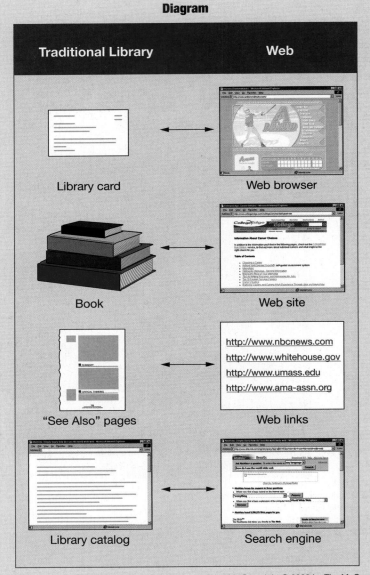

Diagram

Traditional Library   **Web**

Library card   Web browser

Book   Web site

"See Also" pages   Web links

http://www.nbcnews.com
http://www.whitehouse.gov
http://www.umass.edu
http://www.ama-assn.org

Library catalog   Search engine

Source: Robert Feldman, *P.O.W.E.R. Learning,* 4e, p. 290. Copyright © 2009 by The McGraw-Hill Companies, Inc. Reprinted with permission of The McGraw-Hill Companies, Inc.

4. What is depicted in this diagram? _____

_____

5. What is the traditional library counterpart of Web pages? _____

6. What is the Web counterpart to the library catalog? _____

Map

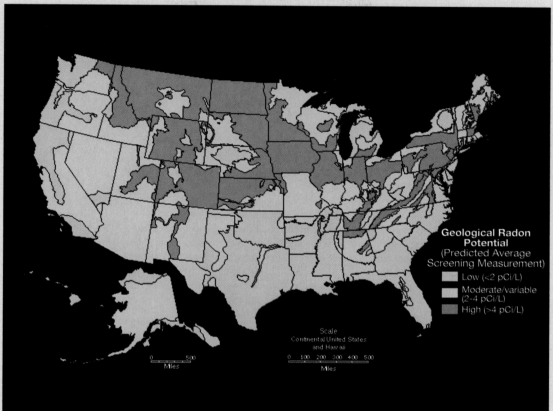

Figure 16.22   Generalized Geologic Radon Potential of the United States   Radon is a naturally occurring radioactive gas that forms in rocks and diffuses into soil and ground water. Because it can be inhaled, it can cause lung cancer. About 10% of lung cancer deaths each year (15,000 deaths) are attributed to radon.

Source: U.S. Geological Survey

Source: Eldon Enger and Bradley Smith, *Environmental Science,* 11e, p. 392. Copyright © 2008 by The McGraw-Hill Companies, Inc. Reprinted with permission of The McGraw-Hill Companies, Inc.

7. What is the topic of this map? _____

_____

8. In which region of the country is the radon potential the lowest? _____

9. Are there individual states that contain low, moderate, and high radon potentials? _____

10. What is the radon potential for the state of Louisiana? _____

11. What is the radon potential for the area in which your college or university is located? _____

Flowchart

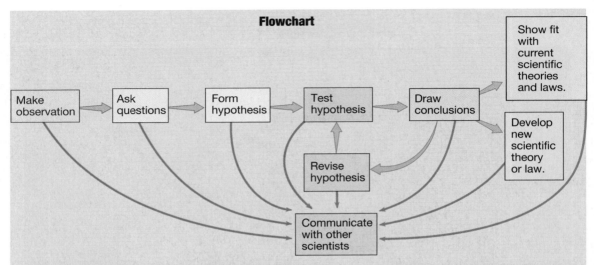

Figure 4.1   Elements of the Scientific Method. Observation of a natural phenomenon is usually the first step. Observation often leads people to ask questions about the observation they have made or to try to determine why the event occurred. This questioning is typically followed by the construction of a hypothesis that explains why the phenomenon occurred. The hypothesis is then tested to see if it is supported. Often this involves experimentation. If the hypothesis is not substantiated, it is modified and tested in its new form. It is important at all times that others in the scientific community be informed by publishing observations of unusual events, their probable causes and the results of experiments that test hypotheses.

Source: Eldon Enger and Bradley Smith, *Environmental Science*, 11e, p. 63. Copyright © 2008 by The McGraw-Hill Companies, Inc. Reprinted with permission of The McGraw-Hill Companies, Inc.

12. What is the topic of this flowchart? _____

13. What occurs after a hypothesis is formed? _____

14. What occurs throughout the process? _____

15. What events can occur after conclusions have been drawn? _____

_____

Cartoon

Source: Frank and Ernest. Reprinted by permission from Tom Thaves.

16. What is going on in the cartoon? _____

_____

_____

17. What general point is the cartoonist making? _____

_____

Timeline

This timeline is from an American history textbook.

Significant Events 1996–2004

1996
- Congress passes and president signs major welfare reform bill, minimum wage increase, and health-insurance reform
- Clinton reelected president; Republicans retain control of Congress

1997
- President and Congress agree on plan to balance budget
- Justice Department files antitrust suits against Microsoft

1998
- Lewinsky scandal rocks Clinton presidency
- Democrats gain in congressional elections
- Clinton impeached by House

1999
- Senate acquits Clinton in impeachment trial

2000
- George W. Bush wins contested presidential election

2001
- Terrorists destroy World Trade Center and damage Pentagon
- United States begins military action against Afghanistan

2002
- Corporate scandals rock business world

2003
- United States invades Iraq

2004
- Prison abuse scandal in Iraq
- Bush defeats Kerry in presidential election

Source: Alan Brinkley, *A Survey of American History,* 12e, p. 909. Copyright © 2007 by The McGraw-Hill Companies, Inc. Reprinted with permission of The McGraw-Hill Companies, Inc.

18. What period of time is covered in this timeline? _____

19. In which year did the United States invade Iraq? _____

20. In which years did George W. Bush win presidential elections? _____

The reading selection in this chapter (Selection 10.1, beginning on page 746) is itself a chapter-length selection from a history textbook. It will give you an opportunity to try out the study skills in Chapter 10 and give you a realistic idea of how much time it takes to master a textbook chapter. With additional practice, you will gain skill and confidence in your ability to master textbook material.

DEVELOPING CHAPTER REVIEW CARDS

Complete the eight review cards for Chapter 10 by supplying the important information about each topic. When you have completed them, you will have summarized important information about the skills in this chapter.

Three Keys to Studying College Textbooks

1.

2.

3.

Card 1   Chapter 10: Selecting and Organizing Textbook Information

---

REVIEW CARDS

CHAPTER **10** Selecting and Organizing Textbook Information

Guidelines for Underlining and Highlighting Textbook Material

Card 2   Chapter 10: Selecting and Organizing Textbook Information

Guidelines for Annotating Textbooks

Card 3   Chapter 10: Selecting and Organizing Textbook Information

Guidelines for Outlining

Card 4   Chapter 10: Selecting and Organizing Textbook Information

Guidelines for Mapping

Card 5   Chapter 10: Selecting and Organizing Textbook Information

Guidelines for Summarizing Textbook Information

Card 6   Chapter 10: Selecting and Organizing Textbook Information

Types of Graphs and Visual Aids

Card 7   Chapter 10: Selecting and Organizing Textbook Information

Guidelines for Interpreting Graphs

Card 8   Chapter 10: Selecting and Organizing Textbook Information

The Age of Globalization

From *American History: A Survey*
by Alan Brinkley

Prepare Yourself to Read

Directions: Do these exercises *before* you read Selection 10.1.

1. First, read and think about the title. What do you already know about globalization?

_____

_____

_____

_____

_____

2. Next, complete your preview by reading the following:

    Introduction: "September 11, 2001"

    "Timeline of Significant Events"

    Section headings and subheadings

    First sentence of each paragraph

    Photos and graphs

    Conclusion

On the basis of your preview, what aspects of globalization does this chapter seem to be about?

_____

_____

_____

_____

_____

3. **Build your vocabulary as you read.** If you discover an unfamiliar word or key term as you read the selection, try to determine its meaning by using context clues.

Internet Resources

Read More about This Topic Online

Use a search engine, such as Google or Yahoo!, to expand your existing knowledge about this topic *before* you read the selection or to learn more about it *afterward*. If you are unfamiliar with conducting Internet searches, read pages 25–26 on Boolean searches. You can also use Wikipedia, the free online encyclopedia, at www .wikipedia.com. Keep in mind that when you visit any website, it is a good idea to evaluate the site and the information it contains. Ask yourself questions such as "Who sponsors this website?" and "Is the information it contains up to date?"

SELECTION 10.1: THE AGE OF GLOBALIZATION

September 11, 2001

At 8:45 A.M. on the bright, sunny morning of September 11, 2001, as tens of thousands of workers—executives and financiers, secretaries and clerks, security guards and maintenance workers, chefs and waiters, citizens of dozens of nations—were beginning a day's work in lower Manhattan, a commercial airliner crashed into the side of one of the two towers of the World Trade Center, the tallest buildings in New York. The collision created a huge explosion and a great fire of extraordinary intensity. Less than half an hour later, as thousands of workers fled the burning building, another commercial airliner rammed into the companion tower, creating a second fireball. Within an hour after that, both towers, their steel girders buckling in response to the tremendous heat, collapsed. The burning floors gave way and fell onto the floors below them, pulling one of New York's (and America's) most famous symbols to the ground. At about the same time, in Virginia, another commercial airliner crashed into a side of the Pentagon, the headquarters of the nation's military, turning part of the building's facade into rubble. And several hundred miles away, still another airplane crashed in a field not far from Pittsburgh.

These four almost simultaneous catastrophes were the result of a single orchestrated plan by Islamic militants to bring terrorism—for years the bane of such nations as Israel, Turkey, Italy, Germany, Britain, Japan, and Ireland—into the United States, which had previously had relatively little recent experience of it. Similarly committed Middle Eastern terrorists had previously attacked American targets overseas—military barracks, a naval vessel, embassies, and consulates. And they had staged a less cataclysmic attack on the World Trade Center in 1993.

On September 11, groups of terrorists boarded each of the four planes armed with nothing more than box cutters and set out to use the aircraft as weapons against important buildings. In three cases, they succeeded. In the fourth, passengers—alerted by cell phone conversations to the intentions of the hijackers—apparently took over the plane and forced it down before it could reach its target. More than 3,000 people died as a result of the September 11 disasters.

The events of September 11 produced great changes in American life. They also seemed to bring to a close an extraordinary period in modern American history—a time of heady prosperity, bitter partisanship, cultural frivolity and excess, and tremendous social and economic change. And yet there was also at least one great continuity between the world of the 1990s and the world that seemed to begin on September 11, 2001. The United States, more than at any other time in its history, was becoming deeply entwined in a new age of globalism, an age that combined great promise with great peril.

Timeline of Significant Events

1977 • Apple introduces first personal computer.

1979 • Nuclear accident at Three Mile Island.

1981 • Existence of AIDS first reported in United States.

1985 • Crack cocaine appears in American cities.

1989 • Human genome project launched.

1991 • Controversy surrounds confirmation of Clarence Thomas to Supreme Court.

1992 • Major race riot in Los Angeles.

• Bill Clinton elected president.

1993 • Congress approves tax increase as part of deficit reduction.

• Congress ratifies North American Free Trade Agreement.

• Clinton proposes national health-care system.

1994 • Congress rejects health-care reform.

• Republicans win control of both houses of Congress.

1995 • New Republican Congress attempts to enact "Contract with America."

• Showdown between president and Congress leads to shutdown of federal government.

• National crime rates show dramatic decline.

• O. J. Simpson trial.

1996 • Congress passes and president signs major welfare reform bill, minimum wage increase, and health-insurance reform.

• Clinton reelected president; Republicans retain control of Congress.

1997 • President and Congress agree on plan to balance budget.

• Justice Department files antitrust suits against Microsoft.

1998 • Lewinsky scandal rocks Clinton presidency.

• Democrats gain in congressional elections.

• Clinton impeached by House.

1999 • Senate acquits Clinton in impeachment trial.

2000 • George W. Bush wins contested presidential election.

2001 • Terrorists destroy World Trade Center and damage Pentagon.

• United States begins military action against Afghanistan.

2003 • U.S. military forces depose Iraqi dictator Saddam Hussein.

September 11, 2001
One great American symbol, the Statue of Liberty, stands against a sky filled with the thick smoke from the destruction of another American symbol, New York City's World Trade Center towers, a few hours after terrorists crashed two planes into them.

Globalization of the Economy

1   Perhaps the most important economic change toward the end of the 20th century, and certainly the one whose impact was the most difficult to gauge, was what became known as the "globalization" of the economy. The great prosperity of the 1950s and 1960s had rested on, among other things, the relative insulation of the United States from the pressures of international competition. As late as 1970, international trade still played a relatively small role in the American economy as a whole, which thrived on the basis of the huge domestic market in North America.

2   By the end of the 1970s, however, the world had intruded on the American economy in profound ways, and that intrusion increased unabated for the next twenty years. Exports rose from just under $43 billion in 1970 to over $789 billion in 2000. But imports rose even more dramatically: from just over $40 billion in 1970 to over $1.2 trillion in 2000. Most American products, in other words, now faced foreign competition inside the United States. America had made 76 percent of the world's automobiles in 1950 and 48 percent in 1960. By 1990, that share had dropped to 20 percent; in 2000, even after a substantial revival of the automobile industry, the American share had risen only to 21.5 percent. The first American trade imbalance in the postwar era occurred in 1971; only twice since then, in 1973 and 1975, has the balance been favorable.

3   Globalization brought many benefits for the American consumer: new and more varied products, and lower prices for many of them. Most economists, and most national leaders, welcomed the process and worked to encourage it through lowering trade barriers. The North American Free Trade Agreement (NAFTA) and the General Agreement on Trade and Tariffs (GATT) were the boldest of a long series of treaties designed to lower trade barriers stretching back to the 1960s. But globalization had many costs as well. It was particularly hard on industrial workers, who saw industrial jobs disappear as American companies lost market share to foreign competitors. American workers also lost jobs as American companies began exporting work—building plants in Mexico, Asia, and other lower-wage countries to avoid having to pay the high wages workers had won in America.

Science and Technology in the New Economy

4   The "new economy" that emerged in the last decades of the twentieth century was driven by, and in turn helped to drive, dramatic new scientific and technological discoveries. Much as in the late nineteenth century—when such technological innovations as modern manufacturing, the railroad, the telegraph, the telephone, electricity, and automobiles—transformed both society and the economy; so in the late twentieth century, new technologies had profound effects on the way Americans—and peoples throughout the world—lived.

The Personal Computer

5   The most visible element of the technological revolution to most Americans was the dramatic growth in the use of computers in almost every area of life. Computers had been important to government and to many businesses since World War II. But their reach expanded with extraordinary speed in the 1980s and beyond. By the end of the 1990s, most Americans were doing their banking by computer. Most retail transactions were conducted by computerized credit mechanisms. Most businesses, schools, and other institutions were using computerized record-keeping. Many areas of manufacturing

were revolutionized by computer-driven product design and factory robotics. Scientific and technological research in almost all areas was transformed by computerized methods.

6   Among the most significant innovations was the development of the microprocessor, first introduced in 1971 by Intel, which represented a notable advance in the technology of integrated circuitry. A microprocessor miniaturized the central processing unit of a computer, making it possible for a small machine to perform calculations that in the past only very large machines could do. Personal computers quickly established a presence in many areas of American life: homes, schools, businesses, universities, hospitals, government agencies, newsrooms. Computerized word processing programs replaced typewriters. Computerized spreadsheets revolutionized bookkeeping. Computerized data processing made obsolete much traditional information storage, such as filing. Some computer enthusiasts talked about the imminent coming of a "paperless" office, in which all information or communication would be stored and distributed through computers, a prediction that failed to materialize. But the emergence of ever smaller and more powerful computers—laptops, notebooks, and palm-sized devices—greatly extended the reach of computer-related technology. At the same time, however, computer scientists were creating extraordinary powerful new forms of networking; and many were predicting that before long the stand-alone personal computer would be obsolete, that the future lay in linking many computers together into powerful networks.

7   The computer revolution created thousands of new, lucrative businesses: computer manufacturers themselves (IBM, Apple, Compaq, Dell, Gateway, Sun, Digital and many others); makers of the tiny silicon chips that ran the computers and allowed smaller and smaller machines to become more and more powerful (most notably Intel); and makers of software—chief among them Microsoft, the most powerful new corporation to arise in American life in generations.

8   But if Microsoft was the most conspicuous success story of the computer age, it was only one of many. Whole regions—the so-called Silicon Valley in northern California; areas around Boston, Austin, Texas, and Seattle, even areas in downtown New York

City—became centers of booming economic activity servicing the new computer age.

The Internet

9   Out of the computer revolution emerged another dramatic source of information and communication: the Internet. The Internet is, in essence, a vast, geographically far-flung network of computers that allows people connected to the network to communicate with others all over the world.

10   In the early 1980s, the Defense Department, an early partner in the development of the Arpanet, the predecessor of the Internet, withdrew from the project for security reasons. The network, soon renamed the Internet, was then free to develop independently. It did so rapidly, especially after the invention of technologies that made possible electronic mail (or e-mail) and the emergence of the personal computer, which vastly increased the number of potential users of the Internet. As late as 1984, there remained fewer than a thousand host computers connected to the Internet. A decade later, there were over 6 million. And in 2001, an estimated 400 million people around the world were using the Internet, including 130 million in the United States.

11   As the amount of information on the Internet unexpectedly proliferated, without any central direction, new forms of software emerged to make it possible for individual users to navigate through the vast number of Internet sites. In 1989, a laboratory in Geneva introduced the World Wide Web, through which individual users could publish information for the Internet, which helped establish an orderly system for both the distribution and retrieval of electronic information.

12   The Internet is still a relatively young communications medium, and its likely impact on society is not yet fully understood. Already, however, it has revolutionized many areas of life. E-mail has replaced conventional mail, telephone calls, and even face-to-face conversation for millions of people. Newspapers, magazines, and other publications have begun to publish on the Internet. It has become a powerful marketing tool, through which people can purchase items as small as books and as large as automobiles. It is a site for vast amounts of documentary material for researchers, reporters, students, and others. And it is, finally, a highly democratic medium through which virtually anyone with access to a personal computer can establish a website and present information in a form that is available to virtually anyone in the world who chooses to look at it. New technologies that make it easier to transmit moving images over the Internet—and new forms of "broadband" access that give more users high-speed connections to the Web—promise to expand greatly the functions that the Internet can perform.

Breakthroughs in Genetics

13   Aided in part by computer technology, there was explosive growth in another area of scientific research: genetics. Early discoveries in genetics by Gregor Mendel, Thomas Hunt Morgan, and others laid the groundwork for more dramatic breakthroughs—the discovery of DNA by the British scientists Oswald Avery, Cohn MacLeod, and Maclyn McCarty in 1944; and in 1953, the dramatic discovery by the American biochemist James Watson and the British biophysicist Francis Crick of the double-helix structure of DNA, and thus of the key to identifying genetic codes. From these discoveries emerged the new science—and ultimately the new industry—of genetic engineering, through which new medical treatments and new techniques for hybridization of plants and animals have already become possible.

14   Little by little, scientists began to identify specific genes in humans and other living things that determine particular traits and to learn how to alter or reproduce them. But the identification of genes was painfully slow, and in 1989, the federal government appropriated $3 billion to fund the National Center for the Human Genome to accelerate the mapping of human genes. The Human Genome Project set out to identify all of the more than 100,000 genes by 2005. But new technologies for research and competition from other projects (some of them funded by pharmaceutical companies) drove the project forward faster than expected. In 1998, the genome project announced that it would finish its work in 2003. In the meantime, in 2000, other researchers produced a list of all the genes in the human body, even if their relationship to one another remained unmapped.

15 In the meantime, DNA research had already attracted considerable public attention. In 1997, scientists in Scotland announced that they had cloned a sheep—which they named Dolly—using a cell from an adult ewe; in other words, the genetic structure of the newborn Dolly was identical to that of the sheep from which the cell was taken. The DNA structure of an individual, scientists have discovered, is as unique and as identifiable as a fingerprint. DNA testing, therefore, makes it possible to identify individuals through their blood, semen, skin, or even hair. It played a major role first in the O.J. Simpson trial in 1995 and then in the 1998 investigation into President Clinton's relationship with Monica Lewinsky. Also in 1998, DNA testing appeared to establish with certainty that Thomas Jefferson had fathered a child with his slave Sally Hemings, by finding genetic similarities between descendants of both, thus resolving a political and scholarly dispute stretching back nearly two hundred years. Genetic research has already spawned important new areas of medical treatment and has helped the relatively new biotechnology industry to grow into one of the nation's most important economic sectors. Eventually, scientists expect the research to open up vast new areas for medical treatment—and also controversial new possibilities for genetically designing foods, animals, and even humans.

16 But genetic research was also the source of great controversy. Many people grew uneasy about the predictions that the new science might give scientists the ability to alter aspects of life that had previously seemed outside the reach of human control. Some critics feared genetic research on religious grounds, seeing it as an interference with God's plan. Others used moral arguments and expressed fears that it would allow parents, for example, to choose what kinds of children they would have. And a particularly heated controversy emerged over the way in which scientists obtained genetic material. One of the most promising areas of medical research involved the use of stem cells, genetic material obtained in large part from undeveloped fetuses, mostly fetuses created by couples attempting *in vitro* fertilization. *(In vitro* fertilization is the process by which couples unable to conceive a child have a fetus conceived outside the womb using their eggs and sperm and then implanted in the mother.)

17 Supporters of stem-cell research—which showed promising signs of offering cures for Parkinson's disease, Alzheimer's disease, ALS, and other previously incurable illnesses—argued that the stem cells they used came from fetuses that would otherwise be discarded, since *in vitro* fertilization always produces many more fetuses than can be used. The controversy over stem-cell research became an issue in the 2000 presidential campaign. George W. Bush, once president, kept his promise to antiabortion advocates and in the summer of 2001 issued a ruling barring the use of federal funds to support research using any stem cells that scientists were not already using at the time of his decision.

A Changing Society

18 The changes in the economy were one of many factors producing major changes in the character of American society. By the end of the twentieth century, the American population was growing larger, older, and more racially and geographically diverse.

The Graying of America

19 One of the most important, if often unnoticed, features of American life in the late twentieth century was the aging of the American population. After decades of steady growth, the nation's birthrate began to decline in the 1970s and remained low through the 1980s and 1990s. In 1970, there were 18.4 births for every 1,000 people in the population. By 1996, the rate had dropped to 14.8 births. The declining birthrate and a significant rise in life expectancy produced a substantial increase in the proportion of elderly citizens. Almost 13 percent of the population was more than sixty-five years old in 2000, as compared with 8 percent in 1970. The median age in 2000 was 35.3, the highest in the nation's history. In 1970, it was 28.0.

20 The aging of the population had important, if not entirely predictable, implications. It was, for example, a cause of the increasing costliness of Social Security pensions. It meant rapidly increasing health costs, both for the federal Medicare system and for private hospitals and insurance companies, and was one of the principal reasons for the anxiety about health-care costs that played such a crucial role in the politics of the early 1990s. It ensured that the elderly,

The American Birthrate, 1960–2000

This chart shows the sharp decline of the nation's birthrate during the period between 1960 and 1975. This was a striking change in the pattern of the nation's birthrate from the twenty years after 1940, which produced the great "baby boom."

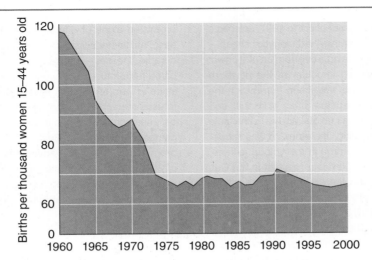

who already formed one of the most powerful interest groups in America, would remain politically formidable well into the twenty-first century.

21   It also had important implications for the nature of the workforce in the twenty-first century. In the last twenty years of the twentieth century, the number of people aged 25 to 54 in the native-born workforce in the United States grew by over 26 million. In the first ten years of the twenty-first century, the number of workers in that age group will not grow at all. That will put increasing pressure on the economy to employ more older workers. It will also create a greater demand for immigrant workers.

New Patterns of Immigration and Ethnicity

22   The enormous change in both the extent and the character of immigration was one of the most dramatic social developments of the last decades of the twentieth century. The nation's immigration quotas expanded significantly in those years (partly to accommodate refugees from Southeast Asia and other nations), allowing more newcomers to enter the United States legally than at any point since the beginning of the twentieth century. In 2000, over 28 million Americans—over 10 percent of the total population—consisted of immigrants (people born outside the United States).

23   Equally striking was the character of the new immigration. The Immigration Reform Act of 1965 had eliminated quotas based on national origin; from then on, newcomers from regions other than Latin America were generally admitted on a first-come, first-served basis. In 1965, 90 percent of the immigrants to the United States came from Europe. By the mid-1980s, only 10 percent of the new arrivals were Europeans, although that figure rose slightly in the 1990s as emigrants from Russia and eastern Europe—now free to leave their countries—came in increasing numbers. The extent and character of the new immigration were causing a dramatic change in the composition of the American population. By the end of the twentieth century, people of white European background constituted under 80 percent of the population (as opposed to 90 percent a half-century before).

24   Particularly important to the new immigration were two groups: Latinos (people from Spanish-speaking nations, particularly Mexico) and Asians. Both had been significant segments of the American population for many decades—Latinos since the beginning of the nation's history, Asians since the waves of Chinese and Japanese immigration in the nineteenth

Naturalization, 1996   On September 17, 1996, ten thousand people, representing 113 different countries, were sworn in as U.S. citizens in Texas Stadium near Dallas, the largest naturalization ceremony in the nation's history. They were part of over 1 million immigrants who became American citizens in 1996, which was also a record (and was more than twice the number naturalized in any previous year). The high number of new citizens was a result of the dramatic increase in immigration over the previous two decades. It was also a result of fears among many immigrants that restrictive new laws would deny them important benefits (including education for their children) if they did not become citizens.

century. But both groups experienced enormous, indeed unprecedented, growth after 1965. People from Latin America constituted more than a third of the total number of legal immigrants to the United States in every year after 1965—and a much larger proportion of the total number of illegal immigrants. Mexico alone accounted for over one-fourth of all the immigrants living in the United States in 2000. In California and the Southwest, in particular, Mexicans became an increasingly important presence. There were also substantial Latino populations in Illinois, New York, and Florida. High birthrates within Latino communities already in the United States further increased their numbers. In the 1980 census, 6 percent of the population (about 14 million) was listed as being of Hispanic origin. By 1997, census figures showed an increase

to 11 percent, or 29 million people. In the 1980s and 1990s, Asian immigrants arrived in even greater numbers than Latinos, constituting more than 40 percent of the total of legal newcomers. They swelled the already substantial Chinese and Japanese communities in California and elsewhere. And they created substantial new communities of immigrants from Vietnam, Thailand, Cambodia, Laos, the Philippines, Korea, and India. By 2000, there were more than 10 million Asian Americans in the United States (4 percent of the population), more than twice the number of fifteen years before. Like Latinos they were concentrated mainly in large cities and in the West. Many of the new Asian immigrants were refugees, including Vietnamese driven from their homes in the aftermath of the disastrous war in which the United States had so long been involved.

Total Immigration, 1961–2000

This chart shows the tremendous increase in immigration to the United States in the decades since the Immigration Reform Act of 1965. The immigration of the 1980s and 1990s was the highest since the late nineteenth century.

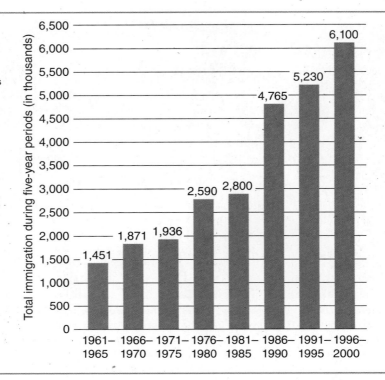

Sources of Immigration, 1960–1990

The Immigration Reform Act of 1965 lifted the national quotas imposed on immigration policy in 1924 and opened immigration to large areas of the world that had previously been restricted. In 1965, 90 percent of the immigrants to the United States came from Europe. As this chart shows, by 1990 almost the reverse was true. Over 80 percent of all immigrants came from non-European sources.

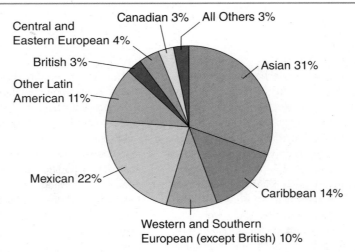

The Black Middle Class

25   The civil rights movement and the other liberal efforts of the 1960s had two very different effects on African Americans. On the one hand, there were increased opportunities for advancement available to those in a position to take advantage of them. On the other hand, as the industrial economy declined and government services dwindled, there was a growing sense of helplessness and despair among the large groups of nonwhites who continued to find themselves barred from upward mobility.

26   For the black middle class, which by the end of the twentieth century constituted over half of the African American population of America, progress was remarkable in the thirty years since the high point of the civil rights movement. Disparities between black and white professionals did not vanish, but they diminished substantially. African American families moved into more affluent urban communities and, in many cases, into suburbs—at times as neighbors of whites, more often into predominantly black communities. The number of African Americans attending college rose by 350 percent in the decade following the passage of the civil rights acts (in contrast to a 150 percent increase among whites); African Americans made up 12 percent of the college population in the 1990s (up from 5 percent twenty-five years earlier). The percentage of black high school graduates going on to college was virtually the same as that of white high school graduates by the end of the twentieth century (although a far smaller proportion of blacks than whites managed to complete high school). And African Americans were making rapid strides in many professions from which, a generation earlier, they had been barred or within which they had been segregated. In increasing numbers, they were becoming partners in major law firms and joining the staffs of major hospitals and the faculties of major universities. Nearly half of all employed blacks in the United States had skilled white-collar jobs. There were few areas of American life from which blacks were any longer entirely excluded. Middle-class blacks, in other words, had realized great gains from the legislation of the 1960s, from the changing national mood on race, from the creation of controversial affirmative action programs, and from their own strenuous efforts.

Poor and Working-Class African Americans

27   But the rise of the black middle class also accentuated (and perhaps even helped cause) the increasingly desperate plight of other African Americans, whom the economic growth and the liberal programs of the 1960s and beyond had never reached. These impoverished people—sometimes described as the "underclass"—made up as much as a third of the nation's black population. Many of them lived in isolated, decaying, and desperately poor inner-city neighborhoods. As more successful blacks moved out of the inner cities, the poor were left virtually alone in their decaying neighborhoods. Fewer than half of young inner-city blacks finished high school; more than 60 percent were unemployed. The black family structure suffered as well from the dislocations of urban poverty. There was a radical increase in the number of single-parent, female-headed black households. In 1970, 59 percent of all black children under 18 lived with both their parents (already down from 70 percent a decade earlier). In 2000, only 38 percent of black children lived in such households, while 75 percent of white children did.

28   Nonwhites were disadvantaged by many factors in the changing social and economic climate of the 1980s and 1990s. Among them was a growing impatience with affirmative action and other programs designed to advance their fortunes. They suffered as well from a steady decline in the number of unskilled jobs in the economy, the departure of businesses from their neighborhoods, the absence of adequate transportation to areas where jobs were more plentiful, and failing schools that did not prepare them adequately for employment. And they suffered, in some cases, from a sense of futility and despair, born of years of entrapment in brutal urban ghettoes.

Modern Plagues: Drugs and AIDS

29   The new immigrants of the 1980s and 1990s arrived in cities being ravaged by two new and deadly epidemics. One was a dramatic increase in drug use, which penetrated nearly every community in the nation. The enormous demand for drugs, and particularly for "crack" cocaine, spawned what was in effect

a multibillion-dollar industry, and those reaping the enormous profits of the illegal trade fought strenuously and often savagely to protect their positions. Political figures of both parties spoke heatedly about the need for a "war on drugs," but in the absence of significant funding for such programs, government efforts appeared to be having little effect. Drug use declined significantly among middle-class people beginning in the late 1980s, but the epidemic showed no signs of abating in the poor urban neighborhoods where it was doing the most severe damage.

30   The drug epidemic was directly related to another scourge of the 1980s and 1990s: the epidemic spread of a new and lethal disease first documented in 1981 and soon named AIDS (acquired immune deficiency syndrome). AIDS is the product of the HIV virus, which is transmitted by the exchange of bodily fluids (blood or semen). The virus gradually destroys the body's immune system and makes its victims highly vulnerable to a number of diseases (particularly to various forms of cancer and pneumonia) to which they would otherwise have a natural resistance. Those infected with the virus (i.e., HIV positive) can live for a long time without developing AIDS, but for many years those who became ill were virtually certain to die.

31   The first American victims of AIDS (and for many years the group among whom cases remained the most numerous) were homosexual men. But by the late 1980s, as the gay community began to take preventive measures, the most rapid increase in the spread of the disease occurred among heterosexuals, many of them intravenous drug users who spread the virus by sharing contaminated hypodermic needles. In 2000, U.S. government agencies estimated that about 780,000 Americans were infected with the HIV virus and that another 427,000 had already died from the disease. But the United States represented only a tiny proportion of the worldwide total of people afflicted with AIDS, an estimated 36.1 million people at the end of 2000. Seventy percent (over 25 million) of those cases were concentrated in Africa. Governments and private groups, in the meantime, began promoting AIDS awareness in increasingly visible and graphic ways—urging young people, in particular, to avoid "unsafe sex" through abstinence or the use of latex condoms. The success of that effort in the United States was suggested by the drop in new cases from 70,000 in 1995 to approximately 40,000 in 2000.

32   In the mid-1990s, AIDS researchers, after years of frustration, began discovering effective treatments for the disease. By taking a combination of powerful drugs on a rigorous schedule, among them a group known as protease inhibitors, even people with relatively advanced cases of AIDS experienced dramatic improvement—so much so that in many cases there were no measurable quantities of the virus left in their bloodstreams. The new drugs gave promise for the first time of dramatically extending the lives of people with AIDS, perhaps to normal life spans. The drugs were not a cure for AIDS; people who stopped taking them experienced a rapid return of the disease. And the effectiveness of the drugs varied from person to person. In addition, the drugs were very expensive and difficult to administer; poorer AIDS patients often could not obtain access to them, and they remained very scarce in Africa and other less affluent parts of the world where the epidemic was rampant. Nevertheless, the new medications restored hundreds of thousands of desperately ill people to health and gave them realistic hopes of long and relatively normal lives.

The Decline in Crime

33   One of the most striking social developments of the late 1990s was also one of the least expected: a dramatic reduction in crime rates across most of the United States. The rising incidence of violent crime had been one of the most disturbing facts of American life for two generations—and a central fact of national politics since at least the 1960s. But beginning in the early 1990s, crime began to fall—in many cities, quite dramatically. The government's crime index—which measures the incidence of seven serious crimes—fell by 19.5 percent between 1992 and 2000, with some of the most dramatic reductions occurring in murder and other violent crimes.

34   There was no agreement about the causes of this unexpected reduction. Prosperity and declining unemployment were certainly factors. So were new, sophisticated police techniques that helped deter many crimes and that led to the arrest of many criminals who would previously have escaped capture. New incarceration

SELECTION 10.1

policies—longer, tougher sentences and fewer paroles and early releases for violent criminals—led to a radical increase in the prison population and, consequently, a reduction in the number of criminals at liberty to commit crimes. Whatever the reason, the decline in crime—when combined with the booming prosperity of the 1990s, which (however unequally distributed) affected most Americans at least to some degree—helped produce an unusual level of social contentment, as recorded in public opinion surveys, in the late 1990s and in 2000. In stark contrast to the late 1970s, and even the 1980s, most Americans expressed general contentment with the state of their society and optimism about the future until at least September 2001.

The Perils of Globalization

35   The celebration of the beginning of a new millennium on January 1, 2000, was a notable moment not just because of the dramatic change in the calendar. It was notable above all as a global event—a shared and for the most part joyous experience that united the world in its exuberance. Television viewers around the world followed the dawn of the new millennium from Australia, through Asia, Africa, and Europe, and on into the Americas. Never had the world seemed more united. But if the millennium celebrations suggested the bright promise of globalization, other events at the dawn of the new century suggested its dark perils.

Opposing the "New World Order"

36   In the United States and other industrial nations, opposition to globalization—or to what President George H. W. Bush once called the "new world order"—took several forms. To many Americans on both the left and the right, the nation's increasingly interventionist foreign policy was deeply troubling. Critics on the left charged that the United States was using military action to advance its economic interests, most notably in the 1991 Gulf War. Critics on the right claimed that the nation was allowing itself to be swayed by the interests of other nations; they opposed such supposedly humanitarian interventions as the 1993 invasion of Somalia and the American interventions in the Balkans in the late 1990s—both because

they insisted no vital American interests were at stake and because they feared that the United States was ceding its sovereignty in these actions to international organizations. But the most impassioned opposition to globalization in the West came from an array of groups that challenged the claim that the "new world order" was economically beneficial. Environmentalists argued that globalization, in exporting industry to low-wage countries, also exported industrial pollution and toxic waste into nations that had no effective laws to control them. And still others opposed global economic arrangements on the grounds that they enriched and empowered large multinational corporations and threatened the freedom and autonomy of individuals and communities.

37   The varied opponents of globalization may have had different reasons for their hostility. However, they were agreed on the targets of their discontent: not just free-trade agreements, but also the multinational institutions that policed and advanced the global economy.

The Rise of Islamic Fundamentalism

38   Outside the industrialized West, the impact of globalization created other concerns. Many citizens of nonindustrialized nations resented the way the world economy had left them in poverty and, in their view, exploited and oppressed. But in some parts of the nonindustrialized world—and particularly in some of the Islamic nations of the Middle East—the increasing reach of globalization created additional grievances, less rooted in economics than in religion and culture.

39   The Iranian Revolution of 1979, in which orthodox Muslims ousted a despotic government whose leaders had embraced many aspects of modern Western culture, was one of the first large and visible manifestations of a phenomenon that would eventually reach across much of the Islamic world and threaten the stability of the globe. In one Islamic nation after another, waves of fundamentalist orthodoxy emerged to defend traditional culture against incursions from the West. The new fundamentalism met considerable resistance within Islam—from established governments, from affluent middle classes that had made their peace with the modern industrial world, from women

who feared the antifeminist agenda of many of these movements. But it emerged nevertheless as a powerful force—and in a few nations, among them Iran after 1979 and Afghanistan in the late 1990s—the dominant force.

40   Islamic fundamentalism is a complex phenomenon and takes many different forms, but among some particularly militant fundamentalists, the battle to preserve orthodoxy came to be defined as a battle against the West generally and the United States in particular. Resentment of the West was rooted in the incursion of new and, in their view, threatening cultural norms into traditional societies. It was rooted as well in resentment of the support Western nations gave to corrupt and tyrannical regimes in some Islamic countries and in opposition to Western (and particularly American) economic and military incursions into the region. The continuing struggle between Palestinians and Israelis—a struggle defined in the eyes of many Muslims by American support for Israel—added further to their contempt.

41   One product of this combination of resentments was individuals and groups committed to using violence to fight the influence of the West. No fundamentalist movement had any advanced military capabilities. Militants resorted instead to isolated incidents of violence and mayhem, designed to disrupt societies and governments and to create fear among their peoples. Such tactics became known to the world as terrorism.

The Rise of Terrorism

42   The United States has experienced terrorism for many years, much of it against American targets abroad. These included the bombing of the Marine barracks in Beirut in 1983, the explosion that brought down an American airliner over Lockerbie, Scotland, in 1988, the bombing of American embassies in 1998, the assault on the U.S. naval vessel *Cole* in 2000, and other events around the world. Terrorist incidents were relatively rare, but not unknown, within the United States itself prior to September 11, 2001. Militants on the American left performed various acts of terror in the 1960s and early 1970s. In February 1993, a bomb exploded in the parking garage of the World Trade Center in New York, killing six people and causing serious, but no irreparable, structural damage to the towers. Several men connected with militant Islamic organizations were convicted of the crime. In April 1995, a van containing explosives blew up in front of a federal building in Oklahoma City, killing 168 people. Timothy McVeigh, a former Marine who had become part of a militant antigovernment movement of the American right, was convicted of the crime and eventually executed in 2001.

43   Most Americans, however, considered terrorism a problem that mainly plagued other nations. Few thought about it as an important concern in their own country. One of the many results of the terrible events of September 11, 2001, was to jolt the American people out of complacency and alert them to the presence of continuing danger. That awareness increased in the weeks after September 11. New security measures began to change the way in which Americans traveled. New government regulations began to alter immigration policies and to affect the character of international banking. Warnings of possible new terrorist attacks created widespread tension and uneasiness. A puzzling and frightening epidemic of anthrax—a potent bacterial agent that can cause illness and death if not properly treated—began in the weeks after September 11 and spread through the mail to media outlets, members of Congress, and seemingly random others.

44   In the meantime, the United States government launched what President George W. Bush called a "war against terrorism." The attacks on the World Trade Center and the Pentagon, government intelligence indicated, had been planned and orchestrated by Middle Eastern agents of a powerful terrorist network known as Al Qaeda. Its leader, Osama Bin Laden—until 2001 little known outside the Arab world—quickly became one of the best known and most notorious figures in the world. Fighting a shadowy terrorist network spread out among many nations of the world was a difficult task, and the administration made clear from the beginning that the battle would be waged in many ways, not just militarily. But the first visible act of the war against terrorism was, in fact, a military one. Convinced that the militant "Taliban" government of Afghanistan had sheltered and supported Bin Laden

and his organization, the United States began a sustained campaign of bombing against the regime and sent in small numbers of ground troops to help a resistance organization overthrow the Afghan government. This first battle in the struggle against terrorism produced a surprisingly quick military victory. Afghanistan's Taliban regime collapsed, and its leaders—along with the Al Qaeda fighters allied with them—fled the capital, Kabul. American and anti-Taliban Afghan troops pursued them into the mountains, but were, at least at first, unable to find Bin Laden and the other leaders of his organization. In the aftermath of this speedy victory, however, American forces found themselves caught up in the instability of factionalized Afghanistan. While continuing to pursue terrorists, they also had to deal with infighting among the new leaders of the nation.

45   In his State of the Union Address to Congress in January 2002, President Bush spoke of an "axis of evil," which included the nations of Iraq, Iran, and North Korea—all nations with anti-American regimes, all nations that either possessed or were thought to be trying to acquire nuclear weapons. Although Bush did not say so, many people—both in America and elsewhere—took his words to mean that the United States would soon try to topple the government of Saddam Hussein in Iraq. In 2003, U.S. military forces did, in fact, invade Iraq and depose Iraqi dictator Saddam Hussein.

A New Era?

46   In the immediate aftermath of September 11, 2001, many Americans came to believe that they had entered a new era in their history. The instability that had plagued so much of the rest of the world for years seemed suddenly to have arrived in the United States, shattering longstanding assumptions about safety and security and opening a period of uncertainty and fear. Prospects for the future were clouded further by a significant weakening of the economy that was already well advanced before September 11 and that the events of that day helped to increase.

47   But fear and uncertainty were not the only results of the September 11 attacks. The reaction to the catastrophe—in New York, in Washington, and in much of the rest of the country—exposed a side of

American life and culture that had always existed but that had not always been visible during the booming, self-indulgent years of the 1980s and 1990s. Americans responded to the tragedies with countless acts of courage and generosity, large and small, and with a sense of national unity and commitment that seemed, at least for a time, to resemble the unity and commitment at the beginning of World War II. The displays of courage began with the heroism of firefighters and rescue workers in New York City, who unhesitatingly plunged into the burning towers of the World Trade Center in an effort to save the people inside. Over 300 such workers died when the towers collapsed. In the weeks after the disaster, New York was flooded with volunteers—welders, metal workers, police, firefighters, medical personnel, and many others—who flocked to the city from around the country and the world to assist with rescue and recovery. Charitable donations to help the victims of the disasters exceeded $1 billion, the largest amount ever raised for a single purpose in such a short time in American history. Open and unembarrassed displays of patriotism and national pride—things that many Americans had once scorned—suddenly became fashionable again. Faith in government and its leaders, in decline for decades, suddenly surged. "Nothing has changed. . . . Everything has changed," wrote one prominent journalist in the weeks after September 11. In fact, no one could reliably predict whether the catastrophe would prove to be a fundamental turning point in the course of American and world history or simply another in the countless changes and adjustments, great and small, that have characterized the nation's experience for centuries.

Conclusion

48   Americans entered the twenty-first century afflicted with many anxieties, doubts, and resentments. Faith in the nation's institutions—most notably, government—was at its lowest point in many decades. Vague resentments over the increasingly unequal patterns of income and wealth in the new economy, which few Americans seemed able to translate into a coherent economic agenda, increased the nation's unease.

49   But the United States at the end of the twentieth century was, despite its many problems, a remarkably successful society. It had made dramatic strides in improving the lives of its citizens and in dealing with many of its social problems since the end of World War II. It entered the new century with the strongest economy in the world, with violent crime—one of its most corrosive problems for more than a generation—in a marked decline, and with its international power and stature unrivaled.

50   The traumatic events of September 11, 2001, changed many aspects of American life, not least the nation's sense of its isolation, and insulation, from the problems of the rest of the world. But both the many long-standing problems and the many long-standing strengths of the United States survived the attacks. It seemed safe to predict that the American people would go forward into their suddenly uncertain future not simply burdened by difficult challenges, but also armed with great wealth, great power, and perhaps most of all with the extraordinary energy and resilience that has allowed the nation—throughout its long and often turbulent history—to endure, to flourish, and to strive continually for a better future.

History
(continued)

Selecting and Organizing Textbook Information: Chapter-Length Selection

Directions: Refer to Selection 10.1 as necessary to complete the following activities.

Option for collaboration: Your instructor may direct you to work with other students on one or more of these items, or in other words, to work collaboratively. In that case, you should form groups of three or four students, as directed by your instructor, and work together to complete the exercises. After your group discusses an item and agrees on the answer, have a group member record it. Each member of your group should be able to explain *all* of your group's answers.

The chapter-length selection "The Age of Globalization" contains the following sections and subsections:

September 11, 2001	Introduction
Timeline of Significant Events	Table
Globalization of the Economy	Paragraphs 1–3
Science and Technology in the New Economy	Paragraphs 4–17
The Personal Computer	
The Internet	
Breakthroughs in Genetics	
A Changing Society	Paragraphs 18–34
The Graying of America	
New Patterns of Immigration and Ethnicity	
The Black Middle Class	
Poor and Working-Class African Americans	
Modern Plagues: Drugs and AIDS	
The Decline in Crime	
The Perils of Globalization	Paragraphs 35–45
Opposing the "New World Order"	
The Rise of Islamic Fundamentalism	
The Rise of Terrorism	
A New Era	Paragraphs 46–47
Conclusion	Paragraphs 48–50

1. Your instructor will give you specific instructions for completing one or more of the following activities in order to apply the skills that you learned in this chapter:

    *   Reread the section "Globalization of the Economy" (paragraphs 1–3), and then **mark** (underline or highlight) and **annotate** it. You should underline or highlight only stated main ideas. If a paragraph has an implied main idea, formulate the main idea and write it in the margin. Number the major details in each paragraph. *See pages 694–97 for guidelines for marking and annotating textbooks.*

    *   Create a detailed **formal outline** of the three paragraphs in the section "Globalization of the Economy" (paragraphs 1–3). Your outline should be titled "Globalization of the Economy." Your outline should consist of the main idea for each of the three paragraphs and the major details for each main idea. *See pages 697–98 for guidelines for outlining.*

    *   Write a one-paragraph **summary** of the section "Globalization of the Economy" (paragraphs 1–3). Your summary should be titled "Globalization of the Economy," and it should consist of the three main ideas in this section. *See page 706 for guidelines for summarizing.*

    *   Create a **study map** of the section "Science and Technology in the New Economy" (paragraphs 4–17). Your study map should contain the three major topics indicated in the three subheadings and also include some of the major details. *See pages 703–5 for guidelines for mapping.*

    *   Create a **topic outline** of the section "A Changing Society" (paragraphs 18–34). Your topic outline should contain *only* the six subheadings of this section and no main ideas or details. Use the Roman numerals I, II, III, IV, V, and VI for your topic outline.

    *   Take **Cornell notes** for the subsection "Modern Plagues: Drugs and AIDS" (paragraphs 29–32). Use the subheading "Modern Plagues: Drugs and AIDS" as the title for your notes. Your notes, which will appear to the right of the review column, should list the four main points (the main idea of each of the four paragraphs) and their major details. The review column should contain the topics of the four paragraphs:

        *   The drug epidemic
        *   The disease of AIDS
        *   AIDS in America and worldwide
        *   AIDS treatment

    See pages 698–702 for guidelines for using the Cornell note-taking method.

2. Your instructor may distribute a practice quiz on one or more sections of the selection "The Age of Globalization." Use any outlines, maps, notes, and summaries you have created to review (study) for this quiz. (Your instructor may also allow you to use your summaries, outlines, notes, and study maps when you take the quiz.)

CHAPTER 11

Rehearsing Textbook Information and Preparing for Tests

In this chapter, you will learn the answers to these questions:

- Why is rehearsal important to memory?

- What are the important guidelines for test preparation?

- What is the five-day test review plan?

- How can I use review cards to prepare for a test?

- How can I consolidate important information on test review sheets?

SKILLS

Rehearsal and Memory

Studying for Tests

- General Guidelines
- Five-Day Test Review Plan
- Creating Review Cards to Prepare for a Test
- Creating Test Review Sheets

CREATING YOUR SUMMARY

Developing Chapter Review Cards

AVAILABLE AT THE ONLINE LEARNING CENTER

Selection 11.1   "Cultural Diversity: Family Strengths and Challenges"
from *Marriages and Families: Intimacy, Diversity, and Strengths*
by David Olson and John DeFrain (Marriage and Family)

Little strokes fell great oaks.

Benjamin Franklin

No great thing is created suddenly.

Epictetus

Memory is the mother of all wisdom.

Aeschylus

REHEARSAL AND MEMORY

long-term memory

Permanent memory.

short-term memory

Temporary memory.

rehearsal

Steps taken to transfer information into long-term memory; techniques include saying the information aloud and writing it down.

As you have undoubtedly discovered, it is difficult to memorize information you do not understand. This is why you must focus on understanding material before attempting to memorize it. But understanding what you read does not mean you will automatically remember it. Thorough comprehension, however, enables you to memorize the material more efficiently.

Even when you understand material, you should not underestimate the time or effort needed to memorize it. You must study information effectively enough to store it in **long-term memory,** or permanent memory. One serious mistake students make is not leaving enough time before a test to transfer material into long-term memory. Instead, they try to rely on **short-term memory,** or temporary memory. If you rely on short-term memory—*cramming*—the information may not be there when you try to recall it during a test.

To understand the difference between long-term and short-term memory, consider a telephone number you have just heard on the radio. It is only in short-term memory and will be forgotten in a matter of seconds *unless you do something to transfer it into long-term memory.* In other words, you will forget it unless you rehearse it in some way.

Rehearsal refers to taking specific steps to transfer information into long-term memory, such as writing it down and repeatedly reciting it aloud. Consider how much information you already have stored in long-term memory: the alphabet; the multiplication tables; names of innumerable people, places, and things; and meanings and spellings of thousands of words. You have successfully stored them in long-term memory because you rehearsed them again and again.

As noted in Chapter 10, rehearsal is the third key to effective studying. When you prepare for a test, you should study over several days. This allows you enough time to transfer information into long-term memory. Psychologists emphasize that both sufficient time and ample repetition are needed to accomplish this transfer.

Before you can rehearse textbook information efficiently, you need to *organize* it. Obviously, the better you organize material, the more efficiently you will be able to memorize it. If you organize the material in your assignments consistently and from the beginning of the semester, you will be prepared to rehearse and memorize material for tests. You can organize material by using any of these techniques:

- Underlining and annotating textbook material
- Outlining or mapping information
- Preparing summaries

Effective rehearsal requires taking specific steps to transfer information into long-term memory.

- Making review cards
- Making test review sheets

Underlining, annotating, outlining, mapping, and summarizing are discussed in Chapter 10; review cards and test review sheets are discussed below. The very act of preparing these study tools helps you store information in long-term memory.

After you have organized material, rehearse it by doing one or more of the following:

- Reciting from review cards
- Reciting from test review sheets
- Reciting from your notes
- Writing out information from memory

Too often, students try to review for a test simply by rereading their notes and textbook over and over again. But rereading is time-consuming and it does not automatically result in remembering. It has been estimated that 80 percent of the time spent studying for a test should be used for memorizing, that is, for transferring information into long-term memory. Here is an example of how you could apply this "80 percent rule." If you need 5 hours to study for a test, you should spend the first hour organizing the material and getting help with things you do not understand. The remaining 4 hours should be spent rehearsing the material in order to memorize it.

How can you tell when you have successfully transferred information into long-term memory? Test yourself. Try writing the information from memory on a blank sheet of paper. If the material is in long-term memory, you will be able to recall it and write it down. If you cannot write it, or can write only a part of it, then you need to rehearse it further.

These steps may sound like a lot of work, but they are necessary if you want to lock information into long-term memory. It is precisely this type of study effort that leads to mastery.

STUDYING FOR TESTS

General Guidelines

This chapter presents a five-day test review plan, but the day to begin studying for a test is the first day of the semester. That means attending all classes, reading every assignment, taking good notes, and reviewing regularly. The review plan described here is designed to complement your careful day-to-day preparation. No review plan can make up for inadequate daily studying and preparation. Following are a few more points you should be aware of before you examine the review plan itself.

First, one reason to start reviewing several days ahead of time is that the amount of material covered is too much to learn at the last minute. In fact, in college you are typically given new material right up to the day of a test.

Second, it is appropriate to ask your instructor what type of test will be given and what will be included on it. Usually, instructors are willing to give a fairly complete description of tests. Don't miss the opportunity to ask questions such as:

- Will the test be based on textbook material, on class material (lectures, demonstrations, etc.), or on both?
- How many textbook chapters will the test cover?
- What will the format be (multiple-choice questions, essay questions, etc.)?
- How many questions will there be?
- Should certain topics be emphasized in studying?

Third, be realistic about test anxiety, or freezing up, when you take a test. Students often complain that they "go blank" on tests, but what really happens is that they discover during the test that they did not prepare well enough. They did not actually forget; after all, you can't forget something you never knew. Good daily preparation and an effective test review plan are the best ways to prevent test anxiety. Knowing what to expect on a test can also leave you feeling calmer, and this is another reason for asking questions about tests.

distributed practice

Study sessions that are spaced out over time; a more efficient study method than massed practice.

Fourth, research studies show that **distributed practice** is more effective than *massed practice.* This simply means that study and review sessions that are spaced out are more effective than a single long session done all at once. Earlier in this chapter, *cramming* was described as trying to rely on short-term memory. Cramming can also be thought of as massed rather than distributed practice. Frantic, last-minute cramming results in faulty understanding, poor recall, increased anxiety, and lower grades.

Fifth, to study and review efficiently, you must be rested. Staying up all night cramming can do more harm than good: It exhausts you, increases stress, and contributes to test anxiety. It also forces you to rely on short-term memory, which can fail under the pressure of fatigue and stress. Try to get at least 8 hours of sleep the night before a test. On the day of the test, eat a good breakfast, such as fruit or juice, whole-grain cereal or bread, and yogurt, eggs, or low-fat milk. It is especially important to get enough protein. Don't rely on caffeine; avoid sugary, salty, and fatty foods. Adequate rest and a nourishing breakfast give you sustained energy and help you concentrate and think clearly.

A final word: Your attitude toward tests can make a big difference. Students often see tests as negative and threatening—even as punishment. Instead, think of a test as a learning experience and an opportunity to demonstrate to yourself and your instructor how much you have learned. When you get a test back, don't look at just the grade. Study it to see what you missed and why. Your performance on a test also gives you an opportunity to evaluate the effectiveness of your test preparation techniques.

Five-Day Test Review Plan

Here is a detailed description of an effective five-day plan for preparing for a test. Although you may need more than five days, that is the least amount of time you should allow.

Five Days before the Test

Get an overview of all the material that will be on the test. This includes text material, class notes, handouts, and so on. Identify important main ideas and details, and prepare review cards and one or more test review sheets for the material. (Such cards and sheets summarize all the important points you expect to encounter on the test. You will learn to construct review cards and test review sheets later in this chapter.) You might also have a study guide that accompanies your textbook. In any case, try to anticipate questions that may be asked on the test. This is also the time to identify questions and problem areas you need further help on. By starting five days ahead, you allow yourself time to get any help you need from the instructor, a classmate, or a tutor. Plan to spend at least 2 hours studying. Take a 5- to 10-minute break at least once an hour.

Four Days before the Test

Briefly overview all the material that will be covered on the test; then review and rehearse the *first third* of the material in detail. First, review all the material on your review cards and your test review sheet or sheets. Then, as you carefully study the first third of the material, use rehearsal techniques to memorize it and test yourself; that is, write and recite it. Plan to spend at least 2 hours studying. If there are problem areas, get help from a tutor, a classmate, or your instructor.

Three Days before the Test

After a brief overview of all the material, review and rehearse the *second third* of the material in detail. Use the rehearsal techniques of writing and reciting to memorize and test yourself on the material. Plan to spend at least 2 hours studying. If any problem areas still remain, this is the time to clear them up. If you still don't understand, make another attempt to get some additional help.

Two Days before the Test

After a brief overview of all the material, review and rehearse the *last third* of the material in detail. Use the rehearsal techniques of writing and reciting to memorize and test yourself on the material. Plan to spend at least 2 hours studying. Rehearse material in the problem areas that you cleared up earlier.

One Day before the Test

Make a final review of all of the material. Rehearse! Write! Recite! Test yourself! This is your final study session for the test, a full dress rehearsal. Study all of your review cards and test review sheets. At this point, you should be feeling confident about the test. At the end of the day, right before you go to sleep, look through the material one last time. Then get a good night's rest. Resist any temptation to celebrate the completion of your review by watching television or going to a movie or a sports event. These activities create interference that make it harder to recall information when you take the test the next day.

Creating Review Cards to Prepare for a Test

As suggested above, one highly effective way to prepare for a test is to make review cards. You already have some experience with such cards since you have been completing chapter review cards throughout *Opening Doors.*

test review cards

Index cards with an important question on the front and the answer on the back.

Review cards, especially useful in preparing for tests, are index cards with an important question on the front and the answer on the back. The question and answer may have to do with a single main idea and its supporting details, a term and its definition, a name and an identification, a mathematical or chemical formula, and so on. Review cards are an efficient, effective, and convenient way to study for tests. They can be prepared from textbook material or lecture notes.

The boxes on page 770 show a sample review card for an important concept in a sociology textbook. Notice how it focuses on one main idea and its two supporting details. Notice also the format of this card: One side presents a probable test question, and the other side answers the question.

Just as outlining, mapping, and summarizing help you organize material, review cards allow you to arrange material clearly and concisely. Most students prefer to use 3×5-inch or 4×6-inch index cards. Cards this size are convenient to carry and can be reviewed whenever you have spare moments. Some students find it helpful to use a different color for each chapter or course. Other students use different colors for different categories of study material; for instance, vocabulary terms might be on cards of one color, and key people and their accomplishments on cards of another color. You can number your review cards so that they can be easily put back in order. For instance, you may want to set aside cards with especially difficult questions so that you can give them special attention before the test.

If you prefer to create review cards electronically, try Studyblue.com or Quizlet.com. These free websites make it easy to produce vocabulary cards, flashcards, and other review cards for any subject at any level. You can share cards with friends, as well as use cards other students have created. Several million existing

SAMPLE REVIEW CARD: FRONT

Card 5

What are the two levels of sociological analysis?

SAMPLE REVIEW CARD: BACK

The two basic levels of sociological analysis are
microsociology and macrosociology.

Microsociology: Small-scale analysis of data derived
from the study of everyday patterns of
behavior.

Macrosociology: Large-scale analysis of data in which
overall social arrangements are
scrutinized.

cards, all developed by other students, are categorized by subject and are available to everyone. Both have mobile apps.

Review cards help you numerous ways. First, preparing these cards involves writing out information, and the very act of making them helps you rehearse material and commit it to long-term memory. Do not assume, though, that simply making the review cards is a substitute for rehearsing the information on them.

Second, review cards let you concentrate on one small, manageable part of the material at a time. Lecture and textbook material can seem overwhelming if you try to review it all at once before a test or at the end of a semester, but it can be quite manageable in small parts.

Third, review cards are especially useful for memorizing key terms, key events, formulas, and the like. Learning 10 definitions, names, or formulas a week is much easier than trying to learn 150 right before a final exam.

Fourth, review cards are also a good way to review with a study partner, because one partner can "test" the other by asking questions based on the cards. Partners test each other, reciting the answers aloud, until the material becomes familiar. Working with a partner can be highly effective.

Fifth, effective students try to anticipate test questions, and review cards are a good way to guide this effort. Writing an anticipated test question on the front of a card, with the answer on the back, allows you to test yourself before the instructor does.

Sixth, review cards help you identify what you know and what you still need to learn or rehearse further.

To sum up, preparing and using review cards to rehearse and learn information can be an important key to success.

Creating Test Review Sheets

Suppose you are going to take a sociology test that covers a chapter of the textbook and the corresponding class sessions. The instructor has announced that you will be allowed to prepare one page of notes (front *and* back) to use while you are taking the test. How could you consolidate an entire chapter's worth of information on one sheet of paper?

To begin with, consolidating the information on a single test review sheet does *not* mean trying to recopy all the lecture notes, handouts, and textbook material in tiny handwriting. In other words, the question really is "What kind of information should you include on this review sheet?" Preparing the sheet would mean being very selective; it would mean summarizing essential information from different sources, such as the chapter, your own class and textbook notes, and your instructor's handouts.

test review sheet

Single sheet of paper consolidating and summarizing, on its front and back, the most important information to be covered on a test.

This example is imaginary, but you should create a real **test review sheet** whenever you prepare for a test. Try to restrict yourself to a single sheet (front and back), consolidating all the crucial information you would bring to the test if you could. For a test that covers several chapters, though, you might want to prepare one sheet per chapter. Preparing review sheets is in itself a way of selecting, organizing, and rehearsing the material you must learn.

Start by identifying the major topics that will be on the test. Be selective, because you cannot include everything. If you have been preparing review *cards* as you went along, then you have already taken the first step in preparing a test review *sheet,* because you have already identified most of the important information you need. However, you will probably have to condense this information even more to create your test review sheet.

Another way to proceed in making a test review sheet is to list the major topics and most important points about each. If your instructor does not identify the major topics for you, check your lecture notes. You should also refer to the textbook's main table of contents or the chapter-opening table of contents. If your textbook does not have these, check the chapter titles, headings, and subheadings since they outline the chapter.

Next, organize the material you want to include on the sheet. There is no one correct way to organize a test review sheet. However, the material itself often suggests logical ways. For example, a test review sheet can be as simple as a list of major topics with key words for each. It can also consist of a grid of rows and columns, a set of mapped notes, a list of formulas, important terms (with or without definitions), a diagram or sketch, or some combination of these. The key is to organize the material in some way that is meaningful to *you*. And since this is your personal review sheet, feel free to use abbreviations, symbols, underlining, and highlighting in different colors to make the information as clear and helpful to you as possible.

The boxes that follow show entries in a table of contents for one chapter of a sociology text (note the major headings and subheadings) and the front and back of a test review sheet prepared for the chapter.

EXAMPLE: CHAPTER TABLE OF CONTENTS USED TO PREPARE A TEST REVIEW SHEET

Chapter One: Approaches to Sociology

The Sociological Perspective	6
Social Facts and Social Causes	6
The Sociological Imagination	8
Science, Sociology, and Common Sense	9
Levels of Sociological Analysis	10
Basic Sociological Questions	11
What Holds Society Together?	12
What Is the Relationship between the Individual and Society?	13
Summing Up	14
The Origins of Social Theory	14
Rational-Choice Theory	16
The Theory of Karl Marx	17
The Theory of Émile Durkheim	18
The Theory of Max Weber	19
Interactionist Theory	20
Comparing the Founding Theories	21
Founding Theories and Contemporary Sociology	22

Source: From Donald Light, Suzanne Keller, and Craig Calhoun, *Sociology,* 5e, p. xi. Copyright © 1989 by The McGraw-Hill Companies, Inc. Reprinted with permission of The McGraw-Hill Companies, Inc.

SAMPLE TEST REVIEW SHEET (FRONT OF PAGE)

CHAPTER 1—APPROACHES TO SOCIOLOGY

1. SOCIOLOGICAL PERSPECTIVE

Social Facts & Social Causes
    Sociology—systematic study of human societies & behavior in social settings
    Sociological perspective—lets us see how our background, social position, time, &
    place affect how we view world & act—also, who we interact with & how others
    see us
    Sociological facts—properties of group life that can't be explained by indiv
    traits, actions, or feelings. Soc facts emerge from social forces (e.g., concept of
    beauty, romantic love)

Sociological Imagination
    Soc imag—ability to see personal experience in world (pers exper is limited, so we
    shouldn't make hasty generalizations)

Science, Sociology, & Common Sense
    Scientific method used by sociologists—collect data (facts, statistics); develop
    theories
    Theory (th)—systematic formal explanation of how two or more phenomena are
    related
    Local th = narrow aspect; middle-range th = broader; general th = most
    comprehensive (explain how several ths fit together). (Contrast w common
    sense—from pers exper, facts not checked, no organization into ths to be tested.)

Levels of Sociological Analysis
    Microsociology—small-scale analysis of data from everyday behavior patterns
    Macrosociology—large-scale anal of data on overall social arrangements

2. BASIC SOCIOLOGICAL QUESTIONS

What Holds Society Together?
    Functional perspective—different parts of society contribute to whole
    Power perspective—those who control resources prob will shape society to their
    own advantage

What Is Relationship btwn Individuals & Society?
    Structural perspective—indiv choices explained by forces arising from social
organization
    Action perspective—society shaped by people's actions

SAMPLE TEST REVIEW SHEET (BACK OF PAGE)

3. ORIGINS OF SOCIAL THEORY

Rational-Choice Th
  Founder—Adam Smith. People choose & decide for own advantage; soc = self-regulating system; all parts act in own interest; market forces mesh pts into whole
  Expanded by Jeremy Bentham—govt intervention needed to help soc function & let peo benefit from resources

Th of Karl Marx
  Economic system shapes social life, breeds conflict; proletariat (workers) should overcome capitalists (oppressors—owners of resources)

Th of Émile Durkheim
  Human behav explained by soc forces binding society (social solidarity); society held together by interrelated working of pts

Th of Max Weber
  Power comes from diff factors—education, soc connections, etc.; society produced by actions of indivs. Stressed politics & culture (not only econ like Marx)

Interactionist Th
  George Herbert Mead—peo interact depending on how they interpret soc situations; we learn our place in world thru soc interactions; th developed from phenomenology

4. FOUNDING THEORIES & CONTEMPORARY SOCIOLOGY

- Sociologists still influenced by ths above—have expanded orig ths to apply to modern issues
- Some to combine functional and power prespective; structural & action-oriented perspective

DEVELOPING CHAPTER REVIEW CARDS

Complete the five review cards for Chapter 11 by supplying the important information about each topic. When you have completed them, you will have summarized important material about the study skills in this chapter.

Rehearsal and Its Importance to Memory

Card 1   Chapter 11: Rehearsing Textbook Information and Preparing for Tests

Studying for Tests: General Guidelines

Card 2   Chapter 11: Rehearsing Textbook Information and Preparing for Tests

Five-Day Test Review Plan

Card 3   Chapter 11: Rehearsing Textbook Information and Preparing for Tests

Test Review Cards

Card 4   Chapter 11: Rehearsing Textbook Information and Preparing for Tests

Test Review Sheets

Card 5   Chapter 11: Rehearsing Textbook Information and Preparing for Tests

Cultural Diversity: Family Strengths and Challenges

From *Marriages and Families: Intimacy, Diversity, and Strengths*
by David Olson and John DeFrain

Applying the Chapter 11 Skills

Selection 11.1, "Cultural Diversity: Family Strengths and Challenges," appears on the *Opening Doors* Online Learning Center (www.mhhe.com/openingdoors). It is a complete chapter from a marriage and family textbook. Use it to apply some or all of these Chapter 11 skills, according to your instructor's directions:

- Creating test review cards
- Creating a test review sheet
- Creating vocabulary cards

In addition, your instructor may distribute a practice quiz on one or more sections of Selection 11.1. To prepare for the practice quiz, use any test review cards, test review sheets, and vocabulary cards you have created. These tools will help you rehearse the material and transfer it into your long-term memory for the quiz. (Alternatively, your instructor may allow you to use any test review cards, test review sheets, and vocabulary cards you have created when you take the quiz.)

Essential Skills
Review Tests

There are 10 Essential Skills Review Tests. Each consists of a short passage followed by 10 multiple-choice items. The tests enable you to assess your progress in applying the following skills:

- Vocabulary in context
- Stated main ideas
- Supporting details
- Implied main ideas
- Sentence relationships
- Author's writing patterns
- Author's purpose, intended audience, point of view, and tone
- Fact and opinion
- Making inferences and drawing conclusions

Your instructor will direct you in using the tests.

Directions: Read the passage below and then select the best answer for each question.

Credit Scores

1   There is a double risk to you associated with credit card debt. The first is the financial threat posed to you if the debt is maintained over a long period of time. The second is your reputation. Your credit rating is a publicly held record that can be accessed by anyone who might be loaning you money. A poor credit rating can impact many aspects of your life. It can stop you from receiving education loans, a home mortgage, a cell phone account, or a car loan. More importantly, it damages your reputation for a long time.

2   Employers often conduct background checks, which include inquiries about a <u>candidate</u>'s credit rating. Employers check credit scores for a variety of reasons. The way you manage your credit can be an indicator of your honesty and character. For example, banks and investment firms and other companies that require handling large sums of money view poor credit as a risk for theft. How you manage your personal finances tells what type of person you are. Because your credit profile also contains your employment history, employers may use it as a way to verify your previous employment. On the other hand, a good credit score can work in your favor.

3   There are simple steps you can take to manage your debt. Maintain a checking account, and try to pay everything you can from that account on a monthly basis. If you need to have a credit card, have only one. It is so easy to be tempted to apply for more cards because there are always great promotions to tempt you to open a new card. Better than a credit card is a debit card. The debit card enables you to draw money or to have the cost of a purchase charged directly to your bank account. It is used as an alternative method to paying cash. Using a debit card is the safest way to manage your spending, as long as you are able to limit your spending to the amount available to you. Credit and debit cards—and checking accounts—are not a threat to your financial reputation if you use them properly.

Source: Donna Yena, *Career Directions: The Path to Your Ideal Career,* 5e, pp. 78–79. Copyright © 2011 by The McGraw-Hill Companies, Inc. Reprinted with permission of The McGrow-Hill Companies, Inc.

1. As used in paragraph 2, *candidate* refers to a person who:

    a. is running for political office.

    b. has nearly completed the requirements for a degree.

    c. is likely to have a certain fate.

    d. is applying for a job.

_____ **2.** Which sentence in paragraph 1 is the *stated main idea*?

    a. the first sentence
    b. sentence 4
    c. sentence 5
    d. the last sentence

_____ **3.** What is the *implied main idea* of paragraph 2?

    a. There are several reasons employers conduct background checks.
    b. The way you manage your credit can be an indicator of your honesty and character.
    c. When you apply for a job, a good credit score works in your favor.
    d. For a variety of reasons, employers often include a candidate's credit scores in a background check.

_____ **4.** With regard to credit cards, it is recommended that you:

    a. only apply for as many as you can pay on each month.
    b. have only one or use a debit card instead.
    c. pay cash rather than use a credit card.
    d. open a new card only if it offers a great promotion.

_____ **5.** The information in paragraph 1 is organized using which *pattern*?

    a. comparison-contrast
    b. definition and example
    c. cause-effect
    d. sequence

_____ **6.** The *tone* in this passage can be described as:

    a. impassioned.
    b. nostalgic.
    c. critical.
    d. unemotional.

_____ **7.** The author's *purpose* in writing paragraph 3 is to:

    a. instruct readers how to prevent or control their debt.
    b. inform readers about techniques credit card companies use to get people to open new accounts.
    c. persuade readers to pay cash instead of using credit cards.
    d. persuade readers to have only a single credit card.

_____ **8.** Who does the author have in mind as the *audience,* or readers, of this passage?

    a. employers who check credit scores
    b. credit score agencies
    c. people who use credit cards
    d. financial advisors who counsel clients about credit card abuse

9. "It is so easy to be tempted to apply for more cards because there are always great promotions to tempt you to open a new card." The preceding sentence presents:

a. a fact.
b. an opinion.

10. What is the *relationship between these two sentences* in paragraph 2: "The way you manage your credit can be an indicator of your honesty and character. For example, banks and investment firms and other companies that require handling large sums of money view poor credit as a risk for theft"?

a. The second sentence presents a contrast with something in the first sentence.
b. The second sentence makes a comparison with something in the first sentence.
c. The second sentence continues a sequence begun in the first sentence.
d. The second sentence illustrates something mentioned in the first sentence.

Directions: Read the passage below and then select the best answer for each question.

1   While on their honeymoon trip to Hong Kong, Thailand, and Bali, Indonesia, Bianca and Michael Alexander got the idea to start a business that would focus on the environment and <u>promote</u> a green lifestyle. Their new business, Conscious Planet Media Inc., offers a weekly broadband TV program as well as green event planning and consulting.

2   Overall, the green economy is worth more than $209 billion annually and is expected to reach $1 trillion by 2020. Many consumers say that concepts such as "all natural," "locally grown," "company donates to causes I care about," and "energy efficient" all positively affect their purchasing decisions.

3   Other ideas for green products and services include:

- a green bed-and-breakfast with recycling bins in the bedrooms, a water-wise garden, green light bulbs, organic meals made from locally grown food, and more;
- low water-use landscaping (xeriscaping) services; and
- green cleaning services that avoid irritating chemicals.

4   You get the idea. There are companies that offer biodegradable products that range from golf tees to coffins. Others offer organic products such as soy-based insulation and worm-fueled compost and composting products. In general, the market for new green products and services seems almost endless.

5   You can use the production and operations management skills discussed in the chapter entitled "Production and Operations Management" to become successful in creating green products and services. The green movement is only beginning. Opportunities are everywhere.

Source: Glenn Croston, "Go Green," *Entrepreneur,* December 2008; "Take a Tour," *Advertising Age,* June 9, 2008; Steve Garmhausen, "Growing a Green Business," *Black Enterprise,* April 2008; Stephanie Simon, "Green Businesses Jump on Opportunity in Denver," *The Wall Street Journal,* August 28, 2008; and Mike Hogan, "An Online Guide to the Green Scene," *Barron's,* March 2, 2009.

Source: Adapted from William Nickels, James McHugh, and Susan McHugh, *Understanding Business,* 9e, p. 231. Copyright © 2010 by The McGraw-Hill Companies, Inc. Reprinted with permission of The McGraw-Hill Companies, Inc.

1. As used in paragraph 1, the word *promote* means:
   a. live.
   b. further the growth of.
   c. benefit from.
   d. learn from.

2. Which sentence in paragraph 4 is the *stated main idea*?

a. You get the idea.
b. There are companies that offer biodegradable products that range from golf tees to coffins.
c. Others offer organic products such as soy-based insulation and worm-fueled compost and composting products.
d. In general, the market for new green products and services seems almost endless.

3. According to the passage, which of the following is available as a soy-based product?

a. insulation
b. light bulbs
c. golf tees
d. compost

4. What is the relationship *within the parts of this sentence* from paragraph 2: "Overall, the green economy is worth more than $209 billion annually and is expected to reach $1 trillion by 2020"?

a. comparison
b. example
c. spatial
d. list

5. With regard to the organization, the information in paragraph 3:

a. compares three things.
b. contrasts three things.
c. lists three things.
d. defines three things.

6. The authors' *tone* in this passage is:

a. arrogant.
b. sentimental.
c. encouraging.
d. pessimistic.

7. Who do the authors have in mind as the *audience*, or readers, of this passage?

a. business owners
b. entrepreneurs
c. people who own green businesses
d. business students

8. With regard to green products and services, the authors' *point of view* is that:

a. there are unlimited opportunities in this growing market.
b. services are more profitable than products.
c. consumers are not influenced by the "green" factor.
d. the next hot field will be green event planning and consulting.

9. Is this sentence from the last paragraph a *fact* or an *opinion*: "Opportunities are everywhere"?

   a. fact

   b. opinion

   c. both fact and opinion

10. Which of the following would be the best *title* for the passage?

   a. Tapping into the Growing Green Movement Market

   b. Developing a Green Lifestyle

   c. Endless Business Opportunities

   d. Customer Loyalty to Green Companies

Directions: Read the passage below and then select the best answer for each question.

1   With regard to toothbrushes, most dentists suggest a flat brushing surface with tufts of about equal length throughout the brush and a head small enough for comfort, regardless of the number of rows. The head of the brush must be small enough to reach all important surface areas of the mouth. Soft nylon bristles are flexible, they clean teeth efficiently, and they usually do not damage the gums. These bristles can make contact below the gum margin to help remove plaque. Toothbrushes with hard bristles should not be used because they can damage the teeth and gums, especially when combined with highly abrasive toothpaste. The type of toothbrush is much less important than the way it is used. To be effective, a brush must be manipulated properly.

2   Electric toothbrushes are useful but are not <u>panaceas</u>. Careful <u>manual</u> brushing can be just as effective as mechanical brushing, although some studies report that certain electric toothbrushes remove plaque more efficiently than manual brushing. An electric toothbrush is particularly helpful to people with poor coordination caused by mental or physical disabilities, patients with orthodontic bands on their teeth, or people who are unwilling to spend sufficient time for proper brushing by hand.

3   Consumers Union's consultants advise replacing one's toothbrush every 4 to 6 weeks because worn bristles are less effective at removing plaque. However, they warn that commercially marketed ultraviolet "toothbrush sterilizers" have no practical value because there is no danger from using a toothbrush that carries germs from one's own mouth.

Source: Stephen Barrett, William London, Robert Baratz, and Manfred Kroger, *Consumer Health: A Guide to Intelligent Decisions,* 8e, p. 127. Copyright © 2007 by The McGraw-Hill Companies, Inc. Reprinted with permission of The McGraw-Hill Companies, Inc.

1. The word *panaceas* in the second paragraph means:

   a. costly devices.
   b. long-lasting implements.
   c. self-care tools.
   d. cure-alls.

2. The word *manual* in the second paragraph means:

   a. thorough.
   b. occurring daily.
   c. done by hand.
   d. slow.

3. Which of the following is the *implied main idea* of paragraph 1?

    a. Dentists have definite ideas about the best type of toothbrush.

    b. Soft, nylon-bristled toothbrushes are able to remove plaque without damaging the gums.

    c. To be effective, a toothbrush should have a certain design, but more importantly, it must be manipulated properly.

    d. The best combination for cleaning the teeth effectively is a soft nylon-bristled toothbrush and a nonabrasive toothpaste.

4. According to information in the passage, toothbrush sterilizers:

    a. are recommended by dentists.

    b. are too expensive for most consumers.

    c. eliminate germs.

    d. are not worth the money.

5. What is the relationship *within the parts of this sentence* from paragraph 2: "Careful manual brushing can be just as effective as mechanical brushing, although some studies report that certain electric toothbrushes remove plaque more efficiently than manual brushing"?

    a. example

    b. spatial

    c. concession

    d. summary

6. The authors' *purpose* in writing this passage is to:

    a. inform readers about toothbrushes.

    b. instruct readers how to brush their teeth and care for toothbrushes properly.

    c. persuade readers to brush their teeth once a day.

    d. persuade readers to purchase an electric toothbrush.

7. It is reasonable to conclude the authors believe that the public:

    a. is changing increasingly to electric toothbrushes.

    b. is careless about toothbrushing.

    c. does not know enough about toothbrushes.

    d. has little interest in proper tooth care.

8. The authors' *intended audience* is:

    a. the general public.

    b. dental school students.

    c. parents with young children.

    d. consumers who are currently using electric toothbrushes.

9. Is the following sentence from paragraph 3 a fact or an opinion: "Consumers Union's consultants advise replacing one's toothbrush every 4 to 6 weeks because worn bristles are less effective at removing plaque"?

    a. fact

    b. opinion

    c. both fact and opinion

10. Which of the following is the best *title* for the passage?

    a. Electric Toothbrushes

    b. How to Brush Properly

    c. Electric or Manual Brushing?

    d. Toothbrushes

Directions: Read the passage below and then select the best answer for each question.

1   Automatic teller machines (ATMs) were introduced in the early 1970s, and their use has grown at a staggering rate since then. Today, there are approximately 12 billion ATM transactions annually.

2   At one point, robberies at these locations were so publicized that critics referred to ATMs as "magnets for crime." However, the ATM robbery rate has dropped from 1 robbery per 1 million transactions during the 1990s to its present 1 per 3.5 million transactions.

3   A combination of factors accounts for this drop in ATM robberies. These include locating ATMs where customers have a high visibility of their surroundings, using landscaping of 24 inches or less in height, and keeping the ATM areas well lit at night. In addition, customers are becoming knowledgeable about self-protection measures and are adopting them. Despite such realities, public fear of being victimized at or near an ATM is substantial.

4   The ATM robbery victim is typically a lone woman who is using the machine between 8 p.m. and midnight. To minimize the time spent with the victim and to avoid having to pressure the victim to make a withdrawal, many offenders simply wait until the transaction is completed before they <u>pounce</u>. Others confront the victim before the transaction, forcing her or him to make large withdrawals. Many victims report that they never saw the robber coming.

5   Offenders are most likely to work alone and are typically armed. They are usually about 25 years of age and tend to position themselves near an ATM, waiting for a likely victim to appear. In addition to taking the cash and any valuables the victim has, offenders may carjack the victim's vehicle to flee the scene.

Source: Adapted from Charles Swanson, Neil Chamelin, Leonard Territo, and Robert Taylor, *Criminal Investigation,* 11e, p. 362. Copyright © 2012 by The McGraw-Hill Companies, Inc. Reprinted with permission of The McGraw-Hill Companies, Inc.

1. As used in paragraph 4, the word *pounce* means:

a. strike someone.

b. attack suddenly.

c. give a loud yell.

d. wave a gun.

2. In a metaphor in paragraph 2, ATMs are described as "magnets for crime." The meaning of this metaphor is that:

a. ATM machines are typically made of metal.

b. robbers are attracted to ATMs as a place to commit robberies.

c. ATMs cheat customers out of their money.

d. customers prefer the convenience of ATMs over going inside a bank.

3. What is the *relationship between the parts of this sentence,* the last sentence in paragraph 3: "Despite such realities, public fear of being victimized at or near an ATM is substantial"?

   a. contrast
   b. summary
   c. example
   d. clarification

4. Which of the following would be the best *title* for the passage?

   a. Safety at Automatic Teller Machines
   b. Victims of Automatic-Teller-Machine Robberies
   c. The Ever-Increasing Use of ATMS
   d. Automatic-Teller-Machine Robberies

5. Which sentence in paragraph 1 is the *stated main idea*?

   a. sentence 1
   b. sentence 2

6. According to the passage, the occurrence of ATM robberies is one robbery per every:

   a. 1 million transactions.
   b. 3.5 million transactions.
   c. 24 million transactions.
   d. 12 billion transactions.

7. According to information in the passage, those who rob ATM users:

   a. are usually female.
   b. work with a partner.
   c. are usually armed.
   d. have been ATM robbery victims themselves.

8. The information in paragraph 3 is organized using which *pattern*?

   a. list
   b. sequence
   c. comparison-contrast
   d. cause-effect

9. Based on information in the passage, it is logical to *infer* that:

   a. women should not use ATMs.
   b. nothing can be done to reduce ATM robberies.
   c. it is safer to use ATMs during daylight hours.
   d. security cameras should be installed at every ATM.

10. Does the following sentence from paragraph 4 represent a fact or an opinion: "Many victims report that they never saw the robber coming"?

   a. fact
   b. opinion

Directions: Read the passage below and then select the best answer for each question.

1   Verbal support materials are vital to the success of a speech. They develop, illustrate, and clarify ideas; they make a speech more interesting and meaningful. Moreover, they can help prove an <u>assertion</u>.

2   There are several popular types of verbal support. These include *definition,* which helps make sure that your listeners understand key terms as you intend them to be understood; *vivid image,* which is a word picture that helps listeners visualize concepts; and *example,* which is an instance that illustrates a statement. Also popular are *narrative,* which is a story that amplifies your message; *comparison,* which shows how two or more things are alike; and *contrast,* which shows how two or more things are different. Finally, there are *analogy,* which explains a concept by likening it to something that seems different; *testimony,* which provides input from experts; and *statistics,* which are numerical ways of conveying information.

3   Of all these types, the narrative (or story) is the favorite of most audiences. People love to hear stories and are more likely to remember them than most other parts of your speech. As with all support materials, you must make sure that a narrative explains, illustrates, or reinforces the message of your speech. Telling a story that is irrelevant to the subject is not appropriate in informative and persuasive speaking.

4   Statistics such as averages, percentages, and correlations can be useful in a speech, but you must be careful to use them accurately and fairly. Adapt statistics to your particular audience, making them as interesting and as meaningful as possible.

Source: Hamilton Gregory, *Public Speaking for College and Career,* 9e, p. 162. Copyright © 2010 by The McGraw-Hill Companies, Inc. Reprinted with permission of The McGraw-Hill Companies, Inc.

1. As used in paragraph 1, the word *assertion* means:

a. a lengthy explanation.
b. a thorough investigation.
c. something stated, but not yet supported.
d. something presented as an example or illustration.

2. What is the *relationship between these two sentences* in paragraph 1: "Verbal support materials are vital to the success of a speech. They develop, illustrate, and clarify ideas; they make a speech more interesting and meaningful"?

a. comparison
b. clarification
c. summary
d. concession

_____   **3.** Which sentence in paragraph 2 is the *stated main idea*?
   a. first sentence
   b. second sentence
   c. third sentence
   d. fourth sentence

_____   **4.** According to the passage, which parts of a speech are audiences most likely to recall?
   a. definitions
   b. vivid images
   c. statistics
   d. narratives

_____   **5.** The type of verbal support that gives information from experts is:
   a. definition.
   b. narrative.
   c. analogy.
   d. testimony.

_____   **6.** Which of the following expresses the *overall main idea* of the selection?
   a. Verbal support materials, of which there are many types, are vital to the success of a speech.
   b. There are eight types of verbal support.
   c. The narrative, or story, is most audiences' favorite type of support.
   d. It is important to adapt statistics to your particular audience.

_____   **7.** The information in paragraph 2 is organized in a:
   a. list pattern.
   b. sequence pattern.
   c. spatial pattern.
   d. cause-effect pattern.

_____   **8.** Is the following sentence from paragraph 1 a statement of fact or an opinion: "Verbal support materials are vital to the success of a speech"?
   a. fact
   b. opinion

_____   **9.** It is logical to *conclude* from the passage that when the author gives a speech, he is likely to:
   a. feel nervous, just like most people.
   b. back up points with statistics.
   c. rehearse it.
   d. include one or more stories.

_____   **10.** Which of the following would be the best *title* for the selection?
   a. Verbal Support
   b. Including Narratives in a Speech
   c. Using Statistics in a Speech
   d. Effective Verbal Support in a Speech

Directions: Read the passage below and then select the best answer for each question.

1   Sloppy people live in Never-Never Land. Someday is their métier. Someday they are planning to alphabetize all their books and set up home catalogs. Someday they will go through their wardrobes and mark certain items for tentative mending and certain items for passing on to relatives of similar shape and size. Someday sloppy people will make family scrapbooks into which they will put newspaper clippings, postcards, locks of hair, and the dried corsage from their senior prom. Someday they will file everything that's on the surface of their desks, including the cash receipts from coffee purchases at the snack shop. Someday they will sit down and read all the back issues of *The New Yorker*.

2   For all these noble reasons and more, sloppy people never get neat. They aim too high and wide. They save everything, planning someday to file, order, and straighten out the world. But while these ambitious plans take clearer and clearer shape in their heads, the books spill from the shelves onto the floor, the clothes pile up in the hamper and closet, the family mementos accumulate in every drawer, the surface of the desk is buried under mounds of paper, and the unread magazines threaten to reach the ceiling.

3   Sloppy people can't bear to part with anything. They give loving attention to every detail. When sloppy people say they're going to tackle the surface of the desk, they really mean it. Not a paper will go unturned; not a rubber band will go unboxed. Four hours or two weeks into the excavation, the desk looks exactly the same, primarily because the sloppy person is meticulously creating new piles of papers with new headings and <u>scrupulously</u> stopping to read all the old book catalogs before he throws them away. A neat person would just bulldoze the desk.

4   Neat people are bums and clods at heart. They have <u>cavalier</u> attitudes toward possessions, including family heirlooms. Everything is just another dust catcher to them. If anything collects dust, it's got to go, and that's that. Neat people will toy with the idea of throwing the children out of the house just to cut down on the clutter.

5   Neat people don't care about process. They like results. What they want to do is get the whole thing over with so they can sit down and watch rasslin' on TV. Neat people operate on two unvarying principles: Never handle any item twice, and throw everything away.

6   The only thing messy in a neat person's house is the trashcan. The minute something comes to a neat person's hand, he will look at it, try to decide if it has immediate use and, finding none, throw it in the trash.

1. As used in paragraph 3, the word *scrupulously* means:

   a. joyfully.
   b. quickly.
   c. carefully.
   d. tirelessly.

2. As used in paragraph 4, the word *cavalier* means:

   a. noble.
   b. unconcerned.
   c. fashionable.
   d. courteous.

3. Which *figure of speech* appears in the sentence "They save everything, planning someday to file, order, and straighten out the world"?

   a. simile
   b. metaphor
   c. personification
   d. hyperbole

4. Which sentence in paragraph 4 is the *stated main idea*?

   a. Neat people are bums and clods at heart.
   b. They have cavalier attitudes toward possessions, including family heirlooms.
   c. Everything is just another dust catcher to them.
   d. Neat people will toy with the idea of throwing the children out of the house just to cut down on the clutter.

5. Overall, the information in the passage is organized as a:

   a. definition.
   b. sequence.
   c. comparison-contrast.
   d. cause-effect.

6. "Neat people are bums and clods at heart" is a statement of:

   a. fact.
   b. opinion.
   c. both fact and opinion.

7. The *tone* in this passage is:

   a. cautious.
   b. humorous.
   c. self-pitying.
   d. solemn.

_____   **8.** The author *implies* that neat people:

      a. care more about order than they care about people or things.
      b. make the world a better place because they are so organized.
      c. save every receipt and balance their checkbooks.
      d. take better care of their children than sloppy people do.

_____   **9.** The author's *intended audience* is

      a. the general public.
      b. neat people.
      c. sloppy people.
      d. sloppy people who want to become neater.

_____   **10.** Based on the passage, which of the following is a reasonable *conclusion*?

      a. The author is neat.
      b. The author is sloppy.
      c. The author is neater than she once was.
      d. The author is sloppier than she once was.

Directions: Read the passage below and then select the best answer for each question.

1   If we divide the world crudely into rich nations and poor nations, two-thirds of them are desperately poor, and only one-third comparatively rich, with the United States the wealthiest of all. Metaphorically, each rich nation can be seen as a lifeboat full of comparatively rich people. In the ocean outside each lifeboat swim the poor of the world, who would like to get in, or at least to share some of the wealth. What should the lifeboat passengers do?

2   First, we must recognize the limited capacity of any lifeboat. For example, a nation's land has a limited capacity to support a population and as the current energy crisis has shown us, in some ways we have already exceeded the carrying capacity of our land. So here we sit, say 50 people in our lifeboat. To be generous, let us assume it has room for 10 more, making a total capacity of 60. Suppose the 50 of us in the lifeboat see 100 others swimming in the water outside, begging for admission to our boat or for handouts. We have several options: we may be tempted to try to live by the Christian ideal of being "our brother's keeper," or by the Marxist ideal of "to each according to his needs." Since the needs of all in the water are the same, and since they can all be seen as our "brothers," we could take them all into our boat, making a total of 150 in a boat designed for 60. The boat swamps; everyone drowns. Complete justice, complete catastrophe.

3   Since the boat has an unused excess capacity of 10 more passengers, we could admit just 10 more to it. But which 10 do we let in? How do we choose? Do we pick the best 10, the neediest 10, "first come, first served"? And what do we say to the 90 we exclude? If we do let an extra 10 into our lifeboat, we will have lost our "safety factor," an engineering principle of critical importance. For example, if we don't leave room for excess capacity as a safety factor in our country's agriculture, a new plant disease or a bad change in the weather could have disastrous consequences.

4   Suppose we decide to preserve our small safety factor and admit no more to the lifeboat. Our survival is then possible, although we shall have to be constantly on guard against boarding parties.

5   While this last solution clearly offers the only means of our survival, it is morally <u>abhorrent</u> to many people. Some say they feel guilty about their good luck. My reply is simple: "Get out and yield your place to others." This may solve the problem of the guilt-ridden person's conscience, but it does not change the ethics of the lifeboat. The needy person to whom the guilt-ridden person yields his place will not himself feel guilty about his good luck. If he did, he would not climb aboard. The net result of conscience-stricken people giving up their unjustly held seats is the elimination of that sort of conscience from the lifeboat.

_____ **1.** The word *abhorrent* in the last paragraph means:

    a. correct, proper.
    b. confusing, perplexing.
    c. satisfying, pleasing.
    d. repulsive, distasteful.

_____ **2.** Which of the following is the *implied main idea* of paragraph 2?

    a. First, we must recognize the limited capacity of any lifeboat.
    b. We must recognize the limited capacity of any "lifeboat" and realize that complete justice can result in complete catastrophe.
    c. To be generous, let us assume it has room for 10 more, making a total capacity of 60.
    d. We have several options: we may be tempted to try to live by the Christian ideal of being "our brother's keeper," or by the Marxist ideal of "to each according to his needs."

_____ **3.** What is the *relationship between these two sentences* in the last paragraph: "The needy person to whom the guilt-ridden person yields his place will not himself feel guilty about his good luck. If he did, he would not climb aboard"?

    a. concession
    b. example
    c. comparison
    d. clarification

_____ **4.** In the *metaphor* in this passage, the people in the lifeboat represent:

    a. people living in wealthy nations.
    b. poor people living in wealthy nations.
    c. people living in poor nations.
    d. wealthy people who nearly drowned.

_____ **5.** According to the passage, a needy person who would take a wealthy person's place in the lifeboat:

    a. would feel guilty.
    b. serves as a safety factor.
    c. is likely to help other needy people survive.
    d. does not have a conscience.

_____ **6.** Which of the following expresses the author's *argument*?

    a. Poor nations should seek the help of wealthy nations.
    b. Wealthy nations cannot and should not help the poor nations.
    c. Poor nations do not appreciate the help given to them by wealthy nations.
    d. Wealthy nations should help only the poorest nations.

_____ **7.** The author supports his argument with:

    a. expert opinions.
    b. facts and reasons.
    c. research findings.
    d. all of the above

_____ **8.** The *tone* in this passage can be described as:

    a. condescending.
    b. ironic.
    c. authoritative.
    d. compassionate.

_____ **9.** It is reasonable to *conclude* that with regard to the poor in our own country, the author would:

    a. not favor helping them.
    b. favor helping them.
    c. advise them to get more education.
    d. tell them to seek help from government agencies.

_____ **10.** The author's *purpose* in writing this passage is to:

    a. inform.
    b. instruct.
    c. persuade.
    d. entertain.

Directions: Read the passage below and then select the best answer for each question.

1   The power of party is at no time clearer than when, election after election, Republican and Democratic candidates <u>reap</u> the vote of their party's identifiers. In the 2008 presidential election, John McCain had the support of more than 85 percent of Republican Party identifiers, while Barack Obama garnered the votes of more than 85 percent of self-identified Democrats. Majority-party candidates do not always do that well with party loyalists, but it is relatively rare—in congressional races as well as in the presidential race—for a party nominee to get less than 80 percent of the <u>partisan</u> vote.

2   When Americans are asked in polls if they are a Republican, a Democrat, or an independent, about a third say they are independents. However, in the follow-up question that asks if they lean toward the Republican Party or toward the Democratic Party, about two in three independents say they lean toward one of the parties. Most of these independents vote in the direction they lean. In recent presidential elections, more than eight in ten leaners have backed the candidate of the party toward which they lean. Less than 15 percent of all voters are "true" independents in the sense that party loyalty plays little to no part in the votes they cast. It is clear that even "independent" voters are less independent than might be assumed.

3   The power of party loyalties is evident in the extent to which straight-ticket voting occurs. Candidates for the presidency and Congress run separately, but voters do not treat them that way. Most voters who cast a ballot for the Republican presidential candidate also vote for the Republican congressional candidate in their district. The same is true on the Democratic side. Less than 29 percent of voters cast a split-ticket, voting for one party's presidential candidate and then voting for the other party's congressional candidate.

Source: Adapted from Thomas Patterson, *The American Democracy,* Alternate Ed., 9e, pp. 207–9. Copyright © 2011 by The McGraw-Hill Companies, Inc. Reprinted with permission of The McGraw-Hill Companies, Inc.

_____ **1.** As used in paragraph 1, the word *partisan* means:

    a. devoted to a political party.

    b. organized.

    c. officially cast.

    d. pertaining to cities.

2. Which sentence is the *stated main idea* of paragraph 2?

    a. When Americans are asked in polls if they are a Republican, a Democrat, or an independent, about a third say they are independents.

    b. In recent presidential elections, more than eight in ten leaners have backed the candidate of the party toward which they lean.

    c. Less than 15 percent of all voters are "true" independents in the sense that party loyalty plays little to no part in the votes they cast.

    d. It is clear that even "independent" voters are less independent than might be assumed.

3. Which sentence is the *stated main idea* of paragraph 3?

    a. The power of party loyalties is evident in the extent to which straight-ticket voting occurs.

    b. Candidates for the presidency and Congress run separately, but voters do not treat them that way.

    c. Most voters who cast a ballot for the Republican presidential candidate also vote for the Republican congressional candidate in their district.

    d. The same is true on the Democratic side.

4. In 2008, the two major presidential candidates:

    a. campaigned hard to appeal to independent voters.

    b. had to overcome split-ticket voting.

    c. did not do well with party loyalists.

    d. received the vast majority of their party identifiers' votes.

5. What is the *relationship between these two sentences* in paragraph 3: "Most voters who cast a ballot for the Republican presidential candidate also vote for the Republican congressional candidate in their district. The same is true on the Democratic side"?

    a. clarification

    b. comparison

    c. summary

    d. concession

6. The information in paragraph 2 is organized as a:

    a. definition.

    b. sequence.

    c. comparison-contrast.

    d. cause-effect.

7. Based on information in the passage, it is logical to *conclude* that:

    a. party loyalty and the vote are not strongly related.

    b. a majority-party candidate is more likely to be elected than an independent candidate.

    c. the way voters are likely to vote cannot be predicted.

    d. more research is needed on the effect of split-ticket voting in presidential and congressional races.

8. The author's *purpose* in writing this passage is to:

  a. inform.
  b. instruct.
  c. persuade.
  d. entertain.

9. Is the following sentence a fact or an opinion: "Less than 29 percent of voters cast a split-ticket, voting for one party's presidential candidate and then voting for the other party's congressional candidate"?

  a. fact
  b. opinion
  c. both fact and opinion

10. Which is the best *title* for this passage?

  a. Republican and Democratic Candidates
  b. Party Loyalty and the Vote
  c. The Impact of Independent Voters
  d. Split-Ticket Voting

Directions: Read the passage below and then select the best answer for each question.

1   We might be tempted to conclude that if we are free to have an opinion, it must be correct. That, however, is not the case. Free societies are based on the wise observation that people have an <u>inalienable</u> right to think their own thoughts and make their own choices. But this fact in no way suggests that the thoughts they think and the choices they make will be reasonable. It is a fundamental principle of critical thinking that ideas are seldom of equal quality. Solutions to problems vary from the practical to the impractical, beliefs from the well founded to the ill founded, arguments from the logical to the illogical, and opinions from the informed to the uninformed. Critical thinking serves to separate the more worthy from the less worthy and, ultimately, to identify the best.

2   Evidence that opinions can be mistaken is all around us. The weekend drinker often has the opinion that as long as he doesn't drink during the week, he is not an alcoholic. The person who continues driving her gas guzzler with the needle on "Empty" may have the opinion that the problem being signaled can wait for another fifty miles. The student who quits school at age sixteen may have the opinion that an early entry into the job market ultimately improves job security. Yet, however deeply and sincerely such opinions are held, they are most likely wrong.

3   Research shows that people can be mistaken even when they are making a special effort to judge objectively. Sometimes their errors are caused by considerations so subtle that they are unaware of them. For example, before Taster's Choice coffee was introduced, it was tested and sampled with three different labels—brown, yellow, and red. People who sampled the brown-labeled coffee reported that it was too strong and kept them awake at night. Those who sampled the yellow-labeled coffee found it weak and watery. Those who sampled the red-labeled coffee judged it to be "just the right strength" and delicious. All this, even though the coffee in each jar was exactly the same. The people had been subconsciously influenced by the color of the label.

Source: Vincent Ruggiero, *Beyond Feelings: A Guide to Critical Thinking,* 9e, p. 61. Copyright © 2009 by The McGraw-Hill Companies, Inc. Reprinted with permission of The McGraw-Hill Companies, Inc.

1. As used in paragraph 1, the word *inalienable* means:
   a. acquired by effort.
   b. cannot be taken away.
   c. temporary.
   d. recently granted.

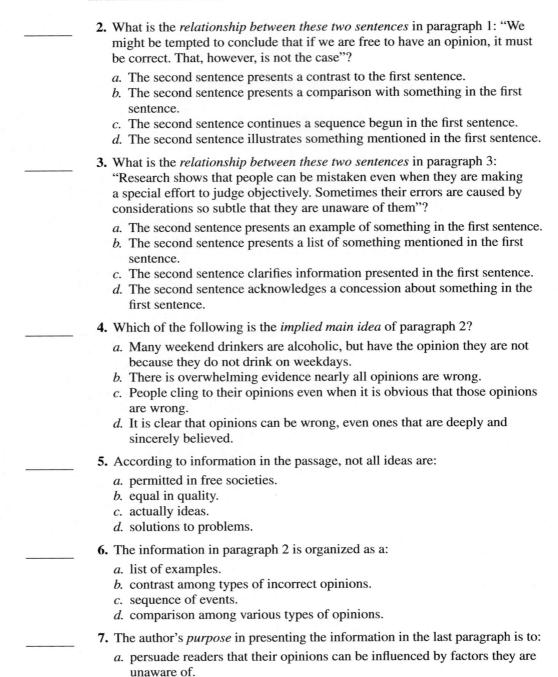

2. What is the *relationship between these two sentences* in paragraph 1: "We might be tempted to conclude that if we are free to have an opinion, it must be correct. That, however, is not the case"?

   a. The second sentence presents a contrast to the first sentence.
   b. The second sentence presents a comparison with something in the first sentence.
   c. The second sentence continues a sequence begun in the first sentence.
   d. The second sentence illustrates something mentioned in the first sentence.

3. What is the *relationship between these two sentences* in paragraph 3: "Research shows that people can be mistaken even when they are making a special effort to judge objectively. Sometimes their errors are caused by considerations so subtle that they are unaware of them"?

   a. The second sentence presents an example of something in the first sentence.
   b. The second sentence presents a list of something mentioned in the first sentence.
   c. The second sentence clarifies information presented in the first sentence.
   d. The second sentence acknowledges a concession about something in the first sentence.

4. Which of the following is the *implied main idea* of paragraph 2?

   a. Many weekend drinkers are alcoholic, but have the opinion they are not because they do not drink on weekdays.
   b. There is overwhelming evidence nearly all opinions are wrong.
   c. People cling to their opinions even when it is obvious that those opinions are wrong.
   d. It is clear that opinions can be wrong, even ones that are deeply and sincerely believed.

5. According to information in the passage, not all ideas are:

   a. permitted in free societies.
   b. equal in quality.
   c. actually ideas.
   d. solutions to problems.

6. The information in paragraph 2 is organized as a:

   a. list of examples.
   b. contrast among types of incorrect opinions.
   c. sequence of events.
   d. comparison among various types of opinions.

7. The author's *purpose* in presenting the information in the last paragraph is to:

   a. persuade readers that their opinions can be influenced by factors they are unaware of.
   b. inform readers about an experiment conducted by Taster's Choice coffee.
   c. instruct readers how to avoid being tricked by advertisers.
   d. persuade readers to have confidence in their opinions.

8. According to the passage, it is reasonable to *infer* that:

   a. every manufacturer uses deceptive practices to market its products.
   b. consumers are easily tricked.
   c. companies package and market products in dishonest ways.
   d. some companies know consumers can be influenced by their subconscious.

9. Does the following sentence from paragraph 3 represent a fact or an opinion: "Research shows that people can be mistaken even when they are making a special effort to judge objectively"?

   a. fact
   b. opinion

10. Which of the following expresses the *overall main idea* of the selection?

   a. Opinions are the right of every free person.
   b. Opinions can provide solutions to problems.
   c. Opinions can be mistaken.
   d. It is not possible to distinguish incorrect opinions from correct ones.

Directions: Read the passage below and then select the best answer for each question.

1   Too much bandwidth on the Internet is devoted to the <u>transmission</u> of porno-graphic and obscene sexual content. The JPEG file format, which makes it possible to include beautiful full-color images on Web pages, also can transmit full-color photos of explicit hardcore pornography and child pornography. The federal gov-ernment has been searching and seizing servers that contain such material.

2   The Supreme Court's 1973 *Miller* ruling gave communities the right to leg-islate obscenity. To help interpret the laws, Godwin (1994: 58) developed the following four-part test for obscenity:

1. Is the work designed to be sexually arousing?
2. Is it arousing in a way that one's local community would consider unhealthy or immoral?
3. Does it picture acts whose depictions are specifically prohibited by state law?
4. Does the work, when taken as a whole, lack sufficient literary, artistic, scien-tific, or social value?

3   Distributing sexually questionable materials over the Internet raises some dif-ficult issues. For example, while an erotic picture might not be immoral in the community where it was uploaded, it may very well be considered obscene in the place it gets downloaded. Screen-capture utilities make it easy to take things out of context; who can prevent users from circulating an image <u>devoid</u> of the supplementary material that made it legitimate? Moreover, children can easily access materials over the Internet that are intended for adults.

4   The U.S. child protection laws forbid any pornographic images that use chil-dren, whether or not they meet Godwin's obscenity test. Individuals convicted can be fined up to $100,000 and imprisoned up to 10 years. For example, as the result of a nationwide FBI investigation of online pornography, a distributor of child pornography was sentenced to five years in prison for sending sexu-ally explicit photos of children via his America Online account (*Tampa Tribune,* 24 February 1996: A6). In 2005, a federal court judge sent an Alabama man to prison for 30 years for possessing, receiving, and producing child pornogra-phy found on his computer, and for offering this material in Internet chat rooms (AP/WKRN News, 17 February 2005).

Source: Fred Hofstetter, *Internet Literacy,* 4e, p. 373. Copyright © 2006 by The McGraw-Hill Compa-nies, Inc. Reprinted with permission of The McGraw-Hill Companies, Inc.

_____   **1.** In paragraph 1, *transmission* means:

    a. creation.

    b. sending.

    c. altering.

    d. tracking.

2. In paragraph 3, *devoid* means:

   a. lacking.
   b. accentuated with.
   c. changed by.
   d. accompanied by.

3. Which sentence in paragraph 3 is the *stated main idea*?

   a. Distributing sexually questionable materials over the Internet raises some difficult issues.
   b. For example, while an erotic picture might not be immoral in the community where it was uploaded, it may very well be considered obscene in the place it gets downloaded.
   c. Screen-capture utilities make it easy to take things out of context; who can prevent users from circulating an image devoid of the supplementary material that made it legitimate?
   d. Moreover, children can easily access materials over the Internet that were intended for adults.

4. For material to be legally classified as obscene, it must:

   a. be considered obscene in the place where it is downloaded.
   b. involve images of children.
   c. be transmitted over the Internet.
   d. meet Godwin's four criteria.

5. Which pattern is used to organize the information in paragraph 3?

   a. list
   b. sequence
   c. definition
   d. cause-effect

6. What is the relationship *within the parts of this sentence* from paragraph 4: "The U.S. child protection laws forbid any pornographic images that use children, whether or not they meet Godwin's obscenity test"?

   a. time order
   b. clarification
   c. summary
   d. example

7. Is the following sentence a statement of fact or an opinion: "Too much bandwidth on the Internet is devoted to the transmission of pornographic and obscene sexual content"?

   a. fact
   b. opinion

8. Based on information in the passage, it is reasonable to *conclude* that anyone associated with child pornography:

a. is protected by the Supreme Court's 1973 *Miller* ruling.
b. could face harsh legal penalties.
c. is devoting too much bandwidth to its transmission.
d. will be caught, fined, and sent to jail.

9. It is logical to *infer* that a painting of a nude woman would:

a. be considered obscene.
b. not be considered obscene.
c. result in the artist going to jail.
d. not be able to be shown on the Internet.

10. Which of the following would be the best *title* for the passage?

a. Child Pornography
b. Pornography
c. U.S. Pornography and Obscenity Laws
d. Pornography and the Internet

Glossary of Key Reading and Study Skills Terms

Appendix 1 lists key terms from *Opening Doors,* with definitions. This list will help you review text material and monitor your understanding of the concepts and skills you have studied. The listing is alphabetical; the numbers in parentheses indicate chapters in which the key terms are introduced.

addition pattern The author simply adds information or elaborates by presenting more details. (*7*)

annotation Explanatory notes you write in the margins of a textbook to organize and remember information. (*10*)

appendix Section at the end of a book that includes supplemental material or specialized information. (*10*)

assessing your prior knowledge Determining what you already know about a topic. (*3*)

auditory learner One who prefers to hear information to be learned. (*1*)

author's argument The author's position on an issue. The author's argument is also known as the author's *point of view*. (*9*)

author's assumption Something the author takes for granted without proof. (*9*)

author's bias The side of an issue an author favors; an author's preference for one side of the issue over the other. (*8, 9*)

average reading rate Rate used for textbooks and more complex material in periodicals (200–300 words per minute). (*2*)

bar graph Chart in which the length of parallel rectangular bars is used to indicate relative amounts of the items being compared. (*10*)

bibliography Textbook feature near the end of the book, giving a list of sources: books, articles, and other works from which the author of the text has drawn information; it may also be called *references, works cited,* or *sources.* Bibliographies sometimes include works the author recommends for further (supplemental) reading. (*10*)

box Textbook feature consisting of supplementary material separated from the regular text; also called a *sidebar.* (*10*)

cause-effect pattern Writing pattern presenting reasons for (causes of) events or conditions and results (effects) of events or conditions. (*7*)

chapter introduction Textbook feature opening a chapter, describing the overall purpose and major topics or "setting the scene" with a case study, anecdote, etc. (*10*)

chapter objectives Textbook features at the beginning of a chapter, telling you what you should know or be able to do after studying the chapter; also called *preview questions, what you'll learn, goals,* etc. (*10*)

chapter outline Textbook feature at the beginning of a chapter, listing the chapter topics or headings in their order of appearance; also called *chapter contents, preview, overview,* etc. (*10*)

chapter review cards A way to select, organize, and review the most important information in a chapter; a study tool and special textbook feature in *Opening Doors;* also called *summary cards.* (*1*)

chapter summary Textbook feature at or near the end of a chapter, in which the author collects and condenses the most essential ideas. (*10*)

classification pattern Items are divided into groups or categories that are named, and the parts in each group are explained; also called *division pattern.* (*7*)

comparison-contrast pattern Writing pattern used to present similarities (comparisons), differences (contrasts), or both. (*7*)

comprehension monitoring Evaluating your understanding as you read and correcting the problem whenever you realize that you are not comprehending. (*2*)

conclusion A decision that is reached after thoughtful consideration of information the author presents. (*9*)

connotation Additional, nonliteral meaning associated with a word. (*2*)

context clues Words in a sentence or paragraph that help the reader deduce (reason out) the meaning of an unfamiliar word. (*2*)

credibility Believability of an author's argument. (*9*)

critical reading Gaining insights and understanding that go beyond comprehending the topic, main idea, and supporting details. Critical reading is also referred to as *critical reasoning.* (*8*)

critical thinking Thinking in an organized way about material you read or hear in order to evaluate it accurately. (*9*)

deductive reasoning A process of reasoning in which a general principle is applied to a specific situation. (*9*)

definition pattern Writing pattern presenting the meaning of an important term discussed throughout a passage. The definition may be followed by examples that illustrate or clarify the meaning. (*7*)

definition with examples pattern See *definition pattern.* (*7*)

denotation Literal, explicit meaning of a word; its dictionary definition. (*2*)

dictionary pronunciation key Guide to sounds of letters and combinations of letters in words. A full pronunciation key usually appears near the beginning of a dictionary; an abbreviated key, showing only vowel sounds and the more unusual consonant sounds, usually appears at or near the bottom of each page. (*2*)

distributed practice Study sessions that are spaced out over time; a more efficient study method than massed practice. (*11*)

division pattern See *classification pattern.* (*7*)

epigraphs Quotations that suggest overall themes or concerns of a chapter; this kind of textbook feature is usually found at chapter openings or in the margins. (*10*)

etymology Origin and history of a word. (*2*)

exhibits Special textbook features such as student papers, plot summaries, profit-and-loss statements, documents, forms, and printouts. (*10*)

fact Something that can be proved to exist or have happened or is generally assumed to exist or have happened. (*9*)

figurative language Imagery; words that create unusual comparisons, vivid pictures, and special effects; also called *figures of speech.* (*2*)

flowchart   Diagram that shows steps in procedures or processes by using boxes, circles, and other shapes connected with lines or arrows. (*10*)

generalization and example pattern   An important concept or general principle, followed by one or more specific examples. (*7*)

glossary   Mini-dictionary at end of a textbook, listing important terms and definitions from the entire text. (*10*)

graphic aids   Illustrations that consolidate information and present it more clearly than words alone; graphic aids include figures, cartoons, and photographs. (*10*)

hyperbole   Figure of speech using obvious exaggeration for emphasis and effect. (*2*)

illustrations   See *graphic aids*. (*10*)

implied main idea   A sentence formulated by the reader that expresses the author's main point about the topic. (*5*)

index   Alphabetical listing of topics and names in a textbook, with page numbers, usually appearing at the end of the book. (*10*)

inductive reasoning   A process of reasoning in which a general principle is developed from a set of specific instances. (*9*)

inference   In reading, a logical conclusion based on what an author has stated. (*9*)

intended audience   People an author has in mind as readers; the people he or she is writing for. (*8*)

intended meaning   What an author wants you to understand even when his or her words seem to be saying something different. (*8*)

intermediate goal   Goal you want to accomplish within the next 3 to 5 years. (*1*)

irony   A deliberate contrast between an author's apparent meaning and his or her intended meaning. (*8*)

kinesthetic learner   One who prefers to incorporate movement when learning. (*1*)

learning preference   The modality through which an individual learns best. (*1*)

line graph   Diagram whose points are connected to show a relationship between two or more variables. (*10*)

list pattern   Series of items in no particular order, since order is unimportant. (*7*)

long-term goal   Goal you want to accomplish during your lifetime. (*1*)

long-term memory   Permanent memory, as contrasted with short-term (temporary) memory. (*11*)

major details   Details that directly support the main idea. (*6*)

mapping   Informal way of organizing main ideas and supporting details by using boxes, circles, lines, arrows, etc. (*10*)

metaphor   Figure of speech suggesting a comparison between two essentially dissimilar things, usually by saying that one of them *is* the other. (*2*)

minor details   Details that support other details. (*6*)

mixed pattern   Combination of two or more writing patterns in the same paragraph or passage. (*7*)

monitoring your comprehension   Evaluating your understanding as you read and correcting the problem whenever you realize that you are not comprehending. (*2*)

monthly assignment calendar   Calendar showing test dates and due dates in all courses for each month of a semester. (*1*)

opinion   Belief or judgment that cannot be proved or disproved. (*9*)

organization   Arranging main ideas and supporting details in a meaningful way. Second of three essential study strategies. (*10*)

outlining   Formal way of organizing main ideas and supporting details to show relationships among them. (*10*)

paraphrasing   Restating someone else's material in your own words. (*6*)

part opening   Textbook feature that introduces a section (*part*) consisting of several chapters. (*10*)

personification   Figure of speech giving human traits to nonhuman or nonliving things. (*2*)

pie chart   Circle graph in which the sizes of the "slices" represent parts of the whole. (*10*)

place order pattern   See *spatial order pattern*. (*7*)

point of view   An author's position (attitude, belief, or opinion) on a topic. (*8*)

predicting   Anticipating what is coming next as you read. (*2*)

preface   Introductory section in which authors tell readers about a text. (*10*)

prefix   Word part attached to the beginning of a root word that adds its meaning to that of the base word. (*2*)

preparing to read   Previewing the material, assessing your prior knowledge, and planning your reading and studying time. (*3*)

previewing   Examining material to determine its topic and organization before actually reading it. (*3*)

prior knowledge   What you already know about a topic; background knowledge. (*3*)

process   A series of actions or changes that bring about a result. (*7*)

propaganda devices   Techniques authors use in order to unfairly influence the reader to accept their point of view. (*9*)

purpose   An author's reason for writing. (*8*)

rapid reading rate   Rate used for easy or familiar material (300–500 words per minute). (*2*)

rehearsal   Saying or writing material to transfer it into long-term memory. Third of three essential study strategies. (*10, 11*)

review   See *rehearsal*. (*10*)

review card   Index card with an important question on the front and the answer on the back. (*11*) Also, throughout *Opening Doors,* a technique for reviewing a chapter; *chapter* *review cards* summarize the most important information in the chapter and therefore are also called *summary cards.*

root   Base word that has a meaning of its own. *(2)*

sarcasm   A remark, often ironic, that is intended to convey contempt or ridicule. *(8)*

satire   A style of writing in which the author uses sarcasm, irony, or ridicule to attack or expose human foolishness, corruption, or stupidity. *(8)*

scanning   Information-gathering technique used to locate specific information quickly and precisely. *(2)*

selectivity   Identifying main ideas and important supporting details. First of three essential study strategies. *(10)*

sequence pattern   List of items in a specific, important order. *(7)*

series   A number of objects or events arranged one after the other in succession. *(7)*

short-term goal   Goal you want to accomplish within 3 to 6 months. *(1)*

short-term memory   Temporary memory. *(11)*

sidebar   See *box.* *(10)*

simile   Figure of speech stating a comparison between two essentially dissimilar things by saying that one of them is *like* the other. *(2)*

skimming   Information-gathering technique that involves moving quickly and selectively through material to find only important material. *(2)*

spatial order pattern   The location or layout of something or someplace is described; may also be called *place order pattern.* *(7)*

SQ3R study system   Systematic approach to studying textbook material utilizing five steps: Survey, Question, Read, Recite, and Review. *(3)*

stated main idea   Sentence in a paragraph that expresses the author's most important point about the topic. *(4)*

statement and clarification pattern   A general statement, followed by explanatory information that makes the statement clearer or easier to understand. *(7)*

study questions and activities   General term for textbook features such as activities, exercises, drills, and practice sections. These features may also be called *questions for study and review, review, ask yourself, self-test, check your mastery, mastery test, learning check, check your understanding, topics for discussion, problems,* etc. *(10)*

study reading rate   Rate used for material that is complex, technical, new, demanding, or very important (50–200 words per minute). *(2)*

study schedule   Weekly schedule with specific times set aside for studying. *(1)*

suffix   Word part attached to the end of a root word. *(2)*

suggested readings   Textbook feature, often at the end of chapters (or parts), listing the author's recommendations for supplemental reading or research, sometimes with annotations (comments); may be called *additional readings, suggestions for further reading, supplementary readings,* etc. *(10)*

summary   Single-paragraph condensation of all the main ideas presented in a longer passage. *(10)*

summary cards   See *chapter review cards. (1)*

summary/conclusion pattern   The author summarizes a preceding section or presents an important conclusion. *(7)*

supplements   Separate aids accompanying a textbook; supplements include *study guides, supplemental readings, student workbooks,* and *CD-ROMs. (10)*

supporting details   In a paragraph, additional information necessary for understanding the main idea completely. *(6)*

table   Material arranged in rows and columns. *(10)*

table of contents   Textbook feature at the beginning of a book, listing chapter titles and sometimes including headings within chapters as well. *(10)*

tactile learner   One who prefers to touch and manipulate materials physically when learning. *(1)*

test review cards   Index cards with an important question on the front and the answer on the back. *(11)*

test review sheet   Single sheet of paper consolidating and summarizing, on its front and back, the most important information to be covered on a test. *(11)*

textbook feature   Device used by an author to emphasize important material and show how it is organized. *(10)*

To Do list   Prioritized list of items to be accomplished in a single day. *(1)*

tone   Manner of writing (choice of words and style) that reveals an author's attitude toward a topic. *(8)*

topic   Word, name, or phrase that tells who or what an author is writing about. *(4)*

underlining and highlighting   Techniques for marking topics, main ideas, and definitions. *(10)*

visual learner   One who prefers to see or read information to be learned. *(1)*

visual literacy   The ability to read (interpret) images, graphs, diagrams, and other visual symbols. *(10)*

visual summary   A textbook chapter summary that contains graphic aids in addition to written information *(10)*

vocabulary aids   Textbook devices that highlight important terms and definitions. Vocabulary aids may be called *key terms, basic terms, terms to know, vocabulary, terms to remember,* etc. *(10)*

webliography   List of websites that feature material related to a topic. *(10)*

word-structure clue   Root, prefix, or suffix that helps you determine a word's meaning. Also known as *word-part clues. (2)*

writing patterns   Ways authors organize and present their ideas. *(7)*

A List of Word Parts: Prefixes, Roots, and Suffixes

Understanding the meaning of various word parts can help you determine the meaning of many unfamiliar words, especially in context. Most of the word parts listed in this appendix are Latin; a few are Greek, Old English, or Slavic.

The first part of this appendix presents the meaning of 215 useful roots, prefixes, and suffixes. Prefixes are followed by a hyphen (for example, *pre-*), and suffixes are preceded by a hyphen (for example, *-itis*).

Try to associate each word part (left column) with its meaning (middle column) as well as with the example word (right column). Associating the word part, its definition, and an example in this way will help you remember word parts that are new to you. Also, if you can associate the word part with a word that you already know, you will strengthen your understanding and recall of the word part even more.

The second part of this appendix presents the most common suffixes. For convenience, these suffixes are presented in categories.

	Word Part	Definition	Example
1.	a-	without, not	amoral, apolitical
2.	ab-	from	abduct, abstain
3.	acou	hear	acoustic
4.	acro	high	acrobat
5.	alter	another	alternate
6.	ambi	both; around	ambidextrous, ambivalent
7.	ambul	walk; go	ambulatory
8.	andr	man (human)	android
9.	annu, anni	year	annual, anniversary
10.	ante-	before, forward	antebellum, antecedent
11.	anthrop	humankind	anthropology
12.	anti-	against	antifreeze
13.	aqua	water	aquarium
14.	arch	ruler; chief, highest	archbishop, archenemy
15.	astro	star	astronomy
16.	aud	hear	auditory
17.	auto-	self	automatic, autobiography
18.	avi	bird	aviator, aviary
19.	belli	war	belligerent, bellicase
20.	bene-	well, good	beneficial
21.	bi-	two	bicycle
22.	bio	life	biology
23.	bov	cattle	bovine
24.	by-	secondarily, secondary	by-product
25.	camera	chamber	bicameral
26.	capit	head	decapitate
27.	card	heart	cardiac
28.	carn	flesh	carnivorous
29.	caust, caut	burn	caustic, cauterize
30.	cav	hollow	cavity
31.	cent-	hundred	century
32.	chromo	color	monochromatic
33.	chrono	time	chronology, chronicle
34.	cide	kill	homicide
35.	circum-	around	circumference
36.	contra-	against	contraceptive
37.	cosm	universe	microcosm, cosmology
38.	counter-	against	counteract, counter-terrorist
39.	crat, cracy	rule	democratic
40.	cred, creed	belief	credibility, creed
41.	crypt	secret, hidden	cryptography, cryptic
42.	cycl	circle	tricycle
43.	dec, deci	ten	decade, decimal
44.	dei	god	deity
45.	demo	people	democracy
46.	dent	tooth	dentist, dental
47.	derm	skin	dermatology

	Word Part	Definition	Example
48.	di-	two, double	dichotomy, divide
49.	dict	speak	diction, dictate
50.	dorm	sleep	dormitory, dormant
51.	dyna	power	dynamo
52.	dys-	bad, difficult	dysfunctional
53.	enni	year	centennial
54.	epi-	upon, outer	epidermis
55.	equ	horse	equine
56.	-esque	like, resembling	statuesque
57.	ethn	race, nation	ethnic, ethnocentric
58.	eu-	good, well	eulogy, euphemism
59.	ex-	out	exit
60.	extra-	beyond, over	extravagant, extramarital
61.	fer	carry, bear	conifer, aquifer
62.	ferr	iron	ferrous
63.	fid	faith, trust	fidelity, fiduciary
64.	fini	limit	finite
65.	flagr	burn	conflagration
66.	flect, flex	bend	reflect, flexible
67.	fore-	before	forewarn, forecast
68.	fort	strong	fortress, fortify
69.	frater	brother	fraternity
70.	gamy	marriage	monogamy
71.	gastr	stomach	gastric
72.	gene, gen	origin, race, type	genesis, genocide, genre
73.	geo	earth	geography
74.	geronto	old	gerontology
75.	grad, gress	go, step	regress, progress
76.	graph, gram	write, record	telegram, photography
77.	gyne	woman	gynecology
78.	helio	sun	heliocentric
79.	hemi-	half	hemisphere
80.	hemo	blood	hemophilia
81.	hetero-	other, different	heterosexual, heterogeneous
82.	homo	same	homosexual, homogeneous
83.	hydr	water	hydrant, hydrate
84.	hyper-	over, above	hyperactive
85.	hypo-	under, less than	hypodermic
86.	ign	fire	ignite
87.	in-, il-, im-, ir-	not	inactive, illegal, impotent
88.	inter-	between	intercept, interrupt
89.	intra-	within	intravenous, intramural
90.	-itis	inflammation	tonsillitis
91.	ject	throw	eject, reject
92.	junct	join	junction, conjunction
93.	kilo	thousand	kilometer, kilogram
94.	later	side	lateral

	Word Part	Definition	Example
95.	leg	law	legal, legislate
96.	liber	free	liberate
97.	libr	book	library
98.	lingua	tongue, language	sublingual, bilingual
99.	lith	stone	lithograph
100.	locu, loqu, log	speak	elocution, colloquial, dialogue
101.	-logy	study of	psychology
102.	luc	light, clear	lucid
103.	macro-	large	macrocosm
104.	magn	great	magnify
105.	mal-	bad, ill	malfunction
106.	mamma	breast	mammal
107.	mania	craving for	kleptomania
108.	manu	hand	manual
109.	matri, mater	mother	maternal, matriarchy
110.	mega-	large	megaphone
111.	meter, metr	measure	thermometer, metric
112.	micro-	small	microscope
113.	milli-	thousand, thousandth	millennium, millimeter
114.	mini-	less	minimal
115.	mis-	bad, wrong	mistreat, misspell
116.	miss, mit	send	dismiss, transmit
117.	mob, mov, mot	to move	mobile, movable, motion
118.	mono-	one	monotone, monopoly
119.	morph	form	amorphous, morph
120.	mort	death	mortal, mortuary
121.	multi-	many	multitude
122.	nat	born, birth	prenatal
123.	naut	sail	nautical
124.	neo-	new	neophyte, neologism
125.	nox	harmful	noxious
126.	noct	night	nocturnal
127.	ob-, oc-, of-, op-	against	object, occlude, offend, oppress
128.	oct-, octo-	eight	octopus, octagon
129.	ocul	eye	oculist
130.	-oid	resembling	humanoid
131.	omni	all	omnipotent
132.	onym	name, word	pseudonym, synonym
133.	ortho	correct, straight	orthodontist
134.	-osis	condition	psychosis
135.	osteo, ost	bone	osteopath, osteoporosis
136.	out-	better than	outrun, outdistance
137.	pac, pax	peace	pacifist, pacific
138.	pan-	all	panorama, pandemic
139.	para-	beside	parallel, parapsychology
140.	path	feeling, illness	sympathy, pathology
141.	patri, pater	father	paternity, patriotic

	Word Part	Definition	Example
142.	ped, pod	foot	pedal, tripod
143.	pel	drive	repel, impel, dispel
144.	pend	hang	pendulum, pending
145.	penta-	five	pentagon, pentathlon
146.	per-	through	perspire
147.	peri-	around	perimeter
148.	petr	rock	petrified
149.	philo	love	philosophy
150.	phobia	fear of	acrophobia
151.	phono	sound	phonics, phonograph
152.	photo	light	photograph
153.	pneum	air	pneumatic
154.	poly-	many	polygon, polyglot
155.	port	carry	portable, porter
156.	pos	place	position
157.	post-	after	postwar
158.	pre-	before	prewar
159.	primo	first	primitive, primordial
160.	pro-	forward, in favor of	progress, pro-American
161.	pseud	false	pseudoscience
162.	psych	mind	psychic
163.	pugn	fight	pugnacious
164.	punct	point	puncture
165.	purg	cleanse	purge
166.	pyre	fire	pyromania
167.	quad-, quar-	four	quadruplets, quartet
168.	quint-	five	quintet
169.	re-	back, again	return, repeat
170.	reg	guide, rule; king	regulate, regal
171.	rupt	break	rupture, disrupt
172.	scend	climb	descend, ascend
173.	scope	see; view	telescope
174.	scribe, scrip	write	scribble, prescription
175.	sequ	follow	sequence, sequel
176.	semi-	half	semicircle
177.	seni	old	senile
178.	simil	like	similar
179.	sol	sun	solar, solstice
180.	sol, soli	alone	solo, solitude
181.	somni	sleep	insomnia, somnolent
182.	soph	wise	sophomore, sophisticated
183.	spect	see	spectator, spectacle
184.	spir	breathe	respiratory
185.	strict	tighten	constrict, restrict
186.	sub-	under	submarine
187.	super-, sur-	over	supervisor, surpass
188.	surg	rise	surge, resurgent

	Word Part	Definition	Example
189.	tang, tact	touch	tangible, tactile
190.	tech	skill	technician
191.	tele-	far	telepathy, telescope
192.	tend, tens	stretch	tendon, tension, extend
193.	terri	earth	territory
194.	tert-	third	tertiary
195.	theo	god	theology
196.	therm	heat	thermometer, thermal
197.	tomy	cut	vasectomy, appendectomy
198.	tors, tort	twist	distort, torture
199.	toxi	poison	toxic
200.	tract	pull, drag	tractor, extract
201.	tri-	three	trio
202.	ultra-	beyond, over	ultramodern
203.	unct, ung	oil	unctuous, unguent
204.	uni-	one	unity, unify, uniform
205.	vacu	empty	vacuum
206.	veni, vent	come	convene, convention
207.	verd	green	verdant
208.	vers, vert	turn	reverse, vertigo, divert
209.	vid, vis	see	video, vision
210.	vinc	conquer	invincible
211.	vit, viv	life	vitality, vivacious
212.	voc, voke	voice, call	vocal, evoke
213.	voli, volunt	wish	volition, volunteer
214.	volv	roll, to turn	revolve, evolve
215.	zoo	animal	zoology

COMMON SUFFIXES

Suffix	Meaning	Examples
Suffixes That Indicate a Person:		
1. -er, -or, -ist	one who (does what the root word indicates)	banker, inventor, scientist, pacifist
Suffixes That Indicate a Noun:		
2. -ance, -ence, -tion, -sion, -ment, -ness, -ity, -ty, -tude, -hood, -age	state of, quality of, condition of, act of	tolerance, permanence, retention, vision, government, happiness, maturity, beauty, gratitude, statehood, marriage
3. -itis	inflammation of (whatever the root indicates)	sinusitis, tonsillitis
4. -ology	study or science of (whatever the root indicates)	psychology, microbiology
5. -ism	philosophy of or belief in	terrorism, Buddhism, pacifism
Suffixes That Indicate an Adjective:		
6. -al, -ic, -ish, -ical, -ive	pertaining to (whatever the root indicates)	normal, hormonal, psychic, selfish, magical, defective, pacific
7. -less	without, lacking (whatever the root indicates)	homeless, toothless
8. -ous, -ful	full of (whatever the root indicates)	harmonious, colorful
9. -able, -ible	able to do or be (whatever the root indicates)	comfortable, comprehensible
Suffixes That Indicate a Verb:		
10. -ify, -ate, -ize, -en	to do (whatever the root indicates)	pacify, meditate, criticize, enlighten
Suffixes That Indicate an Adverb:		
11. -ly	in the manner (indicated by the root)	slowly, heavily, peacefully
12. -ward	in the direction of (whatever the root indicates)	eastward, homeward, backward

Master Vocabulary List

Appendix 3 lists vocabulary words in the Vocabulary in Context exercises in *Opening Doors.* This list will help you locate the Vocabulary in Context exercise where each word appears.

In *Part One,* vocabulary words are listed by selection. In *Part Two,* vocabulary words are listed alphabetically. The numbers in parentheses indicate the reading selection in which the vocabulary word appears.

Credits

Index

Monitoring your comprehension means *evaluating your understanding as you read and correcting the problem whenever you realize that you are not comprehending.* You should monitor your comprehension whenever you read and study college textbooks. Asking yourself comprehension-monitoring questions as you read will guide your reading and enhance your understanding. The comprehension-monitoring questions that are presented throughout *Opening Doors* are listed below.

Vocabulary Chapter 2

Vocabulary in Context: *"Are there clues within the sentence or surrounding sentences that can help me deduce the meaning of an unfamiliar word?"*

Word-Structure Clues: *"Are there roots, prefixes, or suffixes that give me clues to the meaning of an unfamiliar word?"*

Connotative Meaning: *"Is there a positive or negative association in addition to the literal meaning of a word?"*

Figurative Language: *"Should these words or this expression be interpreted figuratively?"*

Reading Comprehension Chapters 4–7

Determining the Topic: *"Who or what is this paragraph about?"*

Stated Main Idea: *"What is the most important point the author wants me to understand about the topic of this paragraph?"*

Implied Main Idea: *"What is the most important point the author wants me to infer about the topic of this paragraph?"*

Identifying Supporting Details: *"What additional information does the author provide to help me understand the main idea completely?"*

Recognizing Authors' Writing Patterns: *"Which pattern did the author use to organize the main idea and the supporting details?"*

Critical Reading and Thinking Chapters 8–9

Determining an Author's Purpose: *"Why did the author write this?"*

Determining an Author's Intended Audience: *"Who did the author intend to read this?"*

Determining an Author's Point of View: *"What is the author's position on this issue?"*

Determining an Author's Tone: *"What do the author's choice of words and style of writing reveal about his or her attitude toward the topic?"*

Determining an Author's Intended Meaning: *"What is the author's real meaning?"*

Evaluating Whether Statements in Written Material Are Facts or Opinions: *"Can the information the author presents be proved, or does it represent a judgment?"*

Making Inferences: *"What logical inference (conclusion) can I make, based on what the author has stated?"*

Evaluating an Author's Argument

    Identifying the Issue: *"What controversial topic is this passage about?"*

    Determining the Author's Argument: *"What is the author's position on the issue?"*

    Determining the Author's Bias: *"Which side of the issue does the author support?"*

    Identifying the Author's Assumptions: *"What does the author take for granted?"*

    Identifying Support: *"What types of support does the author present?"*

    Deciding Whether an Author's Support Is Relevant: *"Does the support pertain directly to the argument?"*

    Evaluating Whether an Author's Argument Is Objective and Complete: *"Is the argument based on facts and other appropriate evidence? Did the author leave out information that might weaken or disprove the argument?"*

    Evaluating Whether an Author's Argument Is Valid and Credible: *"Is the author's argument logical and believable?"*

    Identifying Propaganda Devices: *"Has the author tried to unfairly influence me to accept his or her point of view?"*

ASSIGNMENT SHEET AND PROGRESS RECORD, PART ONE

CHAPTER REVIEW CARDS, CHECKPOINTS, AND TEST YOUR UNDERSTANDING EXERCISES

Due Date	Review Cards, Checkpoints, and Test Your Understanding Exercises	Number of Items	Score
_____	**Chapter 1** Review Cards (7 cards) pp. 21–24		_____
_____	**Chapter 2** Review Cards (8 cards) pp. 83–87		_____
_____	Test Your Understanding: Context Clues, Part 1 pp. 89–90	10	_____
_____	Test Your Understanding: Context Clues, Part 2 pp. 91–92	10	_____
_____	Test Your Understanding: Word Structure, Part 1 pp. 93–96	20	_____
_____	Test Your Understanding: Word Structure, Part 2 pp. 97–99	20	_____
_____	Test Your Understanding: Figurative Language, Part 1 pp. 101–02	10	_____
_____	Test Your Understanding: Figurative Language, Part 2 pp. 103–04	10	_____
_____	**Chapter 3** Review Cards (9 cards) pp. 155–59		_____
_____	**Chapter 4** Checkpoint: Locating the Stated Main Idea pp. 218–21	5	_____
_____	Review Cards (7) pp. 223–26		_____
_____	Test Your Understanding: Determining the Topic and Stated Main Idea, Part 1 pp. 227–30	10	_____
_____	Test Your Understanding: Determining the Topic and Stated Main Idea, Part 2 pp. 231–34	10	_____
_____	**Chapter 5** Checkpoint: Formulating Implied Main Ideas pp. 285–88	5	_____
	Review Cards (7 cards) pp. 289–91		
_____	Test Your Understanding: Formulating Implied Main Ideas, Part 1 pp. 293–96	10	
_____	Test Your Understanding: Formulating Implied Main Ideas, Part 2 pp. 297–300	10	
_____	**Chapter 6** Checkpoint: Identifying Supporting Details pp. 354–56	5	_____
_____	Review Cards (6 cards) pp. 357–59		_____
_____	Test Your Understanding: Identifying Supporting Details, Part 1 pp. 361–64	10	_____
_____	Test Your Understanding: Identifying Supporting Details, Part 2 pp. 365–69	10	_____
_____	**Chapter 7** Checkpoint: Basic Writing Patterns pp. 435–37	5	_____
_____	Checkpoint: Other Writing Patterns pp. 444–46	10	_____
_____	Checkpoint: Relationships within and between Sentences pp. 452–54	10	_____
_____	Review Cards (7 cards) pp. 455–58		_____
_____	Test Your Understanding: Recognizing Authors' Writing Patterns, Part 1 pp. 459–62	10	_____
_____	Test Your Understanding: Recognizing Authors' Writing Patterns, Part 2 pp. 463–66	10	_____
_____	**Chapter 8** Checkpoint: Reading Critically pp. 535–38	5	_____
_____	Review Cards (5 cards) pp. 539–41		_____
_____	Test Your Understanding: Reading Critically, Part 1 pp. 543–46	10	_____
_____	Test Your Understanding: Reading Critically, Part 2 pp. 547–50	10	_____
_____	**Chapter 9** Checkpoint: Thinking Critically pp. 625–28	5	_____
_____	Review Cards (8 cards) pp. 629–33		_____
_____	Test Your Understanding: Thinking Critically, Part 1 pp. 635–38	10	_____
_____	Test Your Understanding: Thinking Critically, Part 2 pp. 639–42	10	_____
_____	**Chapter 10** Review Cards (8 cards) pp. 739–43		_____
_____	**Chapter 11** Review Cards (5 cards) pp. 775–77		_____